The Musical Idea

WALTER E. NALLIN

THE
MUSICAL
IDEA

A Consideration of Music
and Its Ways

THE MACMILLAN COMPANY, NEW YORK
COLLIER-MACMILLAN LIMITED, LONDON

To Mary, Judi, and Mary Kate

Preface

In our time music seems to be everywhere. Mechanically reproduced, it pours from loudspeakers in stores, theaters, restaurants, or amusement parks; performed by amateurs or professionals, it is heard in schools, churches, homes, concert halls, and opera houses. Discussed in magazines, explained in books, and criticized in newspapers, music has had entire industries—concerned with the manufacture of instruments, the publication of scores, or the production of phonograph records—grow up around it.

For centuries music has brought pleasure, solace, inspiration, and edification into the lives of many. Traditionally associated with religious rite, various kinds of ceremonial observance, dancing, the theater, or formal concerts, it has now become a corollary of radio and television shows, motion pictures, or the pageantry at football games. For more than a thousand years it has retained a respected place in the curricula of schools, colleges, and universities, a tradition being brilliantly maintained, and even enlarged, in modern times. Clearly, in many ways, to many people, and over a long period of time, music has been proven useful, meaningful, and important.

This book makes some attempt to describe music, its materials, lore, stylistic evolution, and traditions. Consistently the approach is twofold, for efforts are made (1) to inform a reader's mind, as well as (2) to alert his ear. Of course, the two are inseparable in any well-conceived scheme of musical study. To be enjoyed, understood, and loved, music must be heard. But the really intelligent person is rarely satisfied to let matters rest here, for he wishes to know something about music's syntax, its patterns of design, its communicative possibilities, and its historical evolution.

By no means a compendium, this volume attempts to advance basic information about music as a communicative art, as well as provide background details intended to enrich the numerous listening opportunities available today. Written for the non-musician, it does not avoid technical discussion, but attempts, rather, to explain the totality of music in terms that are clear, precise, and meaningful.

Read it carefully. Make frequent use of the glossaries (one for terminology, the other listing outstanding composers), peruse the bibliography, and enhance your study by reading some of the books listed on its pages. A wealth of wondrous musical experiences lies ahead. Enjoy them!

Over the years, as this volume progressed through its evolutionary stages, so many have been so very generous with their kind assistance and advice that I am reluctant to advance any listing of specific names lest, through inadvertence, some should suffer oversight. Rather, let me express my deep and abiding appreciation to friends, students, and colleagues in the broad realm of music who have given so unstintingly of their time, skills, and knowledge to assist in bringing forth a volume that we hope will find both favor and acceptance in the collegiate community.

Special thanks, however, are due my long-time mentor, confidant, and friend, Dr. Emanuel Saxe, Dean of The City College's Baruch School (soon to become the Baruch College). Consistently, as this bulky manuscript underwent its trial in the crucible of classroom experience, he remained a pillar of strength who sustained, advised, and guided my errant and often stumbling steps. Without his encouragement this project might well have foundered on a hundred different shoals. His constancy shall never be forgotten.

W. E. N.

Acknowledgments

Grateful acknowledgment is made to the following for their kindness in making available illustrative materials that unquestionably enhance the substance of this book.

Photographs:

1. Foto Lala Aufsberg of Nurnberg, Germany, for the frontispiece (facing page 1) and other illustrations used in the end papers.
2. Franco Colombo, Inc. of New York City for the quotation from Edgard Varese's *Ionisation*, cited in Figure 1, page 15.
3. The Metropolitan Museum of Art, New York City, for Figure 2, page 46 (The Crosby Brown Collection, 1889), the facing illustration on page 120 (The Crosby Brown Collection, 1889), the facing illustration on page 218 (The Crosby Brown Collection, 1889), and Figure 19 on page 492.
4. Bryce Bowmar of Bowmar Records, Inc., North Hollywood, California, for the numerous illustrations found in Figure 3, page 81; Figure 4, page 83; Figure 5, page 85; Figure 6, page 86; Figure 7, page 87; Figure 8, page 88; Figure 9, page 90; Figure 10, page 92; Figure 11, page 93; and Figure 12, page 94.
5. The Baldwin Piano and Organ Company, Cincinnati, Ohio, for Figure 13, page 101.
6. Columbia Records Inc. of New York City for Figure 16, page 109.
7. Library of Congress, Music Division, Washington, D.C., for Figure 18, page 409.
8. Louis Melancon of the Metropolitan Opera Association, New York City, for Figure 21, page 542; Figure 22, page 575; and Figure 23, page 578.
9. Maxwell Weaner, New York City, for his extremely skilled work in carrying forth the music autographing.

Musical Examples:

1. Associated Music Publishers, Inc., New York City: *Ein Heldenleben* by Richard Strauss; copyright 1927 by F. E. C. Leuckart. *Mathis der Maler* by Paul Hindemith; copyright 1934 by B. Schott's Soehne. *Variations on a Nursery Song* by Ernst von Dohnanyi; copyright 1922 by N. Simrock. *Pavane pour une infante defunte* by Maurice Ravel; copyright 1910 by Editions Max Eschig. All used by permission of the copyright owners and Associated Music Publishers, Inc., agents for the United States.

2. Belmont Music Company, Los Angeles, California (Universal Edition), for excerpts from the *Wind Quintet,* opus 26, and *Variations for Orchestra,* opus 31, by Arnold Schoenberg. Copyright 1925 and 1929 by Universal Edition. Used by permission of Belmont Music Company.

3. Boosey and Hawkes, Inc., New York City: *First Suite in E-flat* by Gustav Holst; copyright 1921 by Boosey & Co., renewed 1948. Reprinted by permission. *Concerto for Orchestra* by Béla Bartók; copyright 1946 by Hawkes and Son (London) Ltd. Reprinted by permission of Boosey and Hawkes, Inc. *Pictures at an Exhibition* by Mussorgsky-Ravel; copyright 1929 by Edition Russe de Musique, renewed 1956. Copyright renewal assigned to Boosey and Hawkes, Inc. Reprinted by permission. *Art of Fugue* by Bach-Gal, copyright 1951 by Hawkes and Son (London) Ltd. Reprinted by permission of Boosey and Hawkes, Inc. *Rodeo* by Aaron Copland; copyright 1946 by Aaron Copland. Boosey and Hawkes, Inc., sole publishers. Reprinted by permission of Aaron Copland and Boosey and Hawkes, Inc.

4. Broude Brothers Music Publishers, New York City: *Fugue in G minor,* Bach-Stokowski; *Variations on a Tchaikowsky Theme,* Arensky; *Biblical Sonatas,* Kuhnau. Copyright 1950 (Bach) and 1953 (Kuhnau) by Broude Brothers, Inc., New York. Used by permission.

5. Elkan-Vogel Company, Philadelphia, Pennsylvania: *Children's Corner Suite* by Claude Debussy. Copyright 1908 by Durand et Cie., Paris. Used by permission of Elkan-Vogel Co., Inc., sole agents.

6. Elkan-Vogel Company, Inc., Philadelphia, Pennsylvania: *Pop Goes the Weasel,* arranged by Lucien Calliett. Copyright 1938 by Elkan-Vogel Company, Inc. Used by permission.

7. Mercury Music Corp., New York City: *Three Places in New England* and *Variations on America* by Charles Ives. Copyright 1935 and 1949 by Mercury Music Corporation. Used by permission.

8. MCA Music, Inc., New York City: "Sabre Dance" from *Gayne* by A. Khachaturian, copyright 1948. Symphony No. 1 by D. Shostakovich, copyright 1946. Symphony No. 5 by D. Shostakovich, copyright 1946. *The Comedians* by D. Kabalevsky, copyright 1948. All used by permission of MCA Music, a division of MCA Inc., New York, N.Y. All rights reserved.

9. Music Publishers Holding Corporation, New York City: *An American in Paris* by George Gershwin; copyright 1929 by New World Music Corporation. Used by permission.

10. W. W. Norton and Company, Inc., for thematic excerpts from *A Treasury of Early Music*, compiled and edited with notes by Carl Parrish, copyright 1958; and quotations from *Masterpieces of Music Before 1750*, compiled and edited by Carl Parrish and John F. Ohl, copyright 1951.

11. Oxford University Press, New York City: *Façade* by William Walton; copyright 1951 by the Oxford University Press, London. Used by permission.

12. G. Schirmer, Inc., New York City: *L'Histoire du soldat* by Igor Stravinsky; copyright 1924 by J. W. Chester, London. Used by permission of G. Schirmer, Inc.

Contents

The Musical Idea

External view of the organ in the Stiftskirche, Regensburg, Germany.

PART ONE

MUSIC'S FUNDAMENTAL ASPECTS

Every art has its materials. Painting, for instance, requires an artist to make skillful use of pigments, oils, tempera, or water colors. And a writer, whether concerned with poetry, essays, novels, or drama, must handle the words, sentences, and paragraphs that are essential to his craft.

Music, too, has its elements. Existing as auditory images, these are the sounds (that is, tones) that a creative—or, for that matter, a re-creative—musician must manipulate to bring his art into being. Just as painters and writers handle pigments and words, just as sculptors and architects handle stone and steel, musicians handle tones.

On the pages that follow, music's tonal materials are identified, described, and illustrated. Chapter 1 centers on the rhythmic force that impels music forward, Chapter 2 is concerned with its subject matter, melody. And in Chapters 3, 4, and 5, musical texture, musical instruments, and the media of performance come in for a share of attention. Always, verbal description is intermingled with musical illustration, and a reader should exert strenuous efforts to absorb both as the educative process goes forward. Of course, this is not easy. Training one's ear to perceive the musical substance is taxing, and strengthening one's memory to retain its imagery can be arduous and time-consuming. Be patient. Do not attempt to assimilate too much too soon. Willingly listen to the examples repeatedly. Only in this way can you train the ear and, thus, build a solid background for meaningful experiences in the future.

Chapter 1

The Rhythm of Music

Music is an art of motion. Every composition, regardless of its age, complexity, or expressive intent, whether it is written for instruments or voices, has a continuous flow. Pieces of all kinds consistently display a forward thrust, and occasional pauses that may occur as a piece is being performed only confirm the inevitability of this momentum. In a sense, musical motion is comparable to the flow of water in a stream, for in either case, the activity is continuous, usually quite smooth, and seemingly inevitable.

Rhythm (that is, ordered motion) describes the force that drives music forward. Rough and turbulent, tranquil and placid, or broad and majestic, rhythmic motion is an absolute requisite, for without this "heart beat" music simply could not exist.

Anthropologists describe the place that rhythmically oriented activity held in the lives of primitive people.[1] In those early times (from 20,000 to 40,000 years ago) the rituals, so important in an aboriginal society, centered on overt physical movements supported by chanting, wailing, clapping, or beating on crude devices. Examples of music from a later period (c. 1000 B.C.) are now available in recorded form (as are numerous authentic folk dances), and these should be listened to in order to appreciate what early practices were like.[2] Compare, for instance, the music of native African dances with that of folk dances from such European countries as Yugoslavia, Russia, or Greece. And then contrast these with current American dances. Although this music comes from widely divergent cultures and represents eras separated by thousands of years, all are as one in a common reliance on rhythm.

[1] Fascinating details of musical activities in early societies may be gleaned from Curt Sachs, *The Rise of Music in the Ancient World, East and West* (New York: W. W. Norton & Company, Inc., 1943).
[2] An abundance of beautifully illustrative examples from pre-Christian oriental and occidental civilizations is included in the collection, "A History of Music in Sound," issued by Oxford University Press.

MUSIC'S TEMPORAL ASPECT

Because it is founded on continuous rhythmic motion, music is a temporal art. This is to say that any piece has an existence in time represented by the moments needed for its performance. Freshness, an ever-changing façade, and the impression of continuous activity unquestionably stimulate a listener. But this shifting panorama of sound also imposes a burden on anyone listening to the music, for he must remain constantly alert to grasp its substance and meaning.

Consider Franz Schubert's [3] *Marche militaire No. 1* as an obviously rhythmic piece. Listen to its several strains, or melodic segments, and observe how a continual rhythmic thrust is maintained as the piece flows along:

All kinds of movement occur in *Marche militaire.* Near the surface is a succession of tones that can be termed its *melodic rhythm,* while other changes take place in its structural base corresponding to *harmonic rhythm.* Most obvious of all, however, is a reiterated pulse that underscores the piece from beginning to end and is the essential rhythmic force around which the piece is organized.

MUSIC'S PULSATION

These recurrent pulsations are commonly called *beats.* They underscore the forward thrust of virtually all music (an exception is religious chant, discussed in Chapter 3) and progress in a regular, reiterated manner. In this sense they can be compared with the recurrent throb of an engine, or the motions involved in walking, rowing a boat, swimming, or riding a bicycle.

While performing, musicians frequently indicate the pulse by tapping their toes, just as the director of a group indicates a composition's thrust

[3] Brief biographic sketches including dates of birth and death, important works, and other significant data about important creative musicians mentioned on these pages can be found in Appendix A, "A Glossary of Composers."

with motions of his hands and arms. And such instruments as the drum, string bass, or guitar, are often used to mark the beat.

Dances and marches clearly demonstrate the incisive qualities of a regular pulse. John Philip Sousa's *Washington Post March*,[4] for example, has a continuous beat that is attractive but uncomplicated. Listen to it and try to mark the pulse by lightly tapping your fingers. These are quotations from its several melodic strains:

Giuseppe Verdi's "Triumphal March"[5] from the opera *Aida* is another piece that is strikingly rhythmic. Again, you should physically mark the pulse while listening. Principal melodies in this "grand" march are these:

[4] Other representative Sousa marches include (1) *The Stars and Stripes Forever,* (2) *King Cotton,* (3) *Manhattan Beach,* and (4) *Semper Fidelis.*

[5] Also representative are (1) the "Processional March" from *Tannhäuser* by Richard Wagner, and (2) the "War March of the Priests" from *Athalie* by Felix Mendelssohn.

TEMPO

Beats can and do move at different rates of speed, which gives the pulse a quality known as *tempo*. Sometimes the pace is fast, again it may be slow; often it is somewhere between. Simple pieces usually move at an unchanging tempo from beginning to end, but works of greater complexity, particularly those intended for concert or solo performance, often change. Indications concerning a composition's basic pace are given at the beginning of a printed score, and modifications are inserted where needed. Although various languages, including German, French, and English may be used for this purpose, most of music's better-known tempo terms are given in Italian. Here is a list of the most common,[6] with a citation of representative works wherein they are used:

TABLE 1. *Terms Indicating Tempo.*

Term	Meaning	Example
presto	very fast	Glinka: Overture, *Ruslan and Ludmilla*
vivace	lively	Tchaikowsky: "Trepak," *The Nutcracker Suite*
allegro	fast	Tchaikowsky: *Ouverture Miniature, The Nutcracker Suite*
moderato	moderate	Tchaikowsky: "Dance of the Reed Flutes," *The Nutcracker Suite*
andante	moderately slow	Tchaikowsky: "Dance of the Sugar Plum," *The Nutcracker Suite*
adagio	slow	Chopin: "Funeral March," Sonata No. 2 in B-flat minor
largo	very slow	Dvořák: Symphony No. 9 ("New World"), second movement
grave	extremely slow	Bach: Overture, Suite No. 2 in B minor

Each term can be modified. A superlative, indicated by adding the suffix *issimo* to the basic word, heightens its meaning; thus, *prestissimo* is faster than *presto*, whereas *adagissimo* is slower than *adagio*. Each also has a diminutive degree indicated by appending *etto*. Thus, *adagietto* is not quite as slow as *adagio*, whereas *allegretto* is not as fast as *allegro*.

Occasional deviations from an even pace are known as (1) *accelerando*, an increase in tempo; (2) *ritardando*, or simply *ritard*, a slowing of pace; (3) *ritenuto*, a holding back; and (4) *rubato*, literally "robbed time," wherein the pulse may hasten or linger in a give-and-take manner. *Accelerando* is frequently used in climactic moments when tension is mounting; conversely, a *ritard* may appear during moments of relaxation, or near the end of a work. *Ritenuto* and *rubato* are employed to break the rigidity of a

[6] For a more comprehensive listing, see Appendix B, "A Glossary of Musical Terms."

fixed pulse and often appear in solo passages or in works for such individual instruments as piano or organ. Numerous other signs convey interpretative suggestions to a performer, and any well-written score will contain an abundance of them. Appendix B, "A Glossary of Musical Terms," lists those in common use.

Credited to Johann Maelzel, who obtained a patent for the device in 1816, the *metronome* is a precise means of indicating tempo. Equipped with a pendulum, calibrated scale, sliding weight, and clocklike mechanism, this machine is capable of establishing any rate of speed between 40 and 208 beats a minute.[7] Beethoven, more than anyone active during the era (he was a friend as well as a contemporary of Maelzel), adopted the practice of indicating metronomic rates in his scores, and many subsequent composers have followed his example.[8]

Tempo has a great deal to do with expressing the character and mood of a piece, and musicians expend great care in determining the precise speed at which a work should be performed. Compositions in fast tempo, for instance, tend to be joyous and stimulating, whereas those in slower tempos are often profound, dignified, and meditative. As with other musical qualities, however, tempos are influenced by a number of extraneous factors for harmonization, melodic movement, or coloration also assist in conveying altered shades of expressiveness.

METER

In addition to flowing at distinctive rates of speed, the rhythmic pulse may also display degrees of accentual stress. Such an interplay between accented and nonaccented beats gives music an organizational scheme known as *meter*, of which four kinds are primary:

1. Duple, counted as *ONE*, two.
2. Triple, counted as *ONE*, two, three.
3. Quadruple, counted as *ONE*, two, *three*, four.
4. Sextuple, counted as *ONE*, two, three, *four*, five, six.

Note that the first beat in any of these patterns receives the principal accent, while the third and fourth beats, respectively, in quadruple and sextuple meter receive a secondary accent. Because of this, duple and triple are referred to as *simple meter*, while the others are known as *compound meter*. Quintuple meter (with five recurrent pulsations) makes an occasional appearance. Such other metrical units as groups of seven, eight, nine, or more pulses are possible but rare.

[7] Recently, an electronic metronome, which adds a flashing light to the traditional audible clicks, has come on the market; a smaller metronome, similar in appearance to a pocket watch, is also available.

[8] Earlier, Maelzel had constructed a chronometer, at whose rigid ticks Beethoven poked sly fun in the second movement, *allegretto*, of his Symphony No. 8 in F major.

One unit of the meter is called a *measure*. Aural recognition of successive measures is made by perceiving the stress that falls on the first beat of each; their visual separation in a written score is easy, for a heavy upright, called a *barline*, divides one from another. In performance, no pause ensues between measures, for a composition's continuous forward thrust effectively integrates them into a cohesive whole.

Before beginning to write, a composer selects the meter best suited to his expressive intent, and usually adheres to this pattern throughout a work. Consequently, most conventional music has the same meter from beginning to end. But it is possible to interject metrical change along the way, and compositions that are lengthy, complex, or unorthodox may contain a number of shifts. A primary reason for adopting changing meter is to avoid rigid accentual patterns and the singsong effect they tend to induce. Although numerous twentieth-century compositions employ frequent metrical change, the concept of free rhythmic movement is as old as music itself. Beautiful examples of unencumbered rhythmic flow exist, for instance, in the repertoire of ancient religious chants.

Prosaic music usually has rather uniform rhythmic characteristics. Nearly all marches, for instance, are in *allegro* tempo and duple meter (although notable exceptions exist in ceremonial or grand marches). To further illustrate the pervasiveness of common metrical patterns, here are some well-known dances grouped according to the meter each employs:

1. *Duple:* polka, habanera, pavane (some are in quadruple), galop, can-can, trepak, tango (sometimes quadruple).
2. *Triple:* minuet, waltz, sarabande, bolero, mazurka, polonaise, courante, seguidilla.
3. *Quadruple:* fox trot and its various related dances, including the lindy, mambo, charleston, twist, and others.
4. *Sextuple* (with two or six beats in a measure): gigue, tarantella, saltarello.

Particular pieces that demonstrate these meters include:

1. *Duple:* Tchaikowsky: *Ouverture,* "Trepak," "Dance of the Sugar Plums," and "Dance of the Reed Flutes," *The Nutcracker Suite.*
2. *Triple:* Bach: Sarabande, Polonaise, and Minuet, Suite No. 2. Tchaikowsky: "Arabian Dance" and "Waltz of the Flowers," *The Nutcracker Suite.*
3. *Quadruple:* Bizet: *Prélude, Pastorale,* and Intermezzo, *L'Arlésienne:* Suites 1 and 2. Grieg: "Ase's Death," and "In the Hall of the Mountain King," *Peer Gynt Suite.*
4. *Sextuple:* Grieg: "Morning," *Peer Gynt Suite.* Offenbach: "Barcarolle," *The Tales of Hoffman.*

Schubert's *Marche militaire* and Sousa's *Washington Post March* are in duple meter. Another example of this basic pattern is the tangy "Champagne Polka" of Johann Strauss.[9] Its principal melodic strains are these:

"Voices of Spring," one of Strauss' most scintillating waltzes, is an example of triple meter. It is based on this succession of melodies:

[9] Similar pieces by this composer include: "Pizzicato Polka," "Annen Polka," "Tritsch-Tratsch (Chit-Chat) Polka," and "Thunder and Lightning Polka."

Following the *Ouverture miniature* in his *Nutcracker Suite,* Tchaikow-sky includes an invigorating *Marche.* Opening with a brilliant fanfare, it flows at a quick pace (marked *marcia viva*) in quadruple meter (as did Verdi's "Triumphal March" already mentioned). These are excerpts from its important melodic ideas:

For the opening section in his celebrated *Peer Gynt Suite,* Edvard Grieg employs "Morning," an evocative piece in sextuple meter. This is its principal theme:

SYNCOPATION

As we have seen, accentual stress normally falls on the first pulse of a measure, but it is also possible to (1) stress a beat other than the first or (2) accent tones that fall between the beats. In either case, this reassignment of emphasis is known as *syncopation.*

All kinds of music employ syncopation, but its exhilarating drive is especially noticeable in contemporary popular music and jazz. In dances ranging from fox trots to rhumbas, syncopated rhythms abound, and many jazz classics include a near-compendium of syncopated patterns.[10]

As he begins the *Menuet* (third movement) of his Symphony No. 4 in C minor, Franz Schubert effectively employs the bristling effects of syncopation. Placing primary stress on the third beat of the measure, he conveys this dynamic rhythmic pattern:

Bedrich Smetana employs a similar kind of syncopation in the "Furiant" from his opera, *The Bartered Bride*. This is how the dance begins:

RHYTHMIC VARIANTS

For the most part, rhythmic factors (pulse, tempo, meter) remain relatively stable during the course of a composition. Occasionally, however, refreshing change is engendered by shifting from a regular routine. A few of the possibilities include:

1. *Significant and/or abrupt changes in tempo,* notable in (a) the "Acceleration Waltz" by Johann Strauss; (b) "In the Hall of the Mountain King" from the *Peer Gynt Suite* by Edvard Grieg (both of which employ *accelerando*); and in (c) the "Hungarian Dance No. 5" by Johannes Brahms, which presents startling tempo changes while remaining in duple meter.[11]

[10] Leroy Anderson's "The Syncopated Clock," actually a fox trot, aptly demonstrates the effectiveness of an interrupted pulse (i.e., syncopation). Most clocks tick rather monotonously day after day, but Anderson's unregenerate timepiece (simulated in the orchestral score by a wood block) occasionally runs amok and displays interesting deviations from clocklike fidelity.

[11] Four sets of *Hungarian Dances* were compiled by Brahms for piano duet sometime around 1858. Later, in 1874, he arranged several (Nos. 1, 2, 10) for orchestra, a step subsequently followed by other musicians. All twenty-one of these dances are piquantly flavored and display captivating deviations from rhythmic orthodoxy.

2. *Shifting meter,* which appears in (a) the third movement of Beethoven's Symphony No. 6 ("Pastoral") with alternate sections in triple and duple meter; (b) the third movement of Gustav Holst's Suite No. 2 for Military Band, which changes meter from one measure to another (and is also heavily syncopated); and (c) the "Tunis-Nefta" section of Jacques Ibert's *Escales,* which shifts from triple to quadruple meter in successive measures.

3. *A use of quintuple meter,* effectively employed in (a) the lilting second movement of Tchaikowsky's Symphony No. 6 in B minor, or (b) the barbaric "Mars" from Gustav Holst's suite *The Planets.*

4. *Cross-rhythms and cross-accents,* which involve placing a stress on diverse beats in various musical parts, occur classically when a pianist plays different rhythms with his right and left hands, or in orchestral music when sundry instruments appear to work at cross purposes. Commonly used in a great amount of contemporary dance music, this technique can be illustrated by this notation:

5. *Polymeter* superimposes two metrical patterns as, for instance, when duple and triple meter are combined. Such a device has been known to all musical eras, but its use has become particularly prominent in the twentieth century. An example occurs in Charles Ives' "Putnam's Camp" from *Three Places in New England* where (among other examples) the well-known "British Grenadiers," in duple meter, is superimposed at the half measure above a quadruple pattern. [12]

COMPOSITE WORKS

Particular works, ballet scores for instance, often include a number of rhythmically diverse subsections. As an example, consider the ballet music from Charles Gounod's opera *Faust* (1859).[13]

[12] Another example may be found in the Finale (fourth movement) of Gustav Holst's Suite No. 2 in F major for Military Band where duple and triple meter are juxtaposed.

[13] Other representative collections include the "Dance of the Hours" from Ponchielli's opera *La Gioconda,* or the "Polovtsian Dances" from Borodin's *Prince Igor.*

1. After a brusque, preemptory introduction, a smooth-flowing waltz (in triple meter) in *allegretto* tempo appears:

2. More darkly tinged, the second section is an *adagio* in quadruple meter. Its arching melodic line is quite restrained:

3. In succession, a spirited *allegretto* in duple meter appears. After a brief introduction, this melody is sounded:

4. Shifting to quadruple meter, the fourth section moves at a *maestoso* (majestic) pace and presents this theme:

5. Flowing with gay abandon in sextuple meter (with two beats in a measure) and marked *moderato con moto,* this section presents a sweeping tune:

6. An *allegretto* in duple meter is announced over a firm rhythmic base:

7. Finally, a spirit of bacchanalian revelry becomes apparent in a duple meter section marked *allegro vivo*. Its first theme is powerful and driving:

NATIONAL DANCES

Invariably founded on attractive pulsating rhythms, ethnic dances are an important part of any nation's sociocultural heritage. Virtually all countries possess a trove of folk dances, but such lands as Hungary, Spain, Norway, Croatia, Slovakia, Greece, Roumania, and Scotland have them in abundance. And in particular instances, some of these native dances have been edited, arranged, and scored for orchestra by outstanding musicians. Included are the *Hungarian Dances* by Johannes Brahms; the *Slavonic Dances* by Antonin Dvořák; *German Dances* (K. 509 and K. 600), by W. A. Mozart; *Norwegian Dances* by Edvard Grieg; *German Dances* by Joseph Haydn; *Scottish Dances* by Malcolm Arnold; *Spanish Dances* by Moritz Moszkowski; *Roumanian Folk Dances* by Béla Bartók, and the *Galanta Dances* by Zoltan Kodály.[14]

Four of Dvořák's *Slavonic Dances* [15] demonstrate the beauties inherent in works of this kind. Written on the suggestion of Johannes Brahms (whose *Hungarian Dances* had previously won wide acclaim), Dvořák's pieces were originally scored for piano duet but later rearranged for orchestra. Here are details about four representative examples:

1. First in the series of *Slavonic Dances,* Opus 46, No. 1 is a furiant, a characteristic Czech dance in triple meter and *presto* tempo. Vigorously accented and heavily syncopated, it has an abundance of melodies:

---

[14] All are readily available in both printed and recorded form.

[15] Two series, each with eight separate pieces, were compiled and published as Opus 46 (1878), and Opus 72 (1887).

2. Distinctly different, "Slavonic Dance" No. 3, Opus 46 is a restrained Bohemian polka. Although some strains are played with animation, its predominant mood is one of tranquility. In duple meter and marked *poco allegro*, it begins with this melody:

3. Later, a new subject in a quicker tempo appears:

4. And a third idea is subsequently introduced by two trumpets:

5. Cast as a Polish mazurka, "Slavonic Dance" No. 2, Opus 72 is notable for its broad, sweeping lyricism. Established in triple meter and played

Figure 1.   Portion from the score of Varèse's *Ionisation* showing use of rhythmic notation.

allegretto grazioso, it is warm and gracious. These three subjects make frequent appearances:

6. Brisk, crisp, and driving, the fifteenth dance (Opus 72, No. 7) is a climactic Serbian *kolo*. Performed in duple meter at an *allegro vivace* tempo, it reflects the surging, exuberant vitality so characteristic of most folk dances. These are its principal melodies:

RHYTHMIC NOTATION

Properly speaking, music is an aural art communicated from performer to listener through the sense of hearing. And for untold thousands of years this was the method employed in passing pieces from one generation to another. In time, however, graphic methods of indicating musical details were formulated, and a system of notation gradually came into being. Now, anyone having to do with creating and promulgating music—composers, arrangers, editors, teachers—is continually required to inscribe musical symbols on the written page. And anyone having to do with performance—pianists, instrumentalists, singers, conductors, or students—is obliged to translate these symbols into living music. Written scores are extremely important in a flourishing musical culture for they permit easy communication from one musician to another, facilitate a wide circulation of pieces, and provide an accurate means of perpetuating music from one era to another.

Written symbols for musical tones are called *notes*. When imposed on a series of five parallel lines called a *staff*, they convey such information to a performer as: (1) the duration of tones (equated in a rhythmic sense); (2) the rise and fall of tones, as is characteristic of melody; and (3) the simultaneous combination of two or more tones, harmony. Other directions within a written score may deal with dynamic level, tempo and meter, articulations, or expressive directions. Usually, these suggestions are cited above or below the staff.

Parts written for most instruments and voice require only one staff, but some (for example, those for piano, organ, or harp) require two or sometimes three. Although notes are actually multidimensional and can convey a number of different directions to the reader, at this point we shall be concerned only with their rhythmic characteristics. These are the notes and *rests* (symbols for silence) that often appear in music:

TABLE 2.   Symbols for Notes and Rests.

	Note	Rest
Whole	𝅝	▬
Half	𝅗𝅥 𝅗𝅥	▬
Quarter	♩ ♩ ♩ ♩	𝄽
Eighth	♫ ♫ ♪ ♪ ♪ ♪	𝄾
Sixteenth	𝅘𝅥𝅯𝅘𝅥𝅯𝅘𝅥𝅯𝅘𝅥𝅯 𝅘𝅥𝅯𝅘𝅥𝅯𝅘𝅥𝅯𝅘𝅥𝅯 𝅘𝅥𝅯𝅘𝅥𝅯𝅘𝅥𝅯𝅘𝅥𝅯 𝅘𝅥𝅯𝅘𝅥𝅯𝅘𝅥𝅯𝅘𝅥𝅯	𝄿

An important determinant in any scheme of rhythmic valuation is the *meter signature*. This sign, which visually resembles a fraction, is placed at the beginning of a score, and at other points where the meter may be changed, and conveys two important facts: (1) the number of beats in a measure (expressed by the upper figure), and (2) the kind of a note that receives a beat (the lower number). These are common meter signatures:

TABLE 3. *Meter Signatures.*

2	3	4	3	6	2	3
4	4	4	8	8	2	2

Applying this information, it will be seen that the durational value of notes is directly contingent on the meter signature. In a given context— quadruple meter, for instance—a whole note will receive four beats, a half note two, a quarter note one, whereas two eighth notes or four sixteenth notes, respectively, constitute one beat. Of course, these values are equally applicable to rests. When the lower figure in a meter signature changes—to eight or two, for instance—necessary shifts must be accomplished that will give an eighth note (or a half note) one beat; altered valuations are then applied to other kinds of notes and their associated rests.

Rhythmic notation is far more complex than these few details would suggest. For instance, two or more notes may be bound together by a connective called a *tie*, or a note's value may be prolonged (by half its original duration) by placing a dot after it. And numerous other details may be included to assist in conveying a composer's intent. Fluency in reading and interpreting rhythmic notation is gained by training and experience. But handling the niceties and subtleties of music, whether in performance or creation, is strongly dependent on sensitivity and an innate instinct for aesthetic fitness. These, and associated qualities, are embraced in the term *musicianship*.

Some Compositions with Prominent Rhythmic Characteristics

Bartók, Béla. *Hungarian Sketches; Roumanian Folk Dances.*
Beethoven, Ludwig van. Piano Sonata No. 12 in A-flat major, second movement ("Funeral March").
Berlioz, Hector. "Hungarian March" from *The Damnation of Faust;* "The Trojan March" from *Les Troyens.*
Borodin, Alexander. "Polovtsian Dances" from *Prince Igor.*
Brahms, Johannes. Hungarian Dances (particularly Nos. 1, 3, 5, 6, 18, 19, 20).
Chopin, Frederic. Waltzes (15) for piano.
Elgar, Edward. *Pomp and Circumstance Marches* (Nos. 1 to 5).
Falla, Manuel de. "Ritual Fire Dance" from *El Amor Brujo.*
Meyerbeer, Giacomo. "Coronation March" from *Le Prophète.*

Mozart, W. A. Minuets (third movements) from Symphonies No. 35 in D major; No. 39 in E-flat major; and No. 40 in G minor.

Ravel, Maurice. *Boléro*.

Saint-Saëns, Camille. *Marche Militaire Française* from the *Suite algérienne*.

Sibelius, Jean. *Valse triste*.

Shostakovich, Dmitri. Dances from *Age of Gold*.

Smetana, Bedrich. Dances from *The Bartered Bride*.

Strauss, Richard. Waltzes from *Der Rosenkavalier*.

Stravinsky, Igor. Excerpts from *L'Histoire du soldat*.

Tchaikowsky, Peter. Waltzes from *The Sleeping Beauty*.

Chapter 2

The Melody of Music

Music has a remarkable capacity to stimulate human imagination. Naturally, all its qualities are employed to further communicative ends, but one, *melody*, has been proven particularly effective in this regard. Unique to music, melody is the aural substance that falls most readily on a listener's ear; it is a distinctive succession of sounds that becomes firmly implanted in memory (particularly after being heard repeatedly), and is a tonal pattern that almost unfailingly elicits some emotive response from listener and performer alike. In brief, it is the essential subject matter of a composition.[1]

Occasionally referred to as *themes, tunes,* or *airs,* melodies are comprised of individual *tones* that succeed one another in a meaningful sequence. Tones, the musical sounds that fall on a listener's ear as he hears a piece of music, result when vibrations are set up within a prepared body, as, for instance, when strings on a violin or piano, reeds on an oboe or clarinet, or vocal cords in a human throat are called into play. All tones have the specific physical properties of (1) pitch, (2) duration, (3) intensity, and (4) quality (*timbre*). Pitch, perhaps the most essential of these, has to do with the highness or lowness of a sound and is directly related to the size of a vibrating body. Duration defines a tone's length—its expanse in time. Intensity describes the strength of a sound measured in degrees of loudness or softness, and quality is concerned with each tone's distinctive sonority.

Despite its composite nature, a single tone is usually devoid of real artistic meaning. To become expressive tones must move, and if this succession is distinctive and memorable, a melody results. In this process of movement melodic tones may (1) ascend, (2) fall, or (3) be repeated. Some melodies are obviously directional and follow an upward or down-

---

[1] In his *What to Listen for in Music* (New York: McGraw-Hill Book Company, Inc., 1957), the distinguished American composer, Aaron Copland says, ". . . the thing that takes the place of a story in music is, as a rule, the melody." (p. 7) For a longer discourse see Chapter 5 in the same book.

ward path, others tend to hover about a central point. Here are examples showing these several kinds of movement:

Melodies seem to have a destination; they begin, progress in a logical way, attain a climax, and conclude in a manner the ear finds satisfying.[2] In moving forward, tones may flow smoothly to adjacent neighbors, or leap up or down in an angular way. These melodies demonstrate both kinds of progression:

[2] This, of course, is a generalization and we must remember that melodic styles—like modes of dress, forms of government, or standards of conduct—differ decidedly from one era to another, from one culture to another, and even from one artistic strata (that is, the avant garde, jazz buffs, folk music aficionados) to another.

Range or *compass* refers to the over-all expanse of a melody, the distance between its lowest and highest tones. These are melodies of limited compass:

And these are wide-ranging melodies, often, but not invariably, associated with instrumental music:

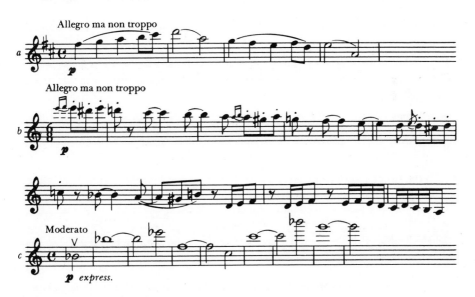

MELODY'S EXPRESSIVE POWER

Covering a broad spectrum of aesthetic suggestiveness, the emotive responses aroused by melody are almost endless. Moreover, the reactions they induce may differ rather considerably from one person to another in both degree and kind. Generally speaking, a pronounced sensitivity to the emotionality of music—that is, one's ability to perceive and react to its stimulus—is a remarkably good index of musicality.

Listen to the melodies in these six pieces. Obviously different in tonal flow and rhythmic activity, each suggests a distinctive emotional mood:

1. *Les Sylphides,* a graceful and poetic work founded on melodies written originally for the piano by Frederic Chopin [3] begins like this:

2. In contrast, the "Sabre Dance" from Aram Khachaturian's *Gayne* has a pulsating brashness that is almost barbaric:

3. On the other hand, Maurice Ravel's *Pavane pour infante défunte* (Pavane for a Dead Princess) is restrained and pensive.

[3] Sections in the best-known arrangement of *Les Sylphides* are taken from (1) the *Prélude* in A major, Opus 28, No. 7; (2) Nocturne in A-flat major, Opus 32, No. 2; (3) *Valse* in G-flat major, Opus 70, No. 1; (4) Mazurka in D major, Opus 33, No. 2; (5) Mazurka in C major, Opus 67, No. 3; (6) a reprise of the *Prélude* in A major; (7) *Valse* in C-sharp minor, Opus 64, No. 2; and the *Grande valse brillante* in E-flat major, Opus 18.

4. Two melodies employed by Serge Prokofiev in the *Gavotte* (third movement) of his *Classical Symphony* (1918) are rather austere in expression. Notice how one discloses a series of wide leaps, whereas the other has a very narrow range:

5. "The Water is Wide," a folk melody of tender charm, has this nostalgic melody:

6. And the "Popular Song" from *Façade* by William Walton, has a melodic freshness decidedly enhanced by crisp and piquant rhythms:

THE TONAL FRAMEWORK

When considered casually melodies seem to enjoy unhampered movement, but this presumed freedom is really an illusion. From first to last, each tone in a melodic sequence exists in a close-knit relationship with its fellows, and the hierarchy thus established assigns rank, function, and status to each. Conventional melodies are almost always organized around a pivotal point called the *tonic*. That point may be their first tone, the tone that recurs with greatest frequency, and more often than not is the tone on which they conclude. All that this association implies in both a melodic and harmonic sense is known as *key* or *tonality*. Although precise differences between the two are somewhat esoteric and technical, in general the key of a composition has to do with relationships existent between tones in a melody (or its correlative harmony), whereas tonality refers to an inter-alliance between two or more different keys.

The foundational tone in any key is its tonic. Examine this simple French folk song (quoted in the key of B-flat), and notice how the melody begins, hovers about, and concludes on this one tone:

And a smooth-flowing Russian folk melody, with a characteristic flavor we shall later identify as minor, shows a similar dependence on the tone A:

Written by Stephen Collins Foster, this melody does not begin on the tonic—D in this instance—but notice how often the latter recurs and how, at length, it becomes the final tone:

If he follows conventional practice, a composer chooses a particular key before beginning to write. Some practical considerations may influence his selection, involving, for instance, (1) ease of performance, (2) limitations of range, or (3) the characteristic "color" that musicians assign to particular keys. Once chosen, the key becomes a focal point for the composition, and its name is often used in identifying the piece—for example, Gershwin's Piano Concerto in F major or Beethoven's Symphony No. 5 in C minor. Lengthy compositions rarely remain in a single key over their entire expanse, however, and shift—by a technique known as *modulation* or key change—to other tonalities. When a melody appears in a new key its tonal alignment is not altered, but the subject is heard on a higher or lower level. To illustrate, consider this melody from the first movement of Schubert's Symphony No. 8 in B minor. Heard first in the key of G major, it appears later in D major:

Key and tonality are not limited to melody, but are significant in a harmonic sense as well. Actually, melody and harmony are strongly interdependent in virtually all kinds of music, and the characteristics of one greatly influence the other. Rhythm, of course, is of abiding importance to both.

MELODIC TYPES

Considered from a broad perspective, two kinds of melody exist: (1) the *theme*, a symmetric subject of perceptible breadth, and (2) the *motive*, a terse musical idea with pronounced rhythmic characteristics.

Themes are tuneful, repetitious, and usually attractive. Smooth and placid or brisk and active, they have an almost limitless expressive range. Themes having perceptible organizational patterns (that is, with balanced and recurrent sections) are called closed, whereas those whose patterns of repetition are nonexistent or haphazard are said to be open. As examples, consider these three beautifully conceived themes by Franz Schubert, the first two closed, the third open:

1. The melody that opens his Symphony No. 9 in C major:

2. The subject from the second movement of his Quartet in D minor ("Death and the Maiden"):

3. The opening theme from his art song "The Erlking":

Impressive, durable, and resilient, motives are constituted from a small cluster of tones—possibly from three to eight. Because subjects of this kind are necessarily terse, an initial quotation does little more than establish their identity; extensive reaffirmation, often called *working out*, is necessary to reveal a motive's full artistic potential. Rarely found in short works, motives are more typically employed in overtures, concertos, chamber music pieces, or symphonies. These are representative examples:

Themes and motives may appear side by side within a single composition, where the latter's succinctness contrasts with a theme's more expansive flow. Such a combination of ideas is illustrated in Glinka's overture to *Ruslan and Ludmilla,* a work founded on three subjects:

Themes appearing as foils to the epigrammatic motives in Beethoven's Symphony No. 5; Schubert's Symphony No. 9; Liszt's *Les Préludes;* and Franck's Symphony in D minor (all quoted on pages 28-29) are these:

MELODIC CHANGE

As lengthy compositions unfold, their melodic material may be modified in a number of ways. Although the techniques of melodic manipulation are many (some are discussed in subsequent chapters), four primary procedures should be mentioned here. Illustrated by passages in J. S. Bach's *The Art of Fugue,* they are concerned with:

1. *Sequential repetition* of a melodic idea on higher or lower scale levels, as is shown in "Contrapunctus IV":

2. *Inversion,* turning a subject topsy-turvy so that its contour progresses in a direction contrary to the original. Bach's subject is this:

3. But when inverted in "Contrapunctus VII," it appears like this:

4. *Diminution,* the constriction of a musical idea to shorten its rhythmic values, as occurs at the opening of "Contrapunctus VII":

5. *Augmentation,* an expanding of rhythmic values, exemplified near the end of "Contrapunctus VII":

MELODIC NOTATION

Tones, which are identified by the first seven letters of the alphabet: a, b, c, d, e, f, g, are brought into being when vibrations are set up within a prepared body, that is, a musical instrument. An a that exists about mid-way in the musical spectrum—near the middle of a keyboard, for instance—results when 440 vibrations per second [4] are actuated on a piano, violin, or similar instrument. Tones that are twice as high, or half as high—said to be an *octave* (eight tones) away from the original—are produced when the vibratory rate is double or halved, to 880 or 220 vibrations, respectively. A similar compounding over a half dozen (or more) octaves may be accomplished by applying this 2:1 ratio. In professional practice, however (piano-tuning, for instance), vibratory rates are trimmed slightly to achieve *tempered tuning.*

Along with indicating rhythmic valuation, notes (previously introduced in Chapter 1) may be inscribed on a staff to show the progression of tones in melodies or harmonies. A *clef sign,* written at the beginning of a staff, assigns letter names to the five lines, spaces between, and any extensions that may be added above or below by a use of *ledger lines.* Widely employed, the *treble* clef (sometimes called the g clef) appears in scores written for such relatively high-pitched instruments as violin, flute, clarinet, or soprano and alto voices. Those of lower pitch—'cello, trombone,

---

[4] Tones ascending from middle c (located at a midpoint on the piano keyboard), have these vibratory rates:

TABLE 4.   Vibratory rates.

c	261.63	f-sharp	369.99
c-sharp	277.18	g	392
d	293.66	g-sharp	415.30
d-sharp	311.13	a	440
e	329.63	a-sharp	466.16
f	349.23	b	493.88

or baritone and bass voices—use the *bass* clef (also known as the f clef).
Instruments of extended range—piano, organ, harp—use both:

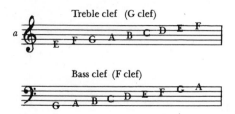

Treble clef (G clef)

Bass clef (F clef)

Known as the *alto* or *tenor* clef (occasionally called the c clef), a third
sign places middle c on either the third or fourth line. It is used mostly
by such middle-voiced instruments as viola or bassoon:

Alto clef   Tenor clef- (C clef)

Middle C   Middle C

THE GRAMMAR OF MELODY

Scales, from the Latin *scala* (ladder), are tonal arrangements whose
steps ascend or fall contiguously. For instance, the progression c, d, e, f, g, a,
b, c, is a scale, as is the sequence *do, re, mi, fa, sol, la, ti, do* (when accurately
sung). In actuality, scales are rearrangements of melodic tones, although
many themes clearly disclose a scalar outline.

An *interval* is the distance from one tone to another. Most are identified
numerically as seconds, thirds, fourths, fifths, sixths, and so on, but two in
particular are identified by name: (1) the half step, the smallest interval
employed in conventional Western music, and (2) the whole step.[5] Numerically, both are seconds. Here are examples of the most common musical
intervals, built upward from f:

2nd   3rd   4th   5th   6th   7th   8th

Precise details of intervallic reckoning are somewhat more complex than
this would indicate, however, for musicians more specifically identify them
as being major, minor, augmented, or diminished.

Each tone can be raised a half step by the use of a *sharp* (written as

[5] Also, the octave (actually an eighth), is conventionally given a title rather than
a number.

♯), or lowered a similar distance by employing a *flat* (written as ♭). A natural (♮) cancels either. Furthermore, a double sharp (x) or a double flat (♭♭) raises or lowers a tone a whole step.

Several scales are used in Western music, and each has an idiomatic sound resulting from the placement of whole and half steps within it. Two are primary: the *major* and the *minor*. Both divide the octave into eight segments but differ in internal organization.

Foundational to the greatest bulk of music heard today, the major scale has this pattern of intervals:

TABLE 5.   *Major Scale Interval Pattern.*

1	1	½	1	1	1	½
(whole-step)		(half-step)				

On a piano, this scale can be performed by playing upward from one c to another, using only white keys. Other major scales may begin and end on tones other than c, but in such instances, accidentals—sharps and flats—must be inserted to create the requisite pattern. In musical notation, a c-major scale looks like this:

Scales based on f and g appear thusly:

Minor scales are more complicated. Three forms exist: *natural, harmonic,* and *melodic* and differ slightly in tonal sequence. Here is an example of each, built on the tone e:

By analyzing the pattern of a harmonic minor scale, you will find its succession of intervals is:

TABLE 6. *Interval Succession for Harmonic Minor Scale.*

1	½	1	1	½	1½	½

Examples of well-known tunes in minor include "This Old Hammer," *B'Shuv Adonai* (When the Lord Restored Zion), "When Johnny Comes Marching Home," "Go Down Moses," or "Greensleeves:"

Some melodies, and many compositions in the larger forms, shift from major to minor (or vice versa) during their course of unfolding. Easily discernible instances appear in "The Erie Canal," a well-known folk melody, or the "Toreador's Song" from Bizet's opera *Carmen:*

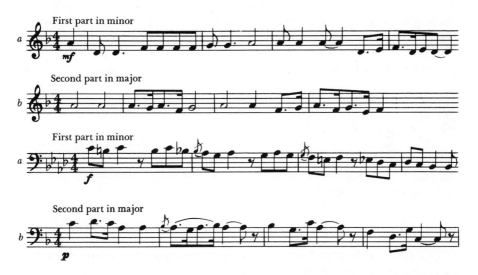

A *chromatic* scale is based on a sequence of half steps. As distinct from the eight-tone major and minor scales, it divides the octave into twelve equal segments. This is how a chromatic scale appears in notation:

As its name implies, the *whole-tone* scale is comprised entirely of whole steps. Here is an example:

Having become prominent in the seventeenth century (although it was actually formulated much earlier), the major-minor system has dominated music for well over three hundred years. In earlier times—among the ancient Hebrews, Greeks, Romans, and early Christians, for instance—other tonal patterns, called *modes,* were used.[6] Identified as *Dorian, Phrygian, Lydian, Mixolydian,* and *Hypodorian,* they have unique sounds resulting from unorthodox intervallic relationships between tones. Some approximation of modal sound may be gained by playing ascending patterns on the piano, starting from d, e, f, g, or b, using only white keys. (Playing from c, of course, would create a major scale, and ascending from a would sound the natural form of a minor scale.) [7] Melodies can be made modal by using a similar tactic: Select a familiar tune—say, "America"—and begin to play it, starting from any tone other than c. Do not strike any black keys, and you are bound to achieve exotic results!

Used in great amounts of ethnic music, the *pentatonic* (five-tone) scale has no half steps. Here is an example:

An easy way to perform a pentatonic scale is to begin on a piano's c-sharp and play upward, using only black keys.

KEYS AND KEY SIGNATURES

Conventional piano keyboards span eighty-eight keys. Here is what a two-octave segment looks like:

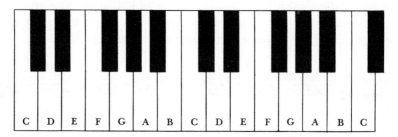

Notice that most white keys are separated by an intervening black key, but that this does not occur between e–f and b–c. Basic tones (a, b, c, d, e, f, g)

---

[6] An excellent explanation of modality, as well as a fine discourse on the general theoretic practice of music up to about A.D. 900, is given in *Man and His Music* by Alec Harman and Wilfrid Mellers (New York: Oxford University Press, 1962). Further information about modes, as well as a fascinating explanation of the melodic patterns most widely used today, can be found in *Harmony and Melody,* by Elie Siegmeister (Belmont, Calif.: Wadsworth Publishing Company, 1965), Vol. I.

[7] Modal melodies, incidentally, are often characterized by an absence of thirds. The thematic material in Ravel's *Pavane pour une infante défunte* (1899), quoted earlier in this chapter, is an example of this.

sound when white keys are struck, whereas many (but not all) of their accidentals (sharps and flats) are produced by striking black keys. Progressing from one adjacent piano key to another produces either a whole or a half step. If the keys are immediate neighbors, as are e–f or b–c, a half step is sounded; if a black key intervenes, as between c–d or a–b, for instance, the interval is a whole step. Progressing from a white key to an adjacent black key (or vice versa) consistently produces a half step.

On the keyboard, that key that sounds the sharp of a tone lies to the right of a primary key; conversely, one sounding the flat of a tone is to the left. For instance, c-sharp is produced by striking the black key immediately to the right of c; and f-sharp is sounded by moving to the right of f; but b-flat is sounded by going to the left of b; and e-flat is to the left of e. Two oddities appear: e-sharp is sounded by striking f, and f-flat is actually e; a similar relationship exists for the altered degrees of b and c. Other tones are also interrelated. Notice, for instance, that both c-sharp and d-flat are sounded by striking the same key, and the same holds true for d-sharp and e-flat, a-sharp and b-flat, and many others. These are known as *enharmonic relations*.

To retain the accepted pattern (1, 1, ½, 1, 1, 1, ½), major scales beginning on tones other than c must employ sharps or flats to alter particular steps. When collated and cited at the beginning of a staff, these accidentals become a *key signature*. Here is a table listing the signatures for all major keys (along with their relative minors): [8]

TABLE 7.   *Signatures of All Major Keys.*

Major Key	Minor Key	Number of Sharps or Flats	Key Signature
C	a	none	
G	e	one sharp	F♯
D	b	two sharps	F♯, C♯
A	f-sharp	three sharps	F♯, C♯, G♯
E	c-sharp	four sharps	F♯, C♯, G♯, D♯
B	g-sharp	five sharps	F♯, C♯, G♯, D♯, A♯
F-sharp	d-sharp	six sharps	F♯, C♯, G♯, D♯, A♯, E♯
G-flat	e-flat	six flats	B♭, E♭, A♭, D♭, G♭, C♭
D-flat	b-flat	five flats	B♭, E♭, A♭, D♭, G♭
A-flat	f	four flats	B♭, E♭, A♭, D♭
E-flat	c	three flats	B♭, E♭, A♭
B-flat	g	two flats	B♭, E♭
F	d	one flat	B♭

[8] *Relative minor* enjoys a common signature with an associated major key. Thus, G major and E minor both have a signature of one sharp and are "related." (See Table **7.**) *Parallel minor* results when major and minor share a common tonic. In this sense, c major and c minor are "parallel" because both begin on c; but they are not related for each has a different signature.

In musical notation, major scales appear like this:

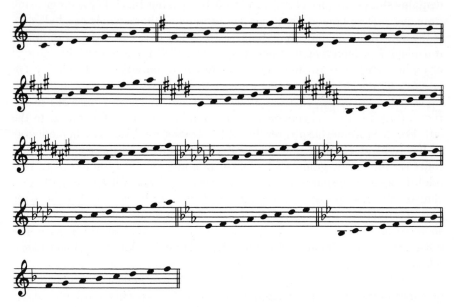

In addition to bearing alphabetical names (a, b, c, etc.) and numbers (1, 2, 3, etc.), scale steps also may be identified by title: (1) tonic, (2) supertonic, (3) mediant, (4) subdominant, (5) dominant, (6) submediant, (7) leading tone, and (8) tonic (an octave higher than the first step). All tones in a key have a role to fulfill, with principal emphasis accorded the tonic, secondary importance given the dominant, and a lesser position assigned the subdominant. This status is important in both a melodic and harmonic sense.

Some steps in a key seem to demand motion, whereas others are comparatively quiescent. Conflict and resolution, the invariable tension and release of all art, result from an interaction between them. To discern this interplay, consider the Scottish melody, "Auld Lang Syne," here laid in the key of F major:

Notice that it begins with a "pickup" on c—dominant in the key—but that the initial tone in the first measure is the tonic f. Observe how frequently the tonic recurs, how it is often preceded by the dominant or subdominant, and how other tones in the key are of lesser consequence. Finally, note that the melody concludes on the tonic.

THE MELODIC CADENCE

Taking its name from Latin where *cadere* means "to fall," the musical cadence is a point in a melodic line where accumulated tensions appear to find temporary or complete repose. Functionally, cadences serve as punctuation in a melody; they separate one segment from another, thereby making the musical flow more comprehensible. A definitive cadence occurs at the end of a piece where the melody almost always comes to rest on its tonic, usually preceded by steps seven, two, or five in the key. Cadences may appear elsewhere in a melody, where they suggest a partial suspension of activity. Identified as *authentic, plagal, perfect* or *imperfect,* various kinds of cadence are used in music. Each has individual characteristics, each serves to implement music's expressive intent, and each has both melodic and harmonic implications. (Details concerning the latter are mentioned in Chapter 3.)

A theme employed by Beethoven in the *Larghetto* (second movement) of his Symphony No. 2 in D major clearly demonstrates cadential use:

Notice how the first interruption, a partial cadence, occurs in the eighth measure, and that similar points of temporary repose appear in measures sixteen and twenty-four. Then, observe how the melody finally concludes on a full cadence in the thirty-second measure.

DYNAMICS

Remarkably effective in an expressive way, musical dynamics are concerned with various degrees of sonorous intensity. Two primary levels exist: (1) *forte* (f), loud, and (2) *piano* (p) soft. Each can be heightened by appending *issimo* to the basic word, or diminished by prefixing *mezzo*— that is, medium. These modifications provide six basic dynamic levels:

TABLE 8.   Basic Levels of Sonorous Intensity.

fortissimo	ff	very loud
forte	f	loud
mezzo-forte	mf	medium loud
mezzo-piano	mp	medium soft
piano	p	soft
pianissimo	pp	very soft

Gradations between these degrees may be used. *Crescendo,* meaning to grow louder, is indicated by the sign ══════ ;   *decrescendo*, becoming softer, is shown by ══════ . A combination of the two, actually an increase and diminution in volume, is indicated: ══════ ══════

Other directions that modify, temporarily, levels of intensity include:

TABLE 9.   Additional Directions to Modify Levels of Intensity.

accent	∧	a sharp, heavy stress
sforzando	sfz	attack in a forcible manner
forte-piano	fp	begin loudly, then fade
smorzando	smorz.	diminish

SIMPLE MELODIC PATTERNS

Meaningful melodic ideas, several measures long, are called *phrases*. Many melodies are constituted from a succession of two or more phrases (which may be either self-contained or related), and the words *antecedent* (for the first) and *consequent* (for the second) are applied to them. Two phrases comprise a *period*, and two of the latter create a *double period*. Phrase length, and the resultant expanse of periods and double periods, cannot be precisely specified. Although many phrases have four measures, others have three, five, six, or even more. Each normally terminates on a cadence (partial or full), which effectively separates one from another.

In the fourth movement of his Quintet in A major for Clarinet and Strings (K. 581), Mozart employs this melody:

Its organizational plan is:

TABLE 10.   *Organization of a Melody by Mozart.*

First Half (played twice)	Second Half (played twice)
first phrase + second phrase (antecedent + consequent) (four + four measures)	third phrase + second phrase (digression + consequent) (four + four measures)

When repetitions are observed, each half has sixteen measures; the melody's total expanse, therefore, is thirty-two measures.

To facilitate identification, alphabetical letters are usually applied to melodic segments: *a* indicates the first idea, *b* the second, *c* the third, and so on. Few melodies extend beyond these limits, however, for dangers are inherent in undue diffuseness. Melodies organized in this manner are said to be in *song form*, which is more accurately described as stanzaic or strophic form. When a subject has two segments (*ab*) it is in *binary* form; when three parts appear (*aba*, or *abc*, for instance) the design is *ternary*. Such schemes as *aa*, *abb*, or *aab*, are obvious permutations of either plan. Here are some well-known melodies that demonstrate the common patterns of simple song form:

1. Binary form, *ab:*

2. Ternary form, *aba:*

3. Ternary form, *abc:*

4. Ternary form, *aab:*

TONAL MEMORY

Individuals differ considerably in their ability to hear and remember melodies, a capacity known as *tonal memory*. For some fortunate persons a single hearing is sufficient to implant a tune so firmly in memory that it can be readily recalled and performed by singing, whistling, or playing on an instrument. Others have a shorter and less vivid memory span, and some are so deficient that they cannot remember a single tone long enough to reproduce it; they are often termed *monotones*.

Most people have a capacity somewhere between these extremes. Nearly everyone finds some enjoyment in listening to music; most hear it with pleasure, retain its imagery reasonably well, and affectionately recall the musical substance when opportunity permits. With training, by acquiring useful listening skills, and especially by cultivating the ability to concentrate on music as it is being performed, one can extend his powers to a remarkable degree. And, of course, deeper perception and greater reward result.

Some Compositions with Notable Melodic Qualities

Arensky, Anton. *Variations on a Theme by Tchaikowsky* (theme).
Bach, Johann Sebastian. Suite No. 2 in B minor for Flute and Strings: *Rondeau, Sarabande, Bourrée I, Menuet*.
Bartók, Béla. *Contrasts for Violin, Clarinet, and Piano* (1938).
Bizet, Georges. *L'Arlésienne:* Suite No. 1.
Chopin, Frederic. *Études* for Piano, Opus 10 and 25.
Debussy, Claude. *Afternoon of a Faun; Suite bergamasque.*
Dvořák, Antonin. *Slavonic Dances.*
Handel, George. Excerpts from *The Water Music.*
Haydn, Franz Joseph. Quartet in C major ("Emperor"), second movement.
Hindemith, Paul. *Kleine Kammermusik*, Opus 24, No. 2.
Mendelssohn, Felix. Music for *A Midsummer Night's Dream.*
Mozart, Wolfgang A. Piano Sonata No. 11 (K. 331), first movement (theme).
Prokofiev, Serge. *Lieutenant Kije Suite* (1934).
Ravel, Maurice. *Mother Goose Suite.*
Schoenberg, Arnold. *Quintet for Wind Instruments* (1924).
Schubert, Franz. Quintet in A major ("Trout"), fourth movement.
Strauss, Johann. "Roses from the South"; "Voices of Spring."
Stravinsky, Igor. *Les noces* (1917–1923); *Symphony of Psalms* (1930).
Tchaikowsky, Peter. *The Nutcracker Suite*, Opus 71a.

Chapter 3

The Texture of Music

In addition to having an existence in time (reflected in a composition's rhythmic aspects) and a rise or fall in pitch (melody), much of the music we hear today has aural depth that, in effect, gives it a third dimension. When melody is heard without any extraneous support it may sound shallow indeed, but when a composition includes several musical lines, or when melody is supported by a full-sounding substructure (that is, harmony), it takes on an obvious density. These can be described as *musical texture*.

Many cultures, modern as well as ancient, have been indifferent to the enrichment that density brings to music. In China, India, and Japan, for instance, as well as in ancient Greece and Rome, only rhythm and melody were employed. And the early Christians, too, used only a single melodic line while uttering the prayerful incantations important in their ritual of worship. But, as the Middle Ages passed into the Renaissance, and as the latter gave way to the Baroque period, innovational changes began to appear in Western music that brought *counterpoint* and *harmony* into being. As a result, three kinds of musical texture subsequently became known:

1. *Monophony,* literally single-voiced music, concerned with the unfoldment of only one melodic line.
2. *Polyphony,* or many-voiced music, which is created when two or more independent, or semi-independent, lines are sounded simultaneously.
3. *Homophony,* or like-sounding music, which results when a melody is supported by a complementary harmonic base.

MONOPHONY

Direct, incisive, often forcefully clear in expression, monophony was (and is) the only musical texture used by aboriginal people. Such *unisonal* music can throb with intensity and convey a variety of fervid emotional states, as in tribal chants, or it can float easily and gracefully to suggest seraphic other-worldliness, as in prayerful incantation. Thousands of monophonic pieces were created by ancient peoples, but, because these melodies were handed down from one generation to another by aural means, virtually all have passed into oblivion. Only in some of the native music available today—in Africa, Australia, or the Far East, for instance— can glimpses of this ancient art be observed.

Centuries before the birth of Christ, monophonic cantillation (oral prayer) was employed in the old Hebrew Temple. When Christianity emerged this same practice, with a linguistic change to Latin, was continued in the new religion. In rather short order, four kinds of Christian psalmody —known as Ambrosian, Mozarabic, Gallican, and Gregorian (Roman) [1]— arose. Although each differs slightly from its associates in melodic flow, modal pattern, or manner of execution, all are as one in being totally mono-phonic. These brief representative samples are included in *A Treasury of Early Music:*

1. Ambrosian chant. *Redde mihi,* a psalmellus for Quadragesima Sunday:

2. Gallican chant. An *Improperia* for the Mass on Good Friday:

3. Mozarabic chant. *Gaudete populi,* an antiphon for the Mass on Easter:

4. Gregorian chant. A hymn, *Veni Creator Spiritus,* for second vespers on Whitsunday:

[1] Further details on these (and others) are mentioned in Chapter 16. Splendid examples of earlier (pre-1750) music in both printed and recorded form are contained within *Masterpieces of Music Before 1750,* by Carl Parrish and John F. Ohl (1951); and *A Treasury of Early Music* by Parrish (1958), both published by W. W. Norton & Co., Inc., New York.

For several centuries this considerable body of Christian chant existed in an unorganized state, but during the pontificate of Gregory I (A.D. 590–604) much of it was collected and inscribed on parchment manuscripts using the neumatic notation that had developed by this time. Through succeeding centuries it has become a treasured legacy, and is today the primary musical language used in rituals of the Roman Catholic church.[2]

Figure 2. Italian 19th century music stand complete with bound volume of Gregorian manuscripts.

For approximately a thousand years in the Christian era, monophony was the only kind of music known in either sacred and secular life. It was used, for instance, by wandering minstrels—known variously as trouvères, troubadours, minnesingers, and (later) meistersingers—who journeyed through Western Europe after the eleventh century singing songs of love and adventure. A trouvère song, *Or la truix trop dure te* [3] (I find it difficult

---

[2] An entire ceremony intoned in Gregorian plainsong, *Missa in Festo Pentecostes*, has been recorded on Archive (ARC 73203).

[3] Quoted in Parrish and Ohl, *op. cit.*

to woo her), a *virelai* (that is, medieval French song) dating from the twelfth or thirteenth century is entirely monophonic and uses this melody:

Representative examples of monophonic instrumental pieces from a later era exist in J. S. Bach's sonatas (3) and partitas (3) for unaccompanied violin, as well as his suites (6) for unaccompanied 'cello. Two specific illustrations, the Bourrées I and II from the Suite No. 3 in the latter collection (written about 1720), demonstrate an unencumbered monophonic flow:

Occurring in a work otherwise notable for harmonic richness, a haunting melody for solo English horn appears near the beginning of Act III in Richard Wagner's opera *Tristan und Isolde* (1865). With simple eloquence it describes the pensive loneliness of a dolorous scene:

Monophonic passages may be used occasionally in large compositions, where their clear-sounding flow suggests vigor, power, or even subtlety.

Occasionally performed by a solo singer or instrumentalist, they are often assigned to members of a chorus or an orchestra who perform in unison. For example, a sizeable group of string and wind instruments performs this incisive unisonal passage during opening measures of the *Prélude* to Bizet's *L'Arlésienne:* Suite No. 1:

Similarly, unisonal passages are contrasted with harmonized ones in the "Intermezzo" of the *L'Arlésienne:* Suite No. 2. As this section begins, alternate four-measure segments—unisonal, harmonized, unisonal, harmonized—are heard:

And in the "Samuel Goldenberg and Schmuyle" section of Mussorgsky's *Pictures at an Exhibition,* woodwinds and strings play this solid-sounding eight-measure passage in unison:

Chopin's *Prélude* No. 14 in E-flat minor (for piano); Debussy's *Syrinx* for solo flute; Varèse's *Density 21.5* for the same instrument; Stravinsky's *Three Pieces for Solo Clarinet;* and Bartók's *Sonata for Violin Unaccompanied* further exemplify monophonic texture in instrumental pieces.

POLYPHONY

Somewhat more than a thousand years ago tentative changes began to appear in music that ultimately transformed the relatively uncomplicated practices of monophony. One of these, *heterophony*—the modification of a melody by adding, omitting, prolonging, or shortening tones—had been known for centuries. But when alterations of this kind developed to a point where different voices (or instruments) were simultaneously sounding diverse tones while ostensibly performing the same tune, aspects of polyphony were in the offing.

In general, two possibilities rest at the heart of polyphonic music: (1) an interweaving of separate strands from a single melody so that two, three, four, or more individual parts (or voices) maintain a semi-independent status as a piece is being performed, or (2) the combining of two or more disparate melodies in simultaneous presentation.

Almost without fail, early polyphonic practices used a pre-existent melody, the *cantus firmus* (fixed song), and set a second line against it note for note. In those times, notes were called *points*, hence the procedure of combining one musical strand with another became known as *counterpoint*, a term still applied to the technique of writing polyphonic music. Then, as the concepts of polyphony spread, diverse designs arose. Naturally, early patterns were comparatively simple, but as centuries passed, other polyphonic designs became more and more complex. Chief among the contrapuntal structures that emerged between the tenth and seventeenth centuries are *organum*, canon and round, quodlibet, motet, madrigal, invention, and fugue.

Organum

Arising as early as the ninth century, *organum* became an important precursor of later polyphonic forms. Virtually all *organa* had a Gregorian melody—the *vox principalis* (principal voice)—to which a second line, the *vox organalis*, was added. Almost without exception, *organa* of this era conveyed religious texts in Latin. Then, over a span of about three centuries, four different kinds became known: [4]

1. *Parallel organum,* wherein a second voice moved at an interval of a fourth or fifth in similar motion with the basic Gregorian melody (except at the beginning and end of phrases).
2. *Free organum,* which arose shortly after 1050, permitted the second

[4] Examples of each that appear in the Parrish and Ohl, *Masterpieces of Music Before 1750* include: (1) *Rex caeli, Domine,* a parallel *organum* from the ninth century; (2) *Agnus Dei,* a twelfth-century free *organum;* (3) *Benedicamus Domino,* a twelfth-century florid *organum,* and (4) *Alleluya* by Perotinus, a measured *organum* in three voices.

voice to move freely (that is, at various distances from the original melody).

3. *Florid organum,* which apparently developed at the monastery of St. Martial in southern France, used a free-flowing and elaborate second voice (*duplum*) to embellish the melody, which was now called the *tenor.*

4. *Measured organum,* practiced by Leoninus (1130–1190), Perotinus (1150–1220), and their associates at Nôtre Dame in Paris, had fixed rhythmic qualities and was usually written in three or four parts.

Canon and Round

Known as early as the thirteenth century as a *rota* (wheel), the canon and round are musical patterns fully dependent on the imitation that results when a melodic line is echoed in one or more subsequent voices. Both designs are very well-known, and since their introduction both have appeared in the music of every age and nation. One of the earliest rounds, "Sumer Is Icumen In," reputed to have appeared in England in 1226,[5] has this melody:

Somewhat more familiar are such beloved rounds as "Three Blind Mice," *Frère Jacques,* and "Row Your Boat." Still another round, "How Lovely Is the Evening" has this melody:

[5] Although a well-known musicologist, the late Manfred Bukofzer, held that it appeared at a later date.

A simple two-part canon, "The Alphabet Song," wherein a second voice imitates the first one measure in arrears, appears like this:

Dona Nobis Pacem (Give Us Peace), an expressive three-voice canon, has lines that can be termed *a, b, c:*

When this piece is performed, each voice begins at *a*. But because the second delays its entrance until the first has reached *b*, and the third waits until the first and second are at *b* and *c*, respectively, the accumulative effect is one of combining three lines to create a polyphonic edifice.

Rounds and canons have several characteristics in common:

1. Any group performing them is divided into sections, according to the number of lines, or voices, in the piece.
2. Each voice is introduced successively, not simultaneously.
3. Voices consistently imitate one another.

But they also differ in a number of ways:

1. Rounds are relatively short and simple; canons tend to be longer and more complex.
2. Rounds are obviously repetitious, canons less so.
3. Rounds employ exact imitation, whereas canons may be "strict" (with precise imitation) or "free" (with scale modifications—that is, "accidentals"—within the melody).
4. Rounds imitate in unison (or at the octave); canons, too, may be unisonal, but in some the imitative voices function on different scale levels—for example, in fourths or fifths above (or below) the original melody.

A brief canon by Wilhelm Friedemann Bach (a son of the great Johann Sebastian), can be played by any two soprano instruments (violins, recorders, clarinets, and so on) to show the design's relatively strict outlines:

Canonic writing appears occasionally within large works. In the finale of his Violin Sonata in A major, for example, César Franck uses this imitative pattern:

And in the Minuet (third movement) of his String Quartet in D minor, Opus 76, No. 2, Joseph Haydn divides his forces so that canonic imitation is carried out between a high voice (played by two violins) and a low one (played by viola and 'cello):

Early in the first act of Beethoven's opera, *Fidelio*, a canonic quartet, *Mir ist so wunderbar* (How wondrous is this mood), is heard. Each voice sings this melody when it enters:

Shortly after opening the Farandole (fourth movement) of his *L'Arlésienne: Suite No. 2*, Georges Bizet presents this brief canon:

The Quodlibet

Simple melodies are occasionally embellished by a descant, from *discantus* (singing away from) wherein a second totally independent melody (or possibly more) is performed simultaneously with the first. Regardless of disparity, these several tunes meet one important criterion: They sound well together. As well-known in the twentieth century as in the twelfth, descants for familiar melodies are often sung in school, church, around the campfire, in the banquet hall, or at hootenanannies.

Pieces employing descant are often called *quodlibets* (do what you wish). Merging two or more melodic lines in either a preconceived or extemporaneous manner, they combine well-known popular or folk tunes.[6] Widely used for generations, "The Orchestra Song" is a gay and charming quodlibet that combines five lines (*a, b, c, d, e*):

[6] Some common combinations in our era are (1) "The Old Folks at Home" with "Humoresque"; (2) "In the Good Old Summertime" with "On the Sidewalks of New York," or (3) "Put On Your Old Grey Bonnet" with "Annie Laurie."

When this piece is sung, the top line is initially performed alone; upon repetition, however, this melody is joined by a second voice singing the *b* tune. Subsequent repetitions enlist the remaining voices (*c, d, e*) in turn.

A more complex *quodlibet,* the sixteenth century *fricassee* (literally, a musical stew) of unknown authorship, is cited in *A Treasury of Early Music.* Employing snippets from dozens of works by then-contemporaneous composers, it is a grand musical mélange, textually as well as musically. This is how it begins:

A far more esoteric quodlibet, which combines two popular tunes of the day, appears as a final variation in J. S. Bach's *Goldberg Variations.*

The Motet

While the polyphonic style was being developed between the thirteenth and seventeenth centuries, musical instruments remained in an imperfect state. But vocal music blossomed as never before. And during this era the motet, a choral design of rare excellence, became exceptionally prominent. Originally sung in Roman Catholic churches during liturgical worship to convey sacred texts in Latin, motets changed so considerably as centuries passed that it is difficult, indeed impossible, to briefly postulate their specific characteristics.

Thirteenth-century motets were based on a Gregorian cantus firmus and written for three voices: (1) the *tenor,* which sang the melody; (2) the *motetus* or *duplum,* a second part; and (3) the *triplum,* a third part. Performed *a cappella* (unaccompanied), these religious pieces initially expressed exalted and profound ideas. Occasionally, however, some were bilingual. In these cases the Gregorian melody was used to convey a Latin liturgical text, but the added parts often employed French to express amorous, or even ribald sentiments.

Subsequently (from about 1300 to 1450), the *isorhythmic* motet, a pattern that maintained fixed rhythmic qualities in each part, became prominent. Constancy gave this kind of design a degree of stability among pieces that otherwise seemed to convey a hodgepodge of diverse subjects. An isorhythmic motet, *Veni Sancte Spiritus* (Come, Holy Spirit) by John Dunstable is contained in *A Treasury of Early Music*. Scored for two voices (with occasional instrumental interpolations), it begins in this manner:

At about this same time, the *conductus* appeared. Akin to the motet, it differed principally in being founded on a nonliturgic melody, and became, consequently, one of the first polyphonic designs to be free of a Gregorian *cantus firmus*. Covering a wide range of poetic matter from satire to amorous adventure, these Latin songs were usually written for one, two, or three voices.[7]

Between 1450 and 1600, the Renaissance motet, an unaccompanied work for four, five, or six voices, emerged. By now it had become an accepted practice to use original melodies in lieu of Gregorian subjects, although most motets continued to retain their sacred character. Of course, the practice of interweaving semi-independent lines in imitative and sequential patterns was retained. Among the outstanding composers of motets (and other contrapuntal works) of this and earlier eras were Guillaume de Machaut (1300–1377); John Dunstable (d. 1453); Guillaume Dufay (1400–1474); Johannes Okeghem (1430–1495); Josquin des Prez (1445–1521); Heinrich Isaac (1450–1517); Adrian Willaert (1480–1562); Nicholas Gombert (1500–1560); Orlando di Lasso (1532–1594); William Byrd (1542–1623); Tomas Luis de Victoria (1540–1613); and Hans Leo Hassler (1564–1612).

---

[7] *De castitatis thalamo* (From this chamber), a *conductus* from the thirteenth century, is included in Parrish and Ohl, *op. cit.*

While writing nearly 180 motets (as well as huge amounts of other vocal music), Giovanni Palestrina (1525–1594) brought the design to a peak of incredible beauty. Representative is his *Song of Songs*, a collection of twenty-nine motets for five voices based on texts from "The Song of Solomon." [8] *Nigra sum, sed formosa* (My beauty is raven but comely), third in the collection, begins like this:

Laudate Dominum (Praise the Lord), a polychoral motet for two four-part groups written by Hassler in 1591, is included in *A Treasury of Early Music*. Its opening subject, which appears successively in the tonic and dominant tonalities, is this:

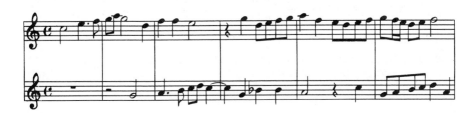

Subsequently, a more homophonic strain is interpolated:

[8] Twenty-one of these have been recorded by the Bach Guild (5059), and scores may be obtained from the World Library of Sacred Music, 2145 Central Parkway, Cincinnati, Ohio.

Shortly after 1720, J. S. Bach wrote six lengthy German-language motets for use at the St. Thomas Church in Leipzig. Requiring instrumental support (from organ or orchestra), four were scored for eight voices, one for five, and one for four. *Lobet den Herrn* (Praise the Lord), shortest in the set, demonstrates Bach's mastery of the polyphonic idiom. This is how it begins:

The Madrigal

Based on a secular poetic form known as the *mandriale,* which had a *ritornello* (recurrent refrain) and three or four stanzas in iambic pentameter, the madrigal made its first appearance in Italy during the fourteenth century. Petrarch (1304–1374) was among the poets who influenced this secular musical pattern, while Francesco Landini (1325–1397) and Jacopo da Bologna (precise dates unknown), two of his contemporaries, attained renown as madrigal composers. Works by these men are contained in the *Historical Anthology of Music* which was compiled by Archibald T. Davison and Willi Apel, and published by the Harvard University Press in 1947.

After 1550, five-part madrigals founded on imitative counterpoint became relatively standard. Although they are unusual in having religious (in Italian) rather than secular texts, a set of eight works published by Palestrina in 1581 based on Petrarch's "Song of the Virgin" aptly demonstrates the beauties of this design. Somewhat later, Carlo Gesualdo (1569–1613); Luca Marenzio (1553–1599); and Claudio Monteverdi (1567–1643) continued this work and wrote collections of madrigals that consistently display fascinating ingenuity.[9]

Spreading rapidly to other lands, the madrigal took firm root in France, Germany, and Spain. In England it attained an unusual state of popularity shortly before 1600 when two variants of the basic pattern were developed: (1) the *ayre,* less contrapuntal than a true madrigal and performed by a solo voice with support from instruments or other voices, and (2) the *ballett,* distinctive in its use of nonsense syllables (for example, fa-las). Among English madrigalists, Thomas Morely (1557–1603): "Now Is the

[9] Recorded examples are contained in Claudio Monteverdi: "Madrigals for Five Voices, Book I (1587)," Lyrichord LL43; and "Don Carlo Gesualdo, Prince of Madrigalists," Columbia KL 5718.

Month of Maying" and "Sing We and Chant It"; John Dowland (1563–
1626): "Come Again, Sweet Love Doth Now Invite"; Thomas Weelkes
(1575–1623): "On the Plains, Fairy Trains"; and Orlando Gibbons (1583–
1625): "The Silver Swan", are especially notable.

The Invention

Modest in intent and distinctly limited in scope, the instrumental invention is a short polyphonic form that nevertheless displays many of the
techniques employed in larger works. Imitation of a subject, exact or
modified, continually occurs in an invention as its basic idea passes through
diverse keys, or appears in inverted form. Some inventions have only a
single subject (sometimes a motive), whereas others have two.

Although others have written inventions, the design is best-known by
the two and three-part works (fifteen in each set) that J. S. Bach published
in 1723.[10] Compact musical vignettes, they have these general characteristics: [11]

1. As each begins, its subject(s) is introduced successively in the two (or
   three) voices.
2. While unfolding, each line consistently maintains its independence.
3. Presented in different registers—medium, high, or low—the subject(s)
   experiences frequent modulation.
4. Melodic alteration, particularly inversion, is common.

As an example consider Bach's Two-Part Invention in C major, whose
subject is introduced successively in the tonic and dominant keys:

A later excerpt shows (1) how the voices have become interwoven, (2)
shifts in key, and (3) inversions of the subject:

[10] Commonly known today as inventions, Bach actually called his collections
Praembula or *Invenzioni* (for the two-part works) and *Sinfonie* (for those in three
parts).
[11] Much common ground exists between the invention and canon. As a matter of
fact, Bach's Two-Part Invention No. 8 in F major is a canon in all but name.

The Fugue [12]

Based on a continual interweaving of horizontal strands and written in two, three, four, five, or even more voices, the fugue is unquestionably the most complex of polyphonic designs. Frequently austere in outline but rich and satisfying in expression, it is primarily concerned with the elaboration of a fundamental musical idea called the *subject*. Fugues also incorporate other ideas, however, including imitations of the theme in different tonal areas (for example, the dominant), which are called *answers*, or the interpolation of a *countersubject,* which may appear in juxtaposition against the main idea.

When a fugue is performed, the first section to appear is the *exposition* wherein the subject and its answers are announced by the several voices. Subsequently, an *episode* presents digressions away from the subject, including announcements of the countersubject. But the dynamic first theme continues to dominate the piece by reappearing frequently in a variety of contexts and keys. Some fugues have a third section known as the *stretto* or *codetta.* Unfailingly, the latter suggests a climactic effect, which occurs near the end of a fugue when the several lines are converging prior to a final citation of the subject.

Within a fugue, these procedures are usual:

1. The subject is introduced by one voice in the tonic key.
2. While the first line continues, the subject is "answered," that is, repeated on higher or lower scale levels (usually in the dominant tonality) by a second voice. This may be a "real" answer (exact), or a "tonal" answer (modified).
3. If material sounded by the first voice over the answer possesses sufficient individuality (and is heard more than once), it is called the countersubject.
4. Subsequent voices enter successively while the lines previously exposed are interwoven around them. Usually, the third voice sounds an octave below the first, the fourth an octave below the second. After the fourth voice has completed its presentation (assuming this is a four-voice fugue) the exposition has been traversed.
5. Succeeding episodes may introduce new material or exploit interesting ideas inherent in the countersubject.

[12] For an eminently readable (and reasonably detailed) treatment of fugue, see Douglass M. Green's *Form in Tonal Music* (New York: Holt, Rinehart & Winston, 1965).

6. Intermittently the subject appears, apparently in alteration with an episode; during this recurrence, modulation, augmentation, diminution, or inversion of the subject may be used.

7. In the episode's later stages, modulations begin to veer toward the home key where the subject and its allied topics are ultimately stated with vigor and finality. Typically the stretto, which suggests a "piling on" effect, occurs here when the subject seemingly becomes impatient and does not wait until the previous voice has concluded before making a new entrance.

8. At the fugue's end (in the codetta), the subject is reaffirmed in strong, resonant terms in the tonic key.

Few have equaled J. S. Bach in the composition of fugues. His *Art of Fugue* (1749), for example, is a definitive compendium of fugal techniques, and his *Well-Tempered Clavier* (1722 and 1744)—forty-eight works for keyboard, two each in all twenty-four major and minor keys—shows an astonishing fertility of invention. As a case in point, consider his Fugue in C minor from Book I of the latter collection, a concise three-voice work that begins in this manner:

Bach's "Little" Fugue in G minor,[13] written originally for organ but now often played in an orchestra transcription, clearly exemplifies characteristic fugal procedures.[14] These are details:

1. Sounded by a lone oboe,[15] the fugue's subject is presented in G minor:

[13] Other interesting examples of fugue may be found in the celebrated "Amen Chorus" (actually No. 52, the Finale) of Handel's oratorio, *Messiah;* the fourth movements of Haydn's Quartet in F minor, Opus 20, No. 5 and the Quartet in A major, Opus 20, No. 6 where they are marked *fugue a due Sogetti* and *fuga a 3 Sogetti,* respectively; "Achieved Is the Glorious Work" in Haydn's oratorio, *The Creation;* the *Kyrie eleison* in Mozart's *Requiem,* K. 626, and the Finale in his Symphony No. 41 in C major ("Jupiter"); the Finale (fourth movement) of Ernest Bloch's *Concerto Grosso No. 1 for Strings and Piano* (1925); and the opening movement of Dmitri Shostakovich's *Quintet for Piano and Strings* (1940).

[14] Another splendid (and relatively brief) example of Bach's craft in fugal writing is the Fugue in G major (known affectionately as "The Jig").

[15] In this analysis, I refer to the orchestral transcription issued by Leopold Stokowski (New York: Broude Bros., 1950).

2. Subsequently, an English horn announces the answer in the dominant tonality (D major), while the oboe weaves this countersubject around it:

3. In succession, the bassoon (in G minor, an octave below the first entry), and a combination of second bassoon, contrabassoon, and bass clarinet (in D, an octave below the answer), bring in the third and fourth voices, respectively. Then, without hesitancy, entry is made into the fugue's second section.
4. Principal emphasis in the episode is placed on this theme:

5. And the working out continues as subject, countersubject, and episode appear in juxtaposition with one another in a variety of keys and registers.
6. At length, after the stretto has introduced accumulative entrances of these several musical ideas, the codetta is attained and the subject is conclusively announced in strong, resolute terms. This fugue's final chord, incidentally, is in major, a characteristic of Bach's time:

Among fugal modifications that have grown up in music, these are reasonably common:

1. The *double fugue*, similar in most respects to a conventional fugue, differs by being based on two primary subjects. Although rare, triple and quadruple fugues have three or four subjects, respectively.
2. The *fughetta*, although shorter than a fugue, is otherwise quite similar. Occasionally found in symphonic movements, overtures, or other large musical structures, the fughetta is demonstrated in the second movement of Bizet's Symphony in C major.
3. The *fugato*, a passage written in a semifugal manner that does not, however, adhere to all the fugue's characteristics. Examples appear in the overtures to Mozart's *Magic Flute* and Smetana's *The Bartered Bride.*

Orchestral Polyphony

When two or more melodies are combined in simultaneous presentation within an instrumental work, orchestral polyphony results. Here are some examples:

1. In the "Farandole" of Bizet's *L'Arlésienne:* Suite No. 2, these two subjects are heard in successive sections:

2. Subsequently, they appear simultaneously.

3. In the second movement of Beethoven's Symphony No. 7, this unusually simple theme appears:

4. Later it is joined by another idea (played by violas and first 'cellos), and the two subjects are heard together:

5. In the March that concludes his First Suite in E-flat major for Military Band, Gustav Holst announces this initial theme:

6. Midway through the piece, a new idea appears:

7. Finally, they are combined:

8. *In the Steppes of Central Asia,* a descriptive work by Alexander Borodin, is based on two themes. Initially, this subject is heard:

9. Later, it is succeeded by another tune:

10. Ultimately, they are combined (in a new key):

HOMOPHONY

As years in the seventeenth century passed, a new texture, *homophony*, became increasingly important in the musical world, a change of the greatest significance to the ultimate emergence of opera, oratorio, the symphony, concerto, and associated patterns. Although polyphonic techniques have continued to appear in all kinds of music, the texture most commonly employed in the majority of works written since 1600 has shifted from an interweaving of horizontal strands to a concern with melody supported by vertical alignments of tones known as *chords*. This has given rise to *harmony*, an art concerned with the creation, manipulation, and linkage of chords.

These compositions clearly demonstrate homophonic texture:

1. During opening measures in the *Largo* (second movement) of his Symphony No. 9 in E minor ("From the New World"), Antonin Dvořák presents this succession of chords:

2. Subsequently, a nostalgic melody is announced by an English horn over a supportive harmony than unquestionably enhances the subject's beauty:

3. As an introduction to his *Marche slave,* Tchaikowsky sounds a series of
reiterated B-flats deep in the bass register. Atop this pulsating foundation, a pensive theme appears:

4. In successive passages, the theme is twice repeated and extended. When
this occurs, the substructure undergoes interesting rhythmic transformations:

5. In the opening strains of the Minuet in his *L'Arlésienne: Suite No. 2,*
Georges Bizet handles his material so that a harp provides an arpeggiated
background (with chordal tones played successively rather than simultaneously) over which a flute sounds this dreamy melody:

In homophonic music, melody and harmony are closely interrelated, and the supportive substructure a composer employs is almost totally governed by the work's thematic material. Often, the latter suggests chordal outlines, as is shown in Strauss' *Blue Danube Waltz:*

In conventional practice, chords are constituted from a series of superimposed thirds, built upward from a root. Those having three different tones are known as *triads;* those with four, five, or six different tones are known, respectively, as chords of the seventh, ninth, or eleventh—because of the scale steps that separate the root and uppermost member. Here are examples of each:

Chords are commonly based on the scale steps in a key and identified by Roman numerals (I, II, III, etc.), as well as by such names as tonic, supertonic, mediant, and so on. In the key of C major, for instance, a succession of triads appears like this:

Various kinds of chords exist; each has a distinctive sound, a stature in the harmonic hierarchy, and an expressive function to fulfill. Among triads there are (1) major, (2) minor, (3) diminished, and (4) augmented chords. Seventh, ninth, eleventh, and other chords may also be major, minor, augmented, or diminished. In any key, the I, IV, and V triads are major; II, III, and VI are minor; and VII is diminished. Numerous other embellishing chords, whose makeup is too complex to describe here, may also enrich a composition's harmonic color.[16]

Chords move in a sequence called a *progression.* As with melodic

---

[16] An excellent treatise on this subject is Walter Piston's *Harmony* (New York: W. W. Norton & Co., Inc., third edition, 1962), which has been written with college students in mind. Consult it for further details. Equally fine is Elie Siegmeister's two-volume *Harmony and Melody* (Belmont, Calif.: Wadsworth Publishing Company, 1965), which gives an even greater amount of information on the subject.

tones, some are active and demand continual movement, whereas others are comparatively quiescent. Interaction between them, in effect an interplay between aural tension and repose, imparts a unique aesthetic quality to homophonic compositions.

Accompaniment

In simple music, chords often move with the same rhythmic motion as melody. This happens, for instance, in "All Through the Night," a favorite Welsh hymn:

A similar circumstance prevails in the chorale (No. 63) "O Sacred Head Now Wounded" from J. S. Bach's *Passion According to St. Matthew:*

More often, however, a homophonic composition is based on a distinctive supporting pattern, actually a combination of harmonic depth and rhythmic thrust termed *accompaniment*. Particularly noticeable in dances and marches, accompaniment may appear in almost any kind of music.[17] As examples, consider the following:

1. A clear, supportive figuration underscores the lilting melodies of Schubert's *Moment Musical:*

---

[17] This is what happened, incidentally, in the *Marche slave;* Bizet's Minuet, and the *Blue Danube Waltz* mentioned here.

2. A standard waltz accompaniment appears in Strauss' *Tales from the Vienna Woods:*

3. Still another kind of accompaniment is used in the "Dance of the Sugar Plums" from Tchaikowsky's *Nutcracker Suite:* [18]

[18] Similar figures can be heard in the *Danse Arabe, Danse Chinoise,* and *Danse des Mirlitons* from this same work.

The Harmonic Cadence

Points of interruption in a composition's flow may suggest a temporary respite, or a complete cessation of activity. These are *cadences,* whose melodic implications were mentioned in Chapter 2. Within melodies, cadences often reflect a drop in pitch that gives the ear temporary release from the tensions that seemingly impel a theme forward. Somewhat more structural, harmonic cadences buttress a melody and greatly implement its scheme of tonal logic. Numerous types of harmonic cadence exist, but the most common are (1) perfect, (2) plagal, (3) imperfect, and (4) deceptive. Here are examples:

Perfect Authentic Cadence		Plagal Cadence		Imperfect Cadence		Deceptive Cadence	
V	I	IV	I	I	V	V	VI

Characteristically appearing at the end of a piece, a perfect cadence engenders a sense of finality as a result of melodic movement from steps seven to eight and a chordal progression from V to I. Often used to conclude hymns with the familiar "Amen," a plagal cadence retains the eighth step in its melody while chords progress from IV to I. Sometimes called a half cadence, the imperfect cadence is commonly used at points of temporary repose; in it, melodic steps go from eight to seven while the chords shift from I to V. Giving a false impression of conclusion, the deceptive cadence proceeds melodically from steps seven to eight (as in a full cadence), but the shift from a V to a VI chord deceives the ear and more musical action must ensue before a piece can be definitively closed.

Consonance and Dissonance

When two or more tones are sounded simultaneouly (as in harmonic intervals or chords), the aural result may be pleasant and tranquil or strident and cacophonous. And the effect they produce may be *consonant* or *dissonant*. Precisely what constitutes consonance or dissonance is variable and often unclear, for what one individual, culture, or era considers dissonant may not be so adjudged by associates or successors.

Both consonances and dissonances are used in all kinds of music. Consonances are stable and secure; the ear receives them with pleasure for their lovely sounds suggest clarity, order, and logic. But the bland pleasantness of unrelieved consonance tends to dull the senses; music also needs the contrast, stimulation, and pungency that dissonance brings.

In Western music, such intervals as thirds and sixths (both major and minor) are considered consonant; seconds and sevenths (also major and minor) are usually held to be dissonant, whereas fourths and fifths (both called perfect) occupy a middle position. Here are written examples of each:

These are only simple intervals, but when such tonal combinations are compounded into chords they express these same qualities. Major and minor chords, for instance, are consonant because they contain major and minor thirds:

But seventh chords—major, minor, dominant, and diminished—suggest dissonant tension for they emphasize the tangy sound of a seventh:

Virtually every composer displays the vitalizing interplay between consonance and dissonance in his pieces, but those active in successive epochs differ widely in their conception of what is dissonant and the frequency with which dissonances may appear. Generally speaking, the passing years have witnessed a liberating trend in this area. Harmonic practices barely tolerable in the eighteenth century became standard in the nineteenth, and are now considered old-fashioned. And because an unremitting quest aimed at the discovery of new sonorities continually beckons composers, it is virtually certain that the limits of music's tonal vocabulary will be greatly expanded in years to come.[19]

RECENT VENTURES

In the twentieth century many notions of conventional tonality have broken down. Seeking newness, some contemporary composers have been attracted to the cultures of earlier times to find exotic tonal flavor in the folk and near-primitive music of pre-Christian times. Modality and the pentatonic scale, for instance, have experienced a greatly renewed use in recent years. And experiments with microtones—intervals smaller than conventional half steps—widely employed in Oriental, Indian, and Near-Eastern music, have been carried out.

Polytonality, the simultaneous use of two (rarely more) keys, is a technique that contributes biting dissonance to a work. Often, it gives the ear an impression of hearing music on two different planes. Sometimes called *bitonality,* it has been used by such twentieth-century composers as Igor Stravinsky, Ralph Vaughan Williams, Béla Bartók, Darius Milhaud, and Charles Ives.

1. Clear examples of bitonality appear in two passages within Ives' Variations on "America" (1891) for Organ. The first occurs in an Interlude between Variations II and III:

2. And the second in an Interlude between Variations IV and V:

[19] For an amusing (and brief) example of a piquantly dissonant work, listen to the Polka from Shostakovich's ballet, *Age of Gold.*

3. Much of the harmonization that Ives uses in this work (and in many of his other pieces as well) is pungent to say the least.[20]

Atonality, literally an absence of tonality, arose as a compositional procedure early in the twentieth century, mostly as a result of efforts expended by Arnold Schoenberg and his followers. Although it denies tonality, a force that appears to be as natural in traditional music as gravity in the physical world, atonality has unquestionably opened exciting new vistas in music. The techniques used in this system are amazingly complex (and their permutations many), but some of its basic points are these:

1. Primacy is denied any one tone, key, or chord; within a composition employing the atonal method, there is no hierarchy of tones.
2. Melodic tones are chosen according to the composer's wishes from the twelve available in a chromatic scale; hence the name *dodecaphonic* (twelve-tone) often applied to this kind of writing.

[20] Further examples of bitonality (polytonality) appear in the "Funereal Vociferation" section of Milhaud's *Les Choëphores* (1916), in his *La Création du monde* (1923), where new keys are continuously imposed above a basic tonality of D minor, and in *Le Boeuf sur le toit* (1919), where a number of South American popular melodies are supported by accompaniments in foreign keys; in Ives' "The Housatonic at Stockbridge" from his *Three Places in New England,* where melodies played by the oboe, English horn and French horn are supported by violins playing in a different key; in the "Games of the Rival Cities" section of Stravinsky's *Le Sacre du printemps* (1913), and in opening measures of Bartók's *Sonata for Two Pianos and Percussion* (1937).

3. A composer may align these twelve tones in any sequence, but none may be repeated until the other eleven have been used. In this manner a *tone row* is created, which becomes, in the broadest sense, a composition's subject.
4. Tones in a row may be given diverse rhythmic values or may be placed in different registers.
5. A tone row may be (1) repeated, (2) inverted, (3) presented retrograde (backward), or (4) inverted retrograde.
6. Depth is acquired by contrapuntally combining two or more lines; each, of course, founded on the same tone row. Dissonances resulting from simultaneously sounding unrelated tones are not avoided but encouraged.
7. A row may be shifted to any step on the chromatic scale and appear in any (or all) of the versions mentioned here.

Despite the system's seeming inflexibility, considerable variety can be injected into a composition by: (1) using various polyphonic devices while combining the lines; (2) alternating versions of the row (retrograde with inversion, and so on); or (3) sounding members of the tone row simultaneously in a chordal rather than a linear fashion. Of course, the tone row is all-important. In atonal pieces it dominates the structure and functions in a role analogous to a *vox principalis* in *organum*, or the cantus firmus in a motet.

One of the earliest pieces to be modeled on the twelve-tone system, Schoenberg's *Quintet for Wind Instruments* (1924) clearly discloses the outline of a tone row in the opening measures of its first movement. Here is the primary idea, quoted in its four positions:

This is how the subject appears when fitted with rhythmic valuations:

Schoenberg's *Variations for Orchestra* (1928) is another example of *serial* (that is, atonal or twelve-tone) music.[21] It is based on this idea, which characteristically appears in the original, inverted and retrograde alignments, as well as on various pitch levels.

Fitted with rhythmic valuations, the subject appears initially like this:

Serial (atonal) compositions tend to be stridently dissonant, but many are unusually colorful and contain passages of striking beauty. Suggesting unrelieved tension, mostly founded on angular melodies, irregular rhythms, and harsh harmonies, they nevertheless reflect the musical syntax of our times. Like space exploration, jet propulsion, or atomic power, they have become an important adjunct of contemporary civilization.[22]

Some Compositions with Notable Textural Qualities

Bach, Johann Sebastian. Fugue in G major ("Great"); Overture from the Suite No. 1 in C major for Orchestra (three-voice fugue); Toccata and Fugue in D minor.

Bartók, Béla. *Concerto for Violin and Orchestra,* first movement (dissonance).

Copland, Aaron. *El Salón Mexico* (1936) (dissonance).

Dvořák, Antonin. Symphony No. 9 in E minor, second movement (homophony).

Haydn, Franz Joseph. Symphony No. 101 in D major ("Clock"), second movement (accompaniment).

Mozart, Wolfgang Amadeus. Serenade No. 12 in C minor, (K. 388), third movement (*Minuetto in canone*).

Paganini, Niccolo. *Caprices for Solo Violin* (monophonic).

Schoenberg, Arnold. *Serenade for Septet and Baritone,* (1923) fourth movement (atonal).

Tchaikowsky, Peter. Symphony No. 5 in E minor, second movement (homophony).

Verdi, Giuseppe. *Libera me* from *Messa da Requiem* (four-voice fugue).

[21] So too, is his Prelude to the *Genesis Suite* (1946).

[22] Delightfully exemplifying this mode of writing are Anton Webern's very brief but extremely colorful *Five Orchestral Pieces* (1913).

Chapter 4

The Instruments of Music

To become communicative, music must be performed. Only then can its substance be enjoyed, understood, criticized, or rejected. And for this purpose music enlists singers and instrumentalists of all kinds. Performance, of course, interpolates a "middle man" between composer and listener (unless an executant happens to be one or the other), and the interpretative factor he necessarily introduces is one of music's most interesting and variable aspects.

All musical instruments (and in this discussion we shall consider the voice as one) produce a characteristic *tonal quality* (their sonority or *timbre*) whose uniqueness makes it possible for a listener to aurally distinguish one from another. Resulting partly from the means employed in producing tone, timbre is also influenced by the instrument's materials (wood, metal, strings), the manner in which it is handled, and the skill of a performer.

"Pure" tone is rare. Except for sounds emitted by a tuning fork or special electronic devices, tones uttered by musical instruments have a composite nature—the result of sympathetic vibrations created above or below a principal tone. Known as *overtones*, these speak with varying degrees of strength when an instrument is handled, and they have a great deal to do with determining an instrument's sonority. To illustrate their mode of behavior, this is what happens when a string on a violin (or similar instrument) is forced to vibrate:

1. A fundamental tone, whose pitch is determined by the string's full vibrating length, sounds.
2. In addition to quivering over its full expanse, the string also oscillates in its several parts: halves, thirds, quarters, and so on.
3. Each vibrating segment produces its own tone; the halves utter a sound an octave higher than the fundamental, the thirds a fifth above the octave, and so on. These are *partials,* or overtones, of the basic sound.
4. Because it is strongest, the fundamental tone predominates, but the

partials make an impression on the ear, too. And their strength, presence, or absence (which differs from one instrument to another) considerably influences the resultant timbre.

A separate overtone series, but one that maintains regular intervallic relationships between its members, exists above each musical tone. Here, for example, are the partials that sound above a low c:

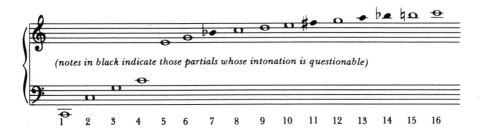

(notes in black indicate those partials whose intonation is questionable)

FAMILIES OF MUSICAL INSTRUMENTS

Orchestral instruments are commonly classified in four family groups: (1) string, (2) woodwind, (3) brass, and (4) percussion. In part, such a listing is based on the material from which an instrument is made, the principles underlying its performing technique, and/or the methods by which tone is produced. Some inconsistencies exist, however. Flutes and saxophones, for instance, although made of metal, are considered members of the woodwind family, whereas the piano, whose tone is produced by vibrating strings, is conventionally classified as a percussion instrument. Various well-known members of the plectrum group—guitar, mandolin, or banjo, and so on—as well as the accordion fall outside the pale of this discussion. Details concerning them should be sought elsewhere.[1]

Exceptions aside, these are the prominent members in each group:

1. *String:* violin, viola, violoncello (usually identified merely as 'cello), string bass (bass viol), and harp.
2. *Woodwind:* flute and piccolo, oboe and English horn, clarinet (which exists in several sizes), bassoon and contrabassoon, and saxophone (also in several sizes).
3. *Brass:* trumpet and cornet, horn (often termed the French horn), trombone and bass trombone, and tuba (manufactured in various shapes and sizes).
4. *Percussion:* timpani, celeste, xylophone, chimes, bells, snare drum, bass drum, cymbals, triangle, gong, and tambourine.

[1] An encyclopedic treatment of virtually all the instruments that have come into being with the forward sweep of Western civilization is contained in Curt Sachs' *The History of Musical Instruments* (New York: W. W. Norton & Co., Inc., 1940).

When considered separately, each group is remarkably self-contained and embraces instruments whose combined sonorities span a full tonal spectrum. Aligned according to compass, this is the range of members in the several families: [2]

TABLE 11. Range of Members in the Families of Instruments.

Voice	String [3]	Woodwind	Brass
soprano	violin	piccolo flute oboe clarinet	trumpet cornet
alto	viola	English horn alto saxophone alto clarinet	horn
tenor	'cello	bassoon bass clarinet tenor saxophone	trombone
bass	string bass	contrabassoon contrabass clarinet baritone saxophone	tuba

STRING INSTRUMENTS [4]

Except for the harp, members of the string family have a related performance technique. They resemble each another in general shape but differ in size. A violin is approximately twenty-three inches long, a viola twenty-six and a half inches, a 'cello forty-nine inches, and a string bass seventy-two inches. Each has four strings securely fastened at one end—on the violin and viola this is the point nearest a player's body when the instrument is tucked under the chin and held in playing position—and affixed to a tuning peg at the other. As each peg is rotated in an instrument's peg box, string tension is increased or decreased, and in this manner a player tunes the several strings to fixed pitches.

Normal performance on string instruments, called *arco,* requires the player to manipulate a *bow* with his right hand. A wooden shaft slightly concave in shape, approximately half an inch thick, and from twenty-four to twenty-six inches long, the bow is fitted with about one hundred strands of hair (horsehair or nylon thread) on its underside. After its strands have

[2] Percussion instruments do not readily fall into such a listing for many do not express pitches at all, whereas others are extremely specialized both in timbre and range.

[3] Because the harp's range spans all four voices (as is also pertinent with the piano or organ), no attempt has been made to include it within this chart.

[4] Two excellent paperback publications about musical instruments are readily available. You are urged to consult *Musical Instruments Through the Ages,* edited by Anthony Baines (Baltimore: Penguin Books, 1961); and *The Instruments of Music,* by Robert Donington (New York: Barnes & Noble, 1962).

Figure 3. Members of the string family (violin, top left; viola, directly below; 'cello, lower left; string bass, right).

been impregnated with rosin (to make them abrasive), a bow is drawn at a right angle across an instrument's strings, an act that causes the latter to vibrate. By stopping the strings (normal performance engages only one string at a time) at various points along the fingerboard with the fingers of his left hand, a player alternately lengthens or shortens their vibrating length, thus providing for the production of various pitches within an instrument's range.

Strings can also be activated by plucking, called *pizzicato*. Produced when a player temporarily lays aside his bow and picks (usually) with the index finger of his right hand, pizzicato produces tones that sound crisp, incisive, and somewhat brittle. Mostly employed as an occasional device, plucking is used at length in the "Pizzicato Polka" by Johann Strauss; in the third movement of Bartók's String Quartet No. 4; and in the third movement of Tchaikowsky's Symphony No. 4.

Although they normally play only single tones, string instruments can produce tonal combinations when two or more strings are simultaneously engaged via a procedure known as double, triple, or quadruple *stopping*. Numerous other techniques can also be employed in articulating tones, or in altering an instrument's sonority. For instance, bow strokes may vary in strength; mutes may be affixed to absorb vibrations from the strings; altered fingerings may be used to produce trills, grace notes, mordents, or other melodic ornaments; and *harmonics* (extremely high partials in the overtone series) may be sounded by particularized action of the bow and fingers.

Violin strings are tuned—progressing upward from the lowermost—to the pitches, g, d, a, e:

Capable of demonstrating extreme agility, with a wide range and remarkable expressive powers, the violin is one of music's most useful instruments. With a clear, sweet, and somewhat penetrating timbre in its upper reaches, like nearly all other instruments it reveals disparate hues in the mid and lower registers. A violin can, for instance, sound dolorous, weighty, and somber when the latter compass is called into play.

Almost identical in appearance with a violin, the viola is approximately one-fifth larger than its associate and has, consequently, a deeper, more resonant timbre. Its strings are tuned to c, g, d, a:

Although it can be eloquent, sensuous, and even passionate in utterance, more conventionally the viola behaves in a restrained manner while assuming a supporting role for the assertive violin.

Generally comparable in sonority with the adult male voice (although its range extends much higher than the latter), the 'cello is an eloquent instrument that sounds especially vibrant in its low register. So sizeable that it must rest on the floor supported by an elongated peg, the 'cello is played from a seated position while an executant cradles the instrument between his knees. Its four strings are tuned one octave below a viola to the pitches c, g, d, a:

Despite its size, the 'cello moves easily and can sound tender, gruff, impassioned, beseeching, or jovial as the occasion requires.

So large that a player must stand beside it while performing, the conventional string bass has four strings tuned to e, a, d, g, but a five-string instrument (which adds a low c) is so widely used that these can be considered the usual open strings:

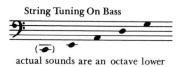

actual sounds are an octave lower

Bass strings are long and thick, they vibrate slowly, and the instrument speaks reluctantly. Consequently, its sonority, although foundational and important, is hardly gracious or pleasant. Occasionally effective in expressing heavy-handed humor, cynical raillery, or various kinds of grotesquerie, the string bass is characteristically assigned to supportive roles that stress its rhythmic and harmonic functions.

Totally divergent from other members of the string family, the harp has

Figure 4.   The harp.

an idiomatic timbre that is delicate, occasionally sensuous, and unfailingly crystalline. Often employed to provide rippling accompaniments supporting the voice or other solo instruments, the harp utters cascading arpeggios, wide-ranging leaps and fluent digital passages with ease. Structural strength is given the instrument's graceful frame by a statuesque front pillar and massive solid maple soundboard (the part that rests against a harpist when the instrument is in playing position). Across its body taut strings (forty-seven is the usual number) are stretched, which a player activates by pluck-ing with the fingers of either hand. By manipulating seven pedals in the instrument's base, he can alter string length to produce (1) a given tone, (2) its sharp, or (3) its flat. Interestingly enough, accuracy in performance is implemented by a simple device: Some harp strings are colored.[5]

WOODWIND INSTRUMENTS

Diverse in many respects, all woodwinds are actually open pipes en-closing a central tube (known as the *bore*), through which a player forces his breath as he engages in performance. Sonorities are brought into being when a player (1) blows across an open hole as on the flute and piccolo; (2) activates a double reed by the force of his breath as on an oboe, English horn, or bassoon; or (3) similarly forces a single reed into motion as on the clarinet or saxophone. Vibrations thus created pass down the tube, where they travel a greater or lesser length depending on how the instrument is fingered. Each instrument is pierced with a series of tone holes, whose precise location is determined by tuning and acoustical factors, from which the air column pours at the first opportunity. Over many of these openings a mech-anism is suspended, whose keys are manipulated by the fingers of a player's right and left hands. By blowing his breath through a woodwind instrument a player creates vibrations; by tonguing he articulates tones, and by finger-ing he causes the instrument to produce sounds of different pitch.

Endowed with a clear and limpid timbre, the flute moves fluently over a compass of three octaves. Vibrant, expressive, and somewhat mysterious in its lower register, the instrument has an eloquent mid-range, and a de-cidedly penetrating upper expanse. Capable of exhibiting extreme agility in performance, the flute is often assigned rapidly paced passages that require nimble dexterity for traversal. Half the size of a flute, the piccolo is operated in precisely the same manner, but tends to be breathy and hollow-sounding in its lower compass and shrill, pungent, and penetrating in the higher register. Rarely used in sentimental or lyric passages, the piccolo more typically plays an irrepressible, semihumorous role and is often used to etch a brilliant silvery edge atop the orchestra's full sonority.

[5] Should you be interested in exotic and/or ancient instruments, be sure to examine *The Showcase of Musical Instruments* (paperback) by Filippo Bonanni (New York: Dover Publications, Inc., 1964), a publication that first appeared in Rome in 1723.

Figure 5. Important members of the woodwind family (oboe, left; clarinet, center; flute and piccolo, right; small insert is a comparison between an oboe's double reed and a clarinet's single reed).

Oboes produce strong resonant tones that are plaintive, exotic, and somewhat nasal in sound. Ancestors of the instrument carry its lineage back to pre-Biblical times, although contemporary oboes are fully perfected and benefit greatly from modern manufacturing techniques. Because of its double reed, the oboe has a middle-voice sonority admirably suited for the conveyance of dolorous and pensive sentiments, but an agile technique and a rather surprising jocose nature also make it useful in lighter passages. Sharing a relationship with the oboe comparable to the violin-viola association, the English horn is a slightly larger and deeper-voiced double-reed instrument. Characteristic English horn sonority is somber and intense, and (especially in the lower register) its rhetorical powers are superb. Consequently, it is frequently employed to sound highly emotional, dark-hued solo passages.

Unquestionably the family's most versatile member, the clarinet has a compass of more than three octaves, a sonority that blends well with other instruments, and a fluency that makes it extremely useful in each register.

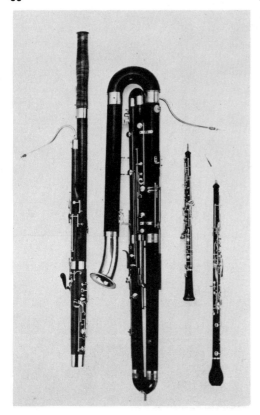

Figure 6. Double reed members of the woodwind family (from left to right: bassoon, double bassoon, oboe, English horn).

The lowermost of these—called the *chalumeau*—has a dark, woody, and rather mysterious quality of sound; the mid-range is full, pleasant, and resonant; and the upper compass is authoritative, ringing, and forceful. Clarinets of standard size are pitched in B-flat and A; but the smaller E-flat soprano and the larger E-flat alto, the B-flat bass, and even a contrabass in either E-flat or B-flat, make occasional appearances in orchestras and bands. Fitted with a beak-shaped mouthpiece to which a narrow strip of cane (that is, a single reed) is firmly affixed, the clarinet speaks when the latter is brought into motion. Because part of its mouthpiece (the face) is cut at a slight angle, a narrow open slit exists between the latter's tip and the end of a reed. Clasping this portion of the assemblage between his lips, the player forces a column of air through the aperture thereby causing the reed (which has been shaved to tissuelike thinness) to vibrate and produce tone. Sweet, pure, and attractive, clarinet sonority is also warm, expressive, and moving. Capable of sounding a ringing *fortissimo*, the instrument can maintain an astonishingly long sustained line, as well as diminish its sound to a barely perceptible *pianissimo*. Because it is so adaptable, the clarinet has become a veritable workhorse in the woodwind family.

Sometimes considered an orchestral clown, the bassoon is nevertheless a valued and versatile musical instrument. Sounding somewhat lugubrious in the extremely low register, it has a noble and clear middle range and an upper compass whose sonority tends to be thin and somewhat comic. Despite its size and rather antiquated fingering mechanism, this double-reed instrument moves with alacrity and finds consistent employment in both sustained and dexterous passages. Twice the size of a conventional bassoon, the contrabassoon is extremely cumbersome, unwieldy in operation, and uncertain in performance. But it contributes an unusually low voice to woodwind sonority and is employed (but infrequently) to obtain special tonal effects.

Comparative newcomers to the families of instruments, saxophones were perfected about 1840 by the Belgian inventor, Adolph Sax, who wished to provide French military bands with instruments that were both practical and fluent. Consequently, he developed a set of winds that could be manufactured from metal (to make them usable out of doors), were conical in bore (so they would speak easily), and were fitted with clarinet-like mouthpieces (so they would have a singing, vibrant tone). During ensuing years saxophones have become fixtures in dance orchestras, concert bands, and similar groups, but they have not gained a fixed place in symphony orchestras. Principal members are (1) the soprano in B-flat, (2) alto in E-flat, (3) tenor in B-flat, and (4) baritone in E-flat. Smaller and larger saxophones

Figure 7. Single reed members of the woodwind family (bass clarinet, left; B-flat clarinet, center; alto saxophone, right).

exist, but are seldom used. Over all, their sonority is vibrant and pleasing to the ear, but an unfortunate tendency to occasionally sound coarse has postponed their full acceptance in serious music.

Figure 8. Saxophones in various sizes (soprano, upper left; alto, upper right; baritone, lower left; tenor, lower right).

BRASS INSTRUMENTS

Constituted from graduated lengths of hollow tubing, each brass instrument is fitted with a cup-shaped metal mouthpiece that a player holds firmly against his lips while playing. By forcing his breath through tautly stretched lips (a formation called the *embouchure*) he causes the latter to vibrate or buzz, and the impulses thus created are passed down the tube from which they ultimately emerge as tone. Flaring outward with a graceful sweep, a *bell* at the far end of a brass instrument's tube serves to project its sound.

Tubing in brass instruments may be *conical*, that is with a gradual swell in circumference from one end of the pipe to the other, or *cylindrical*, with little increase in rotundity short of the bell. Conical brasses include the cornet, horn, and tuba. Each has a full, ingratiating quality of tone, as well as a fluent manner of speaking. On the other hand, the trumpet and trombone are provided with cylindrical tubes and have, consequently, a strong, penetrating timbre well suited for the expression of fanfares, martial music, or climactic effects.

Tones on brass instruments are produced by "buzzing," but a primary method of changing from one pitch to another is by employing partials in the overtone series. By merely varying the tension of his lips, as well as the strength of the air column, a brass player can produce a half dozen different tones. Familiar because of their employment in well-known bugle calls ("Assembly," "Taps," "Charge"), these are natural harmonics above a fundamental tone. Above c, for instance, without varying the length of an instrument's tube, a cornetist could sound:

Bugle Tones Above C

Since early in the nineteenth century, however, all brasses (except the trombone) have been fitted with additional lengths of tubing (usually three) that permit a downward extension of compass. Entrance of the air column into these extra loops is controlled by three piston (sometimes rotary) valves that a player manipulates with the fingers of his right hand (left hand for horns). By depressing the first valve (the one nearest his body), for instance, a cornetist brings enough additional tubing into operation to lower the instrument's pitch a whole step; used alone, the second valve drops it a half step; whereas the third extends the pitch downward a step and a half. When open tones (those played without fingering) are combined with fingered tones, a full range of chromatic sounds within the instrument's compass of more than two octaves can be produced. Here, for instance, is the fingering pattern employed on a cornet:

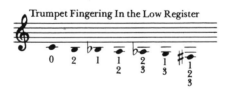

Trumpet Fingering In the Low Register

Additionally, any of the brasses can be fitted with *mutes*, devices that alter an instrument's timbre when firmly inserted into its bell. More than half a dozen different mutes are employed for the cornet, trumpet, and trombone; one does basic service for the horn and tuba (although the latter is rarely muted).

Similar in virtually all respects except bore, the cornet and trumpet are soprano members of the brass family. Perceptibly assertive in sonority, the trumpet is often used in music of a robust nature, whereas the dulcet cornet

Figure 9. Members of the brass family (trumpet, upper left; horn, center right; tuba, lower left; trombone, lower right).

is well-given to the performance of broad, gentle melodies. Fingering, performance technique, and method of blowing are identical, but each has a differently shaped mouthpiece required to coincide with the dimensions of its bore.

Possessed of a warm and attractive sonority, the horn is poetic and reserved in quiet passages, but it can become brassy and assertive when employed in the more sonorous degrees. Circular in shape, with a conical bore and a funnel-shaped mouthpiece, the modern horn is a direct descendent of instruments used in earlier times for signaling and at hunting forays. As the result of an unusual richness in overtones, the instrument has an opulent sound. However, this abundance greatly increases its complexity, for a player is thereby required to exercise great accuracy in performance.

Because it does not have a system of valves,[6] the trombone is operated differently from other brasses. Its mechanism consists of an elongated piece of tubing (called a *slide*), fitted over another tube of slightly smaller dimension (called a *stocking*). In theory, a player can place the slide anywhere on the stocking, but conventional practice assigns seven *positions* to

---

[6] A valve trombone exists, but it can hardly be termed a standard instrument in contemporary performing groups.

the instrument's operational technique. For instance, when the slide is extended outward in regularly ordained positions on a tenor trombone, this descending chromatic scale will sound:

Trombone Positions In the Low Register

As in other brasses, upward extension of the instrument's compass is accomplished by sounding partials above each fundamental tone. In general, the range of tones available to a trombone is comparable with the 'cello or male voice, but its projective power far exceeds either. Able to speak reiterated tones with ease, it moves over rapidly paced passages with remarkable agility. But the instrument unquestionably finds its most exalted use in an utterance of dignified and strongly resonant ideas.

Largest constituents in the family of brasses, tubas exist in diverse shapes and sizes. Some are upright and are comprised of lengths of rectangularly shaped tubing that ultimately flare into an upward pointing bell, whereas others (called bell-front) have a forward tilted bell for better projection of tone. Best-known are the *sousaphones*, instruments named after John Philip Sousa, who is said to have recommended shaping the tuba so that it would encircle a player's body, rest on his left shoulder (for easy portability), and finally expand into a bell directly above his head. As with other large bass instruments, tubas are cumbersome; their voice is gruff but resonant, their technique sometimes lumbering but accurate. Comparative latecomers to the orchestra, they were rarely used in music antedating the late nineteenth century. However, in more recent orchestral works, and as foundational instruments in wind bands, they have been proven extremely valuable.

PERCUSSION INSTRUMENTS

Because of their flamboyant mode of operation, percussion instruments often become a cynosure of attention when heard (and seen) in performance. Situated where they can be easily observed (usually at the rear of a band or orchestra), percussionists are often required to make large physical movements while manipulating their instruments, and this lends an aura of ostentation as well as authority to their acts.

Sound is produced on percussion instruments when some sort of physical blow is delivered to the object. Sometimes the instrument is struck with a stick or mallet (drums, timpani, or xylophone); shaken (tambourine); snapped (castanets); struck against itself (cymbals); or rattled (sleigh bells). Certain percussion instruments produce only idiomatic sounds that are devoid of genuine tonal attributes. These are the *untuned percussion,* a category that embraces a wide variety of apparatus including triangle, castanets, wood block, rachet, whistles of various kinds, whip, popgun, cymbals, tambourine, gong, snare drum, bass drum, and tom-tom.

Figure 10. Various percussion devices (gong, upper left; triangle, upper right; cymbals, lower center; from left on the bottom: maracas, castanets, tambourine, wood-block).

Among these, the drums are particularly useful. Existing in various sizes and shapes, they serve a number of musical purposes and are employed in such widely disparate groups as symphony orchestras, marching bands, or dance "combos." Possessed of a circular body (called the shell), a typical drum has two "heads" (of cowhide or plastic) stretched tautly over this frame and mounted in a manner that leaves the membrane free to vibrate when struck with a stick or mallet. Drum bodies differ in circumference and depth, a circumstance that alters the sound each emits. A bass drum, for instance, is about twenty-four inches in diameter and from fourteen to sixteen inches in depth; when struck with a padded mallet it produces a dull booming sound. About fifteen inches around and from six to eight inches deep, the snare drum utters a crisp, snappy sound because of "snares" (strands of metal wires) affixed to its underside. Scotch, tenor, and bongo drums are other apparatus in this category.

Figure 11. Various drums in the percussion family (top: tympani; center: bass drum; bottom: snare drum).

Cymbals are constituted from a single filament of brass thread circularly spun around a central point until a desired diameter has been attained. Slightly concave in shape, they may be mounted on a supporting pole that passes through their center hole or attached to handles that a player grasps while playing. In either case, cymbals are free to vibrate when struck (against one another, or with a mallet), and produce a clangorous, shimmering sound. Tiny finger cymbals may be only two or three inches in diameter, large gongs (closely akin to huge cymbals) may extend to twenty-eight or thirty inches, but the most commonly employed cymbals are from twelve to fourteen inches in size.

Far more valuable for general musical purposes are the *tuned percussion.* Including such instruments as timpani, glockenspiel, xylophone, chimes, and bells, they are capable of sounding pitches and, by extension, of playing melodies. Of course, each employs a percussion instrument's functional technique—they vibrate when struck.

Timpani are commonly called kettle-drums, which effectively describes their general appearance. Actually, they are shaped like sizeable copper kettles over which the head—formerly made of cowhide, but now more usually manufactured from plastic—is stretched while mounted on an adjustable mechanism. By applying pressure to this device, a player can increase or slacken the head's tension and thus cause it to emit sundry pitches when struck with a mallet. Timpani appear in sets of two, three, or four drums

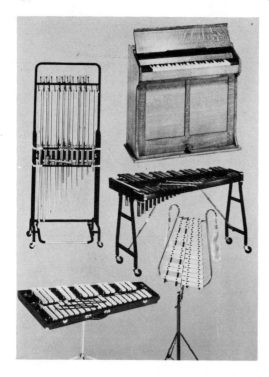

Figure 12. Tuned members of the percussion family (tubular chimes, upper left; celesta, upper right; xylophone, center; orchestra bells, lower left; glockenspiel, lower right).

(each can sound about a dozen different pitches) that graduate in size from twenty to thirty inches. Mallets used by a timpanist are made of different materials: hard rubber, felt, sponge rubber, or plastic. Because their resilience is of considerable importance in determining timpani sonority, a performer keeps several sets readily available.

Other tuned percussion fall into the category of *bar* instruments, for they are comprised of wooden or metal slabs of graduated size fitted over a tablelike frame. Among the most common are:

1. Glockenspiel, often termed the bell-lyre, which has from twenty to thirty chrome-plated metal bars mounted on a lyrelike frame. When struck they emit a high-pitched, penetrating sound.
2. Orchestra bells have bars similar in alignment and size to those on a glockenspiel, but differ by having them mounted in a small rectangular case. Bell sonority is, consequently, less strident.
3. Xylophone and marimba both have wooden bars. Dry-voiced and brash, xylophone timbre is more assertive than the sweet and gentle-sounding marimba. An associate, the vibra-harp (also known as the vibraphone), has metal bars, resonating tubes installed directly beneath them, and small motor-driven disks to assist in sustaining its tonal vibrations.
4. Tubular chimes, actually a set of hollow metal pipes suspended vertically

on a large frame, have a full-sounding timbre that is often employed to simulate a pealing of church bells.

5. Celesta, bearing an external resemblance to a small piano, has a set of metal bars mounted within a wooden case that are struck by hammers as a player manipulates its keys. Resultant tones are subdued, delicate, and rather ethereal in sound.

THE VOICE

Capable of expressing sentiments of the most intimate kind, the human voice is unquestionably music's most eloquent spokesman. Voices were man's first means of musical utterance, and for thousands of years they remained his only means of expression in this area. Interestingly enough, virtually every advance accomplished in perfecting instruments and their mode of performance through the years has resulted from emulating the voice. This has been carried over into pedagogy where students on strings, woodwinds, and brasses are continually admonished to "sing" as they perform in order to achieve a natural and artistic manner of expression.

Voices differ in timbre, sweetness, and accuracy. Many people sing easily and effectively; their voices are true in pitch and a joy to hear. Others are less gifted, and from an artistic viewpoint their efforts may be questionable. Nevertheless, almost everyone gains some enjoyment (to say nothing of emotional release) from singing, which remains today, as it has been for thousands of years, a direct and highly meaningful approach to music.

In choral activity, four categories of voice—determined principally on the basis of compass and partly in accordance with timbre—exist: (1) soprano, (2) contralto (usually abbreviated to alto), (3) tenor, and (4) bass. Because individual capacities vary, precise ranges cannot be specified, but Scholes, writing in *The Oxford Companion to Music* (p. 1099), cites a convenient way of remembering their typical expanse (See Appendix C, "Suggested Bibliography.") He gives the following as middle tones:

Middle Notes for Voices

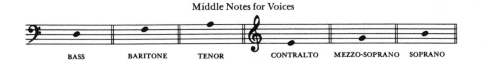

BASS   BARITONE   TENOR   CONTRALTO   MEZZO-SOPRANO   SOPRANO

and says that each voice normally extends an octave above and below these pitches. With training and experience, Scholes says, a voice can extend to a tenth in either direction.

In mature adults, women are sopranos or altos, and men are either tenors or basses. Children of both sexes possess a "childish treble" that hovers somewhere around the soprano and alto ranges until puberty (from age twelve to age fifteen), when boys' voices characteristically fall an octave in pitch.

In professional practice, numerous subdivisions are observed within the categories mentioned here. Primarily important in such areas as the theatre, opera, or broadcasting, these niceties are also pertinent in church music, operetta, or musical comedy. Here is a partial list of specialized voices:

Soprano

1. *Coloratura:* Often asked to execute brilliant pyrotechnics abounding with rapid scale runs and leaping arpeggios, this voice is capable of performing with sweeping bravura in an extremely high register. It is exemplified by the roles of Gilda in Verdi's *Rigoletto* and Violetta in his *La Traviata.*
2. *Lyric:* Required to be less agile than the coloratura, this voice has a warm and eloquent sound. It is demonstrated by Mimi in Puccini's *La Bohème* and Marguerite in Gounod's *Faust.*
3. *Dramatic:* Mostly asked to express passionate intensity, this middle-range voice has a smoldering, glowing intensity. It is effectively employed in parts assigned to Leonora in Beethoven's *Fidelio* and the title role in Puccini's *Tosca.*
4. *Mezzo:* Closely impinging on the contralto range, this vibrant and low-pitched voice is often used to suggest maturity, age, or sensuousness. It is effectively employed for the title roles in Bizet's *Carmen* and Saint-Saëns' *Samson et Dalila.*

Contralto

Variously used to suggest turbulent emotion or exalted dignity, the contralto voice is not customarily separated into subdivisions. Both Ameris in Verdi's *Aïda* and Azucena in his *Il Trovatore* are contralto roles; Brahms created his lovely *Alto Rhapsody* for this voice, and Mahler assigned it an important part in *Das Lied von der Erde* (The Song of the Earth).

Tenor

1. *Lyric:* Possessed of a smooth and pleasing timbre, this male voice may be compared with the lyric soprano in fluency and expressiveness although the two sound an octave apart. The Duke in Verdi's *Rigoletto*, or Rudolpho in Puccini's *La Bohème* are roles for lyric tenor.
2. *Robust:* Sometimes identified as a dramatic tenor, this voice is capable of conveying passionate emotional states ranging from unbridled elation to deep pathos. Don José in Bizet's *Carmen*, and the title role in Verdi's *Otello* illustrate it.
3. *Heroic:* Employed to sing extremely high vocal lines, this voice finds only occasional employment. Richard Wagner was especially fond of its capabilities and used it in the title roles for *Tristan und Isolde* and *Siegfried.*

Bass

1. *Baritone:* Reflecting a composite sonority that combines tenor and bass characteristics, this voice is frequently employed to convey impressions of maturity, courage, or manliness. Important roles for baritone are those of Escamillo in Bizet's *Carmen* and Figaro in Rossini's *Barber of Seville.*
2. *Lyric:* Sometimes known as a bass-baritone (or a *basso cantante*), this smoothly engaging voice is used in the title role of Mozart's *Don Giovanni,* for Sparafucile in Verdi's *Rigoletto,* and for Mephistopheles in Gounod's *Faust.*
3. *Basso buffo:* Used mostly for comic purposes to portray a pompous fool or a frightened clown, this dark-hued voice is employed for Dr. Bartolo in Rossini's *Barber of Seville* and Leporello in Mozart's *Don Giovanni.*
4. *Basso profondo:* Possessing the lowest compass in the vocal spectrum, this voice has been delightfully employed by Mozart for the role of Osmin in his *Abduction from the Seraglio.*

Voices and instruments may be employed separately, of course, but mostly they are combined for joint performance. In the chapters that follow, attention will center on pieces wherein their resources are merged.

Some Compositions that Demonstrate Musical Timbre

Recorded collections illustrating the sounds of diverse orchestral instruments:

Beckett, Wheeler. "The Complete Orchestra."
Britten, Benjamin. "The Young Person's Guide to the Orchestra."
Hanson, Howard. Vol. I: "The Composer and His Orchestra." Vol. II: "Mosaics."
Menuhin, Yehudi. "Instruments of the Orchestra" (issued by Capitol).
Randolph, David. "Instruments of the Orchestra" (issued by Vanguard).
Mitchell, Howard. "Instruments of the Orchestra" (issued by RCA Victor).

Works that feature individual instruments:

Strings

Violin: Beethoven. Concerto in D major.
Viola: Berlioz. *Harold in Italy.*
'Cello: Bloch. *Schelomo* (1915).
String Bass: Saint-Saëns. *Carnival of the Animals* (Elephant Section).
Harp: Ravel. *Introduction and Allegro* (1906).

Woodwinds

Flute: Mozart. Concerto in G major (K. 313).
Piccolo: Vivaldi. Concerto in C major.
Oboe: Cimarosa. *Concerto for Oboe and Strings.*
English horn: *Sibelius.* "The Swan of Tuonela."

Clarinet: Mozart. Concerto in A major (K. 622).
Bassoon: Mozart. Concerto in B-flat major (K. 191).
Saxophone: Ibert: *Concertino da Camera.*

Brass

Trumpet: Haydn. Concerto in E-flat major.
Horn: Mozart. Concertos (4) for horn.
Trombone: Rimsky-Korsakoff. Concerto for Trombone and Military Band.
Tuba: Mussorgsky-Ravel. *Pictures at an Exhibition* (Bydlo Section).

Percussion

All members of the family: Milhaud. Concerto for Percussion and Small
Orchestra (1930).

Operatic arias that exemplify characteristic vocal sonority:

Soprano: Delibes. "Bell Song" from *Lakme;* Rossini. *Una voce poca fa* from
The Barber of Seville; Verdi. *Ah forse lui* and *Sempre libera* from *La
Traviata.*

Contralto: Bizet. "Habanera" and "Seguidilla" from *Carmen;* Saint-Saëns.
Mon coeur s'ouvre a ta voix from *Samson et Dalila;* Verdi. *Stride la
vampa* from *Il Trovatore.*

Tenor: Leoncavallo. *Vesti la giubba* from *I Pagliacci;* Puccini. *Che gelida
manina* from *La Bohème;* Verdi. *Celeste Aïda* from *Aïda.*

Baritone: Bizet. "Toreador's Song" from *Carmen;* Rossini. *Largo al factotum*
from *The Barber of Seville;* Verdi. *Di Provenza il mar* from *La Traviata.*

Bass: Mozart. *La vendetta* from *The Marriage of Figaro;* Mussorgsky. "Mono-
logue" and "Death of Boris" from *Boris Godunov;* Rossini. *La calunnia e un
venticello* from *The Barber of Seville.*

Chapter 5

The Media of Music

Some musicians perform alone. This is especially true of pianists or organists, but others—violinists, 'cellists, clarinetists, or singers—occasionally engage in a solo discourse. More usually, however, most musicians combine their efforts and play (or sing) in orchestras, bands, choruses, or ensembles. Whether performing singly or in groups, they produce an idiomatic quality of sound (sonority) that becomes the actual tonal substance to fall on a listener's ear. In this sense, those who create sonority (the performers) are the means, or *media*, by which music becomes articulate and communicative. Obviously, they are an indispensable link between creator (composer) and receptor (listener).

As old as music itself, performance has been practiced for untold thousands of years. Initially, of course, primitive man used his voice, and wailed, screamed, or shouted as he besought protection in adversity or exulted in triumph. Somewhere in the early stages of human evolution man also learned to beat on hollow logs, scrape on jagged bones, or shake tinkling objects, and began to support his vocal acts with crude and noisy "accompaniments." Little is known about this activity, but information gleaned from art relics, cave drawings, and objects unearthed at excavation sites provides a fertile field for conjecture.

Millennia later (that is, from two to three thousand years before the coming of Christ), ancient Egyptians and their contemporaries supported a flourishing musical practice. Again, no actual musical examples remain, but numerous illustrations from this era show instrumentalists playing on pipes, tambours, and string instruments while others stand nearby obviously engaged in singing. Still later, Scripture narrates interesting details about a variety of musical acts. We learn, for instance, from the Old Testament of how David sang to his own harp accompaniments. And in the copious literature of ancient Greece the artistic proclivities of Homeric bards are precisely detailed.

During the late Middle Ages, wandering minstrels (who sang and occasionally performed on the lute) became extremely important in the social and cultural life of Western Europe, and at this time, soloists and choirs became actively engaged in performing liturgical music at monasteries, churches, and cathedrals. Mostly this was a choral art, engaged in by individuals or groups whose efforts were occasionally supported (accompanied) by keyboard and string instrumentalists. Sometime after 1500, however, instrumental performance gained prominence. An enormous proliferation then occurred that greatly increased the stature of keyboard instruments (organ, virginal, spinet), created an enormous vogue in the use of such string instruments as the lute and various sized viols, and paved the way for an eventual formulation of modern orchestras and associated ensembles.

When musical practices of the last four or five centuries are examined, four primary kinds of performing media become apparent: (1) solo instruments, (2) small instrumental ensembles, (3) large instrumental groups, and (4) various combinations of singers including solo voices, choral ensembles (often termed choirs), voices with instruments, and large choral organizations. Occasionally, two (or more) media may be intermingled (as in opera), when instruments, solo voices, vocal ensembles, and other choral groups are merged.

SOLO INSTRUMENTS

Almost any instrument can be used in a solo role, but some have been proven more effective in this capacity than others. Because of intrinsic limitations in their technique, fluency, or sonority, the trombone, string bass, tuba, contrabassoon, piccolo, several kinds of drum and similar percussion instruments are unable to sustain listener interest and rarely appear alone on the recital platform. On the other hand, these are excellent solo instruments:

Piano

With a compass of over seven octaves, astonishing technical possibilities, and a wide dynamic range, the piano successfully merges melody, harmony, accompaniment, counterpoint, and color in an eminently satisfactory manner. Bartolomeo Cristofori of Florence, Italy, perfected a mechanism in 1709 that allowed existent keyboard instruments to play loudly and softly. And he gave this new device, which incorporated other innovational changes, the name *pianoforte* (later contracted, of course, to piano). Housed in either grand or upright cases (with the frame installed in a horizontal or vertical plane, respectively), a piano is fitted with the familiar keyboard of eighty-eight white and black keys. When these are depressed by decisive motions from a player's fingers, felt-covered hammers deliver a blow to freely suspended (and previously tuned) strings, thus causing the latter to vibrate and produce tone. Piano sonority is greatest at this moment of impact, after which it fades unless renewed by further hammer strokes.

Figure 13.   Open view of a modern grand piano.

Literature for the piano is very extensive and greatly varied. Carl Phillip Emanuel and Johann Christian Bach (sons of Johann Sebastian) were among the first to explore its capabilities, and they were followed by such gifted composers as Franz Joseph Haydn (who wrote fifty-two piano sonatas), Wolfgang Amadeus Mozart (seventeen sonatas), and Ludwig van Beethoven (thirty-two sonatas). In the nineteenth and twentieth centuries, Franz Schubert, Felix Mendelssohn, Frederic Chopin (who wrote almost exclusively for the instrument), Franz Liszt, Johannes Brahms, Claude Debussy, Maurice Ravel, Arnold Shoenberg, Béla Bartók, Serge Prokofiev, and the American, Charles Ives, wrote volumes of unusually fine piano material. To gain some insight into the instrument's multifaceted expressive possibilities, listen to Chopin's *Waltzes* (fifteen), *Mazurkas* (fifty-one), or *Polonaises* (sixteen) for Piano, or Debussy's twenty-four *Preludes* for Piano, Books 1 and 2.

Organ

Even more self-contained than the piano, the organ has enjoyed a long existence. In ancient Greece and Rome a water organ (called a *hydraulis*) was known, and during the Middle Ages precursors of our modern instrument (fitted with a graduated array of pipes and a mechanical bellows to provide the requisite stream of air) became prominent, particularly at theological centers. Twentieth-century organs are of two kinds: wind and electronic. Complexities inherent in the construction and operation of a wind (often called a *pipe*) organ are almost unbelievable. Operated from a console at which the player sits while playing on its several keyboards (called manuals), a wind organ also includes several series of pipes (sizeable organs may have as many as five thousand individual pipes) through which columns of air (provided by electrically operated fans) are passed to produce sonority. Every wind organ is a custom installation, and because of size, initial cost, lack of mobility, and expensive maintenance, such an instrument is used mostly in large auditoriums, churches, or concert halls.

By comparison, the electronic organ is sturdy, compact, and comparatively trouble-free. Substituting transistors and vacuum tubes for a wind organ's cumbersome mechanical apparatus, it projects a diversity of tones through an electronic amplifying system. Because it is relatively modest in cost and yet capable of producing richly variegated music, this new kind of organ is widely used in small churches, homes, schools, restaurants, sports arenas, and similar places of public assembly.

During a "Golden Age" (c. 1600–1750), excellent organ compositions were written by such virtuosi as Jan Pieters Sweelinck (1562–1621); Girolamo Frescobaldi (1588–1643); Dietrich Buxtehude (1637–1707); J. S. Bach; and G. F. Handel. During the Romantic era (and continuing into the twentieth century), Felix Mendelssohn; Johannes Brahms; César Franck; Charles-Marie Widor (1844–1937); Max Reger (1873–1916); and Charles Ives also wrote generously for it. Among the compositions that combine organ with orchestra, Handel's sixteen concertos for organ and orchestra; Mozart's seventeen sonatas for organ and orchestra; Saint-Saëns' Symphony No. 3 in C minor; and Poulenc's Concerto in G minor for Organ, Strings, and Timpani (1938) are notable. In addition to the works of unparalleled excellence that J. S. Bach wrote for this "king of instruments" (e.g., the *Chorale Preludes,* the Toccata and Fugue in D minor), the Toccata from Widor's Symphony No. 5 in F minor and a nimble Scherzo in E minor by Gigout aptly demonstrate the instrument's capabilities.

Other Keyboard Instruments

Important among the piano's precursors are the virginal, clavichord, and harpsichord. Considerable similarity exists between them, for each has a series of strings stretched over a wooden frame housed in a trapezoid-shaped case. Divergent in size, one differs from another primarily in the means taken to activate its strings, and this, of course, causes each to have a distinctive timbre. Popular during the fifteenth and sixteenth centuries (particularly in England), the virginal quickly acquired an extensive literature, including such collections of pieces as "The Parthenia," the "Fitzwilliam Virginal Book," and "My Ladye Nevells Booke." Later, the clavichord became prominent, and numerous Baroque composers began to write for this charming instrument with such a crystalline quality of tone. Particularly distinguished clavichord pieces are the *French Suites* and *English Suites* (c. 1722, 1725) of J. S. Bach.

Somewhat more complex than its associates, the harpsichord has two (sometimes three) keyboards and several *stops*, contrivances that make it possible to vary the instrument's timbre. Important up until 1750, it enjoyed a fine literature whose principal contributors were Girolamo Frescobaldi and Domenico Scarlatti (Italy); François Couperin and Jean Philippe Rameau (France); and Johann Froberger and Johann Kaspar Fischer (Germany). In the twentieth century renewed interest has been shown the harpsichord, and such composers as Manuel de Falla, Francis Poulenc, and Elliott Carter have written for it. Representative harpsichord pieces include Bach's *Goldberg Variations,* his two- and three-part inventions, and the extensive collection of preludes and fugues he issued in the *Well-tempered Clavier.*

Strings

String instruments do not often perform alone. J. S. Bach's three sonatas and three partitas for unaccompanied violin, Bartók's *Sonata for Unaccompanied Violin* (1944); Hindemith's *Sonata for Viola Unaccompanied,* as well as Bach's six suites for unaccompanied 'cello are among the relatively few works written for a lone string performer. More typical is the appearance of a violin, viola (occasionally), or 'cello with keyboard support (mostly from the piano). Ludwig van Beethoven (ten violin sonatas, five 'cello sonatas); Johannes Brahms (three violin sonatas); Claude Debussy ('Cello Sonata in D minor); and César Franck (Violin Sonata in A Major), are only a few of the composers who have written for this combination of instruments.

Winds

As with strings, wind instruments rarely perform alone; their appearance with piano is far more characteristic. Nevertheless, the sweet, dulcet timbre and flexible technique of woodwind instruments has motivated some composers to write solo pieces for them. Among the examples are Claude Debussy's *Syrinx* for solo flute; Edgard Varèse's *Density 21.5* for the same instrument; and Stravinsky's *Three Pieces for Clarinet.*

SMALL INSTRUMENTAL ENSEMBLES

When assembled for group performance, instruments may be drawn from a single family (as in a string quartet), or from two or more families (as is the case, for instance, in Debussy's Sonata No. 2 for Flute, Viola, and Harp). Generically referred to as *ensembles,* such groups are more conventionally identified as duos, trios, or quartets, according to the number of their players. Because ensemble music is intended to reveal an unencumbered flow of musical lines, most groups enlist only a small number of performers (for example, from two to five). Larger bodies (sextets, septets, octets), appear occasionally, however. Their membership may range upward to as many as a dozen players.

Theoretically, any association of instruments can be brought together for ensemble performance (incidentally, this category is commonly known as *chamber music* and is discussed more fully in Chapter 15), but in actual practice certain combinations have been proven more compatible than others. Because of their warm, vibrant expressiveness, string instruments (violin, viola, 'cello) are commonly used, as are a number of woodwinds (flute, oboe, clarinet, bassoon). But others with exotic sonorities (piccolo, harp, English horn), unusual assertiveness (trumpet, trombone), or limited technical and tonal resources (string bass, tuba) are more characteristically reserved for the orchestra or band.

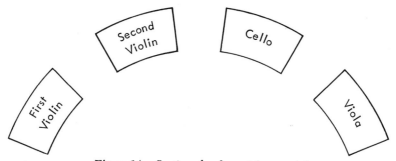

Figure 14. Seating plan for a string quartet.

These small ensembles (with five players or less) have proved most adaptable to changing musical styles and have acquired an interesting repertoire:[1]

1. *Duos*

    a. Two pianos. Poulenc: *Sonata for Two Pianos* (1953).

    b. Violin, viola, or 'cello with keyboard. Beethoven: Violin Sonata No. 5

---

[1] A representative example (or two), accompanies this listing. Further items are cited at the end of the chapter.

in F major ("Spring"); Debussy: Sonata No. 1 in D minor for 'Cello (1915).

    c. Flute, clarinet, oboe, or similar wind instrument, with keyboard. Handel: fifteen sonatas for flute; Brahms: two sonatas for clarinet.

    d. Violin with viola, or violin with 'cello. Kodály: Duo for Violin and 'Cello (1914).

2. *Trios*

    a. Violin, viola, and 'cello (known as the string trio). Beethoven: Trio in D major.

    b. Violin, 'cello, and piano (known as the piano trio). Mendelssohn: Trio in D minor.

    c. Such other combinations (varying from one work to another) as flute, viola, and harp. Debussy: Sonata No. 2. Or 'cello, clarinet and piano. Beethoven: Trio in B-flat major.

    d. Trio sonata (widely employed during the Baroque era), which includes two treble instruments (typically two violins, or violin and flute) with *continuo* (played by 'cello and keyboard). J. S. Bach: Trio Sonata No. 3.

3. *Quartets*

    a. First violin, second violin, viola, and 'cello (known as the string quartet. Dvořák: Quartet No. 6 in F major ("American").

    b. Violin, viola, 'cello, and piano (known as the piano quartet). In lieu of the latter, a woodwind or brass instrument may be employed and the ensemble is then called an oboe (or whatever instrument is used) quartet. Brahms: Piano Quartet No. 1 in G minor. Mozart: Quartet in F major for Oboe and Strings, K. 370.

4. *Quintets*

    a. Two violins, two violas and 'cello (or one viola and two 'cellos); two violins, viola, 'cello, and piano (or one of each plus a string bass). Schubert: Quintet in A major ("Trout") and Quintet in C major.

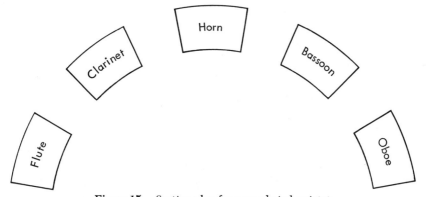

Figure 15.   Seating plan for a woodwind quintet.

  b. Two violins, viola, 'cello and a woodwind or brass instrument (clarinet, horn, etc., and known, consequently, as a clarinet quintet or a horn quintet). Brahms: Quintet in B minor for Clarinet and Strings.
  c. Flute, oboe, clarinet, bassoon, horn (known as the woodwind quintet). Hindemith: *Kleine Kammermusik*, Opus 24, No. 4.

LARGE INSTRUMENTAL GROUPS

Whereas small ensembles include from two to five or six players, large instrumental groups may extend from fifty to one hundred (or more) musicians. Naturally, this difference in size has a great deal to do with the sonority a group produces, the kind of music it plays, and the role it assumes in musical life. Because of their modest size, ensembles are well suited for performance in small concert rooms or perhaps the living room of a home, but large groups are heard to advantage only in sizeable concert halls. Pieces for a small ensemble assign only one player to a part, but in works for large groups the lines are invariably doubled (that is, played by two or more musicians). Normal procedures within a symphony orchestra, for instance, require that the first violin part be executed by as many as sixteen instrumentalists; in a string quartet it is played by only one.

Among the well-established large instrumental groups, three are particularly prominent: (1) the symphony orchestra, (2) the chamber orchestra, and (3) the wind band.

The Symphony Orchestra

Since it began to assume a "modern" instrumentation more than three hundred years ago, the orchestra has developed into an unusually eloquent body. Although termed a *symphony* orchestra its role is not limited to the conveyance of symphonic works, for this group performs suites, concertos, tone poems, overtures, operatic excerpts, and sundry other kinds of very contrasted music. Virtually every important composer active during recent centuries has written for the orchestra, often with incredibly fine results.

Prior to the early seventeenth century, large instrumental groups were haphazardly constituted. Shortly after 1600, however, some of the Italian operatic composers then becoming prominent discovered the advantages of writing for a fixed body of instruments and took steps to formalize the orchestra. Claudio Monteverdi (1567–1643), probably the greatest of these, recognized the violin as a most persuasive voice and placed it (along with other members of its family) at the center of orchestral sonority, although his group also included such other strings as lutes, harps, guitars, and viols, along with numerous wind and keyboard instruments. Then, in succession, such Italian violinist-composers as Giuseppe Torelli, Arcangelo Corelli, and Antonio Vivaldi codified the basic principles of string writing, and incorporated them in a series of concertos, suites, and sinfonias (overtures) that have remained fixtures in the orchestral repertoire.

Subsequent developments occurred intermittently, for the modern orchestra took shape with agonizing slowness. Up to 1750 it was still an ill-defined group, obliged to rely on the *basso continuo* (literally, "continuous bass" provided by 'cello and harpsichord) for rhythmic and harmonic support. Only after Bach, Handel, Rameau, and Vivaldi had been succeeded by Haydn and Mozart, and only after the Baroque had given way to the Classic era, were its iron-bound constrictions loosened. Reduced to a secondary status during the Monteverdi era, such instruments as *chitarroni* (large lutes), *viola da braccio,* and *viola da gamba* (precursors of the violin), as well as *regals* (small organs), disappeared. Parts previously assigned them were given to such relatively modern instruments as violins (playing first and second parts), violas, 'cellos, and string basses (the latter two doubling the same line but sounding one octave apart).

Modern wind instruments (usually in pairs) were added gradually to replace the antiquated relics of an earlier time. First to appear were oboes and bassoons; flutes, horns, and (occasionally) trumpets were later additions. In particular works written between 1700 and 1800, timpani were the sole percussion, but as time passed other drums and devices (cymbals, or triangle) were added. Strangely, the enormously useful clarinets were comparative latecomers to the orchestra. They do not appear in the compositions of J. S. Bach (d. 1750), or of Handel (d. 1759), although both made exemplary use of the flute and oboe. Only after 1780, possibly because Mozart sponsored them so avidly, were clarinets and their deeper voiced cousins the basset-horns used with any frequency. Curiously enough, the venerable trombone found considerable employment outside the orchestra (in sacred music, for instance), but it was not until the early nineteenth century that its powerful voice was added to symphonic scores.

More than anyone else, Franz Joseph Haydn gave the post-1750 orchestra its definitive instrumentation. Sequestered in rural Hungary while working at the court of Prince Nicolaus Esterhazy between 1761 and 1790, Haydn, to use his own words, "was forced to become original." He assigned a composition's melodic line primarily to first violins, used second violins and violas to sound supportive harmonies, and relied on 'cellos and string basses to provide a full-sounding bass. Over these—and often in alternation with them—Haydn imposed the coloristic winds then available.

An unusually large orchestra of this time (for instance, the one Haydn conducted in London in 1791) numbered about forty players, but most Baroque and Classic performing groups had approximately twenty members. During the nineteenth century, however, the large modern symphony orchestra really came into its own. Not only was its numerical strength increased (accomplished, for the most part, by doubling the string parts), but such striking individual voices as the piccolo, English horn, harp, bass clarinet, and celesta were added. In brief, this was an era of vigorous experimentation, when orchestral instrumentation responded to the efforts of Beethoven, Berlioz, Liszt, Wagner, Tchaikowsky, and Brahms. Small wonder that it developed so brilliantly!

Contemporary symphony orchestras differ somewhat in size and makeup, but most professional groups have about one hundred players and display an instrumentation shaped along these lines:

TABLE 12. *Instrumentation of Contemporary Symphony Orchestra.*

Strings
16 first violins; 16 second violins; 12 violas; 12 'cellos; 9 string basses; 2 harps.

Woodwind
4 flutes (one doubling piccolo); 4 oboes (one doubling English horn); 4 clarinets (one doubling E-flat soprano clarinet and/or bass clarinet); 4 bassoons (one doubling contrabassoon).

Brass
4 trumpets; 6 horns; 3 trombones; 1 tuba.

Percussion
3 or 4 musicians performing as required on a variety of instruments. (In addition, large orchestras usually include an organist and a pianist on their staff).

Of these, approximately sixty-seven percent play strings, sixteen percent woodwinds, fourteen percent brass, and three percent percussion. Even when a group's size is increased or reduced, these proportions remain relatively fixed.

Pieces available to a symphony orchestra range from the buoyant dance suites and highly ornamented *concerti grossi* of Baroque composers (early eighteenth century); through the elegant and seemingly fragile symphonies of the Classicists (late eighteenth century); to include the colorful tone poems of the Romanticists (nineteenth century); and the vivid, often stridently dissonant pieces of twentieth-century writers. No other performing group enjoys such a rich and variegated literature, filled with so many unquestioned masterpieces. Of the thousands of splendid compositions available, hearing these six (at least in part) will give a listener some idea of how the orchestra's expressive capabilities have grown over the years:

1. Bach: Suite No. 2 in B minor for Flute and Strings (1723).
2. Mozart: Symphony No. 39 in E-flat major (K. 543, 1788).
3. Berlioz: *Symphonie fantastique* (1830).
4. Tchaikowsky: *Overture: 1812* (1880).
5. Debussy: *Prélude, l'après-midi d'un faun* (1894)
6. Bartók: *Concerto for Orchestra* (1943).

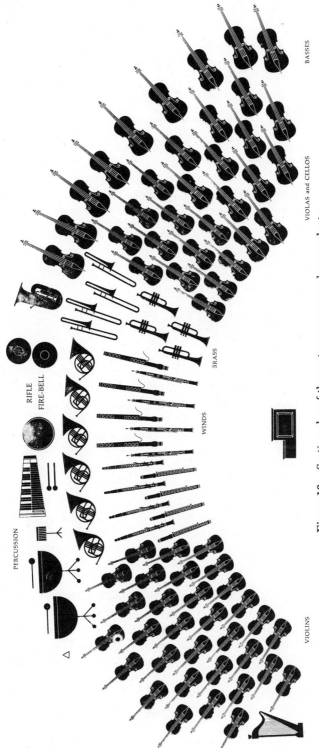

Figure 16. Seating plan of the contemporary symphony orchestra.

BASSES

VIOLAS and CELLOS

BRASS

WINDS

PERCUSSION

RIFLE

FIRE-BELL

VIOLINS

109

The Chamber Orchestra

Comprised mostly of strings (with a few winds and sometimes a piano) and often termed a "little orchestra," the chamber orchestra may number from twenty to thirty players. Naturally, the resonance of such a group is less opulent than that of a full symphony orchestra, and it lacks some of the colorful timbres that are a stock-in-trade of the larger body. But the chamber orchestra is an extremely flexible organization, readily adaptable for use in opera, oratorio, and the theatre, as well as on the concert platform.

Although the instrumentation of a chamber orchestra cannot be specified exactly (it differs from work to work), the alignment of instruments in these two compositions may be considered fairly typical:

1. In his *Pulcinella: Suite* (1920), Stravinsky calls for two flutes, two oboes, two bassoons, two horns, one trumpet, one trombone, and reduced strings; he specifies, furthermore, that the group should number approximately thirty-three persons.
2. While scoring his *Pavane pour une infante défunte* for orchestra in 1912 (he had originally composed it for piano in 1899), Ravel wrote for two flutes, one oboe, two clarinets, two bassoons, two horns, harp, and strings.

Thus, a chamber orchestra reduces its strings and woodwinds, totally ignores the piccolo, English horn, and bass clarinet, sharply curtails the brass, and virtually eliminates the percussion (although this neglect is modified in particular compositions).

Although he did as much as anyone during the Romantic era to expand the orchestra, Richard Wagner also assisted in diverting this flood tide when he composed his *Siegfried Idyll* (1870) for a group of fewer than twenty-five musicians. Scored for flute, oboe, two clarinets, bassoon, two horns, trumpet and strings, Wagner's piece was initially intended for private performance (at home on Christmas morning), but his example was so refreshingly different that others began to emulate the plan. Among the representative pieces written for chamber orchestra during subsequent years are Camille Saint-Saëns' *Carnival of the Animals* (1886); Schoenberg's *Pelleas und Melisande* (1902) and *Chamber Symphony* (1906); Ravel's *Le Tombeau de Couperin* (1917); Richard Strauss' *Le Bourgeois Gentilhomme Suite* (1918); Stravinsky's *L'Histoire du soldat* (1918) and Suites Nos. 1 and 2 for Small Orchestra (1917–1921), Hindemith's *Kammermusik* (1922); and Copland's *Music for the Theater* (1925).

Limited to a single family of instruments, the string orchestra has about twenty players and assigns them to violins (usually divided into first and second parts), viola, 'cello, string bass, and (perhaps) harp. Because of the unusual expressive capabilities of these instruments, the string orchestra has a most opulent sonority. Pieces written for it include Arensky's *Vari-*

ations on a Theme by Tchaikowsky; Dvořák's Serenade in E major; Elgar's Serenade in E minor; Tchaikowsky's Serenade in C major; Vaughan Williams' *Fantasie on a Theme by Tallis;* and Richard Strauss' *Metamorphosen.*

The Wind Band

Since Roman times the wind band has been an adjunct of virtually all military establishments, and in the last half century (particularly in the United States) it has flourished in association with fraternal organizations, municipalities, and schools and colleges. Traditionally employed at parades, military ceremonies, pageants, rallies, outdoor concerts, and sporting events, it has also taken on the more prestigious tasks of performing indoors, making phonograph records, and broadcasting.

Within Roman legions, a band was constituted from a small number of brass instruments (perhaps as few as eight) and used partly for marching purposes at reviews and military exercises, and partly for signalling (via bugle calls). During the Renaissance and later eras, brass instrumentalists employed for similar purposes (pageantry and signaling) were attached to municipal payrolls (particularly in Germany), and called town musicians. As centuries passed, bands continued to remain small so that even as recently as 1825–1850 most groups had only eight, ten, or twelve players performing on a variety of woodwinds and brasses. Since 1850, however, the band has experienced an amazing growth. Disparity still exists in its precise strength and instrumentation, but an average modern group capable of undertaking a well-rounded schedule of activities would include approximately sixty musicians distributed over this instrumentation:

TABLE 13. Instrumentation of the Wind Band.

Woodwinds

3 flutes (1 doubling piccolo); 3 oboes (1 doubling English horn); 3 bassoons (a contrabassoon is possible but rare); 1 or 2 E-flat soprano clarinets; 12 B-flat clarinets (playing first, second, and third parts); 2 alto clarinets; 2 bass clarinets; 4 (or more) saxophones (2 altos, 1 tenor, 1 baritone is typical).

Brass

5 cornets (distributed over first, second, and third parts); 3 trumpets (playing first and second parts); 4 (or more) horns (playing first, second, third, and fourth parts); 6 trombones (playing first, second, and third parts); 2 baritone horns (sometimes called euphoniums); 4 basses (tubas).

Percussion

5 players performing on a variety of drums, cymbals, timpani, glockenspiel, and other instruments.

Of these, about fifty percent perform on woodwinds, slightly over forty percent on brasses, and somewhat less than ten percent on percussion.

Although a band cannot produce the delicate timbre or the glowing resonance of an orchestra, it nevertheless expresses an impressive sonority and has a marvelous capacity to perform well under diverse (and sometimes trying) conditions. Many pieces in the band's repertoire are transcriptions from orchestral works by Johann Strauss, Jacques Offenbach, or Franz von Suppe. But others—John Philip Sousa, Edwin Franko Goldman, Ludwig Tiecke, and Kenneth Alford, for instance—have written an abundance of marches for band. A few—Hector Berlioz, *Symphonie funèbre et triomphale;* Felix Mendelssohn, Military Overture in C major; and Gustav Holst, Suites in E-flat and F major—have written band compositions that approach symphonic proportions. Other representative compositions in band literature are listed at the end of this chapter.

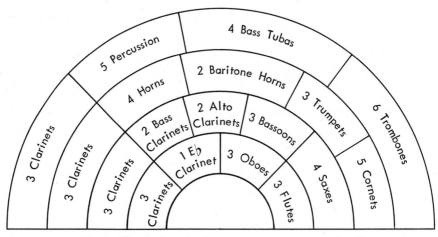

Figure 17.   Seating plan for a contemporary concert band.

VOCAL MEDIA

Literature for solo and group voices is both exceedingly large and of excellent quality. Despite this, and the diverse circumstances in which vocal activity occurs—in schools, churches, the home, opera, theaters, or broadcasting studios—the makeup of choral groups has never become as carefully delineated as that of instrumental organizations. Consequently, singing groups can be described only in general terms.

Choruses

Choral organizations whose membership may range from twenty-five to one hundred or more singers are conventionally identified as *choruses.* Smaller groups, or those fulfilling a special purpose in church, for example, are frequently called *choirs.* Occasionally, the designation choral (pronounced core-ahl) is applied to either kind of organization.

Much vocal music is written in four parts (for soprano, alto, tenor, and bass voices), and the resultant *mixed quartet* assigns women's voices to the two upper parts, and men's voices to the lower lines. When these parts are doubled, perhaps many times over, the *mixed chorus* comes into being. Such choruses may include a dozen or several hundreds of singers, and the sonority they produce may be scaled from a barely audible hushed *pianissimo* to a stentorian *fortissimo*. Generally speaking, small choral groups (choirs), tend to be crystalline and intimate in sound, and their use in expressing deeply felt sentiment (as in religious worship, for instance) approaches the most sublime of musical utterances. Large choruses give an impression of grandeur and monumentality; their massive resonance is well suited for expressions of jubilation, exultation, or the mass emotions associated with crowds of people. With the question of size aside, because the mixed chorus encompasses the full range of pitches available to human voices, it is unquestionably the most flexible, the most satisfying, and the most exciting of choral organizations. Especially notable in the large literature available to mixed choruses are (1) the "Hallelujah Chorus" from Handel's *Messiah;* (2) the "Entry of the Guests" from Act II of Wagner's *Tannhäuser;* and (3) the "Anvil Chorus" that opens Act II in Verdi's *Il Trovatore.*

Other choral groups have a more specialized membership. Among the best-known are (1) the men's chorus, (2) women's chorus, and (3) children's chorus. Each, of course, has a distinctive sonority, each has been found useful in particular musical and dramatic circumstances, and each has its music scored in two, three, four (or more) parts.

Sometimes employing boy sopranos and altos, the men's chorus is more characteristically limited to adult male singers whose voices are organized into first and second tenor, baritone, and bass parts. Even though boys' voices afford the group a fuller vocal range, sonorities produced by young singers tend to be thin and piping, and no match for the robust, virile timbres of mature male voices. Glee clubs, college singing societies, and some church groups are usually limited to men. Numerous opera composers have found apt usage for a male group's rich sonorities as is demonstrated in the "Prisoners' Chorus" from Beethoven's *Fidelio;* the "Soldiers' Chorus" from Gounod's *Faust;* and the "Pilgrims' Chorus" from Wagner's *Tannhäuser.*

Usually divided into the first and second soprano and first and second alto parts, women's choruses express a clear, sweet, and almost ethereal sound in upper ranges of the pitch spectrum. Feminine voices do not express the same robust vibrancy as the lower-pitched male voices, of course, and the characteristic timbre of a women's choral group is dulcet, pure, and gracious. This is beautifully demonstrated in Debussy's cantata, *La Damoiselle élue* (The Blessed Lady, 1888), which uses only women in both solo and ensemble roles. Similarly, Puccini scored his opera, *Suor*

Angelica (Sister Angelica, 1918), entirely for women and marshalls the timbres produced by these light, fluent voices in a most evocative way. Shorter examples of pieces written only for women can be found in the introduction to Act II of Verdi's *Aïda* and in the opening portion of Act III in Mussorgsky's *Boris Godounov*.

Because they have an uncanny way of suggesting seraphic beauty, children's voices are often used in religious music. For centuries, boys' choirs have won a deserved reputation for their pure and soaring sonority, qualities that are demonstrated, for instance, in Benjamin Britten's "A Ceremony of Carols." And numerous opera composers have found fitting employment for their ringing sounds, particularly in scenes where large groups of people are gathered. Examples can be discerned in the "Chorus of Street Boys" from Act I of Bizet's *Carmen* and in the chorus of children that greets Parpignol in Act II of Puccini's *La Bohème*.

The Vocal Craft

Singing techniques, as well as standards determining an ideal vocal sonority, have changed a great deal through the centuries. Among the ancient Greeks, for instance, a pure and rather thin sound was highly prized (according to written documents that describe Hellenic vocal art), and the Orient has consistently acclaimed a nasal, pinched and singsong timbre for more than a thousand years. As far as modern vocal practices are concerned, a movement of special importance in the development of communicative singing began in Italy shortly after 1700, when the *bel canto* concept was formulated. Based on an enunciation of evenly balanced sounds produced by singing with an open mouth and throat, bel canto forced the previously employed declamatory style (which utilized short, clipped sounds articulated at the front of the mouth), into a secondary position. Although varying "schools" of vocal technique have arisen during recent centuries, and the art of singing differs markedly from country to country and on various levels of artistic competence, the liquid-smooth concept of bel canto has now won almost total international acceptance. In today's professional practice both styles of singing have a place: Bel canto is used in performing arias, solo songs, and ensemble pieces, and the declamatory method is used in enunciating recitatives commonly found in opera and oratorio.

Before 1650, copious amounts of polyphonic music were created for voices. Written in three, four, or five parts and based on religious or secular texts, part songs of this era made extensive use of imitative counterpoint and were identified as *frottola, villanella, motet, madrigal, ballet, ayre, canzonet, chanson, lied,* or *villancico* (depending on their character and place of origin). In some cases voices performing them were supported by instruments, but most works were sung *a cappella* (unaccompanied). An abundance of compositions by Giovanni Palestrina (Italy); Tomás Luis

Victoria (Spain); William Byrd (England); and Orlandus Lassus (Germany), to mention only four outstanding musicians of this era, brought this flowering of vocal music to a peak of excellence. In subsequent centuries and in other areas of musical activity, J. S. Bach, *St. Matthew Passion*, Mass in B minor; G. F. Handel, *Messiah, Ode for St. Cecilia's Day*; W. A. Mozart, Mass in C major ("Coronation"); Franz Joseph Haydn, *The Creation*; Giuseppe Verdi, *Requiem*; Richard Wagner, *Tannhauser*; and Georges Bizet, *Carmen* expanded this distinguished choral tradition.

Solo Song

Aside from its use in religious chant or ethnic music, and despite the incontrovertible fact that monophonic vocal practices are really the foundation of all Western music, the unaccompanied solo voice (or unisonal chorus) is now comparatively rare. Vast amounts of music for solo voice with piano exist, however—a good deal of it written during the nineteenth and twentieth centuries. Variously known as the *art song* (England and America), *chanson* (France), or *lied* (Germany), these pieces merge the unlimited imagery of lyric poetry with music's unparalleled expressive beauties. Beethoven, Schubert (who wrote more than six hundred lieder), Schumann, Brahms, Wolf, Mussorgsky, and Richard Strauss are only a few of the composers whom the world has recognized as masters of song. (For a more complete discussion, see Chapter 13).

Chorus and Orchestra

Although the piano (or organ) is often used to support choral performances—particularly when these are given by school, college, church, or community groups—this instrument is often acting as a substitute for orchestra. So considerable are the expressive possibilities inherent in a combination of voices and instruments, that virtually every major composer has attempted to explore their breadth by writing cantatas, masses, oratorios, operas, or associated choral-orchestral works. Originating as early as the times of Andrea Gabrieli (early sixteenth century) and his pupil Heinrich Schütz, an unusually fine literature for dual performing resources has subsequently come into being. Among representative nonoperatic compositions are Mendelssohn's "Hymn of Praise" and his oratorio *Elijah*; Berlioz's *Grande messe des morts* and *Te Deum*; Brahms' *Alto Rhapsody* and "Song of Destiny"; Verdi's *Requiem* and four *Pezzi sacri* (sacred pieces); and Dvořák's *Stabat Mater* and *Requiem*. Arising with a general movement that aimed at discovering new expressive possibilities in the post-Wagnerian era (after 1890), such compositions as Debussy's *La Damoiselle élue* and *Martyrdom of St. Sebastian*; Delius' *Sea Drift* and *Mass of Life*; Vaughan Williams' *Serenade to Music* and Mass in G minor; Prokofiev's *Alexander Nevsky*; Stravinsky's *Les Noces* and *Symphony of Psalms*; Honegger's *King David* and *Joan of Arc;* Bloch's *Sacred Service;* and Kodály's *Psalmus Hungaricus* have greatly enriched the literature for choral-orchestral groups. (Details about these and similar large-scale vocal works are mentioned in Chapter 16).

Recent Innovations

When Schoenberg composed his *Pierrot Lunaire* in 1912, he pioneered in formulating a distinctive musical declamation called *sprechstimme* (literally, "speech song"). Decidedly eerie in sound, this kind of song—which also appears in a modified form in Walton's *Façade* (1926) to convey an Edith Sitwell text—can be moving, frightening, impassioned, or amusing. Certainly, it is different.

Both before and after Schoenberg, other composers employed voices in a multiplicity of ways. Some, for instance, ask singers to intone wordless *melismas* (melodic ideas) on a single syllable, thus obtaining vocal effects while avoiding the enunciation of a specific text. Debussy in *Sirenes* (for women's chorus, 1889); Puccini in the "Humming Chorus" from *Madama Butterfly* (1904); Ravel in *Daphnis et Chloe* (for mixed chorus, 1911); and Vaughan Williams in his Symphony No. 3 (with soprano soloist, 1922) also utilized this technique (which, incidentally, is currently finding extensive use in arrangements of popular American music).

A CONDUCTOR'S ROLE

Because the complexities of musical performance are so formidable, any sizeable organization normally vests its leadership in a single individual, the conductor. Given full authority over a group in marshalling its communicative and expressive resources, his task is to insure an orderly, meaningful, and artistic interpretation of a score. Orchestras, bands, choruses, and choirs benefit from this unilateral direction, but small ensembles substitute individual rapport instead.

When working with a group, the conductor is an undisputed arbiter in determining such niceties as: (1) correct tempo; (2) degrees of dynamic shading; (3) balance and blending between instruments and/or voices; (4) fine points of articulation and phrasing; and (5) the infinite subtleties of nuance. His additional responsibilities extend to: (1) selecting the pieces to be played; (2) determining the group's personnel; (3) training the executants; and (4) arranging performer placement so that all will be heard to advantage.

Standing at a point of vantage where he can be easily seen by performers and audience alike, using gestures, facial expressions, bodily postures, glances, and other pantomimic expressions, a skilled conductor guides his group through the composition at hand. Although most musicians are more than willing to cooperate with a conductor, artistic performance is such an involved matter that untold patience and unlimited obeisance are needed to accomplish satisfactory results.

A good conductor must possess consummate musical insight, the direct result of long training, exhaustive study, and a considerable variety of experience. In addition to being a facile performer on at least one instrument (and perhaps several), he should also be a perceptive person who merges a firm grasp of music's materials with the psychological insight, tact, and unending patience of a born leader. To be adequately prepared for performance, a conductor must fully comprehend every aspect of a score including its style, historic background, and aesthetic intent. In conducting opera, for instance, he should (1) be fluent in the opera's language (which may be different from his own); (2) be able to command an orchestra of near-symphonic dimensions; (3) be fully knowledgeable in the sundry aspects of vocal technique; (4) know virtually every note that each singer and orchestra member is required to perform; (5) have insight into varied matters of stagecraft; and (6) be sufficiently forceful in personality to direct a performing group that may number well over one hundred people.

TRANSCRIPTIONS

When a work is modified so that is can be performed by a group other than the one for which it was originally composed, a *transcription* (colloquially known as an "arrangement") results. Concerned principally with shifts in coloration and an appropriate assignment of lines (that is, musical parts), a transcription does not appreciably affect a composition's melody, texture, harmony, formal pattern, or rhythmic qualities, but it may markedly change its communicative impact (and, consequently, its popular appeal). In today's musical world, transcriptions are common, particularly in the light popular areas where dances, show tunes, favorite ditties, and other bits of musical fluff are given new settings. Sometimes, transcribing a piece has to do with rearranging piano (or organ) works so they can be performed by instrumental groups, but other projects venture farther afield and are concerned with realigning choral or operatic pieces so they can be performed by orchestra or band.

To illustrate, here is a list of well-known compositions that have undergone transcription. Listen to them in both the original and transcribed settings (in each case recordings are available), and note the important differences that realignment brings:

1. *Pictures at an Exhibition* by Modest Mussorgsky. Originally written as a set of piano pieces, this descriptive work (which portrays an imaginary visit to an equally imaginary art museum) was subsequently orchestrated by Maurice Ravel.

2. *Ma mère l'oye* (Mother Goose Suite) by Maurice Ravel. This piece describes five characters from Perrault's timeless fantasy tales; the composer provided two versions: one for two pianos, the other for orchestra.
3. *Variations on a Theme by Haydn* by Johannes Brahms. A beautifully molded composition that was scored (by the composer) for either two pianos or orchestra.
4. *The Children's Corner Suite* by Claude Debussy. This is a whimsical set of musical vignettes composed for piano. But André Caplet (with the composer's approval) later transcribed it for orchestra.
5. *Passacaglia and Fugue in C minor* by J. S. Bach. Originally written for organ, it has been given a number of orchestral transcriptions and at least one for piano.

Additional Compositions for Various Performing Media

Piano, harpsichord or organ [2]

Bach, J. S. *Italian Concerto* in F for Harpsichord; Fantasia and Fugue in G minor for Organ.
Beethoven, Ludwig van. Sonata No. 8 in C minor ("Pathetique") for Piano.
Chopin, Frederic. *Études* for Piano.
Schumann, Robert. *Carnaval* for Piano.
Widor, C. M. Symphony No. 5 in F minor for Organ.

One instrument with piano

Beethoven, Ludwig van. Violin Sonata No. 9 in A major ("Kreutzer"). Sonatas (5) for 'Cello and Piano.
Brahms, Johannes. Sonata No. 3 in D minor for Violin and Piano.
Tartini, Giuseppe. Sonata in E minor for Violin and Piano ("Devil's Trill").

Trios

Beethoven, Ludwig van. Trio No. 6 (piano) in B-flat major, ("Archduke").
Brahms, Johannes. Trio in E-flat major for Horn, Violin, Piano.
Dvořák, Antonin. Trio (piano) in E minor ("Dumka").
Mozart, Wolfgang Amadeus. Trio in E-flat major for Clarinet, Viola, Piano, (K. 498).

Quartets

Beethoven, Ludwig van. Quartet No. 7 in F major ("Rasumovsky").
Debussy, Claude. Quartet in G minor.
Haydn, Franz Joseph. Quartet in D minor ("Quinten").
Schubert, Franz. Quartet No. 14 in D minor ("Death and the Maiden").

[2] Among the works that have been written for two pianos, these are representative: (1) Mozart: Sonata in D major (K. 448); (2) Schumann: Andante and Variations in B-flat major; (3) Rachmaninoff: Suites (opus 5) and Fantasy (opus 17); and (4) Bartók: Sonata for Two Pianos and Percussion.

Quintets

Beethoven, Ludwig van. Quintet in E-flat major for Piano and Winds.
Brahms, Johannes. Quintet in F minor for Piano and Strings.
Mozart, Wolfgang Amadeus. Quintet in A major for Clarinet and Strings (K. 581).
Schubert, Franz. Quintet in A major ("Trout") for Violin, Viola, 'Cello, Bass, Piano.

Symphony orchestra

Beethoven, Ludwig van. Symphony No. 3 in E-flat major ("Eroica").
Liszt, Franz. *Hungarian Rhapsody No. 2.*
Ravel, Maurice. *Boléro.*
Tchaikowsky, Peter. *Capriccio italien.*
Britten, Benjamin. *Young Person's Guide to the Orchestra.*

Wind Band

Grainger, Percy. *Lincolnshire Posy.*
Hindemith, Paul. Symphony in B-flat major for Concert Band (1951).
Milhaud, Darius. *Suite française* (1944).
Vaughan Williams, R. *Toccata Marziale.*

Choral groups

Bach, J. S. Cantata No. 4, *Christ lag in Todesbaden.*
Gesualdo, Don Carlo. Italian Madrigals.
Haydn, Franz J. *Missa in tempore belli* (*Paukenmesse*).
Palestrina, G. *Missa Papae Marcelli.*

For a more extensive listing of vocal works, see Chapters 13 "Song," 16 "Large Choral Works," and 18 "Opera."

Double Flemish virginal, made c. 1600 by Lodewijek Grauwels.

PART TWO

BASIC PATTERNS OF MUSICAL ARCHITECTURE

In one way or another, music continually grows. Sometimes expansion is accomplished by the simple act of repetition (as when a song is sung over and over again), or by the process of addition (as when a number of contrasted segments are bound together under a common heading). Growth of a different kind occurs in lengthy compositions (overtures, concertos, symphonies, or quartets), when music's materials are handled, shaped, and expanded in a number of ways.

Each process differs in technique and complexity. Mere repetition is usually obvious enough; straightforward and appealing, it has the virtue of relative simplicity. Although verbatim recurrence strengthens the impact a work has on a listener, it also brings the dangers of monotony. Contrasting episodes help to relieve this tedium and bring refreshing change. Even more interesting to a perceptive ear, however, are the manipulative processes that composers employ to elaborate on their musical ideas.

On pages that follow, attention is drawn to four primary designs: (1) part form, (2) variation form, (3) sonata form, and (4) rondo form. Found in nearly all kinds of music written during the past three hundred or more years, they have proven flexible, useful, and sturdy. Other designs exist, of course, but they are mostly permutations of these basic forms. As before, you should listen carefully and repeatedly to the musical examples, for by training the ear, you are opening avenues leading to a lifetime of highly enjoyable musical experiences.[1]

[1] For additional information about music's structural patterns see (1) Hugo Leichtentritt, *Musical Form* (Cambridge, Mass.: Harvard University Press, 1951); (2) Douglass M. Green, *Form in Tonal Music* (New York: Holt, Rinehart and Winston, 1965); and (3) Wallace Berry, *Form in Music* (Englewood Cliffs, N.J.: Prentice-Hall, Inc., 1966).

Chapter 6

Growth by Addition:
Part Form

Constituted from a series of independent or semi-independent segments (called strains) that succeed one another in a meaningful way, part form is a frequently used musical design. Each of its sections has a distinctive melody (although familial relations may exist between them), and each terminates on a partial or complete cadence. Precise dimensions for the strains cannot be given: Some may be only a phrase (approximately four to six measures), or a period (twice as long), while others (for example, subdivisions within symphonic movements) may extend to a hundred or more measures. Identified by alphabetical symbols—small letters (*a, b, c*) for phrases and periods, capital letters (*A, B, C*) for lengthy segments—associated strains usually share common rhythmic characteristics (tempo, meter) and related harmonic qualities (tonality), but differ in melody.

Stephen Foster's graceful "Beautiful Dreamer," a short melody in part form, has a sequence of neatly balanced phrases:

Considerably larger, the third movement in Brahms' Symphony No. 3 in F major follows a similar plan. These are the principal melodic ideas used in this piece:

123

BINARY AND TERNARY PART FORM

Foundational patterns used in huge amounts of rather simple music, *binary form,* a two-part design often identified merely as *ab,* and *ternary form,* a three-part pattern with an outline of *aba* or *abc* strains, have been employed for centuries. Often called *song form,* which indicates their original source, both are now commonly used in either vocal or instrumental music.

These brief melodies demonstrate "simple" part form:

1. As he begins the *Prélude* of his *L'Arlésienne: Suite No. 1,* Bizet presents a melody (undoubtedly of folk origin) organized in binary (*ab*) form:

2. In the first movement of his Sonata No. 12 in A-Flat major for Piano, Beethoven uses a theme with nicely balanced phrases in ternary design (*aba*):

3. And in his *Variations on a Theme by Tchaikowsky*, Arensky employs a borrowed melody that demonstrates a ternary pattern in the sequence *abc*:

Aside from obvious divergences in their number of segments, binary and ternary form also have these differences:

1. Closely integrated, binary form's segments are interdependent. Normally, one is separated from the other by a partial cadence, with the result that the second strain seems to be a logical, indeed an inevitable, outgrowth from the first.

2. On the other hand, ternary form is an alliance of relatively independent sections (two in the *aba* alignment, three in the *abc* plan). Each may demonstrate common qualities with its associate(s), but for the most part its strains are contrasted in a number of ways. Often, they are separated by full cadences.

Binary form is the older of the two and reached a heyday during the Baroque era when such dances as the gavotte, minuet, gigue, or allemande were almost always established in a two-part alignment. From 1750 onward, however, ternary form became an increasing favorite and was frequently used in the minuet with trio, scherzo *da capo aria,* or waltz form designs that we shall discuss subsequently.

Because it is a concentric design, binary form has a center of equipoise at the cadential point between *a* and *b.* For the most part, each section is of approximately the same length, each has relatively uniform rhythmic qualities, and each follows a similar melodic curve. Key relationships are usually quite orthodox. After beginning in the tonic key, *a* normally finds its cadence on the dominant; *b* assumes this new key and ultimately makes its way back to conclude in the home key.[1]

Cleanly etched examples of simple binary form appear in the two Menuets Handel included in his *Music for the Royal Fireworks* (1749). Sounding in D minor and D major, respectively, each has two eight-measure strains (*a* and *b*) that are repeated in performance. In both Menuets, *a* has a cadence on the dominant, while *b* returns to the tonic:

---

[1] In particular instances, relative major or minor tonalities may be used in lieu of a shift to the dominant.

Several possibilities of alignment exist within the binary format. Apel,[2] for instance, distinguishes between three types: (1) a symmetric pattern where each section (*a, b*) is of equal length; (2) an asymmetric design where the second section is longer than the first; and (3) *rounded binary form* where *a* reappears after *b* without, however, a full cadence separating the two. The latter, of course, closely impinges on ternary form. Several modified patterns may also appear. The simplest consists of two nearly identical sections (*a, a'*) that differ only at the cadences (*a* usually concludes on the dominant, *a'* on the tonic). Quite obviously, this pattern suffers from a lack of contrast. Far more widely used, the *ab* sequence is relatively standard and is occasionally extended to create such successives as: *aa'b, abb'*, or *aa'bb'*.

Founded on the aesthetically satisfying principle of statement-digression-return, ternary form is used in large and small compositions. Thousands of keyboard pieces (known under such names as ballade, elegy, reverie, étude, impromptu, intermezzo, capriccio, berceuse, or nocturne) have been written in ternary form. And in such extended orchestral works as overtures, large dance forms, or movements within symphonies, concertos, or chamber music compositions, an enlarged version of the design frequently appears. Two cadential points commonly appear in ternary form; the first between *a* and *b*, the second between *b* and the oncoming strain. Often, the first is a full cadence, whereas the second may be either partial (as is usual in the *aba* plan), or full (typical in the *abc* pattern). Within ternary form adventuresome harmonic changes may be interjected. For example, the midsection (b), typically shifts to a related key (dominant, subdominant, or associated minor), but it can venture to a "foreign" key and thereby introduce some extraordinary shifts. Furthermore, melodic ideas usually have a greater scope in the ternary pattern where they may be longer, more independent, or show greater contrast than those in binary form.

THE QUESTION OF DIMENSION: SIMPLE AND LARGE PART FORM

Songs, hymns, patriotic airs, folk melodies, popular tunes, marches, and dances are normally constituted from phrases, periods, or double periods. When these segments are combined (usually in a binary or ternary plan), *simple part form,* whose expanse may stretch from sixteen to thirty-

[2] Apel, Willi, *Harvard Dictionary of Music* (Cambridge, Mass.: Harvard University Press, 1946), p. 87.

two (or more) measures, results. *Large part form* also appears in either the binary or ternary format, but its sections are more expansive and may extend to hundreds of measures, with individual subsections (*abc*) under the major divisions (*A,B,C,*).

A melody Mozart uses in the first movement of his Sonata in A major for Piano (K. 331), has an expanse of eighteen measures (without repeats) and is an example of simple ternary form (*aba*): [3]

On the other hand, the third movement in Dvořák's Symphony No. 8 in G major, which extends to 315 measures, exemplifies large part form.[4] A lilting waltz that follows an *ABA* pattern (with numerous repetitions and extensions of its melodic ideas), it has this outline:

TABLE 14.   *Outline of Dvorak Waltz in ABA Pattern.*

A (G minor)	B (G major)	A (G minor)	Coda (G major)
85 measures	94 measures	da capo [5]	51 measures

[3] With considerable logic, it could also be argued that this is rounded binary form. Actually, the two patterns are very similar.

[4] Similar large-scale designs may be found in the second movements of Mendelssohn's Violin Concerto in E minor; Schumann's Piano Concerto in A minor; or Tchaikowsky's Symphony No. 6 in B minor; furthermore, it is most aptly demonstrated in the third movement of Tchaikowsky's Symphony No. 4 in F minor.

[5] *Da capo*, literally "to the beginning," is a frequently used musical abbreviation. Appended at the end of a *B* section (and often contracted merely to D.C.), it directs the musicians to again play a composition from the beginning. "*Fine*" (finish), usually inserted at the end of *A*, tells them where to stop.

Consistently melodic, the movement is based on two primary ideas. This is the first subject (in A):

And this is the second theme (paramount in B):

EARLY PART FORM

Although the actual beginnings of part form are uncertain, its origins may extend to the Hellenic period. Learned writings from this era—by Plato in the *Republic;* Aristotle in *Politics;* Aristoxenus in *Harmonic Elements*—tell a great deal about the musical practices of ancient Greece, but do not, of course, include any actual musical examples. Conjecturally speaking, however, it seems likely that many Greek songs had a strophic (sectional) organization, and that during subsequent eras (that is, the Roman and early Christian periods), rudimentary part form patterns became known in both sacred and secular music. Manuscripts dating from succeeding epochs—the late Middle Ages and early Renaissance—contain quotations of pieces (both sacred and secular) that reveal aspects of sectional organization.

Virtually all compositions created by the French trouvères and troubadours are organized in part form. So, too, are the songs of such later German musicians as the minnesingers and meistersingers. To their very considerable credit, the latter codified a pattern known as *bar* form (really an *aab* pattern), that was widely employed in songs of the Medieval, Renaissance, and later eras. Eventually, a final *a* was inserted in such works, resulting in an *aaba* design that became very pervasive in the subsequent song literature of nearly all nations.

Examples of this French and German practice are contained in *Masterpieces of Music Before 1750.* (See Appendix C, Bibliography.) For instance a trouvère song from the twelfth or thirteenth century, *Or la truix* has the pattern: *ab cc ab ab,* while a similar item, a minnelied entitled *Willekom-men Mayenschein,* by von Reuenthal, demonstrates typical bar form (*aab*).

FOUR- AND FIVE-PART FORM

Because it is a design that grows by agglomeration, part form can be extended by adding new strains to those already introduced, or by repeating previously heard sections. In this manner, the simple ternary design (*aba*) can be enlarged to include four sections in an *aaba* sequence. Best-known to present-day listeners through its appearance in many popular songs (for example, Irving Berlin's "Easter Parade" and Jerome Kern's "Smoke Gets in Your Eyes"), this sturdy pattern has actually been in use for hundreds of years (in meistersinger songs, for instance). Its outlines are clearly evident in Foster's "Old Folks at Home":

Another plan of sectional recurrence—a five-part design—has the sequence *ababa,* or, in particular instances, *abaca.* (The latter, incidentally, impinges on simple rondo form, discussed in Chapter 9.) Successive strains in five-part form, usually of similar length, are separated by perceptible cadences. Such is the circumstance in the rousing "Soldiers' Chorus" from Charles Gounod's *Faust,* an example of *abaca* design:

1. This theme *a* is sung as the piece begins:

2. In succession two other melodies (*b* and *c*) are heard. Between them, as well as at the end of the piece, *a* reappears:

A similar scheme is used in the March from Serge Prokofiev's opera, *Love for Three Oranges*.

In works of large dimension, the five-part plan (*ABACA*) is often referred to as "part form with two trios" (the trios being, respectively, *B* and *C*). Because of length, its strains may have binary or ternary subdivisions (identified as *a, b, c, d*) and so on. An example exists in the third movement of Brahms' Symphony No. 2 in D major:

1. *A:* As the piece begins, an oboe sounds this lilting waltz-like melody (thirty-two measures long and marked *allegretto grazioso*) over an accompaniment from 'cellos, clarinets, and bassoons:

2. *B* (first trio): In turn, a second section, which retains the same key (G major) while shifting to duple meter and a *presto ma non assai* tempo, appears:

3. *A:* Compressed to nineteen measures and ensconced in a new harmonic setting, a modified version of the first section succeeds.
4. *C* (second trio): While remaining in triple meter, this strain assumes a more rapid tempo (*presto*) as strings articulate a descending theme:

5. *A:* Temporarily (for twenty-five measures) appearing a half step lower, the first subject later shifts upward to the home key (G major) as it brings this tranquil symphonic movement to a close.

THE DA CAPO ARIA

When the outlines of a relatively large-scale ternary pattern (*ABA*) are applied to a lengthy piece for solo voice and orchestra, the *da capo aria* results. Widely used in opera, oratorio, and cantatas, the design gets its name from the direction, *da capo,* normally inserted at the end of *B.* Its outlines are demonstrated in an important aria from the third act of Bizet's opera *Carmen.* Beginning with the words *Je disque rien ne m'épouvante* (Nothing shall deter me), this piece is sung by the cast's leading soprano and, consequently, is often identified as "Micaela's Aria":

1. After a brief orchestral introduction wherein horns are prominent, a flowing melody *A* is sung:

2. Later, in a more animated middle portion, this new theme *B* appears:

3. Still later, the original subject *A* returns to conclude the aria.[6]

---

[6] Another fine example of *da capo* form, the aria *Quoniam tu solus sanctus* (Only you are holy) from J. S. Bach's Mass in B minor, is sung by the bass voice with support from *corno da caccia,* two bassoons, and continuo. *Cara Sposa,* a *da capo* aria from Handel's *Rinaldo,* is included in the collection, *Masterpieces of Music Before 1750.*

Although he did not stringently follow the dictates of standard *da capo* form, Mozart employs the design's outlines in the lilting cavatina, *Se vuol ballare, signor contino* (I'll play the tune, Mr. Count) sung by Figaro (a baritone) early in the first act of his opera *The Marriage of Figaro:*

1. Without preamble, the aria opens with this theme *A*:

2. Shifting to duple meter, *B* adopts a faster tempo and interjects this new idea:

3. Nearing the aria's close, a portion of *A*—limited to twenty measures in lieu of the previous sixty-three—returns to round out the design.[7]

PART FORM IN SHORT WORKS

"Light classics"—marches, dances, and genre pieces so numerous as to defy orderly enumeration—are often organized in part form. Brief and usually well-known, they are constituted from a series of segments that may (or may not) have subdivisions. Quick-step marches,[8] for instance, are usually based on a broadly conceived binary form with these general outlines:

TABLE 15. Outlines of Binary Form for Quick-Step Marches.

Introduction	A	B
(Which may include from 4 to 8 measures)	*a.* 1st strain, repeated *b.* 2nd strain, repeated (each extending from 16 to 32 measures)	*c.* Trio (3rd strain) *d.* Episode *c.* Return to trio (each 12 to 32 measures)

[7] Although it is performed by two singers (and is, therefore, not an aria), a soprano-alto duet in Bach's Cantata No. 78, *Jesu der du meine Seele,* beautifully exemplifies the *da capo* outline.

[8] As specific examples consider: Sousa's *King Cotton, El Capitan,* or *Stars and Stripes Forever;* Goldman's *On the Mall,* or Bagley's *National Emblem.*

Occasionally, a *da capo* (which repeats the A section verbatim) is employed, and this, in effect, creates a large ternary design.

Numerous short piano pieces, some based on dance patterns, employ sectional designs. Mendelssohn's "Songs Without Words" (for piano), for instance, are mostly organized in ternary form. So, too, are Chopin's Nocturnes, which have the sequence: *andante-allegro-andante,* and his Impromptus, which follow the reverse pattern: *allegro-andante-allegro.* Other piano works in ternary form are Brahms' Waltzes, his Capriccios (in fast tempo), and his Intermezzos (in slow tempo).

PART FORM IN LARGER WORKS

Most "concert" waltzes (some for piano, others for orchestra) are organized in four or five sections, each with binary or ternary subdivisions. Sometimes these segments flow directly into one another via connecting passages, but again cleavages may exist between them. Often, such pieces have an introduction (which may be of a nondance nature), and a lengthy concluding section called a *coda.* Representative works organized along these lines include (1) *Tales From the Vienna Woods* by Johann Strauss II, which has a dreamy introduction, five sections (each with binary or ternary subdivisions), and a nostalgic coda; [9] (2) *Valse brillante* in E-flat major (for piano) by Frederic Chopin, which also has an introduction, five sections that are more or less dance-like, and a coda; (3) *Valses nobles et sentimentales* by Maurice Ravel (originally for piano, later scored for orchestra), which has six sections in ternary form, one in binary form (Part II), and a concluding epilogue.

Certain symphonic movements, too, use a waltz pattern (mostly in the ternary sequence). Examples exist in the second movement ("At the Ball") of Hector Berlioz's *Symphonie fantastique;* the third movement of Tchaikowsky's Symphony No. 5 in E minor; and the third movement of Johannes Brahms' Symphony No. 3 in F major.

THE MINUET AND TRIO

Sometime after 1725, a large ternary design known as *minuet and trio form,* became widely adopted. Structurally sound, excellently balanced, and remarkably easy for a listener to assimilate, it found extensive use in many of the suites, sonatas, and symphonies written during this and succeeding eras.

From an architectural point of view, a minuet and trio pattern consists of two relatively large and self-contained parts (A and B) that are charac-

---

[9] Other Strauss Waltzes that are similarly organized include (1) *The Emperor Waltz,* (2) *Voices of Spring,* (3) *Vienna Blood,* and (4) *Roses from the South.* (For an analysis of his *On the Beautiful Blue Danube,* see pp. 144–147).

teristically subdivided into binary or ternary strains (*ab, aba, abc*). Because
A is reaffirmed (usually via a *da capo* marking) after the close of *B*, the
entire design reflects the outlines of ternary form. In general, this is the way
it is set up:

TABLE 16.   Outline of Typical Minuet and Trio Pattern.

A (minuet)		B (trio)		A (minuet)
a;	*b + a*	*c;*	*d + c*	*a; b + a*
(repeated)	(repeated)	(repeated)	(repeated)	(without repeats)

Each subdivision may be a collection of phrases, a period, or a double
period; typically, each is from eight to twenty-four (perhaps more) measures long, and each terminates on a half or full cadence. Perceptible relationships often exist between melodies in the subdivisions, but differences
between *A* and *B* are usually quite pronounced and reflect shifts in rhythm
(meter and tempo), key, orchestration, and expressive intent. Undoubtedly,
the minuet and trio pattern arose as a result of uniting two individual
dances within a single work. Performed by a small body of players (usually
three, hence the designation trio), the second was more restrained, slower in
tempo, thinner in sonority, and darker in color than its associate.

Actually an idealized version of a very popular eighteenth-century
dance, the Menuetto (fourth movement) in J. S. Bach's *Brandenburg Concerto No. 1* (1721) reveals the outlines of a small-scaled minuet and trio
design. Part of a larger structure that also includes a *Polacca* and a Trio II,
this portion has the ground plan: [10]

TABLE 17.   Outline of Bach Menuetto.

A (Menuetto)		B (Trio)		A (Menuetto)
a (12)	*b* (12)	*c* (8)	*d* (20)	*da capo*
(r)	(r)	(r)	(r)	of *a,b*

Often used by Haydn, Mozart, Schubert, Beethoven, and contemporaries
within third movements of their symphonies, the minuet and trio design
became considerably enlarged after 1775. An extended version is exemplified by the Menuetto (third movement) of Mozart's Symphony No. 39 in
E-flat major (K. 543). These are details:

1. *A* (menuetto): *a.* Full orchestra announces a sixteen-measure period
   that begins like this:

[10] Numbers in parentheses indicate the total measures in each strain; the abbreviation (r) indicates repetition.

2. *b + a.* This same group continues with another strain that has a total expanse of twenty-eight measures. Actually, it is comprised of 8 + 20 measures:

3. *B* (trio): *c.* An eight measure strain features the first clarinet:

4. *d + c.* And the next section, with two eight-measure segments, introduces this idea:

5. *A* (menuetto): *a; b + a.* Finally, a verbatim repetition of the first section, without repetition of strains, is accomplished via the *da capo* marking.

THE SCHERZO

Taking its name from the Italian language, where *scherzo* connotes a jesting or sportive behavior, a musical pattern that often expresses sardonic humor, wry witticism, or unbridled exuberance gained a place in the hierarchy of musical designs shortly after 1800. Beethoven, as much as anyone, may be given credit for its formulation, although at least one of his predecessors (Haydn), some of his contemporaries (Schubert, for example), and many of his successors (Mendelssohn, Berlioz, Schumann), made considerable use of this impetuous design. Individual pieces disclose intrinsic differences, of course, but most scherzos have these distinctive characterics:

1. An unusually rapid pace.
2. Angular, craggy, and incisive melodic outlines.

3. A general adherence to triple meter (although some use duple).

4. A common adoption of ternary form.

5. An abundance of syncopation spiced with piquant cross-rhythms.

6. Sudden dynamic changes.

7. A consistent use of crisp, neatly articulated staccato tones.

Within a scherzo, diversity is obtained by shifts in instrumental coloration, a use of contrasted dynamic levels, and an employment of different melodic strains. Thematic manipulation (as in sonata form, for instance) may appear, but it is quite rare; rather, ternary part form, with *ab* and *cd* subdivisions (similar in outline to the minuet and trio pattern already mentioned), is a scherzo's typical plan.

As the fifth movement within his Septet in E-flat major (scored for violin, viola, 'cello, string bass, clarinet, horn, and bassoon), Beethoven employs a pulsating scherzo.[11] Cast in triple meter, but played so rapidly that one feels only a single pulse in each measure, it is marked *allegro molto e vivace* and has these details:

1. *A* (scherzo): [12] *a.* Playing the tones of a descending E-flat major chord the horn begins the first strain, but is soon joined by other instruments that extend the theme over a sixteen-measure expanse:

2. *b* + *a:* Continuing a crisp articulation of tones, the full ensemble presents a brief antiphonal discourse as the second strain begins. An expanse of thirty measures is traversed until an extended version of *a* appears to close the section.

3. *B* (trio): *c.* Playing in its upper register, the 'cello sounds this sustained subject as the trio opens:

[11] Other notable examples, some organized quite differently, include the "Queen Mab" Scherzo from Berlioz's *Roméo et Juliette* symphony, and the Scherzo from Mendelssohn's Incidental Music for *A Midsummer's Night Dream* (discussed in Chapter 9).

[12] Almost invariably, the several subdivisions *a, b, c, d* within a scherzo experience immediate repetition. Just as invariably, they are *not* repeated when reaffirmed in a *da capo*.

4. *d + c:* And this same instrument continues by presenting a lyrical *sostenuto* (*d*) for sixteen measures until the trio's first subject *c* returns:

5. A (scherzo): *a; b + a.* Rounding out a ternary design, the entire first section A is brought back via a *da capo* marking. This time, of course, its strains are played without repetition.

Another scherzo example appears in the third movement of Schubert's Octet in F major. Scored for two violins, viola, 'cello, string bass, clarinet, bassoon, and horn, this excellent chamber music piece effectively combines the piquant sonorities of string, woodwind, and brass instruments. Set in the tonic key, marked to be played *allegro vivace,* and established in a scherzo's usual triple meter, it is organized in a large ternary design. These are details about it:

1. A (scherzo): *a.* Playing in unison, strings introduce the first four measures of a motive-like subject; they are joined by winds for the second four measures (which are harmonized):

2. Much repetition and extension of the subject is accomplished during the remainder of this thirty-six measure strain.
3. *b + a:* Maintaining an obvious thematic relationship with the foregoing, the second strain continually reaffirms a fragment from the first subject. The recurrence of *a* begins in a verbatim manner, but its length is greatly extended by further motivic byplay. In all, this strain has 102 measures.
4. B (trio): *c.* Flowing in a more leisurely manner and shifting to C major, this twenty-measure strain is conveyed almost entirely by the string quartet (only the bassoon intrudes briefly):

5. *d + c:* The prevailing mood of sustained lyricism is maintained (in *d*) for another twenty-four measures before a modified version (sixteen measures long) of *c* appears.

6. *A* (scherzo): *a; b + a.* Verbatim recurrence is maintained via a *da capo* marking when the vigorous scherzo returns to complete the ternary design.

PARTICULAR EXAMPLES OF PART FORM

Johann Sebastian Bach (1685–1750), *French Suite* No. 5 in G major

Written to be performed on the clavichord or harpsichord, typical keyboard instruments of the eighteenth century, in recent times Bach's clavier compositions have become standard items in the literature for piano. Some are contained in the *Clavierubung* (Keyboard Exercises), a four-volume collection of pieces written between 1731 and 1742. Others are in such sets as the *Well-Tempered Clavier,* forty-eight preludes and fugues (two in each major and minor key) written in 1722 and 1744; in the two-part and three-part Inventions collated in 1723; or in the six *English Suites* and six *French Suites,* both dating from about 1720. Essentially stylized collections of well-known dances, each of the latter includes from five to eight independent pieces, most organized in binary form.[13] Why the two sets were termed French and English is something of a mystery. All six *English Suites* begin with lengthy preludes, however, a movement not included in the *French Suites* and this may account for their separate classification.

With a sequence of seven dances, each in the home tonality of G major and each organized in binary form, the *French Suite* No. 5 is an elegant and graceful example of Baroque keyboard music. These are details about its sections:

1. *Allemande:* Established in quadruple meter and marked to be played at a moderate tempo, this opening dance has a florid melodic line considerably enriched by *agréments* (embellishments). After beginning in the tonic, its first strain (twelve measures long) finds a cadence on the dominant (D major); the second (also of twelve measures) begins in the new key and concludes on the tonic. Three lines are perceptible: (1) a soprano melody, (2) a supporting bass, and (3) a harmonic middle voice. This is how the piece begins:

[13] A more extended discussion of the suite (and these pieces) will be found in Chapter 11.

2. *Courante:* Quickly paced and in triple meter, the second section has two
   strains of sixteen measures each. Two lines are apparent, a sprightly
   melody and an equally nimble bass:

3. *Sarabande:* Rather austere in expression, in triple meter, and written
   with three discernible lines, this piece has an opening strain of sixteen
   measures and a second of twenty-four. It begins like this:

4. *Gavotte:* Played in *alla-breve* time (2/2) at a moderately rapid tempo,
   this brisk dance is an effective foil for its sedate predecessor. The first
   section has eight measures; whereas the second has sixteen. Possessing
   an attractive melody, the piece begins like this:

5. *Bourrée:* Rhythmically similar to the gavotte and with *a* and *b* strains
   of ten and twenty measures, respectively, the fifth section continues in
   duple meter and a rapid tempo. Its musical substance is rather spare
   and consists of the melody with a continually moving bass:

6. *Loure:* In compound meter (6/4), played with six beats in a measure, this stately episode has two sections of eight measures each:

7. *Gigue:* Rollicking and irrepressible, the gigue is in compound meter (12/8, with four beats in a measure), and has a first strain of twenty-four measures and a second of thirty-two:

Wolfgang Amadeus Mozart (1756–1791), Menuetto from Quintet in A major for Clarinet and Strings (K. 581)

Written in 1790, when the composer was at the height of his powers (but, unfortunately, with only one year of life remaining), Mozart's clarinet quintet is a beautiful chamber music composition with four contrasted movements. Each is thematically, structurally, and expressively autonomous; yet, the entire composition is a model of beautifully integrated formal elegance.

Returning to the basic tonality of A major (the second movement shifts to the subdominant, D major), the quintet's third movement is a Menuetto with two trios. Throughout, it retains triple meter (as is characteristic of all menuets) and consistently adheres to an *allegretto* tempo. Distinctive contrasts in coloration are effected by shifting from string to wind timbre, a particularly notable divergence between the two trios. For the most part, however, all five instruments perform in an altogether compatible manner. Although the movement's several subdivisions are readily apparent—obvious cadences are interposed between them—the total structure is remarkably synthesized. Seemingly, each new melodic idea grows out of its predecessor, the musical flow appears to be spontaneous, and the total design gives an impression of being irresistibly logical.

1. *A* (menuetto): [14] *a.* Opening without an introduction, the full ensemble presents this initial eight-measure subject:

---

[14] Following usual part-form procedures, the several strains *a, b, c, d, e, f* are repeated immediately after their initial presentation, but they are not reaffirmed when the two *da capos* appear.

2. *b + a:* In succession, strings introduce a digressive strain of sixteen measures, after which a verbatim return is made to *a.*

3. *B* (first trio): *c.* Shifting to A minor, string instruments sound an angular, but restrained, sixteen-measure theme:

4. *d + c:* While maintaining the same somber mood, the subsequent strain presents an eight-measure digression before a modified version of *c* appears.

5. *A* (menuetto): *a;* b + a. By observing the *da capo* marking, a return is now made to the *menuetto.* However, its strains are heard *senza replica* (without repetition).

6. *C* (second trio): *e.* With this jaunty melody sounded by the clarinet over a string accompaniment, the piece enters its fourth section:

7. *f + e:* Strings modify this lilting tune as they move into a succeeding strain of twenty-three measures. After a half cadence, the entire ensemble reaffirms (and slightly extends) *e.*

8. *A* (menuetto): *a;* b + a. Again, the initial section returns and its strains are heard without repetition. This time, of course, it writes *finis* to the movement.

Ludwig van Beethoven (1770–1827), Scherzo from Symphony No. 3 in E-flat major

Written during 1803–1804 as he was entering the so-called second period of his career, Beethoven's third symphony shows a fully matured composer at work. Considerably more expansive than any pre-existent composition of its kind, the "Eroica" Symphony (so-called because the composer designated it a testimonial to the heroic nature of mankind) is filled with noble ideas. Unquestionably, it is one of music's most monumental works.

In lieu of the courtly minuet that had become a conventional interpolation during preceding decades, Beethoven inserted an impetuous scherzo as the third movement in his E-flat symphony. Previously, he had experimented with a similar concept (in the Symphony No. 2 in D major), but despite a quickened tempo and some angular rhythms, this earlier piece retains a minuet's conventional qualities and is lilting rather than dynamic, jovial rather than impassioned. But an invigorating scherzo—replete with tumultuous string passages, vigorously accented cross-rhythms, and abundant syncopation—is a distinctive addition to the Symphony No. 3, and stands as a strikingly novel (for its time) addition to the hierarchy of symphonic designs.

1. *A* (scherzo): *a.* Utilizing the work's home tonality (E-flat major), the first strain opens with a subdued passage of exquisite delicacy. Staccato strings produce a rustle of sound as they play in triple meter (with one pulse to the measure) at an *allegro vivace* pace. Atop this base, an oboe (doubled by first violins an octave lower) introduces this important subject:

2. *b* + *a:* Only thirty measures long, the first strain is succeeded by a passage of 135 measures, whose length is further extended by repetition. Considerable use is made of the first theme in this section, for the initial subject returns repeatedly in a variety of guises. Upon repetition, this section terminates on a full cadence.
3. *B* (trio): *c.* Brilliantly evoking a long-standing tradition of using only three instruments for the midsection (that is, trio) of a work in ternary form, Beethoven employs three horns to sound this fanfare-like subject:

4. Minimal interjections are made by strings and woodwinds during these thirty-two measures.
5. *d* + *c:* Traversed twice, the trio's second strain has sixty-two measures. Initially it is concerned with a soaring woodwind subject supported by angular string figurations, but selected woodwinds (flute, oboe, bassoon) later sound this smooth-flowing idea over a three-octave expanse:

p dolce sempre legato

6. After brief string interjections, horns reaffirm *c*.
7. *A* (scherzo): *a; b + a*. Plunging ahead with precipitous haste, Beethoven reaffirms the scherzo. Obviously similar, this recapitulation deviates only slightly by interpolating three measures in duple meter (*alla breve*) near its end. Over all, of course, scherzo-like staccato articulations, insistent pulsations, and tangy cross-rhythms are maintained.
8. *Coda:* Utilizing the same pace as heretofore and employing melodic-rhythmic ideas previously expressed in other sections, a relatively short (twenty-measure) coda brings this epochal symphonic movement to an incisive close.

Johann Strauss II (1823–1899), *On the Beautiful Blue Danube Waltzes*

Writing for an adulating nineteenth century audience, members of a gifted musical family somewhat humorously called "The Waltzing Strausses," created an abundance of three-quarter time melodies (and almost as many polkas, marches, galops, and similar pieces) that brought them considerable fame and fortune. Sire of the family was Johann I (1804–1849), a Viennese orchestra leader who gained local renown as a composer, but later became internationally celebrated as the father of Johann II (often called the "Waltz King"). Two other children, Josef (1827–1870) and Eduard (1835–1916), also earned glowing reputations as composer-conductors.

Undoubtedly the most facile creative talent in the family, Johann II extended and enlarged a legacy bequeathed by his father and Joseph Lanner, another pioneering writer of scintillating waltzes. Strauss had an uncanny ability for formulating ravishing melodies, luxuriant harmonies, and sparkling rhythms with which to cloak the dictatorial throb of rigid dance forms. In addition to sixteen operettas (the best-known are *Die Fledermaus*, 1874, and *Der Ziguenerbaron*, 1885), he wrote over five hundred unusually attractive compositions. These are details about the five principal sections (each organized in binary or ternary form) within his *Blue Danube Waltzes*, 1867.[15]

1. *Introduction:* Tremolo strings provide a background as the solo horn presents fragments from a beloved and important melody. Opening in

---

[15] Contemporary conductors exercise considerable latitude in observing (or neglecting) repeats or *da capos* in pieces of this kind. Consequently, a listener must be prepared to accept occasional deviations from the composer's original plan.

the key of A major, the introduction is first played at an *andantino* tempo in sextuple meter. Before long, however, this meditative vein is interrupted and a *tempo di valse* appears to establish the work's basic tonality (D major), meter (triple), and tempo (*allegro moderato*).

2. *Waltz No. 1: a.* Upward rising tones announce the familiar *Blue Danube* melody; crisp rhythmic interjections impel the dance on its way:

3. *b:* Detached staccato tones become prominent in the incisive melody of the second strain:

$$\begin{array}{cc}
a & b \\
\text{32 measures (D major)} & \text{16 measures (r) (A major)}
\end{array}$$

4. *Waltz No. 2: c.* Maintaining tangy waltz momentum, 'cellos sound this lilting tune:

5. *d:* But the prevailing expressive mood becomes pensive when first violins interject a new idea:

6. *c:* Verbatim recurrence of the first strain (*c*) is accomplished via the *da capo* marking.

c
16 measures (r) (D major) d
16 measures (B-flat major) c
da capo

7. *Waltz No. 3: e.* Somewhat angular in outline, this opening melody is, nevertheless, attractive:

8. *f:* And a succeeding subject is similarly engaging:

e
16 measures (r) (G major) f
16 measures (r) (G major)

9. *Waltz No. 4: g.* After a brief martial introduction, ascending arpeggio tones dissipate any semblance of solemnity and the lilting dance continues:

10. *h:* Now an unusually agile melody appears:

Introduction, g h
4 measures   16 measures (r) (F major) 16 measures (r) (F major)

11. *Waltz No. 5: i.* Succeeding a ten-measure portentous introduction, a smooth-flowing tune quickly removes any aura of strictness:

12. *j:* But the second strain is resolute and strong:

Introduction,   *i*   *j*
10 measures   16 measures (r) (A major)   16 measures (r) (A major)

13. *Coda:* Concluding segments in Strauss waltzes are usually a lengthy reprise of previously heard material. The *Blue Danube's* coda, for instance, with an expanse of 146 measures, is nearly as long as the five combined waltzes. Familiar melodies reappear in profusion with, however, subtle changes in harmonic background, instrumental color, or contrapuntal involvement. Finally, a spirited passage marked *rascher* (very quickly) concludes.

Dmitri Shostakovich (b. 1906), *Allegretto* from Symphony No. 5

Fluently creative, equipped with a ready fund of innovational techniques and prodigious amounts of imaginative ideas, Dmitri Shostakovich has become one of Russia's most outstanding composers. Although he has written an abundance of chamber music, songs, opera, and concertos, Shostakovich has acquired unusual distinction in the symphonic domain and his (to date) thirteen symphonies are frequently-performed contemporary masterworks. Chief among them is the Symphony No. 5 (1937).

Organized in a traditional four-movement sequence, and skillfully employing the coloristic resources of an enlarged modern orchestra (including the small E-flat clarinet, contrabassoon, and piano), Shostakovich's Fifth Symphony has a dynamic first movement, an eloquent and slowly paced third, and a brusque, tumultous finale. Organized in ternary form, its second movement is a tense, quick-moving, irrepressible scherzo. These are details about it:

1. *A* (scherzo): Moving in a brisk *allegretto* tempo (the metronome marking is 138), the opening segment—in A minor and triple meter, save for occasional quadruple interjections—employs 'cellos and basses to play a heavy-footed passage in octaves (*a1*):

2. Soon thereafter (in measure 13), the shrill E-flat clarinet, with assistance from other high-pitched woodwinds, sounds an impertinent theme (*a2*):

3. After both ideas have been extended, woodwinds announce a new subject (*b1*) that is fully consonant with the section's prevailing mood of gay raillery:

4. In alternation, horns sound a contrasted fanfare (*b2*):

5. *B* (trio): [16] More restrained in utterance, the movement's middle section is decidedly lyric in expression and rather opaque in scoring. Initially, a solo violin sounds this melody (*c*) over a harp and 'cello accompaniment, after which it is repeated by the flute over a bassoon and string background:

6. Brusquely interrupting this idyllic flow, unisonal strings (with assistance from horns) present another idea (*d1*):

---

[16] Using the designation *trio* at this point is my own invention; it does not appear in the Shostakovich score.

7. An extension (*d2*), however, is marvelously refined:

8. *A* (scherzo): Reassigned to bassoon and contrabassoon (in lieu of the previously used 'cello-bass combination) the first theme *a1* harkens a reaffirmation of the scherzo. All four themes *a1, a2, b1, b2* reappear, but this is not a verbatim reaffirmation, for numerous changes are introduced in orchestration and key. The dimensions of each are approximately the same, however, for the first scherzo had eighty-six measures whereas this concluding portion has eighty-three.

9. *Coda:* After a brief two-measure interjection has been sounded by timpani, the solo oboe presents a brief reminiscence of a theme (*c*) from the movement's midsection. Then, with a joyous outburst, the full orchestra sweeps this brash and piquant movement to a clangorous close.

Some Further Examples of Part Form

Bach, Johann Sebastian. Suite No. 2 in B minor for Flute and Strings: (a) Sarabande, (b) Bourrée I, (c) Bourrée II, (d) Polonaise, (e) Menuet, (f) Badinerie (all in binary form).

Beethoven, Ludwig van. Quartet No. 2 in G major, third movement (scherzo with trio). Symphony No. 8 in F major, third movement (menuet with trio).

Bizet, Georges. *L'Arlésienne: Suites Nos. 1 & 2:* (a) Menuetto, (b) Carillon, (c) Pastorale, (d) Intermezzo; Symphony No. 1 in C major, third movement (scherzo with trio).

Chopin, Frederic. Scherzos (for piano); Waltzes (for piano).

Debussy, Claude. *Children's Corner Suite* (for piano): (a) "Doctor Gradus ad Parnassum," (b) "Jimbo's Lullaby," (c) "Serenade for the Doll," (d) "The Little Shepherd," (e) "Golliwogg's Cake Walk."

Dvořák, Antonin. *Slavonic Dances;* Symphony No. 7 in D minor, third movement (scherzo); Symphony No. 9 in E minor, third movement (scherzo).

Handel, George. *Royal Fireworks Suite:* (a) Bourrée, (b) *La Paix,* (c) *La rejouissance,* (d) Menuet I & II (all in binary form).

Haydn, Franz Joseph. Quartet in D major ("Lark"), third movement (menuet with trio); Symphony No. 101 in D major ("Clock"), third movement (menuet with trio).

Mendelssohn, Felix. Octet in E-flat major for Strings, third movement (scherzo); Quartet No. 4 in E minor, second movement (scherzo); Symphony No. 4 in A major ("Italian"), third movement (menuet with trio).

Mozart, Wolfgang Amadeus. Concerto in A major for Clarinet (K. 622), second movement (ABA); Overture, *Abduction from the Seraglio* (K. 384) (ABA); Symphony No. 41 in C major ("Jupiter"), third movement (menuet with trio).

Prokofiev, Serge. Concerto No. 2 in G minor for Violin (1935), second movement.

Ravel, Maurice. *Mother Goose Suite:* "Pavane of the Sleeping Beauty" (ternary form).

Rossini, Gioacchino. Overture, *William Tell*.

Schubert, Franz. *Moments Musicaux* (for piano); Quartet No. 14 in D minor ("Death and the Maiden"), third movement; Quintet in A major ("Trout"), third movement.

Schumann, Robert. Works for piano including: (a) *Carnaval*, (b) *Kinderscenen*, (c) *Waldscenen*; Symphony No. 1 in B-flat major ("Spring"), second and third movements.

Tchaikowsky, Peter. Concerto No. 1 in B-flat minor for Piano, second movement (ABA); *The Nutcracker Suite:* (a) "Dance of the Sugar Plum Fairy," (b) "Trepak," (c) "Arabian Dance," (d) "Chinese Dance," (e) "Dance of the Reed Flutes."

Wagner, Richard. Prelude, Act III of *Lohengrin;* Overture, to *Tannhäuser*.

Chapter 7

Constancy with Change: Theme and Variation Form

Founded on the time-honored principle of constancy with change, theme and variation form successfully merges artistic concepts that may—initially—appear antipathetic. Frequently used by instrumentalists while improvising on a jazz "classic," or by church organists while extemporizing on a congregational hymn (chorale), it has been proven one of music's most durable and useful designs. Anyone who has ever added a few flourishes of his own while whistling a tune knows something about variation form. And he knows, moreover, of the satisfaction to be gained from ornamenting a melody with a few choice roulades and embellishments.

Formal variations, of course, are far more intricate than the casual improvisations of a whistling dilettante, but the techniques used in creating either are quite similar. Beginning with a memorable tune (often established in simple part form), a musician (or whistler) spins a filigree around the subject's outermost limits. Mostly, these embellishments have to do with melodic change (perhaps the most common of all variation procedures), but occasionally they touch on changes in rhythm, tonality, harmony, texture, or coloration.

THE VARIATION THEME

Because it is the foundation for all subsequent variants, a theme used in variation form is of overriding importance. Such melodies must be memorable, attractive, malleable, resilient, and durable. These qualities are demonstrated, for example, in subjects employed by Haydn in the second movement of his String Quartet in C major ("Emperor"); by Handel in the "Harmonious Blacksmith" from his Suite No. 5 for Harpsichord; and by Schubert in his Quartet No. 14 in D minor, often called "Death and the Maiden":

151

When creating a set of variations, a composer may work with an original subject or a borrowed theme. Folk tunes are often used for this purpose (for example, Dohnanyi's *Variations on a Nursery Song* or Kodály's *Peacock Variations*), but themes by other composers see occasional service, too: Brahms' *Variations on a Theme by Haydn*, Rachmaninoff's *Rhapsody on a Theme of Paganini*, or Arensky's *Variations on a Theme by Tchai-*

kowsky. In such instances, acknowledgment is customarily made of the subject's source.

Although they should not be considered formula-ridden, most variation themes are (1) tuneful, (2) regular in structure, (3) comparatively short, (4) direct in expression, and (5) distinctly memorable. On the other hand, themes that are (1) lengthy, (2) irregular, (3) complicated or florid, (4) lacking in simple tunefulness or individuality, or (5) banal do not make satisfactory variation subjects, although they may find apt usage elsewhere.

A clear, concise, and direct statement of the theme normally occurs at or near the beginning of a composition in variation form. Specific statements of this subject may also appear in several (or all) of the subsequently variations when it appears simultaneously with the embellishing lines. Mostly, verbatim affirmation occurs in earlier sections, whereas a shifting away from an exact (or a near-exact) quotation is reserved for later variations. When a theme is clearly stipulated it is said to be *explicit,* but when its precise substance is allusive, vague, or merely suggestive it becomes *implicit.* Both kinds of presentation are commonly used in variation designs.

VARIATION ACTIVITY

Successive variations challenge the constancy of a theme. Typically, most of these adhere to a subject's outlines, contain the same number of measures, retain the same harmonic substructure, and observe identical cadential points. Despite adherence to a common base, however, each variant discloses sufficient individuality to engage a listener's mind and challenge his ear. Variations appear successively (occasionally connected by intermediary bridge passages) and are identified by number (that is, "variation one," "variation two," and so on), although titles are sometimes given them, particularly in descriptive works. For the most part, each variation concludes on a full cadence, and a short pause occurs before its successor is begun. Admittedly, a great deal of activity in this design is technical and concerned with an adroit manipulation of materials (rhythms, melodies, or harmonies). Yet, the primary artistic intent of a piece in variation form is to disclose the full expressive potential of its subject. Without such aesthetic penetration, the undertaking is reduced to a mere mechanical exercise.

Since the early seventeenth century, when modern concepts about variation form were formulated, four primary kinds of design have become prominent:

1. A pattern wherein the theme's tonal outline and harmonic substructure remain fixed. Widely used until about 1750, it mostly relies on rhythmic shifts and the superimposition of ornaments to embellish the melodic line. Grace notes, mordents, grupetti, trills, and agréments are

freely used within the design. J. S. Bach's *Goldberg Variations* are exemplificative.

2. A design that remains harmonically fixed while sustaining wide-ranging melodic change became well-known in the late eighteenth century. Mozart's numerous variations (for instance, his twelve variations on *Ah, vous dirai-je, Maman,* described subsequently) illustrate the type.

3. A plan that recognizes a theme's structural outlines while permitting considerable latitude in a treatment of its melody and harmony moved to the fore about 1850. Brahms' *Variations on a Theme by Haydn* (see p. 170) exemplifies it.

4. A free variation pattern that treats its melodic material in a distinctly casual manner arose sometime around 1890. Neither thematic outlines, harmonic base, nor formal patterns are rigorously observed in works of this kind. Richard Strauss' *Don Quixote* (see p. 163) is a fine example.

Witty and whimsical, the set of twelve variations that Mozart created (in 1778) on *Ah, vous dirai-je, Maman* (I will speak to you, Mama), a folk melody that countless generations of children in English-speaking lands have known as "Twinkle, Twinkle, Little Star," exhibits the neatly balanced outlines characteristic of late eighteenth-century variation designs. Exhibiting a regular phrase structure, the theme has a sequence of eight-measure segments with the outline *a (r), b + a:*

In succession, twelve variants, plus a brief coda, appear. Each scrupulously adheres to the theme's outlines, but each also exhibits a distinctive individuality acquired mostly by an interpolation of melodic embellishments. These are details:

1. *Variation one.* Firmly establishing the home key of C major (used in all the variants except number 8), this section imposes a sixteenth-note figuration above an abstracted version of the theme:

legato

2. *Variation two.* Rhythmic momentum now shifts to the bass register (the pianist's left hand), while an explicit theme is heard in the upper voice:

legato

3. *Variation three.* A triplet figure skips nimbly over a relatively wide expanse while the theme is outlined below:

4. *Variation four.* Almost a total reversal of the previous section, this variant features triplet motion in the bass register while the theme sounds above:

5. *Variation five.* Incipits from the subject are exchanged between the treble and bass voices in a most adroit way:

6. *Variation six.* Scalar motion to adjacent steps soars upward from the lower register as crisp chords in the upper hand mark the beat:

p legato   *cresc.*

7. *Variation seven.* Now the upper line moves fluently over a sustained bass background:

8. *Variation eight.* Exhibiting an important harmonic shift, this variant ventures to the tonality of C minor:

9. *Variation nine.* Back in major, this segment has some contrapuntal involvement readily distinguishable in the successive entries of voices:

10. *Variation ten.* Melodic tones sound amidst fleet sixteenth-note embellishments; later a number of "foreign" chords challenge (temporarily) the work's harmonic structure:

11. *Variation eleven.* Marked to be played *adagio,* this is the composition's slowest section. Initially restrained, the passagework later becomes quite florid:

12. *Variation twelve.* Featuring a shift to triple meter, this variant cleverly imposes a modified version of the theme above a rapidly paced bass figuration:

13. *Coda.* Bound directly to the final variation, this eleven-measure epilogue maintains the same meter, tempo, key, and melodic figuration while bringing the piece to a definitive close.

VARIATION PROCEDURES

Composers invariably display skill, fluency, and remarkable ingenuity when writing in the variation pattern. And because the means by which a theme can be varied are infinitely diverse, no two approach their task in quite the same way. But these are some of the basic procedures that have been widely adopted:

1. *Rhythmic change,* which may involve shifts in tempo, meter, or figures of accompaniment, as well as the augmentation (lengthening) or diminution (shortening) of note values in a theme. Often in this undertaking, a melody may be recast as a march or a dance or be embellished so that it has two, three, four, or more tones on a beat.
2. *Melodic change,* which can be accomplished by adding or deleting tones from a theme. But several other possibilities exist, notably: (a) introducing embellishing tones (that is, higher or lower neighbors, chord tones, or scale runs) into the melodic line; (b) interpolating arabesques (called *obbligatos*) above or below a subject; (c) changing a melody from major to minor (or vice versa); (d) transferring the theme from one register to another; or (e) inverting it so the tonal flow is opposite the original.
3. *Harmonic change,* a subtle but effective kind of shift, that can be used as a corollary with melodic and expressive change. Often, it involves changes in key and mode, or an employment of exotic embellishing chords.
4. *Change in coloration,* which can rather easily be accomplished by shifting from one instrument (or family) to another, by a divergence in register, or by a use of modified dynamic levels. Employing such devices as *pizzicato* (or altered bowings) in strings, or mutes on brasses, is also very effective.
5. *Change in texture,* which may involve an occasional use of monophony (rare) or polyphony (more common) in variation design. Of available

polyphonic patterns, canon and fugue (fugato) are especial favorites.

6. *Altered expressive intent*, which leads a listener toward the discovery of a theme's latent poetic resources. Such character changes are accomplished, of course, by using one or more of the technical devices mentioned here.

Several of these variation techniques are demonstrated in the fourth movement of Schubert's Quintet in A major ("Trout") for Piano and Strings. Based on one of the composer's art songs, *Die Forelle,* and scored for violin, viola, 'cello, string bass, and piano, this lovely piece begins when strings announce the melody in D major: [1]

Encompassing twenty-eight measures, the subject has this pattern:

a	*b*	*c*
(8 meas.) (r)	(4 meas.)	(4 + 4 meas.)

These are details about each variation:

1. *Variation one.* While the bass provides a pizzicato foundation and other strings contribute decorative arabesques, the piano (making its first appearance) plays the theme.
2. *Variation two.* Sounded by the viola in a middle register, with a contributory harmonization from the 'cello, the theme is embellished by violin figurations:

3. *Variation three.* Descending to a low register, the subject is sounded (in octaves) by the 'cello and bass while the violin and viola provide discreet

---

[1] In large works (chamber pieces, concertos, symphonies, or operas) individual movements (or sections) may be shifted to related keys. This change to the subdominant is actually quite orthodox.

rhythmic accompaniments for it. But the piano attracts primary attention in this section by playing rapidly paced octave embellishments:

4. *Variation four.* Moving away from the movement's primary key (D major), the tonality now shifts to D minor. A darker color permeates the music, but the pace does not slacken as the entire quintet conveys a rhythmically marked variant on an implicit theme.
5. *Variation five.* While other ensemble members play a subdued accompaniment, the 'cello sounds a melodic variant in the key of B-flat major:

6. *Coda.* Returning to the home key, this epilogue reaffirms and extends the theme for seventeen measures. Shifts in coloration occur when passages are sounded by the violin-piano combination and reiterated by strings alone (with the 'cello carrying the melody). Shortly thereafter, the work tapers to a gentle close.

CHACONNE AND PASSACAGLIA

Specialized variation designs founded on a brief and simple melody (which is often identified as a *basso ostinato* or *ground bass*), the chaconne and/or passacaglia are used in works for keyboard instruments, ensembles, or orchestra.[2] Actually, the two are so nearly identical that a discussion of one (and we shall speak only of the passacaglia) is sufficient to describe the other.

Passacaglias are often in triple meter and most adhere to such relatively slow tempos as *andante, largo,* or *adagio.* Originally they were ceremonial dances of Spanish or Italian ancestry, but despite this choreographic association, their expression is stately and profound rather than animated and rhythmic. In general, passacaglias have these characteristics:

1. Themes are nearly always explicit and demonstrably present in each variation.

---

[2] As variation designs, both patterns apparently made their first appearance in Spanish lute music of the sixteenth century; later, they were widely used in seventeenth-century English pieces for virginals.

2. Very often passacaglia subjects have only a single tone in a measure, many disclose a limited compass, and tonal movement within them may progress only to adjacent scale steps.
3. Although uncomplicated, passacaglia subjects may have strong harmonic implications that are only gradually realized as the variations progress.
4. Variations are continuous and flow directly into one another. Cadences between sections are minimized or evaded, and perceptible pauses are rare.
5. Because of the theme's brevity, passacaglias usually have a rather large number of variations—perhaps as many as twenty or more.

Composed originally for a two-manual clavicembalo, later arranged for organ, and often heard today in an orchestral transcription (by Respighi, Stokowski, Ormandy, and others), J. S. Bach's Passacaglia and Fugue in C minor is based on this theme: [3]

In succession, twenty variants appear, each clinging to the theme's eight-measure outline. Mostly, the melody lingers deep in the bass, but in two instances it moves into the upper register and occasionally is heard only by implication. As a tour de force with which to conclude his passacaglia, Bach uses a double fugue based on two separate subjects. One is the theme quoted here, the other is this:

Gustav Holst uses a chaconne as the opening movement of his First Suite in E-flat major for Military Band (1909). Based on an eight-measure theme, it begins when the subject is introduced by euphoniums and basses:

[3] Other representative examples of this design appear in the final movement of Bach's Partita No. 2 for Unaccompanied Violin (where it is termed a chaconne); the aria, "Dido's Lament," from Henry Purcell's opera *Dido and Aeneas;* the fourth movement of Brahms' Symphony No. 4 in E minor; the ballet music Gluck wrote for *Orphée et Euridice* (1762); Vitali's *Chaconne for Violin;* the "Crucifixus" in Bach's Mass in B minor; the first movement of William Schuman's Symphony No. 3 (1941); and the fourth movement of Ralph Vaughan Williams' Symphony No. 5 (1943).

Subsequently, fourteen variations and a coda with these characteristics appear:

1. *Variation one.* As trombones sound the melody, cornets weave a smooth-flowing variant around it.
2. *Variation two.* Passing to low woodwinds, the subject is ornamented by a languid clarinet figuration.
3. *Variation three.* While woodwinds and cornets contribute agile flourishes, low brasses sound the subject.
4. *Variation four.* Similarly conceived, this variant requires trombones to reinforce the melody. Percussion are added, and the embellishing figuration becomes more syncopated.
5. *Variation five.* Brasses outline the theme while fleet woodwinds weave a sixteenth-note figuration around it.
6. *Variation six.* Upper brasses play the melody *pesante* (heavily), while low-pitched instruments contribute a steadily paced eight-note figuration.
7. *Variation seven.* A solo horn sings the melody; clarinets embellish.
8. *Variation eight.* Now the alto saxophone sounds the theme as high woodwinds present ornamental interjections.
9. *Variation nine.* Woodwinds and horn play in a smooth, flowing manner as an inverted version of the theme appears.
10. *Variation ten.* Cornets continue with the inverted theme, while tubas provide a distinct rhythmic thrust.
11. *Variation eleven.* Over a firm bass, unisonal trombones restate the theme in its original alignment.
12. *Variation twelve.* Playing in octaves, cornets and euphoniums sound the melody as woodwinds interject a descending line against it.
13. *Variation thirteen.* Building toward a climax, the subject appears in upper voices while instruments of middle range embellish it.
14. *Variation fourteen.* Playing *maestoso* (majestically), low brasses continue to express mounting tension as they reiterate the theme.
15. *Coda.* In a resonant epilogue, the full wind ensemble brings the piece to a climactic close.

EARLY VARIATION DESIGNS

Precisely when musicians began to vary themes is uncertain, but the practice is unquestionably venerable. For instance, church musicians active as early as the eighth century created polyphonic forms (organum) based on Gregorian incipits that were really variants on a plain-song melody. And successors carried this concept well into the Renaissance. Subsequently, Josquin des Pres (1440–1521) based his mass *Pangue Lingua* (published in 1539) on a well-known church hymn; and Giovanni Palestrina (1525–1594) constructed his *Missa Assumpta est Maria* (c. 1570) around another

Gregorian melody. Similarly, "divisions on a ground," variations (mostly for keyboard) that became an often-used pattern during the sixteenth and seventeenth centuries, carried the practice into instrumental music.[4] A *ground* is a composition's subject, and *divisions* are variants formulated by rhythmically compounding the theme. Somewhat later, in Bach's time, related techniques were used to create *doubles* wherein a theme (usually a dance tune) was changed by quickening its rhythmic activity. Doubles often appear within suites and associated eighteen-century instrumental compositions.[5]

During the seventeenth and eighteenth centuries, such German church composers as Dietrich Buxtehude, Johann Pachelbel, and especially J. S. Bach based many of their organ pieces, cantatas, and oratorios on Lutheran chorales (hymns). In so doing, they employed a well-known chorale melody as a theme and wove numerous variants around it. Examples include Bach's chorale preludes, which he issued in such collections as the *Orgelbuchlein* (Little Organ Book) or the *Schubler Chorales*.[6] Many of his church cantatas are similarly organized, with a beloved congregational hymn (chorale) appearing in varied form in many (and often all) of its sections. Bach's Cantata No. 140, *Wachet auf!* (discussed in Chapter 16), is a fine example.

FREE VARIATIONS

In a general collapse of formal patterns that occurred after 1850, *free variations* emerged. Normally, the procedures of variation form are comparatively rigid, but this new concept attempted to set formalism aside and establish pliancy in its stead. In the century's early years, some attempts had been made to loosen the structure by interpolating digressive episodes between variations, or by employing two or more themes within a given piece (a scheme often used by Haydn). Both techniques, incidentally, appear in the second movement of Beethoven's Symphony No. 5.

By using thematic material as an incitement to creativity but not as a limitation of action, the free variation enables a musician to pursue a relatively unfettered course. As with conventional designs, idiomatic themes are employed, but they are not necessarily symmetrical nor are they held inviolate. No effort is made, for instance, to follow an *a priori* design. Variations exploit thematic material, often at great length, but are not constricted by it. Within this pattern, subjects are handled episodically; consequently, some variations are long while others are amazingly brief. Often the treatment accorded thematic material is dictated by extramusical, or programmatic, considerations.

[4] A set of variations for virginals based on the melody, "Loath to Depart," created by Giles Farnaby (c. 1560–1600) and published originally in the Fitzwilliam Virginal Book, is included in *Masterpieces of Music Before 1750* (see Appendix C, Bibliography).
[5] See, for instance, the *Polonaise* from Bach's Suite No. 2 in B minor for Flute and Strings (discussed in Chapter 11).
[6] A particularly good individual example is the chorale prelude, *Vom Himmel hoch.*

Richard Strauss' *Don Quixote* (1897) is a highly regarded (and lengthy) example of free variation form. Employing Cervantes's tale about an elderly (and addled) would-be knight as a focus for his endeavors, Strauss created a brilliant orchestral work that includes an expansive introduction, a presentation of themes, ten variations, and a finale. In the piece, Don Quixote is depicted by a solo 'cello, while a solo viola (with occasional assistance from the bass clarinet and tenor tuba) personifies his ever-faithful servant, Sancho Panza. This is the sequence of sections in Strauss' tone poem:

1. *Introduction.* Presentation of the Dulcinea theme ("The Ideal Woman"); Don Quixote goes mad.
2. *Theme.* Don Quixote, "Knight of the Sorrowful Countenance," and Sancho Panza, his mule-riding squire, are introduced.
3. *Variation one.* "Adventure with the Windmills": Quixote takes to the road, attempts to attack a windmill, and is unceremoniously dumped from his horse by the churning arms.
4. *Variation two.* "Battle with the Sheep": Considering a herd of sheep to be the army of Alifanfaron, he charges and manages to kill seven of the animals. Stoned by the shepherd, Quixote falls to the ground.
5. *Variation three.* "Colloquies of Knight and Squire": In a lengthy exchange of views, Quixote is sentimental, the squire practical; an argument follows.
6. *Variation four.* "Adventure with the Pilgrims": Once again Quixote attacks and is bested; the victorious Pilgrims march on.
7. *Variation five.* "The Knight's Vigil": At night, standing guard beside his weapons, Quixote dreams of Dulcinea.
8. *Variation six.* "Meeting the Three Maids": When the travelers confront three village wenches, an impish Panza tries to persuade Quixote that one is Dulcinea, but Quixote is not fooled. His ideal woman is lovely, and this girl is ugly!
9. *Variation seven.* "Ride Through the Air": Sitting blindfolded on a wooden horse, the two imagine they are riding through the air; an orchestral wind machine implements the illusion.
10. *Variation Eight.* "Voyage in the Enchanted Boat": Finding an oarless boat on the shore of a stream, the two embark for a short sail but ignominiously capsize.
11. *Variation nine.* "Battle with the Benedictines": Seeing two priests, Quixote mistakes them for magicians abducting a fair princess; he attacks and the monks flee.
12. *Variation ten.* "The Defeat of Don Quixote": Ultimately defeated in battle by a neighboring knight, Quixote is obliged to retire for a year in humiliation and disillusionment. During this time sanity returns.
13. *Finale.* "Clearing of the Mind": Now of sound mind, Quixote confronts death at home. His passing is noble, dignified, and touching.

A set of variations that Lucien Calliett created (originally for band, subsequently transcribed for orchestra) on "Pop Goes the Weasel" [7] humorously (and briefly) exemplifies the free variation pattern. These are the details:

1. *Introduction.* Tossed about between brasses and woodwinds, fragments from the well-known folk melody are handled contrapuntally as the piece begins:

2. *Theme.* Familiar the world over, "Pop Goes the Weasel" is announced by the full band:

3. *Variation one.* Called a "Fugue," the first variant presents its subject in a polyphonic setting. First it is announced by clarinets, after which other voices enter to maintain the plan of a typical fugue. Now, however, the theme appears in a new key:

[7] Available recordings present this piece in its orchestral version. Because a college band can easily play it, however, I suggest that a tape be made of its performance and be used for classroom purposes. Consequently, we shall consider only the band arrangement in this analysis.

4. *Variation two.* After a six-measure introduction, a "Menuet" in characteristic triple meter is heard. Presented by upper woodwinds, the subject is
crisp and cheerful:

5. *Variation three.* Evoking the exotic "Near East," this variant returns to
duple meter as heavy brass sound a unisonal passage that prefaces an
agile clarinet cadenza. Afterward, this version of the theme is played at
a slow pace in G minor:

6. At its close, mocking laughter sounds from the trombone as if to suggest
that this tongue-in-cheek music should not be taken too seriously.
7. *Variation four.* Shortest of the sections, the "Music Box" has only sixteen
measures. Of course, its scoring is intended to simulate sounds emitted by
a miniature box organ. Woodwinds, assisted by the glockenspiel, present
this version of the theme:

8. *Variation five.* Brusque trombone smears and snappy brass fanfares interrupt the idyllic flow and announce an eight-measure transition leading
to "In Jazz," the final variation. Sounded briefly in a syncopated manner
by the full band, the subject has this contour:

9. *Coda.* Replete with assorted woodwind trills, the epilogue affirms brief portions of the theme before the entire ensemble concludes the piece with a brisk snap.

Other representative works in free variation form include: Vincent d'Indy's *Istar* (1896); Ralph Vaughan Williams' *Fantasia on a Theme by Thomas Tallis* (1910); Max Reger's *Variations on a Theme by Mozart* (1912); and Serge Rachmaninoff's *Rhapsody on a Theme of Paganini* (1934).

VARIATION FORM IN CONTEMPORARY POPULAR MUSIC

Performers have always been warmly lauded for their ability to extemporize variations on a theme. Mozart, Beethoven, Paganini, Liszt, and Chopin, for instance, known to posterity as composers of distinction, were hailed in their time as executants who won renown for skill in improvisation. Such recognition has continued into the twentieth century where acclaim (and handsome recompense) has been showered on instrumentalists who demonstrate unusual ability in improvising variants on popular tunes. Benny Goodman, Tommy and Jimmy Dorsey, Artie Shaw, Jack Teagarden, George Shearing, Louis Armstrong, Duke Ellington, and Count Basie are only a few who belong in this company.

For the most part, popular improvisation follows the procedures used in formal variations. A familiar melody is used as a theme, and an instrumentalist extemporizes variants as he "rides" through a "chorus," using "riffs," "licks," and other corollaries of the idiom. Thematic limitations are always recognized, and because a performer must "play in the chord," the work's primary harmonic structure is carefully maintained. Mostly, themes are varied by an imposition of spicily syncopated embellishments and altered rhythmic figures. Listening to recordings by the performers mentioned here (and others) will eloquently illustrate these techniques.

PARTICULAR EXAMPLES OF VARIATION FORM

Wolfgang Amadeus Mozart (1756–1791), Finale from the Quintet in A major for Clarinet and Strings (K. 581)

Prior to composing the finale for this superb clarinet quintet, Mozart had used variation form in a number of his keyboard and ensemble works. After employing it in the opening movement of his Piano Sonata in A major (K. 331), for instance, he went on to treat with the design in such dissimilar locations as the Finale (sixth movement) of his Serenade No. 10 in B-flat major for Thirteen Winds (K. 361) and the Finale of his Trio in E-flat major for Clarinet, Viola, and Piano (K. 498). Nowhere else, however, did he demonstrate a greater mastery of form or a deeper sublimity of thought than in the A major quintet. Seemingly, every note is burnished to a high gloss, every phrase is cleanly etched, and the total pattern is a model of rare excellence. Most listeners consider it a flawless work.

Consisting of a theme, five variations, and a coda, the quintet's final movement begins when this crisply articulated subject is played by the full ensemble:

Basically a ternary pattern,[8] the theme has this outline:

a	*b*	*a*
first + second phrase	third +	second phrase
(4 + 4 measure) (r)	(4 + 4 measure)	(r)

1. *Variation one.* Adhering to the theme's phrase structure, cadential points, and general outline (as do all succeeding variations), the first episode employs the clarinet to weave an arabesque around the subject (which is sounded by strings).
2. *Variation two.* Over a triplet figuration played by the second violin and viola, the first violin presents a lyric variant on the implicit subject.
3. *Variation three.* Shifting to A minor and flowing at a slightly slower tempo, this section initially highlights the viola; later (in *b*), the bright-sounding violin offers its contrasting timbre.
4. *Variation four.* Performing at a quick tempo, the clarinet undertakes agile arpeggio embellishments while strings sound the tune. In alternation, the first violin contributes effective changes of color.
5. *Interlude.* A brief four-measure connecting passage demonstrably assists in slowing the tempo.

[8] Although its outlines could be considered within the province of rounded binary form.

6. *Variation five.* Marked to be played *adagio*, this variant becomes the most pensive portion of the piece. Both first violin and clarinet embellish the implicit theme, while associates are assigned to secondary roles. (Because of the slow pace, sections within this variation are not usually repeated.)

7. *Interlude.* Another connective, five measures long, acts as a bridge between the final variation and coda.

8. *Coda.* Extending to thirty-six measures, a brisk coda in *allegro* tempo reaffirms (and slightly extends) the melody. Conclusive chords effectively write finis to the movement.

Ludwig van Beethoven (1770–1827), Finale from Symphony No. 3 in E-flat major

As a pattern for the fourth movement of his "Eroica" Symphony (1804), Beethoven created a variation design that is widely considered to be one of music's most exalted structures. Climaxing a sweeping work notable for its epic proportions, this finale is filled with complex, transcendental beauties. Based on a theme previously used in the ballet *The Creatures of Prometheus* (1801) and in the Variations (15) and Fugue on a Theme from *Prometheus* for Piano (1802), it fully demonstrates the composer's apparently inexhaustible fund of invention.

Beginning with a brief tempestuous introduction (marked *allegro molto*) sounded by strings in the key of E-flat major, the movement presents (in the twelfth measure) the spare outlines of a theme that later (in variation three) takes full-grown form:

On the basis of this extremely simple subject (harmonically founded on the tonic, subdominant, and dominant chords), Beethoven goes on to formulate a design of ten variations (of various length) and a coda. Some sections reveal an extreme economy of means, while others are infinitely more grandiose. Particular variations (the early ones) are formal in outline and follow the theme's exact structure; others are free in form and exceed the subject's dimensions. For the most part, the successive variations are continuous and flow directly into one another, often over brief bridge passages. Here are details:

1. *Variation one.* Utilizing only violins and 'cellos, the first variant is concerned with a rhythmic byplay on harmonies implicit in the theme.
2. *Variation two.* As first violins sound the theme's outlines in a sustained manner, violas (later 'cellos) weave a triplet figuration around it.
3. *Variation three.* Sounded with a clear and ringing sonority by oboe, clarinet, and bassoon, the full-blown theme (quoted here) at last makes an entrance. Around it, strings contribute a supportive configuration.
4. *Variation four.* Departing from E-flat major, this section shifts to C minor as several instruments become involved in a polyphonic discourse. Woven with great skill, it shows Beethoven's mastery of the fugal idiom.
5. *Variation five.* Now the tonality shifts to B minor (a remote key) and violins—doubled by flutes an octave higher—sound the theme in inversion. Later, both violins and flute display nimble agility while embellishing the subject.
6. *Variation six.* In a seeming parade of tonalities, G minor appears next. Suggesting the rhythms of a folk dance, the orchestra sounds a vigorous (but hardly recognizable) elaboration of the theme. Frequent interjections of the ubiquitous bass line, however, remind the listener of where he is.
7. *Variation seven.* Settling briefly in C major, this variation begins with a literal announcement of the subject, but soon (in the ninth measure) it is superseded by an imitative byplay founded on the familiar bass. Only twenty measures are included here.
8. *Variation eight.* Returning to the home tonality of E-flat major (when it does not depart for remaining strains), this expansive polyphonic variant is begun by first and second violins, with violas, 'cellos, basses, flutes, horns, and others gradually added in subsequent measures. At length, it terminates on a half cadence.
9. *Variation nine.* Interrupting the music's steady flow in duple meter, this *poco andante* slows in tempo and shifts to quadruple meter. Discoursing songfully on a lyric abstraction from the theme, woodwinds (oboe, clarinets, and bassoons) are subsequently joined by strings and horns. As measures pass, the full ensemble performs in an attractive, jaunty manner.
10. *Variation ten.* Without pause the movement sweeps into its final variation as the meter, tempo, key, and general expressive mien remain as before. Treated obliquely, semblances of the theme peek through the elaborate orchestral façade.
11. *Coda.* Assuming a *presto* pace, the epilogue plunges frenetically toward a final climax that almost obsessively reiterates the movement's basic harmonic progression. Heavily accented (and continually repeated) E-flat chords conclude.

Johannes Brahms (1833–1897), *Variations on a Theme by Joseph Haydn,* Opus 56a

While he was about it in 1873, Brahms created two versions of this lovely work, one for two pianos, the other for orchestra. For years biographers have puzzled over which was the original setting. But there is no question that the piece has become best-known in its orchestral guise.

Comprised of a theme (which Brahms rather overgenerously ascribes to Haydn, for the tune is very likely of folk origin) and eight variations, this carefully constructed work of near-symphonic proportions concludes with a robust passacaglia. Actually, this is very much like concluding a variation structure with another set of variations. Neither sameness nor monotony is observable, however, for the listener's mind is continually engaged and his ear challenged by the shifting panorama of sound paraded before his ears.

Cast in a loosely conceived *aba* pattern, the theme on which this edifice is built (often called the *St. Anthony Chorale*) has these segments:

a	*b*	*a*
first + second phrase	third + fourth phrase	second phrase + extension
(5 + 5 measure) (r)	(4 + 4 measure)	(5 + 6 measure) (r to *b*)

In musical notation, it appears like this:

1. *Variation one.* Marked *poco piu animato,* the first variation remains in the home key (B-flat major) and maintains the previously established duple meter. While strings weave a configuration around an implicit theme, winds play sustained chords supporting them.
2. *Variation two.* Shifting to B-flat minor, this section is played *piu vivace* (faster). Winds sound an angular idea, while strings add embellishments of their own.

3. *Variation three.* Back in major and played *con moto* (with motion), this variant displays a smooth and placid flow. Initially oboes are prominent, but silky-smooth violins later vie for attention.

4. *Variation four.* Pastoral in character, this section shifts to B-flat minor (as had variation two) and adopts triple meter. Both the oboe and horn are prominent and instructed to play *dolce e semplice* (sweetly and simply). Later, strings carry a variant of the melody, while flute and clarinet embellish.

5. *Variation five.* Played with brusque animation in a *vivace* tempo, this rhythmically complex variant in sextuple meter (with two beats in a measure) suggests unbridled vigor. Fleet woodwinds are featured, while crisply articulated strings provide a supportive foundation.

6. *Variation six.* Also marked *vivace*, this variation is played at a slightly slower pace and suggests a martial spirit as horns sound a series of fanfares. Meanwhile, other instruments present angular arpeggios extracted from the theme.

7. *Variation seven.* In decided contrast, this episode is bucolic in spirit and gentle in flow. Marked to be played *grazioso* (gracefully), it is in sextuple meter and relies principally on the flute and viola to enunciate a light, fluent *siciliano.*

8. *Variation eight.* Dark in color and set in the minor mode, this *presto non troppo* (not too rapid) has an organ-like sonority. As measures pass, its subdued tones sound almost awesome.

9. *Finale.* Based on a five measure subject:

this concluding passacaglia presents seventeen variants of its own before the principal subject reappears to bring the composition to a forceful and militant close.

Anton Arensky (1861–1906), *Variations on a Theme by Tchaikowsky*

When Tchaikowsky died on November 6, 1893, several of his compatriots expressed a wish to memorialize a man who had done much for Russian music. To further this end they wrote a series of compositions dedicated to him. One of these composers was Anton Arensky, a former pupil of Rimsky-Korsakov, who was actually much closer in personal temperament to Tchaikowsky than to his teacher. Within months after Tchaikowsky's passing (but actually in 1894), Arensky completed a quartet scored for the rather unusual combination of violin, viola, and two 'cellos, that had a set of variations for its second movement. Based on the fifth of Tchaikowsky's "Sixteen Children's Songs" (a piece originally entitled "Legend," but more typically known in English-speaking lands as "When Christ Was a Little Child"), this movement from the quartet was later rescored by the composer for a string orchestra that included first and second violins, violas, 'cellos, and string basses. In this form it has subsequently become very well-known.

Flowing graciously at a *moderato* pace in E minor, Tchaikowsky's lovely theme is a model of ternary song form (in the *abc* sequence):

Revealing beautifully balanced phrases, each terminating on a full cadence, it has this structure:

a	*b*	*c*
4 measures (r)	4 measures (r)	8 measures (r)

In succession, seven variations and a coda appear:

1. *Variation one.* Featuring an overlapping entry of voices, the opening variant (which doubles the length of *a* and *b* while keeping the original expanse of *c*) sustains an ambiguous relationship between major and minor.
2. *Variation two.* Playing *cantabile* (lyrically), violas and some 'cellos sound the theme while embellishments are provided from above by violins, and below by other 'cellos and basses.
3. *Variation three.* Observing the direction *andantino tranquillo*, violins sound the melody (in major and with four beats in a measure) while other strings embellish.
4. *Variation four.* Shifting to a pulsating *vivace* tempo and duple meter, this segment bristles with crisp pizzicato effects. Because they are treated freely, the theme's substance and structural outlines are quite obscured.
5. *Variation five.* Back in minor, using quadruple meter, and moving at an *andante* pace, the melody is sounded by 'cellos and basses beneath violin-viola figurations.

6. *Variation six.* Moving energetically at an *allegro con spirito* pace, the full ensemble sounds arpeggiated passages around an implicit theme.
7. *Variation seven.* Adopting an accompaniment used by Tchaikowsky in the *andante cantabile* of his first string quartet, Arensky employs muted violins to sound an inverted version of the theme above a piquant rhythmic figuration.[9]
8. *Coda.* Using eerie-sounding harmonics, violins, violas, and 'cellos begin to play a fragment of the theme, but soon embark on a pensive ten-measure discourse reminiscent of religious chant. Finally, a brief thematic incipit returns to conclude this radiantly colored work.

Ernst Dohnanyi (1877–1960), *Variations on a Nursery Song*

Filled with infectious good humor as well as flip glibness, Dohnanyi's ribald spoof of musical pretentiousness is a delightful treat. Using an innocuous little tune [10] "Twinkle, Twinkle, Little Star", the Hungarian-born composer has fashioned a piece that is by turns, witty, gay, and bitingly satiric. Its prey are the pedants who attempt to becloud music's beauty with their own pomposity. Irreverent (and sometimes irrelevant), parodist Dohnanyi hurls his cynical shaft with uncanny accuracy. Small wonder that *Variations on a Nursery Song* (1913) has become a favorite in the repertoire.

The theme, which should be compared with Mozart's subject quoted on page 154, is this:

[9] Romantics liken this to the practice of reversing rifles (so the weapons are held upside down) traditionally observed by honor guards at military funerals.

[10] The same one, incidentally, that Mozart used in his *Ah! Vous dirai-je, Maman* variations.

Whimsical interpolations at two principal cadential points (marked * in the quotation) are Dohnanyi's own. With tongue in cheek, he even makes fun of this doggerel melody.

For its performance, *Variations on a Nursery Song* enlists a solo piano and orchestra. In the key of C major, it includes a lengthy introduction, an announcement of the theme, eleven variations, and a sweeping finale. These are its salient points:

1. *Introduction.* Marked to be played *maestoso,* the lush sounding preface begins with an aura of mock severity; no symphony could be more portentous, no funeral cortege more solemn. Brasses intone, timpani rumble, and strings scrape frenetically. Lengthy and grandiloquent, the preface concludes with a flourish that apparently presages a disclosure of unusually important ideas.
2. *Theme.* Slyly the piano announces the innocuous subject, almost as a one-finger exercise. Sketchy support is provided by pizzicato strings.
3. *Variation one.* Coyly restrained while presenting the theme, the piano now displays great dexterity by scampering wildly over its upper compass. Strings sound this abstraction of the theme:

4. *Variation two.* Horns, playing in unison, manage a dignified stance while announcing a martial fanfare, but a puckish piano mocks them at every turn.
5. *Variation three.* Opulent strings undertake an espousal of the subject and benefit from the support of cascading piano arpeggios:

6. *Variation four.* Two bassoons and a contrabassoon enjoy a four-measure discourse over the piano's rhythmic foundation; two flutes and a piccolo alternate with them:

7. *Variation five.* Harp and piano depict an eighteenth-century music box as high-pitched bells outline the theme:

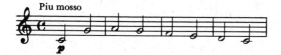

8. *Variation six.* Fluent woodwinds articulate rapidly paced arpeggios with adroit skill; as usual, the piano is not far behind.
9. *Variation seven.* Shifting to triple meter, the piano presents a gushing melody that immediately summons the image of Johann Strauss:

10. *Variation eight.* A stern march succeeds as bassoons and clarinets do what they can to simulate a martial mood. Trumpets and trombones would better suit the purpose, but this would spoil the joke. 'Cellos, string basses, and timpani bumble and thump through the section.
11. *Variation nine.* To a pageant of forms treated unconventionally, Dohnanyi adds a light-footed scherzo. This has the design's usual nimble motion, but incongruous touches succeed in arousing only the specter of a bona fide scherzo.
12. *Variation ten.* A passacaglia's stately pace replaces the scherzo; both are in triple meter, but here the resemblance ends. No one can misread the "Twinkle, Twinkle" theme that wells up from a low register, although it now has three beats on each tone.
13. *Variation eleven.* Beginning with conventional harmonizations, this episode in *maestoso* tempo conveys a chorale with mock dignity. Its harmonic underpinings are shaky, however. Insidiously, foreign tones begin to enter the chordal structure so that ultimately the refulgent harmonic colors of French Impressionism prevail.
14. *Finale, fugato.* Now, contrapuntal treatment feels the flick of Dohnanyi's satirical pen. In the wake of a series of rushing scale passages, fragments from the theme are announced in a fugal manner by violas, clarinet, violin, and oboe. Of course, the ubiquitous piano joins in a melee that causes the subject to undergo unusually involved convolutions. Finally, timpani interrupt with a powerful, sustained roll. An ironic piano quotes

"Twinkle, Twinkle" with mock seriousness, and an irrepressible response arises from the piccolo and bassoon. Then, with an impertinent snap, Dohnanyi brings his lampoon to a brusque close.

Some Further Examples of Variation Form

Bach, Johann Sebastian. Chaconne from Violin Partita No. 2 in D minor; *Goldberg Variations* (for harpsichord).

Beethoven, Ludwig van. Concerto in D major for Violin (second movement); Quartet in A major, Opus 18, No. 5 (third movement); Septet in E-flat major for Violin, Viola, 'Cello, String Bass, Clarinet, Horn, and Bassoon (fourth movement); Sonata No. 9 in A major for Violin and Piano ("Kreutzer"); second movement; Symphony No. 5 in C minor (second movement); Trio in G for Violin, 'Cello, and Piano ("Kakadu"); *Variations on a Theme by Diabelli*.

Brahms, Johannes. Symphony No. 4 in E minor, fourth movement (passacaglia); Variations and Fugue on a Theme by Handel (for piano); Variations on a Theme by Paganini (for piano).

Britten, Benjamin. *Young Person's Guide to the Orchestra* (1946).

Copland, Aaron. *Orchestral Variations* (1957).

Dvořák, Antonin. Symphony No. 8 (formerly No. 4) in G major (fourth movement).

Franck, César. Symphonic Variations for Piano and Orchestra.

Gershwin, George. Variations on "I Got Rhythm."

Goldmark, Karl. Symphony in E-flat major ("Rustic Wedding"), first movement.

Haydn, Franz Joseph. Quartet in C major, ("Emperor") second movement; Symphony No. 94 in G major ("Surprise"), second movement; (also in Symphonies Nos. 88, 95, 97, 103).

Hindemith, Paul. *Symphonic Metamorphosis of Themes by Carl Maria Weber*.

Ives, Charles. Variations on "America" for Organ (1891).

Kodály, Zoltan. *Peacock Variations*.

Mendelssohn, Felix. *Variations sérieuses* (for piano).

Mozart, Wolfgang Amadeus. Serenade No. 10 in B-flat major for 13 Winds (K. 361), sixth movement; Trio in E-flat major for Clarinet, Viola, and Piano (K. 498), Finale.

Prokofiev, Serge. Concerto No. 3 in C major for Piano, Opus 26 (second movement).

Ravel, Maurice. *Boléro* (1927).

Rachmaninoff, Serge. *Rhapsody on a Theme of Paganini* (1934).

Schoenberg, Arnold. *Variations for Orchestra* (1928).

Schubert, Franz. Quartet No. 14 in D minor ("Death and the Maiden"), second movement; Octet in F major for 2 Violins, Viola, 'Cello, String Bass, Clarinet, Horn, and Bassoon (fourth movement).

Schumann, Robert. *Symphonic Études* (for piano).

Tchaikowsky, Peter. Theme and Variations from Suite No. 3; Trio in A minor for Piano, Violin, and 'Cello (second movement); *Variations on a Rococo Theme for 'Cello and Orchestra*.

Chapter 8

Transforming the Musical Idea: Sonata Form

Since about 1750 sonata form has been widely used in sonatas, over-tures, concertos, symphonies, and various kinds of chamber music (trios, quartets, quintets, or serenades) and has become, consequently, a corner-stone in many, perhaps even most, multimovement instrumental pieces. Essentially a tripartite design, it has an *exposition* where a number of musical ideas are announced, a *development* where some (or all) of the subjects undergo some transformation, and a *recapitulation* where the themes are reaffirmed in a decisive manner. As with most other large designs, sonata form may include an introduction and/or a coda.

Care must be taken to distinguish between a sonata and sonata form. Although their names are obviously related, the concept each represents is distinctly different. Sonatas, particularly those written since 1700, are relatively lengthy works for a single instrument (piano or organ), or for one (violin, 'cello, flute, clarinet) that performs with keyboard support. Most sonatas are divided into movements (three or four is the usual number) which may be organized in part form, variation form, sonata form, or rondo form (to be discussed in Chapter 9)[1]. On the other hand, sonata form is an organizational scheme used within individual movements of sonata-based works, a pattern whose qualities we shall now examine.

THEMATIC MATERIAL IN SONATA FORM

Ideas used in sonata form must be distinctly memorable, strikingly indi-vidualistic, and exceptionally rugged, for most of them undergo the most exhaustive kind of scrutiny. Because they are strong and resilient, motives make excellent sonata-form subjects. Succinct and distinctive, these melodic nuggets withstand the rigors of manipulation very well, and their myriad ex-pressive facets continually elicit interest while undergoing development.

[1] Further details about sonatas, their qualities, and mode of organization will be found in Chapter 15.

Consequently, composers have learned to place firm reliance on these compact, epigrammatic ideas.

But concentrating on motives alone would lead to undue terseness, and so broad, smooth-flowing themes are often juxtaposed to provide contrast. Such melodies may be of phrase length (that is, from four to perhaps as many as twelve measures), but they are rarely expansive enough to reveal binary or ternary subdivisions. Of course, the latter are fully liable to thematic development, or, as is often the case, fragments may be excised from them and used in a motivic manner.[2]

Normally, melodic material in sonata form is separated into two (sometimes three) units: the *principal theme* (or group of themes), a subject that is introduced as the exposition opens, and the *subordinate theme* (or group), which appears after the first idea has been sufficiently exposed. In some works a third melody, the *closing theme*, appears as the exposition nears its conclusion. Although early Classicists (Haydn, Mozart, and contemporaries) usually included only a single memorable idea within their principal and subordinated themes, later composers (including Beethoven and his successors) often employed two or more. When this occurs, the several themes generally have common expressive characteristics.

Sonata form's themes are bound together by connecting passages, which gives the ear an impression that the musical fabric is being woven from a continuous thread. Founded mostly on scale runs, broken chords, or fanfares, such episodes normally contain little of intrinsic interest. Occasionally, however, particular transitions may include ideas that a composer examines at greater length in the development or coda.

THE EXPOSITION

Unless an introduction is included, a piece in sonata form begins with the exposition, where much (and usually all) of the composition's essential material is initially announced. In most sonata-form designs, at least two musical ideas (and sometimes more) are presented here.

First to appear, the principal theme (so-called regardless of whether it dominates the piece or not) is likely to be strong, brief, and crisply dynamic. Presented in the tonic key and reaffirmed a number of times (more or less verbatim), it establishes a prevailing mood for the entire composition. Rarely symmetric, principal themes tend to be dramatic, powerful, and aggressive (that is, motivic).

A bridge passage then carries the composition into a new, but related tonality. Often this is the dominant (sometimes the subdominant), but if the piece is in minor the related major may be used. With a new key established, the subordinate theme appears. Normally less vibrant but more

[2] Representative motives and themes were quoted in Chapter 2. Now, it would be appropriate to re-examine them in the light of this discussion.

melodic than the opening subject, it provides contrast and (perhaps) a change of pace. Although it usually possesses little overt intensity, the subordinate theme is not a casual inclusion within the design. Aside from variety, this gracious subject very effectively contributes balance, lyricism, and unhurried gentility. Indeed, in some compositions, it becomes the most memorable idea.

Approaching an area known as the *codetta* (closing section), the exposition may reaffirm its principal subject (a fairly common procedure) or introduce the closing theme. In either case, this segment typically concludes on an incomplete cadence (a chord of the dominant or an inverted tonic chord), which gives the listener a clear indication that further activity is about to ensue. Often, a verbatim repetition of the exposition is accomplished before entry is made into the development.

For the first movement of his Symphony No. 40 in G minor, Mozart created a beautifully molded piece in sonata form. As its exposition unfolds, these successive ideas appear:

1. Prefaced by an innocuous and extremely brief accompanimental figure, the principal theme is introduced in octaves (and in the key of G minor) by violins:

2. After repetition, extension, and the sounding of a *forte* connecting passage, the subordinate theme is heard in the related key of B-flat major:

3. Then, as the exposition proceeds toward a cadence, which occurs on a D-major chord, dominant in the key, fragments of the principal theme reappear to act as the closing subject.

THE DEVELOPMENT

Progressing from the exposition into the "working-out" section (the development) is normally accomplished by means of a bridge passage. Sometimes this transition is handled so smoothly that it is difficult to determine where one leaves off and the other begins. Occasionally called a *free fantasia*, the development has an intent of closely examining the previously announced musical ideas to seek out their latent expressive possibilities. In this undertaking a composer may use both the principal and subordinate themes (and any worthwhile ideas inherent in the transitions), or he may concentrate on one (usually the principal theme) to a neglect of the other. Normally, new ideas are not interpolated here, but this is not inviolate. Mendelssohn, for instance, inserted an important third subject in opening measures of the development in the first movement of his Symphony No. 4 in A major.

Because composers are given (and usually exercise) complete latitude in undertaking their developmental procedures, it is not possible to reduce this activity to formula. Certain basic techniques, however, are common:

1. Subjects can be manipulated by a use of (1) inversion, (2) segmentation, (3) realignment, (4) imitation, (5) sequential repetition, or (6) contrapuntal interplay.
2. Continual modulations maintain the tonality in a state of flux, a fluidity in decided contrast with the stable tonalities in other sections of the piece.
3. Rhythmic shifts may involve a lengthening (augmentation) or a shortening (diminution) of time values; almost unfailingly these sections display a general increase in rhythmic activity.
4. Altered hues of coloration can be accomplished by a use of diverse instruments, an exploitation of extreme ranges, or demands for unusual fluency.
5. Development sections give an impression of being incredibly complex; their lines twist and turn; cross-rhythms, syncopations, and impetuous angular thrusts abound; often, the dynamic level mounts to ear-shattering intensity.

No limits can be prescribed concerning the length of a development. Some composers (Beethoven and Schubert, for instance) linger over the process of thematic manipulation, but their immediate predecessors (Haydn and Mozart) were more cursory. Their developments, and those of most Classic composers, tend to be succinct, clearly molded, and extremely compact.

Upon entering the development section in the first movement of his Symphony No. 40, Mozart turns to an exploitation of the first (principal) theme to a total neglect of the second. These are the steps he follows:

1. After two pre-emptory *tutti* (with all instruments playing) chords and a brief descending woodwind passage have been heard, the principal theme appears in a new key:

2. Embellished with a running filigree from violins, a portion of the theme is announced by the lower strings (viola, 'cello, bass) in this manner:

3. Afterward, it is enunciated by octave-spaced violins over a nimble lower-string accompaniment:

4. The two preceding steps are then reaffirmed, but in descending keys.

5. Violins, with an imitative effect provided by woodwinds, lead a fragment of the theme upward; subsequently, it comes back down:

6. Finally, three tones from the subject are sounded vigorously by upper strings (and imitated by lower-voiced associates), after which a descending passage leads into the recapitulation:

THE RECAPITULATION

Ostensibly concerned with reaffirming a composition's important ideas, the recapitulation is rarely a verbatim reiteration of what has gone before. Similar in outline to the exposition and, of course, based on the same material, it nevertheless has a distinctive architectural role to fulfill. Usually it reveals important individual characteristics. Again the principal theme makes an initial appearance (although in particular works this alignment may be changed) in the tonic key but often in a heavier scoring than heretofore to emphasize finality. In succession, the movement's other themes, including the connectives, are heard; but the sequence of tonalities is shifted. Now the subordinate theme is heard in the tonic key, another step intended to stress an impression of finality. Moreover, the thematic material may be heard only once, for little need exists to repeat subjects that have by now become quite familiar.

To illustrate, here are details of the recapitulation in the first movement of Mozart's Symphony No. 40:

1. Played by first and second violins, the principal theme is heard (in the tonic key) over the previously used lower-string accompaniment (with an added touch from bassoon).
2. After a lengthy transition, the subordinate theme is affirmed (and repeated) in the tonic:

3. In the closing section (codetta), fragments from the principal subject are sounded in a manner that suggests some aspects of thematic development.
4. Finally, a short coda based on the principal theme concludes.

APPENDAGES OF SONATA FORM

An introduction and/or coda may extend sonata form's dimensions. Because both are optional, their inclusion cannot be specified with certainty. Generally speaking, codas are near-fixtures but the utilization of introductions is less frequent.

Two kinds of introduction exist: (1) a short preface consisting of a few chords or a brief rhythmic flourish sufficient to alert an audience, establish the key, and prepare a way for the exposition; or (2) a lengthy prologue that contrasts with other sections in tempo, meter, and thematic material. Short introductions are demonstrated in the first movements of Beethoven's Symphony No. 3 in E-flat major where two stentorian chords do duty, and in Mozart's Symphony No. 40, as we have seen. On the other hand, Schubert employs an introduction of seventy-seven measures in the first movement of his Symphony No. 9 in C major, and both Dvořák and Weber (in the Symphony No. 9 in E minor and in the Overture to *Oberon*, respectively) employ similarly expansive, contrasted prefaces.

When present, codas tend to become an intrinsic part of a sonata form design. Often, they maintain the same meter and tempo as preceding sections and use ideas extracted from the principal or subordinate themes. In particular works (the first movements of Beethoven's Symphony No. 3 or Schubert's Symphony No. 8 in B minor), codas are so lengthy and exhibit so much activity as to become tantamount to a second development. Whether short or long, however, few pieces in sonata form dispense with these epilogues.

A SYNOPTIC OUTLINE OF SONATA FORM

Listed in tabular form, these are sonata form's usual characteristics:

1. *Introduction* (optional). Two kinds exist: (1) the short, terse, and related preface; or (2) the lengthy, lyric, contrasted one.
2. *Exposition* (sometimes called the *statement*):
   a. Announces (and repeats) the principal theme in the tonic key.
   b. Presents a bridge passage leading to the second theme that modulates to a new key (usually the dominant or related major).
   c. Sounds the subordinate theme (usually with repetition).
   d. Closes with a codetta that may (or may not) introduce a new subject.
3. *Development* (sometimes called the *fantasia* or *working-out* section):
   a. Discourses on portions of one or more of the themes previously presented, including a possible use of ideas from bridge passages.
   b. Makes extensive modulations through a number of new keys.
   c. Provides a transition leading to the next section.
4. *Recapitulation* (sometimes called the *restatement*):
   a. Reaffirms the principal and subordinate themes in their usual alignment (although this may be changed, or some material may be omitted).
   b. Stresses the tonic key to strongly affirm the composition's basic tonality.
   c. Employs the codetta as a transition into the finale.
5. *Coda* (optional):
   a. Usually adheres to the tempo, meter, key, and thematic material previously introduced.
   b. Again stresses the primacy of the home key.

SONATA FORM IN CHAMBER MUSIC

Sonatas, quartets, quintets, and other chamber pieces often reveal the outlines of sonata form with crystalline clarity. Well aware of the dramatic and expressive opportunities that exist, composers frequently use this design, often in first movements or finales, while writing for single instruments (mostly piano or organ) or small ensembles.

In the same year (1787) that he was deeply involved in writing his operatic masterwork *Don Giovanni* (K. 527), Mozart composed a Quintet for Strings in G minor (K. 516). Scored for two violins, two violas, and 'cello, it is a deeply emotional work that continually excites the listener's imagination. Details about its first movement, a tautly organized design in sonata form, are these:

1. Beginning without introduction, the piece employs the first violin to sound this upward-arching principal theme over support from the second violin and first viola:

2. Repetition is accomplished by using darker-hued instruments (both violas and 'cello); a subsequent twelve-measure extension calls the full ensemble into play.
3. Over a dance-like figuration provided by the ensemble's four other instruments, the first violin sounds the subordinate theme (whose contour is downward) in B-flat major, a related tonality:

4. In the lengthy extension and codetta that follow, fragments of the principal theme continually appear.
5. As the development begins, this motive from the principal theme (played by the 'cello) sounds repeatedly from deep in the bass:

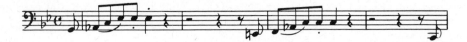

6. The subordinate theme is also used here. Its permutations are too numerous to mention, however, for over and over, in augmentation and diminution, in a shifting panorama of tonalities, at varied dynamic levels, or in diverse registers, the subject is shaped, altered, and transformed.

7. Almost precipitately, the recapitulation appears when upper strings (two violins, one viola) reaffirm the principal theme precisely as before. Repetition is begun by violas and 'cello, just as earlier, but subsequent measures veer in other directions.

8. This, too, is a circumstance with the subordinate theme—it begins in the same manner as in the exposition, then later pursues a modified course. But unfoldment is so inevitable that the ear readily follows the realignment of melodic lines and tonalities.

9. Initially concerned with the principal theme, the coda later allots a share of attention to the subordinate subject. Finally, two crisp chords (dominant and tonic) conclude.

Sonata form is a keystone in the design of many fine keyboard pieces. For instance, in the first movement of Beethoven's Piano Sonata No. 8 in C minor (composed in 1798 and often called the *Pathétique*), it is handled in this way:

1. Prefaced by a portentous introduction (whose tempo is marked *grave*), the movement begins with this thematic idea:

2. But the exposition (and subsequent sections) move at a more animated pace (*allegro di molto e con brio*) in duple meter. Over an agitated tremolo sounded from the instrument's bass register, this principal theme is announced, repeated, and extended:

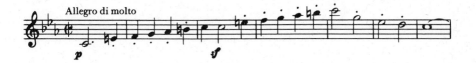

3. Following a similar upward contour, the subordinate theme nevertheless discloses an individual tonal flow:

4. A considerable display of pianistic pyrotechnics then occurs, but as the section nears its terminus semblances of the principal theme can be discerned.
5. Exposition and development are clearly separated in this piece, for Beethoven inserted a four-measure quotation from the introduction to divide them.
6. When the development gets underway (at the *allegro con brio* tempo and with a modified key signature), fragments from the subordinate theme are exposed to initial manipulation, but later the principal theme appears. In both cases the activity is brief.
7. Following usual procedures, the recapitulation presents the principal and subordinate themes in a sequence very much as before, save for modifications in key.
8. Once again, material from the introduction serves as punctuation. This time, four measures in *grave* tempo lead into a brisk and brief coda founded on the principal theme. Four accented chords conclude.

While residing in the United States between 1892–1895, Antonin Dvořák wrote (among others) two works that were influenced in some degree by the music he heard here. One was the Symphony No. 9 in E minor, usually referred to as "From the New World" (discussed in Chapter 17); the other was his String Quartet No. 6 in F major, known as the "American." Composed in the summer of 1893 while Dvořák was vacationing at Spillville, Iowa, the latter has a beautifully conceived first movement in sonata form, whose details are these:

1. Violin tremolos and a solid low f from the 'cello provide a setting wherein the principal theme is announced by the viola and repeated (two octaves higher) by the violin:

Allegro ma non troppo

2. Considerable byplay, based on fragments from this theme, occurs in the extension until a second idea (actually a member of the principal theme group) appears:

3. Sounded by the first violin over sustained chords from other instruments, the subordinate theme (the third idea in this movement) is comparatively languid:

4. And in the brief closing section that follows, fleeting reference is made to the first and third themes.
5. Developmental activity initially requires the viola to sound the first theme; later, fragments from it are taken up by other instruments.
6. Interesting polyphonic activity occurs near the development's close when this subject is successively introduced (and embellished) in four different registers:

7. Within the recapitulation, the principal theme and its second member appear in proper alignment. And the subordinate subject is subsequently heard in the tonic tonality.

8. At length, an eleven-measure coda—based on a new idea—brings this lyric movement to a forcefully expressed close.

SONATINA FORM [3]

Sometimes described as "sonata form without development," sonatina form finds occasional use in a variety of instrumental pieces. Dispensing with one full section (the development) typically included in the parent design, it has only an exposition and a recapitulation, with the added possibility of an introduction and/or coda.

When used in lengthy compositions with elongated time values and slow tempos, sonatina form tends to streamline a work by omitting formal development. Such is the case, for example, in the *adagio* of Brahms' Violin Sonata No. 3 in D minor; the *andante* of Schubert's Quartet in A minor; and the second movement of Schubert's Symphony No. 8 in B minor. Still other examples of sonatina form (although they are buoyant, zestful pieces in quick tempos) exist in Rossini's overtures to *The Barber of Seville*, *La gazza ladra*, and *The Italian Woman in Algiers*.[4]

PARTICULAR EXAMPLES OF SONATA FORM

Franz Schubert (1797–1828), Symphony No. 8 in B minor, first movement

Because it has only two movements in lieu of the conventional four, this beautiful work is sometimes considered incomplete and identified, consequently, as the "Unfinished Symphony." Although evidence exists to show that Schubert intended to carry his composition further (sketches for a third movement have been found), in the five extremely active years of his life that remained he never resumed work on the B minor symphony. Nor did he ever hear it performed.

In September of 1823, Schubert gave a manuscript copy of two completed movements from his Symphony No. 8 to Anselm Huttenbrenner, a friend who was also an official in the *Musikverein* (music society) of Graz, capital city of Styria (one of Austria's Alpine provinces), for conveyance to the organization. Whether through carelessness or design, Huttenbrenner never forwarded the document, and it remained, unrecognized and unperformed, on his shelves until December, 1865. Then, thirty-seven years after Schubert's death, the piece was exhumed (so to speak) and given a premiere in Vienna. Since then, it has become a popular favorite.

Scored for a conventional orchestra of the early nineteenth century

---

[3] Another modification of sonata form, *sonata-rondo form*, is discussed in Chapter 9.

[4] The first two of these are analyzed at some length in Chapter 10.

(except for the composer's rather unusual penchant for trombones), the first movement is organized in sonata form. These are the details:

1. As the piece begins, a somber melody wells upward from a low register, played in *pianissimo* in B minor by 'cellos and basses:

2. Although this introductory theme ultimately becomes the movement's most important idea, it is heard only once in this location.
3. A cleanly articulated sixteenth-note violin accompaniment (over a pizzicato figure from lower strings) supports the movement's principal theme sounded by oboe and clarinet (playing in unison):

4. Immediately repeated and enriched by interpolations from a horn, the theme is then extended. After a sharp break in the musical flow, horns and bassoons play a sustained passage that shifts the tonality to G major.
5. Over a syncopated accompaniment played by clarinets, violas, and basses, this exquisite subordinate theme is announced by 'cellos and subsequently repeated two octaves higher by violins:

6. In the codetta that follows, extensive use is made of fragments from the subordinate theme.[5]
7. After a brief transitional passage (in which *pizzicato* strings are featured), the introductory theme, the only melodic idea used in this fantasia section, appears a fourth higher than previously (played by 'cellos and basses). Initially sounded in E minor, it is executed in an overlapping manner that suggests a use of polyphony. Then, as the

---

[5] Verbatim repetition of the exposition is quite characteristic.

section unfolds, this theme undergoes a startling transformation. Heretofore played in a restrained manner, it now becomes forceful, resolute, and even bombastic. Occasionally the syncopated accompaniment for the subordinate theme is heard, but the subject itself never appears; nor does the principal theme. Considerable use is made, however, of a series of descending passages that suggest the introductory theme in inversion. At length, over a connecting passage of quiet lyric beauty (sounded by clarinets and bassoons), an entry is made into the recapitulation.

8. Following a regular course, this restatement of ideas begins as violins set up the previously heard accompaniment over which the principal theme (and its repetition) is sounded by woodwinds. Now, however, its extension is foreshortened.

9. After a brief modulation, the subordinate theme appears (with repetition) in D major, a related tonality. As before, fragments from this subject are employed to extend the section.

10. In the coda, Schubert again reaffirms his introductory theme. Sounded in the home key, it is treated repetitiously, gracefully, and tenderly, as if the composer were loath to let it pass into oblivion. Finally, three crisply articulated chords bring this ineffably lovely movement to a resonant close.

Carl Maria von Weber (1786–1826), Overture to *Oberon*

Written to preface the composer's final opera, von Weber's *Oberon* Overture was given a premiere performance in London on April 12, 1826. Organized in sonata form and based on a number of themes from the opera, it presents a succinct digest of the latter's dramatic intent. Although the theatrical work is rarely heard in contemporary performance, its overture has become a fixture in the orchestral repertoire. These are its salient points:

1. Mysterious awe is suggested as a solo horn presents this brief ascending figure:

2. Muted strings respond, after which the exchange is repeated and the dialogue extended. Along the way, fleet woodwinds interject sprays of vivid color. After a short pause, the brass articulate a quiet fanfare that sets off a flurry of activity depicting antics in the domain of Oberon, King of the Elves:

3. Shortly thereafter, an extremely loud chord terminates the introduction.
4. Nimble first violins present the principal theme:

5. Agile passagework runs through the orchestra with spontaneous ease during these measures, but in the midst of uninhibited frolic, the solo horn reaffirms its solemn proclamation (once repeated). At a stroke the melee quiets, and a solo clarinet sounds this unusually lovely subordinate theme:

6. Violins repeat the subject and then move on to play a more incisive third theme over a firm accompaniment:

7. Initially concerned with the principal theme, the development relies on first violins to present this subject in sequential passages over a crisp, rhythmic base. Midway, some use is made of ideas from the work's transitional passages. Then, soaring serenely above an agitated string accompaniment, the subordinate theme is sounded *dolce* (sweetly) by two oboes, but its repetition—assigned to violins—is more distinctly accented.
8. After a ringing dominant chord (based on A) has terminated the development, the recapitulation begins with the principal subject played, as before, by violins.
9. Avoiding the subordinate theme entirely, Weber moves directly into a presentation of his third subject, this time sounded by full orchestra at a *fortissimo* level.

10. And this, in turn, leads directly into a brief coda founded on incipits from the first and third themes. With it, the piece comes to an almost ear-shattering close.

Michael Glinka (1804–1857), Overture to *Ruslan and Ludmilla*

Somewhat overgenerously described as "the father of Russian music," Glinka actually did a great deal to foster the emergence of a nationalistic school of composers in his native land. The son of a wealthy landowner, he worked briefly in a government office (1824–1828) before resigning to devote himself to travel and music. Exposure to the musical life of Milan, Berlin, and Vienna persuaded Glinka that definite steps should be taken to espouse an idiomatic art in Russia. And to this end he wrote his first opera, the pioneering *A Life for the Czar* (1836), which was warmly acclaimed. A second, *Ruslan and Ludmilla* (1842), was greeted with indifference bordering on disdain. Only its overture, possessed of idiomatic Slavic flavor, an abundance of verve, and brilliant orchestral color has continued to maintain a place in the literature. These are its details:

1. Articulated by full orchestra, a forceful motive (which recurs with remarkable frequency during the rest of the piece) opens:

2. Here the terse subject is sounded three times: first in the tonic, then in the subdominant, and lastly in the dominant tonalities.
3. Brilliant scale passages played by strings provide a transition into the exposition.
4. After a brief (two measure) accompaniment, an upward rising subject eight measures long and seemingly possessed of irrepressible energy is presented as the composition's principal theme:

5. After repetition, this subject is extended, during which subtle interjections from the opening motive continually reappear. And a sportive
interplay between flute, oboe, clarinet, and bassoon tosses fragments of
the principal theme through the orchestra. Further passagework leads
to the subordinate theme.

6. Obvious contrast exists between the overture's three subjects. Distinctively different from the two ideas previously introduced, the subordinate subject has a restrained demeanor:

7. Announced by violas and 'cellos, it is subsequently repeated two octaves
higher by violins.

8. Soon after this theme has been concluded, the motive reappears—this
time played quietly by clarinets and bassoons—to open the development.

9. Activity begins when a fragment from the final measures of the subordinate theme is played by 'cellos and basses:

10. Other instruments echo this idea with a strata-like interlarding of
lines. Woodwinds then express a similar colloquy, during which the
principal theme makes a powerfully enunciated appearance. Although
the development is short, its procedures are traversed twice, but in
different keys.

11. Presaged by the brilliant scale passages heard previously, the recapitulation begins when the principal theme reappears. After extension, the
subordinate subject is sounded by 'cellos alone (this time a major third
higher than before), and repeated by violins. After its conclusion, the
ubiquitous motive and fragments from the principal theme serve as
closing subjects.

12. Frenetic but relatively brief, the coda is based on an altered version of
the principal theme. Successively surging and plunging, its line is played

by winds and low strings while violins add a pulsating figuration against it. Violent indeed, this activity brings the piece to an exciting close.

Peter I. Tchaikowsky (1840–1893), Symphony No. 5 in E minor, first movement

Premiered during the winter of 1888 at St. Petersburg (now Leningrad), the fifth of Tchaikowsky's symphonies (he wrote a sixth and final work in 1893) was received coolly. But it soon gained in popularity, and is now firmly entrenched in the orchestral repertoire. Like nearly all of this composer's works it is lengthy and sometimes tedious, but an abundance of instrumental colors and piquant melodies makes it easy to assimilate. Established in sonata form, its first movement has these details:

1. Announced by clarinets performing in their low register, a dolorous introductory tune is heard over a sustained string background:

2. Appearance of the principal theme is presaged by a four-measure accompaniment. Over it, clarinet and bassoon announce an angular melody that is repeated and extended at great length:

3. After a number of sequential and climactic passages (mostly founded on excisions from the first theme), an expansive transition presents three additional ideas:

4. After temporizing almost unendurably, Tchaikowsky uses octave-spaced violins to announce this sweeping subordinate theme:

5. In the codetta that follows, considerable use is made of a crisp fanfare from the transition (quoted above).

6. Employing this same two-measure subject, Tchaikowsky then moves into the development and becomes enmeshed in an extensive elaboration of the principal theme. Handled like motives, melodic fragments appear in a sequential alignment at ever-mounting levels of intensity. No perceptible reference is made to the subordinate theme, but ideas from the transitional passages consistently recur. After attaining a shattering climax, the dynamic level abates and the development concludes.

7. Over a quiet accompaniment, a lone bassoon reaffirms the principal theme to usher in the recapitulation. Clarinet, flute, and octave-spaced violin-violas then take up the subject. As before, its presentation is lengthy.

8. The transition is also long, and in the process a series of previously announced subjects are heard (but in new keys).

9. When the subordinate theme finally appears, it is presented a tone higher than before, in the key of E major.

10. Although the recapitulation is less redundant than the exposition, Tchaikowsky cites his subordinate theme at length.

11. Prefaced by the nearly ubiquitous fanfare, the coda is founded on the principal theme. Sounded repeatedly, this subject finally falls deep into the orchestra whence it literally fades into oblivion. Only an extremely quiet E minor chord, marked *ppp,* is needed to conclude the movement.

Paul Hindemith (1895–1963), *Mathis der Maler* Symphony, first movement

In 1930, Hindemith wrote both the text and music for an opera, *Mathis der Maler* (Matthias the Painter), based on the life and times of Mathias Grünewald (c. 1460–1528). An important German artist, Grünewald suffered from the doubts, criticisms, political upheavals, and general tribulations that affect sensitive men in any age. By creating this opera, Hindemith had an intent of revealing these vicissitudes and the artist's triumph over them. Because theatrical performances were slow in coming (the opera did not experience a premiere until 1938), the composer rearranged three important portions from the score for orchestra in the form of a symphony. This work was first performed in 1934.

Originally the opera's overture, the symphony's first movement is organized in sonata form. Termed *Engelkonzert* (Angelic Concert) because it is intended to suggest a nativity scene in Grünewald's famous Isenheim altarpiece in St. Anthony's Church at Colmar, Alsace, it is by turns firm, restrained, powerful, and seraphic. These are the details:

1. As the movement opens, octave-spaced clarinets, succeeded by oboes and flutes, sound a gentle theme:

2. Primary interest in the introduction, however, centers on a medieval-sounding hymnic melody introduced by trombones:

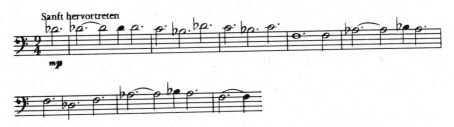

3. When the exposition begins at a more animated pace in duple meter, flutes and first violins announce the principal theme:

4. Repeated and extended, this subject is later supplanted by a second theme assigned to first violins:

5. Repetition is accomplished by flute and oboe (playing in octaves) over an undulating string accompaniment, after which the horn reaffirms it again in a new key. Still later, the subject comes back in the violins, a third higher than when first given out.

6. Flutes are enlisted to convey the closing theme:

7. As the development begins, the first subject becomes involved in the kind of contrapuntal byplay for which Hindemith was internationally famous. When the section presses forward, other themes become similarly engaged. A distinctive touch is added as trombones solemnly intone (in triple meter) the introduction's hymnic melody, while other instruments present their more agile subjects in duple meter.

8. In the recapitulation, Hindemith follows a modified plan; the first theme does not appear in the original tonality but a half tone higher. Later it is heard in other keys.

9. The third theme appears next and undergoes a series of transformations, including an interjection of occasional measures in triple meter. Finally, the second subject—in a crisp, angular format—terminates the recapitulation.

10. Resonant chords, sounded by full orchestra, comprise a succinct (five-measure) coda.

Some Further Examples of Sonata Form

Beethoven, Ludwig van. Concerto No. 5 in E-flat major for Piano ("Emperor"), first movement; Concerto in D major for Violin, first movement; Overtures: *Coriolanus; Leonora No. 3;* Sonata No. 21 in C major for Piano ("Waldstein"), first movement; Symphony No. 3 in E-flat major ("Eroica"), first movement.

Brahms, Johannes. Quartet in A minor, first and fourth movements; Symphony No. 3 in F major, first movement.

Dvořák, Antonin. Symphony No. 9 in E minor ("From the New World"), first movement.

Franck, César. Symphony in D minor, first movement.

Haydn, Franz Joseph. Quartet in C major ("Emperor"), first movement; Symphony No. 101 in D major ("The Clock"), first movement.

Mendelssohn, Felix. Concerto in E minor for Violin, first movement; Overtures: *The Hebrides; A Midsummer Night's Dream;* Symphony No. 4 in A major ("Italian"), first movement.

Mozart, Wolfgang Amadeus. Symphony No. 41 in C major (K. 551), first, second, and fourth movements.

Prokofiev, Serge. Concerto No. 3 in C major for Piano (1921), first movement; Symphony No. 1 in D major ("Classical"), first and fourth movements; Symphony No. 5 (1944), first movement.

Schubert, Franz. Quartet No. 14 in D minor ("Death and the Maiden"), first movement; Overture to *Rosamunde;* Symphony No. 9 in C major ("Great"), first and fourth movements.

Tchaikowsky, Peter I. Symphony No. 4 in F minor, first and fourth movements.

Weber, Carl Maria. Overtures: *Der Freischütz; Euryanthe.*

Some Further Examples of Sonatina Form

Beethoven, Ludwig van. Symphony No. 8 in F major, second movement.
Berlioz, Hector. Overture, *Roman Carnival*.
Brahms, Johannes. Piano Quartet in G minor, *allegro*.
Franck, César. Sonata for Violin and Piano in A major, first movement.
Mozart, Wolfgang Amadeus. Overture, *The Marriage of Figaro* (K. 492);
    Serenade in G major (K. 525, *Eine kleine Nachtmusik*), first movement (with
    a twenty-measure interlude between exposition and recapitulation).
Schubert, Franz. Symphony No. 8 in B minor ("Unfinished"), second move-
    ment.
Shostakovich, Dmitri. Symphony No. 1 (1925), first movement.
Tchaikowsky, Peter I. Serenade in C major for Strings, first movement (*Pezzo
    in forma di sonatina*); *Ouverture Miniature* from *The Nutcracker Suite*.

Chapter 9

Thematic Recurrence:
Rondo Form

Following a plan of sectional recurrence somewhat similar to the scheme used in part form, music's rondo form is an additive design that grows by affixing successive strains one to another. Primarily based on a striking theme (the *principal rondo subject*), it also includes a number of digressive strains (called *episodes*) that may be heard in a sequence of five parts (*abaca*), seven (generally *abacada*), or even nine (likely *abacadaea*). From a structural viewpoint, rondo form differs from part form by having a greater number of sections. Expressively, however, it tends to be quite different from any of the designs we have previously considered.

THE RONDO THEME

As with any musical pattern, rondo form's melodic ideas are of overriding importance, a circumstance especially true of the principal subject. Typically, a first rondo theme (often called the *refrain*) is a jovial, spirited, and exuberant idea filled with gaiety, charm, and good humor. Without fail it sets the design's expressive tone and, because of frequent reappearances, invariably dominates the piece. As an example, consider the subject Mozart employs in the finale of his Sonata in A major for Piano (K. 331):

Some rondo themes are longer than this one (it, incidentally, has *aba* subdivisions). But lengthy subjects are awkward to handle in rondo form; consequently, composers tend to either avoid or foreshorten them in appearances other than the first. For instance, Mozart employs a relatively long subject in the finale of his Concerto in B-flat major for Bassoon (K. 191):

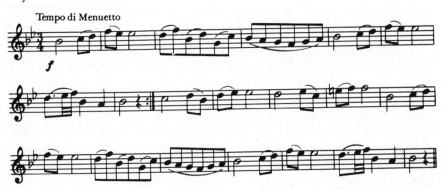

But in three subsequent appearances after the first, he restricts its announcement to the first eight measures.

Although recurrence of the principal theme is a distinctive rondo characteristic, this does not preclude the possibility of occasionally embellishing a subject when it returns. Such alterations, however, are rarely so far-reaching as to obscure the subject's identity.

Inevitably, individual composers differ in the kinds of rondo theme they favor. J. S. Bach's subjects for instance, are usually short, sturdy, and direct, whereas those of Haydn and Mozart (for the most part) are longer and more playful. Beethoven, Mendelssohn, and Brahms often created rondo themes of unusual length. As an example, consider the fifty-six measure subject that Brahms employs in the finale of his Sextet in B-flat major for Strings. It begins with this idea:

Subsequently, this strain is repeated an octave higher; then, a contrasted mid-section (*b*) is interpolated, after which the first idea (modified in its closing measures) reappears.

SOME RONDO QUALITIES

Successive strains within a rondo are known as the refrain, first episode, second episode, and so on, but more conventionally (and succinctly) they are identified as *a, b, c, d*, etc. Sometimes a piece may have as many as nine (rarely more) subdivisions, although works with fewer sections (five or seven) are more common. One fundamental premise of the rondo design, however, a characteristic observed by virtually all who have worked with it, holds that the principal subject should recur at least three times. From Bach (d. 1750) to Bartók (d. 1945), this stricture has been rather carefully maintained.

Key relations in rondo form are usually quite regular. Almost without exception, such pieces begin and end by sounding the principal theme in the home key, and most present their intervening episodes in the dominant, subdominant, or related major and minor tonalities. Daring modulations or sudden shifts to unrelated keys are comparatively rare and occur only in lengthy compositions. Often, a rondo's subdivisions are bound together by means of bridge passages. These gently lead the ear from one strain to another and from one tonality to another.

Most rondos move at a brisk tempo and are brilliant, forthright, taut, interesting, fresh, and invigorating in expression. Rarely serious or complex, the typical rondo is playful, dexterous, and infectiously buoyant. Occasionally, however, particular works in rondo form are slow enough to appear pensive. Examples exist in the second movement of Beethoven's Sonata No. 8 in C minor for Piano (*Pathétique*), or in the "Nocturne" from Mendelssohn's music for *A Midsummer Night's Dream*.

EARLY RONDOS

One of the first musical patterns to acquire a definite outline, rondo form took its name and structure from such medieval poems as the *rondeau* and *rondel* (occasionally known as the *roundelai*). Widely used in French poetry written c. 1000, rondeaus have thirteen lines organized into a first stanza of five lines, a second of three, and a third of five. Taken from the poem's first line, a common refrain is used to conclude both the second and third stanzas. Slightly different in pattern, the rondel has fourteen lines divided into two stanzas: one of eight lines and another of six. In this instance, the first two lines constitute a refrain and reappear as lines seven-eight and thirteen-fourteen. When composers of the pre-Renaissance period began to set these poems to music, they followed an eminently logical course and employed the same tune for the reiterated lines, thus paving a way for the emergence of musical rondo form.

Between 1000 and 1300, the troubadours (songsters active in southern France and northern Italy) and their successors, the trouvères (who practiced mostly in northern and central France), frequently used the rondo plan in their pieces. Mostly their songs were antiphonal (that is, featuring exchanges between a solo singer and a group), and rondo form's refrain-episode plan well suited the purpose. Songs by Adam de la Halle (1220–1287),[1] a prominent trouvère, exemplify the practice, as do similar pieces by such later composers as Giullaume de Machaut (1300–1377); Giullaume Dufay (1400–1474); and Gilles Binchois (1400–1460). A specific example, Machaut's rondeau *Ma fin est mon commencement* (My end is my beginning), appears in the *Music Scores Omnibus*,[2] and a twelfth- or thirteenth-century virelai of unknown authorship, *Or la truix trop du rete* (I find it difficult to woo her), is in *Masterpieces of Music Before 1750*.

In the seventeenth and early eighteenth centuries, numerous French and Italian keyboard composers (known as *clavecinists*), including Jacques Chambonnieres (1602–1672); François Couperin (1668–1733); Jean Philippe Rameau (1683–1764); and Domenico Scarlatti (1683–1757), became espe-

---

[1] Whose *Le Jeu de Robin et Marion* and "Thirteen Rondeaux" have been recorded by Archive (ARC 3002).

[2] William J. Starr and George F. Devine, *Music Scores Omnibus*, Part I: (Englewood Cliffs, N.J.: Prentice-Hall, Inc.), pp. 23–24.

cially partial to rondo form and employed it often in their clavichord and harpsichord pieces. Apparently, Jean Baptiste Lully (1632–1687), an Italian active in France, was the first to apply the concept to orchestral composition.

WHERE RONDO FORM MAY BE USED

Rondos may appear independently or within symphonies, concertos, and chamber music compositions. As we have seen, early examples appeared in vocal and keyboard pieces; later, Bach and Handel (among others) employed the pattern in instrumental works. With these examples before them, the Viennese Classicists (active in the late eighteenth century) began to make frequent use of the rondo within works for orchestra. Because of its exuberant and often ebullient spirit, the rondo found an apt place in the finales of such pieces. But this is not its only location, for the design appears occasionally in second movements (usually played in a slow tempo), as may be discerned in the *adagio* of Beethoven's Symphony No. 4 in B-flat major, or the *Romanze* of Mozart's Serenade in G major (*Eine kleine Nachtmusik*).

Independent rondos are less numerous. Such excellent pieces as Saint-Saëns' *Introduction and Rondo Capriccioso* for Violin and Orchestra (discussed subsequently); Mozart's Rondos in D major (K. 382) and A major (K. 386) for Piano and Orchestra; and Mendelssohn's *Rondo Brilliant* for Piano and Orchestra, however, show that the design can very successfully stand alone.

SIMPLE RONDO FORM

As its name suggests, simple rondo form is the design's most elemental pattern. Essentially a five-part structure (with an *abaca* outline), it begins with a principal theme (*a*) that is regular in outline and rarely longer than eight measures. Presented in the tonic key, this subject is immediately repeated, after which it (usually) concludes on a full cadence. Similarly cast and of approximately the same length, the first episode (*b*) shifts to a related key (perhaps the dominant, perhaps to minor) and is heard without repetition. Concluding on a partial cadence, it is immediately succeeded by the principal theme. Thereafter, the second episode (*c*)—usually an eight-measure idea established in a related key—and a final affirmation of the principal theme (*a*) are heard.

"Amaryllis," a French folk song arranged by Henri Ghys and published in 1868, is organized in simple rondo form. It unfolds like this:

1. An opening refrain *a*, has four full measures (note half measures at its beginning and end) that are repeated:

2. The first episode *b*, comprised of two phrases, shifts to minor:

3. Afterward, the refrain *a* reappears in its original form.

4. A repeated eight-measure period, the second episode *c* modulates to the subdominant:

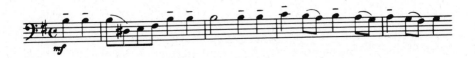

5. After the refrain *a* has been heard a third time, a short coda concludes.

More pensive in mood, the second movement (*adagio cantabile*) from Beethoven's Sonata No. 8 in C minor for Piano (*Pathétique*) is also in simple rondo form.[3] These are its characteristics:

1. Established in A-flat major (a related tonality of the work's home key), the principal theme *a* is announced in the instrument's middle register and immediately repeated one octave higher:

2. Twelve measures long, the first episode *b* appears in the key of F minor:

[3] A further example of simple rondo form, the Finale (third movement) of J. S. Bach's Concerto No. 2 in E major for Violin, has the pattern *abacadaea* (all with sixteen-measure segments save the fourth episode *e*, which is twice as long).

3. Immediately thereafter, the principal subject *a*—limited to eight measures—returns.

4. Shifting to A-flat minor, the fourteen-measure second episode *c* has a long, arching line:

5. Now given in full, the principal subject *a* returns; as before, it is first heard in the middle register, then an octave higher.

6. Finally, a short, seven-measure coda concludes.

THE CLASSICAL RONDO

Similar in many respects to the simple rondo (it usually has, for instance, a five-part sequence), the classical rondo nevertheless incorporates several changes that make it more complex. Among the most significant are these:

1. Classical rondo themes are usually lengthy and may include several different ideas; moreover, these subjects are not always regular in outline (that is, comprised of four, six, or eight-measure phrases).

2. Occasionally, the principal theme may undergo manipulation (development) that markedly extends the design.

3. Segments do not always terminate on perceptible cadences; rather, connecting passages may bind the principal theme with its several digressions.

Within the broad outlines of classical rondo form, three variants (known as first, second, or third rondo form) exist. Each is founded on the principle of thematic recurrence, but one differs from another in (1) the frequency and extent to which a principal theme returns, and (2) the number of their episodes.

The second movement (*largo*) of Beethoven's Sonata No. 2 in A major for Piano exemplifies classical rondo form: [4]

1. Set in D major (subdominant of the home key), the nineteen-measure principal rondo theme *a*, organized in simple ternary form, begins like this:

---

[4] Flexibilities inherent in this kind of rondo may be experienced by examining (and listening to) Beethoven's: (1) *Rondo a Capriccio* in G major (Rage Over a Lost Penny); (2) Rondo in C major; and (3) Rondo in G major, both Opus 51, Nos. 1 and 2. Each reveals interesting permutations of the classical rondo's basic plan.

2. Only twelve measures long, the first episode *b* shifts to B minor (a related tonality):

3. Afterward the principal theme *a* reappears.
4. Revealing interesting harmonic changes and some slight manipulation of the principal theme, the second episode *c*, seventeen measures long, begins like this:

5. Shortened to only eight measures, the principal theme *a* makes a final appearance.
6. And a brief coda (five measures long) closes the movement.

A boisterous Finale (the seventh movement), in Mozart's Serenade No. 10 for Thirteen Wind Instruments (K. 361), is a splendid example of classical rondo form. These are its details:

1. Oboes and clarinets unite to sound the principal rondo theme *a*, a sixteen-measure subject that is immediately repeated:

2. The first episode *b* is indeed lengthy. Organized in ternary form, it has three eight-measure strains (each repeated) that pass, successively, through F major, B-flat major, and G minor. This is how the digression begins:

3. After this forty-eight measure expanse has been traversed, the principal theme *a* returns.
4. Even longer, the second episode *c* has four strains, each of eight measures and each repeated, that progress through E-flat major, C minor, G minor, and D minor. This is the first of them:

5. After a full perusal of these subsections, the principal theme *a* again recurs.
6. Comparatively long (forty-two measures), the coda maintains an exuberant demeanor while bringing the movement to an exciting close.

SONATA-RONDO FORM

When the principles of thematic recurrence are intermingled with the techniques of melodic manipulation, sonata-rondo form results. Initially formulated during the era of Haydn, Mozart, Beethoven, and Schubert (between approximately 1775–1810), it has since been widely accepted as an important compositional design.

Essentially a tripartite structure (as is sonata form), the combined pattern has these divisions:

1. An *exposition* concerned with (1) presenting the principal theme in the tonic key; followed by (2) an announcement of the subordinate theme (or, in rondo parlance, the episode) in a related key; and (3) recurrence (more or less verbatim) of the principal theme.
2. A *development* that centers on an elaboration of previously announced material, as would be characteristic of conventional sonata form.
3. A *recapitulation* that sounds (1) the principal theme; (2) the subordinate theme; and (3) the principal theme all in the tonic key.

Structural differences between conventional sonata form and this design are minimal, of course, and center mostly on a full return of the principal theme in final measures of the exposition and recapitulation. Stylistically, however, distinctive differences do exist. Good-humored, buoyant, and irrepressible, the sonata-rondo pattern is almost always flip and impertinent in expression, whereas sonata form tends to be much more portentous, dramatic, and even epochal in outlook.

A fine example of sonata-rondo form appears in the finale (third movement) of Beethoven's Concerto No. 4 in G major for Piano:

1. Playing with near-military precision, orchestral strings introduce an incisive principal theme *a* that is immediately reiterated by the solo instrument and subsequently expanded by both forces:

2. More lyric than its predecessor, a rather languid subordinate subject *b* is introduced by the piano and later reaffirmed by the orchestra:

3. After considerable colloquy between soloist and orchestra has ensued, the principal theme *a* returns.
4. Concerned at its beginning and end with an exploitation of the principal theme, the development also elaborates on the subordinate subject in its middle portion.
5. Sounded by full orchestra (*tutti*), the principal theme *a* ushers in a compressed recapitulation. In short order, the subordinate subject *b* appears and is played by both piano and orchestra.
6. After a lengthy cadenza (played by the soloist alone), and a connecting passage in which both performing forces become involved, a *presto* coda—based on *a*—brings the movement to a tumultuous close.

PARTICULAR EXAMPLES OF RONDO FORM

J. S. Bach (1685–1750), *Gavotte en rondeau* from Partita No. 3 in E major for Solo Violin

Early in December 1717, Bach moved from a position in the service of Duke Wilhelm August at Weimar to become *Kapellmeister* (music director) for Prince Leopold of Anhalt-Cothen. And while in this new post (where he remained until 1723), he became primarily occupied with writing for keyboard, strings, and orchestra. In the very considerable body of material created during these years, six works for solo violin—variously termed *partitas* (because they are mostly a collection of dances), or *sonatas* (because their segments are not of a dance character)—rank as excellent examples of Baroque string music. One of these, the Partita No. 3 in E major, has seven movements: (1) a lengthy *Prélude* (the work's only nondance section); (2) a dignified *Loure;* (3) a crisp *Gavotte en rondeau;* (4) a stately *Menuet I;* (5) a continuation in *Menuet II;* (6) an incisive *Bourrée;* and (7) a rollicking *Gigue.* Except for the *Prélude* and *Gavotte,* all are organized in binary form, and, as was characteristic of the period, all are in the home key. Incorporating nine segments—organized as *abacadaea*—the *Gavotte en rondeau* reveals these details:

1. Beginning on the third beat of the measure (typical of gavottes), the principal rondo theme *a* makes an immediate appearance as the piece begins:

2. Shifting to the related tonality of C-sharp minor, the first episode *b* presents this melody:

3. Immediately thereafter the principal rondo subject *a* returns.
4. Venturing to B major (dominant of the home key), the second episode *c* introduces a sixteen-measure subject wherein several lines (played by the one instrument) are adroitly combined:

5. Again, the ubiquitous rondo subject *a* returns.
6. Another sixteen-measure section, the third episode *d* is heard in the key of F-sharp minor, a somewhat unorthodox modulatory excursion:

7. Once more, the primary rondo theme *a* returns.
8. Longest of the segments, with twenty measures, the fourth episode *e* remains in the home key:

9. To conclude, the principal rondo theme *a* makes a final appearance in precisely the same format it has retained throughout the piece.

Ludwig van Beethoven (1770–1827), Concerto in D major for Violin, Finale

Now accepted everywhere as an important piece in the repertoire for violin and orchestra, Beethoven's Concerto in D major has not always been so highly esteemed. Written in 1806 and given a premier that same year by Franz Clement, an eminent virtuoso to whom it was initially dedicated, the concerto did not find ready acceptance. Violinists considered its complexities insurmountable, and because publishers were loath to print a controversial work, it languished. Beethoven then made a startling concession to musical ineptitude: In 1808 (but only after considerable revision), he published it as a piano concerto! Ultimately, of course, circumstances were righted. Complete with further revisions and an altered dedication (to Beethoven's long-time friend, Stephan von Breuning), the D major concerto was published in a definitive version for violin in 1809.

Organized in three movements (as are most concertos), this piece has (1) an opening *allegro* in sonata form, (2) an introspective *larghetto* in variation form; and (3) a nimble *allegro* in classical rondo form. Wishing to maintain a direct line of continuity between the second and third movements, Beethoven specified that they be linked with an interpolated (and presumably improvised) cadenza.

1. Established in the home key (D major), the rondo finale begins as the solo instrument announces this principal theme *a* in its low register:

2. Repetition is accomplished two octaves higher, after which the full orchestra reiterates (and extends) the subject, playing *fortissimo*.

3. Enjoying discreet orchestral support (mostly from woodwinds), the solo violin provides a fourteen-measure bridge leading to the next section.

4. Sounded in the dominant tonality (A major), the first episode's comparatively brief theme *b* has a falling contour:

5. During an extensive transition, orchestra and soloist engage in a colorful colloquy. Subtly, near its end, orchestral strings cite fragments from the principal subject underneath ornamental arabesques played by the solo instrument. Eventually, this passage concludes on a quiet violin trill.

6. When the principal theme *a* returns, it follows a pattern Beethoven consistently observes throughout the movement: (1) citation in a low register by the solo violin; (2) repetition two octaves higher; and (3) reaffirmation (sometimes modified) by the orchestra.

7. A second episode *c* shifts to the parallel tonality of D minor, where the violin sounds a rather severe theme:

8. An aura of tranquility hovers over this section, which is preserved as a lone bassoon repeats the theme under a solo violin filigree. Later, a similar dialogue, between violin and bassoon, sounds a modified version of the subject.

9. Again, a bridge passage (sixteen measures long) continues the narrative.
10. Appearing as before (that is, with three citations), the principal theme *a* presents an unchanging countenance.
11. At its end, however, an extensive byplay occurs involving fragments from: the transitions, the first episode *b*, and the principal rondo theme itself *a*.
12. After the full orchestra, using an idea from the first transition, brings the dynamic level to a sonorous *fortissimo*, the soloist interpolates a brief cadenza.
13. Then the principal rondo theme *a* appears, but in a wrong key (E-flat major). Eventually things right themselves, however, and the sportive first subject brings the movement to a brilliant close.

Felix Mendelssohn (1809–1847), Scherzo from Incidental Music for *A Midsummer Night's Dream*

When he was seventeen years of age (in 1826) and strongly influenced by a reading (in German) of several Shakespeare plays, Mendelssohn wrote a piece for two pianos (later orchestrated) which he called Overture to *A Midsummer Night's Dream*. Seventeen years later (in 1843), the already famous composer—by royal command of Frederick William IV, King of Prussia—created other portions of a score intended to support presentation of the drama at Berlin. Included in this series of radiant pieces (mostly for orchestra, but with a few vocal interpolations), were several zesty *Intermezzi*, the poetic Nocturne, a stately Wedding March, and a scintillating Scherzo. Divorced from their original context, many of these are now frequently heard in an orchestral suite.

All sections of the music for *A Midsummer Night's Dream* are, of course, intended to highlight the Shakespearean drama. Some, such as the Wedding March are performed as action ensues on stage, whereas others are inserted as connectives between various scenes. This is a circumstance with the Scherzo, which serves as a bridge between the drama's first and second acts, where it convincingly suggests a never-never land of quite implausible make-believe. Organized in sonata-rondo form, it has these details:

1. Set in G minor, Mendelssohn's Scherzo refutes a widely held misconception that music in a minor mode is necessarily gloomy. Moving at an extremely rapid pace (*allegro vivace*), two each of flutes, clarinets, and bassoons announce the principal rondo theme *a*:

2. Repetition is accomplished in an altered sonorous hue (oboes and horns are added); a third affirmation—to which a lengthy extension is appended—involves the entire orchestra.

3. Announced almost furtively (*pianissimo*), the subordinate theme (equivalent to rondo form's first episode *b*), is sounded with a feather-light touch by violins, violas, and 'cellos:

4. Violins alone present an agile six-measure passage that leads into a reappearance of the principal theme *a*.

5. Under sustained woodwind chords, the principal theme *a* undergoes development as violas, 'cellos, and basses probe its inner recesses. In alternation, upper woodwinds and some strings adroitly toss thematic fragments back and forth. Later, the subordinate subject experiences treatment, handled mostly by violins and violas playing in unison. Then, as the "Fantasia" section nears its end, fragments from both themes sound through the orchestra.

6. Compressed and scored differently, the recapitulation reaffirms both subjects. Now, the subordinate theme appears in a new key (as is conventional), and other traditional tenets are observed by Mendelssohn, who was a superb musical architect.

7. Making virtuoso demands on a solo flutist who must traverse a lengthy and difficult passage (presumably in a single breath), the coda maintains fleet nimbleness to the composition's very end.

Camille Saint-Saëns (1835–1921), *Introduction and Rondo Capriccioso* for Violin and Orchestra

During a lengthy compositional career, Saint-Saëns wrote three symphonies, numerous concertos for piano, violin, or 'cello, several operas of which the best-known is *Samson et Dalila* (1877), the piquantly descriptive *Danse macabre,* and the humorous *Carnival of the Animals.* But one of his most popular works, a great favorite since it was introduced by the Spanish virtuoso Pablo Sarasate in 1863 (when the composer was 28), is a piquant and charming piece for solo violin and orchestra in extended rondo form. Unpretentious and witty, Saint-Saëns' *Introduction and Rondo Capriccioso* has an insouciant charm, a touch of wry humor, and a gentle whimsy that makes it linger in one's memory. These are its details:

1. As the title indicates, the *Rondo Capriccioso* is prefaced by a stately
   introduction, thirty-six measures long. Playing over a restrained harmonic
   background (in A minor), the solo violin introduces this graceful melody:

2. Later, a more animated second subject is announced.

3. Heralded by a crisp accompaniment (and played at an *allegro* tempo),
   the principal rondo theme *a*—which has an unusually wide compass—is
   sounded, repeated, and extended by the solo violin:

4. For the first digression *b*, the solo instrument introduces an impassioned
   subject:

5. Later, this strain becomes filled with extremely active passagework.
6. In characteristic manner, the principal subject *a* is reiterated, repeated,
   and extended by the solo violin.

7. Vigorously asserting itself, the orchestra (with later assistance from the solo violin) sounds the first of several bridge passages.
8. Introduced by the soloist, a second episode *c* is rather melancholy and marked to be played *con morbidezza* (with delicacy):

9. Here the solo instrument performs in duple meter with an accompaniment in sextuple meter (taken two beats in a measure).
10. Again, a bridge passage, this one featuring the solo instrument, is used as a connective.
11. After approaching a reaffirmation of the principal theme *a* over a descending chromatic passage, the solo instrument continues to maintain its prominence while sounding the subject.
12. Bridge number three (performed jointly by orchestra and soloist) leads into a reappearance of the first episode *b* in a new key.
13. And bridge number four leads into a final, but modified, affirmation of the principal rondo theme *a*, this time sounded by oboe, flute, and others over an ornamental violin configuration.
14. Played *piu allegro* (a little faster), the coda elicits extreme dexterity from the soloist. Suitably climactic (and in the major mode), it concludes in a sparkling, animated fashion.

Maurice Ravel (1875–1937), *Pavane pour une infante défunte*

Just whom Ravel had in mind as an *infante défunte* when he wrote this elegiac work is uncertain. From the title it might be supposed that his subject was a Spanish princess long since deceased, yet the composer held warm friendships with a number of young people and it is possible that his pavane was written as a memoriam for one of them. That a commemorative work could be founded on a dance pattern may seem incongruous, yet it is a historical fact that ceremonial dances have been significant in ritual observance, some of them dolorous, since time immemorial. As late as the seventeenth century, for instance, the slow and solemn pavane was employed on state occasions to express sentiments that were both funereal and somber.

After publishing the pavane as a piano piece in 1899, Ravel rescored it in 1912 for a small orchestra consisting of two flutes, two oboes, two clarinets, two bassoons, and two horns, a harp, and the usual strings. Organized in simple rondo form (*abaca*), it is an extremely tuneful musical miniature. Clarity, restraint, and formal elegance stand uppermost in it, but Ravel was an unusually gifted orchestrator, and this piece (along with virtually all his other instrumental works) glows with the most vivid of aural sonorities.

1. Beginning without preamble, the pensive principal rondo theme *a* is announced (in G major) by the horn over a gentle string accompaniment:

2. In direct succession, the first episode *b* shifts to the dominant tonality (D major) and uses a solo oboe (supported by other woodwinds) to present this related subject:

3. Thereafter, this seven-measure idea is repeated by strings.
4. When the principal theme *a* reappears, it is assigned to flutes and clarinets, which play in octaves over an undulating string accompaniment.
5. Several instrumental voices are employed to present the second episode *c*. Divided into two-measure segments, the subject is passed from flute to strings, from clarinet to strings, and then to the full ensemble; its repetition is similarly segmented. Set in the key of G minor, the ten-measure theme is this:

6. For its final appearance, the principal theme *a* is assigned to octave-spaced violins (doubled by similarly separated flutes). Back again in G major, it is played with glowing ardor over a rippling harp accompaniment.
7. Only a few cadential chords (in lieu of a formal coda) are needed to close this unhurried, leisurely, and captivating pavane.

Some Further Examples of Rondo Form

Bach, Johann Sebastian. Suite No. 2 in B minor for Flute and Strings (*Rondeau*).

Bartók, Béla. Concerto No. 3 for Piano (1945), Finale; *Music for Strings, Percussion and Celesta* (1935), Finale.

Beethoven, Ludwig van. Concerto No. 5 in E-flat major for Piano, Finale; Rondo in C major for Piano and Orchestra; Sextet in E-flat major for Woodwinds, fourth movement; Sonata No. 21 in C major for Piano ("Waldstein"), Finale.

Brahms, Johannes. Quartet in G minor for Piano and Strings, Finale; Quartet in C minor for Strings, Finale; Serenade No. 1 in D major, sixth movement; Sextet in B-flat major for Strings, fourth movement; Symphony No. 3 in F major, second movement.

Haydn, Franz Joseph. Quartet in E-flat major ("Joke"), third and fourth movements; Quartet in D major ("Lark"), Finale; Symphonies Nos. 94 in G major ("Surprise"); 101 in D major ("Clock"); and 103 in B-flat major ("Drum Roll"), Finale.

Hindemith, Paul. *Sonata for Clarinet and Piano* (1940), fourth movement.

Lalo, Edouard. *Symphonie espagnole* for Violin and Orchestra, fifth movement.

Mendelssohn, Felix. Concerto No. 1 in G minor for Piano, Finale.

Mozart, Wolfgang Amadeus. Concertos No. 23 in A major (K. 488), and No. 25 in C major (K. 503) for Piano, Finale; Quintet in E-flat major for Piano and Winds (K. 452), Finale; Rondos in D major (K. 382), and A major (K. 386), for Piano and Orchestra; Sonata No. 3 in B-flat major for Piano (K. 281), third movement.

Piston, Walter. Symphony No. 4 (1949), second movement.

Prokofiev, Serge. Concerto No. 3 in C major for Piano (1921), third movement; Concerto No. 2 in G minor for Violin (1935), third movement.

Schoenberg, Arnold. *Quintet for Wind Instruments* (1924), fourth movement.

Weber, Carl Maria. Concerto No. 2 in E-flat major for Piano, third movement.

A collection of 18th and 19th century string instruments, including three viole d'amour (upper row), two violins (lower row), and a viol neck (center).

PART THREE

MUSIC'S PRINCIPAL EXPRESSIVE DESIGNS

Over the last four hundred years, a number of well-defined structures have become firmly established in the hierarchy of musical designs. Covering a wide spectrum of performing media and ranging from pieces for single instruments (partitas, sonatas, or suites), through extended orchestral works (overtures, tone poems, symphonies), to large-scale compositions for voices and instruments (oratorio, some symphonies, and opera), they embrace the most exalted and most extensive ideas conceived by composers in recent times.

Such compositions have a sense of totality, a well-drawn architectonic scheme, and an emotionality that is often overwhelming, occasionally subtle, and unfailingly persuasive. Some are so abstract as to appear austere, while others seeth with the strongest passions imaginable. All are as one, however, in an employment of music's basic materials (rhythm, melody, texture, instruments and/or voices) for communicative purposes. And, in one manner or another, most employ the formal patterns (part form, variation form, sonata form, rondo form) we have discussed in previous chapters.

Understanding and enjoying compositions of this kind brings our study to glorious fulfillment. Of course, a full realization of the beauties inherent in many works may not come immediately, and a lapse of some time may be required before a meaningful understanding of the pieces discussed in Chapters 10 through 18 comes about. But a lifetime lies ahead, and ideas contained in these chapters (including suggestions from the charts appended to the end of each chapter) should provide ample guidance for future experiences in the broad realm of music.

Take time to enjoy your contacts with music—past, present, and future. May they be pleasurable and stimulating. And most of all, may they bring beauty, satisfaction, and emotional release into your life.

Chapter 10

Curtain Raiser, Concert Piece, and Rhapsody

Single-movement pieces variously called overtures, preludes, prologues, rhapsodies, fantasias, or toccatas, are frequently included on today's concert programs. Scored for orchestra, band, or such individual instruments as piano, harpsichord, or organ, many are colorful and imaginative works organized in sonata form, sonatina form, or part form (although free form is far from rare). Best-known of the works in this category are the theatrical overtures used to introduce operas, operettas, or some plays. Although most of these are conceived for instruments, a few (for example, the prologues to Mascagni's *Cavalleria Rusticana* or Leoncavallo's *I Pagliacci*) occasionally incorporate brief vocal passages.

Colloquially termed *curtain raisers*, theatrical overtures alert an audience and inform it that stage action is about to ensue. Moreover, they establish an appropriate aesthetic mood for dramatic unfoldment, and acquaint listeners (often, but not invariably) with important melodies from the complete score. Early overtures bore little thematic relationship with the works they prefaced. So fully independent that they could be passed from one opera to another, some did double or even triple duty—for example, Rossini's *Barber of Seville* Overture (1816) which saw previous service with *Elizabetta, regina d' Inghilterra* (1815), and before that with *Aurelaine in Palmira* (1813). But most later overtures are based on thematic fragments from the parent work (Preludes to Verdi's *La Traviata* or Bizet's *Carmen*) and are thereby tangibly bound to it.

Similar pieces, free of theatrical association, are known as *concert overtures* and often (but not invariably) have a narrative or descriptive intent. An initial formulation of this concept may be credited to Beethoven, who salvaged his *Coriolanus* Overture (1807) from a theatrical fiasco (it had been written originally to introduce a drama by H. J. Collin) and gave it a stature in orchestral literature. Subsequently, he composed other pieces (*King Stephen, Namensfeier, Consecration of the House*) that were overtures in name and format but innocent of dramatic liaison. And these, in turn, established a trend taken up by Mendelssohn (*Hebrides* Overture, *Calm Seas and Prosperous Voyage*); Berlioz (*The Corsair, Roman Carnival*); *and* Brahms (*Academic Festival* Overture, *Tragic* Overture).

OVERTURE BACKGROUNDS

Overtures began to assume their modern shape early in the seventeenth century, shortly after opera was born. Initially little more than flourishes sounded from a theater's orchestra pit, they nevertheless presaged the later emergence of significant compositions. Comparatively few instrumental designs were then extant (that is, around 1600), and most of these were adaptations of such vocal patterns as the motet, madrigal, or chanson. Excluding dances, or such polyphonic designs as the canon or fugue, these were the overture's most important predecessors:

1. *Ricercar:* A sixteenth century form modeled after the motet, it stressed imitative counterpoint and was comparatively restrained in expression. Many had several themes, but the idiom was so flexible that when Bach wrote his *Musical Offering* (1747), he used the name ricercar to identify fugues based on a single theme. An example, the *Ricercar dopo il Credo,* composed for organ by Girolamo Frescobaldi, is included in *Masterpieces of Music Before 1750.*

2. *Fantasia:* Related to the ricercar, this pattern was, nevertheless, more exuberant in expression and freer in form. A later example, Bach's Chromatic Fantasia and Fugue in D minor for Harpsichord (1720), shows the design's luxuriant ornateness.

3. *Canzona:* Sixteenth-century canzonas were polyphonic vocal pieces of dazzling beauty; subsequently, however, the design was modified and applied to works for keyboard or ensemble. Frescobaldi's *Canzoni per sonar* (5) written for keyboard (harpsichord) exemplify the pattern.

4. *Toccata:* Literally "touch pieces" that advantageously display a keyboard performer's digital dexterity, early toccatas were filled with ornate passagework. Later examples became more polyphonic and were largely based on imitation. Bach's Toccata and Fugue in D minor for Organ is a fine example.

5. *Prelude:* Arising in the fifteenth and sixteenth centuries from the practice of instrumentalists "warming up" (that is, limbering their fingers) before performing, this became a freely conceived, extemporaneous form. French organists (François Couperin and Jean Philippe Rameau) codified "preludizing," and established a design later used by Bach, Handel, and others.

COMMON OVERTURE TYPES

Generally speaking, most of today's well-known overtures fall within one of these categories:

1. Works written between 1600–1775 that were conceived in the French or Italian style (see p. 225). Handel's overtures and those that preface Bach's *Four Orchestral Suites* [1] exemplify the former, whereas Mozart's Overture to *The Abduction from the Seraglio* demonstrates the latter.
2. Overtures written during the Classic era—those to Mozart's *The Marriage of Figaro, Don Giovanni,* or *The Magic Flute* are outstanding—were brilliantly conceived orchestral pieces usually cast in sonata form, sonatina form, or part form.
3. Theatrical overtures of the Romantic era based on thematic material from the works they introduce. Most were written in a broadly conceived sonata form: Weber's *Oberon* Overture and Wagner's *Flying Dutchman* Overture.
4. Independent, single-movement compositions initially called concert overtures that were later identified as symphonic poems or tone poems: Mendelssohn's *Hebrides* Overture, Beethoven's *Namensfeier* Overture, and Tchaikowsky's *1812* Overture exemplify the type.
5. Preludes that are (usually) shorter than conventional overtures and organized in part form or a free pattern. Examples include prologues to Verdi's *La Traviata* and *Aïda;* or Wagner's *Lohengrin.*
6. Richly endowed overtures that convey a compressed version of the musico-dramatic work to which they are joined: Wagner's *Die Meistersinger* Overture and Beethoven's *Leonora* Overture No. 3.
7. Light overtures comprised of a succession of scintillating melodies organized in potpourri form: Offenbach's *Orpheus in Hades;* von Suppe's *Beautiful Galatea;* Strauss' *Die Fledermaus;* and Sullivan's *H. M. S. Pinafore.*

RHAPSODY, PRELUDE, AND FANTASIE

Scored for individual instruments (piano, harpsichord, or organ), or such instrumental groups as orchestra, string orchestra, or band, most rhapsodies, preludes, and fantasies are organized in a free (or rhapsodic) manner. Although many in the current repertoire postdate the mid-nineteenth century, progenitors can be traced to pre-Baroque times and beyond. Very likely the name itself dates from an even earlier era, for in ancient Greece, pieces of epic poetry with disconnected episodes or discontinuous parts (for example, the second book of *The Iliad*) were called rhapsodies.

---

[1] As a specific example, consider the Overture to Bach's Suite No. 2 in B minor for Flute and Strings.

In actuality these were a free effusion of words with little or no formal plan, and existed in marked contrast with other examples of highly organized Greek poetry.

Like its linguistic counterpart, the musical rhapsody became a free outpouring of ideas. Franz Liszt, one of the first Romantic composers to work with this concept,[2] published nineteen *Hungarian Rhapsodies* for Piano between 1846–1885 (some were subsequently orchestrated by Liszt and others). Although termed "Hungarian," these are not really nationalistic works. Rather, they are based on traditional Gypsy melodies. Yet the trend had vague nationalistic overtones, and it subsequently enjoyed a considerable vogue. Others who wrote similar works include Edouard Lalo (*Norwegian Rhapsody*); Maurice Ravel (*Rhapsodie espagnol*); Georges Enesco (*Roumanian Rhapsodies*); Ralph Vaughan Williams (*Norfolk Rhapsodies*); George Gershwin (*Rhapsody in Blue*); Edward German (*Welsh Rhapsody*); and Béla Bartók (*Rhapsodies (2) for Violin and Orchestra*).

Among the most venerable of single-movement instrumental forms, preludes were used as early as the fifteenth century to introduce polyphonic pieces for lute or keyboard. Many exude an extemporaneous aura and emphasize freely conceived scale runs and brilliant arpeggio passages. J. S. Bach employed preludes to preface many of his sonatas, suites, and partitas for harpsichord (see, for instance, the forty-eight preludes and fugues in his *Well-Tempered Clavier*). In later years, Frederic Chopin utilized this concept in a series of piano works that are almost improvisatory in character. His twenty-four *Préludes* (1839)—one each in the several major and minor keys—are delightful musical miniatures that emphasize special pianistic problems. Serge Rachmaninoff (*Préludes* for Piano, 1904 and 1910); George Gershwin (*Préludes (3)* for Piano); and Dmitri Shostakovich (*Preludes and Fugues (24)* for Piano) are among those who followed his example. Claude Debussy's twenty-four *Preludes* for Piano, Books 1 & 2, written in 1910 and 1913, are a particularly distinguished set of similar pieces.

Fantasias—the designation has been variously spelled fantasie, phantasy, or fantasy—have existed for centuries as agile, decorative, and effusive compositions in free form. Apparently inaugurated by Italian composers during the fourteenth and fifteenth centuries, the design spread to other lands, particularly England, where it acquired the picturesque title "fancy." Early keyboard fantasias (for harpsichord, clavichord, or organ) often prefaced fugues, where the contrast between free form and strict form was very effective.[3] Fantasias, which tend to be not only free in outline but episodic in structure and kaleidoscopic in mood, experienced renewed life during Classic and Romantic times when composers avidly sought release from rigid formality. Among the exemplificative pieces written during these years

---

[2] His efforts, however, had been anticipated by a host of composers working in the span of years between 1400–1800 (see p. 222).

[3] An excellent example is J. S. Bach's *Fantasia and Fugue in G minor* for Organ.

are Mozart's Fantasia in C minor for Piano (K. 475); Beethoven's *Fantasia in C minor* for Piano, Chorus, and Orchestra ("Choral Fantasy"); Schubert's *Wanderer Fantasie* for Piano; Schumann's Fantasia in C major for Piano; and Ferruccio Busoni's *Fantasia Contrapuntistica* (1910). Late in the nineteenth century the fantasy began to appear in orchestral works, as is shown in Tchaikowsky's *The Tempest* (after Shakespeare, 1872); *Francesca da Rimini* (after Dante, 1876); and *Romeo and Juliet* (1880).

WAYPOSTS IN OVERTURE DEVELOPMENT

The Baroque and Classic Eras

From the tenth to the seventeenth centuries, an instrumental tradition of sorts was maintained in church, castle, theater, and tavern. Initially, this was an extremely casual practice, and pieces—conceived originally for voices—were performed on an assortment of available instruments, chiefly viols. Indeed, compositions written as late as the sixteenth century often bore the inscription: "apt for voices or viols" to indicate they could be either played or sung. In time, however, such specialized instrumental patterns as the ricercar, fantasia, canzona, toccata, and prelude came into being. Polyphonically oriented (for this was the prevailing style of the era) they were performed on keyboard instruments, or by the catch-as-catch-can "orchestras" of the period.

Music's first "overture" was likely the thrice-repeated nine-measure flourish that prefaced Monteverdi's *Orfeo* (1607). Although it was not called an overture, for the designation was then unknown, this "toccata" enlisted available instruments to sound a piece that was an obvious "audience-catcher." Subsequently, Monteverdi (and others) undertook the composition of similar pieces, but it was not until after 1650 that a recognizable overture pattern, known as the "French Style," came into being as a result of Lully's work.[4] Established in a series of compositions written in Paris between 1672–1686, this scheme organized the overture into two (sometimes three) segments. From the *canzona-overture* heretofore largely practiced in Venice, Lully evolved a design consisting of (1) a stately introduction, often marked *grave* in tempo, that moved scalewise in uneven rhythmic figurations (that is, with dotted notes), and (2) a quicker principal section, typically an *allegro*, that was often fugal or, at least, imitative in texture. Based on a short motivelike theme introduced successively in several voices, such a piece unfolded as its main subject passed through various keys and registers in a sequential manner. Sometimes, Lully's overtures had a third section that returned to a slow tempo and suggested one of the era's slow dances (for example, a sarabande or a stately minuet).

[4] As early as 1658, in his ballet *Alcidiane*, Lully used an overture that began with a slow preface followed by a lively, fugue-like allegro. Tangible codification of this practice, however, was reserved for a later date.

Sometime after 1675, the "Italian" overture came into being, largely as a result of efforts expended by Alessandro Scarlatti. Founded on a scheme precisely opposite from Lully's, it had a quick *allegro*, a pensive *largo*, and a *presto* finale. For nearly a century (until after 1750) both styles coexisted. French overtures were often used in nonoperatic works (suites, oratorios, or cantatas), whereas Italian specimens were employed in the theater. After 1750, however, French-style overtures declined and ultimately vanished. But the Italian *sinfonia avanti l'opera* (symphony before the opera), as Scarlatti termed his overtures, continued to flourish.

Despite its name, use of the French overture was not limited to Gallic composers. Purcell's Overture to *Dido and Aeneas* (1689), for example, although written by an Englishman,[5] was conceived in the French style (as were many of Handel's overtures, including those to *Rinaldo*, 1711 and *Messiah*, 1742). And particular works of Bach—his *Suites for Orchestra*, some of the partitas and suites for solo strings, some *French Suites* and *English Suites*, as well as some partitas for keyboard—include French-style overtures.

Christoph Willibald Gluck prefaced his *Orfeo ed Euridice* (1762) and *Alceste* (1767) with comparatively short overtures (the former an *allegro* movement in sonatina form, the latter a sectional structure vacillating between *lento* and *andante* tempos). Noble, dignified, and exalted in expression, they are among the most distinguished overtures to predate those of Mozart. Gluck's contemporary, Jean Philippe Rameau, a native Frenchman who was a prodigious composer of opera-ballet, naturally found considerable use for instrumental prefaces. Interestingly enough, however, his preference in this area extended to Italian-style works.

With the ascent of Classicism (c. 1780), a composite version of the overture became unqualifiedly triumphant. Typically, it had a rather ponderous introduction (possibly adapted from French sources) followed by a quick main section in sonata form (with exposition, development, and recapitulation). In nearly all respects—tempo, formal pattern, melodic material, and expressive intent—it was a near-equivalent of the first movements in most eighteenth-century symphonies. These characteristics are prominent in the operatic prefaces of Mozart, works that must be considered exemplars of the Classic overture. Although his Overture to *Abduction from the Seraglio* (1782) has the perfect outlines of an Italian-style overture, later works (that is, Overtures to *The Marriage of Figaro*, 1786; *Don Giovanni*, 1787; or *The Magic Flute*, 1791)—harken to the new concept and are cast in sonatina form or sonata form.

As Classicism merged with Romanticism, influences emanating from the French Revolution became increasingly decisive in politics, government, philosophy, and the arts. In Western Europe, for instance, activity

---

[5] One, however, who had a French teacher (Pelham Humfrey, himself probably a pupil of Lully).

in the Parisian theaters was watched, discussed, and imitated. Serious opera was in high estate, of course, but the inroads of light French theatrical works were also felt, and pieces by Daniel François Auber (1782–1871); François Boieldieu (1775–1834); and André Grétry (1741–1813) were acclaimed everywhere. Invariably, their witty operas had sparkling overtures, and although both lacked profundity, depth, and complexity, the times welcomed these bits of musical fluff. Such overtures as those to *Crown Diamonds* (Auber) and the *Caliph of Bagdad* (Boieldieu), for instance, established precedents that have been emulated well into the twentieth century.

The Century of Romanticism

When Rossini, Bellini, and Donizetti composed their operas, each followed a centuries-old Italian tradition that considered overtures to be little more than curtain raisers. Actually, those by Bellini and Donizetti are quite perfunctory and find little use outside the theatre today, but Rossini's pieces are different. Because of superior melodic gifts, a facile inventive touch, and a flair for colorful orchestration, Rossini infused his overtures with attractive verve, wit, and charm. Among the most notable are those to *L'Italiana in Algeri* (1813); *The Barber of Seville* (1816); *La Gazza Ladra* (1817); and *William Tell* (1829).

Unquestionably Romanticism's foremost composer, Ludwig van Beethoven marshalled orchestral resources with the skill of a born craftsman. Everywhere in instrumental music—with symphonies, concertos, chamber music pieces, or piano works—his capacity was supreme. And these same qualities were carried over into the composition of overtures. Chief among the latter are those to: *The Creatures of Prometheus* (1801), a ballet; the opera *Fidelio,* including the *Leonora* Overture No. 2 (1805), *Leonora* Overture No. 3 (1806), *Leonora* Overture No. 1 (1807), and the *Fidelio* Overture (1814); *Coriolanus* (1807), a preface to Collin's drama; *Egmont* (1810), part of the incidental music for a Goethe drama; *The Ruins of Athens* (1811), incidental music for a drama by Kotzebue; *King Stephen* (1811), intended to enhance another Kotzebue drama; *Namensfeier* ("Nameday," 1814), a musical salute to Emperor Francis II; and *Consecration of the House* (1822), written for the opening of a theater in Vienna. All maintain a relationship with the theater, but each is also a "character" overture, and in this sense a progenitor of Mendelssohn's concert overtures and Liszt's symphonic poems. Conceived in sonata form, most have awesome introductions, quickly paced principal sections based on two (sometimes more) contrasting themes, and lengthy codas.

Among the best-known overtures by Carl Maria von Weber are those for *Der Freischütz* (1821), *Euryanthe* (1823), and *Oberon* (1826). Each is warmly lyric, filled with an abundance of dramaturgy, and organized in sonata form. His *Jubel* Overture (1818), notable for being one of music's earliest independent concert overtures, is a curious work. Written to commemorate a royal celebration in Saxony, it is particularly noisy in concluding portions (which are based on the English melody, "God Save The King").

Far removed from Beethoven and Weber in statutory miles, Hector Berlioz was, nevertheless, a kindred spirit. Among the Frenchman's important single-movement works are *Waverley* Overture (1827), inspired by Scott's Waverley novels; *Les Francs-Juges* (Judges of the Secret Court, 1827), the preface for a projected opera that was never completed; *Le Roi Lear* Overture ("King Lear," 1831), an orchestral testimonial to a Berlioz passion: William Shakespeare; *Rob Roy* Overture (1832), another work inspired by Scott; *Le Carnaval Romain* ("The Roman Carnival," 1844), intended to preface the second act of his opera *Benvenuto Cellini; Le Corsaire* Overture (1855), motivated by a Byron poem; and three operatic overtures including those to: *Benvenuto Cellini* (1838), *Les Troyens* (1859), and *Béatrice et Bénédict* (1862).

Curiously anachronistic, Felix Mendelssohn was a Classicist working in a Romantic environment. Although he must be considered a traditionalist, this greatly gifted man was capable of exploiting heretofore unrealized possibilities in overture design as is shown in such pieces as the Overture to *A Midsummer Night's Dream* (1826), based on Shakespeare and written when the composer was only seventeen; *Military* Overture in C major (1824), a classically oriented work for wind band; *Hebrides* Overture (1832), also known as *Fingal's Cave,* a musical portrait of islands lying off the Scottish coast; *Calm Seas and Prosperous Voyage* (1832), based on poems by Goethe; *Beautiful Melusina* (1833), the musical tale of a wayward nymph; and the *Ruy Blas* Overture (1839), preface to a drama by Victor Hugo.

Franz Schubert found occasional employment for the single-movement pattern, as is demonstrated by his *Wanderer Fantasie* and the *Fantasia in F minor* (both for piano). Schubert's lovely *Rosamunde* Overture (1823), written to preface a play by Helmina von Chezy, is probably his most frequently performed orchestral composition, but the *Fierrabras* Overture and *Overture in Italian Style* are equally fine. Robert Schumann, a later Romanticist, was not strikingly successful as a composer of dramatic music, but the incidental music he wrote for *Manfred* (after Byron, 1849) was well received, and its overture is an exceptional composition. Schumann's *Fantasia in C major* for Piano is also a particularly fine keyboard work.

In personal life as in professional practice, Franz Liszt was a freebooter. After an extensive career as a piano virtuoso (he is generally considered to have been the most distinguished performing artist of his time), Liszt retired to the ducal court at Weimar where, among other activities, he took up the composer's pen. Although his resultant works are discursive, uneven, and iconoclastic, Liszt formulated the concept for his symphonic poem, which was actually little more than the Mendelssohnian concert overture in a new guise. Where Mendelssohn adhered to sonata form, Liszt ventured toward free form; where illustrative allusions had been previously vague and general, Liszt became increasingly specific. Among his significant works in this area (discussed more extensively in Chapter 14) are thirteen symphonic poems, among which are *Tasso,* after Byron, 1854; *Les Préludes,* after Lamartine, 1854; *Orpheus,* 1854; *Mazeppa,* after Victor Hugo, 1854; and nineteen *Hungarian Rhapsodies.*

Richard Wagner was a composer whose field of specialization (opera) might normally have held him aloof from instrumental music. In the Wagnerian concept of music drama, however, orchestral resources are advanced to a pre-eminent position with a result that overtures and preludes, as well as numerous instrumental passages within the operas themselves, are crucial to a full realization of the composer's intent. Wagner's early operas (*Rienzi, Flying Dutchman,* and *Tannhäuser*) have overtures—the first two in sonata form, the third in part form—that qualify as eloquent curtain raisers. But his subsequent music dramas (*Lohengrin, Das Rheingold,* and *Parsifal*) are prefaced by preludes—introductions that lead directly into the first scene. Those to *Die Meistersinger* and *Tristan und Isolde* are lengthy, emotion-packed works that actually give microcosmic versions of their dramas. Wagner's *Siegfried Idyll,* also a single-movement piece, is *sui generis.* Based on material from the opera *Siegfried,* it was composed for his wife and infant son, scored for small orchestra, and first performed (at their home) on Christmas Day, 1870.

Working contemporaneously with Wagner, but in a land that had long since established its own musical traditions, Giuseppe Verdi did not exert as profound an influence on instrumental music as his German colleague. Many of Verdi's overtures, for instance, do not enjoy a vigorous life outside the theater. Important exceptions are those to: *Nabucco* (1842); *Les vepres siciliennes* (1855); and *La Forza del destino* (1862). Verdi also used preludes extensively, and those to *Rigoletto* (1851); *La Traviata* (1853); *Il Trovatore* (1853); *Aida* (1872); and *Otello* (1887) are superb, passionate, but relatively brief works.

A master of serious composition, Johannes Brahms was also aware of the dazzling beauties inherent in tuneful, popular works.[6] Consequently, melodism abounds almost everywhere in his compositions, and the musical fabric—although often thick and knotty in texture—invariably glistens with a silky, richly hued sonority. Brahms created two single-movement concert pieces, the *Academic Festival* Overture and the *Tragic* Overture, both written in 1880. If the former, Brahms' musical salute to the University of Breslau was, to use his own words, "a potpourri of student songs à la Suppe," his *Tragic* Overture is modeled on the more serious aspects of Beethoven's craft. Precisely what tragedy the composer had in mind as he wrote is not revealed, but the work consistently discloses a serious mien as it progresses through a full-scale sonata form movement.

[6] He was, for instance, a warm admirer of Johann Strauss' music.

Few composers working in the late nineteenth century could match the versatility of Peter I. Tchaikowsky. Equally at home in the concert hall or opera house, Tchaikowsky wrote a number of highly popular single-movement compositions including: *Romeo and Juliet* (final revision 1880), based on Shakespeare's drama; *The Tempest* (1873), another piece stimulated by Shakespeare; *Francesca da Rimini* (1876), motivated by Dante; *Capriccio italien* (1880), musical impressions of a visit to Rome; *Overture 1812* (1880), commemorating Russia's victory over Napoleon; and *Hamlet* (1888), a third work based on Shakespeare.

While Brahms was active in Germany and Tchaikowsky was similarly engaged in Russia, Bedrich Smetana and Antonin Dvořák furthered music's cause in Bohemia. A primary figure in Slavonic nationalism, Smetana became prominent as an operatic composer (*The Bartered Bride*) and also created his illustrious *Ma Vlast* ("My Fatherland," 1879), a set of six symphonic poems on interrelated subjects. Dvořák, a far more capable composer, ultimately acquired international stature and wrote voluminously in both the instrumental and vocal idioms. Among his significant orchestral works are three *Slavonic Rhapsodies* (1878); Overture: *My Home;* ten *Legends* (1881); *Husitska Overture* (1883); and a cycle of three overtures called: (a) *In Nature's Realm* (1891), (b) *Carnival* (1891), and (c) *Othello* (1892).

Successors to Berlioz were slow to arise in France. The arch-romanticist died in 1869, but nearly two decades lapsed before any extensive efforts were expended in behalf of French instrumental music. For ultimately undertaking such a project, France can thank a Belgian: César Franck. An organist and church musician, Franck was not a prolific composer, nor can his work be termed unusually significant, but he had a born teacher's capacity to influence those about him. Consequently, Ernest Chausson, Camille Saint-Saëns, and Vincent d'Indy—pupils and followers of Franck—were encouraged to study and compose. Between them, these men in turn prepared an environment in which the art of Claude Debussy and Maurice Ravel, twentieth-century French composers of distinction, could flourish.

The Twentieth Century

As the new century moved through its first quarter, composers continued to affix instrumental prologues to their opera, ballet, and dramatic scores. In many instances—as with Puccini, Richard Strauss, or Debussy—these were comparatively short pieces bound directly to an opera's opening scene. But concert overtures (in reduced numbers) continued to appear and are represented by Henry Hadley's *In Bohemia* (1900); Edward Elgar's *Cockaigne* Overture ("In London Town," 1910); Serge Prokofiev's *Overture on Hebrew Themes* (for small ensemble, 1919); and William Walton's *Portsmouth Point* (1925).

A dedicated Impressionist, Claude Debussy attempted to depict pictorial imagery in many of his compositions. For instance, the *Préludes* for

Piano (Books 1 and 2, 1910, 1913), works of rare beauty, depict a variety of evocative concepts. These artistic ideas, incidentally, permeate most of his orchestral writing (further details on the latter are mentioned in Chapter 14). But Maurice Ravel, a French compatriot, tended to be more abstract. Ravel's *Pavane pour une infante défunte* (composed for piano, 1899, scored for small orchestra, 1910); the orchestral *Alborado del gracioso* (1912); his *Boléro* (1927); and *Tzigane* (1924) are single-movement pieces primarily founded on dance patterns. And the Viennese Expressionists, who were generally contemporaneous with the French Impressionists, apparently found little to interest them in single-movement patterns. Nor did Igor Stravinsky do much with them. Wishing to present a musical offering to his mentor, Nicholas Rimsky-Korsakoff, Stravinsky wrote an orchestral fantasy, *Feu d'artifice* ("Fireworks," 1908), early in his career. But virtually all his succeeding instrumental pieces were conceived as suites, concertos, or symphonies. On the other hand, Ralph Vaughan Williams wrote a number of works in single-movement format, including a *Fantasia on Greensleeves*, *Fantasia on a Theme by Tallis* (1910), the *Norfolk Rhapsody No. 1* (1906), *Toccata Marziale* (for winds), and an overture to Aristophanes's *The Wasps* (1909).

George Gershwin's jazzy *Rhapsody in Blue* (for piano and orchestra, 1924) became a cynosure of attention soon after its premiere and greatly assisted in directing world attention toward a rising generation of American composers. Also employing piano and orchestra, Serge Rachmaninoff's *Rhapsody on a Theme of Paganini* (1934), couched in a post-Romantic syntax, is actually a set of free variations on a borrowed theme. But Béla Bartók's two *Rhapsodies for Violin and Orchestra* (1928) adhere to Lisztian concepts and present a free effusion of ideas in bisectional designs. Ernest Bloch's *Schelomo* ("A Hebraic Rhapsody," 1916), combines the sensuous luster of musical Impressionism with subjects based on near-Eastern cantillation and is a scintillating masterwork.

With his *Cuban* Overture (1934) Gershwin merged the compelling expressiveness of jazz with popular Latin-American rhythms, and Aaron Copland followed a related path when he wrote his *El Salón Mexico* (1936) so it would suggest choreographic activities in a Mexico City dance hall. Vividly demonstrating the Hispanic influences that have imposed an indubitable stamp on contemporary musical idioms, he employs several Mexican folk melodies in an incandescent, pulsating score. Copland also used the single-movement pattern while composing his *Outdoor* Overture (1938) for a performing group at New York City's High School of Music and Art. William Schuman turned toward nationalistic subjects when he wrote the *American Festival* Overture (1939) and *Chester* (an overture for band, 1956), as did Roy Harris with his jingoistic "When Johnny Comes Marching Home" (1935). Contemporaneous with these are Samuel Barber's Overture to *The School for Scandal* (1933) and Arthur Benjamin's Overture to *An Italian Comedy* (1937). Somewhat later in vintage are Shostakovich's excellent *Festive* Overture (1954) and Bernstein's Overture to *Candide* (1956). Despite their titles, all have now assumed the role of concert overtures.

Within the last decade, avant-garde experimenters working with electronic music have turned toward the single-movement design with unique results. Employing conventional materials in a highly unorthodox manner, Edgard Varèse became a pioneer along these lines with his *Ionisation* (1931) and *Density 21.5* (for solo flute, 1935). Varèse's *Poème électronique* (1958), subtitled "Direct Magnetic Tape Creation," is a bizarre piece that shows the extremes toward which contemporary music has moved. Further examples of such strikingly unusual music can be found in Karlheinz Stockhausen's *Zyklus* (1959) for one percussionist, and his *Refrain* (1959) for three performers. Vladimir Ussachevsky (*Creation—Prologue*, 1962); Milton Babbitt (*Composition for Synthesizer*, 1964); and Otto Luening (*Gargoyles*, 1962) are three contemporary American musicians moving along similar paths. Available on recordings, their pieces show how the malleable single-movement design, formulated more than three and a half centuries ago, has remained flexible, adaptable, and useful through the passing years.

PARTICULAR EXAMPLES OF SINGLE-MOVEMENT WORKS

Ludwig van Beethoven (1770–1827), *Leonora* Overture No. 3

Four overtures became caught up in the tribulations that afflicted Beethoven's lone opera, *Fidelio*. The original preface—now called the *Leonora* Overture No. 2—a curtain raiser of sufficient beauty to please most musicians, did not meet the composer's exacting standards and was discarded after the premier in 1805. *Leonora* Overture No. 3 suffered in the debacle of 1806 when the opera was presented in revised form, and the *Leonora* Overture No. 1 was similarly rejected in 1807, the year of its composition. Ultimately, the *Fidelio* Overture (1814)—fourth in the series—was appended to the opera where it has remained during ensuing years. But the three *Leonora* overtures have not fallen into obscurity; rather, they continue to flourish as independent orchestral pieces. Occasionally, the Overture No. 3 is performed as an interlude between the two scenes in *Fidelio's* second act, where it decidedly does not belong.

Fidelio is a "rescue opera"—a theatrical work wherein a wrongly incarcerated prisoner (Florestan) is freed through the courageous efforts of a self-sacrificing wife (Leonora). Hearing the *Leonora* Overture No. 3 gives a listener considerable insight into the opera's dramatic and musical substance, for it quotes important melodies from the parent work and thereby manages to suggest a gist of its plot. These are its details:

1. Set in C major, the work begins with a slow and profoundly expressive introduction that suggests the descent into a dank and gloomy dungeon:

2. Later, clarinets and bassoons take up a theme from an important tenor aria, *In des lebens fruhlingstagen* (In the days of spring):

3. A dialogue between flute and violins follows, and a similar exchange later engages 'cellos and basses. Characteristically, the introduction concludes on a chord of the dominant.
4. Organized in sonata form, the overture's main section (in *allegro* tempo and duple meter) continues the established C-major tonality as violins and 'cellos present a theme (suggestive of Leonora) over a viola and bass accompaniment:

5. Extension enlists the full orchestra, *fortissimo*. Then, rapidly paced cascading passages serve as a bridge leading to the second subject.
6. More lyric than its companion, the gracious subordinate theme is introduced by flute and first violins in octaves:

7. After this idea has been fully stated, fragments from the first theme, presented in a syncopated manner, bring the exposition to a close.
8. Initial developmental activity centers on material from the principal theme's closing measures, and this idea moves in a descending sequence

through the tones of an E-major chord. Fragments from the subject itself provide contrast and are heard in a variety of keys and orchestral guises. Midway, *Fidelio's* celebrated fanfare is interposed:

9. In the opera, this trumpet call heralds the appearance of an official coming to correct abuses in prison administration; consequently, sounding this subject symbolizes a triumph of virtue over evil. Within the overture the fanfare is first played quietly (as in the opera), whereas its second presentation resounds with greater sonority.
10. Between them, a hushed passage (sounded by woodwinds) seems to question whether this fortunate turn of events can, in actuality, be true:

11. After this highly dramatic interpolation, the development continues, via a spirited duet between flute and bassoon, until a series of sequential passages shifts the work's tonality toward its home key.
12. In the recapitulation, an eloquent orchestra affirms a condensed version of the exposition wherein principal and subordinate themes—the latter now played by clarinet and first violins—are heard only once.
13. Appearing in altered guise in the coda, the subordinate theme sustains a colorful colloquy between orchestral instruments. After the dynamic level diminishes to a barely perceptible whisper, in a sudden dramatic shift, strings build toward a resounding climax. This passage, in *presto* tempo, launches a pellmell rush toward the inevitable conclusion.

Gioacchino Rossini (1792–1868), Two Operatic Overtures

Before he was twenty-one, Rossini had written such operas as *La Cambiale di Matrimonio* (1810) and *Tancredi* (1813), works that marked him as one of Italy's most gifted young composers; sixteen years and thirty-six operas later his prodigious activity came to an abrupt halt. *William Tell,* produced at Paris in 1829, was Rossini's final dramatic composition, after which forty years of near-silence ensued. Why this hiatus in creativity occured is something of a puzzle. It seems likely, however, that the greatly adulated composer may have had a premonition that times were turning against him, that opera-goers were now demanding a more serious fare than he cared to offer, and that the scintillating buffa style of which he was a master was becoming passé. Rather than compete against new arrivals in an unfamiliar métier, Rossini may have felt it politic, indeed expedient, to withdraw with reputation intact.

OVERTURE TO *THE BARBER OF SEVILLE*

Circumstances surrounding the premiere of Rossini's most celebrated work can only be termed a fiasco. Commissioned to write an opera for production at Rome in February of 1816, he procrastinated at such length that, finally, it had to be composed in something like thirteen days. When the work was introduced, audience reaction was hostile; boos and catcalls sounded everywhere in the theater, and objects of all sorts were showered upon the hapless—and inept—cast. In this melee, the opera's original overture was lost. Rather than write another, Rossini merely reached into his trunks to retrieve a preface that had been used twice before, in 1813 and 1815. Without ado or revision, it was appended to the *Barber of Seville* where it has since remained.

1. Sounded by full orchestra, a stentorian chord opens, after which rustling strings, in company with fluent woodwinds, articulate rising staccato scale passages in E major. After a modified repetition of these measures in the dominant tonality, an engaging melody is sounded by first violins:

2. In succession, staccato strings and legato woodwinds enjoy a colorful discourse, after which the overture's introduction closes on a B-major chord.
3. Organized in sonatina form, the main section (in *allegro vivo* tempo and quadruple meter) shifts to E minor. The principal theme is sounded by first violins and piccolo:

4. After this subject has been repeated and extended, a bridge of reiterated trills modulates to G major, where the subordinate theme is announced by oboe:

5. This, too, is repeated and extended, after which the orchestra takes up another idea and becomes engaged in action that suggests aspects of thematic development (this occurs in the exposition's closing measures):

6. As a midpoint in the work is reached, the pace slows temporarily. Then, resuming a quick tempo, the recapitulation presents the principal theme in E minor with its expanse considerably shortened. When the subordinate theme is presented by the clarinet, with assistance from other solo instruments, the tonality shifts to E major, where it remains.
7. Bearing a general resemblance to preceding sections, the coda employs an accelerated tempo to conclude this scintillating piece with a burst of unusual exuberance.

OVERTURE TO *LA GAZZA LADRA*

A mere dramatic bagatelle, the opera *La Gazza Ladra* (The Thievish Magpie) had its premiere in May, 1817. Based on a very casual plot, it deals with accusations leveled at a young girl who allegedly has stolen a spoon. Actually, the item had been purloined by a pet magpie. After exploiting this narrative to the hilt, Rossini cleverly resolves the deception and concludes on a happy note. History delivered the work a blow, however, for aside from its overture, *La Gazza Ladra* has passed from the repertoire. These are details about its orchestral prologue:

1. Three pre-emptory snare-drum rolls, guaranteed to alert even the most recalcitrant audience, announce the overture's opening. In quadruple

meter and marked *maestoso marziale*, the introduction is stately and decorous—save for mischievous interjections at cadential points. Four heavy orchestral chords ultimately close this section, but the use of a partial cadence implies that more activity is about to occur.

2. Again Rossini selected sonatina form as a formal pattern, and again his sequence of keys shifts from E minor to E major. Now, however, the work's main sections are played in triple meter (at an *allegro* tempo). Strings quote the principal theme, first in minor and then in major:

3. Characteristic of Rossini, this subject is immediately repeated with a slightly heavier orchestration. And in the passage that follows, a new subject—actually a second member of the principal theme—surges upward from the low register:

4. Onset of the subordinate theme is anticipated by a series of sustained chords played by bassoons, horns, and trombones. When it is announced, this subject cavorts with unrepressed animation:

5. After the second idea has been heard at length, a different subject, distantly related to the principal theme, is used to terminate the exposition:

6. Comparatively short, the recapitulation presents the first subject only once, and no thematic byplay is appended to its end. Interestingly enough, Rossini shifts to E major as the subordinate theme makes a final appearance. Otherwise, activity here closely parallels the exposition.
7. Obviously climactic and well suited for its task, the animated coda has no discernible thematic relationship with the overture's preceding segments.

Franz Liszt (1811–1886), *Hungarian Rhapsody No. 2*

Although born in Hungary—at Raiding where his father was in the employment of a Count of Esterhazy—Liszt was taken to Paris before the age of ten and became, in effect, a cosmopolite. Returning to Hungary as a renowned pianist in 1839, he discovered that virtually all recollection of that land had slipped from his memory, including any competence in handling its language. Determined to become more firmly tied to his native heath, Liszt plunged into a serious study of Magyar (Hungarian) music with results that were almost spectacular. One tangible offshoot was a book, *The Gypsies and Their Music in Hungary* published in 1859; another was the creation of a series of compositions based on ethnic melodies. Perhaps the most celebrated of these are the nineteen *Hungarian Rhapsodies* (a twentieth remains unpublished) that Liszt wrote for piano (fifteen of them between 1851 and 1854). Then, during subsequent years, assisted by Franz Doppler, he scored six for orchestra (but complicated matters by changing their numbering scheme and shifting their tonalities).

By far the most celebrated piece in this collection, Liszt's second *Hungarian Rhapsody* is shaped in the manner of a *csárdás*, a Hungarian dance with two contrasted sections. First is a *lassú*—dreamy, introspective, and in a minor mode—that employs considerable rubato; second is a *friska*—filled with wild exuberance and breathless gaiety—played (mostly) in a major tonality. The details are these:

1. Appearing without fanfare, a heavily ornamented melody in C minor is announced by violins, violas, and clarinets over rhythmic interjections from other members of the orchestra:

2. In direct succession, a more languid theme is sounded by this same combination of instruments:

3. Then, before the second subject is taken over by high woodwinds, a brilliant cadenza is interpolated by a solo clarinet.

4. Marked *dolcissimo* (sweetly), a new theme (heard later in a new key when the *friska* appears) is introduced by flutes and violas:

5. And an associated subject is interjected by the oboe and first violins:

6. Another clarinet cadenza presages a return of the first melody, heard, as before, in the clarinet-string coloration. When the *lassú* nears its close, the second melody, conveying the sweet refulgent tones often associated with Gypsy music, is played in close harmony by strings and woodwinds.

7. With gleeful abandon, the *friska* unfolds in *vivace* tempo. Continuing in the prevailing duple meter, it shifts temporarily to F minor but later settles in F major where it remains. Four subjects are important in this section. The first is announced in stentorian terms by the full orchestra:

8. Allotted to first violins (with assistance from flutes and clarinets), the second idea features the wide-ranging angular leaps so typical of ethnic music:

9. But the most driving subject in this piece is a heavy-footed theme announced *fortissimo* by the full wind section as strings provide a syncopated accompaniment:

10. Finally a fourth melody, in a score that is almost promiscuously lyrical, starts at the *pianissimo* level when it is introduced *staccatissimo* (crisply) by violas and 'cellos:

11. Over and over these several subjects are heard in diverse alignments. As the composition nears its end, gleeful merriment is interrupted when a dolorous little tune is announced by clarinet and bassoon:

12. Such an exuberant composition is not destined to end on a somber note, however, for a spirited coda (based on the fourth *friska* subject) brings it to a smashing close.

Peter I. Tchaikowsky (1840–1893), *Capriccio italien*

While sojourning at Rome in 1880, Tchaikowsky had rooms at the Hotel Constanzi overlooking barracks occupied by the Royal Cuirassiers. Never one to let an opportunity for musical stimulation pass, he became impressed with the bugle fanfares that sounded periodically from the garrison and seized on one as an introductory subject for an Italian caprice then taking shape in his mind. Furthermore, the Carnival—a period of wild gaiety and uninhibited frolic in Italian urban life—was then in full swing, and from the streets, dance pavilions, and cabarets the temporary Russian *émigré* absorbed enough melodies to stock a dozen compositions.

Organized in a single-movement format, Tchaikowsky's *Capriccio italien* is actually a fantasy on four themes. Acknowledged by the composer as folk melodies, each is an unusually attractive subject possessed of idiomatic Italianate flavor. Within the *Capriccio* they appear in an orderly array, but without adherence to any preconceived design. And although each experiences considerable repetition and occasional extension, none undergoes extensive manipulation. To give his composition as much color as possible, Tchaikowsky employed a somewhat larger orchestra than usual. Such piquant voices as the English horn, piccolo, glockenspiel, trumpet, and cornet intermingle with conventional instruments and adroitly display their unusual sonorities and techniques. These devices are unfailingly effective and do much to give the *Capriccio italien* its scintillating and vivacious character.

1. A summons to festivity is announced by two trumpets, playing loudly and in unison, as the work begins:

2. After a pulsating accompaniment has been set up by several brass instruments, the strings (also playing in unison) present the composition's first important melody, a somewhat dolorous tune in A major:

3. Performed in sextuple meter at an *andante* pace, this subject is pleasantly lyrical, although it vaguely suggests a tinge of somberness.

4. After some repetition—Tchaikowsky is rarely terse—two oboes sound a more animated melody marked to be played *Pochissimo piu mosso* (a little faster):

5. Almost immediately reaffirmed by two cornets with enriched orchestral support, the subject is later greatly extended by the full ensemble.

6. Venturing into the comparatively remote key of D-flat major and assuming an *allegro* moderato tempo in quadruple meter, the *Capriccio* becomes briskly joyful as violins announce a carefree street song:

7. A brief reprise of the somber first theme succeeds this exuberant melody, but pensiveness is felt only momentarily, for a rollicking *saltarello* theme —the final musical idea in this orchestral fantasy—soon appears. In duple meter and *presto* tempo, the new subject is initially quoted in A minor by upper woodwinds:

8. Again and again this irrepressible tune is tossed about through the orchestra, much as a tumbler is thrown by fellow acrobats in a gymnastic exhibition. A reprise of the work's second theme—this time presented in triple meter—punctuates the dance, but its appearance is fleeting for the *saltarello* soon returns to impel the composition toward a final cadence. As the coda appears, mounting tempos (indicated in the score as *presto, piu presto,* and *prestissimo*), continually increase the pace. At its conclusion, the *Capriccio italien* is both riotous and frenetic.

Georges Enesco (1881–1955), *Roumanian Rhapsody No. 1* (1901)

At the turn of the century, Georges Enesco began collecting Roumanian folk melodies with a view toward using some in compositions he was then planning. He found—as had Liszt, Brahms, and Dvořák before him—that many, indeed most, of the presumed Magyar and Slavonic tunes so dear to his countrymen were thoroughly permeated by haunting Gypsy melodies of Asiatic origin. Actually Orientals (Indians and Egyptians) whose ancestors were brought to central Europe more than a thousand years ago as slaves and servants for their Roman conquerors, the Gypsies have clung tenaciously to a fine heritage of extremely colorful loristic traditions. And their music— languid, sensuous, dramatic, and consistently lyric—has found a way into considerable amounts of folk and art music in France, Italy, Spain, and Russia, as well as in the Balkan countries. Unquestionably, its syntax has imposed an imprint on Enesco's *Roumanian Rhapsody No. 1*.

1. Organized in a freely conceived manner, this piece remains in the key of A major over its considerable length. As it begins, a solo clarinet (with assistance from flute and oboe) presents fragments from a melody heard later at greater length:

2. In turn, a sturdy folk tune (the composition's first complete melody), is announced by violins who perform over a solid quadruple meter accompaniment:

3. Shortly thereafter a smooth transition to sextuple meter (performed with two beats per measure) is accomplished, and strings sound a sweeping melody of great beauty:

4. This is succeeded by a gracious folk song with two disjunct parts:

5. These two subjects—one in sextuple meter, the other in duple—occupy the rhapsody's midsection. No development occurs here (or anywhere else in the piece); rather, the listener's ear is continually regaled with a plethora of new melodic ideas.

6. Assuming a faster pace, marked *plus vite*, a spirited tune is sounded by flutes and first violins:

7. As the tempo accelerates, still another melody—suggestive of the *hora*, a Roumanian national dance—is introduced by a single flute:

8. A thoroughly aroused orchestra now assumes the burden and passes the tune from one instrumental voice to another, consistently maintaining its rollicking gait.

9. With no interruption, but at an accelerated tempo (*très vif*), the rhapsody sweeps onward as the full ensemble announces a new subject:

10. In one manner or another this idea is reaffirmed, always in four-measure phrases, until still another melody (actually the composition's seventh distinctive theme) is sounded by first and second violins playing in unison:

11. Fully entrapped by the mounting momentum of an orgiastic folk dance, these last several subjects are reaffirmed a dozen times (or more) until the music is brusquely interrupted by a long pause.

12. At a slower pace in quadruple meter, oboe and clarinet present the rhapsody's final subject over a pizzicato accompaniment:

13. Pent up energies cannot be denied, however. Again assuming an extremely fast pace (*très vif*), the piece rushes helter-skelter toward a final boisterous cadence.

Single-Movement Compositions
(Including overtures, preludes, fantasies, and rhapsodies)

Bach, Johann Sebastian (1685–1750)
   Chromatic Fantasy and Fugue in D minor for Harpsichord (1723). A bravura piece that contrasts brilliant passagework with strict polyphony; its lines are fluent and often breathtakingly beautiful.
   Toccatas for Harpsichord (1708). Five extremely digital works, each with three to four contrasted sections.
Balakirev, Mily (1837–1910)
   Islamey, an oriental fantasy (1869). (Originally for piano, orchestrated in 1908.) A virtuoso display piece founded on three Caucasian themes; it is strong, ebullient, fanciful, and distinctly grandiose.
Barber, Samuel (b. 1910)
   Adagio for Strings (1936). Pensive, solemn, and relatively short, it is somewhat liturgical in spirit and richly harmonic in sound.
Bartók, Béla (1881–1945)
   Rhapsodies (2) for Violin and Orchestra (1928). Each has a *lassú* (slow) and a *friss* (fast) section; the first uses a cimbalom; both are modal, folkish, and employ much rubato.
Beethoven, Ludwig van (1770–1827)
   Various overtures including: *Prometheus* (1800); *Coriolanus* (1807); *Egmont* (1810); *King Stephen* (1811); *Fidelio* (1814); *Leonora,* Nos. 1 (1807), 2 (1805), and 3 (1806); *Namensfeier* (1814); and *Consecration of the House* (1822). Stalwarts in the orchestral repertoire; all are in sonata form, and most include a slow, profound introduction followed by an *allegro* main section; oriented around the theatre, they now exist independently. Without exception all are impressive, strong, and very dynamic.
Berlioz, Hector (1803–1869)
   Various overtures including: *Les Francis-Juges* (1823); *Waverley* (1827); *King Lear* (1831); *Rob Roy* (1832); *Benvenuto Cellini* (1837); *Roman Carnival* (1844); *Le Corsair* (1855), and *Béatrice et Bénédict* (1862). Orchestral showpieces of uneven cast, most are organized in individual patterns. Broadly descriptive, they feature colorful scoring, memorable melodies, and an exuberant spirit.
Bloch, Ernest (1880–1959)
   Schelomo, Hebraic Rhapsody for 'Cello and Orchestra (1915). Iridescent in color, this exotic concerted piece is in free form and concerned with a personality study of Scripture's King Solomon.
Brahms, Johannes (1833–1897)
   Academic Festival Overture (1880). Based on a wealth of German student songs, it is a gay and jovial orchestral potpourri.
   Tragic Overture (1880). Elegiac, pensive, and somber, it is organized in sonata form.

Bruch, Max (1838–1920)

    Kol Nidrei, for 'Cello and Orchestra (1880). Modal, luminous, and intro-spective, it is mostly based on excerpts from Hebraic cantillation.

    Scottish Fantasy for Violin and Orchestra (1880). A virtuoso display piece in free form that uses numerous semifolkish Celtic melodies.

Chabrier, Emanuel (1841–1894)

    España (1883). Brilliant orchestral showpiece based on Spanish dance tunes, it is attractive and delightfully rhythmic.

Chavez, Carlos (b. 1899)

    Toccata for Percussion (1942). Intriguing display piece for an unusual group; it is scintillating, brash, and organized in three sections.

Chopin, Frederic (1810–1849)

    Ballades 1, 2, 3, 4 for Piano (1835–1842). Lyric and occasionally melancholy, these romantic piano pieces are vaguely associated with poems by Mickiewicz.

    Fantasie in F minor (1841). A lengthy (for Chopin) piano work with several contrasted sections; actually, it is a galaxy of mood pictures.

Copland, Aaron (b. 1900)

    El Salón Mexico (1936). Bright and snappy, it uses folk melodies and odd rhythms to depict the environment of a Mexican dance hall.

Debussy, Claude (1862–1918)

    Préludes for Piano, Books 1 and 2 (1910, 1913). Impressionistic miniatures (24), that are delightfully evocative and wonderfully descriptive.

Delius, Frederick (1862–1934)

    Brigg Fair, An English Rhapsody (1907). In the Dorian mode, it employs variation form to elaborate on a Lincolnshire folk song.

Dvořák, Antonin (1841–1904)

    Carnival Overture (1891). Part of a triptych, it is filled with verve and abandon and effectively hints at wild Bohemian revelry.

    Scherzo Capriccioso (1883). Surging, irrepressible, and in ternary part form, it employs a wealth of intoxicating melodies.

Elgar, Edward (1857–1934)

    Cockaigne Overture (1902). London depicted in orchestral terms; the piece is occasionally humorous and noisy, but mostly dignified and realistic.

Enesco, Georges (1881–1955)

    Roumanian Rhapsodies Nos. 1 and 2 (1901–1902). Ethnic music clothed in a compelling artistic dress; catchy tunes and gypsylike rhythms are included.

Gabrieli, Giovanni (1557–1612)

    Five *Canzoni per sonar,* and *Sonata pian' e forte* (late sixteenth century) for brass. Renaissance works in polychoral style that are modal and majestic. Originally, they were used in church.

Gershwin, George (1898–1937)

    Cuban Overture (1934). Racy and carefree, it mingles Hispanic idioms with modern jazz; organized in loose sonata form, it is pulsating and frenetic.

    Preludes (3) for Piano (1926). Diverse moods expressed in a jazz idiom, these musical vignettes include provocative harmonies and intriguing tunes.

    Rhapsody in Blue (1924) for piano and orchestra. Ragtime clothed in symphonic attire, it is in free form with an abundance of carefree melodies.

Glinka, Michael (1804–1857)

> Overture to *Ruslan and Ludmilla* (1841). A short, dynamically powerful operatic preface founded on a motive and two themes; it is organized in sonata form.
>
> *Kamarinskaya* (1848); *Summer Night in Madrid* (1848); and *Jota Aragonesa* (1845). Orchestral fantasies founded on Russian or Spanish subjects, they are colorful, allusive, and free in outline.

Gluck, Christoph (1714–1787)

> Overtures to *Orfeo ed Euridice* (1762); *Alceste* (1767); and *Iphigenie en Aulide* (1774). Short sectional works infused with deep pathos, they are unfailingly serious, grave, and elegant.

Handel, George F. (1685–1759)

> Overtures to *Ariadne* (1734); *Alexander's Feast* (1736); and *Jepthe* (1752). In French style, their fast sections are polyphonic, others homophonic; all combine profundity with wit.

Lalo, Edouard (1823–1892)

> Overture to *Le Roi d'Ys* (1888). A glistening operatic preface with a plethora of themes; musically, it introduces three characters from the drama.

Liszt, Franz (1811–1886)

> *Hungarian Rhapsodies* (1846–1885). (Originally for piano, some are now orchestrated.) Gypsy epics (19) founded on Magyar melodies; they are strikingly modal, with continually shifting rhythms.

Mendelssohn, Felix (1809–1847)

> Various overtures, including the *Military* Overture in C major for Winds (1824); *A Midsummer Night's Dream* (1826); *The Hebrides* (also known as *Fingal's Cave*) (1832); *Calm Sea and Prosperous Voyage* (1832); *The Beautiful Melusine* (1833); and *Ruy Blas* (1839). Most are descriptive pieces organized in beautifully balanced sonata-form patterns; stylistically, they combine Classic and Romantic elements; all are filled with glowing tasteful orchestral color; all have sweeping, memorable melodies, and clean, incisive harmonies.

Mozart, Wolfgang Amadeus (1756–1791)

> Various overtures including those to: *Idomeneo* (1781); *Abduction from the Seraglio* (1782); *The Impressario* (1786); *The Marriage of Figaro* (1786); *Don Giovanni* (1787); *Cosi fan tutti* (1790); and *The Magic Flute* (1791). Elegant operatic prefaces, some in sonata form, others in sonatina form or part form; all are neat, precise, and well balanced with an abundance of lyricism; string color predominates with occasional flecks of contrasting woodwind sonority.
>
> Fantasias for Piano in C minor (K. 396); D minor (K. 397); C minor (K. 475), and for Organ in F minor (K. 608). Free-form keyboard works that require extreme dexterity for successful performance.

Rachmaninoff, Serge (1873–1943)

> *Rhapsody on a Theme of Paganini* for Piano and Orchestra (1934). Actually a set of free variations (24) based on a theme from Paganini's violin caprices, this keyboard work is filled with stunning bravura.

Ravel, Maurice (1875–1937)

> *Alborado del gracioso* (1905, 1912). A "morning song" expressed by orches-

tra; suggesting rueful mockery, it is complex, scintillating, and typically Spanish.

Boléro (1927). Popular Spanish-dance pantomime that employs an obvious rhythmic ostinato, a continually mounting crescendo, one theme, and extremely vivid orchestration.

Pavane pour une infante défunte (1899, 1910). Pensive, nostalgic, and resigned, it is gently rhythmic and organized in simple rondo form.

Tzigane, Rhapsody for Violin and Orchestra (1924). A virtuosic, fiery gypsy fantasy, that is diabolically difficult to play.

Rimsky, Korsakoff, Nicholas (1844–1908)

Russian Easter Overture (1888). Founded on Orthodox Church themes, it is fervent, ecclesiastic, and robed in shimmering orchestral colors.

Rossini, Gioacchino (1792–1868)

Various overtures including those to: *Scala di Seta* (1812); *Signor Bruschino* (1813); *Italiana in Algeri* (1813); *Barber of Seville* (1816); *La gazza ladra* (1817); *Cenerentola* (1817); *Semiramide* (1823); and *William Tell* (1829). Captivating operatic preludes mostly organized in sonatina form and filled with bubbling themes, they are founded on fundamental harmonies and crisp rhythms; expressively they are witty, spontaneous, and irresistible.

Sarasate, Pablo de (1844–1908)

Zigeunerweisen. A free effusion of languid and fiery gypsy melodies handled in a sparkling, adroit manner.

Schubert, Franz (1797–1828)

Wanderer Fantasie for Piano, (1822) (arranged for piano and orchestra by Franz Liszt, 1851). Established in four linked sections and based partly on an art-song melody, it employs several interconnected themes; an epochal, pioneering work.

Overture to *Rosamunde* (1823). Intended to preface a short-lived drama, it is chaste and classically oriented but warm and lyric in expression.

Schuman, William (b. 1910)

Chester, (Overture for Band, 1956) and *George Washington Bridge* (also for band, 1950). Modern wind works based on American subjects; acrid and pungent in sound, they are also sonorous and impressive.

Schumann, Robert (1810–1856)

Fantasia in C major for Piano (1836). Lengthy and impassioned with numerous subdivisions, this extremely pianistic piece elaborates freely on one basic theme.

Overture to *Manfred* (1849). Based on Byron's poem, it is murky, emotional, profound, and founded on an ambivalent pattern.

Suppe, Franz von (1819–1895)

Various overtures (1865–1880) including: *Beautiful Galatea; Light Cavalry; Morning, Noon, and Night in Vienna; Poet and Peasant;* and *Pique Dame.* Light melodic potpourris that were originally used to preface comic operas but now usually performed independently; they are tuneful, zesty, gay, and mostly organized in part form.

Tchaikowsky, Peter (1840–1893)

Marche slave (1876) and *Overture 1812* (1882). Patriotic *pièces d'occasion* that use numerous Slavic melodies and extravagant effects; they are powerful, tuneful, noisy.

Capriccio italien (1880). Sunny Italy painted by a sentimental Russian; established in free form, the piece is unusually melodic and effectively variegated.

Varèse, Edgard (b. 1885)

Ionisation (1931). Bizarre sonoric discourse for thirteen percussion; *sui generis*, it is eccentric, revolutionary, and cacophonous.

Vaughan Williams, Ralph (1872–1958)

Fantasia on a Theme by Tallis (1910). Scored for double string orchestra plus four solo strings, it has a silky, glistening sonority and features some polyphony; mostly, it is gothic in spirit.

Toccata Marziale (for band, 1924). Showcase for winds; weighty, resonant, and based on one subject, it is technically involved.

Verdi, Giuseppe (1813–1901)

Various overtures and preludes including those to: *Nabucco* (1842); *Luisa Miller* (1849); *La Traviata* (1853); *Les vespres siciliennes* (1855); and *La Forza del destino* (1862). Impassioned pieces that summarize the musical essence of their respective operas, their themes are broad, gracious, and expansive. The works are filled with pathos and sweeping emotion; most are in part form.

Wagner, Richard (1813–1883)

Various overtures and preludes including those to: *Rienzi* (1840); *Flying Dutchman* (1841); *A Faust Overture* (1844) (a concert overture); *Tannhäuser* (1844); *Lohengrin* (1848); *Tristan und Isolde* (1859); *Die Meistersinger* (1867); and *Parsifal* (1882). Rich-sounding orchestral masterpieces that, for the most part, anticipate the drama's emotive substance. They are complex, lengthy, demanding and founded on diverse patterns and broad melodies. Some are grand (*Tannhäuser*); sensuous (*Tristan*); Romantic (*Lohengrin*); or good-humored (*Meistersinger*).

Walton, William (b. 1902)

Portsmouth Point Overture (1926); *Scapino* (a comedy overture, 1940); and *Johannesburg Festival* Overture (1956). Glittering contemporary works in free form; virtuostic, vivacious, and generally descriptive.

Weber, Carl Maria von (1786–1826)

Various overtures including those to: *Peter Schmoll* (1803); *Der Freischütz* (1821); *Euryanthe* (1823); and *Oberon* (1826). Romantic, poetic, and ardent, all are organized in sonata form; their abundance of memorable melodies makes them outstanding.

Chapter 11

Additive Designs: The Suite and Associated Forms

Suites and their associates are constituted from a series of relatively short, contrasted, and obviously independent pieces. Although the number of their sections cannot be determined beforehand (some have as few as three while others have a dozen or more), typical suites usually include from four to six pieces. Sometimes these subdivisions are referred to as movements, but more commonly they are identified by tempo marking (*allegretto, adagio. largo*); by rhythmic characteristics (polonaise, waltz, march); by title ("Anitra's Dance," "Waltz of the Flowers," "On the Trail"); or by the role they fulfill (overture, intermezzo, finale, and so on).

Characteristically, each section of a suite is thematically independent, and it is atypical for melodies from one to appear in another.[1] Contrast, not uniformity or sameness, is the suite's most prominent hallmark, and the several subdivisions within one may differ sharply in tempo, meter, form, expressive intent, or orchestral coloration as well as thematic substance.[2] In effect, then, a suite is an association of disjunct pieces brought together by the will of the composer or arranger, and its lack of internal cohesion, and consequent freedom, is not a weakness but a distinctive quality.

Many suites are based on newly composed material, but others are founded on music previously used in ballet, opera, theater, or motion picture scores. When this occurs, worthwhile musical ideas often experience renewed life and gain enhanced prominence in a new format. Such is the case, for instance, with Bizet's *L'Arlésienne* music, Kabalevsky's *The Comedians,* or Kodály's *Hary Janos.*

Typically, suite sections are comparatively brief, symmetrical, and regular in structure. Their melodies often reveal regular phrase patterns of

---

[1] Although, as we shall see, certain seventeenth-century variations suites use the same material in their sections (of which there are usually two).

[2] Suites written in the nineteenth and twentieth centuries often employ different keys in their subdivisions. But this was rarely the case in works written prior to 1750 when a uniform tonality was maintained throughout.

four, eight, or sixteen measures. And many reflect the rhythms of such dances as the minuet, polka, gigue, waltz, or hoedown. Consequently, many have acquired far-reaching popularity: Grieg's *Peer Gynt Suite,* Tchaikowsky's *Nutcracker Suite,* and Grofé's *Grand Canyon Suite.*

ASSOCIATED FORMS

Suites are not the only musical designs to grow by adding one piece to another. Such other patterns as the divertimento, serenade, *sonata da camera, partita, ordre,* or cassation also have additive propensities. Generally speaking, these are substitutes for the suite that appeared in various eras and countries as the course of music developed. Each contains a number of relatively short sections (again, four to six is typical) assembled with due regard for independence and contrast. As with the suite, they are scored for instruments (strings, winds, or keyboard), make some use of dance patterns, and (especially the divertimento, serenade, or cassation) are serious enough in mien to have acted as important precursors for the symphony.

PERFORMING MEDIA FOR SUITES

Almost without fail, suites are written for instruments. Few indeed are those that even occasionally use voices (for example, sections of Grieg's *Peer Gynt* music or Ravel's *Daphnis et Chloé:* Suite No. 2), and those primarily concerned with choral forces are so rare as to be negligible. Vocal works organized along additive lines are more usually cast as song cycles, cantatas, or oratorios. Keyboard suites for harpsichord, clavichord, or piano are common; so, too, are those for orchestra, string orchestra, or band. Less frequent are those for such individual instruments as violin, 'cello, clarinet, or flute, and relatively few suites have been written for chamber groups. Works in these categories are more likely to be conceived along sonata lines.

Precise dating is difficult, of course, but it seems that suite-like pieces began to appear sometimes after 1500. For instance, an early example, *Der Prinzen-Tanz: Proportz* (1550) (included in *Masterpieces of Music Before 1750,* see Appendix C: Bibliography), gives an idea of what these works were like. Cast in a bisectional pattern of dance and afterdance, it shows how the suite began by linking two distinctive pieces under one heading.[3]

Keyboard suites were the undoubted precursors of orchestral works. Between 1600 and 1750 the clavichord and harpsichord became standard household instruments and were provided with an urgently needed literature by enterprising composers of the era. Froberger's Suite in E minor for

---

[3] It also demonstrates the expressive possibilities of a lute.

Clavichord (c. 1650)[4] shows how the suite had developed into a multi-sectioned design by this time. And in an apparently ceaseless stream, keyboard pieces, ranging from the *French* and *English Suites* (c. 1720) of J. S. Bach through the piano pieces of Robert Schumann (*Kinderscenen, Carnaval*), to the contemporary works of Bartók (*Out of Doors Suite*), have continued to appear through the years.

Suites for orchestra, however, are unquestionably the design's best-known examples. Few works can rival the popular acceptance of Rimsky-Korsakoff's *Scheherazade*, for instance. Other pieces extending from Bizet's *L'Arlésienne:* Suite No. 1 to Leonard Bernstein's suite from *West Side Story* have consistently captured listener imaginataion. Less celebrated, but extremely delightful nonetheless, are suite-like pieces for string orchestra (for example, Tchaikowsky's Serenade in C major for Strings).

THE DANCE SUITE

Perhaps the era's most important instrumental design, the seventeenth-century dance suite had a fixed sequence of pieces that most composers were at pains to observe. Based on a pattern credited to J. J. Froberger (1616–1667), it included the:

1. *Allemande:* A dance in moderately slow tempo that was rather austere in expression but possessed of a pleasing and smooth-flowing melody. Considering its name, the *allemande* would seem to be of German origin, although it had much in common with the *pavan*, a dance of Italian ancestry.
2. *Courante:* Performed at a rapid tempo in triple meter, this dance featured a great deal of adroit passagework. In those times (c. 1600–1700) two kinds of *courante* were known, the Italian and French. Similar in many respects, French works differed from their associates by having added rhythmic subtleties occasioned by a use of sextuple meter.
3. *Sarabande:* A noble and dignified dance of Spanish (some say Mexican) origin founded on a homophonic texture, this stately piece was typically performed at a slow tempo in triple meter.
4. *Gigue:* Very likely taken from English sources (where it was called a jig), this carefree dance in sextuple meter (taken with two beats to the measure), or in such other compound meters as 3/8, 9/8, or 12/8, made an admirable finale for the suite. Not untypically, much contrapuntal activity occurs within it that may, at time, reach near-fugal proportions.

As time passed, efforts were made to relieve the sameness of this plan by adding additional dances. Known as *galanteries*, such interpolations were usually placed between the sarabande and gigue. Even though almost any kind of dance could be used, these found common acceptance:

[4] Also included within *Masterpieces of Music Before 1750*.

1. *Minuet:* A popular triple-meter dance that, in this era, was performed in a decorous manner. Often, a second minuet (called the trio because it included only three lines played by as many musicians) was appended; afterward a return was made to the first minuet via a *da capo* marking.

2. *Gavotte:* Cleanly accented, beginning on the half-bar, and performed with a stiff and regular pulse in *alla breve* time, the gavotte was an incisive, near-metronomic piece. Certain specialized patterns featuring a drone bass were called *musettes.*

3. *Bourrée:* Rhythmically similar to the gavotte but moving at a quicker tempo, the bourrée begins with only a brief (usually an eighth-note) pickup.

4. *Passapied:* Sometimes organized in rondo form, this is a fast dance in triple meter.

5. *Loure:* Founded on a pattern of dotted notes that give it a rather regal expression, this slow dance in sextuple meter brought stateliness and dignity to the design.

6. *Polonaise:* Somewhat martial in expression, this dance had a set rhythmic pattern and was performed at a moderate pace in triple meter.

7. *Air or Aria:* A nondance piece very likely adopted from the theater, this was less rhythmically marked and consequently somewhat freer in its tonal flow than overt dances.

THE THEATRICAL SUITE

Late in the nineteenth century, an associative form combining segments from previously composed works acquired new life. For more than a century (from about 1750 to 1860), the suite had lain dormant as composers turned their attention elsewhere. But when Bizet reorchestrated music previously composed for Daudet's drama, *L'Arlésienne* (The Woman from Arles) and published it as a suite in 1872, he began a practice that others were quick to follow.

Known as the "theatrical" or "dramatic" suite, this kind of suite is unquestionably best-known today. Here is a listing of sections in two well-known works that show how it is organized:

Peer Gynt Suite No. 1 by Edvard Grieg

An eloquent orchestral piece based on a score composed in 1876 as incidental music for a drama by Henrik Ibsen, it has four movements.

A. "Morning Mood": In slow sextuple meter and the key of E major, this opening section has a gentle, repetitive melody initially stated by flute over a sustained chordal background. Expressively, it represents the gradual break of day.

B. "The Death of Ase": Marked *andante doloroso,* in quadruple meter and the key of B minor, this section has a melody comprised of repeated four-measure phrases. Poignantly, it suggests the passing of Peer Gynt's mother.

C. "Anitra's Dance": Animated and compelling, this clear-cut dance pattern is in triple meter and the key of A minor. Seemingly a waltz, it is actually a mazurka and is intended to suggest the sensuous movements of dancing slave girls.

D. "In the Hall of the Mountain King": Obsessively redundant but continually building to a powerful climax, this march-like finale is in B minor, quadruple meter, and *moderato* tempo. Descriptively, it depicts the rather clumsy antics of gnomes and trolls.

Nutcracker Suite No. 1 by Peter Tchaikowsky

Originally composed for a ballet in 1892, portions of this extremely attractive score were later realigned within an orchestral suite.

A. *Ouverture Miniature:* Comparatively expansive and organized in sonatina form, this buoyant preface is in the key of B-flat major and performed in duple meter at an *allegro* tempo.

B. *Six Characteristic Dances:* actually the heart of the suite, they include
  1. March—in G major, quadruple meter, quick tempo, and ternary form.
  2. "Dance of the Sugar Plum Fairy"—in E minor, duple meter, slow tempo, and binary form.
  3. "Russian Trepak"—in G major, duple meter, *vivace* tempo, and ternary form.
  4. "Arabian Dance"—in G minor, triple meter, moderate tempo, and based on a single theme.
  5. "Chinese Dance"—in B-flat major, quadruple meter, fast tempo, with only one theme.
  6. "Dance of the Reed Flutes"—in D major, duple meter, moderate tempo, and ternary form.

C. *Waltz of the Flowers:* A rather lengthy piece in large waltz form, it is performed at a lilting tempo (of course in triple meter) and is set in the key of D major.

THE DESCRIPTIVE SUITE

More expansive than an overture, more episodic than a symphonic poem, and more malleable than a symphony, a large-scale version of the suite became prominent very late in the nineteenth century when the *descriptive* or symphonic suite was formulated. Conceived for the modern virtuoso orchestra, it merges the suite's additive principles with a narrative intent. One of the first pieces of this kind to appear, Rimsky-Korsakoff's *Scheherazade* (1888), based on four episodes from *The Thousand and One*

Nights, shows how this design is formulated. By using a combination of sensuous melodies, lush harmonies, stunning orchestral colors, and clever sound effects, Rimsky-Korsakoff succeeds in capturing the listener's imagination with a narrative about: (1) "The Sea and Sinbad's Ship," (2) "Story of the Kalander Prince," (3) "The Young Prince and Young Princess," and (4) "Festival at Bagdad." So that no one would misread his intent, the composer astutely appended a brief essay to the first page of his score describing the work's discourse.

Once again a pioneering work opened new paths that others were quick to follow. With his *Mother Goose Suite* (1908), for instance, Maurice Ravel created an enchanting work based on five excerpts from the seventeenth-century fairy tales of Perrault. Written originally for piano duet and later orchestrated, it includes sections entitled (1) "The Sleeping Beauty," (2) "Tom Thumb," (3) "Empress of the Pagodas," (4) "Beauty and the Beast," and (5) "The Fairy Garden." Brief quotations from Perrault are cited over each portion of the score. When Gustav Holst wrote *The Planets* (1915) he wished to convey, via music, impressions of seven celestial bodies. His exciting descriptive suite, considered a model of contemporary orchestration, has these subdivisions: (1) "Mars, the Bringer of War," (2) "Venus, the Bringer of Peace," (3) "Mercury, the Winged Messenger," (4) "Jupiter, the Bringer of Jollity," (5) "Saturn, the Bringer of Old Age," (6) "Uranus, the Magician," and (7) "Neptune, the Mystic."

Complex and lengthy (the Ravel less so than Holst), these scores carry the suite well into the twentieth century. Whether concerned with depicting a visit to an imaginary art gallery (Mussorgsky's *Pictures at an Exhibition*), describing areas within a great city (Coates' *London Suite*), or a voyage on the Mediterranean (Ibert's *Escales*), in its new guise the suite has been proven a most welcome addition to the family of musical designs.

WAYPOSTS IN SUITE DEVELOPMENT

Emergence

Late in the fifteenth century an important precursor of the suite arose when performing musicians began to link one dance with another. Termed *dance and afterdance,* this coupling opened with a dignified slow dance in which everyone, young and old, participated; in turn, it was followed by a fast and vigorous dance in which only the young engaged. Tentatively construed at first, by the early sixteenth century the pattern had settled on a pairing of the *pavan* (a dance of Spanish origin performed in slow duple meter) with a *galliard* (a lively dance in triple meter). Patterns of acceptance continually change in music, however, so that the *pavan-galliard* association was later superseded by a union of the *allemande* (in slow duple meter) with the *courante* (in lively triple meter). Later, a third combination was formulated when a *passamezzo* (in quadruple meter and moderate tempo) was merged with a *saltarello* (a spirited Italian folk dance in fast triple meter).[5] In any case, the rhythmic differences between these dances was paramount, whereas divergences in melody and harmony were less important. Indeed, the two pieces were often based on the same tune, played, of course, in different rhythms.

Contrasting a slow dance with a fast one and enhancing their divergence by shifts in meter and melody produced a design that amused and stimulated dancers. But even more important as far as the future of serious music was concerned was the interest it aroused in bystanders who merely watched and listened. From this practice, of course, the nascent suite adopted its fundamental principles.

Just who the suite's actual formulators were is impossible to determine. Dozens of musicians created hundreds (and perhaps thousands) of suites in those early times, but virtually all remain anonymous. However, a Venetian printer, Ottaviano Petrucci (1466–1539), who had sufficient enterprise to issue a collection of suite-like pieces for the lute in 1507–1508, must be considered an important sponsor who immeasurably aided in establishing its early literature. Much later, in 1612, the *Parthenia,* a collection of twenty-one keyboard pieces (many of them suites) by various British composers was issued. And shortly thereafter (during the early seventeenth century) another great English collection, the *Fitzwilliam Virginal Book,* was compiled. Taken as a whole, material in these volumes—and in numerous other collections that now began to appear—indicates the style and scope of instrumental composition in the sixteenth and early seventeenth centuries. Many pieces within these folios adhere to the dance and afterdance patterns, some are extended by the simple device of adding a prelude, whereas others incorporate sets of variations.

The Baroque Era

After about 1650, the four-movement dance suite (allemande, courante, sarabande, gigue) became standard. Inclusion of the latter two pieces—one from Spanish sources, the other from England—shows the international stature the suite had acquired by this time. Then, in direct succession, the practice of interpolating galanteries (which were mostly French in origin) became so widely adopted that most Baroque suites came to include from six to as many as ten movements.

Several sets of suites created by J. S. Bach, an unusually prolific composer even in an era notable for musical fecundity, exemplify the period's pattern. His two collections of six works each for the harpsichord (or clavichord), known as the *English* or *French Suites* and written between 1720–1722, are particularly outstanding. (So, too, are his *Six Partitas for*

---

[5] Later examples of the saltarello (e.g., in the Finale of Mendelssohn's Symphony No. 4, "Italian") are most often in 6/8 time, taken with two fast beats in a measure.

Harpsichord, part of a collection known as the *Clavierubung—*"Keyboard Studies"—composed sometime after 1726.) This is how they are organized:

TABLE 18.   French Suites.

No. 1 (D minor)	No. 2 (C minor)	No. 3 (B minor)	No. 4 (E♭ major)	No. 5 (G major)	No. 6 (E major)
Allemande	X	X	X	X	X
Courante	X	X	X	X	X
Sarabande	X	X	X	X	X
Menuet	Air	Menuet *	Gavotte	Gavotte	Gavotte
	Menuet	Anglaise	Air	Bourrée	Polonaise
				Loure	Bourrée
					Menuet
Gigue	X	X	X	X	X

* With Trio and *da capo.*

TABLE 19.   English Suites.

No. 1 (A major)	No. 2 (A minor)	No. 3 (G minor)	No. 4 (F major)	No. 5 (E minor)	No. 6 (D minor)
Prélude	X	X	X	X	X
Allemande	X	X	X	X	X
Courante *	X	X	X	X	X
Sarabande	X	X	X	X	X †
Bourrée ‡	Bourrée ‡	Gavotte ‡	Menuet ‡	Passepied ‡	Gavotte ‡
Gigue	X	X	X	X	X

* In this suite only: I, II, with two doubles.
† With double.
‡ In each case: I, II, with *da capo.*

In addition, Bach wrote six suites for solo 'cello and a similar collection (also six in number) for solo violin, which he called sonatas (3) and partitas (3). Of even greater importance, however, are his excellent Suites (4) for Orchestra. Probably written between 1717 and 1723 while the composer was serving as musical director to the Prince of Cöthen, these suites (or *ouvertures* as the composer termed them) are multimovemented pieces with distinctive patterns.[6] All begin with an overture in the French style, and then sound a succession of dances:

1. *Suite No. 1 in C major:* Scored for two oboes, bassoon, strings, and continuo, it has (1) Overture, (2) Courante, (3) Gavottes I, II, (4) Forlane, (5) Menuetto I, II, (6) Bourrée I, II, and (7) Passepied I, II.
2. *Suite No. 2 in B minor:* Scored for flute and strings (with continuo), it

[6] Notice that these orchestral works set aside the tradition-bound allemande-courante-sarabande-gigue sequence.

includes (1) Overture, (2) Rondeau, (3) Sarabande, (4) Bourrée, I, II, (5) Polonaise (with a double), (6) Menuet, and (7) Badinerie.
3. *Suite No. 3 in D major:* Scored for two oboes, three trumpets, timpani, strings, and continuo, it has (1) Overture, (2) Air, (3) Gavotte, (4) Bourrée, and (5) Gigue.
4. *Suite No. 4 in D major:* Scored for three oboes, bassoon, three trumpets, timpani, strings, and continuo, it includes (1) Overture, (2) Bourrée I, II, (3) Gavotte, (4) Menuet I, II and (5) Rejouissance.

As active as his colleagues in composing suites, George Frideric Handel was less rigid in his conception than most Germans and tended to follow examples then (c. 1725) being postulated by the Italians. Few of Handel's suites follow an established sequence and most intermingle dance and non-dance patterns with originality and boldness. His keyboard suites, for instances, are polyglot compositions termed *lessons,* after the English practice, and are closely related to the *sonata da camera.* With distinctive *élan,* Handel intermingled French dances with Italian arias in his suites and produced an exemplary series of works for flute, oboe, keyboard, and strings. His *Water Music* (c. 1715 with about twenty movements) and *Music for the Royal Fireworks* (1749), both written to commemorate royal occasions, are excellent suite-like compositions conceived primarily for winds.

Constituent movements within Baroque suites are usually organized in binary form. Contrast between the *a* and *b* strains is mostly provided by shifts to new keys (moving from the tonic to dominant or from major to minor and back again is typical). Composers expended little effort toward interjecting divergent material within movements, nor were themes "developed" as became typical of the sonata in a later era. Nomenclature was notoriously inexact during these times, too, and names given to suite-like compositions varied from one country to another. In England the design was usually identified as lesson, in Italy as *sonata da camera,* in German lands as *partien* (later changed to *partita*), while French pieces were known as *ordres.* Although confusing, this abundance of names shows the suite's prolix nature and widespread diffusion.

The Rococo and Classic Eras

French composers became unusually active in writing suites during the Rococo era, a period extending from about 1710 to 1775, which marks a gradual transition from the Baroque to Classic styles. Basing their craft on practices pioneered by Jacques Champion de Chambonnières (1602–1672), such musicians as François Couperin (1668–1733) and Jean Philippe Rameau (1683–1764) then created a wealth of keyboard suites. Typically written for harpsichord, their *ordres* had a large number of movements (perhaps as many as twenty) that often bore descriptive titles and were intended to serve picturesque and vaguely narrative ends. Heavily laden with embellishments (trills, mordents, and *grupetti*) they were charming and pretty rather than monumental. Couperin's *Pièces de clavecin,* and a similar set issued by Rameau under the same title, are exemplificative.

When the Baroque era passed into history with the death of J. S. Bach (1750) and Handel (1759), the suite also went into eclipse. Sons of Bach— Carl Philipp Emanuel, Wilhelm Friedemann, and Johann Christian—as well as virtually all other composers active between 1760 and 1800 became fascinated with the sonata. Now the suite became passé; apparently its direct manner of expression was too naive to survive in a sophisticated era singularly concerned with thematic manipulation. But the wheels of artistic change turn slowly, and many Classicists continued to find interest in such suite-like patterns as the serenade, divertimento, and cassation.[7] Constituted from a series of independent movements (more, incidentally, than was typical of a suite), they were quite adventuresome in exploring the possibilities of instrumental coloration and thematic manipulation. Many were written for wind ensemble (with one player to a part) with an intent of outdoor performance, while others intermingled strings with winds.

During his lengthy and productive career, Haydn wrote over seventy divertimentos (which he variously called cassations, *feldpartiten, scherzandi,* or *notturni*), whereas Mozart wrote twenty-two (which he sometimes called serenades). Along with Mozart's Serenade in G major (K. 525) for Strings, *Eine kleine Nachtmusik,* these three pieces for winds are especially fine examples of the design:

1. Serenade No. 10 in B-flat major (K. 361): Composed in 1780 and scored for thirteen winds (two oboes, two clarinets, two bassett horns, four horns, two bassoons, and contrabassoon), it has the sequence: (1) *Largo,* (2) *Menuetto,* (3) *Adagio,* (4) *Menuetto,* (5) *Romanze,* (6) *Tema con Variazioni,* and (7) *Rondo.*
2. Serenade No. 11 in E-flat major (K. 375): Written in 1781 for woodwind octet (two horns, two oboes, two clarinets, two bassoons), it has five movements: (1) *Allegro maestoso,* (2) *Menuetto I,* (3) *Adagio,* (4) *Menuetto II,* and (5) *Allegro.*
3. Serenade No. 12 in C minor (K. 388): Dating from 1782 and scored for the same combination as No. 11, it has a four-movement pattern: (1) *Allegro,* (2) *Andante,* (3) *Minuetto in Canone,* and (4) *Allegro.*

Works of this kind lean heavily toward the symphony. Within them overtures (or preludes) are abandoned; contrasting thematic material is employed in many of the movements; sections are comparatively lengthy (as are, indeed, entire compositions); and a previous preoccupation with dance patterns is reduced to a point where only one (usually a minuet) is used.

[7] Designs, incidentally, that veer in directions ultimately taken by the symphony. As is pointed out in Chapter 17, they are important symphonic progenitors.

The Romantic Era

Virtually none of the early Romanticists showed interest in the suite. This was an era when the symphony, concerto, opera, and lieder reigned supreme, and composers turned their primary endeavors in those directions. Representative of the few suite-like works that appeared during those years are such pieces as the compilation of material Beethoven wrote for Goethe's drama *Egmont,* the music for his ballet *Prometheus,* and Mendelssohn's music for Shakespeare's *A Midsummer Night's Dream.* According to earlier concepts, of course, these are not suites at all, but a collection of material from a common source that had been previously written for a specific purpose. Now, of course, they are commonly performed in suite format.

In this desert of neglect, the keyboard suites of Robert Schumann stand as flourishing oases. Memorable by any standard, their exceptional qualities shone with especial brilliance during years when the suite was in eclipse. In the considerable body of piano music he wrote, three of Schumann's suites are particularly distinguished. *Carnaval* (1834), consisting of twenty-one short pieces that depict scenes and characters at an imaginary masked ball, has individual sections identified as "Pierrot," "Arlequin," "Eusebuis," "Florestan," or "Chiarina"; *Kinderscenen* (Scenes from Childhood) written in 1838, has thirteen sections bearing such titles as "From Foreign Lands and People" (No. 1); "Entreating Child" (No. 4); "Knight of the Rocking Horse" (No. 9); and "The Poet Speaks" (No. 13). Still another, *Kreisleriana,* also dates from 1838. Its eight sections do not bear titles, but each reveals Schumann's imaginative flair and remarkable penchant for poetic writing.

Prior to approaching the symphony, Johannes Brahms flexed his compositional muscles by writing two serenades, probably the first pieces of consequence to bear this name since the time of Mozart. Created in 1859 and 1860, respectively, Brahms' orchestral Serenades No. 1 in D major and No. 2 in A major (the latter scored without violins) have six and five movements. Symphonies in all but name, they are exquisite lyric works that clearly presage the eminence Brahms was later to attain as a symphonist.

Little-known when he was asked to write incidental music for Alphonse Daudet's drama *L'Arlésienne* in 1872, Georges Bizet (whose *Carmen* appeared in 1875) subsequently acquired considerable repute for the theatrical suite he extracted from this score. And four years after Bizet's death (which occurred in 1875), his close friend and associate, Ernest Guiraud, compiled a second suite from the *L'Arlésienne* music. In this modest and unheralded manner, the theatrical suite was formulated as the nineteenth century entered its final quarter. Whether he knew of Bizet's work in Paris is a matter of conjecture, but Edvard Grieg followed a curiously similar path in fashioning his celebrated *Peer Gynt Suites.* Commissioned by Henrik Ibsen himself (in 1874) to write incidental music for a poetic satire then being readied for theatrical presentation, Grieg approached his task with some reluctance. After the drama had its premiere in 1876, however, he wasted no time in rearranging portions of the score into two orchestral suites that have since become world famous.

Working contemporaneously with Bizet in Paris, Leo Delibes scored signal success with his ballets *Coppelia* (1870) and *Sylvia* (1876). In both instances, however, their music has gone on to enjoy even greater popularity in the form of orchestral suites. Filled with geniality and striking rhythmic verve, the *Coppelia Suite* includes a (1) Prelude-Mazurka, (2) Ballade, (3) *Scène et Valse*, (4) *Csárdás*, and (5) *Valse lente*. Somewhat more austere in expression, the *Sylvia Suite* is nevertheless vibrant with dramatic life and includes a celebrated passage for pizzicato strings as well as the brash *Cortège de Bacchus*.

Numerous parallels are apparent in the careers of Dvořák and Brahms. A protégé of the older man, Dvořák benefited greatly from Brahms' example and advice, and like his mentor, also wrote two serenades. Composed in 1875, Dvořák's Serenade in E major, filled with a warm and glowing lyricism, is an outstanding showcase for strings. And his Serenade in D minor (1878), scored for two oboes, two clarinets, two bassoons, contrabassoon, three horns, 'cello, and double bass, is a superb chamber work infused with the majestic sweep usually associated with a symphony.

Although none of his four *Suites for Orchestra* (except for a portion of the Suite No. 3) holds a firm place in the repertoire, Tchaikowsky turned this design to good account when he reshaped portions of his ballets along additive lines. Best-known, of course, is his *Nutcracker Suite* (1892), but two others, *Swan Lake* (1877) and *The Sleeping Beauty* (1889), have all the crystalline elegance, glowing color, and abundant lyricism that typically mark this composer's works. Somewhat more ornate than a similar piece by Dvořák, Tchaikowsky's Serenade for Strings in C major (1880) is an excellent item in the literature for strings.

The Contemporary Era

With three scores composed for the Ballet Russe early in the century, Igor Stravinsky blazed a brilliant trail into the modern era. Working under the aegis of Serge Diaghilef, an unusually astute impresario, he delighted the music world with *The Firebird* (1910), charmed it with *Petrouchka* (1911), and shocked it with *Le Sacre du printemps* (1913). Nor was he less epochal in writing *L'Histoire du soldat* (1918) and *Pulcinella* (1920). Brash and jazzy, *L'Histoire* is scored for a small ensemble (clarinet, bassoon, cornet, trombone, percussion, violin, and string bass) and founded on the ragtime that United States Army bandsmen carried to Europe during World War I. *Pulcinella* is taken mostly from the works of Giovanni Pergolesi (1710–1736), an Italian composer of scintillating *opera buffa* whose melodies Stravinsky adroitly transformed while bringing neoclassicism to the fore as a stylistic idiom in the contemporary period. All of these works, of course, were written originally for theatrical presentation. But it is now far more conventional to hear them performed in the concert hall in suite format.

Almost obsessively concerned with the conveyance of evocative ideas, Claude Debussy brought the allusiveness of Symbolist poets and the suggestivity of Impressionist painters to music. His *Nocturnes for Orchestra* (1899), for instance, include three distinctive descriptive sections (*Nuages, Fêtes,* and *Sirenes*). So, too, does his dazzling orchestral masterwork *La Mer* (1905), whose movements are titled "From Dawn to Noon on the Sea," "Play of the Waves," and "Dialogue of the Wind and Sea." In three other sets of pieces, Debussy more specifically applied the name suite to identify the contents. His *Petite Suite* (1888), also called *Jeux d'enfants* (Children's Games), is a composition for piano duet in twelve sections (of which five were later scored for orchestra). And his *Suite bergamasque* (1905), an extremely haunting work that includes the well-known *Clair de lune,* and the *Children's Corner Suite* (1908), written in six sections for piano and later transcribed for orchestra by André Caplet, are works of ravishing beauty.

Few scores have the luminous transparency of Ravel's *Daphnis et Chloé* (1911). Another ballet written for Diaghilef, it is based on subjects from classic mythology but its musical substance is undeniably Impressionistic. Stunning in every respect, the Suite No. 2 extracted from this music has three sections entitled: (1) "Daybreak," (2) "Pantomime," and (3) "General Dance." Originally written (in 1908) for two pianos, Ravel's *Ma mère l'oye* (Mother Goose Suite) was later scored for orchestra and produced as a ballet in 1915. Delightfully whimsical, it has a restrained and gentle charm fully consonant with the five episodes it portrays. Two other works by Ravel employ a suite's general outlines. *Le Tombeau de Couperin* (1917), a musical memoriam for a celebrated eighteenth-century French composer and written originally for piano in six movements, was later compressed and orchestrated in 1919 to include (1) "Prelude," (2) "Forlane," (3) "Menuet," and (4) "Rigaudon." Ravel's *Rapsodie espagnole* (1908), a seminationalistic work generally expressive of the Iberian environment, also has four movements that brilliantly exploit modern-day orchestral resources.

As with the French Impressionists, Viennese Expressionists found the suite very useful. Foremost, of course, was Arnold Schoenberg whose *Five Pieces for Orchestra* (1909) and *Three Little Pieces for Orchestra* (1910) adhere to additive concepts. Alban Berg, perhaps the most gifted of Schoenberg's disciples, applied the name to his *Lyric Suite* (1926) but this piece could, with equal validity, be termed a string quartet. Berg's *Three Pieces for Orchestra* (1914) is obviously modeled on his mentor's example. Anton Webern, a third member in the atonal triumvirate, also observed the practice by writing *Six Pieces for Orchestra* (1910) and *Five Orchestral*

Pieces (1913). Couched in strongly dissonant terms, these Expressionistic works tend to be stark and ascerbic, but strangely beautiful.

Gustav Holst gave impetus to an important twentieth-century movement when he composed his Suite No. 1 in E-flat major (1909) and Suite No. 2 in F major for Military Band (1911). A precedent for this step existed in the several wind serenades of Mozart, as well as in the numerous band transcriptions of orchestral works that had been made during preceding years. But Holst's pieces inaugurated a trend in writing for winds that has borne significant results. His compatriot Ralph Vaughan Williams, for instance, followed a similar bent with his *English Folk Song Suite* for band, based on a collection of British ethnic melodies. Then, as World War II was drawing to a close, the French composer Darius Milhaud wrote his *Suite française* (1945) for band as a gesture of gratitude for efforts expended by American soldiers in freeing his homeland. Based on a plethora of authentic folk melodies, its five movements enumerate the French provinces wherein United States forces fought: (1) *Normandie,* (2) *Bretagne,* (3) *Ile de France,* (4) *Alsace-Lorraine,* and (5) *Provence.* Still another fine contemporary work for winds based on the additive concept is Vincent Perischetti's humorous *Divertimento for Band* (1950).

Béla Bartók and Zoltan Kodály, both illustrious twentieth-century Hungarian composers, also made apt utilization of the suite format. Aside from his pungently flavored *Dance Suite* (1923), Bartók follows additive principles in his *Divertimento for String Orchestra* (1939) and in the brilliant *Music for Strings, Percussion, and Celesta* (1935). Even more relevant, however, are his *Hungarian Sketches* and the invigorating *Roumanian Folk Dances* (1915), pieces that capture the depth and plasticity of the venerable dance suite and cloak it in new attire. Similarly conceived, Kodály's *Marosszek Dances* (1930) and *Dances from Galanta* (1933), although theoretically united within a single through-composed work, are collections of ethnic dance patterns set in suite format. All are brilliantly conceived, reveal an exciting emotional tension, and are scored with lavish orchestration.

While still a fledgling composer, Serge Prokofiev wrote his *Scythian Suite* (1914). Exceedingly complex and at times almost offensively raucous, this dazzling score was originally conceived as a ballet. Depicting activities in the lives of an ancient nomadic people who lived along the north shore of the Black Sea, it deals with: (1) "Invocation to Veles and Ala," (2) "The Evil God and Dance of the Pagan Monsters," (3) "Night," and (4) "The Glorious Departure of Lolli." On the other hand, Prokofiev's *Lieutenant Kije Suite* (1934) is witty and satirical rather than orgiastic. Based on music created originally for a film, it has five movements that describe (1) "The Birth of Kije," (2) his "Romance," (3) "Kije's Wedding," (4) "Troika," and (5) "The Burial of Kije." Although Prokofiev's opera *The Love of Three Oranges* is not widely performed today, a suite of excerpts compiled by the composer in 1925 has earned warm popularity. Similar pieces arranged by this sophisticated Russian composer are taken from the ballets *Romeo and Juliet* (1937) and *Cinderella* (1944).

Crammed with syncopated rhythms and zesty (and occasionally folkish) melodies expressed in sparkling orchestral hues, the suites of Aaron Copland are among the brightest in contemporary musical literature. Constituted from music written for ballet, the theater, or motion pictures, they intermingle the jazzy devices of popular music with the more recondite aspects of serious composition. Based on a well-known saga of America's Old West, Copland's *Billy the Kid Suite* (1938) narrates details in the pursuit and capture of that notorious outlaw. But his *Rodeo* (1942), cast in four separate sections, is tender and sentimental rather than epic and violent. Additional suites by this distinguished American composer include *Appalachian Spring* (1944), based on music from a Martha Graham ballet; *Our Town* (1940), whose music was originally conceived for a film based on the Thornton Wilder drama; *The Tender Land* (1954), from an opera by Copland; and *The Red Pony* (1948), comprised of excerpts from a motion picture score.

Contemporary suites are both numerous and popular: Grofé's *Grand Canyon Suite* (1931), which depicts aspects of an immense natural wonder; Richard Rodgers' motion picture score for "Victory at Sea"; and Leonard Bernstein's suites from *On the Town* (1944) and *West Side Story* (1957) are only a few representative examples. In the time-honored manner of suites, each includes a number of episodes wherein contrast, independence, directness, and color—the suite's important attributes—are paramount. They demonstrate how this sturdy and venerable form remains viable, useful, and meaningful into the present day.

PARTICULAR EXAMPLES OF THE SUITE

J. S. Bach (1685–1750), *Suite No. 2 in B minor for Flute and Strings*

While serving as *Kapellmeister* at Cöthen during the so-called "second period" in his career (between 1717–1723), Bach was primarily concerned with composing secular music, much of it for keyboard, strings, and orchestra. Judging from available evidence, it seems likely that his four suites for orchestra were written then, although a possibility exists that the last two were composed later (between 1729 and 1736).

Prince Leopold, Bach's employer at Cöthen, maintained an orchestra of about eighteen players for which these works (at least the first two) were written. As with most groups of the time, it required a *continuo*, usually a harpsichord, to supply vital rhythmic and harmonic support during performance. But its center of sonority actually rested with the strings, while winds were used to provide occasional changes in timbre.

Organized in seven contrasting movements, Bach's Suite in B minor shows the state of excellence this design had acquired by the early eighteenth century. Although each of its sections clings to the home key and most are organized in binary form (*ab*), remarkable diversity is engendered by a consistent use of contrasting melodies and rhythms. These are its details:

1. *Overture:* Cast in French style, this introductory movement has three distinctive parts:
   A. An opening *grave* in quadruple meter that is ponderous and dignified in expression;
   B. A brisk *allegro* in *alla-breve* meter with a pronounced fugal texture (this is the longest section in the suite's most extensive movement), and
   C. A *lentement* in triple meter that suggests portentous gravity.
2. *Rondeau:* Gracious in expression, organized in simple rondo form (with the pattern *abaca*), in duple meter, and played at a moderately fast tempo, this section has an eight measure principal theme:

3. Its first episode *b* is twelve measures long; the second *c* sixteen. Of course, the principal theme returns after each digression.
4. *Sarabande:* In *andante* tempo and triple meter, this stately dance is cast in simple binary form (*aa′*). Particularly noteworthy in this section is Bach's use of canonic imitation wherein the melodic line (played by flute and first violins) is echoed by lower-pitched instruments at the interval of a fifth and three beats in arrears:

5. *Bourrée:* Clearly delineated under separate headings, two examples of this dance comprise a fourth portion of the suite. Both are in duple meter,

binary form, and *allegro* tempo, but each has individual melodic lines. After the second bourrée has been performed—it is, incidentally, only half as long as the first—a return is made to the initial segment via a *da capo* marking.

6. *Polonaise:* Exemplifying the strong rhythmic thrust of a firmly accented dance pattern, this section in triple meter and *moderato* tempo has a twelve measure theme:

7. An excellent example of doubles—that is, the reaffirmation of a theme with florid embellishments—follows. In this instance, the melodic line is assigned to low strings ('cellos, basses, and continuo) while a solo flute engages in the agile pyrotechnics incidental to variation. After the double, the polonaise is repeated, thus establishing a broad ternary design.

8. *Menuet:* Almost ubiquitous in works of this kind, this crisply articulated dance retains typical triple meter, an *allegro* tempo, and a binary pattern. Its first section of eight measures has this theme:

9. *Badinerie:* So light as to seem playful, this jocose finale is also appropriately climactic. Organized in binary form and played at a rapid tempo in duple meter, it calls on the solo flute for extremely active work:

Georges Bizet (1838–1875), Suite No. 1 from *L'Arlésienne*

Fraught with such classic elements of high tragedy as passion, madness, and death, Alphonse Daudet's drama *L'Arlésienne,* (The Woman from Arles), was introduced in Paris on October 1, 1872. Hardly a success, it was withdrawn after a mere fifteen performances, and has since been mounted only at widely spaced intervals. But Bizet's incidental music for the drama has been proven more durable. After the theatrical failure, he chose four pieces from the twenty-seven originally written and organized them to constitute the first *L'Arlésienne Suite*, which had its initial performance on November 10, 1872. Because resources at the *Théatre du Vaudeville* (where the drama was performed) were extremely limited, the original orchestration was written for only twenty-six players, but these proscriptions were not imposed on the subsequent suite. Consequently, the new setting is scored for a full symphony orchestra.

1. *Prelude:* Strings in a low register, buttressed by selected winds, sound this theme in unison as the suite begins:

2. Set in C minor, this sixteen-measure subject, organized in a binary pattern *ab*, becomes the basis for a set of variations that has these qualities:
   a. *Variation one:* Expressing quiet charm, four woodwinds (flute, English horn, clarinet, and bassoon) play in a smooth and flowing manner.
   b. *Variation two:* Rising from a subdued *pianissimo* to a roaring *fortissimo*, the full orchestra presents this variant with animated gusto.
   c. *Variation three:* Shifting to C major and allocating the theme to 'cellos, this section (in *andante* tempo) uses horns and bassoons to weave an arabesque about the melody.
   d. *Variation four:* Strings, doubled by winds, present a full-throated reaffirmation of the melody.
3. As the *Prelude* enters into its second section, the alto saxophone sings a graceful melody, supported by quiet strings and woodwinds:

4. Enunciated by violins and violas, an insistent and passionate third melody appears later:

5. But the energies of this last subject are soon spent, and the movement comes to a gentle close on a series of sustained chords.

6. *Minuetto:* Transformed from earlier examples of this dance by a quickening tempo, Bizet's minuet (which ultimately settles in C minor) follows the outlines of ternary form *ABA* with rounded binary segments in each section. It begins like this:

7. Shifting to A-flat major, the Trio opens with an accented figure that soon subsides to support a legato melody played by the saxophone:

8. Violins embellish this subject, and later repeat it against flute and harp arpeggios. Along the way, a digression is provided by a short staccato theme. Then, with a final appearance of the entire first section (that is, both first and second strains), the movement comes to a close.

9. *Adagietto:* Scored for strings alone, this elegiac movement in triple meter shifts to the key of F major. First violins present its somber melody over sustained harmonies:

10. *Carillon:* Playing *fortissimo,* orchestral horns simulate a tolling of bells during opening measures in the Finale. Set in E major, it contrasts vividly with the foregoing section as first violins impose their vigorous subject atop the chiming horn *ostinato* (a constantly reiterated idea) that continues for fifty-six bars:

11. Midway the mood becomes more tender as flutes, later joined by oboes and strings, convey a lyric melody in sextuple meter:

12. Soon the carillon's spirited exuberance returns, however, to sweep away any semblance of introversion. Expressed in loudest terms, its affirmative optimism concludes both the movement and the suite.

Claude Debussy (1862–1918), *The Children's Corner Suite*

Graciously entering a nonadult world of whimsy, wonderment, and make-believe, in 1908 Debussy created a gorgeously transparent set of piano pieces as a gift to his five-year old daughter, Claude-Emma. Without descending to triviality and everywhere maintaining the glistening aural colors of musical Impressionism, he subtly evoked images fascinating to a child and beguiling to even the most sophisticated adult.

Enigmatic, aloof, complex, and mysterious to his contemporaries, Debussy was a unique composer. A musician to the core, he nevertheless reached outside its bounds for sources of inspiration. An intimate in the company of Symbolist poets and Impressionistic painters so important on the Parisian scene in his day, he successfully transferred their muted colors, veiled allusions, and poetic transports to pieces for piano, voice, and orchestra. Not a prolific composer by any means, Debussy wrote with painstaking care, refining and polishing each tone, phrase, and idea to a lustrous sheen. As a result, nearly every one of his compositions is a masterwork, widely respected and warmly acclaimed.

Curiously enough, titles quoted above sections in *The Children's Corner*

Suite are given in English, but the dedication to Claude-Emma (known affectionately as *Chouchou*) reads: *A ma chère petite Chouchou, avec les tendres excuses de son père pour ce qui va suivre.* (To my dear little Chouchou, with her father's affectionate apologies for what follows.) Because he was a gifted pianist, Debussy had a consummate insight into the instrument, but these pieces rarely resort to virtuosic display. Rather, they are lovely vignettes, filled with a crystalline elegance. Restraint, unhurried geniality, and understated charm are apparent in each section. These are their details:

1. *Doctor Gradus ad Parnassum:* Suggesting (in a parodistic manner) the tedious finger exercises embryonic pianists practice in order to acquire facility, this piece relies on an abundance of arpeggios (broken chords) played in the right hand while the left provides supportive harmonies. Designated *modèrement animé*, the movement is performed at a rapid tempo in quadruple meter. Organized in a basic *aaba* design, it begins in C major but shifts to B-flat (major and minor) for the brief midsection. This is how it opens:

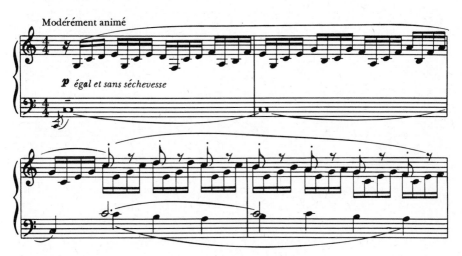

2. *Jimbo's Lullaby:* Apparently an instance of quaint misspelling, this tender ballad alludes to Jumbo the elephant, whose likeness Claude-Emma may have possessed in a toy. Played at a rather rapid but flowing pace (*assez modère*) in quadruple meter, it is in G minor and founded on this basic tune:

3. *Serenade of the Doll:* Crisp, light, and played staccato, this ternary design (*aba*) is in E major and played quickly (*allegretto ma non troppo*) in triple meter. A testimonial to almost any doll a child might have in her collection, this lilting tune appears after a two-measure introduction:

4. *The Snow is Dancing:* Longest section in the suite, this episode suggests the cavorting demeanor of snowflakes as they fall before a child's eager gaze on a wintry afternoon. Performed crisply in the instrument's upper register at a rather rapid tempo (marked *modèrement animé*) in triple meter, it is in the key of F major and begins like this:

5. *The Little Shepherd:* Very likely a wallpaper figure, the subject of this piece was Chouchou's cherished friend. As expressed in Debussy's music, the shepherd had a placid demeanor that could, at times, become impish. In A major, moderate tempo (*trés modère*) and quadruple meter, it opens with this theme:

6. *Golliwogg's Cakewalk:* Negro minstrels then appearing in Paris music halls were known as "golliwoggs," and one of their dances, based on a popular choreographic exercise from far-off America, was the cakewalk.

Beloved by young and old (so much so that doll replicas were made of them), these minstrels provided Debussy with a splendid subject for his finale. Expressing pert, syncopated rhythms (and in duple meter, fast tempo—marked *allegro giusto*—ternary form, and the key of E-flat), the cakewalk begins with this catchy idea:

Dmitri Kabalevsky (b. 1904), Suite from *The Comedians*

In the furtherance of his duties as a Soviet Peoples' Artist, in 1938 Dmitri Kabalevsky composed incidental music for a play, *Inventor and Comedian,* then being staged by the Children's Theater of Moscow. Revolving around the lives of itinerant entertainers (circus clowns), the theatrical work is flip, cheerful, and farcical. And the music Kabalevsky wrote for it fully implements this spirit of rowdy festivity.

Scored for a relatively small orchestra (woodwinds, horns, trumpets in pairs, one trombone, a tuba, sundry percussion, piano, and reduced strings), the *Comedians Suite* realigns portions of the original score without regard for dramatic continuity. Compiled in 1939 and given a premiere the following year, it is a collection of short, boisterous, and extremely attractive musical vignettes. Everywhere Kabalevsky displays his gifts as a superb orchestrator, and he consistently paints the suite's several sections in iridescent hues. His tunes are direct and simple and, surprisingly for a contemporary composer, nearly all the movements are organized in such basic designs as part form or rondo form. Filled with piquant flicks of gay raillery, as well as passing moments of irony and satire, the ten episodes in the *Comedians Suite* have these qualities:

1. *Prologue:* In sextuple meter (with two beats in a measure) and *allegro vivace* tempo, the first section begins as a striking rhythmic figure is sounded by brass instruments. Over its compulsive thrust, a rollicking tune is announced by high woodwinds and piano:

2. Between two appearances of this subject, a short theme whose apparent function is merely to separate portions of the principal melody is heard. Surprisingly, the Prologue closes on a quiet, almost furtive, note.

3. *Comedians Galop:* So well-known as to be notorious, this episode is performed at a *presto* tempo in duple meter. As it races forward at a pell-mell pace, this subject is heard time and again:

4. *March:* Almost somber in comparison with the foregoing, this segment is in duple meter and *moderato* tempo. Clarinet and bassoon introduce the principal theme:

5. Later, an oboe—doubled and supported by clarinets—interpolates a second melody.

6. With a return of the first subject, this time played by strings, this section in ternary form concludes.

7. *Waltz:* Over a characteristic three-quarter time accompaniment, clarinet and oboe perform a lilting melody in a crisp, staccato manner:

8. Later, first violins play a smooth and lyric subject in the midsection:

9. Finally, woodwinds and strings join forces as they reaffirm the first theme.

10. *Pantomime:* Marked *sostenuto e pesante* (sustained and heavy), this contrasting episode is played in quadruple meter. Low strings, bassoon, and snare drum sound the initial subject:

11. A more flowing theme follows, after which both ideas are reaffirmed to create a repeated binary pattern *abab*. Four measures of heavily accented chords conclude.

12. *Intermezzo:* Upper woodwinds present a catchy subject at an *allegro scherzando* pace in duple meter:

13. A single horn and two trumpets repeat, after which the idea is passed to other instruments. Closing measures in this agile romp, however, are sustained and quiet.

14. *Little Lyrical Scene:* This, the suite's most tender movement, is in sextuple meter and marked to be played *andantino semplice* (slowly and simply). Its most important idea is heard as a solo clarinet sings this engaging melody over sustained harmonies:

15. *Gavotte:* Crisply rhythmic, this quaint dance from an earlier era begins as strings announce a cleanly etched principal subject:

16. Although some digression occurs, this theme dominates the section and returns as the end nears.

17. *Scherzo:* Moving with the speed of a rocket (in *presto* tempo), this duple-meter section discloses a feather-light touch as first violins introduce the principal subject in a rondo-form design *abaca*:

18. As a foil, strings sound the second theme *b* whose flow is deceptively slow:

19. Then, after the first theme recurs, a smooth third subject *c* appears:

20. *Epilogue:* The longest section in the suite, this *allegro molto e con brio* in *alla breve* time begins with a powerful theme:

21. Although other subjects appear, they are distinctly subservient to this primary theme. Over and over, its sonorous tones (and resonant sup-

portive chords) are heard until the full orchestra finally concludes with a ringing, climactic *fortissimo*.

Aaron Copland (b. 1900), Four Dance Episodes from *Rodeo*

When he accepted an invitation from Agnes de Mille to create music for a ballet concerned with activities at a Western ranch, Aaron Copland had already established a reputation as an exponent of musical Americana. His *Billy the Kid* (1938), based on the saga of notorious Brooklyn-born Billy Bonney, had clearly demonstrated a mastery of the métier. As outlined by Miss de Mille, however, *Rodeo* was to follow a somewhat different bent than the pulsating, brash, and totally masculine *Billy the Kid*. She envisaged a story filled with young romance, tender sentiment, unrequited affection, rejection, and ultimate acceptance. Cloaked in Western overtones, the substance of her story was both simple and timeless: A woman gets her man.

At first bemused and skeptical, Copland later became enchanted with the scenario. Subtitled "The Courting at Burnt Ranch," it tells this tale: Saturday afternoons on many ranches are given over to the fun of a rodeo. From miles around, the country gentry come to watch exhibitions of skill and daring as adventuresome young folk vie with one another in roping contests and feats of horsemanship. On just such an occasion, a young cowgirl (dressed in Western attire) attempts to compete with men. At first tolerant, the cowboys later consider her a nuisance and try to ignore her. This neglect becomes especially crushing when the head wrangler shows an obvious preference for the rancher's daughter (who is dressed in feminine garments). Lonely and depressed, the cowgirl wanders near the corral after darkness has fallen, but later she decides to attend a dance at the ranch house. Despair turns to anger, however, when she gazes into the building and sees her rival (the rancher's daughter) dancing cheek-to-cheek with the wrangler. Rushing away in a fury, she soon returns clad in a pretty frock with a ribbon in her hair. Formerly ignored, the cowgirl now becomes a center of attention as all the men (including the wrangler) ask that she dance with them in a spirited hoedown.

Witty, gay, and infectiously buoyant, Copland's score for *Rodeo* (1942) is as charming as the narrative it relates. Vibrant with youthful vigor, it has spicily syncopated rhythms and bright, sophisticated colors. Many melodies are Copland's own, but others have been drawn from such compilations of folk material as *Our Singing Country* and *Traditional Music of America*. This is no mere pastiche of Western tunes, however, for Copland transforms his materials as he shapes them into an unusually jaunty score. These are its details:

1. *Buckaroo Holiday:* Summoning folks from miles around to a jubilant carnival, the suite's opening section suggests that fun and excitement are in store for everyone. Two folk melodies, "If He'd Be a Buckaroo by His

Trade" and "Sis Joe" are woven into this *allegro con spirito* episode, which opens with a brisk descending subject:

2. The longest section in the suite, "Buckaroo Holiday" employs a series of rhythmic figures that suggest, in one manner or another, dances associated with America's West. Among the thematic fragments that appear, these are especially notable:

3. *Corral Nocturne:* After the afternoon's exciting activities the quiet of evening descends on the ranch, and a luminous August moon rises over the nearly deserted corral where the cowgirl comes to ponder her problems. Played at a *moderato* tempo, this flowing section enjoys a number of meter changes. Its principal melody is a rather dolorous little tune:

4. *Saturday Night Waltz:* Meanwhile, rodeo guests turn their attention to the dance floor where a fun-filled party is underway. Sounds suggesting

the tuning of string instruments open this section, but their brash vigor soon subsides as a slow waltz is heard:

5. *Hoedown:* An exuberant folk dance in *allegro* tempo and duple meter finds apt realization at Copland's hands in the finale of this suite. Again using a folk melody ("Bony-parte"), he makes imaginative use of the stomping, accented rhythms of an old-fashioned square dance. Near its beginning, clarinets and upper strings play in emulation of country fiddlers:

Selected Suites [8]

Albeniz, Isaac (1860–1909)
 Iberia (1906–1909). A set of twelve pieces originally for piano but now orchestrated, it vividly describes Andalusian life and places.
Bach, Johann Sebastian (1685–1750)
 English Suites (6); *French Suites* (6); Partitas (6) for Harpsichord (after 1720, 1722, and 1731, respectively). Including eighteenth-century dance and nondance forms, their segments are dexterous, short, rhythmically contrasted, and mostly in binary form.
 Sonatas (3), Partitas (3) for Unaccompanied Violin; and Suites (6) for Unaccompanied 'Cello, (c. 1720). Virtuoso pieces for solo string instruments, some segments are dances, others abstract; primarily monophonic, a few are occasionally polyphonic.
 Suites (4) for Orchestra (c. 1725). Superb eighteenth-century dance suites prefaced by nondance overtures; they are scored for strings, a few winds, and continuo and are expressively gracious and dignified.
Bartók, Béla (1881–1945)
 Dance Suite (1923). Includes five idiomatic dances plus a finale; its melodies are angular, but the scoring is extremely colorful.

---

[8] Fine examples of early suites, in recorded and printed form, are included in *Masterpieces of Music Before 1750.*

Divertimento for String Orchestra (1939). A modern string classic with a glistening sonority; it is almost regal in expression.

Music for Strings, Percussion, Celesta (1935). Esoteric, dissonant, and remarkably contrapuntal, it has four movements that explore unusual timbres, patterns, and expressive devices.

Bennett, Robert Russell (b. 1894)

Suite of Old American Dances (for band) (1949). Jazzy and bright, it includes a cakewalk, schottische, one-step, waltz, and rag.

Berg, Alban (1885–1935)

Lyric Suite for String Quartet (1926). Atonal, extremely complex, and organized in six sections, it is biting, pungent, and richly expressive.

Three Pieces for Orchestra (1913–1914). Austere, glowing, and dissonant, they suggest Viennese Expressionism wreathed with captivating lyricism.

Bernstein, Leonard (b. 1918)

On the Waterfront Symphonic Suite (1955). A pulsating cinema score in suite format that depicts New York's dockside; it includes a galaxy of mood pictures, and is extremely colorful and tangy.

Ballet music from *West Side Story* (1957). Bright, brash, and filled with zestful dance episodes, it is clothed in a brilliant orchestral garb.

Bizet, Georges (1838–1875)

L'Arlésienne: Suites Nos. 1 and 2 (1872). Based on music written for a Daudet drama, these pieces are melodic, clear, and exceptionally well-written.

Suite of excerpts from *Carmen* (1874). Contains a series of instrumental interludes and dances from a fine opera; it abounds with dazzling melodies and intoxicating rhythms.

Brahms, Johannes (1833–1897)

Serenade No. 1 in D major (1860). Classically conceived and cast in six sections, it employs a small orchestra and is expressively dignified and interesting.

Chopin, Frederick (1810–1849)

Les Sylphides (1909). A rearrangement of pieces written originally for piano, it is gracious, elegant, and almost sensuous.

Copland, Aaron (b. 1900)

Billy the Kid (1938); *Rodeo* (1942). Balletic musical vignettes concerned with depicting America's West, they are rhythmically solid, somewhat folkish, crisp, bright, and stunning.

Debussy, Claude (1862–1918)

Children's Corner Suite (for piano, 1906; orchestra, 1908). Child's naiveté beautifully described in six whimsical episodes; its sections are fragile, perfectly balanced, and beguiling.

Suite bergamasque (for piano, 1890–1905). Impressionistic and allusive; among its six sections is the lush *Clair de lune.*

Delibes, Leo (1836–1891)

Coppelia; Sylvia (ballet suites, 1870 and 1876). Tuneful, rhythmically striking, and established in clear patterns, these French scores are both sweet and handsome.

Dvořák, Antonin (1841–1904)

Serenade in D minor for Winds, 'Cellos and Double Basses (1878). Lyrical, neatly balanced, and in four movements, this fine piece has an unusually opulent sonority.

Falla, Manuel de (1876–1946)

Dances from *The Three Cornered Hat* (1919). Taken from a ballet founded on a humorous Spanish subject, it features sparkling rhythms and languid melodies.

Gounod, Charles (1818–1893)

Ballet Music from *Faust* (1859). Seven dances from the French opera that are delightfully contrasted, sentimental, and lovely.

Grainger, Percy (1882–1961)

Lincolnshire Posy (folk melodies arranged for band, 1940). A piquant work for winds in six sections; it is rhythmically complex but contains a plethora of excellent tunes.

Grieg, Edvard (1845–1907)

Peer Gynt Suite, No. 1 (1888). Unusually popular, it contains music originally written for an Ibsen drama; in four sections, it is both eloquent, direct, and descriptive.

Grofé, Ferde (b. 1892)

Grand Canyon Suite (1931). An aural portrait of America's immense natural wonder, it has five sections and is musically lush, opulent, and impressive.

Handel, George Frideric (1685–1759)

Water Music (1717); *Royal Fireworks Music* (1749). Unusual eighteenth-century suites written originally for a boating party and peace celebration; each had numerous segments (twenty or more) that are usually reduced to four or five in contemporary performance.

Holst, Gustav (1874–1934)

The Planets (1914–1916). A stunning score in seven sections that brilliantly depicts as many celestial bodies; it is powerful, incisive, and richly sonorous.

Suite Nos. 1 and 2 in E-flat and F major for Military Band (1909, 1911). Band stalwarts in three and four segments, respectively; movements are folk-like, with well-wrought patterns.

Ibert, Jacques (1890–1962)

Escales (Ports of Call) (1922). A Mediterranean cruise taken via music, it has three titled sections and is sensuous, exotic, and melodic.

Ippolitov-Ivanov, Michael (1859–1935)

Caucasian Sketches (1894). An eastern-Russian province is aptly described in semioriental, colorful, and evocative language.

Ives, Charles (1874–1954)

Three Places in New England (1914) A contemporary masterwork that portrays historic American vistas; it is iconoclastic, brash, and shocking, but always interesting.

Kabalevsky, Dmitri (b. 1904)

The Comedians (1940). Comprised of ten short sections from a drama score, its patterns are mostly in part form; the writing is clever, obvious, and glittering.

Khachaturian, Aram (b. 1903)

Gayne, Ballet suites 1 and 2 (1942). From a Russian ballet, these pieces use daemonic rhythms and sensuous melodies to constitute a pulsating, vibrant, and exciting work.

Kodály, Zoltan (1882–1967)

Hary Janos Suite (1926). Narrating a Hungarian legend, it has folkish and attractive melodies and vivid instrumental coloration.

Mendelssohn, Felix (1809–1847)

Incidental music to *A Midsummer Night's Dream* (1826, 1843). Rapturous and occasionally pensive, this superb score is founded on the Shakespearean drama.

Milhaud, Darius (b. 1892)

Suite française (1944). A French composer's tribute to American soldiers, it uses folk tunes from five provinces and is driving, powerful, resonant, and occasionally brusque.

Suite provençale (1937). Including eight brief sections founded on a plethora of folk tunes, it is occasionally polytonal, but mostly vivacious.

Mozart, Wolfgang Amadeus (1756–1791)

Serenades Nos. 10, 11, 12 (K. 361, 375, 388) (1780–1782). Wind classics with multimovements (7, 5, 4) established in superb formal designs; tuneful and pleasant.

Serenade in G major, (K. 525), *Eine kleine Nachtmusik* (1787). A near-symphonic work for strings that is continually gracious and elegant.

Perischetti, Vincent (b. 1915)

Divertimento for Band (1950). Modern work for winds in six sections, it is mischievous, whimsical, and occasionally pungent.

Piston, Walter (b. 1894)

The Incredible Flutist (ballet suite, 1938). Depicting a pied piper in orchestralia, it is unusually jaunty and has a tango, minuet, waltz, and other dances.

Prokofiev, Serge (1891–1953)

Lieutenant Kije Suite (1934). Satirical, humorous, and in five sections, it is concerned with the life and death of a nonentity; brash, fluent, and clever.

Scythian Suite (1914). Unusually expansive ballet score in four bitingly dissonant sections; it is complex and almost overwhelming.

Ravel, Maurice (1875–1937)

Daphnis et Chloé, Suite No. 2 (1910). Three excerpts from a scintillating French ballet, these pieces are consistently evanescent, vivid, and strikingly Impressionistic.

Ma Mère l'Oye (Mother Goose Suite, 1908). Charming musical fairy tale in five sections; it is fragile, limpid, and extremely lyric.

Rapsodie espagnole (1907). A hauntingly lovely Iberian portrait that most effectively employs an Impressionistic syntax.

Le Tombeau de Couperin (1914–1917). A musical tribute to an eighteenth-century composer, it robes four dances from an earlier era in contemporary attire.

Rimsky-Korsakoff, Nicholas (1844–1908)

Capriccio espagnol (1887). A Russian view of Spain that is an orchestral tour de force; it is cast in five scintillating, exhilarating sections.

Suite from *Coq d'or* (1907). Four operatic excerpts that are pompous, sweeping, and occasionally shallow.

Scheherazade (1889). Orientalism in music, it narrates four Arabian Nights tales and is very melodic with unusually opulent orchestration.

Schoenberg, Arnold (1874–1951)

Five Pieces for Orchestra (1908). Excitingly dissonant and extremely unorthodox, its sections nevertheless have evocative titles.

Schubert, Franz (1797–1828)

Incidental music from *Rosamunde* (1823). Expressing warm Viennese Romanticism, it includes an overture, several entr'actes, and ballets.

Schumann, Robert (1810–1856)

Carnaval (1835); *Kinderscenen* (1838); *Kreisleriana* (1838); and *Waldscenen* for Piano (1849). Superb piano works with numerous short sections (21, 13, 8, 9) in part form, virtually all with titles; these pieces are lyric, sentimental, and engagingly pianistic.

Shostakovich, Dmitri (b. 1906).

Age of Gold (ballet suite, 1930). A witty Soviet work that lampoons capitalism; it is hilarious and saucy, and has four sections that include: waltz, adagio, polka, and finale.

Stravinsky, Igor (b. 1882)

Firebird Suite (1910). Narrative ballet that is excitingly rhythmic and melodically glowing; it has six charming sections.

Suite from *L'Histoire du soldat* (1918). Jazzy pantomime with narration, it uses seven players and is quirky, sparkling, and dramatic.

Petrouchka (1911). A large work in four sections that depicts a clown's romance and death; it uses a big orchestra and has a series of interconnected dances.

Pulcinella Suite (1920). Neoclassicistic, lean, spare, and catchy; it includes eight sections with titled subheads.

Tchaikowsky, Peter (1840–1893)

Nutcracker Suite (1892). Unparalleled favorite that is whimsical, sweetly melodic, and based on an abundance of dances.

Serenade in C major for Strings (1880). Opulently melodic and organized in a classic four-movement pattern, it has an unusually rich string sonority.

Suite from *The Sleeping Beauty* (1889). Narrative ballet in five episodes, it is consistently gracious and lyrical.

Telemann, Georg Philipp (1681–1767)

Suite in A minor for Flute and Strings (c. 1725). A Baroque suite in seven sections that begins with a French overture, it is clear, neat, and incisive.

Vaughan Williams, Ralph (1872–1958)

English Folk Song Suite (for band, 1924). Based on sturdy folk melodies, it has three sections and is solid, dynamic, and tuneful.

Walton, William (b. 1902)

Façade Suites, Nos. 1 and 2 (1926, 1938). Devastatingly witty, its original version employs a small ensemble and a narrator to deliver Edith Sitwell poetry; over all it is flip, saucy, and impertinent.

Webern, Anton (1883–1945)

Six Pieces for Orchestra (1901, rev. 1928). Short musical vignettes that use an unusual pointillistic technique; they are Expressionistic, cacophonous, and stunning.

Chapter 12

Musical Dialogue:
The Concerto

Concerned with exploiting the sonorous differences between two musical forces (rarely more) since its formulation late in the sixteenth century, the concerto has become one of music's most important instrumental designs. Contrast is used in music of all kinds for a variety of purposes, of course, and is reflected in rhythmic, melodic, harmonic, coloristic, formal, and expressive differences. But a concerto raises this juxtaposition to the highest possible level, and thereby gains its uniqueness.

Conversational exchanges are a common mode of communication. People meet and talk, discuss ideas, and disseminate information. Music, too, has had its forms of exchange for an amazingly long time. *Antiphony*, for instance, a dialogue between singers and instrumentalists or—as is more common—between performing groups, has been known and practiced since Biblical times.[1] From antiphony and a host of other techniques formulated over a span of many centuries, the instrumental concerto ultimately arose.

As its *raison d'être*, the concerto emphasizes a duality of performing forces. Certainly the idea of having one musical body vie with another in sportive interplay in simple enough, but its consequences are often far-reaching. For instance, such a discourse almost inevitably creates a benign kind of antagonism between performers (and even a natural "stereo" effect) as musical repartee is bandied back and forth. Although different kinds of concertos exist (and are discussed subsequently), the solo concerto, which contrasts a single performer (perhaps a pianist, violinist or 'cellist) with an ensemble (most often the orchestra) is undoubtedly best-known. Sheer weight of sonority is important in a solo concerto, of course, but it is not the only significant factor in such a work. If this were so, the numerically preponderant orchestra could easily overcome a lone soloist. Of greater conse-

---

[1] Scripture tells, for instance, of how men and women gathered on opposite hillsides and sang hymns to one another. And in churches and synagogues, responsorial exchanges between a celebrant (priest, minister, cantor) and a congregation or choir are obviously antiphonal.

quence from an artistic point of view, however, is an individual's ability to capture and hold listener attention, which greatly assists in correcting any numerical imbalance.

THE SOLO CONCERTO

Most solo concertos have a formal plan that divides the piece into three contrasted movements: an architectural scheme that calls for sonata form in the first movement, part form or variation form in the second, and rondo form, sonata form, or modified sonata-rondo form in the finale. Moreover, concerto movements invariably include a number of interpolated solo passages called *cadenzas*.

Usually so dynamic as to appear ebullient, a typical concerto's first movement flows at a moderately rapid pace (sometimes after a slow introduction) over a comparatively lengthy course. Firmly rooted in the composition's home key, it is carefully organized and normally follows this plan:

1. After an introduction (optional), the movement's principal theme is announced by the orchestra. Material from the subordinate theme may be included, ignored, or given in part. Usually this section closes on a tonic chord.
2. Now the soloist enters and reaffirms the previously stated ideas; this episode typically concludes in the dominant key.
3. A short orchestral *tutti* leads into the development where the soloist becomes a principal protagonist. After both forces have been used to express elaborate thematic manipulation and wide-ranging modulations, a return is made to the home key.
4. Although the recapitulation may begin with the orchestra sounding a compressed version of the principal theme, the soloist soon becomes prominent. Both, in turn, present the subordinate theme and the closing strain.
5. Somewhere in the recapitulation's latter stages, perhaps in the coda or, as is often the case, at a juncture between the two, an important cadenza is inserted.
6. Within the coda a final *tutti* is elicited from the orchestra in which the soloist may or may not participate; this writes *finis* to the movement.

Concerto second movements are usually elegiac and subdued. Less rigidly organized than their predecessor, they contrast with it in meter, tempo, melody, formal pattern, key, and expressive intent. Almost invariably played at a slow tempo, second movements may be marked *adagio, largo, largetto,* or *andante*. Mostly, they represent a pensive interlude between the first movement's forcefulness and the finale's jaunty cheerfulness. Although second movements may adhere to part form or variation form, sonata form is occasionally employed. Usually related to the work's basic key but not identical with it, the movement's tonality may shift to the dominant (sometimes the subdominant) or to minor. As befits a leisurely pace, its melodies are often expansive and lyric, and the quiet discourse that ensues is tantamount to an intimate conversational exchange between friends.

Many concerto finales (that is, the third movement) employ rondo form. Sonorous repartee falls readily into place within this pattern, for it allows the two bodies to engage in a chatty and light-hearted colloquy. Some concertos retain sonata form here, however, and a few employ the variation design. Regardless of structure, final movements are almost always in a quick tempo, and have the intent of bringing the composition to a climactic close.

In particular concertos, the several movements may be bound to one another. In this way, composers attempt to avoid the diffusion that a succession of separate episodes necessarily brings. One of the first to attempt such a synthesis was Felix Mendelssohn, who linked the three movements of his Violin Concerto in E minor with brief transitional passages. Franz Liszt created a similarly integrated work in his Concerto No. 2 in A major for Piano, and some years later Camille Saint-Saëns followed a like path when he wrote his Concerto in B minor for Violin. In the main, however, most solo concertos retain a separation into distinctive movements.

THE CONCERTO GROSSO

Sometime after 1550, the idea of contrasting sonorities between instrumental groups became increasingly important to musicians. Previously, polychoral works had featured an exchange between singers, and in early *concerti ecclesiastici* (sacred concertos) voices and instruments (mostly keyboard or strings) had been effectively deployed one against the other. But now, in the *concerto grosso* (large concerto) that began to take shape, it became standard practice to contrast one instrumental force with another.

Soon after its formulation this design acquired remarkable stability. Employing two groups of players known as the *concertino* and *ripieno*, it had these general characteristics:

1. *Concertino* (sometimes called the *soli*): smallest of the groups, which rarely had more than six or seven instrumentalists (and often as few as two or three) who performed on winds, strings, or harpsichord in any combination. However, many eighteenth-century *concerti grossi* were written for a concertino of two violins and a 'cello. Naturally, this smaller group provided effective tonal contrast with the larger body and it allowed some degree of specialization, for parts assigned its players were often comparatively difficult.

2. *Ripieno* (sometimes called the *concerto* or *tutti*): a body generally equivalent to an orchestra although eighteenth-century ensembles rarely included more than strings. Parts assigned the ripieno were nearly always doubled (played by more than one performer), whereas those given the concertino were not. Consequently, the former had a heavier and more resonant sound than its smaller associate.

In concerto grosso performance, the ripieno usually begins the first movement (most of these pieces have three) and discourses at some length. As the movement unfolds, the first theme returns occasionally in abbreviated form and is distinguished as the *ritornello* (literally "return to"). Interjected between ripieno quotations are passages played by the concertino that are more technically involved and have a lighter sonority. Most first movements conclude with a forceful presentation of the ritornello in the tonic key. In direct succession the second (slow) movement, usually in part form, and the third (fast) movement, often in a rondo pattern, are heard. Mostly, they are not as elaborate in substance, as lengthy, nor as formal in outline as the first movement.[2]

Three (from a total of six) of Johann Sebastian Bach's *Brandenburg Concertos* (1721) are distinguished representatives of the Baroque concerto grosso (the others do not maintain a clear division between concertino and ripieno). Following a general three-movement sequence, but scored for diverse forces, they reveal these structural details:

TABLE 20. *Structural Details of Three Brandenburg Concertos.*

Title	Movements	Scored for
Concerto No. 2 in F major	1. *Allegro* 2. *Andante* 3. *Allegro assai*	*Concertino:* trumpet, flute, oboe, violin *Ripieno:* strings and harpsichord
Concerto No. 4 in G major	1. *Allegro* 2. *Andante* 3. *Presto*	*Concertino:* violin and two flutes *Ripieno:* strings and harpsichord
Concerto No. 5 in D major	1. *Allegro* 2. *Affettuoso* 3. *Allegro*	*Concertino:* solo harpsichord, flute, and violin *Ripieno:* strings (violins in unison), and harpsichord

Although different in pattern and apparently modeled after earlier pieces by Arcangelo Corelli, Handel's twelve *Concerti Grossi*, Opus 6, written in 1740, are equally notable. These are details about three pieces in this set:

---

[2] For a reasonably detailed analysis of a representative concerto grosso, Bach's *Brandenburg Concerto No. 2* see p. 300.

TABLE 21.   **Structural Details of Three of Handel's Twelve Concerti Grossi.**

Title	Movements	Scored for
Concerto No. 1 in G major	1. *A tempo giusto* 2. *Allegro* 3. *Adagio* 4. *Allegro* 5. *Allegro*	*Concertino:* violin I and violin II *Ripieno:* violins I, II, viola, 'cello, bass, and continuo
Concerto No. 2 in F major	1. *Andante larghetto* 2. *Allegro* 3. *Largo* 4. *Allegro ma non troppo*	(as in No. 1)
Concerto No. 3 in E minor	1. *Larghetto* 2. *Andante* 3. *Allegro* 4. *Polonaise* 5. *Allegro ma non troppo*	(as in No. 1)

When the concerto grosso evolved to the point where its concertino was reduced to a single player, it became, in effect, a solo concerto. Precisely when this occurred is difficult to date, but several works by Antonio Vivaldi written early in the eighteenth century employ only one soloist and must be considered among the earliest of solo concertos.[3] Once introduced, the solo concerto quickly outstripped its predecessor, and a final *coup de grace* was delivered the concerto grosso concept by the rise of sonata form, a design that became extremely important in the solo concerto organization.

THE CADENZA

Not entirely unique to the concerto (they also appear, for instance, in arias), cadenzas are extended passages that a soloist performs alone after the orchestra has subsided into discrete silence. Providing limitless opportunities for technical display, they are usually replete with cascading arpeggios, scale runs of dazzling brilliance, wide leaps, and brilliant trills. Several cadenzas are usually present in a concerto, with the most important interpolated near the end of the first movement. Cadenzas do not have a rigid formal outline and vary considerably in length. Most are based on thematic fragments from the parent composition that are treated in a free, almost improvisatory manner. Interpolated between such thematic excisions are artfully contrived virtuoso passages that require extreme dexterity for satisfactory performance.

[3] These pieces, incidentally, retain sufficient intrinsic interest to make them regular members in the contemporary repertoire.

Like many other instrumental acquisitions, cadenzas appear to have sprung from a sixteenth-century vocal tradition that arose when soloists inserted flourishes between the cadential dominant (V) and tonic (I) chords used to conclude most arias. Instrumentalists of the period, many of whom were better-than-average composers, were not slow to adopt this practice for their own use. But much time had to elapse before tangible evidences of cadenza usage began to appear in scores. Handel's twelve *Concerti Grossi*, Opus 6 (1740) are among the first printed works that require executants to improvise such solo passages, and the same composer's organ concertos (written initially for his own use) call for similar abilities from keyboard performers.

When creating a concerto in the eighteenth century, a composer merely indicated the place at which he wished a cadenza inserted and relied on an instrumentalist to extemporize the passage. In an era when nearly all performers were composers, this enabled an executant to display his ability in improvisation as well as performance. But many nineteenth-century virtuosos were less adept in a creative sense, and cadenza improvisation became burdensome. Consequently, many composers (Beethoven, Mendelssohn, Schumann, and Liszt, for example) began to write cadenzas as a part of their compositional endeavor. If nothing else, this established a closely knit relationship between concerto and cadenza. An initial milestone in this area appeared in 1809 when Beethoven composed cadenzas for his Concerto No. 5 in E-flat major for Piano ("Emperor"). At the place where an extemporized passage would normally have been performed, he inserted the direction: *Non si fa una cadensa, ma attacca subito il seguente* (Do not insert a cadenza but attack the following directly). No one could misread his intent, and performers were careful to follow the instruction. Then, with such a precedent established, the practice became widely emulated. Consequently, most concertos postdating the early nineteenth century have composer-provided cadenzas.

CONCERTO PERFORMING MEDIA

Since its inception, the concerto's form has been considerably altered. And so, too, has the concept of what a satisfactory performing media might be. Sixteenth and seventeenth century concertos were almost entirely in the grosso format, of course, and were written for strings with continuo. Then, as the solo concerto emerged, individual string instruments became widely used, as were such keyboard instruments as harpsichord (initially) and piano (later).

In our time nearly all orchestral instruments have had concertos written for them, but piano and violin unquestionably enjoy the most extensive repertoire. Partly because of the instrument's unexcelled performance capabilities, and partly because of the tonal contrasts that may be obtained when its sonority is pitted against that of an orchestra, concertos for piano have proliferated. Mozart gave definitive status to such keyboard works late in the eighteenth century by composing twenty-seven concertos for his personal instrument. The Concerto No. 24 in C minor (K. 491) is a particularly beautiful example. Beethoven's five piano concertos are similarly excellent, and his Concerto No. 5 in E-flat major, subtitled "Emperor," is a towering giant in the repertoire. Less epic in substance, but richly infused with an endearing romantic ardor, are piano concertos by Robert Schumann and Edvard Grieg (both in A minor) and Peter Tchaikowsky (No. 1 in B-flat minor, discussed subsequently).

A near-rival are violin concertos. Although well represented in the orchestra, the violin can effectively assume a soloist's role because of its superb technical and expressive powers. Violin concertos are numerically abundant and extend from the early pieces of Tartini, Corelli, and Vivaldi to the latest compositions of Prokofiev, Stravinsky, and Hindemith. Among representative examples are concertos by Beethoven (in D major); Mendelssohn (in E minor); Tchaikowsky (in D major); and Brahms (in D major).

Like the violin, the 'cello is important in the orchestra, and this makes it necessary for a solo 'cellist to speak clearly and with persuasive eloquence. And because the 'cello's compass is in the mid and lower ranges, its sonority must be vigorously projected to rise against the more massive orchestral timbre. Despite these limitations, however, the 'cello repertoire includes a number of fine works including concertos by Boccherini (in B-flat major); Schumann (in A minor); and Dvořák (in B minor).

Concertos for flute, oboe, clarinet, bassoon, harp, viola, saxophone, horn, or trumpet exist in varying numbers. Some are excellent compositions, but the total literature for each instrument is limited. Representative examples are listed at the end of this chapter.

In addition to solo concertos, *double* or *triple concertos* also exist. Comparatively rare, works of this kind usually treat their solo instruments as a unit and contrast the sonorities of a small group (comprised of two or three players) against the orchestra. Among the representative examples are Vivaldi's Concertos for Two Trumpets; J. S. Bach's Concerto in D minor for Two Violins (his concertos for two, three, and four harpsichords are also notable); Mozart's Concerto in C major for Flute and Harp (K. 299) and Concerto in E-flat major for Two Pianos (K. 365); Beethoven's Triple Concerto in C major for Violin, 'Cello, and Piano; and Brahms' Double Concerto in D major for Violin and 'Cello.

When a design becomes as ubiquitous as the concerto, it cannot always be held within conventional limits. Consequently, a number of unorthodox concerted works have recently appeared in the literature. Here are some examples:

1. *Ebony Concerto* by Igor Stravinsky. Couched in modern jazz idioms, it
   is scored for a solo clarinet and dance orchestra.

2. *Concerto for Timpani and Brass* by Jaromir Weinberger. Featuring an unusual solo instrument, its three movements exploit unusual rhythms sounded against pungent brass sonorities.
3. *Concertino da Camera* for Alto Saxophone by Jacques Ibert. Sportive and racy, it is one of the few works that successfully exploit the saxophone's expressive potential.
4. *Concerto for Coloratura Voice and Orchestra* by Reinhold Glière. Requiring unusual vocal virtuosity, this taxing work (for voice) effectively contrasts vocal-instrumental coloration.
5. *Concerto for Percussion and Small Orchestra* by Darius Milhaud. Saucy, pert, and colorful, this piece abounds in unusual effects elicited from a battery of percussion instruments.

Then, too, twentieth-century composers have rediscovered the brilliant effects inherent in "concertos for orchestra" that Baroque musicians had initially explored. Rather than project a single soloist or group against a larger body, these compositions highlight, in turn, multiple instruments in the modern orchestra. Embracing a kaleidoscope of color with constantly changing hues, they excite the ear as the focal point shifts from one instrument or family of instruments to another. Among the composers who have recently created concertos for orchestra are Albert Roussel (1927); Paul Hindemith (1935); Zoltan Kodály (1939); Béla Bartók (1943); and Samuel Barber (*Capricorn Concerto*, 1944).

CONCERTO MODIFICATIONS

As the concerto developed, a number of peripheral forms arose that tended to simplify the design, merge it with other compositional types, or constrict its expanse. Among these, the *concertino,* actually a diminutive version of the concerto; the *concertante,* which amalgamates symphonic and concerto characteristics; and such single-movement forms as rhapsodies, fantasies, poems, or nocturnes have become important.

Closely resembling its parent form, a concertino (known in German as *konzertstück*) is theoretically contained within a single movement, although it often has distinctive subdivisions (typically three) linked by transitional passages. Concertino sections differ in tempo, meter, melodic substance, and expressive intent, and most are organized in a comparatively free manner. Carl Maria von Weber's *Concertino for Clarinet* is a fine example of the design, as are Dohnanyi's *Konzertstück for 'Cello and Orchestra* and Honegger's insouciant *Concertino for Piano and Orchestra.*

When the concerto grosso went into temporary eclipse shortly after 1750, the conjoint *sinfonia concertante* emerged. Actually an application of concerto principles to a symphonic design, the concertante employs a small group of players (usually from three to six) to perform in juxtaposition with an orchestra. Haydn's *Sinfonia Concertante in B-flat major,* and Mozart's two

Sinfonia Concertantes in E-flat major (K. 297b and K. 364) are representative.

After 1850, single-movement works for solo instrument and orchestra experienced a heyday. Evocative and poetic, they usually unfold along episodic lines, and because of their exciting beauty, flip manner of delivery, and emotional intensity, many have become great favorites. Examples include Chausson's *Poème for Violin and Orchestra;* Fauré's *Ballade for Piano and Orchestra;* Ravel's *Tzigane for Violin and Orchestra;* Saint-Saëns' *Havanaise for Violin and Orchestra;* and Richard Strauss' *Burleske for Piano and Orchestra.*

WAYPOSTS IN CONCERTO DEVELOPMENT

To 1750

From antiphonal interchanges that occurred in Biblical times, a continuation of similar responsorial practices during succeeding centuries, the advent of polychoral activities at Venice late in the sixteenth century, and a subsequent rise of *concerti ecclesiastici,* concerted pieces for instruments ultimately arose. More than a thousand years in the making, this heritage came to glorious fruition late in the sixteenth century.

Although it is known today as an instrumental pattern in which voices rarely appear, the concerto's roots rest on pre-existent vocal pieces. Particularly important among its predecessors were certain motets written by Andrea Gabrieli and his nephew, Giovanni, late in the sixteenth century. Capitalizing on a circumstance that placed two choir lofts in the Cathedral of St. Mark in Venice, they initially required their choirs to sing in an antiphonal manner and later began to write in a similar way for divided instrumental forces. At this same time, when most music was not only written for voices but performed *a cappella* (without accompaniment), *concerti ecclesiastici* (church concertos) became important. Written primarily for voices, the latter also used accompaniments provided by organ (with or without string assistance). Adriano Banchieri's *Concerti ecclesiastici a 8 voci* (1595) were among the first such pieces to appear. They were followed by Lodovico Viadana's *Concerti ecclesiastici a un, a due, a 3 & a 4 voci, con il basso continuo per sonar nell'organo,* published in Venice in 1602. As the title indicates, this collection specifically requires the organ to supply a *basso continuo,* then a relatively little-known device.

Important work in concerto formulation during the seventeenth century occurred in Italy. Although still dominated by vocal concepts, concerto-like pieces for voices and orchestra began to appear that occasionally used solo instruments, particularly the violin, in passages interpolated between choral sections. Because terms of identification were loosely applied in those times, lines of distinction between such designs as the canzona, sonata, concerto, or sinfonia scarcely existed. But before the century closed, each began to acquire unique attributes.

Between 1675 and 1750, when the Baroque era was in full flower, the concerto came to prominence. Thousands of concerted compositions were written during this span and included (1) concertos so closely associated with the nascent sinfonia that distinction between them was all but impossible; (2) works in concerto grosso format that featured an exchange between groups of instrumentalists; and (3) compositions that contrasted one instrument, typically the violin or harpsichord, against an "orchestra" (mostly strings) of the period. Of these, the first soon passed into oblivion, although vestiges of it arose later in the *sinfonia concertante*. But the concerto grosso prospered, and the solo concerto gathered the strength necessary to carry it to fame in succeeding years.

A triumvirate of Italian composers consisting of Arcangelo Corelli, Giuseppe Torelli, and Francesco Geminiani became important in refining the concerto grosso late in the seventeenth century (the latter during the eighteenth). Based mostly on the pre-existent instrumental *canzona*, Corelli's pieces were usually divided into five or more movements, whereas Geminiani clung to a four-movement sequence related to the *sonata da chiesa*. Torelli published one of the first sets of purely instrumental concertos (the *Concerti da camera*, 1686, scored for two violins and bass), and began to emphasize the concertino's two violins in a design that obviously veered toward the solo concerto.

Regardless of composer, however, concertos of this era were primarily scored for two groups of strings (that is, they were concerti grossi). Their *ripieno* normally included any available string performers, whereas the smaller group, the *concertino, soli, concertato,* or *concertante,* numbered two or three musicians (two violins and a 'cello was typical). A lengthy title Corelli appended to one of his sets of concerti grossi describes their mode of performance: *Concerti grossi con duoi violini e violin-cello di concertino obligati, e duoi altri violini, viola e besso di concerto grosso ad arbitrio che si potranno radoppiare.* [A set of concerti grossi with two violins and 'cello as a required concertino with two other violins, viola, and bass as the concerto grosso (ripieno) with an added possibility of doubling.]

Numerous other Italians, including Alessandro Scarlatti, Tomaso Albinoni, Pietro Locatelli, Francesco Veracini, and Giuseppe Tartini assisted in perfecting a solo concerto design at this time that has remained remarkably stable during ensuing eras. Each was a practicing violinist who knew the instrument and its expressive possibilities intimately; consequently, their works not only reveal superb technical fluency and unusual sonorous effects, but eloquent communicative power as well. At their hands, the solo concerto in three movements with a just and equable balance between soloist and orchestra became firmly established. Interestingly enough, earlier solo concertos had tended to emphasize the orchestra with a consequent neglect of the soloist.

It is hardly possible to overrate the influence of Antonio Vivaldi on concerto development. Not only an extremely prolific composer, the "Red Priest," as he was affectionately known because of his flaming red hair, was unconventional and enterprising. Based on a three-movement scheme (usually with *allegro-adagio-allegro* tempos), Vivaldi's extremely abundant concertos quickly became widely accepted models. J. S. Bach, for instance, made handwritten copies of many and transcribed several of the Italian's violin works for harpsichord or organ. In addition to writing for such accepted instruments as strings or keyboard, Vivaldi also composed concertos for bassoon, piccolo, oboe, trumpet, lute, and mandolin, singly and in varied combinations. Among his masterworks are *The Four Seasons,* a set of piquantly descriptive concertos for violin and orchestra and twelve concertos for one, two, or four solo violins, issued under the title *L'Estro armonico.*

None were more energetic in concerto composition in northern lands than Bach, Handel, and Telemann. Some of the very first keyboard concertos (for harpsichord or organ) were written by Bach, who began by transcribing previously composed violin works of his own and those by Vivaldi and others. Although few were originally conceived for this instrument, Bach's harpsichord concertos (for one, two, three, or four instruments) are important milestones in concerto development. Based on Vivaldi models, Bach's six organ concertos are also fine representatives of the Baroque keyboard concerto. His two violin concertos (in A minor and E major), as well as the Concerto in D minor for Two Violins, are outstanding virtuoso string pieces. And his six *Brandenburg Concertos* are without peer.

Nor are Handel's concertos less worthy. His sixteen Concertos for Organ and Orchestra (originally played during oratorio intermissions) are magnificent display pieces that wrote *finis* to the Baroque solo-keyboard concerto; no others could surpass their noble grandeur. Handel's twelve *Concerti Grossi,* Opus 6 (1740) follow Corelli's pattern of multiple movements and are similarly excellent. And his three Concertos for Oboe are clever and interesting pieces conceived on a smaller scale. Highly inventive, Georg Philipp Telemann turned out prodigious amounts of concertos as the Baroque era came to a close. Like Vivaldi, he was an enterprising composer who delighted in exploring the sonorous possibilities of unusual instruments. Among Telemann's works that experience rather frequent contemporary performance are several Concertos for Flute and Orchestra, a number of Concertos for Oboe and Orchestra, a Concerto in D major for Trumpet and Strings, and the Concerto in D major for Three Trumpets, Two Oboes, and Orchestra.

During the Classic Era

After 1750, German composers became the primary custodians of instrumental music as attention in Latin lands shifted to a concern with vocal works written for the opera house and church. Outstanding among northern composers active during the Rococo period (the years intervening between the Baroque and Classic eras) were Carl Philipp Emanuel Bach and Johann Christian Bach, sons of the great Johann Sebastian. Abandoning the concerto grosso format, C. P. E. Bach wrote a sizeable number of punctiliously conceived solo concertos (the Concerto in A major for 'Cello, for example). His brother, an even more prodigious composer, created thirty-seven solo concertos for clavier and thirty-one *sinfonie concertante*. Charming and somewhat fragile in substance, these pieces can hardly be termed monumental; rather, they show the concerto in transition and presage greatness without actually attaining it.

Classic concertos, like symphonies composed during the same era, are models of artistic restraint. Literally every line in them gives evidence of being finely tailored, with obvious care taken to insure a true rapprochement between the sonorous bodies. This did not prevent particular works from becoming challenging vehicles for digital display, however. The concertos of Mozart, to cite a particular instance, are superbly conceived compositions that give soloists ample opportunity to divulge the full pyrotechnics of their craft. Yet, together with many of the beautifully proportioned and skillfully constructed works of the period, they rarely permit display to become an end in itself.

Classicism's concertos tend to be somewhat more melodic than their older Baroque cousins. Often, the latter were based on stiff, angular, motivic themes (particularly in the first and final movements) that were endlessly manipulated in long sequential passages. Although not uncommon during the Baroque, lyric melodies were employed with discretion and typically assigned to pensive second movements. Seemingly, an unqualified acceptance of lyricism during these times meant a subjugation of polyphony's remaining vestiges to the gathering forces of homophony. But such proscriptions could not persist and were ultimately swept aside in the century's later decades.

Franz Joseph Haydn was one of Classicism's most distinguished musicians, but despite the impressive work he accomplished in establishing the symphony's basic principles, his concerted compositions are disappointing. Haydn wrote dozens of concertos for clavier (a generic term for available keyboard instruments), violin, 'cello, double bass, horn, trumpet, flute, and "lira," known vernacularly as the hurdy-gurdy, but comparatively few have become firmly established in the repertoire. Exceptions are a radiant Concerto in D major for 'Cello; a nimble Concerto in D major for Harpsichord; and an impish Concerto in E-flat major for Trumpet. By Haydn's time, of course, the concerto grosso had become passé, but his *Sinfonia Concertante* in B-flat major (for oboe, bassoon, violin, 'cello, and orchestra) is somewhat similar to the earlier design in the sense that it pits a small instrumental group against a more massive one.

Wolfgang Amadeus Mozart was the greatest concerto composer of his period, if not of all time, and wrote between forty and fifty concertos, most (twenty-seven) for his beloved piano. Other instruments were not neglected, however, and in a body of works for which musicians shall be ever-grateful, he composed (1) the Concerto in B-flat major for Bassoon (K. 191); (2) seven concertos for violin—No. 3 in G major (K. 216), No. 4 in D major (K. 218), and No. 5 in A major (K. 219) are outstanding; (3) the Concerto in A major for Clarinet (K. 622); (4) Concertos Nos. 1 in G major (K. 313) and 2 in D major (K. 314) for Flute; (5) the Concerto in C major (K. 299) for Flute and Harp; and (6) Four Concertos for Horn. As with Haydn, Mozart ignored the concerto grosso but his *Sinfonia Concertante* in E-flat major (for oboe, clarinet, bassoon, horn, and strings, K. 297b) and the *Sinfonia Concertante* in E-flat major (for violin and viola, K. 364) are works of great individuality and charm.

During the Romantic Era

Concertos written during the nineteenth century show individual musicians exercising the era's well-known penchant for subjectivity. Introspective composers (Schumann and Chopin), in company with their more flamboyant contemporaries (Berlioz and Liszt) wrote works—concertos among them—that alternately plumb the depths or scale the heights. Seemingly, poetry was everywhere, and composers no less than painters or philosophers consistently attempted to evoke a poetic muse. Such orientation inevitably leads to excessive lengths, of course, but when sheer expression is the only desideratum, other artistic virtues are unhesitatingly cast aside.

Nevertheless, the age began on a plane of rigorous artistic veracity. Ludwig van Beethoven, a composer thoroughly indoctrinated in the precepts of Classicism, was its first outstanding exemplar. A remarkable pianist, Beethoven brought a penetrating insight of the resources of this instrument as well as consummate creative mastery to bear on the writing of five piano concertos. Like his celebrated nine symphonies, these are strong and decisive works, filled with militant affirmativeness. Each follows the Mozartean three-movement plan, but their restless rhythms, abrupt cadences, and epic contrasts give them an emotionality heretofore unknown. His Concerto No. 4 in G major is a particularly fine work filled with lovely melodies and a kind of relaxed geniality, but his Concerto No. 5 in E-flat major ("Emperor") is a brilliant virtuoso piece laden with staggering bravura passages. Beethoven's Concerto in D major for Violin, his lone venture in writing for solo strings, is beautifully sculpted. With interconnected second and third movements (the former in variation form, the latter in rondo form), it is one of the finest concerted pieces in the literature. His Concerto in C major for Violin, 'Cello, and Piano (the "Triple Concerto") harkens to the earlier concerto grosso concept. Unusual in several respects, it has a dry and rather severe style that makes taxing demands on each of the soloists. Unquestionably, this has limited its frequency of performance.

Also steeped in the tenets of Classicism, Felix Mendelssohn neverthe-less maintained a curious rapport between two antipathetic styles. His hauntingly lovely Concerto in E minor for Violin is one of the most gracious and lyric pieces in the repertoire, and his Concerto No. 1 in G minor for Piano is a charming small-scale piece that pales only in comparison with the towering keyboard works surrounding it. One of these is the rapturous Concerto in A minor for Piano by Robert Schumann. A "Prince of Romanti-cists," Schumann was a less distinguished musical architect than Mendels-sohn, but his unabashed harmonic ardor, sweeping melodic inventiveness, and mastery of complex rhythmic devices are used with singular effectiveness in this almost celestial piece. Similarly, Schumann's Concerto in A minor for 'Cello is a glowing Romantic work filled with imaginative melodic ideas and deeply felt poetic sentiment.

Few composers have written more effectively for the piano than Frederic Chopin, yet this gifted musician was essentially a miniaturist who became ill at ease when writing in the larger designs. Chopin's Concertos No. 1 in E minor and No. 2 in F minor are the most extended pieces this frail and sensitive man attempted. Although they reveal his superb key-board mastery, both evidence a disconcerting weakness in handling the orchestra and a less than perfunctory interest in exploiting its resources. Im-balance between soloist and orchestra, along with a pronounced architectural weakness and an inability to create themes that stand up well under symphonic bombardment, cause the Chopin concertos to be less than totally satisfactory.

Judging from contemporaneous accounts, Franz Liszt was a wizard at the keyboard. Perhaps the greatest performing artist ever to mount the concert platform, this pianistic necromancer set himself the task, in which he brilliantly succeeded, of emulating the demonic virtuosity Nicolo Paganini exhibited on his violin. Although Liszt's early piano pieces tend to be superficial and tawdry, his Concerto No. 1 in E-flat major (revised 1856), and the Concerto No. 2 in A major (revised 1861) are well conceived. Crisply melodic and organized in four movements, the first is quite orthodox in substance and outline except for the composer's somewhat obsessive use of the triangle. But the second is distinctly unusual. Encompassed within a single beautifully integrated movement (with, however, three perceptible subsections), it is closely knit, filled with exciting emotional tension, and gorgeously lyrical.

Two piano concertos by Johannes Brahms, No. 1 in D minor and No. 2 in B-flat major, veer in directions noticeably different from those taken by

Chopin or Liszt. Written for the composer's own use and, consequently, fiendishly difficult to perform, both are devoid of extraneous display or sheer exhibitionism. Rather, in company with Brahms' Concerto in D major for Violin, and the Concerto in A minor for Violin and 'Cello (the "Double Concerto"), they are tightly knit, glowingly impassioned, and immensely vibrant works.

During Romanticism's waning years the concerto flourished with undiminished vigor, and a number of unique and impressive works were written just prior to 1890. Quite obviously influenced by Germanic traditions, although he resolutely filled his pieces with an idiomatic Slavic flavor, Peter Tchaikowsky brought his emotion-laden Concerto No. 1 in B-flat minor for Piano and the richly lyrical Concerto in D major for Violin to international attention during these years. Contemporaneously working with deft skill and impeccable craftsmanship in Bohemia, Antonin Dvořák then published his warm and tender Concerto in B minor for 'Cello and the lyrically engaging Concerto in A minor for Violin. Somewhat earlier (1868), Norway's Edvard Grieg created his atmospheric Concerto in A minor for Piano that is comparable in every respect to Schumann's superb concerto in the same key.

In the Twentieth Century

No less than symphonies, operas, sonatas, or suites, concertos of the contemporary era freely employ such devices as the whole-tone scale, chromatic harmony, twelve-tone patterns, polytonality, and polyrhythm. As in the past, concertos for piano or violin remain favorites, but solo pieces for 'cello, viola, clarinet, harp, and other instruments are far from rare. Among the century's innovations has been a renascence of interest in the harpsichord, as evidenced by Manuel de Falla's Concerto for Harpsichord (1927); Francis Poulenc's *Concert champêtre* (1929); and Elliott Carter's Sonata for Flute, Oboe, 'Cello, and Harpsichord (1952)—which, despite its name, is not distantly removed from the concerto grosso.

Filled with unusual effusiveness, four piano concertos by Serge Rachmaninoff claimed attention early in the century. A virtuoso pianist of unusual ability, Rachmaninoff wrote with knowing insight for his personal instrument, but these compositions are obviously founded on the syntax of an earlier era. Refulgent with opulent nineteenth-century lyricism, his Concertos No. 1 in F-sharp minor (1891), No. 2 in D minor (1901), No. 3 in D minor (1909), and No. 4 in G minor (1927) exhibit broad, flowing themes, thick, almost turgid harmonies, and fulsome sonorities that tend to weary the ear after being heard repeatedly.

Claude Debussy did not write any concertos, but his contemporary, Maurice Ravel, composed two unusually fine pieces for piano. An indifferent pianist himself, Ravel nevertheless created a glowing Concerto in G major (1931) that is filled with brash syncopated rhythms and the exciting, breathless quality of jazz. And his Concerto for Left Hand (1931), written for virtuoso Paul Wittgenstein who lost his right arm in World War I, requires prodigious technical feats from a one-armed soloist. Like its associate, it is an invigorating work that has won just renown in our era.

Of the three well-known proponents of Viennese Expressionism active early in the century, two contributed to the concerto repertoire. Anton von Webern did not enter this domain, but Arnold Schoenberg and Alban Berg both wrote bold, mercurial, and dazzling concerted works. Composed comparatively late in his career, Schoenberg's Concerto for Violin (1936) and Concerto for Piano (1943) are uncompromising pieces that require a great deal from both performer and listener. Couched in atonal terms, they have spare and angular melodies, spectacular sonorities, and extremely dissonant harmonies. As with many examples of surrealistic art, they are unorthodox, sometimes shocking, but uniquely beautiful. Although he was a younger man, Berg's Chamber Concerto for Violin, Piano, and Thirteen Winds (1925) and his Concerto for Violin (1935) predate Schoenberg's concertos. More of a melodist than his mentor, Berg softened his pieces with a songful lyricism, but at heart remained an avowed atonalist. Gifted with a superb sense of color, he fully exploited the instrumental timbres available in the chamber piece and delved deeply into virtually all the known resources of virtuoso string writing in his violin concerto.

Twentieth-century Russian composers effected a curious amalgam between the opulent melodism of the Tchaikowsky-Rachmaninoff tradition and the ascerbic, percussive sonorities of the contemporary era. One of the most outstanding, a man extraordinarily gifted as a pianist and composer, Serge Prokofiev wrote five concertos for piano [No. 3 in C major (1921) and No. 5 in G major (1932) are especially fine] and two for violin. Most remarkable is the Concerto No. 2 in G minor (1935). Surprisingly enough, Prokofiev remained something of a traditionalist and consistently retained the concerto's conventional frame while pouring adventuresome new ideas into it. Organized in the traditional three-movement sequence, his concertos are handsome, spell-binding works that sometimes stun the senses with reckless bravado but always please the ear with vivid colors and sparkling melodies. Aram Khachaturian followed a similar course while writing his radiant Concerto for Piano (1936) and the lilting Concerto for Violin (1940). Although attractive, these are ambivalent works that do not show Prokofiev's imaginative flair but shrewdly intermingle Slavic exoticism with the prosaic clichés of modern popular music.

George Gershwin's jazzy Concerto in F major for Piano (1925) was one of the first virtuoso pieces by an American composer to attract international attention. Some background for this emergence had been laid by the placid scores of Edward MacDowell (Concertos Nos. 1 and 2, 1885 and 1890) and by an issuance of similarly bland works from several other composers during the first quarter of the century. But the glittering sheen of Gershwin's score was perfectly suited to the era in which it was born, and it became, consequently, a model for subsequent generations of composers. Similarly reflective of the "roaring twenties," Aaron Copland's Concerto for Piano (1927) also contains pulsating jazz rhythms and the brisk, businesslike clarity of popular music. Two decades later, Copland wrote an impressive Concerto for Clarinet (1948) in response to a commission from Benny Goodman. By turns pensive and easy-going, it also has an edgy, restless virtuosity fully expressive of the anxiety-wracked society in which it appeared.

One of the most gifted creative musicians of this era, Béla Bartók wrote several concerted works. His three concertos for piano (No. 3, 1945, is exceptional) are craggy, impassioned, and overwhelming scores, and his Concerto for Violin (1938) is everywhere accepted as a contemporary masterpiece. Even loftier heights were attained when Bartók composed his Concerto for Orchestra (1943), an exemplary five-movement piece that successfully exploits the myriad sonorous hues available to a modern orchestra.

Extremely agile and filled with demanding pyrotechnical devices, Igor Stravinsky's Concerto in D major for Violin (1931) is another modern-day classic. And his Concerto for Piano and Wind Orchestra (1924) juxtaposes wind and piano sonorities in a dazzling array. A somewhat later arrival to orchestra desks, Samuel Barber's Concerto for Piano (1962) is a glowing piece by an important American composer that merges old-fashioned charm with a bristling, modern syntax. It is, perhaps, the decade's most outstanding solo concerto.

Despite the popularity of solo concertos, the concerto grosso staged a remarkable comeback in recent years. That this is not a mere hankering for antiquarianism is exemplified by Ernest Bloch's Concerto Grosso for String Orchestra and Piano (1925), a work whose materials are imaginative, modish, and modern. With his Concerto Grosso in E-flat major ("Dumbarton Oaks," 1938) and the Concerto Grosso in D major for Strings (1948), Stravinsky implemented this revival, as have several other contemporary writers.

As the century moves onward, the concerto literature continues to grow. New pieces capture attention, notoriety, and acclaim just as their predecessors continue to hold a place in listener affection. Because the new arrivals represent an art in transition, their directions are those of music itself: uncertain, experimental, unpredictable, but always engrossing and exciting.

PARTICULAR EXAMPLES OF THE CONCERTO

J. S. Bach (1685–1750), *Brandenburg Concerto No. 2* in F major

After meeting with Christian Ludwig (1677–1734), music-loving Margraf of Brandenburg in 1719, Bach determined to compose a set of concertos for the nobleman that would tangibly demonstrate his creative ability. Titular ruler of Berlin and its environs, the Margraf indulged in the unusual hobby of collecting musical works—particularly concertos—written for him by living composers. Wealthy, unencumbered, cultured, and well educated, he maintained a private orchestra that was, of course, readily available to perform the commissioned works.

With his position as *Kapellmeister* to the Duke of Cothen becoming insecure, and the need to secure a new position pressing on him, Bach wrote six concertos with meticulous care and dispatched them to Berlin in 1721 with the usual obsequious letter of transmittal. Unquestionably, he wished to win a position in the Margraf's service, but in this respect was doomed to disappointment, for court records show that the compositions were received, filed in the archives, and promptly forgotten. During ensuing years, manuscript copies of the *Brandenburg Concertos* (as they had become known) passed through various hands, but the pieces were not actually published until 1850.

While engaging in orchestral performance, musicians of the eighteenth century characteristically gathered about a keyboard instrument, either a harpsichord or clavicembalo, where their director presided as he contributed the necessary "filling in" to buttress the piece. When a concerto grosso was at hand, the concertino and ripieno groups were separated, with solo instruments taking a position near the director's right and the larger body occupying a more distant location. Accordingly, modified antiphonal effects were obtained as the two groups engaged in concerto-like colloquy. Signals were communicated to the musicians visually or orally, and not infrequently a *Kapellmeister* "led" the group simply by playing loudly on his instrument.

Because it reveals a clear separation between the concertino and ripieno (a distinction not consistently maintained in all the associate works), the second *Brandenburg Concerto* is an excellent example of the grosso plan. Comprised of flute, oboe, violin, and trumpet, its concertino has an abundance of sonorities to contrast against the ripieno's full string timbre, differences that Bach astutely emphasized in a remarkable way. These are further details about the piece:

First movement. As the concerto begins, both concertino and ripieno unite in sounding the basic theme:

Totally dominating the movement, this subject (the ritornello) reappears frequently but displays sufficient modifications in key and coloration to offer a continually changing countenance. Played at a reasonably rapid tempo (*allegro*) in quadruple meter, the movement is firmly rhythmic and benefits considerably from the ritornello's pulsating thrust. Naturally, repartee between concertino and ripieno is important, but the latter is decidedly more assertive.

Second movement. Few movements in Baroque concertos stray far from the basic tonality, and Bach observes convention in this instance by shifting to D minor, a related key. Overshadowed during much of the first movement, the concertino instruments now discourse eloquently over a continuo accompaniment (provided by harpsichord and 'cello). In successive order, violin, oboe, and flute engage in a polyphonic interplay that begins like this:

As the movement unfolds at a gentle pace (marked *andante*) in triple meter, ripieno strings are held in total abeyance. Although in minor, the movement's final cadence rests on a D-major chord, a standard procedure in Bach's time.

Third movement. Utterly neglected during the second movement, the trumpet becomes vigorously assertive in the finale, which is in duple meter

and marked to be played *allegro assai* (very fast). Without ado, it initiates
the movement by sounding the subject of a four-voice fugue:

Herculean efforts are here required of a trumpeter, for his part is cruelly
high and unusually exposed. In succession, oboe, violin, and flute join in
fugal exposition as the subject is heard in the tonic (F) and dominant (C)
keys. Underneath this nimble polyphonic discourse, the ubiquitous continuo jogs blithely along. Concertino instruments consistently stand in the
foreground during this movement, and their voices are actively employed
in combining the fugue's several lines. Expressing a robust spirit of carefree gaiety, this section brings the piece to an unusually impressive close.

Wolfgang Amadeus Mozart (1756–1791), *Concerto in A major for Clarinet* (K. 622)

Many, perhaps even most, concertos have been written for particular
virtuosos. Such was the case, at any rate, with Mozart's clarinet concerto,
composed for Anton Stadler (1753–1812), a distinguished soloist who, late
in the eighteenth century, greatly assisted in establishing this instrument as
a standard member of the orchestra. Both Mozart and Stadler were active
in Vienna at about the same time, and a warm friendship ultimately grew
up between them. An important artistic consequence of this liaison was the
composer's Trio in E-flat major for Clarinet, Viola, and Piano (K. 498), his
Quintet in A major (K. 581) for Clarinet and Strings, and this concerto.

Mozart's sponsorship of the clarinet had few precedents. J. S. Bach
apparently never used the instrument, Handel virtually ignored it, and
Vivaldi gave it only passing attention. But the "Mannheimers," particularly
Johann Stamitz, were devoted to a promulgation of literature for woodwind
instruments, and it is likely that Mozart became impressed with the clarinet's
possibilities while visiting this German city. Once begun, this cultivation
was so successful that before the century closed, clarinets had become firmly
established in the hierarchy of instrumental groups.

Along with the *Requiem* (K. 626), which remained unfinished at his
tragically early death, Mozart's clarinet concerto (1791) was one of his last
pieces. Actually, however, it had been begun earlier, in 1789, as a single-
movement work for basset horn, a near-relative of larger size than the conventional clarinet. These are salient details about the completed masterwork:

First movement. In the accepted manner of classical concertos, the orchestra
begins this sonata-form movement with an abridged version of the exposi-

tion. Written in quadruple meter and performed at an *allegro* tempo, it is primarily based on these four melodic ideas:

When the clarinet enters, these themes are reaffirmed in a modified manner.

Developmental activity uses excisions from both the principal and subordinate themes, and in the process each is marvelously transformed. Indeed, the entire section becomes so lyric that thematic exploitation seems a natural, almost an inevitable act. Although the solo instrument's communicative resources are fully exploited during its brilliant dialogue with the orchestra, the development is remarkably succinct; within it, everything is clear, crisp, and compact.

Foreshortened, the recapitulation avoids any redundant presentation of melodies by soloist or orchestra. Midway through, Mozart provided for the insertion of a cadenza but relied on a performer to extemporize the passage. Today, the cadenza is either avoided or held within modest bounds to prevent compromising the pristine beauties of this classically oriented score. Finally, a concluding coda, based on the first subject, terminates the movement.

Second movement. Shifting to the subdominant tonality (D major), this segment begins as the solo instrument plays an exquisite *adagio* theme in triple meter:

Supported by strings as it introduces the subject, the clarinet surrenders its prerogative to the full ensemble when the theme is repeated. Throughout this movement in ternary form (ABA), principal emphasis is placed on the presentation of long, arching melodic lines by both forces.

Although the dialogue between soloist and orchestra is continually gracious, the clarinet discloses dazzling agility during the second section (B) which begins like this:

At length, the initial section (A) returns, after which a fifteen-measure coda rounds out one of the most beautifully balanced movements in all of music.

Third movement. Neither aloofness nor restraint is observable in the finale. Cast in sextuple meter (taken with two beats to the measure) this sprightly movement in sonata-rondo form launches immediately into a presentation of the principal theme (*a*):

Back in the home key (A major), the finale has an impish spirit whose effectiveness is enhanced by the composer's adroit intermixture of instrumental colors. Although artistic balance is observable everywhere, the piece has a whirlwind of ideas. For the first digession (*b*), this lyric theme is used:

Throughout, as each new theme is announced, it is first sounded by the clarinet and then taken up by the orchestra. Because it is both brief and gentle, the theme of the second digression (*c*) remains comparatively obscure:

In typical rondo manner, the principal theme (*a*) returns after each episode.

A short development, based on the principal and first intermediate themes, occurs within this movement. But musical byplay is short-lived and thematic manipulation is readily abandoned as the piece nears its end. After a final appearance of the principal rondo theme, a coda, which enlists the full ensemble, brings the concerto to a distinctive close.

Felix Mendelssohn (1809–1847), *Concerto in E Minor for Violin*

Although his radiant Concerto for Violin did not have its public premiere until September, 1844, Mendelssohn began talking about the piece as early as July, 1838. Ferdinand David (1810–1873), an excellent violinist and close personal friend for whom the work was written, assumed the role of gadfly and continually urged the onset of work. But the usually facile and accommodating Mendelssohn required much prodding before actually embarking on his task. Then, as the concerto underwent its gestation, David was frequently consulted, sometimes in a technical way, sometimes about an artistic matter. Among his more obvious contributions is a handsome cadenza, heard as the first movement nears its close.

Ostensibly cast in a single movement, the E minor Violin Concerto nevertheless shows perceptible cleavages between its sections. Mendelssohn linked its three movements with brief transitional passages, and even employed aspects of thematic recurrence within sections to provide greater cohesion, but synthesis is more theoretic than actual. To a perceptive ear, a concerto's conventional outlines are readily apparent:

First movement. Speaking effortlessly above subdued orchestral strings, the solo violin introduces this lovely principal theme:

Subjects of this kind are necessarily expansive, and Mendelssohn gives the melody a full presentation during these early measures. Marked *allegro molto appassionato* and cast in sonata form, the movement is played in duple meter. After the soloist interjects some agile passagework between incisive orchestral chords, the orchestra is allowed to repeat the principal theme in a resonant and emphatic manner. Then, in succession, massed violins announce a transitional theme, which is really the principal theme's second part:

Again, virtuoso passagework serves as a connective. This time it leads to the tranquil subordinate theme, sounded by flutes and clarinets over a sustained violin pedal point:

Subsequently, this subject is repeated in a higher register by the solo violin; after some melodic byplay, the closing section, based on the principal theme, brings the statement to a close.

Opening with a motive derived from the principal subject, the development plunges into an impassioned musical discourse. Although dramatic and evocative, it is comparatively short and concerned with only the two ideas from the principal theme. At a musical crossroads between the development and recapitulation, a cadenza is interpolated. Filled with brilliant passagework, mostly arpeggios and trills, this solo passage also makes occasional allusions to the principal theme.

Played by the full orchestra in a restrained manner, the principal theme provides a background for fleet violin pyrotechnics as the recapitulation begins. Later, sonority grows to a resonant *fortissimo* as the principal theme's second idea is announced by the orchestra and repeated by the soloist. Now heard in E major, the subordinate theme is again presented by woodwinds over the soloist's sustained pedal point. But this excursion into major is temporary, for the minor mode returns as the movement heads toward its conclusion. Slightly faster than preceding sections, the coda is characterized by an exciting *accelerando*.

Second movement. Because he intended this second section to follow hard on the first, Mendelssohn provided a short connecting passage leading directly into an *andante* movement in sextuple meter. Set in C major, it expresses Romantic sentiments in warm poetic terms. After a quiet introduction has been gracefully spelled out by orchestral instruments, the soloist presents this first theme (A) of a ternary pattern:

Although gentle and gracious, the subject is actually as sturdy as a stout oak.

Possessing more momentum, the movement's second portion (B) involves both forces in a firm, forceful presentation. Soloist and orchestra enjoy an eloquent exchange during these measures, but the prevailing mood of poetic lyricism is never dispelled. Returning so subtly as to be hardly perceptible, the first theme (A) is reaffirmed almost without listener awareness. Ultimately, the movement closes quietly in C major.

Third movement. Founded on an allusion to the first movement's initial theme, a brief transitional passage leading into the finale is interrupted when a brusque fanfare is sounded (in major) by horns, trumpets, and bassoons. An arpeggio figure rises several times from the solo violin, and ultimately breaks into an elfin-like theme that becomes the movement's principal subject:

Marked *allegro molto vivace* and played in quadruple meter, this passage imposes virtuosic demands on a soloist. Ultimately these actions are halted when a march-like subordinate theme is sounded from the orchestra:

In the development that follows, for this movement is in sonata form, the second theme receives initial treatment. But the first subject comes bounding into the discourse occasionally to find adept transformation at the soloist's hands. Subsequently, the recapitulation appears, and although foreshortened, it manages to encompass both themes.

Based on the second theme, a comparatively lengthy coda treats its subject so extensively as to nearly become a second development. Only brief fragments from the first theme are allowed to appear in this final episode, however, for the ebullient march is precisely the right idea with which to conclude a stunning concerto.

Peter I. Tchaikowsky (1840–1893), *Concerto No. 1 in B-flat minor for Piano*

For a work that was to become so successful, Tchaikowsky's Piano Concerto in B-flat minor had a decidedly inauspicious beginning. On Christmas Eve, 1874, the eager composer, hardly able to restrain his enthusiasm, played the newly composed piece for his mentor, patron, and friend, Nicholas Rubinstein. An excellent pianist as well as head of the Moscow Conservatory, Rubinstein was piqued because Tchaikowsky had not sought his advice while writing the work. Consequently, he acted singularly unimpressed while hearing it played and, afterward, became so vehement in his denunciation that the hypersensitive composer was reduced to tears. Filled with humiliation, Tchaikowsky rushed from the room when Rubinstein went to the piano and began to burlesque his manner of writing. But he remained loyal to the concerto and steadfastly refused to abandon it. In time, certain changes were incorporated, and its dedication was shifted from Rubinstein to Hans von Bulow (1830–1894), a well-known German pianist, conductor, and champion of Tchaikowsky's music, who gave the piece its premiere in Boston on October 25, 1875. These are details about this brilliant work:

First movement. After a *fortissimo* prefatory passage sounded by the orchestra's sonorous horns, a sweeping theme in D-flat major appears, played in octaves by first violins and 'cellos:

Allegro non troppo e molto maestoso

Although heard several times in the introduction, this memorable idea
does not recur elsewhere in the concerto. Shifting from triple to quadruple
meter and assuming an *allegro con spirito* pace, the main portion of the
movement unfolds in sonata form. Its first subject, a sprightly little
motive, is announced by the piano, after which it becomes the basis for
a jaunty repartee between soloist and orchestra:

Allegro con spirito

Consisting of two distinct ideas (quoted separately below), the subordinate theme is introduced by woodwinds in a smooth and placid
manner:

Such melodies make it possible for a composer to fully exploit the possibilities of orchestral dialogue. In this instance, Tchaikowsky assigns the
theme to such colorful instruments as flute or clarinet while the soloist
weaves a series of arabesques around it.

A lengthy development utilizes all the themes, with particular emphasis
accorded the second subject. While the latter opens and dominates the
development, the rakish first theme continually intrudes, almost in the

manner of a thoughtless buffoon interrupting a serious conversation. Near the end of the development, after the solo instrument has entered via one of the work's several short cadenzas, a discourse occurs between the piano and orchestra that may well be one of music's most unrestrained emotive outpourings.

Primary emphasis in the recapitulation is placed on the second subject. Treated at length—mostly in the form of orchestral solos for oboe, violin, or clarinet—this melody is consistently enriched by piano embellishments. Where recapitulation and coda unite, the movement's principal cadenza, based mostly on the subordinate theme, is inserted. In the manner of cadenzas, this is a brilliant showpiece that totally overshadows the subsequent brief coda.

Second movement. Shifting to D-flat major, the second movement, the work's shortest, is marked to be played *andantino semplice* in sextuple meter. Cast as a three-part design (ABA), it is an island of quietude between the first movement's powerful aggressiveness and the finale's unrestrained frenzy. Pizzicato strings sound a four-measure rhythmic figuration that presages the appearance of a sweet atmospheric subject played by a solo flute and then reaffirmed by the piano:

Later, a more active idea attempts to interrupt the idyllic flow, but the first melody continues to peek through openings in the musical façade until 'cellos give it another quotation. Midway through the movement, a scherzo-like touch is interjected when the pace changes to *prestissimo* and a curiously banal expression (in F major and almost like a waltz) is presented by violas and 'cellos:

After another short cadenza (seemingly they proliferate throughout this piece), the piano reaffirms the first theme (A). With a short coda wherein upper woodwinds are prominent, the movement concludes on a succession of *pianissimo* chords.

Third movement. So riotous as to suggest an impassioned Cossack dance, the concerto's finale is almost ear-shattering. Based on three themes, it is in B-flat minor, triple meter, and marked *allegro con fuoco*. After a short four-measure introduction, the piano sounds this principal theme:

Twisting, turning, writhing, and leaping, this agile idea is repeatedly thrown back and forth between piano and orchestra.

Introduced by upper strings and subsequently repeated (with embellishments) by the piano, the second theme is more restrained:

Seeming superfluous in the midst of this melodic abundance, the angular third subject is easily overwhelmed and heard only infrequently:

From thence onward, Tchaikowsky follows an unfettered course. Because the first two subjects recur frequently, semblances of rondo form are suggested, but these are only fleeting allusions. Aspects of thematic development involving all three subjects appear near the end of the movement, but this working-out actually proves to be a free fantasia. Ultimately, piano and orchestra join in an eloquent presentation of the subordinate theme, after which a buoyant coda (marked *allegro vivo*) brings this glowing piece to an intensely exciting close.

Béla Bartók (1881–1945), *Concerto for Orchestra*

One of the twentieth century's most impressive scores, Bartók's *Concerto for Orchestra* (1943) runs an expressive gamut from pensive introspection to witty joviality. Composed at a time when the ravages of a fatal illness were grievously taxing the composer's strength, it is nevertheless strong, militant, and assertive. Genuinely symphonic in dimension, it aims at exploring the sonorities and expressive resources of the orchestra's many diverse instruments.

First movement. Marked *andante non troppo,* the opening movement begins when a somber subject is sounded deep in the low strings. Three trumpets offer a contrasting commentary until, at length, richly sonorous upper strings assume leadership. In *allegro vivace* tempo, the movement's main section has a distinctly different character. Far more dynamic, it begins with this angular melody (the first subject), which actually includes two ideas:

In contrast, a smooth-flowing second theme is introduced by oboe and repeated by clarinets and strings:

Throughout, trumpets, horns, and trombones are highlighted, and their resonant sonority eloquently suggest breadth, vigor, and dignity.

Second movement. Opening with a short drum solo over which a crisp, folk-like melody is sounded by two bassoons, this *allegretto scherzando* is delightfully expressive. Its principal melody is taken up, in turn, by oboes, clarinets, flutes, and trumpets:

Brasses interject a pompous note midway through the movement, but woodwinds later return in a manner similar to the opening measures. Conjointly, brasses and strings conclude.

Third movement. As befits its designation "Elegia," the third movement is solemn and somewhat murky as it sounds material from the introduction of the first movement. A lone oboe sings this pensive theme embellished by clarinet, flute, and harp figurations:

Later, strings present the section's most important subject:

Clever rhythmic subtleties, plus an effective register change, provide an abundance of contrast as this theme is repeated and extended. Finally, the movement closes as it began, this time with the piccolo as soloist.

Fourth movement. Called an "Interrupted Intermezzo," this section gives the impression of being continually punctuated. Some of its angularity is illusory, however, and can be attributed to the metric changes that occur in nearly every measure. Opening the movement, a single oboe presents this principal theme:

Strings extend the subject and pass it from violas to violins. Later, a spirited folk dance interrupts the intermezzo and injects a touch of gaiety. After a reappearance of the first theme and a short flute cadenza, a tapering of sonority brings the section to an extremely quiet close.

Fifth movement. By turns fleet of foot, richly expressive, and unusually agile, orchestral strings become a center of display in the concerto's finale. Few techniques in the lexicon of advanced string writing are neglected by Bartók in these measures as he imposes extreme virtuosic demands on the instrumentalists. This is a portion of the scintillating principal subject, initially introduced by second violins:

Brightest of the concerto's five movements, the finale is in *presto* tempo and, according to the composer, is intended to be symbolic of "life-assertion." Although lengthy, it is continually exuberant and concludes the work on an exciting and affirmative plane.

Selected Concertos
(*Including associated designs*)

Bach, Jøhann Sebastian (1685–1750)
  Brandenburg Concertos, Nos. 1–6 (1721). Fine Baroque concerti grossi with an individual scoring for each; all are well constructed, mostly homophonic, but occasionally polyphonic.
  Concerto No. 1 in D minor for Harpsichord (1730). One of seven, this has the pattern *allegro-adagio-allegro* and employs considerable rococo ornamentation to embellish its lines.
  Concertos No. 1 in A minor, and 2 in E major for Violin (1717–1723). Early solo works for violin, they employ continuo and are frequently motivic; each has three movements.
  Concerto in D minor for Two Violins (1717–1723). Based on a responsorial discourse between soloists, as well as violin-orchestra colloquy, this piece is often strikingly polyphonic.
Barber, Samuel (b. 1910)
  Concerto for Piano and Orchestra (1962). A splendid contemporary bravura piece with a three-movement plan; I is technically complex, II is a canzone, and III, the finale, unusual for being in quintuple meter; undoubtedly one of the era's best.
Bartók, Béla (1881–1945)
  Concerto for Orchestra (1943). An unsurpassed five-movement contemporary work that most effectively contrasts individual and sectional sonorities.
  Concerto No. 3 for Piano (1945). Austere (I), almost pious (II), and playful (III), this is a brilliant technical showcase for piano.
  Concerto No. 1 for Violin and Orchestra (1938). Often-performed and lyrical (for Bartók), it is harmonically astringent with a sturdy design; variation form (II).
Beethoven, Ludwig van (1770–1827)
  Concertos for Piano: No. 1 in C major (1797); No. 2 in B-flat major (1795); No. 3 in C minor (1803); No. 4 in G major (1808); and No. 5 in E-flat major, ("Emperor," 1809). Cornerstones in the piano repertoire, these

are strong, determined, and powerful works that employ the usual three-movement pattern: fast-slow-rondo. Founded on succinct motives or broad themes, they use conventional designs within movements to disclose a fine balance between soloist-orchestra; cadenzas are provided by the composer.

Concerto in D major for Violin (1806). One of the best in the literature, it has sonata form (I), variation form (II), and rondo form (III) movements that are lyric, but expressively strong and assertive.

Concerto in C major for Violin, 'Cello and Piano (1805). Written for a comparatively rare combination of instruments, it has a superb *largo* (II) and a polonaise in the finale.

Berg, Alban (1885–1935)

Concerto for Violin and Orchestra (1935). Expressionistic and dissonant, but occasionally sweet and lyric, it employs the usual pattern; architecturally, this piece is superb.

Boccherini, Luigi (1743–1805)

Concerto in B-flat major for 'Cello and Orchestra (c. 1790). Established in Classical-rococo style with a very ornate solo line, it has an excellent rondo (III) and is expressively warm and pleasant.

Brahms, Johannes (1833–1897)

Concertos No. 1 in D minor and No. 2 in B-flat major for Piano (1858–1881). Romanticism incarnate, the first has an extended three-movement design, whereas the second, in four movements, is more virtuosic; both are unusually songful.

Concerto in D major for Violin (1878). Sensitive and lyrical, it exhibits some elements of Hungarian flavor; mostly it is reflective, fervent, impassioned.

Concerto in A minor for Violin and 'Cello (1887). Venturing close to the concerto grosso plan it is sturdy (I), balladlike (II), and exuberant (III).

Bruch, Max (1838–1920)

Concerto No. 1 in G minor for Violin (1866). Often called a fantasie, it has a *vorspiel-adagio-finale* plan; founded on numerous long arching tunes, it is glowing and cheery.

Chopin, Frederic (1810–1849)

Concertos No. 1 in E minor and No. 2 in F minor for Piano (Both 1830). Romantic works that effectively exploit the piano, but minimize the orchestra, they are infused with lyricism, rubato, and astonishing bravura.

Copland, Aaron (b. 1900)

Concerto for Clarinet and Orchestra (1948). An unusual modern work with two movements (slow-fast) linked by an extended cadenza; it is tuneful and jazzy.

Corelli, Arcangelo (1653–1713)

Twelve concerti grossi (1712) (No. 8 is the "Christmas Concerto."). Consistently antiphonal, they are expressively chaste and abstract; all employ a concertino of two violins and 'cello.

Dvořák, Antonin (1841–1904)

Concerto in B minor for 'Cello (1895). Impassioned, sentimental, and robust, it employs many folk melodies and features a cyclic treatment of themes.

Concerto in A minor for Violin (1880). Flashingly violinistic and occasionally rhapsodic, it is based on an abundance of Czech tunes; the finale is a fine rondo.

Gershwin, George (1898–1937)
> Concerto in F major for Piano (1925). Cast in the American idiom of symphonic jazz, it is fresh, vital, and structurally fine.

Glazounov, Alexander (1867–1936)
> Concerto in A minor for Violin (1904). Permeated with Romantic melodies that are rhapsodic and occasionally epic, the work is unfailingly poetic and radiant.

Grieg, Edvard (1843–1907)
> Concerto in A minor for Piano (1868). Nostalgic, occasionally tempestuous, it is a popular Romantic concerto with numerous broad and flowing themes.

Handel, George Frideric (1685–1759)
> Twelve Concerti Grossi (1739). Contrasting two solo violins with strings, these pieces have multimovements (4, 5, 6) that are short, buoyant, and cleanly hewn.

> Three Concertos for Oboe (two in B-flat, c. 1740; one in G minor, c. 1703). Peerless works for a little-exploited instrument, they are suite-like in plan and modest in scope.

> Sixteen Concertos for Organ (1736, 1739). Written by and for the composer, they are notable Baroque solo works, somewhat irregular in form.

Haydn, Franz Joseph (1732–1809)
> Concerto in D major for 'Cello (1783). One in a set of six, it is a fine Classically oriented piece conceived on a relatively small scale.

> Concerto in E-flat major for Trumpet and Orchestra (1726). A stunning solo piece for a robust instrument that is technical (I and III), lyric (II), and always playful.

Honegger, Arthur (1892–1955)
> Concertino for Piano and Orchestra (1924). Pert, insouciant, and relatively short, it is technically adroit.

Kodály, Zoltan (1882–1967)
> Concerto for Orchestra (1940). Sturdy, piquant, and different, it exploits sectional sonorities and has an obvious Hungarian focus.

Lalo, Edouard (1823–1892)
> *Symphonie espagnole* for Violin and Orchestra (1875). Glowingly melodic, it delightfully exploits the Spanish-Gallic idiom; in five movements, it is extremely virtuosic.

Liszt, Franz (1811–1886)
> Concertos No. 1 in E-flat major (1857) and No. 2 in A major for Piano and Orchestra (revised 1856, 1861). Superb concertos by a master pianist; the first in four movements is song-like and rhapsodic, the second has a single movement and is fanciful and rather discursive.

MacDowell, Edward (1861–1908)
> Concertos No. 1 in A minor and No. 2 in D minor for Piano (1885, 1890). Written by a pioneering American composer, these are Romantic, flowing, but rather quaint pieces.

Mendelssohn, Felix (1809–1847)
> Concerto No. 1 in G minor for Piano (1831). Charming rather than brilliant, it is structurally clear, short, and almost Classic in outlook.

> Concerto in E minor for Violin (1844). Rapturous and Romantic, organized in three interconnected movements, it is consistently warm and melodic.

Mozart, Wolfgang Amadeus (1756–1791)

> Concerto in B-flat major for Bassoon (K. 191) (1774). Highlighting a little-exploited solo instrument, it employs a small orchestra and is dextrous (I), song-like (II), and agile (III).

> Concerto in A major for Clarinet (K. 622) (1791). A matchless Classic work that is persuasive, tuneful, elegant, and founded on unusually clear patterns.

> Concerto No. 1 in G major for Flute (K. 313) (1778). Graceful and Classic, its three sections are neat, delicate, and well-balanced.

> Concerto in C major for Flute and Harp (K. 299) (1778). Calm and serene, it suggests the French rococo style and features an unusual combination of solo instruments.

> Concertos Nos. 1, 2, 3, 4, for Horn (K. 412, 417, 447, 497) (1782–1786). Humorous, occasionally petulant, they are musically unproblematic but require a skilled executant.

> Concerto No. 20 in D minor for Piano (K. 466) (1785). Fervid, restless, and somewhat tragic, this enlarged work very effectively juxtaposes piano-orchestra sonorities.

> Concerto No. 24 in C minor for Piano (K. 491) (1786). Declamatory, poised, and sharp in outline (with a finale in variation-form), it stresses an enhanced role for the orchestra.

> Concerto No. 5 in A major for Violin ("Turkish") (K. 219) (1775). Folkish (for Mozart) and based on polyglot melodies, that is, Turkish, it is quite free and almost improvisational in outline.

Paganini, Niccolo (1782–1840)

> Concerto No. 1 in D major for Violin (1820). Packed with bravura and requiring a dazzling technique, this showcase has an abundance of ardent, fiery melodies.

Poulenc, Francis (1899–1963)

> Concert champêtre for Harpsichord (1928). A contemporary solo work that persuasively reaffirms a seventeenth-century French keyboard style; it is very tuneful with taut harmonies and sparkling sonorities.

> Concerto in G minor for Organ, Strings, Timpani (1938). Based on a single theme and cast in one movement with several subsections, it is stately and exuberant and adroitly emulates a Baroque fantasia.

Prokofiev, Serge (1891–1953)

> Concertos No. 1 in D-flat major (1911) and No. 3 in C major (1921) for Piano. Impressive contemporary works conceived within traditional outlines with flowing melodies, secure patterns, and brilliant passagework; they are glowing, boisterous, and tangy.

> Concertos No. 1 in D major (1913) and No. 2 in G minor (1935) for Violin. Conventional in outline but unique in content, the first is witty, melodic, and occasionally grotesque. The second is restrained, tender, and lyric. Both are logical and well-balanced.

Rachmaninoff, Serge (1873–1943)

> Concertos No. 1 in F-sharp minor (1891), No. 2 in C minor (1901), and No. 3 in D minor (1909) for Piano. Suggesting a late manifestation of musical Romanticism, these are discursive and rambling works founded

on sweeping melodies and involved piano passagework; they are perfervid but shallow.

Ravel, Maurice (1875–1937)

Concerto in D major for the Left Hand (1931). Written for a one-armed pianist and organized in a single subdivided movement, this is jazzy, improvisatory, and exceptional in content.

Concerto in G major for Piano and Orchestra (1931). Mozartean, but with a twentieth-century syntax, it is supple, vivacious, and syncopated.

Saint-Saëns, Camille (1835–1921)

Concerto No. 2 in G minor for Piano (1868). Requiring phenomenal fluency, this brilliant piece is buoyant, intense, and exciting.

Concerto No. 3 in B minor for Violin (1880). Charming and graceful, it has a lilting barcarolle (II), and a crisp-brusque finale (III).

Schoenberg, Arnold (1876–1951)

Concerto for Piano and Orchestra (1942). Employing the twelve-tone system, this one-movement piece with four subsections is mostly acrid and pungent in sonority but occasionally charming in appeal.

Schumann, Robert (1810–1856)

Concerto in A minor for 'Cello (1850). Smooth, Romantic, and dark in color, it has three integrated movements and is euphonious, touching, and sentimental.

Concerto in A minor for Piano (1845). Effusively Romantic, it is sweeping (I), pensive (II), and robust (III).

Sibelius, Jean (1865–1957)

Concerto in D minor for Violin (1903). Filled with rhapsodic passages that are mostly poetic and poignant, this solo work uses a unique kind of Nordic lyricism.

Stravinsky, Igor (b. 1882)

Concerto for Piano and Wind Orchestra (1924). Contrasting the piano with winds, basses, and timpani, this spectacular showcase is neoclassic in style and includes a toccata (I) and fugue (III).

Concerto in E-flat major ("Dumbarton Oaks," 1938). For fourteen instruments, this heavily contrapuntal piece in Baroque style has three linked movements; it is a fine example of the modern concerto grosso.

Tchaikowsky, Peter (1840–1893)

Concerto No. 1 in B-flat minor for Piano (1875). Lengthy, dynamic, and extremely digital, it is flamboyantly colorful; by turns it exults, glowers, and romps.

Concerto in D major for Violin and Orchestra (1881). Warm and passionate, it personifies Slavic melodism; architecturally excellent, it abounds with radiant allure.

Torelli, Giuseppe (1658–1709)

Concerti Grossi (1709). Probably the first published concerti grossi, they contrast two solo violins with other strings. They are antiquated but interesting.

Vivaldi, Antonio (1678–1741)

Numerous concertos for such instruments as bassoon, 'cello, flute, guitar, mandolin, and others, singly or in combination. Myriad and diverse, these pieces use various instrumental combinations; usually they are short, in three movements, and mostly motivic; historically important, they are now much in vogue.

The Four Seasons (c. 1700). Four descriptive works that use continuo, solo violin, and strings. Each is in three movements; quaint and lovely, they employ sectional forms and are among the earliest concertos in today's active repertoire.

Chapter 13

The Lyric Art: Song

Song is unquestionably man's oldest means of musical expression. Early in the span of human existence he learned to grunt, groan, screech, wail, and ultimately to sing as tribulation, anguish, exultation, sorrow, or pain pressed on him. And these impassioned utterances soon became a part of such rituals as fertility rites, burial observances, wedding festivals, and ceremonial dances. As centuries passed, song marched steadily forward, hand-in-hand with civilization's sociopolitical development. Whether in primitive society or the Atomic age, many of man's deeds, aspirations, innermost thoughts, prayers, love lyrics, and laments have been eloquently described in song.

Virtually everyone sings. Children are almost continually surrounded by song, and most quickly learn to imitate the rise and fall of tones, the flow of rhythm, and the enunciation of words. At home, in school, in social groups, around campfires, at the banquet table, or while riding in an automobile, both adults and children sing. It makes no difference whether their songs are silly or serious, whether the results are artistic or atrocious, or whether the pitch is true or uncertain. What really matters is that enjoyment, satisfaction, a sense of accomplishment, and gratifying emotional release almost invariably accompanies the act of singing.

Naturally, song literature differs considerably. From one age to another, from one society to another, from one nation to another, subjects treated in song, their mode of performance, and their syntax show distinctive traits. On the nature of primitive song, we can only speculate although ethnomusicologists are certain that it was (1) monophonic, (2) limited in compass, (3) vividly emotional, and (4) performed with a nasal resonance markedly different from today's normal voice timbre. Cantillation (the chanting of prayer texts) used in conjunction with worship in the old Hebrew Temple centuries before the birth of Christ is the first vocal activity described (very incompletely) in early documents, but even here very little is really known about its techniques or substance.

Early song was unquestionably "word-born," for its melody was formulated from a repetitious recitation of words. Words have a rhythm engendered by their syllabic sequence, and because some syllables are intuitively stressed while others remain comparatively quiescent when a text is declaimed, there is a natural tendency for a voice to rise or fall in pitch as it follows a poem's cadenced flow. When this occurs in a language richly endowed with speech inflections, song becomes a foreordained result.

FOLK SONG

In theory, folk melodies are the product of a people and are presumed to result from spontaneous creation by a group, but in fact this is rarely the case. A group does not create; masses of people accept, modify, and propagate, but they do not originate. However loosely construed, musical composition results from the efforts of a single individual with, perhaps, assistance from a collaborator. He may be a song leader who extemporizes in public or a temporary recluse working privately at home. But he is one person, not many.

Regardless of origin, folk songs are unique in their capacity to express the joys, sorrows, traditions, or aspirations of a people. Without fail, they convey deeply felt sentiments that the inarticulate can repeat with conviction. Rarely complex, florid, or esoteric, most folk songs are sturdy, direct, and comparatively simple. Many employ the musicotextual vocabulary of particular ethnic groups (for example, Gypsies, Cossacks, American Indians, southern Negroes); and, along with being surprisingly unsophisticated, their poetic material often uses such ingenuous nonsense syllables as fa-la-las, or ei-ei-os.

Most of the folk melodies well-known in modern times date from no earlier than the mid-nineteenth century, although their precursors (and the genre itself) extend backward over thousands of years. Until quite recently, most folk music existed as a kind of wild flower; it was a natural phenomenon, an art form loved and enjoyed by masses of people, but one that existed in a pristine state. Now this has changed, and folk melodies from various nations and cultures have been collected, edited, published, and issued on phonograph records. And lorists deeply interested in ethnic melodies of all kinds have become an important cult in contemporary musical life.[1]

PARTICULAR KINDS OF FOLK SONG

Because the folk song has been in existence for thousands of years, it has naturally come to enfold a wide diversity of material. Yet, particular

[1] Recorded examples of folk music are so numerous as to defy a meaningful listing here. Well-organized record catalogues (for example, Schwann's) will provide an abundance of helpful listening suggestions for the interested student.

kinds of song maintain an obvious appeal for successive generations. Love songs, narrative or epic songs, drinking songs, nursery and children's songs, work songs, songs of celebration, patriotic songs, songs of lament, and songs associated with dancing, for instance, penetrate the literature of every era. Of course the primacy each type attains varies from one culture, nation, or age to another; but their relative constancy shows a continuing human interest in certain basic aspects of life. None of these subjects is abstract or greatly removed from everyday living; instead, each reflects a concern with broadscale emotions—courtship and love, the lives and activities of children, national allegiance, work, play, worship, and finally, death. Obviously, this is a microcosm of life expressed in song, pertinent everywhere in the world.

During its long span of existence, folk song has never been scrupulously concerned over the sources of its text and/or tunes. Rarely fastidious or censorious, this facet of music does not deign to observe the laws of copyright or the niceties of plagiarism. Sometimes ribald, crude, and even uncouth, sometimes grim, heroic, or noble, folk song is the voice—*vox populi*—of a people.[2]

Within the incredibly rich trove of international folk songs these are notable types.

Ballads

Based on unsophisticated narrative poems that rarely display any measure of complexity but lean instead on an impersonal disclosure of notable events, ballads usually have a series of four-line stanzas separated by an interpolated refrain. Virtually all nations have a ballad literature, but their subjects differ considerably. In America, for instance, ballads commonly center on cowboys; such beneficent outlaws as Jesse James; folk heroes such as Casey Jones; outstanding events in the lives of mountain folk; or activities of southern Negroes. Many are entirely lacking in self-consciousness, and their scope of credibility may range from simple to fanciful. Full credence cannot be given historical tales described in ballads, for many contain errors in chronology of hundreds of years and reflect wild flights of imagination, wishful thinking, and unbridled ambition. Some well-known American ballads include "Sweet Betsy from Pike," "John Henry," "Barbara Allen," and "Tom Dooley." The text of "A Cowboy's Lament," taken from Carl Sandburg's *The American Songbag*, runs like this:

>   I. As I walked out in the streets of Laredo,
>   As I walked out in Laredo one day,

[2] Printed collections of folk songs are numerous. Some (Sandburg's *American Songbag*) are library items in hardcover. But *A Treasury of Folk Songs* by Sylvia and John Kolb (New York: Bantam Books, 1948); the *Burl Ives Song Book* and *Burl Ives Sea Songs* (New York: Ballantine Books, 1953) and the *Lancer Sing Along Song Book*, compiled by Robert Stein (New York: Lancer Books, 1961) are available in paperback and may warrant inclusion within your personal collection.

I spied a poor cowboy wrapped up in white linen,
Wrapped up in white linen as cold as the clay.

II. "I see by your outfit that you are a cowboy,"
These words he did say as I boldly walked by;
"Come sit down beside me and hear my sad story,
I'm shot in the breast and know I must die."

III. "Get six jolly cowboys to carry my coffin,
Get six jaunty maidens to sing me a song,
Take me to the valley and lay sod over me,
For I'm a young cowboy and know I've done wrong."

IV. "Oh, beat the drum slowly and play the fife lowly,
Play the dead march as you carry me along;
Put bunches of roses all over my coffin,
Roses to deaden the clods as they fall."

Work Songs and Chanteys

Burdensome tasks become lighter and weary hours pass more quickly when workers sing—a fact as well known to Phoenecian galley slaves as to modern industrial technicians. Consequently, a salty uninhibited song literature has grown out of the activities of prison work parties, longshoremen, lumbering crews, or track-laying gangs. Sea chanteys, associated with seafaring men physically engaged in hoisting canvas, swabbing decks, and unloading cargo also fall within this category. In many cases, work song texts are sung by a single individual who is interrupted at the end of each stanza when the full crew (or the group) interposes an unchanging refrain. "Blow the Man Down," "Pick a Bale of Cotton," "Cape Cod Chantey," and the "Night Herding Song" exemplify work songs of the sea, river levee, sailing vessel, and Great Plains. As a specific example, consider "The Drunken Sailor":

What shall we do with the drunken sailor,
What shall we do with the drunken sailor,
What shall we do with the drunken sailor,
Early in the morning?

Chorus: Hooray and up she rises,
Hooray and up she rises,
Hooray and up she rises,
Early in the morning!

Hymns

Although most hymns have a known authorship, the widespread practice of hymn singing—carried out at church services, camp meetings, or sim²lar religious observances—has given them a status nearly equivalent to folk song. Sung in the vernacular, hymns are regular in outline, predictably metric, based on religious poetry (which is sometime Scripturally oriented), and unfailingly inspiring. For untold generations they have brought solace into the lives of many. Hymn singing is a venerable practice, for history reports that early Christians adopted it from pre-existent Jewish worship, and succeeding generations have perpetuated its observance throughout the world. Many Protestant sects, especially those founded on the doctrines of Luther and Calvin, have made hymn singing a focal point in their ritual of worship. Among cherished hymns are "We Gather Together" (Old Dutch), "For the Beauty of the Earth" and "God of Our Fathers" (United States), "Faith of Our Fathers" and "Now the Day is Over" (English). "Nearer My God To Thee," a splendid American hymn, has words by Sarah Adams and music by Lowell Mason:

> Nearer, my God to Thee, nearer to Thee!
> Even though it be a cross that raises me
> Still all my song shall be, nearer, my God, to Thee,
> Nearer, my God, to Thee; nearer to Thee.

Carols

Generally comparable with hymns, carols have the distinction of being devoted to a narration of the Christmas story, although a few are concerned with Easter and other religious holidays. Carols are usually easy to sing, but some disclose considerable complexity as, for instance, Praetorius' "Lo How a Rose Ere Blooming" (seventeenth century). Virtually all Christian nations possess a trove of carols that makes an annual reappearance during the Christmas season, and among the international favorites are "Mary Had a Baby," "Silent Night," "Go Tell It on the Mountain," "O Tannenbaum," and "The First Noel." "Adeste Fideles," well-known the world over, has this text:

> O come all ye faithful, joyful and triumphant,
> O come ye, O come ye to Bethlehem.
> Come and behold Him, born the King of Angels;
> O come let us adore Him, O come let us adore Him,
> O come let us adore Him, Christ the Lord.

Spirituals

Closely associated with the socioreligious life of American Negroes, spirituals are often based on Scriptural subjects (treated, however, very freely), and many are devoted to Old Testament episodes concerned with oppression. Although particular spirituals are performed in a sentimental and melancholy manner, others have a lilt that is almost jazz-like. Spiritual singing is widely practiced throughout the United States, and its pieces are among the country's most authentic specimens of folk music. Included are "Joshua Fit The Battle," "Ezekiel Saw the Wheel," "Lonesome Road," "The Old Ark's A-Moverin'," "Wayfaring Stranger" and "Lonesome Valley." In "Go Down Moses" a Negro singer equates the Jewish captivity in Egypt with the bondage of his own race:

> When Israel was in Egypt's land,
>   Let my people go.
> Oppressed so hard they could not stand,
>   Let my people go.
> Go down, Moses, 'way down in Egypt's land;
>   Tell ole Pharaoh, Let my people go!

FOLK SONG IN COMPOSED SETTINGS

When the natural beauties of folk melody are blended with the more recondite techniques of formal composition, the "arranged" folk song results. More than an occasional employment, this practice has become increasingly prominent since the early nineteenth century. Some composers with an intuitive feeling for folk music (Dvořák, Grieg, Vaughan Williams, and Bartók, for example) have gained particular renown in this area. But others more generally acknowledged as art composers (Haydn, Beethoven, Chopin, and Brahms) have also compiled collections of folk melodies that effectively intermingle elements of both a native and a learned craft.

Representative of the folk songs that have been given art settings [3] (mostly with piano accompaniment) by well-known composers are:

1. *Twelve Irish and Scottish Songs* arranged by Beethoven and published in three volumes between 1814 and 1818. In his endeavors, the composer was stimulated by a Scottish office clerk, George Thompson (1757–1851), who commissioned him to arrange the melodies for violin, 'cello, piano, and voice. Earlier, Haydn had been engaged for a similar project.
2. *Deutsche Volkslieder* (German Folk songs), a collection of twenty-one songs arranged for voice and piano by Brahms and issued in 1894.
3. *Songs of the Auvergne*, twelve songs (others have also been arranged) indigenous to an agricultural area in south-central France, collected (in 1924) and scored for voice and orchestra by Joseph Canteloube (1879–1957).
4. *Seven Popular Spanish Songs*, melodies from a number of Spanish provinces arranged for voice and piano by Manuel de Falla in 1914.
5. *Folk Songs of the British Isles*, compiled in six volumes between 1943 and 1961 by Benjamin Britten. Concerned with native melodies from

---

[3] Less obviously folkish than many other pieces in this genre, Ravel's *Cinq mélodies populaires grecques* (1907) and *Deux mélodies hébraïques* (1914) are, nevertheless, based on authentic ethnic melodies.

France, Britain, and Ireland, they are arranged for voice and piano in books that contain from five to ten songs apiece.

Aaron Copland has gathered together two sets of *Old American Songs* that are certain to appeal to listeners in the United States. Compiled in 1950 and 1952, respectively, they were initially arranged for voice and piano and subsequently orchestrated. Splendid examples of musical Americana, their range of subjects extends from tangy minstrel tunes to soothing lullabies. A listing of titles gives an indication of their scope; but, of course, the songs must be heard to gain a full appreciation of their beauty:

1. "The Boatmen's Dance," a music-hall tune published in 1874 by Dan Emmett (who later wrote "Dixie").
2. "The Dodger," a political campaign song of the 1880s.
3. "Long Time Ago," a quiet, sentimental melody from unknown sources that was issued originally in 1837.
4. "Simple Gifts," a favorite song of the Shaker religious sect that dates from about 1837.
5. "I Bought Me a Cat," a nonsense tune of uncertain origin.
6. "The Little Horses," a pensive children's lullaby with a sweet and gentle melody.
7. "Zion's Walls," a pulsating and exciting tune initially used as a stimulant at revival meetings.
8. "The Golden Willow Tree," a narrative ballad.
9. "At the River," a hymn tune dated 1865.
10. "Ching-a-Ring-Chaw" another bumptious minstrel song mostly founded on nonsense syllables.

ART SONG

Characteristics separating art song from folk song are subtle but significant. For one thing, art songs have an acknowledged authorship and an obvious enrichment resulting from the artistic insight a trained composer brings to their creation. Even more important, however, is art song's alliance with lyric poetry, an association that provides this genre with tender, compassionate, and well-wrought texts. Lines in a folk song may be salty, crude, pious, or unbridled, but the poetry of art song is more generally sentimental, compassionate, and restrained. Although particular art songs may be satirical, dramatic, narrative, or humorous, most are gently suggestive and convey deeply felt sentiments.

Just as many other kinds of music have grown from this common root, art song emerged from folk song. But precisely how or when one kind of song gave way to the other is difficult to determine. In ancient Greece, for instance, singing was all-important in musical culture, and Greek bards were renowned for their prowess in creating pieces that may well have been the precursors of modern art song. But whether their works were, in fact, Hellenic equivalents of modern song is impossible to say, for extant fragments are so minuscule that reconstruction is out of the question. We do know, of course, that Greek poetry was superb.

Art song as we know it today reached a point of unquestioned excellence in Germany during the early nineteenth century. At this moment in history, a fortunate confluence of poets possessed of unusual gifts (Goethe, Schiller, Heine) and composers of uncommon lyric ability (Schubert, Schumann, and Brahms) produced a flowering that brought this lyric art to a pinnacle of rare beauty. As revealed in thousands of art songs (known in German as *lied*, plural *lieder*) written during this period, these pieces were conceived for a single voice, were based on excellent lyric poetry, and enlisted the piano as a coperformer (other instruments were occasionally employed). In time, three patterns were formulated: (1) *the strophic song*, a design that repeats the same melody (often a part-form pattern with sixteen, twenty-four, or thirty-two measures) for each poetic verse, as is shown in Schubert's "Hedge-Rose"; (2) *the modified strophic song*, similar to the foregoing except that it employs a different melody for particular portions of the poem, as is demonstrated in Schumann's "Two Grenadiers"; and (3) *the through-composed song* (known in German as *durchkomponiertes lied*), which is nonrepetitive in its musical line, as exemplified by Schubert's "Erlking." (Texts for these songs are quoted on pp. 342–344).

This was only a beginning for modern art song, however, for in subsequent years and in diverse nations an abundance of beautiful pieces appeared. Written for solo voice, many were greatly expanded to encompass a series of semi-independent pieces, some enlisted more than one instrument for accompaniment, and others were developed to the extent of requiring a full orchestra for support.

THE SONG CYCLE

Few art songs take longer than several minutes to perform. Because the emotional imagery of lyric poetry has an almost searing intensity, it must be quickly and succinctly expressed before its poignancy is consumed. Consequently, art songs usually have the distinctive characteristics of brevity and intimacy. Other kinds of verse have a greater breadth, however; their subjects are more expansive and their language is more rhetorical. Narrative or epic poetry, for instance, requires an enlarged pattern when set to music. To meet their demands, as well as to serve a craving for artistic expansion, the *song cycle*—really a series of songs on related topics—was formulated.

Characteristically, a song cycle has the additive properties of a suite, for it unites a succession of disparate pieces under a single heading. Typically, these differ in meter, tempo, melody, key, structure, and text. Each song in a cycle—whose number cannot be precisely specified, for works exist that include from six to twenty-four or more pieces—is autonomous. Yet, these several pieces are also associated, for each deals with a particular aspect of an integrated text. Like individual members in a social community, these associated songs assist in creating an edifice greater than themselves.

Robert Schumann's *Frauenliebe und Leben* (Woman's Love and Life) with eight songs based on a poem by Adelbert von Chamisso, is a fine example of the song cycle. Within it, individual songs tell of a woman's devotion to her beloved. In succession they describe such events as courtship, marriage, and motherhood, to ultimately conclude this miniature drama with the sadness of bereavement. Here is a listing of pieces within the cycle:

1. "Ever Since I Saw Him"—a buoyant piece describing the thrill of early infatuation.
2. "He, of All Mankind"—a glowing description of her beloved's many fine qualities.
3. "I Can't Believe It"—expressing disbelief that she has been found worthy of marriage.
4. "O Ring Upon My Finger"—a warmly expressed promise to dutifully assume mature responsibilities.
5. "Help Me, Dear Sisters"—concerned with eager preparations for marriage.
6. "Dearest Man"—reflective of the exuberant joy of approaching motherhood.
7. "Here at My Breast"—vividly expressing the parental delight experienced when a boy is born.
8. "Now You Have Hurt Me"—pensively recounting the final anguish a woman feels when her beloved dies.

Prior to the early nineteenth century, song cycles were little known. Then, in short order, the form reached a point of unusual excellence at the hands of such composers as Beethoven, Schubert, and Schumann. These are the important cycles they wrote:

1. Ludwig van Beethoven: *An die ferne Geliebte* (To a Distant Beloved, 1816), a collection of six songs based on poetry by Aloys Jeitteles.
2. Franz Schubert: *Die Winterreise* (The Winter Journey, 1827), twenty-four songs founded on a poem by Wilhelm Muller. *Die schone Mullerin* (The Maid of the Mill, 1823), twenty songs also on Muller texts.
3. Robert Schumann: *Liederkreis* (that is, song cycle, 1840), nine songs on Heinrich Heine texts. *Liederkreis* (1842), twelve songs based on poems by Josef Eichendorff. *Frauenliebe und Leben* (A Woman's Love and Life, 1840), eight songs on poetry by Adelbert Chamisso. *Dichterliebe* (A Poet's Love, 1844), sixteen songs based on Heine texts.

Other examples of the song cycle are mentioned at the end of this chapter.

THE ORCHESTRAL SONG

Essentially an intimate utterance, song differs in many ways from such musicodramatic works as opera and oratorio. Always the lone singer has remained important in song presentation, and early bards—as well as such successors as the troubadours, trouvères, minnesingers, or meistersingers— implemented this singleness by accompanying themselves on a lute or similar instrument. When the German lied attained an apogee in the nine- teenth century, song characteristically became united with the piano, and two musicians (singer and pianist) became partners in performance.

As Romanticism entered its second phase sometime after 1830, how- ever, the *orchestral song*—which substitutes richly hued instrumental sono- rities for the piano's monochromatic and somewhat acrid timbre—came into being. Hector Berlioz, a French musician with a ready fund of imaginative ingenuity, was one of the first to experiment along these lines. His *Nuits d'été* (Summer Nights), a set of six pieces for solo voice and orchestra based on texts by Théophile Gautier, was begun in 1843. But after composing the first song, entitled "Absence," Berlioz laid the project aside until 1856 when he completed the remaining five. Berlioz's cycle was not without precursors, however, for during an earlier period other similarly conceived pieces had been issued. Beethoven's *Ah, perfido!* (1796), for instance, although unmis- takably aimed toward the theater and called, in fact, a scena is one example. And Mozart's concert arias are others.

Orchestral songs have some of the cycle's external characteristics. Most include a number of independent songs (from three to six or seven is usual) that succeed one another in an orderly sequence. Over-all continuity is maintained by the text's narrative discourse, but musically and structurally each song has distinctive qualities. Any of the art song's three organizational patterns may be used, but the through-composed type with its "endless melody" is particularly well suited to this enlarged form. A fine example of orchestral song appears in Gustave Mahler's *Lieder eines fahrenden Gesellen* (Songs of a Wayfarer, 1883), for which the composer created both words and music. Suggesting melancholic resignation, it tells a sad tale of un- requited love. These are its words:

I. *On My Love's Wedding Day*

It will be a sad day when my beloved marries,
For then I shall go into a dark room and mourn.
Flowers bloom, and birds sing in the meadow.
How beautiful is the world! But for me they bloom and sing no more.
The time of spring is past, and there is no more singing.
When I go to sleep I shall think only of sorrow.

II. *Today I Walked Across the Field*

Today, walking across the fields, I found dew on the grass.
Happy birds sang good morning to me.
Truly the world is beautiful, and everyone sings!
Bluebells are swinging their heads in the fields,
And the world is filled with sunshine.
Music, flowers, and birds are washed by the golden sun.
It is a happy world, but will happiness ever come to me?
No! I know it will never come.

III. *A Sharpened Dagger*

A sharpened dagger cuts deep into my breast,
And fills me with the pain and joy of happiness.
Why must I endure this cruelty? It never stops.
When I look to the heavens I see two blue eyes;
As I walk in the fields I see golden tresses.
When I am awake, I hear only her happy laughter.
I wish I were dead, never to open my eyes again!

IV. *My Love's Two Blue Eyes*

My love's two blue eyes send me roaming through the world,
And I must say farewell to my beloved land.
Why did you ever look toward me? Now I am torn by remorse.
At night I roam the dark countryside, but no one bids me adieu.
My only companions are love and despair.
On the highway I found peace in sleep under a tree.
Blossoms fell on me, and I was happy again.

WAYPOSTS IN ART SONG DEVELOPMENT

Early Song

Abundant literary documents attest the skill and inventive power of Greek poets (many of whom were also musicians), but only such fragments as (1) two "Hymns to Apollo" (mid second century B.C.), engraved in stone at Delphi; (2) "Seikilos' Song" (second or first century B.C.); and (3) Mesomede's "Three Hymns" to Helios, Nemesis, and the Muse (second century A.D.) remain as bona-fide examples of the Greek's extensive musical practice. Subsequently, of course, Rome became the center of cultural and political life. Music in this city on the Tiber, as well as throughout the Empire, was derived from Greek models, and it may have flourished as extensively here as in Hellas, but again a cloak of more than a thousand years hides tangible evidence. Only religious chant, utilized in the early Christian Church, continues to exist into our time.

And so it was with virtually all other music created during a span that extends from the early Christian era through the late Middle Ages. People lived and died, they fought and tilled the soil, they worshipped God and raised children; inevitably they must have danced and sung. But meaningful evidence of their musical proclivities is so fragmentary as to be merely suggestive. Treatises dealing with musical theory, however, some dating from Grecian times, have been handed down to us and reveal the penetrating work of astute scholars. Ranging from Aristoxenos of Tarentum (fourth century B.C.), including Boethius (c. A.D. 500), and extending to Guido of Arezzo (c. 995–1050), theoreticians studied music carefully and established its scholarly aspects in sufficient depth to warrant the subject's inclusion within the curricula of medieval universities. Along with arithmetic, geometry, and astronomy, music became a part of the *quadrivium* (mathematical arts), as distinct from the *trivium* (rhetorical arts), which included grammar, dialectics, and rhetoric.[4]

Folk music flourished everywhere. In village and castle, field and forest, tavern and home, people played on crude instruments, moved in stylized dances, and sang. Mostly their music was gay and spirited—pictorial illustrations and prose writings tell us this—but sometimes it was meditative and profound as singers pondered aloud the verities of life. Few examples of this literature have been preserved, for medieval minstrels were unlettered men, unable to write even in the simple, crude, and inexact notation of the time. Song of this era was an oral art, passed from one generation to another by word of mouth, and in this casual transmittal much was inevitably lost, transformed, or corrupted. Only a few specimens of medieval secular music —inscribed, oddly enough, by priestly hands—have been preserved in monastery libraries, repositories that were comparatively free from the sack and destruction of that troublous period. These songs are not in the least religious; indeed, some are surprisingly ribald as they narrate witty tales about uninhibited human behavior.

Much early secular music was carried from one community to another by mendicant songsters who roamed the countryside as itinerant musicians. In an age (between the tenth and thirteenth centuries) when human communication was difficult if not impossible, these peripatetics were welcome guests at manor houses, castles, taverns, and homes; they brought news, gossip, entertainment, and that touch of cosmopolitanism inevitably acquired by constant travel. Others, the *goliards*, who were more learned and better trained than these itinerants, became active sometime during the tenth century, and practiced song creation on a more complex scale. Goliards and *jongleurs* (the latter term indicative of professional status), were expected to create and perform songs on the spur of a moment. Although the accompaniments they extemporized on the lute or an associated

---

[4] Fascinating excerpts from treatises written during these and later times are included in Oliver Strunk's *Source Readings in Music History* (New York: W. W. Norton & Co., Inc., 1950), available in paperback.

string instrument while singing were quite simple, the general artistic capabilities of these songsters should not be underestimated.

Sometime after 1150,[5] a subsequent bardic movement arose that kept secular music alive during a period when arts and letters were not otherwise cultivated. As the movement attained ever-widening scope, these men (there were also a few women within their ranks) sang of love, courtship, and marriage; but later efforts turned toward more recondite subjects as the craft of minstrelsy became increasingly complex.[6]

During these centuries, thousands of songs were created. Most were irretrievably lost, but some, particularly German pieces, were collected in *liederbucher* (songbooks). Among the most significant of these documents are the *Lochamer Liederbuch* (1450); the *Glogauer Liederbuch* (1460); and the *Münchner Liederbuch* (1460), each of which contains sizeable numbers of fifteenth-century monophonic folk songs, many fine examples of early part songs, some canons, and numerous dances.

Up until the end of the thirteenth century, most songs—secular as well as sacred—were sung in Latin, but later vernacular languages became more widely employed. Unaccompanied sacred songs, *laudi spirituali*, were widely used in Italy, whereas similar works, known as *cantigas*, were favorites in Spanish lands. Secular songs of the time were variously identified as *ballades, ballatas, madrigals, rondeau,* or *virelais*.[7] Particularly important among the composers of late Renaissance song were such Burgundians as Guillaume Dufay and Gilles Binchois; such Englishmen as John Dowland, Thomas Morley, and William Byrd; and such Franco-Italians as Guillaume Machaut and Francesco Landini.

Lines of demarcation between solo and part songs were seldom observed during this era, for many pieces could be performed by a lone singer or a group. For instance, the *frottola*—a strophic Italian song based on an amorous text—was often performed in a harmonized version with three or four parts, but it could also be given by a solo voice with lute accompaniment. And a similar circumstance pertained with the madrigal. Organizational patterns in these pieces were symmetric and uncomplicated, and most followed a plan somewhat akin to the later strophic design. Textual matter was often amatory, but songs could, on occasion, relate deeds of valor, chivalry,

[5] Minstrels of the Middle Ages and Renaissance were known at various times and in diverse lands as trouvères (northern France during the twelfth and thirteenth centuries); troubadours (Provence from the eleventh to the thirteenth centuries); minnesingers (Germany and Austria from the twelfth to the fourteenth centuries); and meistersingers (Germany in the fifteenth and sixteenth centuries). All were poets and musicians who created and performed pieces that were direct forerunners of the art song.

[6] Samples of this song literature are included in: (1) *Masterpieces of Music Before 1750* (a trouvère song, *Or la truix*, from the twelfth century and a minnelied, *Willekommen Mayenschein*, from the thirteenth century); (2) *A Treasury of Early Music* (a troubadour canso by Bernart de Ventadorn, who died in 1195, entitled *Be m'an perdut*); and (3) the *Music Scores Omnibus* (*O Roma nobilis*, a goliard song).

[7] Again, interesting examples are included within the collections mentioned previously.

or adventure. Distinctions between secular and sacred pieces (aside from obvious divergences in text) were hardly noticeable, for the melodic lines, modes, and scales in secular music were greatly influenced by the Church's musical practice.

Song from 1500 to 1800

As the Renaissance flowered, so, too, did the vocal craft. True, wandering minstrels had passed from the scene, but songs introduced by the troubadours, trouvères, minnesingers, and meistersingers continued to persist in memory. Taking the place of yesteryear's redoubtable bards were "gentlemen" who cultivated the fine art of minstrelsy with the same eager passion they displayed toward swordsmanship, geographic exploration, and courtship. Consequently, in France, England, and Italy, solo and concerted vocal music flourished in an age when instruments had not yet attained mechanical perfection. And it was then (c. 1500–1600) that such kinds of polyphonic song as the *frottola, villota, villanella, ballett,* and *falala* flourished, particularly in Italy.

In the growth of Western music, three forces exerted a significant influence on the development of song: (1) the establishment of a musical liturgy within the Christian Church that was primarily derived from Oriental and Near Eastern sources—that is, the Hebrew Synagogue; (2) adherence to a feudal system of government that gave both master and servant some degree of security and an opportunity to cultivate the leisure art of music-making; and (3) the formulation of opera (c. 1600) and associated designs and the ascendency it gave monody over previously used polyphony.

How monody and polyphony continued to coexist is shown, for instance, in the works of Giulio Caccini a well-known operatic composer, who published a collection of songs entitled *Nuove musiche* in 1602 which effectively demonstrated the close liaison existent between these two kinds of writing.[8] Subsequently, Peri, Monteverdi, and Alessandro Scarlatti demonstrated a similar proficiency.

Despite the importance that art song had now attained almost everywhere in Europe, its significance in Germanic lands was matched, and even surpassed, by the *volkslied* (folk song). Some of the latter were religious, many were secular, some were of venerable age, while others were newly composed. All, however, became unusually popular. Among northern composers of volkslieder Heinrich Issac is especially notable, and his lovely *Innsbruch ich muss dich lassen* (Innsbruch, I Must Leave Thee) is a fine example of what these pieces are like.

Then, as years passed (from c. 1600–1800) such large-scale vocal works as Masses, cantatas, oratorio, and, of course, opera flourished (as did instrumental music), but song writing declined. Haydn and Mozart, outstanding

---

[8] As a song writer, however, Caccini had been anticipated in Elizabethan England by John Dowland who published his epochal *First Book of Songs* in 1597.

composers during the second half of the eighteenth century, were active in a multitude of musical tasks, but song occupied them little. In his magnificent corpus of works, for instance, Mozart wrote only two notable songs, *Abend-empfindung* (An Evening Song) and *Das veilchen* (The Violet). Opera had now become a cynosure of attention. It was discussed, praised, or ridiculed, but it could not be ignored. Subsequently, during the century of Romanticism, the stylistic pendulum swung in a more evenly balanced arc, and song once again attained a position of prominence.

Song During the Nineteenth Century

Unquestionably, the most important era of art song development coincided with a rise of musical Romanticism, and from 1810 to 1890, while this movement blazed with feverish intensity, composers created an abundance of unusually beautiful pieces. Germany became a focal point for this renascence, and here the lied rose to a state of near perfection. Fortunately, the period had an abundance of such lyric poets as Friedrich Gottlieb Klopstock (1724–1803); Johann Wolfgang Goethe (1749–1832); Joseph Christoph Schiller (1759–1805); William Wordsworth (1770–1850); Samuel Taylor Coleridge (1772–1834); Joseph Eichendorf (1788–1857); Wilhelm Muller (1794–1827); and Heinrich Heine (1797–1856).[9] And as a corollary, the comparative state of perfection the piano had attained by this time became significant. Songs of the Renaissance had employed a lute to support the voice, and although it was monochromatic and rather weak in sonority, this instrument's gentle suggestiveness made it most acceptable for song accompaniment. Succeeding epochs shifted the emphasis somewhat and used such keyboard instruments as the virginal, clavichord, harpsichord, and even the organ to support the voice. But the piano proved to be ideal for song accompaniment. Remarkably versatile, it could articulate tones in a phenomenal manner, and had more than sufficient sonority to match any solo voice. Consequently, most Romantic songs came to rely very heavily on the instrument. Many begin with a short piano introduction and conclude with an appropriate postlude. Moreover, the instrument is used throughout to provide occasional interludes and underscore a text's emotional substance with colorful harmonies and invigorating rhythms.

Franz Schubert, who was one of music's most peerless composers of song, lived only briefly past the age of thirty but wrote over six hundred songs (656 is given as the definitive number). He had a musical instinct that can only be compared with Mozart's and a penchant for poetry that enabled him to read a poem, perceive its innermost substance, and set it to music with incredible facility. Contemporaries report that Schubert's reading a poem was tantamount to composing a song; one grew directly out of the other. Despite this copiousness, however, he was rarely redundant in song

[9] Verses by such earlier poets as Shakespeare, Dante, Tasso, Villon, and numerous other non-Germans were also used.

composition, for his fertile mind was capable of creating songs hour after hour without resorting to stereotype or formalism. For him, each piece was an individual creation, and he scrupulously avoided clichés absorbed from himself or another composer. The content and forms of his great cycles— *Die Winterreise* (the Winter Journey) and *Die schöne Müllerin* (The Maid of the Mill)—are charged with depth, beauty, and individuality. And such shorter jewel-like pieces as *Der Erlkönig* (Erlking), *Gretchen am Spinnrade* (Margaret at the Spinning Wheel), or *Der Tod und das Madchen* (Death and the Maiden) are miniature masterpieces infused with subtle intensity, joyous brio, or profundity touched with shadow.

Beethoven and Schubert were approximate contemporaries, but they viewed music from a different perspective. A man of profound intellect, Beethoven had little patience for banalities and caprice; consequently, his songs are mostly concerned with a penetrating study of human emotion. He searched carefully and critically for texts (a similar quest was devoted to obtaining suitable opera librettos) and discovered satisfactory poems in the works of such gifted German writers as Goethe, Schiller, and the earlier Gottfried Burger (1747–1794); Heinrich Holty (1748–1776); and J. H. Voss (1751–1826). Beethoven's best-known songs are *Adeliade,* an impassioned love song based on a poem by Matthisson; *An die ferne Geliebte* (To A Distant Beloved),[10] with poetry by Jeitteles; *Ah, perfido!,* a *scena* that presages the orchestral song; and the catchy "Scottish Songs," arrangements of Celtic folk melodies for voice, piano, violin, and 'cello.

Lieder by Robert Schumann are much in accord with Schubertian traditions. Founded on a revelation of strong personal emotion, they are sensitive musicopoetic jewels that bring the art song to new levels of expressiveness. Most of Schumann's predecessors refrained from displaying strong personal involvement in their songs; they tended to assume a detached attitude, occupying, as it were, the role of a narrator who offered commentaries on human existence. But Schumann, like the poets whose texts he used, was concerned about his place in the continuum of human existence, his emotions, and his reactions to the demands of life. And he was not the least reluctant to express these sentiments in song. In a sense, Schumann was an emancipator. He made far more extensive use of declamation than had previously been the case and provided piano accompaniments that forcefully and eloquently limned the text of a song. And in passages for piano alone, he expressed poetic ideals in purely musical terms. Schumann's songs are numerous and widely diverse in substance, length, and expression. Among them are *Du Bist wie eine Blume* (You are Lovely as a Flower); *Die Lotosblume* (The Lotus Flower); *Fruhlingsnacht* (Spring Night), and *Die beiden Grenadiere* (The Two Grenadiers). His superb cycles include *Dichterliebe* (A Poet's Love), two sets of *Liederkreis* (that is, song cycle), and *Frauenliebe und Leben* (A Woman's Life and Love).

[10] A work that is one of Romanticism's earliest song cycles.

Few Romanticists ignored the song, despite a penchant many had for the larger forms. Hector Berlioz and Franz Liszt, for instance, are notable for their expansive orchestral compositions, but they also turned occasionally to writing small lyric miniatures. Berlioz's songs have a rare and gentle beauty, and his orchestral cycle *Nuits d'été* is a most provocative work. Liszt's songs are not often heard today, but several reveal unexpected pools of poetic depth. Contemporaneously, from 1850–1875, Robert Franz (1815–1892),[11] Peter Cornelius (1824–1874), and Edvard Grieg[12] were also active as composers of excellent lieder.

Johannes Brahms' serious intent, keen perceptiveness, and compassionate outlook on human affairs enabled him to bring a nobility to the song found nowhere else save in the pieces of Beethoven. After studying the songs of Schubert and Schumann (he was a close friend of the latter), Brahms began to compose works based on these proven models. In all, he wrote 197 songs, which, for the most part, are comparatively short, have regular outlines, and are organized in strophic patterns. Well acquainted with folk art, (e.g., the forty-nine *Deutsche volkslieder*), Brahms occasionally incorporated native melodies within sets of songs. Most of his composed songs feature broad themes enriched by opulent harmonies that are balanced by beautifully conceived contrapuntal lines. Special interest rests with their piano introductions and concluding passages, for these often contain, in germinal form, important musical ideas on which the piece is founded. Among Brahms' better-known songs are *Am Kirchof* (In the Churchyard); *Vier ernste Gesange* (Four Serious Songs); *Feldeinsamkeit* (In Fields of Summer); *Immer leise wird mein Schlummer* (May Your Slumber Be Gentle); and *Vergebliches Standchen* (The Futile Song).

Croats, Slavs, Poles, Letts, and other European ethnic groups possess a priceless legacy in their native music. Hence, it was inevitable that Romanticists active in Bohemia and the general Balkan area should become concerned with art song. One of these was Antonin Dvořák, an unusually facile musician with rare melodic gifts. Markedly influenced by folk music, Dvořák carried his penchant for warm, flowing melody into song—qualities that are delightfully exemplified, for instance, in the strikingly beautiful "Songs My Mother Taught," from a collection called *Seven Gypsy Songs* (1880).

Many Russian composers of this and later generations created songs in emulation of German writers (Schubert, Schumann, Brahms), and lyric pieces by Tchaikowsky ("None but the Lonely Heart"), Alexander Gretchaninoff ("Cradle Song"), Alexander Glazounov, or Serge Rachmaninoff reveal the lied's pervasive influence. Theirs was a learned craft, little concerned with native lore. But songs by Modest Mussorgsky, some carefree

---

[11] Whose "Dedication," and "To Music" are delightful.

[12] Best-known in this area for *Ich liebe dich,* he was actually a prodigious song writer.

and joyous, others weighted with melancholy, are more genuinely reflective of the Russian temperament. Among the better-known of his sixty art songs are "The Seminarist," "A Garden by the Don," such cycles as *The Nursery* (seven songs), *Sunless* (six songs), and his extremely touching *Songs and Dances of Death* (four songs). In actuality, Mussorgsky was little concerned with lyric sentimentality; to him song was an expression of life's vagaries, particularly as the uncertainties of human existence affected common folk. Always intense and effective, his art is occasionally so barbaric as to appear crude.

Three song composers brought the golden age of lieder to a close and, at the same time, opened a way into the new century. Richard Strauss, Hugo Wolf, and Gustav Mahler—heirs to the mantle of German musical Romanticism—were richly endowed in many ways. Unusually versatile, Strauss wrote stunning instrumental and operatic scores that literally set the musical world agog, but he was also a superb lyricist whose songs place much emphasis on music's harmonic and rhythmic implications. Seemingly little concerned with an unfoldment of symmetric melodic lines, their musico-poetic image may appear to be episodic and disjointed, but many have a sparkling countenance, a charming exuberance, or a profoundly deep level of poignance. Wolf's compositional output was almost totally centered on song. Strongly influenced by Richard Wagner, he lived a short, hectic, and tragic life. But like Schubert before him, Wolf possessed a poetic instinct that enabled him to create songs with an artistry comparable only to the earlier master. Restless, tortured, and occasionally convoluted, they have a punctilious concern for structure and are unfailingly strong, vital, and forceful in expression. Noted as a virtuoso conductor, Mahler wrote songs, some scored for orchestra, that express deeply felt emotions. His *Des knaben wunderhorn* (The Youth's Magic Horn), *Kindertotenlieder* (Songs on the Death of Children), and *Lieder eines fahrenden Gesellen* (Songs of a Wayfarer) seem to be based on a folkish musical language, yet they rarely employ actual folk melodies. Nearly every one is a gem, rich in sentiment and deeply expressive of profound human compassion.

Song in the Twentieth Century

Appropriately enough, the "new music" of such composers as Arnold Schoenberg, Alban Berg, and Paul Hindemith (all of Germanic descent) was used to create songs startlingly different from their Romantic predecessors. Schoenberg's pieces, as exemplified in the cycle *Pierrot Lunaire* (1912) for instance, are so unusual as to appear bizarre. Based on twenty-one short poems by Albert Giraud, this set uses *sprechstimme* (that is, a semi-declamatory speaking voice) as well as five players who perform on eight instruments via doubling to convey a discourse that has been a petrel of controversy since the day of its composition. Eerie, exotic, but startlingly evocative, this work is a landmark in twentieth-century composition. Schoenberg's *Book of the Hanging Gardens* (1907), however, an earlier cycle of fifteen songs for voice and piano based on poems by Stefan George, is comprised of jewel-like miniatures (each piece takes less than two minutes to perform). More lyric than pieces in *Pierrot Lunaire,* its songs are avant-garde works that are almost spellbinding in evocative beauty. Berg's songs, too, are unusual. Along with being piquant, and occasionally shockingly dissonant, they are lyric and gracious. Particularly so, are the *Altenberg Lieder,* five humorous vignettes based on picture postcard texts. Berg's *Der Wein* (1930), a sweeping concert aria for voice and orchestra is conceived along the epic lines of Beethoven's *Ah, perfido!,* but his *Seven Early Songs,* written between 1905–1908, are more modest in scope. Hindemith's great contribution to the song repertoire is a vast cycle *Das Marienleben* (Song of Mary), originally written in 1923 and extensively revised in 1948. Based on a sequence of fifteen poems by Ranier Maria Rilke, it is probing in metaphysical content, angular in melodic contour, and extremely difficult to perform. *Herodiade* (1944), a verse drama for narrator and chamber orchestra (wind quintet, string quintet, and piano), is based on three occult poetic fragments from the writings of Stephane Mallarmé. Unusual in syntax, its rhythmic flow clings to the syllabic progression of the text, which the voice declaims while avoiding any tendency to break into the sustained lyricism of song.

A climate warmly receptive to song had been established in France during the late nineteenth century through the efforts of Gabriel Fauré (1845–1924) and Henri Duparc (1848–1933). Subtly allusive, gently poetic, and exquisitely expressive, the French *chanson* (art song) is beautifully exemplified by Fauré's cycle *La Bonne Chanson* (1892). Similarly conceived, Duparc's songs represent the writing of a specialist whose output was almost exclusively contained within this idiom. His *l'Invitation au Voyage,* founded on a poem by Baudelaire, is particularly representative. But to attain its fullest flowering, the chanson had to await the arrival of Claude Debussy, a musician endowed with remarkable individuality. All of Debussy's forty-eight songs appear to be episodic and extremely fragile, but they have an inner strength, spacious melodic arcs, and richly variegated harmonic hues that make them evocative in the highest degree. Virtually all are based on the vague evanescence of Impressionistic verse. Exemplificative are *Ariettes oubliées* (1888), a setting of six poems by Verlaine; *Proses Lyriques* (1893), four songs based on Debussy's own poetry; *Chansons de Bilitis* (1897), founded on the poetry of Pierre Louys, and *Three Ballades to Poems of François Villon.*

Maurice Ravel's songs are somewhat less Impressionistic. Often taut, terse, and laconic, they are unfailingly whimsical, sardonic, and witty. Where Debussy is distant, poetic, and suggestive, Ravel tends to be precise, punctilious, and explicit. His *Cinq mélodies populaires grecques* (Five Popular Greek Songs, 1907), *Deux mélodies hébraïques* (Two Hebrew Songs, 1914), and *Chansons madecasses* (Songs of Madagascar, 1926), for instance, charmingly combine the exoticism of folk melodies with the erudite opulence of art song. And his *Don Quichotte à Dulcinée* (1932), a humorous setting of the timeless Cervantes classic for solo voice and piano, as well as *Shéhérazade* (1903), a dazzling orchestral song, are infused with rare depth, beauty, and tonal radiance.

In England, Ralph Vaughan Williams became an exemplar of twentieth-century song writing whose pieces merge gracious melodism with the ineffable loveliness of English poetry. Vaughan Williams was an ardent lorist who collected and edited much British folk music; consequently, it was all but inevitable that strains of ethnic tunes would occasionally appear in his songs. Particularly notable among them is a cycle, *On Wenlock Edge*, based on Housman's poem "A Shropshire Lad," which he scored for tenor voice, piano, and string quartet. England's younger generation of song composers is ably represented by Benjamin Britten, whose sensitivity for vocal lyricism is eloquently demonstrated in the *Serenade for Tenor* (voice), *Horn, and Strings* (1943); the esoteric *Les Illuminations* for solo voice and orchestra (based on the poetry of Rimbaud); six *Songs from the Chinese* (1958), and a sizeable collection of *Folk Song Arrangements* (from France, England, and Ireland) for voice and piano.

Although song writers in France, Germany, Russia, England, and the United States tend to dominate the field during the modern era, composers in Latin lands, Italy and Spain, have not been idle. Ottorino Respighi can be considered Italy's best-known representative. His *Il tramonto*, for soprano and quartet (1918) is a full-bodied lyric work more akin to the solo cantata than art song, but many of his individual songs show the indisputable melodic gifts often associated with Italian composers. Spain's best-known song composer in this period is Manuel de Falla. Particularly adept at expressing fascinating folk idioms within lyric works, Falla aptly demonstrated his craft when he combined the pristine melodic flow of ethnic tunes with sophisticated harmonies and accompaniment in his *Seven Popular Spanish Songs* (1914).

Still in the process of formulation, an idiomatic art song literature is nevertheless beginning to flourish in America. Springing from heterogeneous sources, American song has tended to grow along imitative lines. Shortly after 1850, Stephen Collins Foster emerged as a figure of talent who might have laid the foundations for an enduring literature in the United States but he was, unfortunately, short-lived. Subsequently, Ethelbert Nevin, Edward MacDowell, and Oley Speaks appeared as a second generation of song composers. Their works are pretty rather than significant, however, and few possess enduring qualities. In the popular field—an apparent American specialty—Jerome Kern, George Gershwin, W. C. Handy, and Irving Berlin are only a few among the hundreds who have contributed prolifically to swell the stream of American popular music.[13]

America's great promise in twentieth-century song writing unquestionably rests in the hands of such men as Aaron Copland (*Twelve Poems of Emily Dickinson*); Samuel Barber (*Hermit Songs*); Roy Harris ("Abraham Lincoln Walks At Midnight"); Charles Ives (selected songs including "At The River," "At Sea," "In Summer Fields"); Silvestre Revueltas, a Mexican composer (*Five Songs of Childhood*); Heitor Villa-Lobos, a Brazilian ("The Crab Song"); and Igor Stravinsky ("In Memoriam, Dylan Thomas").[14] Strong in individuality, continually affirmative in their viewpoints, wise and experienced in the ways of poetry and music, they write with a sure and steady skill. Around them have grown the experimentalists, Lukas Foss (*Song of Songs*, 1947; *Time Cycle*, 1960); Luciano Berio (*Circles,* based on e. e. cummings); and Luigi Nono (*Polifonica*) who use avant-garde techniques to attain an ultimate in newness. From the efforts of these men and others, song in the United States (and elsewhere throughout the world, for that matter) continues to flourish in our time as one of music's most richly communicative facets.

PARTICULAR EXAMPLES OF SONG

Franz Schubert (1797–1828): Three Songs

Life did not last long for Franz Peter Schubert, son of a schoolmaster, nor was his existence easy. Money was always in short supply for this shy and diffident man, and artistic recognition—aside from the adulation given by a small circle of friends—did not really come until he had been dead for nearly half a century. Still, a typical Bohemian in mind and manner, Schubert enjoyed life and delighted in the easy camaraderie of fellow musicians, singers, and painters. Most satisfying of all was the reward gained from incessant creativity, for seemingly he was never idle. In the song idiom alone, Schubert is known to have written eight songs in a single day; in one year he wrote over 140 songs, and before death removed him (at age thirty-one), he had composed more than 650.

Few Schubert songs are either long or complex, but anyone who sings them must be a fine communicative artist, fully able to project their tender beauty, gentle lyricism, and deeply felt sentiment. In the beautifully simple

[13] From a musicocultural point of view, twentieth-century popular songs can hardly be considered latter-day equivalents of the folk song, for they are catchy but synthetic products of "Tin Pan Alley." George M. Cohan, Gus Kahn, Leo Feist, Cole Porter, Frank Loesser, the teams of Rodgers and Hammerstein and Lerner and Loewe, are only a few of the writers who have created much of America's popular music for well over fifty years.

[14] *The Art Song in America,* in both recorded and printed form, has been recently published at Durham, North Carolina, by Duke University Press. This splendid collection sheds a great deal of light on the growth of song in our nation.

"Hedge-Rose," the endearing "Margaret at the Spinning Wheel," and the intensely dramatic "Erlking," whose texts follow, Schubert's musicopoetic powers are convincingly demonstrated. Each reveals a different facet of his ability for they differ in length, expressive intent, and organizational pattern; but they are as one in possessing an ineffable charm and irresistible appeal. Here is a paraphrase of their texts: [15]

THE HEDGE-ROSE
(A strophic song)

Text by Goethe   *Music by Schubert*

Once a boy saw a hedge-rose, a hedge-rose in the heather,
Tipped with dew and very fair,
Swift he ran to pick it there, in the golden weather.
Hedge-rose pretty, hedge-rose red, hedge-rose in the heather.

Said the lad: "I'll pick you now, hedge-rose in the heather."
Said the rose: "I'll stab you now.
My thorn is sharp, pluck me will you never!"
Hedge-rose pretty, hedge-rose red, hedge-rose in the heather.

But the boy in scorn, broke a hedge-rose in the heather.
Though she stabbed him with her thorn,
Yet she died that summer morn, in the golden weather.
Hedge-rose pretty, hedge-rose red, hedge-rose in the heather.

MARGARET AT THE SPINNING WHEEL
(A modified strophic song)

Text by Goethe   *Music by Schubert*

All my rest is gone, my heart is sore, I'll find it never, never more.
If he is not here, the world is a tomb, for life is drear and wrapped in gloom.
My aching brain seems on fire, with wild regret and mad desire.
All my rest is gone, my heart is sore, I'll find it never, never more.

To see only him I gaze down the street, it is he I go out to meet.
His manly form and handsome face, his rippling laughter and noble grace.
The sound of his voice brings magic bliss, the touch of his hand and, oh, his kiss!
All my rest is gone, my heart is sore, I'll find it never, never more.

My heart is straining to meet his embrace, that I may hold him with warmth and grace!
And kiss him as I would be kissed, with emotion so strong, I would die of bliss!
All my rest is gone, my heart is sore, I'll find it never, never more.

[15] In performance, art songs are usually sung in their original language. For purposes of study, however, on succeeding pages some attempt has been made to suggest, in English, the gist of their linguistic flow. In no case, however, are these literal or even complete translations.

THE ERLKING
(A through-composed song)

Text by Goethe   *Music by Schubert*

Who rides through the night, so dark, so wild?
A father rides with his beloved child.
He holds the lad closely within his arm,
He guards him safely, he keeps him warm.

"My son, why do you hide your face in fear?"
"Father, can you not see that the Erlking is here?
The Erlking calls me with crown and shroud!"
"No, son, that is but a passing cloud!"

"My lovely boy, come with me.
From morning until night I'll play with thee.
I shall give you jewels and wealth untold,
You shall walk in robes of shining gold."

"Oh father, my father, do you not hear?
The Erlking is whispering in my ear!"
"No, rest you, rest my child,
These are only sounds of the night wind wild."

"Oh, my darling boy you must come with me,
And my fair daughters shall wait on thee.
All their midnight revels you shall gaily keep,
And then gently and tenderly fall to sleep."

"Oh, father, my father, do you not see,
The Erlking's daughters looking at me?"
"My son, my son, be not afraid,
Those are only willows waving in the glade."

"I love you child, I love you; but I'll show no remorse,
If you resist, I'll take you by force."
"Oh, father, my father, now he grips my arm!
The Erlking has done me a dead harm!"

The father shudders and speeds through the night,
The child is terrified and shakes with fright.
He reaches home in doubt and in dread,
Within his arms the child lays dead.

Robert Schumann (1810–1856): A Song and a Song Cycle

After 1820, a literary muse seemingly influenced the stream of music
in Germany, for many creative musicians not only composed but wrote
prose and poetry as well. Robert Schumann, primarily a musician but a man
who possessed indisputable literary gifts, was foremost among them. As an
essayist, critic, and magazine editor he encouraged the spread of Romanticism's tenets, and as a composer he wrote works heavily imbued with the

emotionalism, lyricism, and sentimentality that were this style's outstanding characteristics.

Schumann apparently inherited his love of literature. The son of a bookseller who is said to have maintained a bookstore so that he would have an opportunity to read the volumes on its shelves, he matured in a bibliophilistic environment. Volumes of every sort fell under his eager gaze, but the collections of Romantic poetry then being circulated in Germany struck a most responsive chord. Unquestionably, this literary orientation became extremely important in shaping the flow of Schumann's subsequent pieces, particularly his lieder. Not as plentiful as those of Schubert, his songs are longer, more complex, and almost obsessively concerned with arousing vivid emotional imagery. Here is a transliteration and condensation of the texts in two examples:

THE TWO GRENADIERS
(A modified strophic song)

Text by Heine   *Music by Schumann*

To France there journeyed two grenadiers,
Returning, in sorrow, from Russia.
At last they came to the German frontier,
Each anticipating a return to his homeland.
There, in despair and sorrow, they learned
Of how France was lying in ruins.
Its army subdued and its might overcome,
While its Emperor had been taken a captive.

Weeping together, the two grenadiers sat,
Each anticipating the relief death would bring.
Said one: "I'm weak and tired, my wound is burning like fire."
The other spoke: "Your grief is mine, even in death we are comrades.
Thoughts fly to my wife and children;
Yet, what is a wife or a child to me?
They must call to Heaven in their hour of need,
My thoughts are possessed by a stronger grief,
For my Emperor and his triumphs exist no longer."

"Give me this last wish, dear friend: When I am sleeping in death,
See that I am taken to my native land, let France have her soldiers to keep.
Lay a red ribbon and the gleaming cross of honor on my chest,
Place a sword in my hand, and a musket near my side.

Thus, I'll lie like a sentinel, awaiting the sound of battle.
Until the horses, neighing and tramping around,
Respond to a mighty barrage of the guns.
Then will the victor ride to conquest again,
For the clashing swords tell the story.
Seizing my weapons, I'll rush from the grave,
To share in my Emperor's glory!"

DICHTERLIEBE (A Poet's Life) [16]
(A cycle of songs)

Text by Heine   *Music by Schumann*

1. *In the Beautiful Month of May*
In the beautiful month of May, when buds open,
Love also awakens within my heart.
In the beautiful month of May, when birds sing,
I told my secret love of the delight she brings.

2. *My Tears Turn to Flowers*
My tears turn to flowers and blossom in the valley,
And my sighs turn into the music of a nightingale.
If you love me, all flowers shall be yours,
And a nightingale will thrill you with its song.

3. *The Rose and Lily*
Rose and lily, sun and dove, I love them all.
But none so deeply, or so completely, as her.
The holy, lowly, lovely, lonely, are my love.
But of all—rose, lily, sun, or dove—I love only her.

4. *When I Gaze into Your Eyes*
When I gaze into your eyes, grief departs,
And when I know your kiss, I fill with bliss.
Within your embrace, my heart fills with rapture.
When you love me, my eyes fill with tears.

5. *I Will Dip My Soul*
I will dip my soul into a lily's chalice,
And it shall breathe a song to my fairest.
It thrills with delight, as I know idyllic bliss.

6. *On the Rhine*
On the Rhine, our holy river, there is mirrored
An image of the Cologne cathedral's nave.
Inside there is a painting of our lady,
Whose eyes, lips, and features are like my love.

7. *I'll Not Complain*
I'll not complain, though my heart breaks in two.
Love is lost and no light falls on my deep night.
In dreams I see you, but a serpent eats my love.
But no matter how unhappy, I'll not complain.

[16] This cycle contains a total of sixteen songs, whose texts are too lengthy to permit their full inclusion here. Lines from the first eight are contained on these pages; titles for the remainder, numbers 9–16, are: 9. "There's Flute and Fiddle A-skirling"; 10. "When I Hear Others Singing"; 11. "A Lover Loves a Maiden"; 12. "On a Sunny Summer Morning"; 13. "In a Dream I Lay Weeping"; 14. "Each Night in Dreamland"; 15. "From Realms of Ancient Story"; and 16. "The Old Ugly Songs."

8. *If the Flowers Only Knew*

If the flowers only knew how my heart is hurt,
They would weep and help heal the wound.
If the nightingales knew how sad I am,
They would sing and aid a hapless poet.
If they knew my story, golden stars would descend,
Only I know sadness; she has broken my heart.

Songs by Johannes Brahms (1833–1897); Modest Mussorgsky (1839–1881); Hugo Wolf (1860–1903); and Richard Strauss (1864–1949)

Approximately one year before his death, Brahms composed *Vier ernste Gesange* (Four Serious Songs), his final compositions in this idiom. These are very nearly his last works for only the eleven chorale preludes for organ bear a later opus number. Turning to Scripture, he selected four passages: two from Ecclesiastes, one from the Apocrypha, and one from St. Paul's Epistle to the Corinthians as a textual base. Revealing this composer's well-known melodic gifts, his instinct for musical narration, and an uncanny ability to support the lyric flow with luxuriant harmonies, these pieces contemplate the profundities that have concerned perceptive men in all ages. Here is a compressed version of their texts:

1. *Ecclesiastes* (III)

Both beasts and the sons of men must die. One breath is given to
each, and both must ultimately pass.
All go to one place; they are dust and return to dust.
Therefore, man should rejoice; who knows what happens after him?

2. *Ecclesiastes* (IV)

I returned and considered the oppressions. There was weeping
and wailing but none came to comfort.
Then I gave praise to the dead.
They know not of the evil wrought on earth.

3. *Ecclesiasticus* (XLI)

O Death, how bitter you are to one who lives in peace,
To him who has joy and is prosperous in many ways!
O Death, how welcome you are to those in want,
Whose life is filled with pain and have little comfort.

4. *Corinthians* (XIII)

Though I speak with the tongues of men and angels,
And have not love, I am as sounding brass or tinkling cymbal.
Though I can prophesy and understand all mysteries,
Though I have faith and can move mountains,
And have not love, I am nothing.
For now we see the world darkly as through a glass,
But then we shall see it face to face. Now abideth faith, and hope,
and love;
But of these three, the greatest is love.

Nearly all Mussorgsky's songs are conceived in a nationalistic idiom, use the Russian language, and express typical Slavic subjects. Many are founded on texts by Russian poets (Mussorgsky also provided some himself), but a few use verses by such German writers as Goethe, Heine, and Ruckert. Perhaps the most celebrated Mussorgsky song in the repertoire in his witty "Song of the Flea" (1879), whose textual substance is this:

SONG OF THE FLEA

Text by Goethe   *Music by Mussorgsky*

Reigning in royal splendor, a king had raised a flea.
A flea? A flea! Ha, ha, ha, ha,
As flesh and blood he loved him, his dearest kin was he.
The flea? A flea! The flea.

The monarch called his tailor to let him know his wants.
He said: "I want my flea well dressed, so measure him for pants!"
A pair of pants? Ha, ha. A flea? ha, ha. A pair of pants!

He wore the finest velvet, and silken clothes bright.
They gave him highest orders and made him a noble knight.
Ha, ha. A flea? Ha, ha. A flea!

He wore a star of jewels as minister of state;
His relatives were favored; at court they all were great.
The courtiers and the ladies from bites were very sore.
The queen and her attendants could bear those pests no more.

They dared not even scratch them, they scarcely could stand or sit,
While we can scratch and kill them as soon as we are bit!
Ha, ha, ha, ha, ha, ha.

Planned as a cycle of twelve pieces, the full expanse of Mussorgsky's *Songs and Dances of Death* was never completed. Only four were written, three in 1875 and one in 1877. Obviously concerned with the grisly subject of death, they are noble, dignified, moving, and profound rather than maudlin or funereal. Seemingly, the composer treats death as an inexorable event whose occurrence cannot be compromised, evaded, or postponed. And in these songs he takes a realistic view of the inexorable tread of fate as Death makes a grim visitation to: (1) a village toper who is attempting to wend his way home through a wintry forest; (2) a mother who greets the forbidding spectre with anguished fear when it appears at dawn to take her sick child; (3) a young girl, incurably ill, who leans from a window to hear a fascinating serenade; and (4) a battlefield where the grim reaper appears as a conqueror whose victories are irresistible. This is a summary of their texts:

SONGS AND DANCES OF DEATH

Text by Golenishchev-Kutuzov   *Music by Mussorgsky*

1. *Trepak*
Here my sturdy worker, bent and grey and laden with vodka,

Why are you wandering through this snowy, trackless forest?
What is life to you but work, sorrow, and wretchedness.
Come with me and rest easy, at least until tomorrow.

2. *Lullaby*

Be calm and quiet my good woman, you cannot help the child.
My song is far more beneficial than yours, so be silent.
Death begone! Although he is in pain, my baby shall sleep.
Yes, he shall sleep, but it will be in the stillness of death.

3. *Serenade*

Do not waste your beauty and youth on others,
I shall be your knight, truly and entirely devoted to you.
Let me clasp you in firm embrace, for I am bewitched.
Be still in my arms, for now you are mine.

4. *The Field Marshal*

Lay down your arms, stop the struggle, victory is mine.
Rise up, fall into ranks, and march before your leader.
When mere men forget you, death shall remember valor.
Come with me, and nevermore return to earth.

Among the more frequently performed Wolf songs (approximately 220 were published during his lifetime, while another one hundred awaited posthumous issuance) are those within his "collections," that is, pieces from a common textual source. Included are the *Morike-Lieder* (1889); *Goethe-Lieder* (1890); *Spanisches Liederbuch* (1891); and *Italienisches Liederbuch* (1892), some of which include more than forty individual songs. Comparatively brief, Wolf's *Three Songs from Michelangelo* (1898) fittingly summarize his craft. Reaching backward in time for more than three hundred years, he selected fragments from the poetry of a greatly gifted Renaissance Italian and employed them in songs that are tender, nostalgic, and extremely beautiful. Here is a summary of their substance:

THREE SONGS

Text by Michelangelo   Music by Wolf

1. *I Think Often*

I think often of my past life, as it was before I met you.
No one noticed me then, but it didn't matter,
For I lived only to compose my songs.
Now, I am well-known. Whether in praise or blame,
My name is spoken everywhere.

2. *All That Exists*

All that exists must come to an end.
As time passes, all living things perish.
Everything that we create is like a shadow
That quickly fades in the daylight.
Like you, we were once happy men,
But now we are only dust in this place.
For all that is created must come to an end.

3. *Does My Soul Long for Blessings?*
Does my soul long for blessings from God?
Do I seek beauty that arises everywhere?
Is it an illusion that pleases my mind and eye,
With an attraction that gladdens me to tears?
My aspirations, my longings are mysterious,
How can I find and hold them close?
These must be achieved in my love for you,
Through your eyes I shall attain my goal.

Richard Strauss' life was long, he died at the age of eighty-five, and richly productive. Aside from other kinds of composition (opera, tone poems, occasional chamber music), he wrote well over one hundred art songs and fifteen orchestral songs. Nearly all were conceived within collections, and many are based on the poetry of Clemens Bretano, Nicholaus Lenau, Richard Dehmel, and Friedrich Ruckert. Representative of his craft is a set of eight songs that Strauss wrote during 1882–1883, based on poems by Herman von Gilm entitled *Letzte Blatter* (Last Words). Although the subjects are pensive, Strauss' music is far from gloomy. Seemingly, his artistic attitude is one of cheerful practicality, with the result that these pieces are affirmative, forthright, and almost optimistic. Here are texts for two songs in the set:

DEDICATION
(Zueignung)

Text by von Gilm   *Music by Strauss*

You know the anguish I feel when we are apart,
Now I thank you for the love in my heart.
Once I delighted in freedom
And drank deeply of unrestrained pleasure,
But you changed all this, and I thank you.
Your love has redeemed my spirit,
And I am filled with adoration.
I thank you for the love in my heart.

ALL SOULS' DAY
(Allerseelen)

Place the varicolored flowers by my side,
And let us recall the days when love was young,
As once it was in May.
Let me caress your hand as I quietly hold it,
And give me your tender affectionate glances,
As once you did in May.
Today there are flowers on every grave,
On this single day those who have died are free.
So come to my heart and let me hold you,
As once I did in May.

Songs by Claude Debussy (1862–1918) and Maurice Ravel (1875–1937)

As it grew (c. 1880), Impressionism exerted an influence on such Parisian litterateurs as Stephane Mallarmé, Paul Verlaine, Pierre Louys, Arthur Rimbaud, and Maurice Maeterlinck, writers who subsequently became known as the "Symbolist Poets." Theirs became a unique literary art wherein verse subjects lived in a transcendental world, a strange "never-never" land that was, at least, partly hallucinatory. Syllabic flow in their poetry is so liquid as to suggest music's melodic stream, and specific intelligibility is often sacrificed in favor of allusion and suggestiveness. Debussy's art, too, flowered in this environment, and nowhere else is his Impressionist bent more perceptible than in the chansons he wrote based on Symbolist texts. These are examples:

ARIETTES OUBLIÉES (1888)
(A song cycle)

Text by Verlaine   *Music by Debussy*

1. C'est l'extase (This Is Ecstasy)

This is languishing ecstasy, this is amorous weariness,
This is a rustling in the forest amid caresses of the breeze.
Through gray boughs a chorus sounds; it speaks with a distant
    murmur.
Sometimes it speaks like rustling grass, or rippling water
As it flows over stones in a stream. My soul is melancholy
In this quiet lament. Is it yours or mine?
Whence comes this sweet song on a soft summer evening?

2. *Il Pleure dans Mon Coeur*
(There Are Tears in My Heart)

When it rains on the city there are tears in my heart.
What is this melancholy that penetrates my heart?
I hear the gentle sound of rain falling on the grass and roof.
For a weary heart the sound of rain is dismal.
There is weeping without reason when a heart is filled with anguish.
No betrayal? Then there is lament without cause;
This is the worst pain of all—not to understand the reason.
I exist without love, without hate—and yet I am filled with grief.

3. *L'Ombre des Arbres*
(Shadow of the Trees)

The shadow of the trees along the misty river bank is vanishing.
In the air, perched on branches, turtle doves sing a plaintive song.
Weary traveler, how much does this landscape reflect your pain?
How much do rain and mist weep for your abandoned hope?

4. *Chevaux de Bois*
(Wooden Horses)

Around and around go the wooden horses, they turn a thousand times.
They turn, but do not stop as they whirl to the music.
A child is dressed in red, his mother in white; a boy in black,
  and a girl in rose.
One is self-possessed, the other pretending, but everyone pays.
Round and round turn the horses, while a sly one casts glances.
The whirling of a machine intoxicates one's senses.
We move in a land of make-believe with an empty stomach,
For there are many troubles and few rewards.
The horses never need spurs to make them gallop;
They revolve without any hope of hay.
Night falls and the crowds disperse; the gay drinkers are filled
  with torment.
Stars shine in a velvety sky, and church bells toll plaintive sounds.
But without cessation, round and round go the horses.

5. *Green*

Here are fruit, flowers, and a heart which beats only for you.
Do not tear it apart with your lovely hands; may my gift please you.
I come in the early morning hours, let me rest at your feet.
Let me lay my head upon your breast to sleep and be quiet.

6. *Spleen*

The roses were red and the ivy dark
If my loved one moves, my despair will rise again.
The sky was too perfect, the sea too great, the air too gentle.
I fear for what the future holds!
May you escape from its fears, for I grow weary
Of the forest, the flowers, the countryside, of everything except you.

Ravel's *Shéhérazade* is sheer fantasy. Opulent in sound, exotic in syntax, and erotic in substance, it has a semi-Oriental suggestiveness that is at once vague, evanescent, and strangely endearing. This is a condensed version of its text:

SHÉHÉRAZADE (1903)
(An orchestral song)

Text by Tristan Klingsor   *Music by Ravel*

1. *Asia*

O Asia, land of tales renowned in ancient lore,
Where fancy dwells like an empress within a mysterious forest.
O Asia, I long to sail in that schooner gently rocking in the harbor.
At dawn she will unfurl red sails, and sail toward the golden sky.
I wish to sail to the isle of flowers,
Where all listen while the sea chants its song.
I long to see Damascus and the cities of Persia;

To see silken turbans entwined about dusky faces with glistening teeth;
I long to see dark eyes burning with love, pupils shining with joy.
I long to see velvet garments and calumets hidden by snowy beards.
I long to see sour merchants, the cadis, too, and viziers
Who grant life or death, as it is their will.
I long to see Persia, India, and China,
To observe mandarins and princesses with tiny hands.
To hear learned men debating over poetry and beauty.
I would linger a while at an enchanted palace
And, like some traveling foreign sage,
Contemplate old landscapes at my ease.
Done in rare colors on lovely textures framed with pine.
Or talk with someone in the midst of an orchard.
I long to see murderous wretches who smile,
While the headsman chops off innocent heads
With a deadly scimitar of genuine Eastern shape.
I long to see poor beggars, rich queens, the rose, and a trace of blood;
I would die of love, or of hate.
Returning home, I would relate my story
To those who believe in dreams,
From time to time raising my old Arabian cup, like Sinbad of yore,
Only to break off, and begin anew with another tale.

2. *The Enchanted Flute*

Cool is the shade and deep my master's sleep,
As he slumbers wearing his soft silken cap,
His long nose protrudes through a white beard.
But I, who patiently keep vigil, can hear, far away,
Sweet music of a flute which creates a yearning to laugh or weep.
A tune now of languorous charm, again quite gay,
Which my beloved can play, when I draw near the casement.
Then each note, it would seem, flies away
From the flute to touch my face in a sweet embrace.

3. *L'Indifferent*
(The Heedless One)

Your sad eyes are as soft as those of a young girl,
And your classic features are covered with down,
In form and grace you are enchanting.
When you sing a song at my door, the language is sweet,
Like certain music it is false in sound. But enter!
Perhaps a cup of wine will give you courage.
No, you go away and I see you leave the doorway,
Giving a sign that you will not stay.
You leave with the light, graceful step of a girl.

Songs by Manuel de Falla (1876–1946)

With impeccable taste, Falla merged learned compositional techniques
with the pristine beauties of folk music while creating his flavorful "Seven

Popular Songs" (1914). Conveyed by a single singer (with piano support), they establish an atmosphere reminiscent of cool gardens, bubbling fountains, and twanging guitars. Most reflect the restrained sentimentality of Andalusia, an area in the south of Spain whose centers are Seville and Cadiz. Because Andalusia felt the brunt of the Moorish occupation, which lasted from the eighth to the thirteenth centuries, an abundance of near-eastern influences are generally perceptible in this music. Two songs in Falla's collection, however—a "Seguidilla" from Murcia (in Spain's southeast), and an "Asturiana" from Asturias (in northwestern Spain)—are filled with pulsating vigor and unbridled animation. Eloquent in musical substance, all the songs are, by turns, subtle, thrilling, boisterous, and beguiling—reflective, perhaps, of the Spanish people themselves. Here is a transliteration of their texts:

SIETE CANCIONES POPULARES ESPAÑOLAS
(Seven Spanish Folk Songs)

Texts: Traditional   *Music by de Falla*

1. *El Paño Moruno*
(The Moorish Cloth)

If once blemished by a stain, this fine cloth on the counter,
Will sell for little, and shall never regain its value.

2. *Seguidilla Murciana*
(Seguidilla from Murcia)

Those who live in glass houses should take this warning:
Beware of how you throw stones at neighbors.
For we are travelers, and someday we shall meet again.
Because you are so flighty, I will compare you
To a penny that passes from hand to hand until worn smooth.
It looks false, and none will take it.

3. *Asturiana*
(From Asturia)

As I sought consolation, I drew near a verdant pine,
To see me weep, it wept again. So green was the verdant pine.
That to see me weep, it wept again.

4. *Jota*

They say we don't love each other, for we keep our secret sealed.
But if they probe your heart and mine, true love will be revealed.
Now I must part from you, and from your house I go in sorrow.
Though it does not please me, farewell until tomorrow.

5. *Nana*
(Lullaby)

Sleep softly, child; sleep, sleep, my angel.
Softly sleep, little starlet, gleam of the morning.
Nanita, mana, softly sleep, little starlet, gleam of the morning.

6. *Canción*
(Song)

Shame on your eyes, those traitors, let me despatch them!
You cannot tell what anguish (have mercy!) it is to watch them.
Mother of sorrows! My love to watch them!
They say you do not want me, although I was once your lover.
Yet gains exceed the losses (have mercy!)
Now all is over (Mother of sorrows!) Now all is over.

7. *Polo*

In my heart I keep my sorrow, which none shall ever surprise.
Accursed be love, and the one who made me wise!

Selected Art Songs and Song Cycles
(*Including orchestral songs*)

Barber, Samuel (b. 1910)
   Hermit Songs (1953). Based on texts by anonymous Irish monks (c. 700–
   1300), these ten sweetly lyrical pieces are sometimes profound, occasionally
   ribald.
   Knoxville: Summer of 1915 (1948). Founded on the James Agee text, these
   nostalgic orchestral songs describe childhood in an American town.
Beethoven, Ludwig van (1770–1827)
   Ah, perfido! (1796). Termed a dramatic *scena* and written for soprano and
   orchestra, this is an impassioned, sweeping piece.
   An die ferne Geliebte (1816). With a text by Jeitteles, this early example of
   the cycle, with six songs, describes the lament of a lovers' separation.
   Twelve Scottish and Irish Songs (1814–1818). Folk melodies arranged for
   piano, violin, 'cello, and voice; this is a lilting and altogether charming
   collection.
Berg, Alban (1885–1935)
   Altenberg Lieder (1912). Five songs based on picture-postcard texts that
   are waggish, clever, and amusing.
   Seven Early Songs (1907). Using texts by different poets extending from
   Lenau to Rilke, these pieces are pensive and mostly tonal.
   Der Wein (1930). An exceptionally brilliant concert aria for orchestra and
   soprano, founded on three Baudelaire-George poems.
Berlioz, Hector (1803–1869)
   Mort de Cléopâtre. Cantata-like in outline and based on an inferior text by
   Vieillard, the work nevertheless is surprisingly dramatic, intense, and
   exotic.
   Nuits d'été (1843–1856). Mystic, nostalgic, and evocative, this cycle of six
   pieces (with texts by Gautier) is a fine example of the early orchestral song.
Brahms, Johannes (1833–1897)
   Alto Rhapsody (1869). Using a Goethe text (from the "Winter Journey")
   and scored for alto, men's chorus, and orchestra, this cantata-like piece is
   fervent, dark, and profound.
   Vier ernste Gesang (Four Serious Songs, 1896). Deeply introspective and

founded on Scriptural excerpts, these are majestic, rather long, but warmly melodic.

Selected songs: *Standchen* (Serenade); *Auf dem Kirchhofe* (In the Church-yard); *Vergebliches Standchen* (Vain Pursuit); and *Immer Leiser* (Always Loving). Representative examples from a collection of more than two hundred Romantic, sentimental and melodically glowing works; most are based on texts by contemporary poets and can be considered the most exemplary lieder successors to appear following the Schubert-Schumann tradition.

Britten, Benjamin (b. 1913)

Les Illuminations for Solo Voice and Strings (1939). Founded on Rimbaud's poetry, these nine songs employ the French language and are allegoric, symbolic, and cynical in substance.

Serenade for Tenor, Horn, and Strings (1943). With texts from Tennyson, Blake, Keats, and others, this cycle of six songs is warm, witty, and whimsical.

Canteloube, Joseph (1879–1957)

Songs of the Auvergne (1924). French rural folk melodies (twelve in this collection) placed in splendid orchestral settings; some are playful, amorous, and naive; others are angry, bitter, and desperate.

Copland, Aaron (b. 1900)

Twelve Poems of Emily Dickinson (1950). Angular, tart, and unpredictable texts that suggest American abstractionism are wedded to music that is stark, strange, and iconoclastic.

Old American Songs (1950; 1952). Hymns, minstrel songs, and others from the nineteenth century arranged in two sets of five pieces each. They are quaint, authentic, and enjoyable.

Debussy, Claude (1862–1918)

Chansons de Bilitis (1897). Allusive and suggestive, these three songs founded on Pierre Louys' poetry are erotic, vague, and evanescent.

Promenoir des Deux Amants (1904–1910). With poetry by Tristan l'Hermite, this cycle of three songs is beautifully conceived and wondrously written.

Selected songs: *Beau Soir* (Beautiful Evening); *Mandoline;* and *La Chevelure* (The Tresses). Representative but early lyric pieces by a greatly gifted writer of chansons; each is independent, short, and haunting.

Duparc, Henri (1848–1933)

Selected songs: *Extase* and *l'Invitation au Voyage* (1868–1884). Delicate chansons that are clearly Impressionistic in syntax and ethereal, erotic, and touching in substance.

Dvořák, Antonín (1841–1904)

Biblical Songs (1894). Pious, exultant, occasionally pensive, these ten songs based on Scripture are short, flowing, and beautifully balanced.

Falla, Manuel de (1876–1946)

Seven Popular Spanish Songs (1914). Obviously Iberian in outlook, these pieces effectively capture an authentic provincial spirit; folk-like, they are many-sided and zestful.

Fauré, Gabriel (1845–1924)

La Bonne Chanson (1891–1892). Verlaine's "eternal poem of youthful love" expressed in nine songs that are tender, ardent, and graceful.

Foss, Lukas (b. 1922)

Song of Songs (1947). Based on the *Song of Solomon* and organized in four sections, this piece for soprano and orchestra is cantata-like, mystic, and sensual.

Time Cycle (1960). Unorthodox, atonal, and often stridently dissonant, this collection of four songs based on Auden-Housman-Kafka-Nietzsche texts expressed in English-German, uses free ensemble improvisation between pieces and is a very bizarre but strikingly unique work.

Granados, Enrique (1867–1916)

Tonadillas. Describing Andalusian life and based on poetry by Periquet, these songs are zesty, buoyant, and piquantly dramatic.

Grieg, Edvard (1843–1907)

Selected songs: "I Love Thee"; "In the Boat"; "And I Shall Have a True Love"; and "A Swan." Based on poetry by Andersen, Krag, and Ibsen, these lieder in the German tradition are infused with an authentic Norwegian flavor; mostly they are restrained, tender, and pensive.

Harris, Roy (b. 1898)

"Abraham Lincoln Walks At Midnight" (1955). A cantata of lament for mezzo-soprano, violin, 'cello, and piano, based on a poignant Vachel Lindsay text.

Hindemith, Paul (1895–1963)

Marienleben (revised 1948). Concerned with the travail of the Virgin Mary, these fifteen songs on a Rilke text are dignified, remorseful, and resigned.

Ives, Charles (1874–1954)

Selected songs: "Evening"; "At Parting"; "General William Booth"; and "In Summer Fields." Samples from the more than one hundred songs written by an erratic American composer; they are unusual, uneven, odd, but often extremely beautiful.

Loewe, Karl (1796–1867)

Ballades. Published in seventeen volumes, more than three hundred sixty eight semifolk-like pieces were issued by this composer between 1820–1860; all are simple, direct, and engaging.

Mahler, Gustav (1860–1911)

Kindertotenlieder (1902). Based on poems by Ruckert that lament the tragic death of children, these five songs are almost devotional, resigned, and intensely affectionate.

Das Lied von der Erde (1908). Scored for alternate use of tenor-contralto in six sections and employing Bethge poetry (from Chinese), this magnificent piece has vivid orchestration and is noble and sweeping, yet pensive in outlook.

Lieder eines fahrenden Gesellen (1883). With texts by the composer and cast in four sections, this piece is resigned and sad, but engagingly lyrical.

Youth's Magic Horn (1888). Superb orchestral songs in two sets of five, these pieces founded on folk poetry are unusually tuneful.

Mussorgsky, Modest (1839–1881)

Nursery (1868–1872). Employing composer texts, this cycle of seven songs is coy, whimsical, and obviously folkish.

Songs and Dances of Death (1875–1877). Russian texts by Golenishchev-

Kutuzov set in a cycle of four songs that is expressively resigned and dark, but eloquently dramatic.

Poulenc, Francis (1899–1963)

Selected songs: *Hotel; Voyage à Paris;* "C"; *Reines des mouettes;* and *Eleurs.* Superlative French chansons that are intimate, subtle, and enigmatic; mostly they are based on licentious poetry by Apollinaire, Aragon, and Vilmorin.

Prokofiev, Serge (1891–1953)

Five Poems by Anna Akhnatova (1916). Contemporary Russian mood pictures that adhere to the Mussorgsky tradition; their texts are variegated; and the music is unconventional, somewhat radical, and vaguely Impressionistic.

Ravel, Maurice (1875–1937)

Chansons madecasses (1925–1926). Three native songs in Parisian attire that use flute and 'cello in addition to piano and voice; their texts are folk-like narrative, and strikingly exotic.

Cinq mélodies populaires grecques (1907). Hellenic melodies with texts by Calvocoressi, they describe wedding joys and festivities; naturally, they are pulsating and exuberant.

Deux mélodies hébraïques (1914). Using traditional Jewish melodies and texts—one a Kaddish, the other an "eternal enigma"—these songs are somber and dignified.

Don Quichotte à Dulcinée (1932). Knight-errantry enacted in three short pieces that are touching, humorous, and glowing.

Shéhérazade (1903). Exotic orchestral songs based on three Tristan Klingsor poems; they are sweeping, sensuous, and excellent.

Schoenberg, Arnold (1874–1951)

Pierrot Lunaire (1912). Based on twenty-one poems by Giraud, this cycle is sung in speech-song and supported by five instruments; it is eerie, extremely bizarre, and shockingly dissonant.

Schubert, Franz (1797–1828)

Die schöne Müllerin (Fair Maid of the Mill, 1823). Superb Romantic cycle of twenty songs founded on Wilhelm Muller texts; each is tender, beseeching, and altogether lovely.

Schwanengesang (Swan Song, 1828). Composer's final songs that use fourteen incipits from Rellstab-Heine-Seidl poetry; but the collection is not a cycle. Expressively the pieces are dramatic, quizzical, and occasionally gloomy. The best-known is "Serenade."

Selected songs: *Fruhlingsglaube* (Spring Faith), poem by Uhrland; *Die Forelle* (The Trout), Schubart; *Die Krahe* (The Crow), Muller; *Die Junge Nonne* (The Young Nun), Craigher; *Rastlose Liebe* (Restless Love), Goethe; *Die Allmacht* (The Omnipotence), Pyrker; *Nacht und Traume* (Night and Dreams), Collin; *Der Schmetterling* (The Butterfly), Schlegel; *Heidenroslein* (Hedge-rose), Goethe; *An die Musik* (To Music), Schober; *Ganymed* (The Cup-Bearer), Goethe; *Gretchen am Spinnrade* (Margaret at the Spinning Wheel), Goethe; *An Sylvia* (Who Is Sylvia), Shakespeare. Representative examples from the more than six hundred lieder written by this genius during his tragically brief life. By turns they are allegorical, questioning, or amorous and convey emotions advanced by the era's leading poets. Set with impeccable taste, they have gracious, flowing melodic lines, subtle and tasteful harmonies, and delightful piano accompaniments.

Die Winterreise (The Winter Journey, 1827). A cycle of twenty-four songs arranged in two parts and based on Wilhem Muller's poetry, it describes a rejected lover's bleak existence and is, consequently, despairing and pensive.

Schumann, Robert (1810–1856)

Dichterliebe (A Poet's Love, 1840). A rapturous, introspective cycle of sixteen songs based on Heine's poetry that discusses, allegorically, various phases of a "poet's love."

Frauenleibe und Leben (A Woman's Life and Love, 1840). Describing eight episodes in a woman's life, this cycle of Chamisso's poems is nostalgic, extremely touching, and tenderly intimate.

Selected songs: *Die Lotosblume* (The Lotus Flower), poem by Heine; *Widmung* (Dedication), Ruckert; *Fruhlingsnacht* (Spring Night), Eichendorff; *Der Nussbaum* (The Walnut Tree), Mosen; *Du Bist wie eine Blume* (You Are Lovely As a Flower), Heine; *Die Soldatenbraut* (The Soldier's Bride), Morike. Direct successors to the lieder of Schubert, these representative pieces have impassioned texts, asymmetrical melodies, and glowing harmonies; within them, the piano's role is greatly expanded.

Sessions, Roger (b. 1896)

Idyll of Theocritus (1954). A huge (forty minutes) dramatic aria for voice and orchestra that is tragic, frenzied, and vibrant.

Sibelius, Jean (1865–1957)

Selected songs: "The Tryst" (Runeberg); "The First Kiss" (Runeberg); "Was It a Dream" (Wecksell); "Sigh, Rushes, Sigh" (Froding); and "Black Roses" (Josephson). Written by a Finnish composer who speaks compellingly of the land, customs, and culture of his people, these pieces are lyrical, whimsical, and occasionally stern.

Strauss, Richard (1864–1949)

Four Last Songs (1948). Based on texts by Hesse (3) and Eichendorff (1), these orchestral songs have angular melodic lines and meditative texts.

Selected songs *Allerseelen* (All Soul's Day), von Gilm; *Schlagende Herzen* (Throbbing Hearts), Bierbaum; *Freundliche Vision* (A Welcome Vision), Bierbaum; *Cacilie* (Cecily), Hart; *Morgen* (Tomorrow), Mackay; *Heimliche Aufforderung* (Secret Invitation), Mackay; *Zueignung* (Dedication), von Gilm; and *Standchen* (Serenade), von Schack. Lieder that merge warm nineteenth-century sentimentality with a pungent twentieth-century musical syntax; their melodies are angular and their harmonies often biting, but their substance and emotionality are exceptionally striking.

Stravinsky, Igor (b. 1882)

Three Japanese Lyrics (1913). Stressing Oriental exoticism, with texts by Akahito, Maztsumi, and Tsaraiuki, they use string quartet, two flutes, and piano to support the voice.

Four Russian Songs (1918). Using flute, harp, and guitar to support a solo voice, these eloquent songs merge Slavic pensiveness with Western avantgarde dissonance.

Three Songs from William Shakespeare (1953). Scored for soprano, flute, clarinet and viola, these pieces are, by turns, spare, eloquent, and melodic; all employ a tone row and tend to be dissonant in sound.

In Memoriam Dylan Thomas (1954). An atonal triptych scored for voice, string quartet, and four trombones, this lament for a Welsh poet is antiphonal, taut, and dirge-like.

Vaughan Williams, Ralph (1872–1958)

On Wenlock Edge (1909). Based on Housman's poem, "A Shropshire Lad," this cycle uses a string quartet with piano and voice to convey an English text in a highly expressive, folk-like way.

Villa-Lobos, Heitor (1887–1959)

Bachianas Brasileiras No. 5 for Soprano and 8 'Celli (1938–1945). In two sections, an aria and dance song, this unique piece blends classic artistic purity with Latin American nationalism; it tends to be sensual and showy.

Wagner, Richard (1813–1883)

Five Wesendonck Songs (1858). Smoldering and intense orchestral songs that suggest unrequited love between poetess and composer; the best-known is *Traume* (Dreams).

Wolf, Hugo (1860–1903)

Goethe-Lieder (1888–1889). Fifty-one short, searing, and passionate songs, many based on well-known texts; all stress the piano's role.

Italienisches Liederbuch (1892–1896). Based on poetry by Heyse, these were issued in sets of twenty-two and twenty-four songs each; they feature a discourse between plebeian lovers, and are robust, racy, and humorous.

Selected Morike songs (1889): *In de Fruhe* (At Daybreak); *Lobe Wohl* (Farewell); *Verborgenheit* (Secrecy); *Nimmersatte Liebe* (Insatiable Love); *Das verlassene Mägdlein* (The Forsaken Maiden); *Der Gartner* (The Gardener); and *Auf ein Altes Bild* (To an Old Picture). Individual poems by Eduard Morike given an inimitable musical treatment; some are quaint, coy, and curiously detached, whereas others are intense, passionate, and fervid; in them the piano and voice act as one.

Spanisches Liederbuch (1891). Forty-four songs based on translations from Iberian poetry by Heyse and Geibel; most are short, lively, and occasionally coy.

Chapter 14

Aural Portraiture:
Illustrative Music

When composers handle the materials of music with an intent of serving normal communicative purposes, *absolute* or *pure* music results. Most symphonies, concertos, string quartets, sonatas, suites, dances, and marches fall within this category, for they are meaningful and enjoyable in and of themselves. This is "music for music's sake," a genre whose ideas, expression, and color fulfill purely musical ends.

Not all compositions are so conceived, however. *Illustrative* (sometimes known as descriptive, narrative, or programmatic) music uses these same materials with an intent of serving extramusical ends. Pieces of this kind tell a story, describe a personality, relate a historical episode, or depict a natural phenomenon. Evocative, colorful, and attractive, descriptive pieces are usually quite easy for a listener to assimilate. Consequently, many have become extremely popular.

Virtually all compositions that employ a text (songs, operas, oratorios, and cantatas) are descriptive to some degree, for words almost always convey specific images and meaningful ideas. Ballet music, too, is usually descriptive,[1] for a dancer's pantomimic gestures convey tangible impressions, particularly in modern ballet. Thus, song and dance speak directly and comprehensibly to a listener without much difficulty. Orchestral music slanted along narrative lines, however, has a number of problems to overcome.

SOME OF THE PROBLEMS

An important question confronting anyone who works with illustrative music centers on the nature of the imagery it arouses. Composers who have devoted themselves to descriptive endeavors are as one on the validity of program music, but they differ considerably over the kind of ideas it may

[1] Except, of course, for classical ballet.

express. Franz Liszt, for instance, wanted his descriptive compositions to be poetic, suggestive, and generally allusive. But Richard Strauss claimed a realism so well developed in his music that precise states of mind, specific occurrences, and finely drawn personalities could be described in tone.

Some chronological periods have exploited illustrative concepts more than others. During the Baroque era, for instance. such composers as Johann Kuhnau (*Biblical Sonatas*) and Marin Marais (*The Gall Bladder Operation*) delighted in depicting a variety of verbal, intellectual, or semiscientific topics in their works. Classicism's composers (Haydn, Mozart, and their contemporaries) were less interested in such an undertaking, however, and wrote few illustrative works (exceptions are Mozart's *Musical Joke* and particular portions within Haydn's two oratorios *The Seasons* and *The Creation*). Subsequently, nineteenth and twentieth century composers became intensely interested in the possibilities of descriptive writing, with a result that an abundance of illustrative works were written during these years.

AESTHETIC CONSIDERATIONS

Purists tend to view program music with skepticism. In their opinion, only musical ideas should be suggested within a composition, and efforts that lead a listener or a performer in extraneous directions amount to travesty. Much logic unquestionably supports this view, for the greatest bulk of pieces within music's repertoire falls within the abstract category. Because nondescriptive compositions almost unfailingly elicit some emotional response, however, proponents of program music hold that a distinction between illustrative and nonillustrative works is not so much a question of kind as of degree. Bach's four orchestral suites and Mozart's sonatas for piano, for instance, are beautifully conceived abstract pieces that delight anyone who hears them, but they unquestionably elicit some form of emotional response.

When a listener is confronted with descriptive music, the presence of an extramusical element necessitates an evaluation of the program—that is, the narrative discourse—as well as the musical substance. Thus, in formulating a judgment, he must consider both the appropriateness of the extraneous subject and the composition's worth as a musical design. To be artistically valid, of course, such a piece should be meaningful from both points of view.

WHENCE THE SUBJECT MATTER?

Ingenious composers continually seek subjects that can be adapted to the purposes of narrative music. Satisfactory topics vary considerably, of course, and range from personality studies (Richard Strauss' *Don Quixote*), to a description of natural wonders (Smetana's *Moldau*). Within the broad range of available subjects, these categories (listed with pieces that exemplify them) have been found especially useful:

1. Literature and Art: *Romeo and Juliet* (Shakespeare), given a musical setting by both Berlioz and Tchaikowsky; *Through the Looking Glass* (based on *Alice in Wonderland*), Deems Taylor; *Harold in Italy* (from Byron's "Childe Harold"), Berlioz; *Scheherazade* (from the "Thousand and One Nights"), Rimsky-Korsakoff; *Francesca da Rimini* (after Dante's *Divine Comedy*), Tchaikowsky; *Pictures at an Exhibition* (based on Victor Hartman's paintings), Mussorgsky.

2. History: *Wellington's Victory*, Beethoven; *Overture 1812*, Tchaikowsky; *Battle of the Huns*, Liszt; *Marche slave*, Tchaikowsky.

3. Drama: Music for *Peer Gynt* (Ibsen), Grieg; for *L'Arlésienne* (Daudet), Bizet; for *Rosamunde* (Wilhelmine de Chezy), Schubert; for *Manfred* (Byron), Schumann and Tchaikowsky; for *A Midsummer Night's Dream* (Shakespeare), Mendelssohn.

4. Personalities: A "*Faust*" *Symphony* (after Goethe), Liszt; *Enigma* Variations, Elgar; *Don Juan* (after Lenau), *Don Quixote* (after Cervantes), and *Ein Heldenleben* (autobiographical), R. Strauss.

5. Geography: *In the Steppes of Central Asia*, Borodin; *Nights in the Gardens of Spain*, de Falla; *The Pines of Rome*, Respighi; *Escales* (Ports of Call), Ibert; *Iberia*, Debussy; *Caucasian Sketches*, Ippolitov-Ivanov.

6. Legend and Folk Lore: *The Swan of Tuonela*, Sibelius; *Till Eulenspiegel's Merry Pranks*, R. Strauss; Overture, *The Russian Easter*, Rimsky-Korsakoff; Suite from *Hary Janos*, Kodály; "Rustic Wedding" Symphony, Goldmark.

7. Satire, Whimsy, and Humor: *Adventures in a Perambulator*, Carpenter; *A Musical Joke*, Mozart; *Lieutenant Kije Suite*, Prokofiev; *Carnival of the Animals*, Saint-Saëns; *Album for the Young*, Schumann; *Children's Corner Suite*, Debussy.

8. Nature: "Pastoral" Symphony (No. 6 in F major), Beethoven; *Moldau*, Smetana; *Out of Doors Suite*, Bartók; *La Mer* (The Sea), Debussy; *Grand Canyon Suite*, Grofé; *The Planets*, Holst; *Waldscenen* (Forest Scenes) for Piano, Schumann.

9. Fantasy: *Symphonie fantastique*, Berlioz; *A Night on Bald Mountain*, Mussorgsky; *Danse macabre*, Saint-Saëns; *Death and Transfiguration*, R. Strauss; *Poem of Ecstasy*, Scriabin; *The Enchanted Lake*, Liadov.

10. Physical Objects: *Pacific 231*, Honegger; *The Iron Foundry*, Mossolov; *George Washington Bridge*, William Schuman; *Little Train of the Caipira*, Villa-Lobos.

MUSICAL SATIRE

Often the butt of literary satire, human foibles occasionally endure musical lampooning. Particular composers (Wagner and Richard Strauss, for example) employed satire as a means of striking at critics; others (Prokofiev, Mussorgsky) used it to deride pompous officialdom; whereas still others (Gilbert and Sullivan) ridiculed outmoded customs. Musical satire is usually subtle but incisive; often, it is devastating. Here are several witty compositions that indicate directions musical satire may take:

1. *Ein musikalischer Spass* (A Musical Joke) by Mozart, which lampoons the ineptitude of village musicians who play irritatingly out of tune, sound false notes, and create a general debacle because they cannot keep together.
2. Passages in Wagner's *Die Meistersinger,* where Beckmesser (a caricature of Edward Hanslick, the composer's severest critic) is portrayed as a fool who carps, lies, cheats, and steals.
3. Shostakovich's ballet *The Golden Age,* which mercilessly jeers at capitalism and its failings.
4. *La Valse* by Ravel, which satirizes the popular craze for waltzes. (Stravinsky also burlesques this dance in *Petrouchka.*)
5. Prokofiev's *Lieutenant Kije* music, wherein a confused Czar (and, for good measure, the sycophants who cater to him) is ridiculed in a subtle but effective manner.
6. *Symphonie fantastique* by Berlioz, which turns to grotesque parody in its finale where the *Dies Irae* (Chant for the Dead) is tortured almost as cruelly as condemned souls must be tormented in Hell.

IMPLEMENTING THE DESCRIPTIVE PROCESS

Normally, the expressive intent of a narrative composition is disclosed by its title. Unlike abstract pieces that usually bear nonspecific designations such as Concerto in F or Symphony No. 5 in C minor, descriptive works have meaningful names (*Hebrides Overture, Moldau*) that immediately establish a frame of reference within a listener's mind. Often, this association is continued in a number of ways:

By Title and Subtitle

Verbal descriptions carried out in headings and subheadings within a piece are very definitive, and the images they create in a listener's mind are unavoidable. Smetana's symphonic poem *Moldau,* a work that describes a river's flow and the countryside surrounding it, shows how this is accomplished. Its seven sections, each with distinctive characteristics, are identified by title: [2]

[2] Other pieces that employ subtitles include (1) the Ravel-Mussorgsky *Pictures at an Exhibition;* (2) Beethoven's Symphony No. 6 in F major ("Pastoral"); (3) Ravel's *Mother Goose Suite;* and (4) Saint-Saëns *Carnival of the Animals.*

1. *Sources of the River:* With minimal support from pizzicato violins and harp, two flutes depict dual streamlets that converge to become the source of a great river. Gradually, more and more instruments are added until the full orchestra announces this surging theme:

2. *Forest Hunt:* Continuing its flow, the river passes through a wooded area where a hunting party seeks game; horns sound, exemplifying activities of the chase:

3. *A Peasant Wedding:* Now the river passes a small village in which wedding festivities are being held; the music alludes to dances typical of such a convivial occasion:

4. *Moonlight, Nymphs Dance:* Nightfall finds the river quiet and placid; this is an occasion for nymphs and elves to come from the forest and dance. After this quiet and gentle subject has been heard, the first theme returns, presumably denoting the river's continual flow:

5. *St. John's Rapids:* At daybreak the stream falls into a turmoil as it passes over a rocky bed. Now the music becomes agitated to suggest the river's turbulent countenance.

6. *The River at Its Greatest Breadth:* Attaining full grandeur, the music portrays a broad and stately river upon which vessels of all kinds sail.

7. *Vysehrad Castle Near Prague:* As it nears the capital city, the Moldau flows past an aged castle symbolic of momentous events in Bohemian history, and the music becomes appropriately majestic:

Shortly thereafter, this river—as all rivers ultimately must—passes out of existence by flowing into a larger body of water (the Elbe). Smetana's piece becomes richly climactic as its descriptive role comes to an end.

Via Program Notes

Considerably more expansive than a mere listing of titles, descriptive essays may be provided (usually by the composer) to assist a listener in comprehending a work's narrative intent. And to fully serve their intended purpose, these "program notes" are printed in concert programs or on record jackets where they can be read before, during, or after a performance. For instance, Berlioz prefaced the score of his *Symphonie fantastique* (1830) with an essay about the work's descriptive aim,[3] and such other scores as Borodin's *In the Steppes of Central Asia;* Rimsky-Korsakoff's *Scheherazade;* Kodály's *Hary Janos Suite;* and Schoenberg's *Verklarte Nacht* also contain brief prefatory comment. More extensive remarks can be found in two works by Ottorino Respighi, *The Fountains of Rome* and *The Pines of Rome.* Perhaps the longest set of descriptive notes intended to aid musical understanding (they extend to more than two pages) is appended to Glière's symphony *Ilya Mourometz*, where adventures in the life of a legendary Russian hero are narrated in considerable detail. As an example of what such essays are like consider the paragraphs Rimsky-Korsakoff inserted within the score of his *Scheherazade* (1889):

The Sultan Schahriar, convinced of the duplicity and infidelity of all women, vows to slay each of his wives after the first night. The Sultana Scheherazade, however, saved her life by the expedient of recounting to the Sultan a succession of tales over a period of a thousand and one nights. Overcome by curiosity, the monarch postponed from day to day the execution of his wife, and ended by renouncing altogether his sanguinary resolution.

[3] Others, particularly certain Baroque composers, had anticipated him, however

Many were the marvels recounted to Schahriar by Scheherazade. For the telling of these she drew from the verses of the poets and the words of folk songs and tales, connecting her stories one with the other.

With Poetry or Illustrations

In the main, a liaison between poetry and instrumental music is somewhat unique. Still, this has not deterred enterprising composers from seeking to link the gentle suggestivity of verse with the orchestra's very considerable expressive resources. And in these instances, the poems that motivate an illustrative composition are usually cited, in whole or in part, on the initial pages of a score. Saint-Saëns' *Danse macabre* (based on a poem by Cazalis); Liszt's *Les Préludes* (after Lamartine); Dukas' *Sorcerer's Apprentice* (derived from Goethe); d'Indy's *Istar* (from a poem of Izdubar); Strauss' *Don Juan* (from Lenau's poem); Tchaikowsky's *Francesca da Rimini* (after Dante); and Bernstein's "Jeremiah" Symphony (which uses excerpts from the Book of Lamentations) exemplify this procedure.

Deems Taylor's *Through the Looking Glass* bears a poetic incipit before each of its four sections. Whimsical, charming, and altogether amusing, texts and music complement one another in a remarkable way. Here are brief quotations from verses included within three sections of this score: [4]

The Garden of Live Flowers

"O tiger-lily," said Alice, addressing herself to one that was waving gracefully
    about in the wind, "I wish you could talk."
"We can talk," said the tiger-lily, "when there's anybody worth talking to."

Jabberwocky

'Twas brillig, and the slithy toves
    Did gyre and gimble in the wabe;
All mimsy were the borogoves,
    And the mome raths outgrabe.

"Beware the Jabberwock, my son!
    The jaws that bite, the claws that catch!
Beware the Jubjub bird, and shun
    The frumious Bandersnatch!"

The White Knight

This time it was a white knight. He drew up at Alice's side, and tumbled off
    his horse just as the red knight had done.

"Thank you very much," said Alice. "May I help you off with your helmet?"

"Now one can breathe more easily," said the knight, putting back his shaggy
    hair with both hands and turning his gentle face and large mild eyes to
    Alice. She thought she had never seen such a strange looking soldier in all
    her life.

---

[4] For a full understanding of what the composer is attempting to express, one should read the poems in their entirety and, indeed, the whole of *Alice in Wonderland*.

On the other hand, some works with an obvious literary association do not carry poetic inscriptions on their scores. Several compositions based on Shakespeare's *Romeo and Juliet*—by Berlioz, Tchaikowsky, and Prokofiev—illustrate this point. And Debussy's *Afternoon of a Faun,* derived from a poem by Mallarmé, does not include any textual citations. Apparently, composers feel that when a tale is well-known, its affirmation would be redundant. Ravel's *Mother Goose Suite* rests at midpoint: Short quotations, but not the entire poem from Perrault, top most of its sections.

Comparatively few compositions have been inspired by paintings, although several musical landscapes (Debussy's *Iberia;* Respighi's *Pines of Rome;* Falla's *Nights in the Gardens of Spain;* and Grofé's *Grand Canyon Suite*) are justly celebrated. Among pieces that link pictorial imagery with music, Rachmaninoff's *Isle of the Dead* (based on Bocklin's painting); Hindemith's *Mathis der Maler* (stimulated by the famous Grünewald altarpiece); the Mussorgsky-Ravel *Pictures at an Exhibition* (suggested by Victor Hartman's water colors); and Walton's *Portsmouth Point* Overture (suggested by an early print of Thomas Rowlandson) are notable.

MUSICAL SYMBOLISM AND THEMATIC ASSOCIATION

Thematic association, a technique wherein melodies are assigned to principal figures or objects in a narrative, greatly implements the descriptive process. When personages—animate or inanimate—appear in the musical discourse, their themes are sounded; and as the dramatic situation changes, the melodies are sufficiently altered to suggest new activities, a change of mood, or a different environment. Interesting examples occur in Gershwin's *An American in Paris;* Saint-Saëns' *Danse macabre;* and Liszt's *Les Préludes* (each to be discussed subsequently).

Not only persons, but natural phenomena and man-made wonders have become favorite subjects for musical portrayal. The sea, for instance, has been frequently treated in descriptive works, and its tides, limitless expanse, and changing moods are depicted in Debussy's *La Mer,* Rimsky-Korsakoff's *Scheherazade,* and Mendelssohn's *Hebrides Overture.* Sometimes, these subjects are suggested by musical figures that have degenerated into mere "sound effects"; still, the technique of thematic association has been proven an important adjunct of the descriptive process.

Personality changes, transformed appearance, or acquired age can also be effectively depicted by musical symbolism. An excellent example occurs in the mood pictures that Richard Strauss drew of an aged knight in his cleverly conceived *Don Quixote.* At various times the Don is shown to be heroic, pensive, melancholy, courageous, or resigned, as the music reveals shifts of his changeable (and sick) mind. In another work *Till Eulenspiegel,* this same composer depicts an irrepressible rogue who impishly shifts from amorous, heroic, or satiric attitudes, to others that are macabre and fatalistic. And again the music underscores these changes. Conversations between two or more individuals are very effectively simulated in orchestral works by employing an exchange between instruments. Fine examples of such colloquy occur in the "Samuel Goldenberg and Schmuyle" section of Mussorgsky's *Pictures at an Exhibition* and in the "Beauty and the Beast" episode of Ravel's *Mother Goose Suite.*

FORM IN ILLUSTRATIVE MUSIC

For the most part, descriptive compositions have little regard for the standard patterns of musical design. Within them, the recital of a story is foremost, and other considerations (formal balance, structural symmetry, or tonal logic) are readily sacrificed to implement the narrative. Adherence to an *a priori* pattern would, in these instances, seriously shackle a composer's eloquence.

Few illustrative pieces follow the theme and variations pattern, although exceptions exist in Elgar's *Enigma* Variations, Strauss' *Don Quixote,* and d'Indy's *Istar,* which are mostly cast in the free variation design. Particular works, most of them written early in the nineteenth century, adhere to the general outlines of sonata form: for example, Mendelssohn's *Hebrides Overture,* movements in Beethoven's "Pastoral" Symphony, or parts of Berlioz's *Symphonie fantastique.* On the other hand, descriptive pieces that observe the outlines of part form, usually in the ternary pattern, are reasonably common: Debussy's *Afternoon of a Faun,* parts of Ibert's *Escales,* sections within Ravel's *Mother Goose Suite.* But rondo form is rare, an exception is Strauss' *Till Eulenspiegel.*

Avoidance of conventional patterns in programmatic writing means an adoption of "free form," which is tantamount to saying that such works usually have no fixed design. Abrogating the inner laws of balance and symmetry could lead to confusion, of course, but chaos is usually avoided by adhering to the strictures of an extramusical discourse.

TYPES OF ILLUSTRATIVE PIECES

Flexible enough to easily encompass extraneous topics, the smaller forms are well given to illustrative purposes. Piano pieces, for instance, often have programmatic connotations. Excellent examples exist in Schumann's *Album for the Young, Carnaval,* and *Scenes from Childhood.* Similarly superb descriptive pieces for keyboard are Debussy's *Children's Corner Suite* (as well as his *Préludes*). Reaching almost to epic proportions, Balakirev's *Islamey* and Mussorgsky's *Pictures at an Exhibition* (in their original versions for piano) are also glowingly eloquent.

Variously known as concert overtures, symphonic poems, or tone poems, some single-movement orchestral compositions effectively exploit the sonorous hues available to modern instrumental groups while engaging in musical portraiture. Mendelssohn's *Hebrides Overture, Tale of the Beautiful Melusine,* or *Calm Sea and Prosperous Voyage* are early and excellent examples.

From Beethoven to Shostakovich, numerous composers have written for the theater or ballet and their works in this idiom, naturally, have programmatic connotations. Well-known examples include Beethoven's music for Goethe's *Egmont;* Mendelssohn's pieces for Shakespeare's *A Midsummer Night's Dream;* Bizet's contributions to Daudet's *L'Arlésienne;* and Grieg's music for Ibsen's *Peer Gynt.* In recent times the writing for motion pictures, radio, and television has burgeoned. Among the musical compositions that have attracted unusual attention in this area are Prokofiev's *Lieutenant Kije,* Richard Rodgers' *Victory at Sea,* and Virgil Thomson's music for the documentary film *Louisiana Story.*

Some symphonies are avowedly descriptive. Beethoven was one of the first to experiment along these lines, and his Symphony No. 6 in F major, subtitled the "Pastoral," is a tangible result.[5] Subsequently, Berlioz with his *Symphonie fantastique* and his *Roméo et Juliette* and *Harold in Italy* symphonies expanded the concept. And still later, Franz Liszt created his "Faust" and "Dante" Symphonies, which are filled with vivid color, passionate intensity, and high drama. In the years postdating 1900, program symphonies have grown to occupy an important niche in musical literature. Narrative works extending from Vaughan Williams' "London" Symphony (1914) to Bernstein's Symphony No. 3—"Kaddish" (1963) are now fixtures in the present-day repertoire.

THE SYMPHONIC POEM

A direct outgrowth from the Beethoven-Mendelssohn concert overture, the single-movement symphonic poem became important during the mid nineteenth century. Because of its tangential nature, immense coloristic possibilities, and extremely buoyant personality it was soon proven well suited to the purposes of story-telling. Exemplified in an abundant collection of pieces ranging from Liszt's *Les Préludes* (1850) to Gershwin's *An American in Paris* (1928), it has grown to a position of unusual significance in orchestral literature. Apparently it was Liszt who first coined the term symphonic poem, for he used it to identify several of his single-movement orchestral pieces (*Hungaria, Mazeppa, Orpheus*) that had a manifest narrative intent. Proclaiming that adherence to a program was a laudable and challenging compositional practice (although he did not always follow this dictum), Liszt then proceeded to vigorously promulgate the cause of illustrative music in the years between 1850 and 1880.

[5] Among earlier examples are Leopold Mozart's piquant "Toy" Symphony (often erroneously ascribed to Joseph Haydn) and his "Hunting" Symphony (which is complete even to a part for baying hounds.) This composer, incidentally, should not be confused with his more illustrious son Wolfgang.

Ostensibly similar to the symphonic poem in purpose and outline, Richard Strauss' tone poems (*Don Juan, Don Quixote, Death and Transfiguration*), differ from their precursors mostly in subtle details. Because Strauss wished his works to travel along stringently realistic paths, his intent was to be specifically evocative whereas Liszt had been essentially poetic. Both chose subjects from literature, legend, history, or folklore and depicted them in compositions that are unusually rich in luxuriant detail. Even today, their pieces dominate the area of illustrative music.

WAYPOSTS IN THE GROWTH OF PROGRAM MUSIC

From Its Emergence to 1800

Although most of the programmatic works well-known to contemporary audiences were written after 1825, illustrative concepts are probably as old as music itself. So little is known about the music of ancient times that it is impossible to precisely specify its scope, but it is not entirely conjectural to realize that a close liaison existed between music and the story-telling so important in the lives of aboriginal people. Tangible evidence concerning musical practice in societies predating the era of ancient Greece is nowhere to be found, but numerous artifacts, relics, and graphic illustrations suggest that illustrative connotations were associated with much music-making in pre-Biblical times. And this same evidence plus the allusions that continually appear in poetry and prose writings show that music was "functional" (that is, narrative to some degree) in ancient Greece and Rome. But actual musical examples are nowhere to be found.

Interestingly enough, particular portions of the chant repertoire employ a naive kind of musical imagery, and this undoubtedly exerted an influence on many secular works created during the Medieval and Renaissance periods. In the fullest sense, of course, such Gregorian incipits can hardly be considered genuine examples of program music, for they do little more than make fleeting references to sounds associated with wind, rain, hail, or thunder. Fragmentary and sketchy though they are, however, these unsophisticated pieces comprise our earliest known examples of descriptive music.

For more than a thousand years thereafter (until the Renaissance), descriptive effects were undoubtedly employed in the songs, dances, and musical entertainment that comprise a backbone of the repertoire in any era, but tangible examples are rare. After the sixteenth and seventeenth centuries, however, circumstances began to change. Written (and, consequently, printed) scores for secular pieces then began to appear, and these provide clear-cut evidence of the period's musical activity. For instance, in the sixteenth century (c. 1529), the Frenchman Clément Jannequin (1485–

1564) wrote (and published) a number of long pictorial chansons with such titles as "The Song of Birds," "The Hunt," and "The Battle" that include appropriate effects to implement their expressive intent. Later, the Englishman William Byrd (1542–1623) used descriptive sounds symbolic of war in "The Battell," a suite of fifteen pieces for keyboard (undoubtedly written with an intent of performance on the virginal). Sections within this piece bear such titles as "The Earle of Oxford's Marche," "The Souldiers' Sommons," "The Marche to the Fighte," "The Retraite," "The Buriing of the Dead," and "The Souldiers' Delight." Along with its other qualities, Byrd's composition is one of the earliest known examples of *battaglia* (battle piece), a specific kind of descriptive work that was to attain considerable notoriety in later years.

Some of this era's program music includes passages wherein the sounds of nature, bird songs, or the movements of animals are imitated, while others attempted to depict such bodily gestures as running, jumping, or falling. Later generations consider these descriptive attempts merely ingenuous, but such effects were important ventures into a then little-exploited resource. After 1600, descriptive techniques became more sophisticated, and ideas of striking originality began to appear within narrative compositions, particularly those destined for theatrical performance.

An altogether charming programmatic work was created by Johann Kuhnau (1660–1722), the immediate predecessor of J. S. Bach as Cantor at the St. Thomas Church in Leipzig, when he published his *Biblical Sonatas* in 1700. Actually a set of six independent pieces, each bearing a descriptive title, they are keyboard works of quaint excellence. Included are (1) "Goliath," (2) "Saul Cured by David's Music," (3) "The Marriage of Jacob," (4) "The Healing of Hezekiah," (5) "Gideon," and (6) "The Funeral of Jacob." On the score of each, descriptive phrases are inscribed to further clarify the work's narrative intent, and these are usually read by a narrator when the pieces are performed. Bearing the full title, "The Fight Between David and Goliath," the first *Biblical Sonata* is a work in seven sections, each identified with a descriptive verbal phrase. These are its details:

1. "Goliath's stamping and ranting." Suggestive of the giant's ungainly movements and frightening ire, the music adopts heavy accents and an angular figuration as it begins:

2. "Trembling of the Israelites." When the fearful subjects of Israel pray to God for assistance, the music reveals their disquietude and heart-felt supplication:

3. "The steadfastness of David." As the Israelites' unlikely champion steps forward to defend them, the music assumes a simple, almost childlike flow that suggests David's unquestioning trust in God's guidance:

4. "Uttering the challenge, the fight, David's slaying of Goliath, and the Israelites' pursuit of the Philistines." Charmingly picturesque, this section depicts the bellicose antagonists stalking one another:

the trajectory of David's stone:

the fall of Goliath:

and the flight of the Philistines:

5. "Rejoicing of the Israelites." Safe now that the threat of terror is past, the happy citizens can hardly believe their good fortune:

6. "Concert to the glory of David." Women in the community sing paeans of praise:

7. "Joyful dancing amongst the people." Finally, everyone joins in celebrating their release from oppression:

In the time of François Couperin (1668–1733), several French composers wrote a number of programmatic works for keyboard. Many of Couperin's harpsichord pieces, for instance, are descriptive and bear such titles as "The Frightened Linnet," "Jugglers," "The Little Windmill," and "Butterflies." And Jean Philippe Rameau (1683–1764), one of Couperin's most distinguished successors, wrote picturesque compositions for the harpsichord, as is exemplified by his *La Poule* (The Hen). That the twentieth century has no monopoly on musical realism is revealed by a composition of Marin Marais (1656–1728): Written for viol and harpsichord, it bears the title *Tableau de l'opération de la taille* (1717) and narrates (but, of course, in musical terms) the procedures involved in a surgical operation! Nor was this Marais' lone excursion into illustrative writing; his operas are among the first stage works to depict storm scenes, battle episodes, and similar momentous events.

Often considered the Baroque era's greatest composer, J. S. Bach did not write independent illustrative works, but occasionally employed descriptive effects within his large choral-orchestral compositions (for example, a rendering of the "Veil of the Temple" in his *St. Matthew Passion*). Bach's contemporary, George Frideric Handel, was somewhat more interested in musical narration and created cleverly conceived passages in his oratorio *Israel in Egypt* that have since been accepted as a *locus classicus* of effective programmatic writing. In it he used angular rhythms, piquant orchestral coloration, and exotic melodic turns to suggest leaping frogs, falling hail, or the infestation by flies that afflicted the Egyptians when they denied freedom to Moses and his Jewish people.

Rarely heard today, symphonies by Karl Dittersdorf (1739–1799) based on quotations from Ovid's *Metamorphoses* (three were published in 1785, six others on the centenary of his death in 1899) are excellent examples of program music practiced during the age of Classicism. Although Dittersdorf's descriptive effects constitute a compendium of devices known to musicians of the time, his illustrative techniques are consistently used to serve artistic purposes. His *Simphonies dans le genre de cinq nations* (Symphony on Customs of Five Nations, published 1770)—Germany, Italy, England, France, and Turkey—predates the Ovid works by some years but shows the same inventiveness in eliciting novel effects from the orchestra.

But the Age of Classicism, basically concerned with restraint, formalism, and gracious elegance, frowned on the excesses of descriptive writing. Haydn and Mozart—witty, urbane, and polished composers though they were—occupied themselves little with illustrative music. One example that appeared during these years, the "Toy" Symphony—once credited to Haydn but now generally ascribed to Leopold Mozart, father of the great composer —is not really a symphony at all, but a humorous little suite replete with bird calls, whistles, rattles, and similar extraneous effects. Spurious or not, it indicates that musicians of this era saw little need to venture outside conventional boundaries in search of expressive ideas. And the great Mozart, one of music's most sublime composers, aside from *The Musical Joke* (K. 522), virtually ignored descriptive concepts (except in his operatic writings).

In the Nineteenth Century

Battaglia (battle pieces), although known in earlier eras (for example, Byrd's "The Battell"), rose to unusual popularity early in the new century. Within them, sounds of war—drum rolls, cries, fanfares, clashes of weapons, a thunder of guns, and the turmoil incidental to general commotion—are imitated. Of course these effects are noisy, and the music is often banal and trashy. Yet, battaglia captured public imagination so forcefully that even Beethoven was persuaded to compose his notorious *Wellington's Victory* (*Wellingtons Sieg oder Die Schlacht bei Vittoria*, 1813; published, 1816). Admittedly a bizarre work, it was written originally for Maelzel's mechanical hurdy-gurdy (called a panharmonicon) to commemorate the Iron Duke's triumph over the forces of Napoleon, in 1813, in a battle that climaxed the peninsular war. Subsequently, the piece was scored for orchestra by the composer and performed in 1813 at a benefit for Austrian soldiers wounded in the battle. Included within it are such tunes as "Rule, Britannia!," "Malbrouck" (better known under the title "For He's a Jolly Good Fellow"), and "God Save the King." These are its details.[6]

1. "English Drums and Trumpets, English March": To the neatly chiseled pulse of snare drums and the crisp fanfare of trumpets, English soldiery march into alignment for combat (it must be remembered that battle maneuvers circa 1813 were almost equivalent to a dress parade). Their resolute tread and firm confidence in ultimate victory are clearly reflected in the music. As the columns are drawn up, strains of "Rule Britannia" are heard:

[6] Historically minded American listeners will find pleasure in listening to James Hewitt's "Battle of Trenton," a battaglia concerned with George Washington's victory over the Hessians at Trenton, New Jersey on December 20, 1776. It is available on a recording made by the Goldman Band (in an album entitled "Cavalcade of the American Band," Capitol SW 1688).

2. "French Drums and Trumpets, French March": From an opposite side of the field, marching with equal assurance in the righteousness of their cause, French veterans come into position as winds and percussion sound. Facing the English, they stand at attention as the band plays "Malbrouck":

3. "Challenge and Acceptance": Again, the code of military etiquette is observed as a formal summons to combat is uttered by the English, figuratively flinging down the gauntlet with trumpets acting as spokesmen. Almost joyously accepted by the French, the challenge is quickly followed by an onset of hostilities.

4. "The Battle": By far the noisiest portion of this work (and also the most exciting), this depiction of battle elicits a diversity of effects from the orchestra. Cannons are cranked into position, rifle fire crackles as salvos are laid down, big guns boom intermittently, and noises that defy precise description are elicited from the severely taxed instrumentalists. Even cavalry charges are suggested. This is war!

5. "The Symphony": Purchased at a terrible price in slain, maimed, and wounded men, victory ultimately comes to the British and the music suggests their exultation, just as it sounds a lament for the fallen. Interwoven into the strains of jubilation is "God Save the King," England's national anthem (known to Americans as "My Country 'Tis of Thee").

6. Finale: Powerfully articulated by a resonant orchestra playing at full sonority, the closing section not only depicts the glory of war, but somehow suggests the futility of combat. What, after all, has been gained by the frightful holocaust to which these heroic men have been exposed? Beethoven points his moral with convincing eloquence.

In his earlier Symphony No. 6 in F major (the "Pastoral," 1808), Beethoven did not slavishly follow narrative lines. Primarily a symphony and only secondarily concerned with following an illustrative discourse, it is, nevertheless, an important milestone in a general proliferation of descriptive writing that began to arise early in the Romantic era. A suggestive rather than realistic work, it has five movements titled (1) "The Awakening of Cheerful Feelings on Arrival in the Country"; (2) "Scene by the Brook"; (3) "Merry Meeting of Country Folk"; (4) "Thunderstorm"; and (5) "Thankful Feelings After the Storm." An often-quoted statement Beethoven appended to his score, "more an expression of feelings than sound painting," reflects a conservative view of the role fulfilled by descriptive music. His Piano Sonata No. 26 in E-flat major (1809), whose movements are called *Les adieux, l'absence et le retour* (The Farewell, Absence and Return), is an emotion-ridden piece in which the composer sensitively expresses a sense of loss over separation from a beloved patron, the Archduke Rudolph. Although its early movements are pensive and restrained, later pages— when Beethoven anticipates an early reunion with his friend—are more affirmative.

Compositions by Hector Berlioz brought program music into unusual prominence as the century approached its midpoint. Possessed of a fevered imagination, a prodigious technique, and apparently unquenchable energy, this ebullient Frenchman found a congenial mode of expression in the extravagances of illustrative music. One of the most imaginative pieces in all of musical literature, his *Symphonie fantastique* (1830) is a semiautobiographical work whose five movements are entitled (1) "Reveries, Passions"; (2) "At a Ball"; (3) "Scene in the Fields"; (4) "March to the Scaffold," and (5) "Dream of the Witches' Sabbath." So that none could misunderstand his intent, Berlioz wrote four sets of program notes explaining the exquisite details of his score. Similarly, *Harold in Italy* (1834), which features a prominent part for solo viola, narrates details from Byron's poem "Childe Harold." Its four movements are entitled (1) "Harold in the Mountains"; (2) "March of the Pilgrims"; (3) "Serenade"; and (4) "Orgy of the Brigands." And within his *Roméo et Juliette* Symphony (1839), scored for solo voices, chorus, and orchestra, Berlioz effectuated a marvelous liaison between Shakespeare's dramatic concepts and the symphony. His work is highly unusual—its structure, for instance, is decidedly at odds with the usual symphonic format—but the eloquence of his language, the compelling dexterity with which his very considerable forces are deployed, and the powerful emotionality he consistently displays make this composition a masterpiece. Employing a smaller canvas, Berlioz also followed programmatic precepts in such single-movement orchestral pieces as the *Waverly* Overture (1827), based on Scott's novels; *Le Roi Lear* Overture (1831), founded on Shakespeare; *Le Carnaval romain* (1844); part of his opera *Benvenuto Cellini;* and *Le Corsaire* Overture (1855), taken from another Byron poem.

Decidedly more conservative, Felix Mendelssohn restrained his programmatic bent within poetic bounds. Mendelssohn's last three symphonies, identified as the "Scotch," "Italian," and "Reformation," might be mistaken for sweeping musical landscapes, but they are really cameos whose descriptive substance is limited to mere suggestions of local color. On the other hand, some of his overtures are wondrously illustrative, and it has been said that sounds surging through the *Hebrides Overture* are so realistic that a listener almost feels the sting of salt spray and hears cries from sea gulls as the piece is played. Equally poignant is the subtle evocativeness of Mendelssohn's *A Midsummer Night's Dream* music—a particularly felicitous nuptial between German Romantic music and a play by Shakespeare—and the piquant descriptiveness inherent in such concert overtures as *A Tale of the Beautiful Melusine* and *Calm Seas and Prosperous Voyage.*

Far more than any predecessor, Franz Liszt found interesting topics for musical portrayal in the myriad vagaries of human personality. His *Les Préludes,* for instance, investigates the aspirations, frustrations, and ultimate triumph of man over forces that seemingly weigh on him. Such other works as *Tasso* or *Orpheus* consider personages somewhat removed from contemporary times, but their narration unfolds along lines displayed in *Les Préludes.* Even when he approached the symphony, Liszt did not abandon program music. His "Faust" Symphony, for instance, is a brilliant musico-psychological study of three important persons in Goethe's drama; and the "Dante" Symphony, a musical study of portions of the *Divine Comedy,* is concerned with questioning and reaffrming life's eternal verities.

It is not generally recognized that Liszt's son-in-law, Richard Wagner had much to do with influencing the course of narrative music, but many of his music dramas contain extended orchestral passages that are a near-equivalent to symphonic poems. "Siegfried's Rhine Journey" and the "Funeral Music from *Götterdämmerung;* the "Forest Murmurs" from *Siegfried;* the "Magic Fire Music" and "Ride of the Valkyries" from *Die Walküre;* and the "Good Friday Music" from *Parsifal* use orchestral resources with distinctive virtuosity to attain illustrative ends. When these passages are played in the theater, singers' voices are stilled (or minimized), stage action becomes nearly static, and only an eloquent orchestra is used to depict the narrative. By orchestral means alone a listener is taken on a journey down the Rhine, visits the mysterious depths of a German forest, sees a lonely mountain crag on which a young girl's recumbent figure is surrounded by spectral flame, or senses the mystic spell surrounding rituals practiced by pious men during Holy Week.

Existing in a cultural milieu vastly different from other Romanticists, Peter Tchaikowsky materially expanded the horizons of descriptive music in Russia. Some of his pieces are lyric, dramatic, and poetic; consider, for instance, *Hamlet, Francesca da Rimini,* or *Romeo and Juliet.* Others, such as *Marche slave* and the *Overture 1812,* are epic, nationalistic, and even jingoistic. The latter piece, incidentally, is a late (1880) outcropping of the battaglia, written to commemorate a celebrated Russian victory over Napoleon. Unusually flamboyant, it is scored for large orchestra, brass band, cathedral bells, and even has a part for cannon. Another side of Tchaikowsky's artistic personality is more whimsical. His music for *The Nutcracker,* for instance, is tender, graceful, and lyric; so too, are the scores to such companion ballets as *Swan Lake* and *The Sleeping Beauty.* And his *Capriccio italien* is not only quaintly picturesque, but blazes with an abundance of emotional fervor.

Particular members of the Russian Five—Alexander Borodin, Modest Mussorgsky and Nicholas Rimsky-Korsakoff (others were Mily Balakirev and Cesar Cui)—contemporaries of Tchaikowsky, differed from him in aesthetic outlook. And this divergence is naturally reflected in their compositions. A physician-scientist, Borodin cultivated music as an avocation and, aside from the many colorful episodes in his opera *Prince Igor,* caught the spell of vast spaces, exotic lands, and strange customs with *In the Steppes of Central Asia.* Mussorgsky was even more successful when writing pictorial works. His *Night on Bald Mountain* (1867) is a pulsating, barbaric musical narration of a Gogol tale in which spirits of the nether world emerge at midnight for frolic and revelry. And his *Pictures at an Exhibition,* written originally as a set of piano pieces and later orchestrated by diverse hands, is a stunning work conceived as a memorial to a deceased friend. Connected by a recurring "promenade" theme, its ten sections are continually charming and evocative. Greatly influenced by exoticism, Rimsky visited the Orient, musically speaking, via his ever-popular *Scheherazade* (a symphonic suite) and the less well-known tone poem *Sadko.* He was too much of a nationalist to neglect his native land, however, and the *Russian Easter* Overture (dedicated to Mussorgsky and Borodin) portrays a duality of Easter observances in Christian and pagan terms. Furthermore, his *Capriccio espagnol* reveals still another Russian trait: an interest in far-off, sun-drenched lands. Organized in five movements, this scintillating orchestral work suggests the mysterious allure of Iberia viewed through the entranced eyes of a foreigner.

In Bohemia, the programmatic concept frequently traveled on nationalistic paths. Bedrich Smetana, an ardent Czech patriot, memorialized his native land in a series of six symphonic poems published under the collective title *Ma Vlast* (My Fatherland). One of these, *Moldau,* is an often-performed composition, and *From Bohemia's Meadows and Forests,* another excerpt from the set, is almost as well-known. Smetana's String Quartet No. 1 in E minor, subtitled "From My Life," ventures into autobiography, a pursuit

seldom followed by musicians. Antonín Dvořák, Smetana's younger compatriot, also touched on programmatic ideas. In the latter stages of a richly
productive career, (that is, after 1895), he created such symphonic poems
as: *The Water Sprite, The Noon-Day Witch, The Golden Spinning Wheel,*
and *The Forest Dove* (1896), all based on K. J. Erben's tragic folk ballads.
A fifth work, *A Hero's Song,* is not directly related to the others and expresses a philosophical view of man's control over the forces surrounding
him. Earlier (1892), Dvořák had composed a triptych of concert overtures
—*Amid Nature, Carnival,* and *Othello*—that embody (according to Dvořák's
own words) the "Three great creative forces of the universe—Nature, Life,
and Love."

Brilliant illustrative works were conceived by Camille Saint-Saëns, a
French composer whose deft command of creative techniques was guided
by a witty, sardonic, and penetrating intellect. His *Danse macabre* (1874),
a lugubrious discourse on "The Dance of Death," takes its point of departure
from a poem by Henri Cazalis and, despite its title, emerges as a dazzling
orchestral tour de force. *Omphale's Spinning Wheel* (1871), however, is
more restrained. But the puckish *Carnival of the Animals* (1886) is a masterly
assault on double-entendre. Pretending to be a depiction of sundry animals,
this *grande fantasie zoologique* actually lampoons several of the composer's
overweening contemporaries. Fourteen sections (scored originally for two
pianos, string quintet, flute, clarinet, and xylophone) bear such titles as
"Royal March of the Lion," "Tortoises," "The Elephant," "Personages with
Long Ears," "Fossils," and "The Swan." Because of its satiric content, Saint-
Saëns directed that the piece not be given public performance until after
his death. Since then, of course, it has become a great favorite.

Richard Strauss was the last great tone poet of the Romantic era and
a most ingenious creator of descriptive music. As much at home amidst
oboes, bassoons, and tubas as he was in the theater surrounded by singers,
stage settings and costumes, Strauss created a brilliant series of illustrative
works (and an equally distinguished series of operas) that demonstrate
unusual deftness, skill, and imagination. Facility caused his descriptive
works to be more realistic—his critics said more banal—than had heretofore
been considered possible, and his adroitness pushed the programmatic concept to its furthermost limits. Strauss' subjects are not common folk: *Don
Juan* (1888), *Till Eulenspiegel's Merry Pranks* (1895), *Thus Spake Zarathustra* (1896), and *Don Quixote* (1897), for instance, are concerned with
extraordinary characters. But circumstances surrounding them, events in
which they become involved, and emotions affecting them—including im-
pishness, love, melancholy, introspection, and insanity—are understandably
human. Strauss' *Death and Transfiguration* (1896), a dignified disquisition
on the fate that awaits every man, is narrated in profound and compassionate terms, but *Ein Heldenleben* (1898), a musical autobiography told
without undue modesty, and the *Symphonia domestica* (1904), a musical

depiction of everyday life in a bourgeois family, are witty, uninhibited, and occasionally brash. Collectively, these brilliant works bring an important era in the development of program music to a close.

In the Twentieth Century

As the new century began, Impressionism affirmed a strong liaison between painting, poetry, and music. Claude Debussy, the movement's outstanding musician, was singularly successful in suggesting Impressionism's vague allusiveness in many of his compositions. His *Afternoon of a Faun* (1894), based on a poem by Mallarmé, for instance, is a languid work depicting the indolent dozing of a tawny animal on a warm summer afternoon. And *La Mer* (The Sea), subdivided into three movements entitled (1) "From Dawn to Noon on the Sea," (2) "Play of the Waves," and (3) "Dialogue of the Wind and Sea," is a vast seascape washed in variegated hues of light and shade. *Images* (that is, "Pictures") is similarly evocative and alive with a diversity of moods. Two sets of three pieces each were published for piano under this title, as was a collection of three works for orchestra (1909–1911). Within the latter, *Iberia,* itself with three subsections ("On the Streets and Highways," "The Perfumes of Night," and "Morning of the Festival Day"), is an especially brilliant piece.

Maurice Ravel leavened the tenets of Impressionism with gentle irony and a decided feeling for classic restraint. Some of his programmatic works were originally conceived for ballet (for example, *Daphnis et Chloé,* produced 1912) or written for keyboard (*Ma Mère l'Oye,* piano duet, 1908) but have since become well-known in orchestral versions. Much of Ravel's illustrative music is whimsical (*Alborado del gracioso,* 1905); some has historical overtones (*Le Tombeau de Couperin,* 1917); whereas other portions are geographically oriented (*Rapsodie espagnole,* 1908).

Nordic subjects came into the stream of descriptive music via the pen of Jean Sibelius, a distinguished Finnish symphonist who also composed highly original narrative works. Significant are *En Saga* (revised, 1901), a ballad-like tone poem; the *Karelia* Overture (1893), which deals with a storied area in Finland's south; *Four Legends* from the *Kalevala* [7] (1894); *Finlandia,* a popular nationalistic work (1900); *Pohjola's Daughter* (1906), a fantasia based on the *Kalevala; Night-Ride and Sunrise* (1909); *The Oceanides* (1914), which recalls the sea nymphs of Greek mythology; and *Tapiola* (1925), a portrait of certain Scandinavian forest gods. Sibelius' style reflects the man and his land. A rugged individualist, he created granitic compositions in which moments of tender beauty are interwoven with bold, tumultuous, and exciting passages.

Nor have American composers been inactive during this era. John Alden Carpenter, for instance, with his *Adventures in a Perambulator* (1915),

[7] Finland's national epic whose verses include a collection of folk tales.

reveals the whimsical chain of events that can occur when baby is taken for a stroll through the park. Deems Taylor ventures into a world of Disney-like fantasy with his *Through the Looking Glass* (revised, 1922); Charles Martin Loeffler engages in nostalgic youthful musings in *Memories of My Childhood* (1924); Charles Tomlinson Griffes evokes pictures of far-off exotic lands in his *Pleasure Dome of Kubla-Khan* (1919); and Ernest Schelling reveals a firm belief in the ultimate triumph of justice in his semibellicose *A Victory Ball* (1923, based on Alfred Noyes' poem). George Gershwin brought a new syntax to descriptive writing in a humorous depiction of events surrounding a trip abroad in *An American in Paris* (1928). Buoyant and lively, this tone poem intermingles clichés from America's popular music (jazz, the blues) with adroitly drawn suggestions of mood painting. And Ferde Grofé takes an armchair listener touring through an immense natural wonder in his *Grand Canyon Suite* (1931). Separated into five contrasted movements ("Sunrise," "Painted Desert," "On the Trail," "Sunset," and "Cloudburst"), it is a rich-sounding uncomplicated work that has earned great popularity.

Charles Ives, unquestionably America's most original talent in illustra-tive writing, was an unorthodox experimentalist. Freed from the necessity of pleasing popular taste (he composed as an avocation while becoming a successful insurance broker), Ives wrote a series of iconoclastic and vividly picturesque compositions early in the century that have only recently gained public renown. Because he composed only when released from professional commitments, Ives' musical output is not large, but his works have a rugged uniqueness that is seemingly an essential part of the American national char-acter. Among his illustrative writings is a symphony, *Holidays* (1904–1913), whose four movements give a depiction (often via popular folk melodies and occasionally with some rather startling sound effects) of "Washington's Birthday," "Decoration Day," "Fourth of July," and "Thanksgiving." Other piquant orchestral works that are similarly startling include "Central Park in the Dark" (1907); "The Pond" (1906); and "Hallowe'en" (1911). His Sonata No. 2, "Concord, Mass., 1840, 1860" (written between 1909 and 1915) for piano, with modest assistance from viola and flute is a musical salute to four New England transcendentalists; its movements are entitled "Emerson," "Hawthorne," "The Alcotts," and "Thoreau." Recondite and obtuse, as well as extremely difficult to play, it is an excellent character study of important people in American cultural history.

Ives' *Three Places in New England* (1903–1914) is an American classic. With three sections entitled "The St. Gaudens' in Boston Common" (with the subtitle "Col. Shaw and his Colored Regiment"), "Putnam's Camp, Redding, Connecticut," and "The Housatonic at Stockbridge," it portrays vignettes of American history in the first two and a fragment of geography in the third. These are details about the second piece in the set ("Putnam's Camp"), which musically depicts thoughts passing through a child's mind

(Ives') as he attends, "some time ago," a Fourth of July picnic at a Revolutionary War campsite: [8]

1. After a brief *allegro* introduction, first violins (with support from other strings) sound this march-like melody, apparently a favorite with Ives:

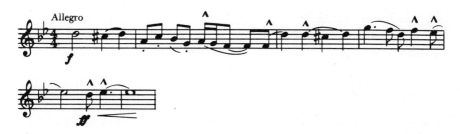

2. After some extension, the subject is reaffirmed, *fortissimo*.
3. Into this boisterous outpouring, a gentle folk-like tune (again played by first violins) is interjected to suggest the onset of a dreamy state:

4. And in the ensuing passage, fragments from a diversity of well-known American tunes are heard. With fine disregard for historical continuity, Ives intermingles Civil War melodies with airs from the Revolutionary era.
5. After a precipitous break in the composition's flow, strings sound sustained chordal harmonies while woodwinds (flute, oboe, and clarinet) present these ideas in a section marked *andante animato*:

[8] An explanatory essay that Ives appended to his score says (in part): "Wandering away from the rest of the children past the camp ground into the woods, he hopes to catch a glimpse of some of the old soldiers . . . tunes of the band and the songs of the children grow fainter . . . over the trees . . . he sees a tall woman . . . the Goddess of Liberty . . . she is pleading with the soldiers . . . but they march out of camp. Suddenly a new national note is heard. Putnam is coming . . . the soldiers turn back and cheer. The little boy awakes . . . runs down past the monument to 'listen to the band' and join in the games and dances."

6. Meanwhile, in a beautiful display of polyorchestral writing (featuring both polyrhythm and polytonality), piano, drums, bassoon, and brass instruments (notably the trumpet) sound fragments from "The British Grenadiers":

7. Other melodies (for example, bits from "Columbia, the Gem of the Ocean") are added to this mélange and the music mounts in intensity until, in a sudden reversal of mood, a previously heard theme reappears *pianissimo* (and *dolce*) in a new key:

8. Quietude does not last for long, however. Assuming a pulsating march tempo and using the first theme (with an occasional interpolated measure in nine-eight meter), orchestral forces coalesce as they drive toward a conclusion. Here the texture becomes exceedingly dense, cacophony abounds, and all instrumentalists seemingly work at cross purposes. (While attending parades in his youth, Ives was fascinated by the clashing timbres produced when two or more bands played different marches simultaneously, and this multilayered activity is reproduced here.) Marked to be performed *con fuoco* with the parenthetical direction "as fast as playable," the coda concludes at an intense dynamic level marked "ffff!"

Such other contemporary American composers as Aaron Copland (*The Red Pony*, 1948) and Leonard Bernstein (*On the Waterfront*, 1955) have written descriptive motion picture scores of unusual beauty. So, too, have composers of other nationalities (for example, Prokofiev's music for *Lieutenant Kije*, 1934 and *Alexander Nevsky*, 1939). Some have found stimulation in ethnic subjects (Ernest Bloch in *Schelomo*, 1915 or the *Israel Symphony*, 1916); travel (Copland's *El Salón Mexico*, 1936); folk customs, lore, and tales (Revueltas' *Sensemaya*, 1938); mechanical wonders (Honegger's *Pacific 231*, 1923, Villa-Lobos' *Little Train of the Caipira*, 1930; and Mossolov's *Iron Foundry*, 1928); and man-made structures (Schuman's *George Washington Bridge*, 1950). Displaying enterprise and ingenuity, they consistently reveal consummate mastery in handling the infinitely varied timbres of the modern symphony orchestra, as well as such associated sonic devices as electronic gadgets, tape recorders, and sound effects machines. In this way, ranging widely over a vast aesthetic perspective, modern-day composers are busily engaged in creating the illustrative scores of today and tomorrow. Seemingly, their goals and opportunities are limitless.

PARTICULAR EXAMPLES OF PROGRAM MUSIC

Franz Liszt (1811–1886), *Les Préludes*

In 1848 Liszt was appointed *Kapellmeister* (Music Director) by the Duke of Weimar and was charged with the responsibility of maintaining a musical establishment of sufficient merit to bring renown and enhanced prestige to the principality. Residing in Weimar for more than ten years, Liszt bent his very considerable talents to the task and shocked the town's burghers with his flamboyant personal life just as he impressed the world with a brilliant series of artistic accomplishments. Among the important fruits of the creative activity that occupied him during these years was a series of orchestral works including thirteen symphonic poems, written mostly between 1848 and 1857. Of these, the third, *Les Préludes,* has become one of Liszt's best-known works. Composed in 1848 but extensively revised in 1854, its programmatic ideas are ostensibly taken from the *Méditations poétiques* of Alphonse Lamartine (1790–1869), one of the first French writers to embrace literary Romanticism. Whether Liszt's composition had its genesis in Lamartine's poem or was merely fitted with a related title and meaningful textual quotations after being completed is a moot point. It cannot escape listener attention, however, that the music follows a narrative summarized in this paragraph from Lamartine's poem, which Liszt appended to his score:

What is life but a series of preludes to that unknown song whose initial solemn note is tolled by death? The enchanted dawn of every life is love; but where is the destiny on whose first delicious joys some storm does not break?—a storm whose deadly blast disperses youth's illusions, whose fatal bolt consumes its altar. And what soul thus cruelly bruised, when the tempest rolls away, seeks not to rest its memories in the calm of rural life? Yet man allows himself not long to taste the kindly quiet which first attracted him to Nature's lap; but when the trumpet gives the signal he hastens to danger's post, whatever be the fight which draws him to its lists; that in the strife he may once more regain full knowledge of himself and all his strength.

Preceded by a quietly restrained introduction and concluded with a vigorous coda, *Les Préludes* has five central sections. Each leads directly into another, although clear differences in expressive intent exist between them. Throughout, a remarkable inner synthesis is implemented by Liszt's use of two germinal motives that continually reappear in altered guise.

1. *Introduction:* After two preliminary *pizzicato* chords have been sounded by orchestral strings, a brief melodic idea appears deep in the low register. Initially announced in the work's primary tonality of C major, this subject is subsequently repeated one tone higher. Later, it passes through a sequence of chromatically ascending keys, beginning on A-flat. Basically, this subject consists of three tones: [9]

But its total expanse is more extensive:

As the piece unfolds, Liszt causes this germinal figure to grow in a number of ways—he termed the process *thematic metamorphosis*—and a remarkable development of it occurs in subsequent portions of *Les Préludes.*

2. Part I, "Man As a Mortal Being," depicts its subject in broad, sweeping terms. An eloquent orchestra sounds a resonant *fortissimo* (the passage is marked to be played *andante maestoso*), and lower brass instruments (trombones and tuba) articulate this modification of the principal theme:

Later, after a transition in which fragments of the motive are heard, the subject is expanded when a solo horn sounds it in this manner:

[9] Curiously enough, the French composer César Franck uses a nearly identical motive in his Symphony in D minor.

Speaking very persuasively, the music suggests that man is well-adjusted and finds pleasure as well as satisfaction in life.

3. Part II, "Happiness in Love," indicates that joy has attained a penultimate degree. Here a second subject, a perfect foil for the masculine first theme, is introduced by a quartet of horns (supported by similarly divided violas) in a passage marked *espressivo ma tranquillo:*

Flowing at a gentle pace, the music is fully expressive of idlyllic tranquility.

4. Part III, "The Storms of Life," brings man into contact with tumult. Premonitions of conflict are suggested by 'cellos when they sound this agitated figure:

In later passages (marked *allegro tempestoso*), the full orchestra becomes engaged in a discourse that writhes and twists as man is repeatedly buffetted by the gale winds of adversity. This is no short-termed tribulation, for the music's course is lengthy; but eventually the pace slackens and sonority abates. Temporarily, it would seem, man has solved his problems.

5. Part IV, "Return to Nature," shows that man has fled from contention to discover peace in a sequestered sanctuary. In a rural retreat he finds quiet and security. With a gentle undulating motion, various instruments (horn, oboe, clarinet, and flute) discourse on a languid theme suggestive of contemplation and repose:

Later, the ardent second theme ("Man in Love") is expressed by violins and full orchestra.

6. Part V, "Man Returns to Strife," shows that problems cannot be solved by ignoring them or by running away. As trumpets sound (in a section marked *allegro marziale animato*), man returns to battle against adversity, and an aroused orchestra sounds music that is tumultuous, pulsating, and frenetic. Ringing through this sonorous melee is the second theme, which has now renounced its reticent demeanor to assume a martial guise:

The first theme, too, joins in the fray as man gains an ascendancy over antagonistic forces. Ultimately, triumph!

7. *Coda:* Because he has conquered both fear and foe, man finds a rightful place in the firmament. Consequently, this concluding epilogue is affirmative and exultant.

Camille Saint-Saëns (1835–1921), *Danse macabre*

A variety of macabre subjects—including a morbid interest in death, purgatory, and life in the hereafter—fascinated many nineteenth century litterateurs. Edgar Allan Poe (1809–1849) in his *Tales of the Grotesque and Arabesque* and Thomas de Quincy (1785–1859) in *Confessions of an English Opium-Eater,* are only two of the writers who were sent on wild flights of creative fancy by such bizarre topics. And several composers joined in a parade that followed—figuratively speaking—a path to the grave. One of the earliest was Hector Berlioz, who conceived his *Symphonie fantastique* (1830) as an elaborate excursion into phantasmagoria (its finale is particularly orgiastic). Later, Franz Liszt depicted aspects of death in his *Todtentanz* (Dance of Death) for piano and orchestra, and visited Hell and Purgatory in his "Dante" Symphony. Gounod was concerned with the supernatural in his opera *Faust;* Mussorgsky treated listeners to an orgiastic rendezvous with the denizens of iniquity in *A Night on Bald Mountain;* and Rachmaninoff journeyed via music to *The Isle of the Dead.* One of the most attractive musical works to pursue this rather gruesome subject is Saint Saëns' *Danse macabre* (1874), a tuneful, spirited, and delightfully organized piece.

Cast in a single movement, *Danse macabre* is a radiant symphonic poem whose colors glisten vividly as a variety of instruments (harp, xylophone, oboe, flute, and low strings) are used for evocative purposes. Particularly effective in this respect is the composer's employment of a solo violin to emulate the spectre of death. Third in a series of descriptive works by Saint-Saëns, *Danse macabre* is based on this poem by Henri Cazalis:

Zig, zig, zig, Death in cadence,
Strikes with his heel on a tomb,
Death plays a dance-tune at midnight,
Zig, zig, zig, on his violin.

The winter wind blows, and the night is dark;
Moans are heard among the linden trees,
Through the gloom, white skeletons pass,
Running and leaping in their shrouds.

Zig, zig, zig, each one is jumping,
The bones of the dancers are heard rattling.

But hush! Suddenly they quit the melee,
And push forward, they fly, for the cock has crowed!

These are its details:

1. Twelve reiterated *D*'s, intended to simulate the striking of midnight, are sounded by the harp as *Danse macabre* begins. In the background sustained string harmonies are heard. After 'cellos and basses (playing *pizzicato*) announce a series of eight tones, the solo violin presents this dolorous little tune in open fifths:

Immediately thereafter, the principal theme is sounded by a low flute over string accompaniment:

Orchestral violins repeat this subject in a higher octave, and the solo violin returns with a graceful little dance tune—the second subject—which is quite different from the previous melody:

f largamente

2. Along with its descriptive intent, *Danse macabre* is also a travesty on the waltz, a dance then (c. 1870) enjoying uncommon popularity. Set in triple meter (and marked *mouvement modère de valse*), it is witty, sardonic, and amusing, despite a presumed macabre descriptive intent.

3. The three subjects already mentioned comprise the basic thematic material of *Danse macabre*. Repeated innumerable times, they are heard with changes in color, shifts in tonality, or modifications of texture. Saint-Saëns' virtuosity in handling this material is truly astonishing.

4. Building with irresistible force, *Danse macabre* grows in intensity as motions of a hypothetical dance become increasingly frenetic. Ultimately, orgiastic merriment and grisly abandon mount to a climactic pitch as the spirits cavort with uninhibited pleasure. In latter stages, a melodic sequence from the *Dies Irae* (Day of Wrath), an incipit from the Gregorian repertoire, booms with sepulchral force from the orchestra to further buttress the eerie intent.

5. But the night of celebration is passing, and streaks of dawn begin to brighten a patch of sky. When this happens, the music breaks sharply, a rooster (impersonated by the oboe) crows, and orchestral sonority falls to a gentle murmur. Acting as spokesman for the revelers, the solo violin somberly sings a touching farewell. After a few restrained measures of the first dance melody have been played, the music quietly fades into oblivion as participants in this riotous "Dance of Death" steal furtively away.

Modest P. Mussorgsky (1839–1881), *Pictures at an Exhibition* (Orchestrated by Maurice Ravel)

Possessed of a wondrously original creative sense, Mussorgsky was, unfortunately, shackled by inferior training. And this lack of technical competence occasionally made it necessary for a second person to edit, or arrange, his compositions. Such is the circumstance with his masterly opera *Boris Godounov,* where several compatriots including Rimsky-Korsakoff and, in later years, Shostakovich, applied finishing touches. And this is also pertinent to *Pictures at an Exhibition,* a set of piano pieces that others, most notably Maurice Ravel, have arranged for orchestra.

Intended as a memoriam to Victor Hartman (d. 1873), a dear friend and painter with whom Mussorgsky worked in furthering the cause for artistic nationalism in Russia, this work attempts to depict a visit to an imaginary art gallery in which several of the artist's illustrations are hung. Beginning with an ambulatory theme known as the "Promenade" (which is also used as a connective between several subdivisions), *Pictures at an Exhibition,* particularly in the orchestral version, describes its subjects in glowing, radiant colors. Consistently melodic, it unfailingly compels listener attention over a rather lengthy course. These are its details:

1. *Promenade:* Suggesting the casual locomotion of a museum visitor, the initial subject in this composition is weighty, yet curiously free. Sounded initially by brass instruments, it convincingly leads a listener through the doors of an art gallery:

    (In shortened versions and with altered orchestration, this subject later recurs between sections 1–2, 2–3, and 4–5).

2. *Gnomes:* An elfin-like dwarf, really a wooden toy fashioned after one of Hartman's designs, is the first subject for musical portrayal. Ungainly and awkward, the plaything is depicted in music that is furtive, halting, angular, and agitated:

3. *The Old Castle:* An ancient edifice before which a troubadour appears to be singing a serenade appeared in Hartman's collection of drawings, and Mussorgsky was moved to create an especially lovely piece of music about it. Particularly effective use is made here of the alto saxophone, which plays this attractive tune:

4. *Tuileries:* Subtitled "Children At Play," this section depicts a garden in Paris where youngsters (supervised by nursemaids) gather to play an

assortment of children's games. Woodwind instruments suggest the taunting songs they sing to tease one another:

5. *Bydlo:* A Polish oxen cart, fitted with huge wooden wheels, is suggested in music that has heavy, ponderous rhythms. Its driver (simulated by the solo tuba) sings a beautiful folk song as the vehicle lumbers along:

In later passages, this melody is repeated by the entire ensemble.

6. *Ballet of The Unhatched Chicks:* In 1870 Hartman designed costumes for a ballet in which some children were to be dressed as canaries, while others impersonated eggs. Mussorgsky's music symbolizes the gestures these youthful ballerinas would make while dancing in such unusual costumes:

7. *Samuel Goldenberg and Schmuyle:* Two senior citizens, one well-dressed and secure, the other—a far different personality—so impecunious that he wheedles beseechingly for alms, engage in a colloquy. In Ravel's orchestration, the rich man is portrayed by low strings playing in unison, while the beggar is delineated by a muted trumpet supported with woodwind harmonies:

Presented successively, the two ideas are later combined in a beautifully conceived example of orchestral polyphony.

8. *Limoges—The Market Place:* Again verbal discourse is the subject of musical depiction, but this is a lively conversation between gossiping habitués—mostly feminine—who gather in the open market place of a French city. Appropriately the music is chatty, crisp, and witty:

9. *Catacombs—Sepulchrum Romanum:* More than elsewhere in this set of pieces, Mussorgsky now expresses deep grief over Hartman's death. Its stimulus was an illustration, drawn by the artist, in which Hartman is shown examining the catacombs in Paris by lantern light. A verbal inscription in the score, *Cum Mortuis in Lingua Morta* (Speaking to the dead in a dead language), indicates the communion Mussorgsky felt toward his deceased friend.

10. *The Hut on Fowl's Legs:* In what may well have been an early example of surrealism, Hartman drew an illustration showing a clock encased within the frame of a hut occupied by Baba Yaga, a celebrated Russian witch. To carry fantasy even further, he mounted the entire structure on fowl's legs! Mussorgsky's music describing this apparition is appropriately bizarre:

11. *Great Gate at Kiev:* Some years prior to his death, Hartman submitted the design for a proposed city gate at Kiev. Conceived in massive style,

it featured a typical Russian bulb-shaped cupola. Mussorgsky's music describing it is sonorous and weighty, as if to emphasize the gate's ponderous size:

Particularly opulent in sound, this becomes a most appropriate and majestic finale.

Richard Strauss (1864–1949), *Ein Heldenleben* (A Hero's Life)

Few composers engage in musical autobiography. In the final episode of his *Enigma* Variations Elgar follows such a course briefly, and Smetana is somewhat more discursive in his String Quartet No. 1 in E minor, subtitled "From My Life." But compared with painters or authors, musicians are quite reticent about describing themselves in their own media. Richard Strauss, however, is an exception, for his lengthy symphonic poem *Ein Heldenleben* (1898) is an unabashed self-portrait of arresting beauty. Rather brashly calling himself a hero, Strauss proceeds to disclose the joys, tribulations, encomiums, frustrations, and carping that befall those active in public life. Professional critics heaped pages of abuse on the piece, but this did not prevent Strauss from composing his subsequent *Symphonia domestica* ("Domestic" Symphony, 1904), which is also autobiographical.

Contained within a single movement and scored for an unusually large orchestra including four each of woodwinds (flute, oboe, clarinet, and bassoon), eight horns, a total of five trumpets, three trombones, two tubas, two harps, percussion, and a full string section, *Ein Heldenleben*—even aside from its uninhibited portrayal of Strauss' personal life—is a remarkable work. Segmented into six subdivisions, it ponders and probes, questions and affirms, examines, and ultimately exults in the "hero's" intrepid personality. All sections, of course, are devoted to an embellishment of the principal subject, all are based on related thematic material, and all are interconnected by transitional passages. These are further details:

1. "The Hero": Without preliminary fanfare, the hero is introduced when a vigorous upward-rising theme is sounded by 'cellos, violas, and horns:

Within moments, a more restrained side of the hero's personality is revealed by a flowing subject with three subsections. Played by first violins in a high register, its initial portion is this:

Continuation enlists middle-voiced violas:

And, finally, 'cellos round out the idea:

In the following measures, each theme is marshalled in a variety of ways to display the hero's complex nature. But the virile first subject consistently dominates the discourse.

2. "The Hero's Adversaries": Every great man has his critics, of course, but Strauss seemingly had more than a fair share. He finds retribution against their polemics, however, in this "Critic's Section," where antagonistic commentators are depicted in the most unflattering terms. Initially, a flute begins:

Soon it is joined by other winds who snarl, snap, and bark in strident cacophony. Contrasting with this discordant unpleasantness, the hero's theme (sounded in minor) rises with gracious serenity from 'cellos and basses. Seemingly, the composer maintains an unruffled demeanor, even in the face of vicious backbiting and innuendo! Precisely at the end of this section a new theme is sounded by winds:

3. "The Hero's Courtship": Gracious and lovely, the hero's wife brings joy and beauty into his life, as this theme (played by a solo violin) suggests:

Another subject assists in describing his lady and the affection husband and wife hold for one another. It too is sounded by the solo violin:

Lengthy passages akin to cadenzas abound in this section, indicating that the wife is comforting, consoling, and advising her consort. Later, a rapturous love duet is heard. What are enemies in the face of such bliss?

4. "The Hero's Battlefield": A new theme (seventh in the work) describes the composer before he clashes with his adversaries:

Once the battle has been joined, however, the affray is vigorous. Instruments associated with combat, drums and trumpets, sound with martial fervor. Amidst the melee, a new theme, rather incongruous in this setting, is heard:

From the latter's gentle nature we learn that the hero much prefers amity to contention. But, as a man of courage, he will not flee from strife; rather, he stands firm and vigorously jousts with enemies. Although the struggle is protracted, his adversaries are finally vanquished and the hero turns toward reconstruction.

5. "The Hero's Works of Peace": With a cessation of hostilities, a new mood seizes the hero. Second violins sing a quiet subject suggestive of compassion, magnanimity, and generosity:

Seemingly this theme suggests that mankind can live in friendly concord, with justice and honor for all. So that no one will misunderstand who is promulgating these doctrines, Strauss quotes themes from his earlier *Till Eulenspiegel, Don Juan,* and *Don Quixote.*

6. "The Hero's Release From the World": As it must for every man, the hero's end of life approaches. Meditative, tender, and sad, he prepares for departure from the world. Critics remain hostile, and some still question his efforts. But, he reflects, this has been a good life; one filled with joy, pleasure, and love. In all, it has been "A Hero's Life!"

George Gershwin (1898–1937), *An American in Paris*

Gershwin's story is the tale of one who "made it the hard way." Born on New York City's lower East Side, he came to composition via "Tin Pan Alley," a cluster of metropolitan publishing houses from which most of America's popular tunes emerge. After casual employment as a song plugger, Gershwin progressed to creating melodies of his own; more exalted work followed when he wrote the scores for such Broadway productions as: *Lady Be Good, Strike Up the Band, Girl Crazy,* and *Of Thee I Sing.* At the suggestion of Paul Whiteman, he composed the *Rhapsody in Blue* (1924) and initiated a style of writing that combined elements of popular jazz with recondite and traditional creative techniques. Four years later (1928), Gershwin was commissioned by Walter Damrosch to write *An American in Paris.*

Formulated as a symphonic poem, Gershwin's piece depicts the nostalgic yearnings of a youthful visitor to the "City of Light." Written for a conventional symphony orchestra, it also calls for an enlarged percussion section and three saxophones. Not the least of its innovations is an employment of French taxi horns that intermittently honk in the music's very midst. These are details about a brilliant musical travelogue:

1. As the work opens, a brisk walking theme symbolizing a stroll down a Parisian boulevard, perhaps the Champs Elysées, sounds from the orchestra:

When crossing streets in the French capital a traveler must be wary, as the Yankee pedestrian discovers when taxi horns sound to warn of imminent danger. Safety is attained on the boulevard's far side, however, and the visitor resumes his stride. Progressing down the avenue he passes a cafe and hears strains of "La Sorella," a melody that provides backgrounds for *La Maxixe*, a tango-like dance much in vogue during the 1920s. With interest alerted the American stops, for hearing this tune enkindles a spark of homesickness. But one cannot tarry wrapped in introspection while in Paris on a spring day, and so the visitor soon resumes pacing as the orchestra utters a second walking theme:

2. Open portals leading into a cathedral beckon the sight-seer, and the music slows as he weighs the possibility of a digression, but the American does not enter this edifice. Rather, he continues and the walking theme resumes its original pace. Soon, however, a new subject sounds, suggesting that the neighborhood changes as the American nears the river:

Ultimately, the Seine is reached. Walking over one of its numerous bridges, he crosses to the Left Bank.

3. New sights distract the American, and the music suggests a continually shifting panorama. As may happen in such circumstances, he meets a young lady and the two strike up a conversation, indicated by coy expressions from a solo violin. But the friendship is short-lived; the tête à tête breaks off and the man walks on alone. Now, he is in a disconsolate

frame of mind; the pace slows and the music loses its walking motion. As the orchestra adopts a blues tempo, a wailing trumpet expresses the American's increasing sense of loneliness:

Eloquently discoursing on this subject, the full ensemble repeats it at considerable length.

4. Spells of melancholy in a young person pass quickly, however. Within a few moments, the American meets a fellow countryman and a spirited exchange of pleasantries occurs. Now the music assumes an *allegro* pace as strains of a Charleston deftly chase away clouds of gloom:

Wailing trumpets, moaning saxophones, and pulsating percussion convey music reminiscent of the "roaring twenties." Gershwin knew this style well and exploits it at considerable length.

5. Two young Americans visit the exotic quarters of a fabulous city and have a holiday they will never forget. And the music remains spirited and tuneful as both walking themes and the blues melody are reaffirmed. As fresh and attractive as a bright sunny day in the city it describes, closing pages of *An American in Paris* become a glowing riot of musical color.

Selected Descriptive Compositions

Beethoven, Ludwig van (1770–1827)
    Sonata No. 26 in E-flat major (*Les Adieux*) for Piano (1809). With three movements titled "Farewell," "Absence," and "Return," it depicts the lament and joy of a friend's departure and return.
    Symphony No. 6 in F major ("Pastoral," 1808). This piece is an early program symphony in five movements that is expertly written, very appealing, and highly picturesque.
    Wellington's Victory ("Battle Symphony," 1813). A battaglia based on well-known French-English airs and battle sounds, it depicts combat, a lament for the fallen, and ultimate exultance in victory.
Berlioz, Hector (1803–1869)
    Harold in Italy (1834). Based on Byron's "Childe Harold," this is a tuneful and engaging work that features a solo viola.

Roméo et Juliette (a dramatic symphony, 1839). Impressive, dramatic, and of epic proportions, it uses soloists, chorus, and orchestra to narrate episodes from a Shakespearean drama.

Symphonie fantastique (1830). Autobiographical, in five movements, and based on a prominent *idée fixe*, it is lyric, occasionally bombastic, but consistently brilliant.

Bloch, Ernest (1880–1959)

Schelomo (Hebrew Rhapsody for 'cello and orchestra, 1916). A personality study of King Solomon in one movement that is luminous, pensive, and complex.

Borodin, Alexander (1833–1887)

In the Steppes of Central Asia (1880). Geographical pictorialism conveyed via semioriental Slavic tunes; it is clear, folk-like, and exotic.

Carpenter, John Alden (1876–1951)

Adventures in a Perambulator (1915). An American composer's baby-carriage view of a visit to the park; witty, light, and amusing.

Copland, Aaron (b. 1900)

Lincoln Portrait (1948). Founded on two traditional American melodies, it uses a narrator and orchestra to convey selected Lincoln texts.

Debussy, Claude (1862–1918)

"Iberia" from *Images* for orchestra (1911). An Impressionist's travelogue to Spain, set in three sections that are gay, nostalgic, and extremely colorful.

La Mer (Three Symphonic Sketches, 1905). An aural seascape bathed in shimmering hues; by turns it is glowing, freely conceived, and tangy.

Prélude à l'après-midi d'un faune (1894). Amorous, sensual, and languid, it is based on a Mallarmé poem and adroitly contrasts glowing strings with limpid woodwinds.

Nocturnes (*Nuages, Fêtes, Sirenes* for orchestra, 1899). Three kaleidoscopic symphonic poems with vibrant sonorities; the third uses a wordless women's choir.

Dukas, Paul (1865–1935)

The Sorcerer's Apprentice (1897). Founded on a Goethe ballad, this humorous and farcical piece depicts an enchanted broom diligently hauling water.

Elgar, Edward (1857–1934)

Enigma Variations (1899). Thirteen personality studies of the composer's friends plus an autobiographical sketch; it is incisive, witty, and occasionally trenchant.

Falla, Manuel de (1876–1946)

Nights in the Gardens of Spain (1915). An Iberian Impressionist's landscape set for piano and orchestra in three movements; alluring, poetic, and evocative.

Franck, César (1822–1890)

Le Chasseur maudit (1882). Because of his transgressions, a Sabbath huntsman (a nonchurchgoer) becomes accursed; this work is emotive, slightly satiric, and based on a Burger ballad.

Gershwin, George (1898–1937)

An American in Paris (1928). This work depicts peripatetic occurrences on a Parisian boulevard; it is bright and vivacious and uses blues, jazz, and a host of unusual effects.

Granados, Enrique (1867–1916)
Goyescas (1914). These are two sets of piano pieces (4-3 each) inspired by Goya etchings; they are exquisite miniatures.

Grofé, Ferde (b. 1892)
Grand Canyon Suite (1931). America's immense natural wonder vividly described in five movements; mostly the music is brash, brilliant, and spectacular

Holst, Gustav (1874–1934)
The Planets (1916). Seven cosmic wonders are portrayed in musical attire; they are colorful, contrasted, and cleanly etched.

Honegger, Arthur (1892–1955)
Pacific 231 (1923). This is the saga of an American steam locomotive; it is noisy, energetic, and incessantly pulsating.

Ibert, Jacques (1890–1962)
Escales (Ports of Call, 1922). A Mediterranean voyage with stops at three ports; it is expressively indolent, exotic, and intriguing.

Ives, Charles (1874–1954)
Sonata No. 2 for Piano ("Concord, Mass., 1840–1860," 1915). New England transcendentalism expressed in four movements; it details the philosophy of Emerson and his associates and is extremely dissonant and complex.
Three Places in New England (1903). Vistas of an area expressed in geographic-historic terms; it is compassionate, nostalgic, and occasionally iconoclastic.

Kuhnau, Johann (1660–1722)
Biblical Sonatas (c. 1700). Six classics for harpsichord that describe David, Goliath, Hezekiah, Gideon, and others; they are puissant, quirky, and quaint.

Liadov, Anatol (1855–1914)
Baba Yaga (1904); *The Enchanted Lake* (1910); and *Kikimora* (1909). Each describes a world of fantasy where magic spells, make-believe, and enchantment reign; they are charming, short, and fanciful.

Liszt, Franz (1811–1886)
Tasso—Lament and Triumphant (Symphonic Poem No. 2, 1849). Founded on a Byron poem and a personality study of an important Italian author, it is expressively morbid, plaintive, and bitter.
Les Préludes (Symphonic Poem No. 3, 1854). Vaguely associated with a Lamartine poem, it is introspective, philosophical, and employs much melodic metamorphosis.
Mazeppa (Symphonic Poem No. 6, 1854). Concerned with an Ukrainian Cossack chief described in a Victor Hugo poem, this composition is frenetic, wild, and boisterous.

Mendelssohn, Felix (1809–1847)
Hebrides Overture ("Fingal's Cave," 1830). Inspired by the composer's visits to Scotland, this piece portrays an immense natural cavern; organized in sonata form, it is lyric, imaginative, and engaging.
Tale of the Beautiful Melusina (1834). This piece portrays a bemused girl

who is changed into a mermaid on Saturdays; founded on Ludwig Tieck's
tale, it is graceful, flowing, and sweet.

Milhaud, Darius (b. 1892)

Le Boeuf sur le toit (1919). A jazzy pantomime with music that describes a
Cocteau setting in an American bar, it uses much Brazilian folk music,
and is quite surrealistic, wildly rhythmic, and exciting.

Création du monde (1923). Motivated by Negro jazz, this ballet score is
based on a Cendrars scenario; it uses five sections and eighteen instruments to depict the origins of genus homo sapiens.

Mossolov, Alexander (b. 1900)

The Iron Foundry (1928). This is an exuberant portrayal of a totalitarian
factory in operation; it is bombastic, crude, and explosive.

Mozart, Wolfgang A. (1756–1791)

Ein Musikalischer Spass (A Musical Joke, K. 522, 1787). Scored for strings
and two horns, it satirizes the incompetence of provincial musicians in a
hilarious way; it is raucous (for Mozart) and occasionally coy.

Mussorgsky, Modest (1839–1881)

A Night on Bald Mountain (1886). Based on a Gogol story, "St. John's
Eve," it is almost monothematic, uninhibited, and frenzied.

Pictures at an Exhibition (1874; orchestrated, 1923). A musical tour through
a gallery where a listener "views" ten sketches by Victor Hartman; initially
for piano, it was later orchestrated by Ravel (and others).

Prokofiev, Serge (1891–1953)

Peter and the Wolf (1936). An amusing orchestral fairy tale that uses narrator and small orchestra to depict a small boy's triumph over a predatory
wolf.

Rachmaninoff, Serge (1873–1943)

Isle of the Dead (1907). Stimulated by a Boecklin painting, this probing
and funereal work depicts a melancholy abode for departed souls.

Ravel, Maurice (1875–1937)

Ma Mère l'Oye (Mother Goose Suite, 1908). Five episodes from Perrault
fairy tales are told with vivacity and charm; each is short, piquant, and
colorful.

Respighi, Ottorino (1879–1936)

The Fountains of Rome (1917). Four landmarks in the Eternal City are depicted in Impressionistic terms; it is restrained, poetic, and tasteful.

The Pines of Rome (1924). A companion piece that depicts four landscapes
in this city, it is austere, audacious, and striking.

Roman Festivals (1929). This piece describes four unbridled celebrations in
the Italian capital; the work is blatant, almost paganistic, and an orchestral tour de force.

Rimsky-Korsakoff, Nicholas (1844–1908)

Capriccio espagnol (1887). A dazzling collection of five pieces redolent with
Iberian tunes and rhythms conceived by a non-Spanish composer.

Scheherazade (1888). An opulent narrative depicting four tales from the
Arabian Nights, so rich in orchestration and melody as to be fulsome.

Saint-Saëns, Camille (1835–1921)

Carnival of the Animals (1886). This is a satiric zoological fantasy that ironically depicts a bevy of animals in fourteen short sections; all are cheery, clever, and entertaining.

Danse macabre (1874). Unworldly denizens dance gleefully at midnight in an elaborate orchestral fantasy in which prominent solo passages are given the violin and xylophone; it is based on a poem by Cazalis.

Schumann, Robert (1810–1856)

Kinderscenen (1838). Thirteen nostalgic episodes recall the composer's childhood; these are short, simple, and delicate piano pieces.

Waldscenen (1849). Nine whimsical studies of forest environs that are exceptionally lyric, poetic, and allusive piano works.

Sibelius, Jean (1865–1957)

Finlandia (1899). Almost a national epic, it includes a sturdy hymn and is granitic, brassy, and exciting.

Swan of Tuonela (1896). Based on a Kalevala legend, it depicts the Finnish Hades and features the English horn in a murky and melancholic discourse.

Valse triste (1903). A slow, pensive waltz originally written for a Jarnefelt play that depicts a son's bedside vigil and the appearance of Death.

Smetana, Bedrich (1824–1884)

Moldau from *My Fatherland* (1882). A nationalistic epic that describes a river's rise and flow, it is sweeping, tuneful, and mostly gay.

String Quartet No. 1 in E minor ("From My Life," 1876). An autobiographical chamber music piece in four movements that suggests life's stages; it is vital, zestful, and ultimately tragic.

Strauss, Richard (1864–1949)

Also sprach Zarathustra (1896). Concerning the Nietzsche-Zoroaster superman, this philosophical discourse has numerous divisions and is long and sometimes dreary.

Death and Transfiguration (1889). This composition narrates four fantasies occasioned by Death's approach; they are pensive, agitated, inquiring, and resigned.

Don Juan (1888). An idealist's view of an infamous roué derived from a Lenau poem, it has broad lovely melodies and is serious and dignified.

Don Quixote (1897). Knight-errantry is portrayed in variation form via solo 'cello; based on Cervantes, it is lengthy but attractive.

Ein Heldenleben (1898). The hero (Strauss) vanquishes critics, performs good works, earns his wife's love, and is portrayed as being courageous, immodest, and bold.

Till Eulenspiegel's Merry Pranks (1895). An irrepressible rogue is depicted as being continually embroiled in prankish episodes; it is mischievous, whimsical, and occasionally pensive.

Stravinsky, Igor (b. 1882)

Petrouchka (1911). The saga of a clown's life, love, and death at a Russian fair; it is clever, varicolored, and continually engrossing.

Le Sacre du printemps (1913). A ballet score depicting sacrificial rites in pagan Russia; with two subdivisions, it is primitive, barbaric and pulsating.

Song of the Nightingale (1919). An oriental fairy tale concerning an emperor's favorite songbird, it is told with sweet melodic charm.

Tchaikowsky, Peter (1840–1893)

Francesca da Rimini (1876). A tragic tale about the life and death of Countess Malatesta as related by Dante; the music is lyric, tempestuous, and ardent.

Overture 1812 (1882). Depicting Napoleon's ignominious defeat in Russia, this jubilant and clangorous piece employs cannon, bands, church bells, and national melodies.

Romeo and Juliet (1881). The poignant Shakespearean tragedy is set in symphonic dress; it is overly sentimental but engrossingly melodic.

Wagner, Richard (1813–1883)

"Entry of the Gods into Valhalla," from *Das Rheingold* (1854). Massive and sonorous, it depicts an awesome processional of immortals over a rainbow bridge into a city of marble.

"Ride of Valkyries" and the "Magic Fire Music," from *Die Walküre* (1856). Rugged daughters of Wotan sweep the sky in a tumultuous outpouring of sound. Later, the fire music is insidious, flickering, and ultimately somnolent.

"Siegfried's Rhine Journey" and "Funeral Music" from *Die Götterdämmerung* (1874). A combined personality study and travelogue that uses numerous leitmotives. The first piece is granitic but restless; the second expresses remorse and deep despair.

"Good Friday Spell" from *Parsifal* (1882). Knights of the Grail observe Holy Week in music that depicts repentance as well as seraphic salvation.

Chapter 15

Chamber Music:
An Intimate Art

Small groups of instrumentalists, which may include from two to eight or nine players, are the usual performing ensemble for chamber music. Although the term is occasionally used semihumorously to identify folk singers or jazz combos, its real meaning concerns serious musicians and the pieces they play. Chamber groups are often called duos, trios, quartets, and so on—dependent, of course, on the number of participants—and may include such instruments as piano, violin, 'cello, flute, oboe, clarinet, and harpsichord. In contemporary concert life chamber music is regularly performed by highly skilled professionals, but the amateur is also significant in this field. Indeed, during its early history between the tenth and sixteenth centuries, chamber music was almost always performed by dilletantes attached to court retinues or by gifted amateurs from various walks of life, students, clerics, or minstrels. In a modified fashion, this practice has continued into our own time.

A consensus holds that chamber music should (1) be primarily concerned with instrumental performance; (2) be performed in a small room (hence the designation chamber); and (3) assign only one player to a part. In a string quartet, for instance, each of four instrumentalists performs individual lines, and there is a notable absence of doubling (sounding a part by more than one player). This is important, for it greatly influences the opaqueness of an ensemble's timbre and places it in diametrical opposition to the massed sonorities of an orchestra. Because of its emphasis on the individual performer, chamber music (along with song) can be considered an unusually intimate art. Rhetorical utterance, dramatic flamboyance, and spectacular effect are foreign to its nature.

THE ESSENCE OF CHAMBER MUSIC

Writing late in the eighteenth century, the English historian, Dr. Charles Burney, spoke of chamber music as including ". . . cantatas, single

405

songs, solos and trios, quartets, concertos, and symphonies of few parts." [1] During ensuing generations, however, this concept has become somewhat modified. Now excluded are works for orchestra, band, or other large groups, and virtually all vocal compositions. Some disputation has arisen whether pieces for single instruments (piano or violin sonatas, for example) should be included, and it has been questioned whether these, in effect, are not too individualistic for the chamber art. Yet, sonatas are a keystone in the chamber music repertoire and probably should be accepted without reservation.

Regardless of the group for which they are scored, most chamber pieces have an organizational plan similar to the sonata (see Chapter 8 and p. 407). Usually they have several movements—typically three or four—each contrasted with its associates in rhythm, melody, key, formal design, and expressive intent. And most of these subdivisions are organized in such patterns as part form, variation form, sonata form, or rondo form and consistently demonstrate a serious expressive mien. Chamber compositions may be lively and witty, but they are rarely trite or obvious.

A *sine qua non* holds that an ensemble's instruments shall exist on an equal plane. Their sonorities, dynamic ranges, technical capabilities, and communicative resources must be commensurate so that one readily comingles with others. When called on, however, each should be fully capable of demonstrating its unique color and facility.

Relatively few chamber pieces are descriptive. Evidently this mode of writing is too serious for the purposes of illustrative music. But a few exceptions exist. Smetana's Quartet in E Minor, subtitled "From My Life," for instance, is an interesting autobiographical work, and Johann Kuhnau's *Biblical Sonatas* (c. 1695) as well as Charles Ives' *Concord Sonata* (1909–1915) follow narrative lines. In the aggregate, however, chamber compositions tend to be abstract in substance and relatively formal in outline.

PERFORMING MEDIA FOR CHAMBER MUSIC

In theory any combination of instruments can be used to perform chamber music. In actuality, however, several rather well-defined groups (see p. 407), find the most widespread employment. Inevitably, different historical periods have tended to emphasize particular groups. During the sixteenth and seventeenth centuries, for instance, chamber pieces were written for an assorted group of string instruments known as a *consort* or a *chest* of viols; the seventeenth and early eighteenth centuries featured the *trio sonata;* and Classicists active after 1750 discovered the *string quartet.* Late in the nineteenth century the *woodwind quintet* gained some prominence, and *percussion ensembles* have similarly become important in the

---

[1] Quoted in Percy A. Scholes, *The Oxford Companion to Music,* ninth ed., (New York: Oxford University Press, 1963), p. 167.

contemporary era. Considering the field at large, these are undoubtedly the best-known chamber ensembles:

Duos
1. One string instrument (normally a violin, viola, or 'cello) with piano.
2. A wind instrument (flute, oboe, clarinet, bassoon, or saxophone) with piano.
3. Two string instruments—that is, two violins; a violin and viola; or a violin and 'cello.

Trios
1. String trio: violin, viola, and 'cello.
2. Piano trio: violin, 'cello, and piano.

Quartets
1. String quartet: two violins, a viola, and a 'cello.
2. Piano quartet: violin, viola, 'cello, and piano.
3. Oboe quartet, Flute quartet, or similarly named group: one wind instrument with violin, viola, and 'cello.

Quintets
1. String quintet: string quartet plus a second viola or 'cello.
2. Piano quintet: string quartet plus piano.
3. Clarinet quintet, or similarly named group: string quartet with an additional wind instrument.
4. Woodwind quintet: flute, oboe, clarinet, bassoon, and horn.

Sextets
1. String sextet: two violins, two violas, and two 'cellos.

Other combinations find occasional employment, of course. Along with a grouping of similar instruments—for instance, a horn quartet—chamber ensembles may unite members of a compatible family as with the brass quintet (two trumpets, horn, trombone, and tuba) or the percussion ensemble (drums, bells, chimes, tympani, and similar devices). Some compositions merge disparate instruments as is demonstrated in Beethoven's Septet in E-flat major (for clarinet, horn, bassoon, violin, viola, 'cello, and string bass) or in Debussy's Sonata No. 2 (for flute, viola, and harp, 1916).

THE SONATA

For nearly three centuries the sonata has existed as a peerless compositional pattern, and nowhere has it found more apt utilization than in chamber music. In external characteristics it is a multimovement piece for a single instrument or, by extension, for one instrument (violin, 'cello, flute clarinet, or others) with keyboard. Few designs equal the sonata in expressive power and none stand above. It is not only important in chamber music; suitably modified, its outlines are commonly applied to such other pieces as the symphony and concerto.

Since about 1750, the sonata has developed into a four-movement pattern with these general characteristics: [2]

1. *First movement:* Usually organized in sonata form, a typical opening movement has an (1) exposition, (2) development, and (3) recapitulation. Frequently its main section, which is usually played at an *allegro* tempo, is preceded by a slow and weighty introduction and concluded with a coda. Set in the home key, the movement is often aggressive, forceful, and dynamic. For the most part, this is a sonata's longest and most important section.

2. *Second movement:* In contrast, this subdivision is normally restrained, quiet, and organized in part form or variation form. Somber, elegiac, and lyric in expression, it may be set in a minor tonality, which further strengthens an aura of introspection.

3. *Third movement:* Spirited and quick, this section may be a minuet, a waltz, or, in works written since c. 1825, a scherzo. Normally the shortest of sonata movements, it is often cast in three-part form and established in triple meter.

4. *Fourth movement:* Typically organized in rondo form or sonata rondo form, the finale is often exuberant and buoyant. (Other formal possibilities are variation form or sonata form.) Normally, such a concluding section moves with impassioned bravura as it sweeps the entire composition to a dramatic close.

Sonatas have been written for nearly all instruments, although the piano has unquestionably acquired the richest and most extensive repertoire. String instruments, particularly violin and 'cello, have been favored, too, but wind instruments are less fortunate. While the modern sonata was being perfected (c. 1700–1750), they existed in an ill-developed state, which may account for their neglect. Only after 1775, when Mozart wrote so exquisitely for winds, did woodwind instruments begin to come into their own.

In the sixteenth and seventeenth centuries, the term sonata (from *sonare* meaning "to sound") was employed to differentiate an instrumental work from a toccata, that is, a "touch piece" conceived mostly for keyboard, or a cantata, one that was sung. In an era when music was basically oriented toward keyboard or voice, such distinctions served an eminently useful purpose. Later, after 1650, two kinds of instrumental composition arose, the *sonata da camera* (chamber sonata), and the *sonata di chiesa* (church

---

[2] It necessarily follows, of course, that these qualities are generally applicable to such "sonata-based" patterns as the string trio, string quartet, woodwind quintet, symphony, and concerto (the latter two with modifications).

sonata). Strikingly similar to the early dance suite, the *sonata da camera* ultimately lost its identity, while the *sonata di chiesa*, which included both dance and nondance patterns, became an important model for later instrumental works.

From 1700 onward, two patterns, based primarily on the *sonata di chiesa*, came into focus. Employed by Bach, Handel, Vivaldi, and their contemporaries, the *Baroque Sonata* was a design used in works for small ensembles, that is, "trio sonatas," or in pieces for a single instrument with keyboard support (Bach's six sonatas for violin and harpsichord or Handel's sonatas for flute and harpsichord). Mostly, it included from four to six rather short movements based on such dances as the bourrée, gavotte, minuet, or gigue. After 1750, the *Classical Sonata* arose. More expansive than any instrumental design heretofore known, it normally had three (sometimes more) movements that were, for the most part, nondance in character. Within it, individual segments became longer and began to exhibit the

Figure 18. A quartet of string instruments—two violins, viola and 'cello—made by Antonius Stradivarius.

workings of thematic manipulation. This was the design promulgated by Haydn, Mozart, Beethoven, Schubert, and a host of successors.

In the twentieth century, sonatas continue to hold a favored position. Such composers as Igor Stravinsky (*Sonata for Piano*, 1924; *Sonata for Two Pianos*); Béla Bartók (*Sonata for Piano*, 1926; *Sonata for Two Pianos and Percussion*, 1937; *Sonata for Unaccompanied Violin*, 1944; Sonatas Nos. 1 and 2 for Violin and Piano, 1921 and 1922, respectively), and Paul Hindemith (with a formidable list of sonatas for bassoon, 'cello, clarinet, flute, harp, oboe, organ, piano, trombone, trumpet, viola, and violin) have cultivated the design with distinction. And their efforts are being continually emulated by dozens of younger writers.

WAYPOSTS IN THE RISE OF CHAMBER MUSIC

Most of today's well-known chamber pieces were written after 1775, and it is often assumed, but erroneously, that such music had its beginnings in the era of Haydn and Mozart. Actually, progenitors of this idiom date from well before the sixteenth century. Considering the field as a whole, chamber music and its performance has passed through three principal stages:

1. A formative period in the sixteenth century and earlier when small vocal groups were common. Then, the madrigal, chanson, motet, and similar designs became models for pieces that were subsequently modified for instrumental performance.
2. An era marked by a rise of the trio-sonata concept. This extended from the early seventeenth to the mid-eighteenth century.
3. The latest epoch which began after 1750 when it was discovered that chamber ensembles no longer needed continuo support. As a result, the string quartet, piano trio, woodwind quintet, and sundry other groups came into being.

The Early Period

Chamber music, as this field is known today, had its beginnings early in the sixteenth century when compositions, essentially vocal in nature, were modified so they could be played by viols, important precursors of the violin family. Inscribed as being "apt for voices or viols," these pieces were written so they could be either played or sung. In keeping with styles of the time, they were fundamentally choral in equality and their range of tones or degrees of technical involvement were governed by vocal considerations. These were the beginnings of an important instrumental art, however, that was soon marked by an appearance of such forms as the fantasia, canzona, and ricercar. And these, in turn, became important progenitors for the trios, quartets, and sonatas of a later era.

During this early era (prior to 1600), composers worked in widely scattered centers. In Italy, Andrea Gabrieli (1515–1586) and his nephew,

Giovanni (1555–1612) were outstanding. Both composed at Venice where they created a series of unusually fine chamber compositions for strings and winds, particularly brasses, that stressed antiphonal interchanges between two or more groups. At about this same time, William Byrd (1543–1623) and Orlando Gibbons (1553–1625), working in England, created their splendid instrumental fantasies, often quaintly termed *fancies*.

In the Baroque Era [3]

Virtually all chamber works written prior to 1750 placed firm reliance on the continuo. Mostly they were trio sonatas with two upper (treble) parts—played by two violins; violin and flute; or violin and oboe—and a continually reiterated bass articulated by 'cello and harpsichord. Between the treble and bass lines nothing was provided by the composer, and when filling parts were added—mostly via extemporization by the harpsichordist— the results ranged from sublime to ridiculous. Composers were legion in this era, and their works so abundant as to defy enumeration. But among the most significant were such Italians as Arcangelo Corelli, Alessandro Scarlatti, and Antonio Vivaldi; the Englishman, Henry Purcell; the Frenchman, François Couperin (*Le Grand*); and the German-born Johann Sebastian Bach and George Frideric Handel.

In particular respects, the Baroque trio sonata was a superbly wrought art work. Finely chased and restrained in expressive power yet curiously intimate in appeal, it comprises an important link in the centuries-old tradition of chamber music. Typically, a trio sonata is cast in four movements and, despite its name, uses four instruments (most commonly two violins, 'cello, and harpsichord) for performance. So that a harpsichordist (who was often the work's composer) might embellish a composition's lines and thus enrich the musical fabric, his score included details written in a kind of musical shorthand known as *figured bass*. During a span extending from the time of Arcangelo Corelli (1653–1713) to that of Johann Sebastian Bach (1685–1750), harpsichordists engaged in almost unlimited improvisation as they "realized" continuo parts. This technique is beautifully demonstrated in the trio sonata from Bach's *Musical Offering* (see p. 426).

Shifted to another age, however, when the harpsichordist became a mere performer (perhaps one possessed of few creative gifts), the realization of a figured bass sometimes imposed indignities difficult to endure.

---

[3] Fine examples of pre- and early Baroque chamber music appear in Parrish's *Treasury of Early Music*. (See Appendix C, "Suggested Bibliography.") They include (1) *In Nomine* for viol consort (in four parts) by Orlando Gibbons; (2) *Tombeau de Mademoiselle Gaultier* for lute by Denis Gaultier; (3) *Capriccio uber dass Hennengeschery* for harpsichord by Alessandro Poglietti; and (4) *Fantasie* for Solo Violin by Georg Philipp Telemann. Other pieces appear in the Parrish and Ohl *Masterpieces of Music Before 1750* (see Appendix C), including (1) *Canzona per l'epistola* for keyboard, presumably written by Ercole Pasquini; (2) *Loth to Depart*, a set of variations for virginals by Giles Farnaby; (3) Suite in E minor for clavichord by J. J. Froberger; (4) *Sonata de chiesa* in E minor (a trio sonata for two violins, 'cello, and keyboard) by Arcangelo Corelli; and (5) Sonata in C minor for harpsichord by Domenico Scarlatti.

Moreover, the harpsichord itself had serious shortcomings that made its inclusion within later ensembles somewhat impractical. Like an organ, it is
fitted with "couplers," which enable the instrument to sound in several registers at once. During solo performance, octave doubling unquestionably imparts enhanced sonority, but in ensemble work the resultant thickness of
sound often negates the ideals of clarity and balance. Consequently, the use
of figured bass, or the harpsichord itself, in chamber works written after
1750 is comparatively rare.

The fifteen sonatas—seven for flute, two for oboe, and six for violin—
that George Frideric Handel composed early in the eighteenth century aptly
disclose the sonata's development up to this time. Published collectively in
Amsterdam in 1724 under the heading of "Opus 1," they actually are totally
independent and diverse pieces assembled merely to serve the expediencies
of publishing. Modeled after sonatas by Corelli, Handel's works are delightfully fresh and original in substance. Cast in four, five, or six short movements, they have soaring melodic lines, occasional bold harmonies, and a
continuously vibrant rhythmic thrust. In each, the solo instrument plays
without cessation, supported by the ubiquitous harpsichord. These are
details concerning an example, the Sonata No. 1 in E minor for Flute:

1. *First movement:* Highly ornate, and founded on a repeated articulation
   of dotted rhythms, this opening *grave* is played at an inordinately slow
   tempo with eight beats in a measure. Flowing in a dignified manner, it
   suggests a vocal arioso in three sections concerned with: (1) the presentation of a musical idea, (2) its extension in a new key, and (3) an altered
   return. As the movement begins, the flute plays this subject:

2. *Second movement:* Energetic in pace and more agile in activity, the
   second section is a brisk *allegro*. Giving the appearance of following a
   unilateral course, it is based on a sportive interplay between motivic
   fragments. At its outset, the solo instrument establishes these ideas:

3. *Third movement:* By comparison restrained, elegiac, and brief, the
following thirteen-measure *adagio* (the sonata's third movement) is a
moment of quietude in the midst of a bustling virtuoso work. This is the
first part of its melody:

4. *Fourth movement:* Assuming an incisive pace in triple meter, the finale is
a spirited dance movement in *allegro* tempo. Organized in binary form
(with thirty-one and forty-nine measures, respectively), it requires the
utmost in lithe dexterity from a flutist. This is how it begins:

In the Classic Era

A more modern concept of chamber music came into being after 1750.
Then, Haydn and Mozart gave definitive status to the string quartet and
established a standard toward which all subsequent chamber composers have
aspired. From the luxuriant sonorous base provided by a quartet's versatile
string instruments, they evolved a whole new plan for writing. In this new
musical environment, reliance heretofore placed on keyboard instruments
via the continuo tradition was abandoned. At this time, too, the sonata
rose to prominence. Henceforth, most chamber pieces, identified as trios,
quartets, quintets, and so on, were to bear a sonata's characteristic outlines.

Although Haydn is credited with being in the forefront while its format
was perfected, precisely when the quartet's instrumentation of two violins,
a viola, and a 'cello was determined—and by whom—is uncertain. Such distinguished musicians as Giuseppe Tartini, G. B. Sammartini, F. X. Richter,
and Luigi Boccherini must be considered innovators whose preliminary
work in formulating the design's outline's was accomplished before Haydn's
important quartets began to appear shortly after 1780.[4] Building on this
established base, and following his sublime instincts, the latter applied

[4] Prior to this time (between 1755–1781), Haydn had written thirty-six quartets.
But his important pieces in this genre were composed in the century's final quarter.

expert finishing touches to the design and created a total list of eighty-three wondrous quartets. Haydn's conception placed each instrument on an equal plane and allocated them parts that were mutually complementary as well as individually interesting. An example of his writing, the Quartet in C major, identified as the "Emperor," will be discussed later.

Of his numerous contemporaries, Haydn's only peer in chamber music writing was W. A. Mozart. Although the caprice of unpredictable fate caused him to predecease Haydn by nearly two decades, Mozart enjoyed a warm friendship with his senior colleague during the years both were active in Vienna. For his part, Haydn was lavish in praising Mozart's abilities, and the latter reciprocated by showing deference, admiration, and great respect for the older man. Particularly notable among Mozart's chamber works, for instance, are the six *Haydn Quartets*—numbers fourteen through nineteen in the composer's total of twenty-three—that he dedicated to Haydn with a warm expression of esteem and affection. Mozart's string quintets, of which there are six, are unusually beautiful works that gain enhanced opulence by having an additional viola as the fifth instrument.

A natural fecundity led Mozart to write for a variety of ensembles. As a matter of course, many of his chamber pieces are for strings alone, some are scored for strings and piano, whereas others use winds in an altogether novel manner. Mozart was one of the first to recognize the unusual expressive possibilities inherent in the latter, and he wrote as unhesitatingly for clarinet, oboe, flute, bassoon, or horn as his predecessors had for strings and keyboard. Splendid examples are his Serenades No. 10 in B-flat major for Thirteen Wind Instruments (K. 361); No. 11 in E-flat major (K. 375); and No. 12 in C minor (K. 388). Both of the latter are scored for woodwind octet (two each of horn, oboe, clarinet, and bassoon).

Mozart's piano trios—eight works written between 1776 and 1788—as well as his piano quartets—in G minor (K. 478) and E-flat major (K. 493) —show a remarkable flair for balancing diverse instrumental parts. Still, whenever the piano is used in chamber works it tends to become a favored instrument and force its associates into comparative obscurity. His Quintet in E-flat major for Piano and Winds (K. 452)—Beethoven wrote for a like combination in the same key—clearly reveals this circumstance although it is a sparkling work that beautifully juxtaposes brightly hued wind sonorities against brittle and acrid piano timbres. Among the chamber works this remarkable man wrote for strings with a lone wind instrument, the four Quartets for Flute and Strings (K. 285, 285A, 285B, and 298), the Quartet in F major for Oboe and Strings (K. 370), the Quintet in A major for Clarinet and Strings (K. 581), and the Quintet in E-flat major for Horn and Strings (K. 407) stand as models of what the fine art of chamber writing can be. Few approach Mozart; none surpass him.

Inevitably, the chamber compositions of Haydn and Mozart are compared. Unquestionably, Mozart learned much from the older man and, armed with this knowledge as well as his own distinctive creative gifts, carried the genre to heights previously unknown. His string quartets, for instance, have a wealth of polyphonic involvement, a rich harmonic fabric, and unusually memorable melodies that none of his predecessors, including Haydn, demonstrated. And his architectural patterns—superb models of musical balance and lucidity—contain a wealth of innovational thought. At Mozart's hands, chamber music came of age.

In the Romantic Period

Among treasured items in chamber music literature, the quartets of Beethoven, sixteen in number, stand supreme. Viewed as a whole, they reflect the three periods into which his creative life is customarily divided. Six quartets composed between 1798–1800, identified as Opus 18, mark his entry into this domain. Later, during the middle portion of his career, the three *Rasumovsky* Quartets, Opus 59 (1806), and the quartets Opus 74 (1809) and Opus 95 (1810) appeared. Finally, as his life neared an end, Beethoven turned with increasing devotion to the quartet with a result that five magnificent works—Opus 127, 130, 131, 132, and 135, plus the Great Fugue in B-flat, Opus 133—were composed between 1822–1826. In every respect, they are monumental capstones to an extraordinary career.

As an example of what Beethoven accomplished in this area, consider his Quartet No. 5 in A major. Cast in the usual four-movement pattern, it differs somewhat from associates by having a minuet as the second movement and a theme-and-variation structure as the third. These are further details about the piece:

1. *First movement:* Moving at a brisk *allegro* pace in A major (and utilizing 6/8 meter taken two beats to the measure), this sonata form movement begins with a brief four-measure introduction, after which this principal theme appears:

Shortly thereafter, a more restrained subordinate subject is heard in a lower register:

In the development, several ideas from the principal theme are shown in a myriad of ways, but no overt reference is made to the second subject. Reasonably orthodox in outline, the recapitulation brings back the introduction and the two themes in regular alignment. A closing coda is neat, crisp, and precise.

2. *Second movement:* While maintaining the same tonality (A major), this Menuetto (of course in triple meter), follows the usual *da capo* outline of menuet-and-trio form. These are its two primary subjects:

3. *Third movement:* Founded on a neatly symmetrical subject, this *andante cantabile* in D major flows gracefully with four beats in a measure (although it is written in duple meter). This is how the theme begins:

In succession, five variants are heard:

   Variation one: Features consecutive instrumental entrances from bottom to top, and has, consequently, a semipolyphonic veneer.

Variation two: Moving adroitly, the first violin weaves a triple figuration above firm rhythms sounded by the other instruments.

Variation three: An undulating pattern masks (but does not obscure) melodic fragments heard in the background.

Variation four: Playing in a sustained manner, all four instruments give the theme a hymnic aura.

Variation five: In decided contrast, this section suggests carefree joviality and vigorous good humor.

Extension: Treating the subject rhapsodically, this thirty-two measure section is provocative and intense.

Coda: Marked *poco adagio,* a brief (ten measure) epilogue concludes the movement.

4. *Fourth movement:* Quietude is nowhere observable in this lithe, extremely rapid finale. Although marked *allegro,* it is usually performed at a breathtaking *presto* pace. The principal theme in a sonata form pattern appears almost immediately:

Then, seemingly as a temporary respite from frenetic activity, the subordinate theme suggests tranquil detachment:

Naturally, the principal theme's pre-eminence in the development cannot be denied, but the second subject manages to make its presence felt. At length, a recapitulation of materials is accomplished in the usual manner, and an animated coda, based on the principal theme, sweeps the quartet to an exuberant close.

Of course, string quartets were not Beethoven's sole contribution to chamber music literature. Notable among his other compositions in this area are the: (1) Rondino in E-flat major for two each of oboe, clarinet, horn, and bassoon; (2) Quintet in E-flat major for piano, oboe, clarinet, horn, and bassoon; (3) Octet in E-flat major for two each of oboe, clarinet, horn, and bassoon; (4) Septet in E-flat major for clarinet, horn, bassoon, violin, viola, 'cello, and bass; (5) Sextet in E-flat major for two each of clarinet, bassoon, and horn; (6) nine piano trios, of which one—No. 4 in B-flat major—is often performed by piano, clarinet, and 'cello; (7) three string trios; (8) thirty-two incomparable sonatas for piano; (9) ten sonatas for violin and piano; and (10) five sonatas for 'cello and piano.

That Franz Schubert was not a slavish follower of tradition is shown by his String Quintet in C major, scored for the conventional quartet with a second 'cello. By adding this fifth instrument, he provided an enriched sonority in the ensemble's lower register and also gave the first 'cello an opportunity to pursue a lyric role. An earlier departure from orthodoxy occurred in 1819 when Schubert scored his Quintet in A major—often called the "Trout" Quintet—for piano, violin, viola, 'cello, and bass.

Among string quartets Schubert's fifteen rank with the finest. Connoisseurs everywhere are agreed that his Quartet No. 14 in D minor, "Death and the Maiden," is a work of exquisite beauty. And his Octet in F major for strings and winds is a radiant piece written with impeccable craftsmanship. Scored for two violins, viola, 'cello, string bass, clarinet, horn, and bassoon, it is conceived on a scale (although with seven movements) that is almost symphonic in dimension. In addition, Schubert's two piano trios, two string trios, three violin sonatas, and fifteen piano sonatas greatly enlarge—and immeasurably enrich—chamber music literature.

Just as they were the immediate successors of Haydn and Mozart, Beethoven and Schubert, in turn, were followed by Mendelssohn and Schumann. Although piano compositions by both of these men are unusually fine, and Schumann's songs are among the priceless treasures of music, their chamber compositions show little distinctiveness or individuality. Notable exceptions, however, are Mendelssohn's Octet in E-flat for strings (actually scored for a double quartet), a glowing work with an incandescent vitality that few can resist, and Schumann's Quartet in E-flat for piano and strings, which is intense, poetic, and beautifully organized.

Shortly after 1850, Johannes Brahms brought new life into the chamber music idiom. Almost single-handedly he sustained its concepts—and, generally speaking, that of all music in abstract designs—during the second half of the century. In the chamber area Brahms' position is unusually exalted. A superb musical poet with an apparently infallible instinct for design, he brought impeccable logic, lyricism, and distinction to the field. Rigorously self-critical, Brahms unhesitatingly destroyed any work he considered inferior, with a consequence that the bulk of his chamber music is not large. But two piano trios in B and C major (a third, in C minor, is less distinctive), three piano quartets, three string quartets, a superb clarinet quintet, an equally superior piano quintet, and two string quintets eloquently attest the excellence he attained. And his two sextets for strings—

scored for two each of violin, viola, and 'cello—are probably the finest extant works in the literature for this combination of instruments.

Working contemporaneously with Brahms but removed from him by geographical distance, several other composers created a wealth of beautiful chamber music as the Romantic era entered into its final decades. In Russia, Tchaikowsky was an acknowledged exemplar, and this amazingly versatile man, skilled and admired as a symphonist, tone poet, and opera composer, also wrote chamber compositions that reveal warmth, facility, and a remarkable skill in melodic invention. Particularly notable are his Quartet No. 1 in D major, the Quartet No. 3 in E-flat minor, and a Piano Trio in A minor. Alexander Borodin, Tchaikowsky's compatriot, was a physician and scientist whose creative efforts inevitably suffered from a diffusion of energies. Nevertheless, his Quartet No. 2 in D major (he wrote a total of three) is an excellently conceived work with a wealth of tonal beauties.

Antonín Dvořák, Bohemia's most outstanding Romantic musician, composed eight string quartets, a great Piano Quintet in A major, four string quintets, three piano trios—including the "Dumka" Trio (1891), perhaps the most celebrated work for this combination of instruments in the literature— one string trio, and a sextet for strings. Notable among these is the Quartet No. 6 in F major, affectionately dubbed the "American" because it was written in 1893 while the composer resided in the United States. Dvořák consistently assumed a lyric approach to music, and his chamber compositions —no less than his numerous other works—are unfailingly melodic, well constructed, and written with obvious professional skill. An emphasis on Dvořák, however, should not obscure the recognition due his mentor, Bedrich Smetana. Busily engaged in multitudinous tasks, some musical, some political, Smetana did not contribute abundantly to the chamber repertoire. But his autobiographical Quartet No. 1 in E minor, subtitled "From My Life," is distinctive for being revelatory, descriptive, and more than a bit tragic. Smetana's Piano Trio in G minor is not as well-known as Dvořák's "Dumka" Trio, but the two have a great deal in common, including a frequent use of idioms—rhythms, melodies, and scale patterns—common to the composers' homeland.

Prior to 1900, few French composers exhibited much interest in chamber music. Berlioz, for instance, was almost entirely concerned with writing large orchestral works, and his contemporaries and successors—Gounod, Massenet, and Bizet, to mention only three—devoted their primary attention to the theater. Only César Franck, a Belgian by birth but a long-time resident of Paris, found occasion to explore the not inconsiderable possibilities of chamber writing. His Violin Sonata in A major, with a fine canon in its finale, is an outstanding work, and his Piano Quintet in F minor is worthy to stand beside a similar piece by Brahms. A mystic in philosophic and intellectual thought, Franck was a gentle and serious man who experimented boldly with musical chromaticism, unusual modulations, and little-exploited harmonizations. He attracted a small band of devoted pupils—d'Indy, Chausson, and Saint-Saëns, among others—who revered his spirit and emulated his writing. From the latter three, Fauré, Debussy, and Ravel, France's most outstanding musicians in the twentieth century, gained their musical legacy.

In the Twentieth Century

Chamber music in recent times has been brought to a peak of excellence by such diverse composers as the Frenchmen, Claude Debussy and Maurice Ravel; the Austrians, Arnold Schoenberg and Alban Berg; the Hungarians, Béla Bartók and Zoltan Kodály; the Americans, Charles Ives and Elliott Carter; and the Russians, Serge Prokofiev and Igor Stravinsky. In many respects this has become a chamber music age, and a wealth of startling, iconoclastic, and distinctly worthwhile compositions has appeared since 1900. Building on precedents established by Brahms, Franck, and Dvořák —and before that by Mozart, Haydn, Beethoven, and Schubert—a newer generation of composers has infused its works with vibrance, newness, and meaningful intensity. They have, in the main, turned toward a more astringent style of writing than heretofore, have tended to emphasize a free flow of contrapuntal lines, and have made a determined exploration of dissonance. As in preceding centuries, the string quartet remains paramount, but pieces for string trio, various combinations of piano with winds, and woodwind quintet have become prominent. Less lustrous in tonal opulence than most string groups, wind ensembles nevertheless have a vigorous timbre that many contemporary writers find useful.

Directly in the wake of Romanticism, musical Impressionism arose. Primarily concerned with a composer's reactions to external stimuli, it employs a strangely ethereal syntax uniquely suited to the intimate charm of chamber music. Many of its ineffable beauties are demonstrated in Claude Debussy's Quartet in G minor (1893), a work written just prior to the new century, filled with an abundance of refreshing ideas. Conceived at a time when the composer was busily engaged in creating his epochal opera *Pelléas et Mélisande* and the extremely colorful tone poem *Afternoon of a Faun,* the G minor Quartet brings Impressionism's transcendental vocabulary into chamber music for the first time. These are its details:

1. *First movement:* Marked to be played *animé et très décidé* (lively and decisively), the principal theme (whose outline suggests the Phrygian mode) appears immediately. Actually, it embraces two ideas:

expressif et soutenu

Virtually ubiquitous, the first of these appears in a variety of guises throughout the quartet and becomes, in effect, a "cyclic theme." Subsequently, this dreamy subordinate theme is announced in a new key:

doux et expressif   *dim.*

Fragments from both subjects are used extensively in the development that follows, as the composer passes them through a galaxy of shifting tonalities at altered rates of speed. Abridged, the recapitulation reaffirms both themes, but in slightly altered guises. Played *très animé* (very fast), the coda is both brief and climactic.

2. *Second movement:* Opening in sextuple meter with two beats in a measure, this pulsating scherzo is clean, crisp, and witty. The first subject (derived from the cyclic theme) is announced by the viola:

While a second idea is announced immediately thereafter by the first violin:

Structurally the movement has a first section A, two trios B and C, and a coda, all played with elfin-like lightness. Its latter part shifts to 15/8 time, with alternate measures of three and two beats, respectively.

3. *Third movement:* Flowing gently at a moderate pace (*andantino*), this nostalgic movement is suggestive of both a lullaby and the style of César Franck. Its first subject is announced in D-flat major:

A more animated mid-portion shifts to C-sharp minor and presents two ideas based on the cyclic theme:

Affirming the outlines of a ternary pattern *ABA*, the first section reappears before the movement concludes.

4. *Fourth movement:* Opening with a reminiscence of previously heard themes treated in a rhapsodic manner, the finale ultimately assumes a *très mouvemente* (very agitated) pace in duple meter as this principal subject is played:

Respite from a tumultuous outpouring of sound is provided by an almost serene subordinate theme:

In succession, both subjects become involved in the byplay conventionally associated with musical development, although the second seems to have pre-eminence. Debussy eschews a regular recapitulation in this movement, and in its stead substitutes a final appearance of the cyclic theme, along with some of its satellites. Interestingly, the coda is concerned with the version of this theme that appeared in the scherzo (second movement).

In addition to a wealth of piano music and an abundance of songs, Debussy also created a Sonata No. 1 in D minor for 'cello and piano; Sonata No. 2 for flute, harp, and viola; and Sonata No. 3 in G minor for violin and piano, all written between 1915 and 1917. Couched in Impressionism's exquisitely refined vocabulary, they are, nevertheless, more formal, more restrained, and more traditional in focus than the composer's usual iconoclastic approach to music might indicate. Seemingly, as he approached the end of life (he died in 1918), Debussy became more conservative in his views and was apparently deeply concerned with preserving the conventions and practices of his predecessors.

Maurice Ravel easily effectuated a liaison between traditional techniques and the strange idioms that appeared in the new century. Somewhat younger than Debussy, he lived and worked in the same Parisian milieu while producing a relatively small collection of highly polished works. In chamber music Ravel paralleled Debussy by writing a sparkling Quartet in F major (1903), but he moved into an area peculiarly his own with the stunning *Introduction and Allegro for Harp, Flute, Clarinet, and String Quartet* (1906). Almost classic in outline, Ravel's Piano Trio in A minor (1914) is another brilliant piece with an astonishingly wide expressive focus; hearing it is a delight.

All the Viennese Expressionists were totally revolutionary in their approach to creativity as they launched into a penetrating exploration of the acrid timbres of atonality. Although he worked in other areas including orchestral composition and opera, Arnold Schoenberg made chamber music an especially favored medium. His four string quartets (written between 1904 and 1936), for instance, are taut, bitingly dissonant, abstract pieces with few resemblances to anything previously written. But they were harbingers of a new era, and an abundance of successive pieces by other composers were soon shaped along similar lines. Schoenberg's *Serenade for Septet and Baritone* (voice), written in 1923, and his *Suite for Strings, Winds, and Piano* (1927) carry the cacophony of merging angular contrapuntal lines to even greater lengths. Alban Berg and Anton Webern, pupils and disciples of Schoenberg, also based their works on the system of atonality. Berg's *Chamber Concerto for Violin, Piano, and Thirteen Winds* (1925) represents a very successful merger of the dichotomous elements in concerto and chamber music writing. His comparatively late *Lyric Suite for String Quartet* (1926) is a starkly dissonant lexicography of modern string writing, but his *Quartet* (1910), and the *Four Pieces for Clarinet and Piano* (1913) are less astringent, less pungent, and therefore more appealing. Webern was a miniaturist. Working with painstaking care, he polished every phrase, every line, and every tone to the highest possible lustre. Consequently, his pieces are amazingly brief but wondrously beautiful. In chamber music Webern's *Five Movements for String Quartet* (1909) reflect an obsessive concern with musical terseness, and his *Six Bagatelles for*

String Quartet (1913) are similarly oriented. Jewel-like and extremely brief, both are unlike anything else in the literature.

Béla Bartók created a wealth of distinctive chamber music. Gifted with an unusual command of the métier, he often suggests folkish turns of melodic phrase as well as the pulsating rhythms of ethnic dances. Bartók's *Contrasts for Violin, Clarinet, and Piano* (1938), for instance, is a three-movement work that includes a vigorous *verbunkos* (recruiting dance), a *piheno* (a relaxed, nondance pattern), and a rapid, angular Bulgarian *sebes* (fast dance). Both melodically and harmonically this piece is piquant, ascerbic, and exciting. With his *Sonata for Two Pianos and Percussion* (1937), also in three movements, Bartók performed the dextrous feat of pouring new wine into old bottles by clinging to conventional sonata outlines while writing for double keyboard and thirteen percussion devices, all manipulated by a single player. Once again his syntax is unusual, and the textures, in particular, show his consummate command of contrapuntal writing. Bartók's six string quartets, written between 1908 and 1939, are bold, mercurial, and very unusual. Forceful in expression, unorthodox in substance, occasionally pensive in outlook, they require the utmost in string virtuosity from executants. Quartets Nos. 1 and 2 are contained within three movements; the third has only a single, subdivided movement; the fourth and fifth have five movements; and the sixth reverts to a four-movement pattern. Bartók's *Sonata for Unaccompanied Violin* (1944), and his Sonatas No. 1 (1921) and No. 2 (1922) for Violin and Piano have big declamatory themes and irregular rhythmic patterns that show the strong, primitive energies he possessed while a young man. And his piano music—including the encyclopedic *Mikrokosmos* (1935), the rhythmically complex *Out of Doors Suite*, and similar other works—bring modern keyboard writing to its apogee.

As these momentous pieces were being written in Europe, the American, Charles Ives, composed quietly and industriously. Content to practice composition as an avocation while pursuing a business career in New York City, Ives wrote a series of iconoclastic compositions, many for chamber ensembles, that have only recently come to public attention. His Quartets No. 1 (1896) and No. 2 (1913), for instance, are taut, tense, and sometimes flamboyant compositions that show experimentalist Ives pioneering in such techniques as polytonality, polyrhythm, and unusual harmonizations. Ives' Piano Sonata No. 2, "Concord, Mass., 1840–1860" (written between 1909–1915) is an extremely difficult *magnum opus* that minutely describes the personalities of several important New England Transcendentalists (Emerson, Hawthorne, the Alcotts, and Thoreau) while involving a performer (assisted by flute) in the most exhaustive convolutions of which a piano is capable. His four sonatas for violin and piano (1908–1914) are less epochal (but just as difficult to perform) and consistently discloses Ives' wry sense of humor, quaint dedication to American melodies, and superb sense of structure.

Amazingly versatile, Igor Stravinsky has been proven no stranger to the chamber music idiom. His *Octet for Wind Instruments* (1923) updates and extends a mode of writing pioneered by Mozart and Beethoven, and *Ragtime for Eleven Wind Instruments* (1918) is cast in the jazz style abroad in an era postdating World War I. His *Septet* (1953) is more classically conceived, and such other ensemble pieces as the *Duo Concertante for Violin and Piano* (1932), the *Sonata for Piano* (1924), and the *Sonata for Two Pianos* continue well-established principles while reflecting the composer's unique personal bent.

Contemporary Russian chamber music is excellently exemplified in pieces by Serge Prokofiev. His ten sonatas for piano (written between 1910–1948) brilliantly display his prowess in writing for keyboard; two sonatas for piano and violin (1938 and 1945, respectively); and one—composed in 1932—for two violins; the *Sonata for 'Cello and Piano* (1949); and the *Sonata for Flute and Piano* (1943) show these same creative powers applied to strings and winds. Prokofiev's Quartets No. 1 (1930) and No. 2 (1941) are structurally splendid, and the *Quintet for Winds and Strings* (1942) is an unusual work radiant with warmth and lyricism. Dmitri Shostakovich, a younger compatriot, has also been remarkably fecund (but somewhat less successful) in writing chamber music, as is aptly demonstrated by his eight quartets. The *Quintet for Piano and Strings* (1940), the *Sonata for 'Cello and Piano* (1934), and the Piano Trio No. 2 in E minor (1944) are Shostakovich's best works in this area.

Traditions established by Smetana and Dvořák in mid-European lands (Hungary, Rumania, Bulgaria, and Czechoslovakia) passed initially into the hands of Leos Janáček (Quartet No. 2, 1923, and No. 3, 1928) who, in turn, bequeathed them to Bartók and Kodály. Combining a deep scholarly penetration into the ethnic backgrounds of music with rare compositional prodigality (as did Bartók), Kodály made himself one of the twentieth century's most eloquent spokesman. His *Duo for Violin and 'Cello* (1914) is a cleanly hewn and beautifully molded work, and his *Sonata for 'Cello Unaccompanied* (1915), as well as the *Sonata for 'Cello and Piano* (1910), have astonishingly wide expressive powers.

Contemporary America does not lack in gifted chamber music composers. One of the most enterprising, Elliott Carter, has written such pieces as *Eight Etudes and Fantasy for Woodwind Quintet* (1950); *Quartet* (1951), *Sonata for Piano* (1946); and *Sonata for Flute, Oboe, 'Cello, and Harpsichord* (1952) that speak in strong, invigorating terms. The latter, in particular, is a landmark in modern chamber music literature. As Carter may be considered a representative of the progressive wing in American composition, so Samuel Barber may be named an exemplar of the conservative group.

Solidly constructed, strongly etched, often couched in dark and resonant colors, Barber's Quartet No. 1 (1936), his *Summer Music for Woodwind Quintet* (1956), and *Sonata for Piano* (1949) effectively counterpoise the more spectacular efforts of experimentalists with the traditional beauties we have come to expect in music. Others in America who have contributed to the chamber repertoire include Aaron Copland, Ned Rorem, Henry Cowell, Alvin Etler, David Diamond, Andrew Imbrie, and Leon Kirchner.

PARTICULAR EXAMPLES OF CHAMBER MUSIC

J. S. Bach (1685–1750), Trio Sonata in C minor, from *The Musical Offering*

This single excerpt from a collection of thirteen pieces the elder Bach wrote for Frederick William, King of Prussia, a trio in name but not in fact, is a beautiful example of Baroque chamber music. In this instance, the trio sonata's two upper parts are assigned to flute and violin, while the continuo is sounded by a bass instrument (a viola da gamba or 'cello) with harpsichord. Ubiquitous in virtually all Baroque instrumental pieces, the continuo sounds continuously but discreetly in the background as the work is being played.

In 1747, as he entered the twilight of life at age sixty-two, Bach, then the respected Cantor of Leipzig's St. Thomas Church, was summoned to the Imperial Presence. Frederick William IV—usually called "The Great" because of his diplomatic, political, and military accomplishments—was a music-loving monarch who had long been conversant with Bach's music and now wished to meet him. As a result of royal command, Bach undertook this journey—perhaps the most extensive peregrination of his life—and traveled to Potsdam, Frederick's seat of empire located on the outskirts of Berlin. According to contemporaneous reports, composer and monarch got along very well. Frederick was properly solicitous toward an elderly man whose musical proclivities he deeply admired, while the deferential Bach handled one of the world's most powerful rulers with a skill he normally applied to keyboard performance.

As a direct outgrowth of the Potsdam sojourn, Bach created *The Musical Offering*, a collection of ricercari, canons, a fugue, and this trio sonata, all ostensibly based on a theme suggested by Frederick. In actuality, however, he found it necessary to reshape the subject considerably after returning to Leipzig. When the work was fully completed, Bach sent an inscribed copy to the monarch as a gesture of homage and respect.

Cast in four movements (all, incidentally, in the key of C minor), this trio sonata makes extensive use of the *style galant*, a manneristic method of executing the numerous ornaments found in melodic lines of Baroque and Rococo compositions. These are further details about it:

1. *First movement:* Imitation, free or exact, is a characteristic in much of Bach's writing, and he effectively demonstrates his skill in this opening *largo* as violin and flute perform atop a firm and secure continuo. Set in triple meter but performed with six beats to the measure, this section follows the general outlines of ternary form. This is how it begins:

2. *Second movement:* Longest of the work's sections, this *allegro* is also a three-part design (achieved via the *da capo* procedure). Its rhythmic flow, in duple meter, has the jogging tempo characteristic of many Baroque instrumental works. A basic eight-measure theme, initially presented by violin over continuo support, actually recurs six times. This is how the subject first appears:

3. *Third movement:* Almost elegiac in tone, this *andante* in quadruple meter moves at an unusually sedate pace. In the main it is not as contrapuntal as companion movements, for the flute and violin mostly complement one another with compatible harmonic parts. This is how it begins:

4. *Fourth movement:* Cast as a vigorous gigue, the trio sonata's finale, performed at an *allegro tempo,* has an unusually active bass line over which
   the two upper instruments move with dextrous agility. Again thematic
   imitation is plentiful, and the resultant dialogue is colorful and gay. As
   the section begins, continuo and flute lead off with this idea:

Franz Joseph Haydn (1732–1809), Quartet in C major ("Emperor")

With more accuracy than is applicable to a *bon mot* usually associated with his name (that is, "father of the symphony"), Haydn might be termed a "father of the string quartet." In 1755, at the age of twenty-three, he began writing quartets, and nearly fifty years later, in 1803, after having attained the age of seventy-one, he completed his eighty-third and final piece in this category. During the intervening half-century music changed a great deal, and a goodly amount of its progress had been stimulated by this fabulously prolific composer. At Haydn's hands, for instance, the quartet's pattern had been greatly expanded, its outlines were drawn taut, and its expressive scope clearly defined. Long since the continuo had been banished and equalitarian roles assigned all four instruments. Additionally, however, Haydn modified the first violin's melody-bearing propensities, brought the second violin into greater prominence, and granted full emancipation to the viola and 'cello.

While writing chamber music, Haydn almost unfailingly adhered to sonata outlines. His quartets, for instance, observe the usual four-movement pattern with the customary formal designs in each; their harmonic schemes, key successives, modulatory excursions—even rhythmic characteristics—tend to be remarkably uniform. Yet each is wondrously fresh, seemingly spontaneous, and vigorously exciting. To a rare degree, Haydn had an extraordinary capacity for expressing emotional intensity, a depth of understanding, and a provocative view of basic human values in virtually all the music he wrote. And these qualities are readily apparent in his fine C major Quartet, (Opus 76, No. 3):

1. *First movement:* Choosing the bright, radiant key of C major as a tonal locus for this quartet, one in a group of six composed in 1799, Haydn begins a brisk sonata-form movement (played in *allegro* tempo) with a presentation of the principal theme:

Less memorable, the second subject serves as a foil for its more assertive associate:

Of course the principal subject is important in the development, where it experiences a series of interesting transformations. Subsequently, the recapitulation reaffirms both subjects with, however, some interesting harmonic changes. Finally, a vigorous coda, based on fragments from both themes, brings the movement to a close.

2. *Second movement:* While visiting England in 1791, Haydn became impressed with the British national anthem, "God Save the Queen" (1744). Shortly thereafter he created a similar melody for his native Austria, *Gott erhalte Franz den Kaiser* (God Preserve Emperor Franz), written in 1797 for four-part chorus. Subsequently, this melody was also used as the basis for a set of variations in the C major Quartet. And its inclusion supplies the work with a title: "Emperor" Quartet.

   Haydn's hymn, a stately subject marked *poco adagio cantabile,* is set in quadruple meter, and, in this instance, the key of G major. It has a ternary pattern *abc:*

In succession, four variations appear, each citing the theme explicitly while sustaining a series of adroit configurations woven around it. By turns, the melody progresses from: (1) second violin to (2) 'cello, (3) to viola, and finally to (4) first violin.

3. *Third movement:* Typical of the period's sonata-based designs, a vigorous menuet (in *allegro* tempo and menuet-and-trio form) appears as the third movement. These are details:

A—Menuet

(a) Comprised of twenty measures (repeated), the first strain begins with this tune:

(*b* + *a*) Thirty-six measures long, the last twenty-four similar to *a*, this repeated second strain has a related contour.

B—Trio

(*c*) The third strain, an eight-measure phrase, has this melody:

($d + c$) And a succeeding thirty-six measure strain (the fourth) adds a new tune and repeats c in its last part.

A—*Return of Menuet* (da capo)

(a) First strain, as before, but without repeat.

($b + a$) Second strain, as before, but without repeat.

4. *Fourth movement:* An *alla breve*, taken with two beats to the measure in *presto* tempo, sweeps the "Emperor" Quartet to a rousing conclusion. Opening in C minor, this sonata form pattern intersperses running triplets between quotations of its principal theme:

Because the movement is virtually monothematic, the first subject dominates the development where its elaboration is contrasted with frequent references to the agile triplet figuration. Within the recapitulation most of the activity is predictable, except for a shift to the major tonality which occurs when the section is half over. Then the piece drives toward a resonant close, accomplished on a series of C-major chords.

Ludwig van Beethoven (1770–1827), Violin Sonata No. 9 in A major ("Kreutzer")

Few works experience the vicissitudes that have beset this sonata. Written in 1803 for George Augustus Bridgetower, probably music's first Negro violin virtuoso, it soon became exposed to a series of disquieting events. Bridgetower (1779–1860) was a well-known soloist when he met Beethoven, then a young man twenty-three years of age. Impressed with the violinist's capabilities, the composer agreed to write a sonata for him that would be featured at a forthcoming recital in Vienna. And, in order to enhance the sale of tickets, Beethoven consented to act as pianist. In due course the recital was held and the work performed, but a falling-out between the two men then occurred. Later, the sonata was issued with a dedication to Rodolphe Kreutzer (hence the name by which it is commonly identified) who, far from being pleased with the accolade, pronounced the work "outrageously unintelligible." As if this were not enough, this same piece later supplied its subtitle, "Kreutzer Sonata," to a novel by Leo Tolstoy, who made it an important factor in a murder perpetrated by a man whose senses were inflamed by the music's emotionality! These are the details of the work:

1. *First movement:* Opening at an *adagio sostenuto* pace in A major, the solo violin engages in a discourse heavily laced with multiple stops that sets a lofty tone for the entire sonata. When the exposition appears, it discloses: (1) a new tempo marked *presto,* (2) a shift from triple to duple meter, and (3) a change to A minor. Sounded in opening measures, its principal theme is a typical Beethoven subject richly infused with dramatic vigor:

On the other hand, the subordinate theme is solemn and chorale-like in its smooth elegiac flow:

But a third theme, the closing subject, is unusually dynamic:

Periodic respite from the movement's incisive drive is given by a frequent interpolation of *ritardandos* and brief pauses. In effect, they greatly assist in highlighting the work's thematic ideas.

Obsessively concerned with the third subject, Beethoven devotes his energies in the development to elaborating on its multiple facets. Over and over it appears in a variety of guises, while no apparent reference is made to either of the other subjects. After some abatement in flow, the recapitulation appears, runs an orthodox course, and reaffirms the three themes in prescribed order. Finally, the brief coda is animated, brisk, and conclusive.

2. *Second movement:* Shifting to the remote key of F major and moving at an *andante* tempo in quadruple meter, this succeeding segment is cast as a superb variation design. Its theme, fifty-four measures long, has the broad outlines of ternary form:

a	*b*	*a*
8 measures	11 measures $+$ 8 measures	
(repeat)	(repeat)	

This is how the subject begins:

Variation one assigns triplet figurations to each instrument, but particular prominence is accorded utterances from the piano.

Variation two brings the violin into an agile virtuosic display that frequently leads it into an extremely high register.

Variation three adopts a dark hue and shifts into F minor where the melodic line becomes smooth-flowing and sustained.

Variation four resumes a quick pace and the major tonality as the piano performs with agility and power; soon the violin joins in a brilliant colloquy.

A short *adagio* passage connects this final variation with the coda. As violin and piano play over the latter's length, no reference is made to previously heard material.

3. *Third movement:* Cast in sonata form the work's finale, a gay and sparkling *presto,* returns to the basic tonality of A major. No preamble is observed, for the principal theme is sounded by the violin immediately after a ringing A major chord has been enunciated by the piano. In all, three themes comprise the movement's subject matter, the first two rondo-like in their playfulness, whereas a third—which occupies a comparatively minor role in the discourse—suggests a tinge of somberness. This is a quotation of each:

In the development, Beethoven centers his attention on the second theme, and only brief mention is made of the first. In succession, the recapitulation runs a regular course and restates the three themes in their usual order. Some contrast is provided when the headlong flight is occasionally interrupted by short rubato passages. When the coda appears, four measures in *adagio* tempo are inserted to provide contrast. Then the work rushes toward a close that is bright, climactic, and sonorous.

Johannes Brahms (1833–1897), Quintet in B minor for Clarinet and Strings

As he neared the end of a distinguished career, Brahms turned quite regularly to writing for the clarinet. An important reason was his friendship with Richard Muhlfeld (1856–1907), an important clarinet virtuoso of this era who was gifted with rare interpretative insight. Accordingly, Brahms' Sonatas for Clarinet—No. 1 in F minor, No. 2 in E-flat major (1894)—his Trio in A minor (1891) for Clarinet, 'Cello, and Piano, and this quintet were composed with Muhlfeld in mind.

By any standard, Brahms' clarinet quintet is outstanding. Imbued with sweeping emotional intensity and an almost austere architectonic plan, it continually excites the imagination just as it delights the ear. Composed in 1890, the work was given its premiere in December, 1891, played by Muhlfeld and the Joachim Quartet. Despite its relatively complex nature, the piece was so well received on this occasion that portions had to be repeated to satisfy insistent demands from a rapt audience. And in subsequent years it has continued to please hundreds of listeners. These are specific details:

1. *First movement:* Although marked to be performed at an *allegro* tempo, this section suggests tranquility and restraint as strings sound a flowing subject later taken up by the clarinet:

Organized in sonata form, this movement in sextuple meter progresses at a sedate, even pace. After its first theme has been sufficiently exposed, this rhythmically marked second subject appears:

During the ensuing development, both subjects undergo transformation. First is the languid opening theme, whose initial measures are portrayed in a variety of instrumental colors. Later, the second subject is treated so quietly as to appear furtive. Ultimately, as the movement flows onward, a full recapitulation reaffirms both themes in regular alignment, although shifts in harmonic color—a Brahms characteristic—add freshness and interest. A coda, derived from the first subject, discourses on this restrained idea at some length before bringing the movement to a quiet close.

2. *Second movement:* Flowing at an exceedingly slow pace (in triple meter), this *adagio* ventures into the related tonality of B major. The clarinet becomes a principal melody-bearer as it sounds this arching theme:

Organized in a large ternary pattern *ABA,* the movement emphasizes a sustained melodic line in its corner sections. Perhaps to provide needed contrast, perhaps to give the clarinetist an opportunity to flex his digital muscles, Brahms created a glittering midsection in B minor replete with unusually brilliant passages. Here, strings do little more than provide a discreet chordal background. After this vibrant display of virtuosity, an epilogue that seems almost anticlimactic reaffirms the opening *adagio.* Similar in substance and dimension to the first section, it continues to sustain the quintet's spirit of gentle lyricism.

3. *Third movement:* Avoiding an overt dance form, Brahms now turns to a scherzo-like design. Marked *andantino,* the opening strain is laid in the key of D major (a related tonality of B minor) and set in quadruple meter. The clarinet leads in expressing this subject:

With a *presto non assai, ma con sentimento,* the movement's trio is reached and a more rapid tempo (in duple meter and the key of B minor) is introduced. Strings now have ample opportunity to display the elfin-like effects that are seemingly inherent in scherzo writing, and they gambol gaily through the subject assigned them. Brahms apparently became so engrossed in this sportive interplay that he barely allowed time for a reaffirmation of the first theme before bringing the movement to a close.

4. *Fourth movement:* Although the variations that close the B minor Quintet are charming rather than monumental, they fully exemplify the composer's mastery of this design. Set in duple meter, the key of B minor, and marked to be played *con moto,* the structure is based on a restrained thirty-two measure subject comprised of two sixteen-measure segments:

In succession, five variations appear:

Variation one features the 'cello while fragmentary embellishments are added by the ensemble's other members.

Variation two gains momentum from a syncopated figuration sounded by the second violin and viola, while higher and lower pitched ideas are contributed by clarinet, first violin, and 'cello.

Variation three is more florid than preceding sections, and both the first violin and clarinet display unusually agile technique.

Variation four shifts to B major and smoothly blends the ensemble's five voices.

Variation five changes to triple meter and utilizes 'cello *pizzicato* to mark the pulse as the smooth-flowing viola sings a melodic variant.

Other instruments join later and swell the sonority to full resonance. No conventional coda is appended to the fourth movement. Rather, Brahms uses this opportunity to reaffirm the principal theme from the first movement in a thirty-measure quotation, thus engendering a "returning home" feeling. As before, the subject is lyric and darkly resonant as it concludes the work on a plane of quiet resignation.

Igor Stravinsky (b. 1882), Suite from *L'Histoire du soldat*

Although Stravinsky's music for *L'Histoire du soldat* (The Soldier's Tale) was originally intended for the theater, a suite of excerpts arranged by the composer and scored for a small ensemble of seven players (as was the original), brings it very close to the sphere of chamber music. And it is so imaginatively conceived, so filled with infectious vigor, so vibrant and alive, and so reflective of a kaleidoscope of rhythmic patterns that one is disinclined to cavil about its origins.

When Stravinsky began this piece in 1917, he was attempting to free himself from the constrictive influences imposed by Serge Diaghilev, a beneficent but dictatorial impresario of the Ballet Russe for whom Stravinsky had written the elaborately conceived *Firebird* (1910), *Petrouchka* (1911), and *Le Sacre du printemps* (1913). Now with a great war raging, times had changed. There was a need to conserve resources, to exercise economy, to abandon broad-scale rhetoric, and to exercise ingenuity. Deliberately restricting himself, Stravinsky created both the *Ragtime for Eleven Instruments* and *The Soldier's Tale* in 1918, and scored them for small groups of players. In the latter's orchestration, each of four instrumental families is represented, as well as the bass and treble ranges:

TABLE 22. *The four instrumental families represented in* L'Histoire du soldat.

Range	Woodwind	Brass	String	Percussion
Treble	Clarinet	Cornet	Violin	One player who performs
Bass	Bassoon	Trombone	String bass	on numerous devices

With impeccable artistry, Stravinsky elicits a maximum of musical effect from this small group. Throughout the work extremities of instrumental range are exploited, various bowings, harmonics, muted effects, tremolos, or altered tunings are required. Consistently, the woodwinds and brasses are required to play with unusual agility, but the lone percussionist in particular, is expected to expend almost herculean endeavors. Moreover, jazz influences are everywhere apparent. Stravinsky heard this kind of music—in those days it was called ragtime—played by bandsmen who came to Europe with the American Expeditionary Forces and, like many of his contemporaries (for example, Maurice Ravel), was fascinated by its exciting elemental vigor. Brash, pulsating, syncopated rhythms abound in *The Soldier's Tale* and their virtuoso use discloses Stravinsky's remarkably facile assimilative powers.

When used within a suite, that is, with an intent of concert performance, numbers of this pantomimic score [5] are usually realigned. In such a circumstance, this is their typical sequence:

[5] Simply stated, the discourse that unfolds on stage when *L'Histoire du soldat* is enacted (created by C. F. Ramuz), concerns a soldier returning disenchanted from the wars, who swaps a battered violin, symbolic of his soul, with an elderly man—Satan in disguise—for a magic book in which answers to every question are written. After extensive travels, including marriage to a princess, the weary and jaded soldier again journeys homeward. As before, he is greeted by Satan, this time without disguise. With compelling insistence sustained by an irrefutable compact, Satan claims the soldier's soul and whisks him away while an entreating princess waves a tearful farewell.

1. *The Soldier's March:* Moving with a firm rhythmic beat in duple meter, but with occasional interpolated ⅜ and ¾ measures, this opening section suggests the plodding movements of a weary man. Cornet and trombone play the melody:

2. *The Soldier's Violin:* Over a quickly paced *pizzicato* bass, the violin plays an undulating tune that begins like this:

3. *Music to Scene II:* Now the pulse becomes less incisive (the tempo is marked *lento*); clarinet and bassoon sound a plaintive subject over sustained violin tones:

4. *The Royal March:* Flamboyantly alive, this vigorous march uses all the ensemble's instruments, but particular stress is given brass sonorities. The trombone plays an introductory theme, but the principal melody is assigned to cornet:

5. *The Little Concert:* Moving at an animated pace (*allegro*), the cornet introduces a figure whose essence is picked up by other instruments and endlessly repeated:

6. *Three Dances:*

    (a) *Tango:* Seductively alluring, this characteristic dance requires the percussionist to sound a pulsating background as the violinist plays:

    (b) *Waltz:* Directly bound to the preceding section, this lilting dance uses the bassoon and string bass to underscore the violin as it sounds this attractive tune:

    (c) *Ragtime:* Played at a moderate tempo, this zestful rhythmic exercise again features the violin:

7. *The Devil's Dance:* Appropriately diabolic, this extremely animated section, which makes occasional reference to melodic figures heard in earlier sections, shifts meter from measure to measure. This is the way it begins:

8. *The Great Choral:* Hymnic in utterance and solemnly paced, this section, marked *largo,* uses the cornet to enunciate a simple, sturdy tune:

9. *Triumphal March of the Devil:* Placing firm reliance on a variety of rhythmic figures articulated by the percussionist, this closing epilogue is angular, episodic, abrupt, and based mostly on thematic fragments previously heard. It begins with this idea sounded by the trombone:

Selected Chamber Music Compositions

Bach, Johann Sebastian (1685–1750)

Art of the Fugue (1750). A superb polyphonic work in nineteen sections that ingeniously demonstrates the devices of imitative counterpoint; its media are unspecified, but the work is usually performed by keyboard or small ensembles.

The Musical Offering (1747). An excellent polyphonic work for small ensemble that includes two ricercars, canons, a fugue, and a trio sonata.

Sonatas and Partitas (6) for Unaccompanied Violin (c. 1720). Taxing pieces for a solo instrument that are occasionally polyphonic; their numerous movements are occasionally abstract but often dance-like.

Well-Tempered Clavier (1722, 1744). A collection of forty-eight preludes and fugues in all major and minor keys; it requires an extremely dextrous technique for performance.

Barber, Samuel (b. 1910)

Summer Music for Woodwind Quintet (1956). This is a single-movement contemporary work that mostly employs a conventional syntax; it is semi-impressionistic and pleasant.

Bartók, Béla (1881–1945)

Contrasts for Violin, Clarinet, and Piano (1938). An unusual trio in three movements; they emphasize sonorous differences, and are ascetic, rhythmically vital, and occasionally tuneful.

Mikrokosmos for piano (1935). A present-day *Gradus ad Parnassum* that includes 153 short pieces, it eloquently explores contemporary compositional techniques.

String Quartets: No. 1 (1908); No. 2 (1917); No. 3 (1927); No. 4 (1928); No. 5 (1934); and No. 6 (1939). Considered among the century's best, these are unusual in outline and continually surprising in substance; they explore the limits of quartet writing, use much polyphony, and are fresh and vivid.

Sonata for Two Pianos and Percussion (1937). Pitting thirteen percussion instruments (manipulated by one player) against two keyboards, it has three movements, and is plangent, incisive, and trim.

Sonata for Unaccompanied Violin (1944). Modern-day monophony in Bachian format, it is tightly knit and incredibly difficult.

Beethoven, Ludwig van (1770–1827)

Octet in E-flat major for Winds (1792); Quintet in E-flat major for Piano and Winds (1796); Septet in E-flat major for Strings and Winds (1800). Outstanding ensemble pieces that are almost symphonic in substance. The octet has four movements, the quintet three, and the septet six. All are very attractive, beautifully molded, and distinctly memorable.

String Quartets: Nos. 1–6 (1798–1800); Nos. 7–9 (1806); Nos. 10–16 (1809–1826). Among the finest in quartet literature, the early pieces are classic in outline and substance, whereas the later ones tend to be iconoclastic, highly individual, and deeply personal in utterance.

Sonatas for Piano, Nos. 1–32 (1783–1822). Often called the pianist's "New Testament," they thoroughly exploit keyboard resources, and are lordly, intricate, and epochal.

Sonatas for Violin, Nos. 1–10 (1797–1812) and Sonatas for 'Cello, Nos. 1–5 (1796–1813). Uniformly excellent, these string pieces reflect a neat balance between instruments; sonata form and variation patterns are frequently employed and their themes and harmonies are strong, affirmative, and masculine.

Trios for Piano, Violin, 'Cello, Nos. 1–7 (1793–1811) and Trios for Violin, Viola, 'Cello (1792–1797). Generally speaking, these are less exalted than the sonatas or quartets; nevertheless, they bear the indisputable stamp of one of music's greatest creative minds.

Berg, Alban (1885–1935)

Chamber Concerto for Violin, Piano, and Thirteen Winds (1925). A highly unusual work that extends well beyond the conventional chamber concept, it is based on the twelve-tone system, has three movements, and is bitingly dissonant.

Quartet (1910). Stringently atonal, it has two movements and abounds with linear polyphony.

Lyric Suite for String Quartet (1926). A modern-day masterpiece that includes a veritable compendium of string devices, it is imaginative, piquant, and occasionally shocking.

Borodin, Alexander (1833–1887)

Quartet No. 2 in D major (1881–1885). A gracious work heavily infused with Russian lyricism, it has a simple structure, an intimate spirit, and lovely harmonies.

Brahms, Johannes (1833–1897)

Quartets for Piano and Strings, Nos. 1–3 (1861, 1875). These are delightfully variegated chamber pieces that include intermezzi, rondos, and occasional folk melodies; all are attractive and structurally excellent works.

Quartets for Strings, Nos. 1–3 (1873, 1875). Massively harmonic, occasionally polyphonic, resonant, and strong in expression, these adhere to the usual pattern. Probably they are the best quartets written in the post-Beethovenian era.

Quintet in B minor for Clarinet and Strings (1891). Extremely lyric and occasionally somber, this superb chamber work has four movements and an abundance of well-integrated sonorities.

Quintet in F minor for Piano and Strings (1866). By turns savage, pensive, petulant, or tragic, it uses alternating themes and relatively free melodic-rhythmic patterns.

Sextets in B-flat major and G major for Strings (1860, 1866). Resonant and organ-like (first) or delicate and fragile (second), these ensemble pieces have glowing melodies and are a quintessence of chamber music.

Sonatas for Clarinet and Piano, Nos. 1–2 (1894); Sonatas for Violin and Piano, Nos. 1, 2, 3 (1879, 1886, 1888). Radiant chamber works with concise designs that abound in Viennese-Romantic melodism, their rhythms are complex and their harmonies stately.

Carter, Elliott (b. 1908)

Sonata for Flute, Oboe, 'Cello, Harpsichord (1952). This is an outstanding contemporary piece that reflects prodigious learning; it is masterly but somewhat austere, esoteric, and forbidding.

Chopin, Frederick (1810–1849)

Ballades (4) (1831–1842); Etudes (1833, 1837); Impromptus (4) (1834–1842); Mazurkas (56) (1824–1849); Nocturnes (19) (1827–1846); Polonaises (12) (1817–1842); Preludes (24) (1836–1839); Sonatas No. 2 in B-flat minor and No. 3 in B minor (1839, 1844); and Waltzes (15) (1826–1848). Widely accepted keyboard works that discover and exploit previously unrecognized poetic resources in the piano. Graciously melodic, they are soft, yielding, stern, demanding, or austere as the composer's expressive intent shifts. All are single-movement pieces (except the sonatas), and amazingly variegated as well as consistently rhythmic. All glow with warm Romantic ardor.

Debussy, Claude (1862–1918)

Images pour Piano, Books 1 and 2 (1905, 1907). Evocative miniatures of rare beauty, these exist in two sets of three pieces each; all are descriptive, fetching, and exquisite.

Preludes for Piano, Books 1 and 2 (1910–1913). Superb keyboard works published in two books of twelve pieces each; they are gently evocative and filled with iridescent colors and ineffable harmonies.

Quartet in G minor (1893). The most original quartet since the time of Brahms, this daring Impressionistic piece is beautifully constructed, exquisitely melodic, and very beautiful.

Sonata No. 1 in D minor for 'Cello and Piano (1915); Sonata No. 2 for Flute, Viola and Harp (1916); and Sonata No. 3 in G minor for Violin and Piano (1917). These final pieces show the composer in a formal pose;

each has three movements and a diversity of content; they are excellent, but the lesser works of a great composer.

Dvořák, Antonín (1841–1904)

Quartet No. 6 in F major, Opus 96 ("American," 1893). A warm, tuneful, Romantic piece written in America; idyllic and strongly homophonic, it is cast in the usual four movements.

Quintet in A major for Piano and Strings (1887). Pervaded by the composer's vibrant personality, it is unquestionably Slavonic in spirit and outlook; now gloomy, now buoyant, it is mostly amiable.

Trio in E minor ("Dumka," 1891). At times fiery, again melancholy (à la dumka), it has six movements and is energetic, harsh, playful, and melodic.

Franck, César (1822–1890)

Quintet in F minor for Piano and Strings (1878). Introspective, cyclic, and in three movements, it is architecturally excellent and shows unusual strength and grandeur.

Sonata in A major for Violin and Piano (1886). A masterly application of the cyclic method to chamber music and in four movements, it is mystical, chaste, and superior in spirit and substance.

Handel, George Frideric (1685–1759)

Sonatas for Flute and Harpsichord (published 1724). These are Baroque works of august beauty with diverse patterns that are lithe, terse, and finely chiseled; similar pieces exist for violin (6) and oboe (2).

Haydn, Franz Joseph (1732–1809)

Quartets in D major ("Lark," 1790); in D minor ("Quinten," 1799); in C major ("Emperor," 1799); and in F major (1799). Representative examples of the composer's eighty-three quartets, these buoyant and vivacious pieces are cast in the Classic, four-movement mold; all are strongly homophonic with cleanly etched structural patterns; generally evoking less emotion than Mozart's quartets, they are, nonetheless, splendid chamber music pieces.

Hindemith, Paul (1895–1963)

Kleine Kammermusik (1922). An excellent woodwind quintet, pungently modern in harmonic and melodic substance, it is continuously linear, restless in unfoldment, and angular in contour.

Sonatas for: Clarinet and Piano (1940); Oboe and Piano (1938); Organ (3), (1937–1940); Trombone and Piano (1942); and Trumpet and Piano (1940). These exemplify a wide collection of chamber works the composer wrote for various instruments; each has an individual pattern and exploits newer compositional concepts. Few modern instrumental works can match their freshness, vitality, or craftsmanship.

Kodály, Zoltan (1882–1967)

Duo for Violin and 'Cello (1914). Employing a now little-used combination of instruments, this four-movement piece is ardent and melodic, but occasionally harsh.

Sonata for 'Cello Unaccompanied (1915). Exemplifying modern-day monophony, this glowing, taut, and occasionally tart piece fully exploits the instrument's expressive richness.

Liszt, Franz (1811–1886)

Sonata in B minor for Piano (1852–1853). A vast single-movement work that is both rhetorical and rhapsodic; mostly its passages are cascading, thundering, and virtuosic.

Mendelssohn, Felix (1809–1847)

Octet in E-flat major for Strings (1825). Written when the composer was only sixteen, this radiant four-movement piece is charming and intimate in appeal but rather symphonic in substance and outline.

Songs Without Words (for piano) (1832–1847). Forty-eight works for piano that are pretty, song-like, small-scaled, and mostly serene in expression.

Trio No. 1 in D minor for Strings and Piano (1839). Conceived in Classic-Romantic styles, it is bright, tuneful, buoyant, and altogether enjoyable.

Mozart, Wolfgang Amadeus (1756–1791)

Quartets Nos. 14–19 ("Haydn"), K. 387, 421, 428, 458, 464, 465 (1782–1785). Representative of the twenty-three quartets written by this fabulous musician, they delightfully reveal his instinct for dramatic pathos; in four movements and occasionally polyphonic, they are brilliant, forthright, fresh, and deeply gratifying to hear.

Quintet No. 5 in G minor for Strings, K. 516 (1787). Profound and almost despairing, this chamber work for two violins, two violas, and 'cello is austere, abstract, and lengthy.

Quintet in A major for Clarinet and Strings, K. 581 (1789). Unusually song-like, with four beautifully contrasted movements, this sweet *cantabile* work beautifully highlights the clarinet's dulcet sonority.

Quintet in E-flat major for Piano and Winds, K. 452 (1784). Written in a concertante style that juxtaposes piano and wind sonority, this is a tasteful, relatively uncomplicated, and vibrant work.

Sonatas for Piano, Nos. 1–17 (1774–1789). Sparkling, radiant, and charmingly individual in pattern and substance, these exceptional keyboard works are both eloquent and excellent.

Nielsen, Carl (1865–1931)

Quintet (1922). A gifted Danish composer's neo-Romantic work for woodwinds in three movements; it is swift, imaginative, and exciting.

Poulenc, Francis (1899–1963)

Sextuor for Piano and Woodwind Quintet (1932). Gamin-like, contradictory, and organized in three movements, it is sardonic, impudent, and occasionally outrageous in a puckish, satiric way.

Prokofiev, Serge (1891–1953)

Quartets No. 1 and No. 2 (1930, 1941). Serene and profound—for this composer—each has three movements; the first is mostly spiritual and aesthetic in outlook; the second, based on Caucasian folk songs, is more whimsical, vital, and obvious.

Rachmaninoff, Sergei (1873–1943)

Préludes for Piano (10 in 1904, 13 in 1910). Extremely lyric, dramatic, and rhapsodic, these keyboard works are not unduly digital; some have become very popular.

Ravel, Maurice (1875–1937)

Introduction and Allegro for Harp, Flute, Clarinet and String Quartet (1906). Intended to highlight the harp, this piece has two obvious sections. Transcendental and multicolored, it is quietly spectacular and iridescent.

Quartet in F major (1903). Classically organized, this pleasingly lyric work is fresh, spontaneous, and distinctly gracious.

Trio in A minor for Piano and Strings (1914). Exercising a determined economy of means, this four-movement piece is cleverly conceived, beautifully molded, and decidedly original.

Sonatine for Piano (1905). Slight in dimension but great in artistic concept, this excellent keyboard piece suggests musical Classicism in Impressionistic attire.

Schoenberg, Arnold (1874–1951)

Quartets Nos. 1–4 (1905, 1908, 1926, 1936). Contemporary quartets of great import, the first is post-Wagnerian in outlook; the second uses untraditional tonality and a soprano voice; the third employs the twelve-tone idiom; and the fourth is clear in outline but very Expressionistic in syntax. Dissonances and unusual effects abound in all.

Quintet for Wind Instruments (1924). Bitingly dissonant, using classic forms but problematic sonorities, this pungent four-movement work for winds is bold, imaginative, and more than a bit disturbing.

Serenade for Septet and Baritone (1923). One of the first pieces to reflect the twelve-tone technique in operation, this work employs some unusual instruments (mandoline, guitar) and baritone voice; esoteric and occult, it is also strangely beautiful.

Verklarte Nacht (1899). A one-movement work for six string instruments (in its original version), this is actually an opulent sounding symphonic poem for chamber ensemble with a semidescriptive intent.

Schubert, Franz (1797–1828)

Octet in F major for Strings and Winds (1824). Scored for string quartet, clarinet, horn, bassoon, and bass, it has a suite-like pattern and is almost orchestral in concept; over all it is spirited, exuberant, and altogether splendid.

Quartet No. 12 in C minor ("Quartettstatz," 1820). Quartet No. 14 in D minor ("Death and the Maiden," 1824). Representative of the fifteen quartets by this composer, these show a masterful grasp of the idiom. Filled with deep feeling, occasionally dark but mostly exuberant, they sparkle with Schubert's glowing harmonic eloquence and incomparable melodism.

Quintet in A major for Piano and Strings ("Trout," 1819). Scored for the unusual combination of violin, viola, 'cello, bass, and piano, this splendid work is massive in scope, very tuneful, and extremely well-organized.

Quintet in C major for Strings (1828). Employing the standard quartet with a second 'cello, this restless and anguish-ridden work is the composer's last chamber music piece.

Trios No. 1 in B-flat major and No. 2 in E-flat major for Piano and Strings (1827). Differing in spirit, both emphasize the piano. They are exuberant, zestful, and use occasional folk melodies.

Schumann, Robert (1810–1856)

Quartet in E-flat major for Piano and Strings (1842). Charming rather than epic, this is a reserved and somewhat naive piece in four movements.

Quintet in E-flat major for Piano and Strings (1842). Probably the composer's finest chamber work, it is spontaneous and inspired; its somber funeral march and stunning scherzo are especially good.

Symphonic Etudes for Piano (1837). Essentially in variation form plus a lengthy finale, this is an extremely digital and brilliant work.

Stockhausen, Karlheinz (b. 1928)

Zeitmasse for five woodwinds (1956). Serial in syntax, unorthodox, angular, nonmelodic, but expressive of beautiful woodwind sonorities, it is a different and arresting work.

Strauss, Richard (1864–1949)

Serenade in E-flat major for Thirteen Winds (1881). Written for woodwinds and four horns, this single-movement, admittedly minor, work is sweetly gracious and pleasant to hear.

Stravinsky, Igor (b. 1882)

Octet for Wind Instruments (1923). A contemporary three-movement piece cast in neoclassic style and scored for four woodwinds and four brass, this is a terse, taut, and carefully organized masterwork.

Ragtime for Eleven Instruments (1918). A chamber music portrait of jazz, it is short, uses a cimbalon, and suggests popular music of the World War I era.

Septet (1953). Ascetic, austere, and set in three movements, it is scored for a mixed ensemble; based on a sixteen-note tone row, it contains a passacaglia and a gigue.

Tartini, Giuseppe (1692–1770)

Sonata in G minor for Violin ("Devil's Trill," c. 1714). An exceptionally agile representative of the Italian Baroque sonata, it uses figured bass, motivic thematic material, and is distinctly manneristic in substance.

Varèse, Edgard (1885–1965)

Octandre (1924). So extremely pungent as to be cacophonous, this highly unorthodox work in three movements is scored for woodwinds, brass, and bass.

Density 21.5 (1935). Conceived to explore the sonorities of a solo flute, it is unusually angular and requires unbelievable dexterity for performance.

Weber, Carl Maria von (1786–1826)

Quintet in B-flat major for Clarinet and Strings (1815). An unusual bravura piece that tends to overemphasize the clarinet, it nevertheless is ingenious, well-constructed, and likeable.

Webern, Anton (1883–1945)

Five Movements for String Quartet (1909). Terse models of musical brevity —one has fourteen measures, another thirteen—they are intensely felt, poetic, and painstakingly written.

Six Bagatelles for String Quartet (1913). Even more concentrated than the preceding—sections in the piece have ten, eight, nine, eight, thirteen, and nine measures, respectively—this set of pieces contains pointillistic miniatures of rare beauty.

Chapter 16

Music and Religion — Large Vocal Forms

We have seen that music very likely had its beginnings in the crude incantations that accompanied ritualistic acts in primitive times.[1] Although a reconstruction of details is almost totally conjectural, music was undoubtedly a handmaiden in rites that predate the formulation of organized religion by thousands of years. Even now, aboriginal peoples chant, wail, shout, and "sing," as they leap, gesticulate, and posture in ceremonial observances. It seems likely, then, that these actions have origins extending backward for tens, possibly hundreds, of centuries.

Religion has engaged the minds of men from times immemorial, and the objects of worship have been varied, ranging from stone idols, cattle, or the sun, to Buddha, Allah, and Christ. Apparently, some kind of "music" was used in all of these instances, but synagogical practices observed in the Old Hebrew Temple constitute the first musical procedures about which we know anything today. There, during an era that predates the emergence of Christianity by approximately one thousand years, prayer texts were chanted aloud during worship. And it became customary to embellish their written versions (in ancient scrolls) with simple signs that gave the reader some idea of how the pitch should be varied in cantillation. From these extremely simple beginnings, religious chant and the rites that use it ultimately spread throughout Christendom.

THE MASS

Prayers comprising the Mass, a ritual of worship observed in Catholic churches for nearly two thousand years, have been taken from such sources

[1] In a wise and witty book entitled *40,000 Years of Music* (New York: Farrar, Straus, and Giroux, 1964), Jacques Chailley, an eminent French musicologist, cites as the earliest extant evidence of a musical act, a wall painting found in a cave in the Ariège, the Pyrenees area of southwest France, which archaeologists estimate to be 40,000 years old. It shows a man wearing an animal's mask and robe (appanages often used in primitive rituals), playing a musical bow and dancing behind several reindeer. Evidently he is trying to charm them.

as the Old and New Testaments, the Psalms, and diverse Scriptural writings. Regardless of source, however, these versicles have been skillfully integrated into a body of prayers that give meaning and drama to a Eucharistic rite where, in Catholic belief, the bread and wine used as sacramentals by a celebrant undergo transubstantiation to become the body and blood of Christ. It necessarily follows, therefore, that consumption of the Eucharist by both celebrant and laity, in what is known as Holy Communion, symbolizes the Last Supper, whereas a celebrant's breaking the Host (the communion wafer) represents Christ's sacrifice on the Cross. Catholics are obliged to attend Mass on all Sundays of the year as well as on special Holy Days of Obligation, and everything associated with this rite—its body of prayers, vestments worn by the celebrant and his assistants, appointments surrounding the altar, and the music that supports this service—are intended to implement and enhance its meaning and impact.

Although other rituals exist in Catholic worship, as we shall see, High Mass and Low Mass transcend all others. From a musical point of view, the former is much more important for its texts are sung, whereas those in a Low Mass are merely recited. In either case the body of prayers is identical, although—because of musical expansiveness—High Mass takes longer to celebrate. While the latter ritual unfolds, an interesting responsorial activity occurs between celebrant (priest) and choir. The former intones his prayers—mostly in Gregorian Chant—from a position on or near the altar, while the choir—usually located in a loft at the rear of a church—makes appropriate responses. Aside from participating in these antiphonal interchanges, the choir also sings portions of the Mass, using either chant or composed music. Latin has been used for centuries in this discourse, but of late there has been an increased stress on vernacular languages. Consequently, a combination of Latin and English is now widely used in this country.

Liturgically viewed, a High or a Low Mass can be separated into the

1. *Ordinary:* that body of prayers common to every day of the church year.
2. *Proper:* those portions whose texts change with each day of an ecclesiastical year.[2]

Both sets of prayers are contained in the *Missal,* a volume from which a priest reads aloud as he celebrates Mass. Members of a congregation are encouraged to read silently and to occasionally respond aloud as a Mass proceeds. Music for Masses is published separately: composed music in individual scores, and Gregorian Chant in the *Liber Usualis.* Subdivisions of the latter include (1) the *Gradual,* a collection of chants used only at Masses, and (2) the *Antiphonal,* which contains chants utilized during

---

[2] Moreover, special Propers are used whenever Mass is celebrated at nuptials, funerals, or on feast days.

various Canonical Hours including Lauds, Vespers, Matins, and Compline.

Outlines limning the Mass were established early in the Christian era, but a full codification of its prayers required more than a thousand years. Initially formulated at Rome sometime prior to the third century, by about A.D. 500 Mass liturgy had developed to a point where it included most of the Proper (see below), between whose segments *lections* (readings from the Epistles and Gospels) were interpolated. During another six or seven hundred years various portions of the Ordinary were successively introduced so that, by about 1300, when the communion prayers were finally added, the rite had been given a reasonably definitive format. Since the sixteenth century only minor changes have been introduced, some within the last year or two.

In all, a Mass has these eighteen parts; some, as we shall see, are further subdivided for particular liturgical purposes:

TABLE 23. Parts of a Mass.

Proper	Ordinary
1. Introit	
	2. *Kyrie*
	3. *Gloria*
4. Prayer	
5. Epistle	
6. Gradual	
7. Tract	
8. Gospel	
	9. *Credo*
10. Offertory	
11. Secret	
	12. Preface
	13. *Sanctus*
	14. Canon
	15. *Agnus Dei*
16. Communion	
17. Post-Communion	
	18. Last Gospel

Only nine of these sections, sometimes known as *hymns*—although they should not be confused with chorale-like songs usually identified by this term—are sung.[3] Because four are contained within the Proper, they are usually expressed in chant, but the remaining five from the Ordinary have

[3] Except for the Requiem, a special Mass for the Dead described subsequently, composers have been understandably reluctant to set portions of the Proper to music. Because these prayers are employed only once a year, any music using them would have limited performance possibilities. Thus, for the most part, musical settings of the Proper have remained in chant.

been set to music by legions of composers. Often, the latter are subdivided to comprise this sequence:

1. *Kyrie* [4]
2. *Gloria:*
   (a) *Gratias Agimus*
   (b) *Qui Tollis*
   (c) *Quoniam*
   (d) *Cum Sancto Spiritu*
3. *Credo:*
   (a) *Et Incarnatus*
   (b) *Crucifixus*
   (c) *Et Resurrexit*
4. *Sanctus:*
   (a) *Hosanna*
   (b) *Benedictus*
5. *Agnus Dei:*
   (a) *Dona Nobis*

STYLES IN MASS COMPOSITION

Hundreds and hundreds of Masses have been composed over the last eight or nine centuries. Naturally they differ greatly in musical substance, but all are as one in a strict adherence to the prescribed text. Within this broad repertoire, four stylistic trends can be discerned:

1. *Masses in Gregorian Chant:* Significant in a period extending from the founding of Christianity to about A.D. 1000, these are exquisite monophonic works. During earlier centuries, chant incipits said to include more than five hundred separate pieces were widely scattered until the pontificate of Gregory the Great (590–604), when individual items were collected and inscribed on parchment manuscripts. Frequently known as *plainsong*, this unisonal music (which now includes more than 1100 items) with an exotic modal flavor, an unencumbered rhythmic flow, and a striking pristine beauty, strongly influenced the subsequent development of both sacred and secular music. Today, entire Masses may be sung in chant, although it is more characteristic to perform four segments of the Proper (Introit, Gradual, Offertory, and Communion) in this style and use composed music for the rest.
2. *Polyphonic Masses:* The period of importance of these ranged from about the twelfth to the fifteenth centuries. As distinct from Gregorian Masses, these composed works gave a musical setting to selected portions

---

[4] In the main, these texts have been taken from the *Psalms*.

Sequence of Prayers	Portions usually set to music	Mass of The Angels (Gregorian)	Palestrina: Marcellus Mass	Bach: B Minor Mass	Mozart: Requiem	Beethoven: Missa Solemnis	Berlioz: Requiem	Verdi: Requiem*
1. Introit								
2. Kyrie	X	X	X	Kyrie Christe Kyrie	Requiem & Kyrie	X	Requiem & Kyrie	Requiem & Kyrie
3. Gloria	X	X	X	Gloria Laudamus Gratias Domine Deus Qui tollis Qui sedes Quoniam Cum sancto		X		
4. Prayer					Dies irae Tuba mirum Rex trem. Recordare Confutatis Lacrymosa		Dies irae Quid sum Rex trem. Quaerens Lacrymosa	Dies irae Tuba mirum Liber Quid sum Rex trem. Recordare Ingemisco Confutatis Lacrymosa
5. Epistle								
6. Gradual								
7. Tract								
8. Gospel								
9. Credo	X	X	X	Credo Patrem Et in Unum Incarnatus Crucifixus Resurrexit Spiritum Confiteor		X		*After Mass has been concluded, the Libera me is sung.
10. Offertory					Domine Jesu Hostias		Domine Jesu Hostias	Domine Jesu Hostias
11. Secret								
12. Preface	X	Sanctus & Benedictus	Sanctus & Benedictus	Sanctus Hosanna Benedictus	Sanctus & Benedictus	X	X	X
13. Sanctus								
14. Canon	X	X	I & II		X	X	X	X
15. Agnus Dei	X	X		Agnus Dei Dona nobis	X	X	X	X
16. Communion					Lux aeterna			Lux aeterna
17. Post-Communion								
18. Last Gospel								

A Chart Showing How Particular Masses Are Organized

of the Proper. Midway in this span of years, however, attention shifted to the Ordinary, some of whose sections were set in accordance with the period's prevailing polyphonic style—that is, in two or three voice parts. An early example is the *Messe de Tournai,* probably the Ordinary's first complete musical setting, whose authorship is unknown. More exact details surround the *Messe Notre Dame,* composed by Guillaume Machaut (1300–1377).

3. *Renaissance Masses:* An immediate outgrowth of polyphonic Masses, these became notable between the fifteenth and seventeenth centuries. Mostly, their thematic material was borrowed from chant or adopted from secular sources, and many employed a primary melody in each section as a *cantus firmus* (fixed song). Among examples are the numerous Masses based on a secular song, *L'Homme Armé* (The Armored Man). As an adjunct, the so-called "Parody Mass" developed, whose melodies were derived from the period's numerous chansons and motets. But a Parody Mass usually had distinctive melodies for each section of the Ordinary, which separated it from a *cantus firmus* Mass. Outstanding among Mass composers during these centuries were (1) Guillaume Dufay (1400–1474), active in the Netherlands; (2) Giovanni Palestrina (1525–1594), an Italian often called the father of church music; (3) Josquin des Prez (1440–1521), one of the most gifted of fifteenth-century Burgundians; (4) Tomás Luis Vittoria (1548–1611), a Spaniard who specialized in church music; and (5) Orlando di Lassus (1530–1594), undoubtedly the era's most celebrated Flemish musician.

4. *Masses after 1600:* As the seventeenth century gave way to the eighteenth, the *a cappella* (unaccompanied style) all but disappeared. Some composers continued to write polyphonic Masses, but their works can be considered the twilight of a fading style. Orchestral music advanced with increasing impetus, and secular patterns that had proven their worth in opera—arias, choruses, and ensemble numbers—were emphasized. Like virtually every musical form then extant, the Mass underwent an enormous expansion. Bach's glorious Mass in B minor (1733–1738), for instance, shows how the Ordinary's five basic segments (see chart on p. 451) were subdivided so that an edifice of twenty-four numbers was created. Other compositions of these and later times demonstrate a similar enlargement.

WAYPOSTS IN MUSICAL SETTINGS OF THE MASS

Formulating the Mass liturgy did not occur easily for these were troublous times marked by persecution and oppression. Nearly three centuries passed in the early Christian Era before its outlines were even tentatively established. During these years cantillation in Latin was adopted for a recitation of its prayers from earlier Jewish practices (which, of course, used Hebrew). Initially transmitted from one generation to another by oral means, late in the sixth century Roman chant (which then became known as Gregorian chant, in the pontiff's honor) was collected and inscribed, so legend goes, in a book bound to the main altar of St. Peter's Cathedral at Rome with a golden chain.

But Gregorian chant is not the only unisonal music known to Christendom. In other areas, wherever the religion penetrated, similar kinds of musical prayer arose. Each differed from the Roman (Gregorian) chant in its use of diverse melodic formulas, individual turns of phrase, or an idiomatic manner of performance. Among them are

1. *Ambrosian chant:* Named after Ambrose, Bishop of Milan (appointed 371, d. 397), it was used mostly in the environs of this city.
2. *Gallican chant:* A French manifestation that arose in Provençe; subsequently, portions from its literature were incorporated within Roman chant.
3. *Mozarabic chant:* This chant developed in Spain, probably in the fourth century. It remained in vogue until after the eleventh century.
4. *Byzantine chant:* Strongly influenced by Oriental (Jewish) models, this was the East's ecclesiastical music. Most of its texts are in free verse.
5. *Syrian chant:* Particularly venerable (Syria was one of the first countries to be Christianized), the substance of this chant influenced both Byzantine and Gregorian models. Some Syrian practices—for example, hymn writing—were widely adopted in the West.
6. *Armenian chant:* Primarily based on hymn singing, this cantillation ultimately developed a more complex rhythmic base than the others.
7. *Anglican chant:* A different kind of musical prayer that developed when special rites were established for the Church of England in the sixteenth century. Unlike others (and aside from its use of English), it utilizes four-part harmony and a comparatively strict metric rhythm.

Chant has never ceased to exert a powerful influence on musical practices within the Catholic Church, but as the Middle Ages passed into the Renaissance, enterprising composers began to move toward newer goals by setting Mass texts to music of their own invention. Initially, these efforts were crude, and only fragmentary bits of the liturgy (that is, a *Sanctus* or an *Agnus Dei*) were composed. But a trend was established, and the practice grew rapidly. Strangely enough, prior to this time (the twelfth century) the advantages of combining several segments from the chant repertoire to comprise a single Mass had not become apparent. Then, various items were merged so they would comprise a continuous, if not an interrelated, whole. One of these, the *Mass of the Angels,* is still in standard use in Catholic churches. By this time, too, composed Masses began to employ some of the well-known polyphonic forms. First was organum, widely used from the ninth to the thirteenth centuries. Then, as years passed, the canon, conductus, motet, and ultimately the fugue, were brought into the design.

One of the earliest composed Masses known today is Guillaume Machaut's *Messe Notre Dame,* which dates from about 1350. Although Machaut's example set a standard, it was not until nearly a century later that the idea of composing Masses, unified in style, spirit, and substance, was generally adopted by other musicians. Then, by about 1450, such Netherlanders and Burgundians as Guillaume Dufay, Johannes Ockeghem, Jacob Obrecht, Josquin des Prez, and Orlando di Lassus became active; in England, at the same time, the "Tudor Composers," Robert Fayrfax, John Taverner, Christopher Tye, and William Byrd, placed their considerable talents at the service of Mass composition.

Almost single-handedly, Giovanni Palestrina established the validity of composed church music (as opposed to chant) in the sixteenth century. At this time the Council of Trent (first convened in 1545 and adjourned in 1563) was deep in a consideration of all ecclesiastical matters, including music's role in religious rite. Some theologians held that only chant was acceptable for liturgical use and that other music suffered from secular influences and was, therefore, corrupt. Clerics who held an opposite view had their position buttressed by Palestrina's compositions which demonstrated, by pragmatic means, that composed Masses could be undeniably devotional. In the end, the Council affirmed that chant should be considered the church's official musical language, but a use of other compositions was not proscribed. Among Palestrina's Masses that assisted in establishing this policy are his *Missa Papae Marcelli* and *Missa Assumpta est Maria,* the latter with a common *cantus firmus* in each of its five sections.

Interestingly enough, instrumental music had a decisive influence on sacred works after 1600. For instance, Lodovico Viadana, a Franciscan friar, published his *Concerti ecclesiastici* in 1605 and opened dual paths along which the secular concerto and orchestral Mass subsequently journeyed. Five in number, Viadana's pieces employ voices and organ and are much concerned with a juxtaposition of vocal and instrumental sonorities. Although these *Concerti ecclesiastici* are far distant from the orchestral Masses of later eras, they nevertheless portend avenues along which subsequent sacred works would pass.

Luther's historic revolt from the Church of Rome occurred in 1517 when the reformer nailed his ninety-five theses to a door of the castle church at Wittenberg. Subsequently, the rift widened, and the one-time Augustinian monk ultimately found himself deep in the throes of establishing a new form of worship. In so doing, he retained two sections from the long-established Roman Mass, the Kyrie and Gloria, which many Protestant composers began to set to music as a *Missa brevis* (short Mass). Ultimately, the Lutheran service became even more musically oriented as the church cantata was perfected.

Early in the eighteenth century it became an accepted practice to subdivide the *Gloria* and *Credo*. By this time, too, the aria, particularly the *da capo* type, became a fixture within composed Masses. In brief, religious works were now becoming increasingly operatic. Italy continued to be a center of Mass composition just as it excelled in operatic writing, and two groups of Italian composers (both of whom employed small orchestras in their Masses) became prominent. In Rome, Adriano Banchieri and Alessandro Scarlatti were especially notable, while Giovanni Pergolesi, Leonardo Leo, Francesco Durante, and Leonardo Vinci gained distinction in Naples. But one of the era's most prominent landmarks in Mass composition appeared in the north, in Germany, where J. S. Bach wrote his Mass in B minor (1733–1737). Begun as a *Missa brevis*, it was ultimately recast to include the full text of a Catholic Mass. Although length precludes its performance in conjunction with religious rite (it is now typically heard in concert performance), Bach's magnum opus is everywhere accepted as one of music's most sublime compositions. Unfailingly, it casts a devotional spell over any audience that hears it.

Masses by W. A. Mozart, Franz Joseph Haydn, and Franz Schubert established new tenets for religious music during the Classic era. Progenitors of a distinguished Viennese tradition, theirs are extended works that merge solo voices, chorus, and orchestra in a design fully compatible with the majestic pageantry associated with a seat of empire. Haydn's "Mass in Time of War" (*Missa in tempore belli*), often called the *Paukenmesse* or his "Lord Nelson Mass"—a Requiem—beautifully express the exalted religious spirit of this Imperial City. Mozart's "Coronation Mass" (Mass in C major, K. 317) is similarly oriented, as is his Mass in C minor, K. 427, termed "The Great" because of its grandiose sweep and regal power. Schubert's Masses have a gracious, seraphic charm. His Mass No. 6 in E-flat major, for instance, is delightfully lyric, sensitively cast, and almost heavenly in its expression of exalted fervor.

From the times of Giacomo Carissimi (1605–1674) to those of Luigi Cherubini (1760–1842), Masses in the contrapuntal and *a cappella* styles continued to maintain an existence, but powerful currents were ultimately arrayed against them. As Classicism gave way to Romanticism, the orchestral Mass, which employs a large retinue of vocalists and instrumentalists, all but banished its predecessors. Secular influences apparently could not be avoided, and musicians wrote grandiloquent pieces more suited for large auditoriums than small parish churches. In this environment the *concerted Mass*, one that employs florid arias, stentorian choruses, and extended orchestral numbers, flourished. Beethoven's *Missa solemnis* reveals this trend toward expansiveness, but others, including Berlioz's *Grand Messe des Morts*, Franz Liszt's *Missa Choralis*, Giuseppe Verdi's *Requiem*, Antonín Dvořák's *Requiem*, and Anton Bruckner's Masses in D minor, E minor and F minor are similarly designed.

A Papal Bull, *Motu Proprio* (by his own wish), issued by Pius X in 1903, attempted to stem the tide of secularization that was washing over church music. In his encyclical the Pontiff called attention to chant as the musical language best suited for the Roman rite; he stressed beauties inherent in the polyphony of Palestrina's Masses and suggested these as models worthy of emulation. Pius X forbade further divisions of the Mass text into disjunct parts (to stifle mere expansiveness), he discouraged the use of instruments in liturgical music and, in general, took a stand intended to re-establish vigor, authenticity, and integrity in church musical practice. Generally speaking, his words have been heeded down to the present time.

Perhaps because of these proscriptions, or perhaps because it has been proven a difficult idiom in which to work, twentieth-century Masses are not numerous. Among outstanding newer religious compositions that reveal exemplary musical and spiritual qualities are the Mass in G minor (1923) by the English composer Ralph Vaughan Williams; the *Mass* (1948) by Igor Stravinsky; and the unusual *War Requiem* (1962) by Benjamin Britten.

THE REQUIEM MASS

Requiem aeternam dona eis, Domine (Grant them eternal rest, O Lord), is the Introit's opening phrase in a "Mass for the Dead," the *Missa pro defunctis,* and has given this rite its best-known name: Requiem. In general, prayers included within a Requiem are similar to those in conventional Masses, save for a few special devotions. Perfected by the Church over centuries of time, the obsequies for a deceased person convey expressions of profound sorrow and deep compassion. And because of the text's intense emotionality, many composers have been motivated to set it to music. This is the alignment of sections in a Requiem Mass: [5]

1. Introit: *Requiem aeternam* (Grant them eternal rest).
2. *Kyrie eleison:* (Lord have mercy).
3. Sequence: *Dies irae* (Dreaded day of wrath).
4. Offertory: *Domine Jesu Christie.*
5. *Sanctus:* (Holy, holy, holy).
6. *Benedictus qui venit* (Blessed is He).
7. *Agnus Dei:* (Lamb of God have mercy).
8. Communion: *Lux aeterna* (May eternal light).

After a Requiem Mass has been concluded, the celebrant lays some of his vestments aside, dons a black cape and, in joint action with the choir, prays over the catafalque using the text *Libera me, Domine, de morte*

[5] However, a perusal of the chart on p. 451 will disclose that composers occasionally subdivide Requiem texts. Furthermore, both the Gloria and Credo are omitted, for their jubilant texts are hardly appropriate in a Mass for the Dead.

aeterna (Deliver me, O Lord, from eternal death). Many composers consider this an integral part of the rite and include it in their Requiems.

Within a Requiem's series of musical numbers, particular prominence is allotted the hymn *Dies Irae* (Day of Wrath), a rather lengthy sequence whose inclusion immediately after the Tract is permitted by ecclesiastical law. A prayer whose origins date from the thirteenth century, the *Dies Irae* has fifty-seven lines that are often elaborately set. Verdi, for instance, subdivided the *Dies Irae* in his "Manzoni" Requiem so that it comprises nine separate numbers.

Of the many Requiems currently prominent in the literature, those by Orlando Lassus (1589), Giovanni Palestrina (1591), Tomás Luis Vittoria (1603), W. A. Mozart (1791), Hector Berlioz (1837), Giuseppe Verdi 1874, Gabriel Fauré (1887), Antonín Dvořák (1890), and Benjamin Britten (1962) are especially fine. Moreover, they demonstrate the paths of development this specialized form of the Mass has taken during recent centuries.

TEXT FOR THE ORDINARY OF A MASS

Kyrie

Kyrie eleison!	Lord, have mercy upon us!
Christe eleison!	Christ, have mercy upon us!
Kyrie eleison!	Lord, have mercy upon us!

Gloria

Gloria in excelsis Deo,	Glory to God on high,
Et in terra pax hominibus *bonae voluntatis.*	And peace on earth to men of good will.
Laudamus te. Benedicimus te.	We praise Thee. We bless Thee.
Adoramus te. Glorificamus te.	We adore Thee. We glorify Thee.
Gratias agimus tibi propter magnam *gloriam tuam.*	We give thanks to Thee for Thy great glory.
Domine Deus, Rex coelestis,	O Lord God, O heavenly King,
Deus Pater omnipotens.	O God, the Father almighty.
Domine, Fili unigenite Jesu *Christe.*	O Lord Jesus Christ, the only-begotten Son.
Domine Deus, Agnus Dei, Filius Patris.	Lord God, Lamb of God, Son of the Father.
Qui tollis peccata mundi,	Thou who takest away the sins of the world,
Miserere nobis.	Have mercy upon us.
Qui tollis peccata mundi,	Thou who takest away the sins of the world,
Suscipe deprecationem nostram.	Receive our prayer.
Qui sedes ad dexteram patris	Thou who sittest at the right hand of the Father
Miserere nobis.	Have mercy upon us.

Quoniam tu solus sanctus.   For Thou only art holy.

Tu solus Dominus. Tu solus Altissimus, Jesu Christe,   Thou alone are Lord. Thou alone are most high, Jesus Christ.

Cum Sancto Spiritu in gloria Dei Patris. Amen.   Together with the Holy Ghost in the glory of God the Father. Amen.

Credo

Credo in unum Deum   I believe in one God,

Patrem omnipotentem, factorem caeli et terrae, visibilium omnium, et invisibilium.   The Father Almighty, maker of heaven and earth, and of all things visible and invisible.

Et in unum Dominum Jesum Christum, Filium Dei unigenitum.   And in one Lord Jesus Christ, the only-begotten Son of God.

Et ex Patre natum ante omnia saecula.   Born of the Father before all ages.

Deum de Deo, lumen de lumine,   God of Gods, light of light,

Deum verum de Deo vero.   True God of true God.

Genitum, non factum, consubstantialem Patri: Begotten, not made, consubstantial with the Father;

Per quem omnia facta sunt.   By whom all things were made.

Qui propter nos homines, et propter nostram salutem, descendit de coelis   Who for us men and for our salvation came down from Heaven,

Et incarnatus est de Spirito Sancto ex Maria Virgine, et homo factus est.   And was incarnate by the Holy Ghost of the Virgin Mary, and was made man.

Crucifixus etiem pro nobis: sub Pontio Pilato, passus et sepultus est.   He was crucified for us; Suffered under Pontius Pilate, and was buried.

Et resurrexit tertia die, secundum Scripturas.   On the third day He rose again, according to the scriptures.

Et ascendit in coelum: sedet ad dexteram Patris.   He ascended into heaven and sitteth on the right hand of God the Father.

Et iterum venturas est cum gloria judicare vivos et mortuos: cujus regni non erit finis.   And He is to come again with glory to judge the living and the dead, Whose kingdom shall have no end.

Et in Spiritum Sanctum, Dominum, et vivificantem, qui ex Patre Filioque procedit;   And I believe in the Holy Ghost, Lord and Giver of life, who proceedeth from the Father and the Son;

Qui cum Patre et Filio simul adoratur, et conglorificatur; Qui locutus est per Prophetas.   Who, with the Father and the Son, together is worshipped and glorified. Who spoke by the Prophets.

Et in unam sanctam catholicam et apostolicam Ecclesiam.   And I believe in one Catholic and Apostolic Church.

Confiteor unum Baptisma in remissionem peccatorum.   And I confess one baptism for the remission of sins.

Et expecto resurrectionem mortuorum,   And I expect the resurrection of the dead,

Et vitam venturi saeculi.   And the life of the world to come.

Amen.   Amen.

Sanctus

Sanctus Dominus Deus Sabaoth.	Holy is the Lord God Sabaoth.
Pleni sunt coeli et terra gloria tua.	Heaven and earth are full of Thy glory.
Osanna in excelsis.	Hosanna in the highest.

Benedictus

Benedictus qui venit in nomine Domini.	Blessed is he who cometh in the name of the Lord.
Osanna in excelsis.	Hosanna in the highest.

Agnus Dei

Agnus Dei, quo tollis peccata mundi:	Lamb of God, who takes away the sins of the world,
Miserere nobis.	Have mercy upon us.
Dona nobis pacem.	Grant us peace.

ORATORIO

Often textually concerned with intensely felt and deeply emotional subjects, oratorio is a large-scale vocal design that enlists soloists, diverse vocal ensembles (duets, trios, and quartets), a chorus (sometimes more than one), and a sizeable orchestra. Most oratorios are separated into divisions known as *parts* that are generally comparable with acts in an opera, and these, in turn, are usually subdivided into individual numbers. Normally, oratorio is presented on a concert platform—sometimes in a church—without scenery, costuming, or dramatic action. Many of these musicodramatic compositions are concerned with a narration of Biblical texts, often taken from the Old Testament, although secular works occasionally appear. And because oratorio and opera have coexisted side-by-side for hundreds of years, they share a number of common characteristics.

Oratorio's foundations rest on the liturgical dramas that were important in religious and social life in Western Europe during the Medieval era. Known as Mystery or Miracle Plays, these dramas, whose existence extended from about the tenth to the sixteenth century, brought enlightenment and entertainment into the lives of many in a period when poverty, pestilence, and oppression were a common lot. Far more than mere theatrical ventures, such plays were also an effective means of promulgating religious doctrine among an illiterate populace. Because they were the only rooms then available in which to house large gatherings, church naves became improvised theaters in which Mystery Plays were enacted.

Sometime after 1550 liturgical drama became even more distinctive when St. Philip Neri (1515–1595) joined them with sermons he was delivering to his Roman congregation. Urging that sacred hymns, called *Laudi Spirituali*, be performed between sections of his discourse, St. Philip also sponsored a staging of plays to further enhance its meaning. Because they were given in the oratory[6] of a church, such works became known as oratorios. Thus, a new combined form, primarily religious in orientation, acquired a structure and a name as the sixteenth century neared its close.

WAYPOSTS IN THE RISE OF ORATORIO

Early Oratorio in Italy, Germany, and France

Written by Emilio di Cavalieri (1550–1602), *La Rappresentazione di anima e di corpo* (A Representation of the Body and Spirit), first performed at Rome in 1600,[7] is a principal forerunner of modern oratorio. With a text reflective of the subjects in many morality plays, *La Rappresentazione* was given in a theatrical manner and included in its cast characters with such names as Time, Life, the World, Pleasure, Intellect, Soul, and the Body. A modest-size orchestra supported vocal lines uttered in a declamatory style, while a chorus occasionally contributed a sequence of popular hymns. Unfortunately, Cavalieri's immediate successors were unable to sustain his efforts. However, shortly after the century's midpoint, Giacomo Carissimi (1605–1674) issued a collection of five pieces, including his superb *Jepthe,* which may be considered music's first bona-fide oratorios.[8] By Carissimi's time, the practice of performing oratorios in a theatrical manner had subsided, and most of these religious dramas began to find a congenial habitat in the church or concert hall. Probably the greatest of this period's Italian oratorio composers, however, was Alessandro Scarlatti whose important works, written between 1680 and 1717, honored the Virgin Mary as the Mother of Christ. Important among his contemporaries and successors were Antonio Caldara, Leonardo Leo, J. A. Hasse, Giovanni Pergolesi, Benedetto Marcello, Nicola Porpora, and Niccolo Jommelli.

Consistently over the years, Italian oratorio showed theatrical leanings that it never successfully sloughed away, but this was not true in northern lands, especially Germany, where sacred drama soon became strongly entrenched. And the further north one traveled, the more redoubtable this spirit of pietism became. Vienna, a Catholic stronghold, was little disturbed, but in Leipzig and Hamburg, to mention only two northern cities, the Reformation's apostolic zeal was inescapable. Among German composers who created important sacred works during the seventeenth and eighteenth centuries were Heinrich Schütz (Dresden); Reinhard Keiser (Hamburg); Dietrich Buxtehude (Lubeck); Georg Philip Telemann (Hamburg);

---

[6] Strictly speaking, the oratory is not an integral part of a church, but a side chapel where private religious services (weddings, funerals, and baptisms) or Benedictions and *Te Deums* are conducted.

[7] A scene from this important work appears in *A Treasury of Early Music.* (See Appendix C.)

[8] *Afferte gladium* (Go take the sword), a scene from Carissimi's *Judicium Salomonis* is in *Masterpieces of Music Before 1750.* (See Appendix C.)

Johann Sebastian Bach (Leipzig); and George F. Handel (Hanover, then England).

Of these, Heinrich Schütz was the earliest, and in many respects, the most significant. Under the patronage of the Margrave Maurice of Hesse-Cassel, he was sent to Italy at the age of twenty-four to study with Giovanni Gabrieli at Venice. Devout in his own religious convictions, Gabrieli not only gave his gifted pupil a sound musical training but a desire to be pious and sincere in sacred expression. Consequently, while writing six oratorios that are obviously Germanic in substance and outlook—the most notable is *Historia der Gerburt Jesu Christi* (The Story of the Birth of Jesus Christ, 1664)—Schütz firmly established the integrity of German oratorio. This *Christmas Oratorio* employs a small orchestra, a soprano soloist (representing an angel), a tenor (Evangelist), a bass (Herod), and a mixed chorus. It contains eight musical numbers, plus an introduction and an epilogue, both performed by choir. Schütz's use of associative scoring—in which flutes and bassoons accompany the shepherds, violins support the Wise Men, trombones add authority to utterances of the High Priest, and trumpets buttress the proclamations of Herod—is particularly convincing.

In comparison, French and Italian oratorios were inclined to be more narrative, historic, and epic. Although none can be termed secular, most tended to view their subjects with something less than devotional solemnity. During a period in French music identified as "The Age of Lully," only a few Gallic composers wrote oratorios. Of them, Marc Antoine Charpentier (1634–1704), a pupil of Carissimi, was undoubtedly the most notable.[9] But French composers of this and later times were primarily interested in bringing Biblical subjects to the stage, a trend discernible, for instance, in writings of the long-lived Jean Philippe Rameau.

Oratorio in the Late Baroque

While he was incumbent Cantor at the St. Thomas Church in Leipzig, J. S. Bach wrote numerous cantatas (to be discussed later in this book) and four compositions in oratorio format. Three of these are examples of Passion music and center on events leading to the Crucifixion, and one, the so-called *Christmas Oratorio*, relates details of the Nativity. In the Reformed Churches of Northern Germany during his time, the Festival of Christmas was not confined to observances on a single day; rather, it began on December 25 and continued until January 6. Bach's *Christmas Oratorio* (1734) is, consequently, a collection of six cantatas intended for rites on December 25, 26, and 27, New Year's Day, the Sunday following, and the Feast of the Epiphany, an event marking the Magi's journey. Scored for chorus, orchestra, and soloists (soprano, alto, tenor, and bass), it has six fully independent divisions that, in turn, include from seven to thirteen numbers.

[9] An example of his work, a scene from *Le Reniement de St. Pierre* (The Denial of St. Peter), may be found in *A Treasury of Early Music*. (See Appendix C.)

Bach's contemporary, Georg Philipp Telemann, was an extremely prolific composer, but his religious works represent a dilution of the German
mystical spirit. This cannot be said of the superb masterpieces written by
Bach's other colleague, George Frideric Handel. Produced privately for the
Duke of Chandos, who was then his patron, Handel's first oratorio, *Esther*,
known originally as *Haman and Mordecai*, was mounted in 1720. Given a
public performance twelve years later (in 1732) at the Royal Opera House
in London, and emblazoned with all the theater's accouterments, it attracted
both warm acclaim and penetrating criticism. Much of the latter was contributed by clerics who objected to the costumed and dramatized performance of a work based on Scripture. Showing adroit inventiveness, Handel
promptly modified this scheme so that henceforth his oratorios would be
given in concert form. Although based on Biblical subjects, Handelian
oratorio nevertheless retains a searing emotional intensity, an impassioned
heroic ardor, and a grandiose cast that is almost secular in outlook. It has,
for instance, little of the mysticism that abounds in works by Bach or
Schütz. Even *Messiah*, unquestionably the most philosophic of Handel's
oratorios, is thoroughly forthright in theological utterance. Seemingly,
while writing oratorio Handel maintained a stance more in accord with
theatrical requirements than in an observance of religious solemnity. Chief
among his oratorios are *Esther* (1732); *Israel in Egypt* (1739); *Saul* (1739);
Messiah (1742); *Judas Maccabeus* (1747); *Joshua* (1748); *Solomon* (1749);
and *Jephtha* (1752).

Oratorio in the Classic and Romantic Eras

Although he was an acknowledged master in nearly every phase of
musical creativity, Mozart seldom ventured into sacred composition, save
for his glorious Masses. Two works in this area, a Passion cantata entitled
Grabmusik and *La Betulia Liberata*, an oratorio, are rarely performed today.
On the other hand, Haydn became acquainted with Handel's oratorios while
visiting England after 1790, and under this stimulus wrote two superb
works, *The Creation* (1798) and *The Seasons* (1801).[10] Despite an original
utilization of German texts,[11] both compositions have their roots in English
literature. Derived partly from *Genesis* but mostly from Milton's *Paradise
Lost*, the text of *The Creation* was organized into a workable libretto by an
English poet named Lidley and subsequently translated into German by
Baron von Swieten. Similarly, *The Seasons* was based on a poem by an
English author, James Thompson (1700–1748). Again von Swieten bent his
literary talents to the task and shaped a libretto that narrates charming,

---

[10] Even earlier, Haydn composed his *Seven Last Words of Christ* (1785) for use
in the Cathedral at Cadiz, Spain on Good Friday of Holy Week. Based on a portion of
the Passion story, it employs a bass soloist to articulate Christ's words in recitative; between them a bishop delivers a short sermon and the orchestra concludes each episode
with a sonata.

[11] Nowadays, they are performed in either English or German.

and rather naive, details about the year's changing seasons. Lyric and contemplative rather than portentous or religious and organized in four major divisions representing winter, spring, summer, and fall, *The Seasons* includes a total of thirty-nine numbers.

Harbinger of the spirit of Romanticism, the great Ludwig van Beethoven created a single oratorio, *Christus am Oelberg* (Christ On The Mount of Olives) in 1802 (published in 1811). Based on a text by Franz Xavier Huber, Beethoven's choral drama contains much fine music, including a well-known chorus: "The Heavens Are Telling." However, some of its other numbers tend to be overly ornate and the composition unquestionably suffers from an outlandish text. Felix Mendelssohn's oratorios, on the other hand, have been proven more enduring. He created four, of which two, *St. Paul* (1836) and *Elijah* (1846), are outstanding. A third, *Lobegesang* (Hymn of Praise, 1840), falls more within the bailiwick of a choral symphony, for it assigns unusually important parts to the orchestra. And a fourth work, *Christus,* remained unfinished at the composer's death. Mendelssohn was a first-rate craftsman, and in the company of large choral works his *Elijah* ranks especially high. Organized in two parts and subdivided into thirty-nine numbers, it is based on fragments from the Old Testament. Everywhere it stands immediately behind Handel's *Messiah* in public approval and acceptance.

With two oratorios of a strangely uneven cast, Franz Liszt, an emissary from Romanticism's avant garde, wrote *finis* to the creation of large choral works in German environs during the century's second half. Liszt's *Christus* (1855–1866), which employs Latin to convey texts from Scripture and the Catholic liturgy, is mystic and unusually religious; but his *Legend of St. Elizabeth* (1865), despite its title, is a lesser work primarily concerned with depicting secular aspects of the Saint's life.

When Hector Berlioz created *L'Enfance du Christ* (1854), he brought French oratorio to its highest point of attainment. Wisely holding his penchant for ostentation in abeyance, Berlioz allowed meaningful details of Christ's infancy to unfold in a simple yet eloquent manner. Organized in three divisions: (1) "The Dream of Herod," (2) "The Flight into Egypt," and (3) "The Arrival at Saïs," *L'Enfance du Christ* is gentle, poignant, and altogether beautiful. Berlioz's secular oratorio, *The Damnation of Faust* (1846), is strikingly different, however, for here the flamboyant musician imposed no restrictions on either his imagination or the choral and orchestral forces at his disposal. Termed "a dramatic legend in four parts," *The Damnation of Faust* undertakes the narration of a popular Romantic topic—Schumann, Liszt, Wagner, and Gounod also wrote on it. In it, Berlioz involves a listener in: (1) Faust's wanderings through Hungary; (2) a visit to a gloomy study where the introspective scientist is about to poison himself; (3) an assignation between Faust and the lovely heroine Marguerite; and (4) the signing of a final compact wherein Faust's soul becomes condemned to hell. Nearly all its music is colorful, brash, and attractive, but several indi-vidual numbers have become particularly well-known including: "Hungarian March," "Song of the Flea," "Dance of the Sylphs," and "Minuet of the Will-o-the-Wisps." Although several subsequent Gallic composers continued in Berlioz's footsteps, none could attain his stature. One, César Franck, wrote five sacred musical dramas between 1846 and 1881, of which *Les Béatitudes* (1879), based on a subject more mystic than religious, has become comparatively well-known. But choral works by such other French musicians as Charles Gounod, Jules Massenet, Camille Saint-Saëns, and Vincent d'Indy have failed to attain lasting stature.

Oratorio in Modern Times

Since Handel's time, oratorio has prospered greatly in England. But it is unfortunate that English oratorio (that is, sacred musical drama by native composers) became mired in a trough of mediocrity between 1750 and 1900. Meanwhile, the nation actively imported its oratorio with a result that during the nineteenth century works by Spohr, Berlioz, Mendelssohn, and Liszt became well-known in the British Isles. Late in the Edwardian age, however, this trend was reversed when Edward Elgar (*The Dream of Gerontius*, 1900; *The Apostles*, 1903; *The Kingdom*, 1906) and Gustav Holst (*The Hymn of Jesus*, 1917) undertook a cultivation of modern English oratorio. Later British composers who were to write fine large-scale English-language choral works include Ralph Vaughan Williams (*Sancta Civitas*, 1926) and William Walton (*Belshazzar's Feast*, 1931).

Among twentieth-century oratorios, Zoltán Kodály's *Psalmus Hungaricus* (1923); Arthur Honegger's *Le Roi David* (1921) and *Jeanne d'Arc au Bûcher* (1938); and Serge Prokofiev's nationalistic *Alexander Nevsky* (1939)—actually the reworking of a motion picture score—have been proven unusually good. In respective order, their composers are Hungarian, Swiss-French, and Russian. Igor Stravinsky's *Oedipus Rex* (1927), based on Sophocles' ancient Greek drama, is a splendid secular oratorio often given in the theater with stylized stage action. And Randall Thompson's *Testament of Freedom* (1943) represents numerous oratorios by American composers that explore patriotic topics.

MESSIAH BY GEORGE FRIDERIC HANDEL

When he began composing his most celebrated oratorio, Handel's renown was in eclipse. A succession of reverses had struck several theatrical ventures in which he was interested, tides of musical taste were apparently turning, and the ornate Italian style of which he was a foremost representative in England was being mercilessly ridiculed by satirical polemics delivered by such essayists as Addison and Steele. Still, in August of 1741 Handel set to work on *Messiah,* and he persevered without respite for twenty-three days. But then it lay among his unperformed manuscripts until April 13, 1742, when it was given a premiere in Dublin.

Compiled by Charles Jennens, the text of *Messiah* is separated into three principal divisions: Part One, frequently termed the "Christmas Section," is concerned with the prophecies and a narrative of the Nativity; Part Two, the "Easter Section," centers on details of Christ's Passion and Resurrection; and Part Three describes man's heavenly aspirations and ultimate salvation. In true oratorio fashion, *Messiah* relies heavily on its chorus, while between numerous sturdy choral numbers (well-suited for amateur choirs) a series of comparatively difficult arias for solo voice is interpolated. Support is provided by a modest-size orchestra, which, in addition to the usual strings, calls for trumpets and kettledrums. During Handel's time it was customary to double the string parts with oboes and bassoons, and in later years, W. A. Mozart, among others, rescored the orchestration to include horns, trombones, flutes, and clarinets.

Of fifty-two numbers in *Messiah*, only two—the Overture, organized in French style with a *grave* introduction and a fast contrapuntal *allegro*, and the "Pastoral Symphony"—are for orchestra alone. There are sixteen arias, and the chorus is allocated twenty-one pieces, of which the celebrated *Hallelujah Chorus* is undoubtedly best-known. Vocal ensembles are minimized; there is only one short number for mixed quartet and one duet for alto and tenor. Between these diverse musical numbers, continuity is provided by accompanied recitative. Here is an outline of the entire work:

Part One
Overture (Performed by orchestra)

1. *Recitative* (Tenor): Comfort ye, my people.
2. *Aria* (Tenor): Every valley shall be exalted.
3. *Chorus:* And the glory of the Lord.
4. *Recitative* (Bass): Thus saith the Lord.
5. *Aria* (Bass): But who may abide the day of His coming.
6. *Chorus:* And He shall purify the sons of Levi.
7. *Recitative* (Alto): Behold, a virgin shall conceive.
8. *Aria* (Alto) & *Chorus:* O thou that tellest good tidings.
9. *Chorus:* O thou that tellest good tidings.
10. *Recitative* (Bass): Behold, darkness shall cover the earth.
11. *Aria* (Bass): The people that walked in darkness.
12. *Chorus:* For unto us a Child is born.
13. *"Pastoral Symphony"* (Played by orchestra).
14. *Recitative* (Soprano): There were shepherds.
15. *Chorus:* Glory to God in the highest.
16. *Aria* (Soprano): Rejoice greatly, O daughter of Zion.
17. *Recitative* (Alto): Then shall the eyes of the blind.
18. *Aria* (Alto): He shall feed His flock like a shepherd.
19. *Chorus:* His yoke is easy and His burden is light.

Part Two

20. *Chorus:* Behold the Lamb of God.
21. *Aria* (Alto): He was despised and rejected of men.*
22. *Chorus:* Surely He hath borne our griefs.
23. *Chorus:* And with His stripes we are healed.
24. *Chorus:* All we like sheep have gone astray.
25. *Recitative* (Tenor): All they that see Him.
26. *Chorus:* He trusted in God that He would deliver Him.
27. *Recitative* (Tenor): Rebuke hath broken His Heart.
28. *Aria* (Tenor): Behold, and see if there be any sorrow.
29. *Recitative* (Tenor): He was cut off out of the land.
30. *Aria* (Tenor): Thou didst not leave His soul in hell.
31. *Chorus:* Lift up your heads.
32. *Recitative* (Tenor): Unto which of the angels.
33. *Chorus:* Let all the angels of God worship Him.
34. *Aria* (Bass): Thou art gone up on high.†
35. *Chorus:* The Lord gave the word.
36. *Aria* (Soprano): How beautiful are the feet.
37. *Chorus:* Their sound is gone out into all lands.
38. *Aria* (Bass): Why do the nations so furiously rage.
39. *Chorus:* Let us break their bonds asunder.
40. *Recitative* (Tenor): He that dwelleth in heaven.
41. *Aria* (Tenor): Thou shalt break them with a rod.
42. *Chorus:* Hallelujah! for the Lord God omnipotent reigneth.

Part Three

43. *Aria* (Soprano): I know that my Redeemer liveth.
44. *Chorus:* Since by man came death.
45. *Recitative* (Bass): Behold, I tell you a mystery.
46. *Aria* (Bass): The trumpet shall sound.
47. *Recitative* (Alto): Then shall be brought to pass.*
48. *Duet* (Alto and Tenor): O death, where is thy sting.*
49. *Chorus:* But thanks be to God.*
50. *Aria* (Soprano): If God be for us, who can be against us.*
51. *Chorus:* Worthy is the Lamb that was slain.
52. *Chorus:* Amen.

* The latter part of this aria is usually omitted.
† This aria is usually omitted.

THE CANTATA

Although it is more modest in dimension than either the Mass or oratorio, the cantata nevertheless ranks as a near equal in beauty and expressiveness. All three have common organizational plans (that is, they are essentially additive), but cantatas usually include fewer than a dozen subsections and take less than thirty minutes to perform. Most of the latter employ a relatively small body of performers including one or two soloists, a modest-size chorus, and a reduced orchestra. Typically, a cantata juxtaposes arias for solo voice with concerted choral numbers and recitative with song, while the orchestra underscores all vocal activity and occasionally contributes sections of its own. Although cantatas may be based on either religious or secular subjects, sacred works are far more common. When they appear, secular cantatas usually deal with historical personages, great events in the development of a nation, or similar patriotic topics. Religiously oriented pieces on the other hand, which are often prominent in Protestant worship, often treat with portions of Scripture. In either case, the vernacular language is employed.

WAYPOSTS IN CANTATA DEVELOPMENT

Although some cantata-like works predate 1600, it was only in the early seventeenth century that such Italian composers as Jacopo Peri, Giulio Caccini, Claudio Monteverdi, and Marc Antonio Cesti evolved an integrated design (usually scored for solo voice with ensemble accompaniment) that included recitative, arioso, and aria. Textual subjects in their cantatas were mostly concerned with historical figures of the Greek and Roman past, or deities and mythological creatures from ancient cultures. Maintaining a careful distinction between secular and religious works, these pieces were called *cantata da camera* (a chamber cantata based on secular material) or *cantata da chiesa* (a church cantata with a pronounced religious viewpoint).[12] For nearly fifty years such solo cantatas were an Italian specialty, but about 1650 works scored for two voices, usually soprano and contralto, were introduced. Essentially contrapuntal in nature, except for declamatory portions wherein monody was requisite, these duo cantatas were distinctly secular in substance and dealt with subjects ranging from amorous to satirical. Many show surprising creative ingenuity, and some include an early variation technique in which a fixed bass line (known as a *strophic bass*) is repeated a number of times and embellished with a new melody (sometimes extemporized by the performer) with each repetition.

Well-known as a composer of oratorio and opera, Giacomo Carissimi also became Italy's outstanding writer of cantatas after 1650, and a few years later Henry Purcell gained similar renown in England. Pieces by these men occasionally include motets, but in time the aria totally vanquished this venerable polyphonic design. In Britain the *anthem*, quite similar in plan, substance, and intent to the cantata, arose as a religiously

---

[12] A brief excerpt from a secular work (c. 1720), the second recitative and aria (from a total of three) in *Stravaganze d'Amore* (The Extravagances of Love) by Benedetto Marcello, is contained in A *Treasury of Early Music*. (See Appendix C.)

oriented work to occupy an important position in Anglican worship. Exceptionally fine examples are Handel's *Chandos Anthems,* twelve works composed between 1716 and 1718 for the then Earl of Carnarvon, who later became Duke of Chandos.

Because it was sponsored by such distinguished musicians as Handel, Giovanni Pergolesi, and Domenico and Alessandro Scarlatti, the solo cantata continued to prosper during the first half of the eighteenth century. Scarlatti alone is credited with having composed approximately five hundred such pieces. Such a prolific outpouring was possible during this era, for most solo cantatas adhered to a relatively fixed form: (1) each usually included six individual numbers—three arias preceded by as many recitatives; (2) each was based on subject matter—often humorous, amorous, or preferably both—taken from classical sources; and (3) each used a string ensemble plus any available winds to support the voice.

Some of Handel's works, however, are more expansive and exemplify a large-scale version of the cantata. His *Acis and Galatea* (1720), for instance, originally designated a masque (an English court entertainment of near-operatic proportions), is a secular work with a text from Greek mythology that centers on activities in the lives of: (1) Acis, a tenor; (2) Galatea, a soprano; (3) Damon, a tenor; and (4) Polyphemus, a bass. Divided into two "acts," it has a total of twenty-one numbers of which eleven are arias. Because it has an English-language text (by John Gay) of unusual quality and a superb musical score, Handel's piece merits attention from contemporary listeners.[13]

As the cantata traveled north after 1700, it took on an increasingly serious outlook so that, in Germany at least, sacred cantatas became much more numerous than secular works. This was, of course, just a reverse of the situation in Italy. Extremely important in this scheme of shifting emphasis was the cantata's almost total acceptance within the Lutheran rite. As exemplified in hundreds of cantatas written by J. S. Bach and his contemporaries, the typical church cantata of this era tends to follow a relatively fixed sequence:

1. It begins with a presentation by the choir of a rather lengthy number often written in fugal style. Occasionally, however, this choral piece is prefaced by an instrumental *sinfonia* (an overture).
2. In succession, a series of arias, duets, and recitatives are performed whose texts are based on a gospel reading appointed for the day. Even a brief cantata has three or four such numbers which are, of course, accompanied by a small orchestra. In particular pieces, a selected instrument (flute, oboe, or violin) may interweave an obbligato around the vocal line.
3. At the cantata's conclusion, usually tantamount to a cessation of the

---

[13] Furthermore, it is currently available in a fine modern recording on the *Oiseau-Lyre* label.

service, a chorale is performed in which soloists, choir, orchestra, and congregation join.

Somewhere within this sequence, at an appropriate juncture between musical numbers, a sermon is preached. Because it is normally based on the same gospel as the cantata, a minister's discourse elaborates on this same subject, and gives the service a remarkable degree of unity. Furthermore, numbers within a cantata are often founded on a traditional chorale melody, which becomes the near equivalent of a *cantus firmus.* And this gives the musical work remarkable cohesion.

J. S. Bach wrote the most outstanding German cantatas of this period, and probably of all time. As a practicing church musician, he had a continuing need for sacred cantatas and wrote more than three hundred, most of them after becoming Cantor at Leipzig's St. Thomas Church in 1723. But he occasionally wrote secular works, as is shown by *Phoebus and Pan* (1731), the witty *Coffee Cantata* (1732), and the charming *Peasant Cantata* (1742).

Considerable divergence exists between one Bach cantata and another, and they can in no sense be considered stereotypes. Their performance time varies rather considerably, although most take less than thirty minutes. Some have only a few concerted choral numbers, and highlight, consequently, arias sung by individual soloists, while others place firm emphasis on the choir's role. Many of the church cantatas are based on Scriptural texts, whereas others employ religious poetry created by contemporaneous writers. Withal, however, their musical substance, formal patterns, expressive intent, instrumental coloration, and textual material are as diverse as one of music's greatest creative minds could make them. Of course Bach was not alone in cultivating the Lutheran Church cantata during these years. Georg Philipp Telemann, to cite only one colleague, wrote somewhat over five hundred such pieces. Few of these experience twentieth-century performance, however, for Telemann's gift lay in fecundity rather than profundity with a result that most of his choral works have now passed from view.

Beethoven's *Ah, perfido!,* which may be considered a late outcropping of the solo cantata, appeared in 1796. Termed a scena or concert aria by its composer, this piece—which is really *sui generis*—employs a single voice supported by a small orchestra to convey a sequence of recitatives and arias. Similarly, Mendelssohn's *Walpurgisnacht* (revised, 1843), the musical setting of a Goethe text, is another representative cantata from the Romantic era. Neither, however, can be considered a major work; neither was emulated by other writers; and neither opened a door to the future.

All during the nineteenth century and well into our own time, the cantata has remained in decline. In 1899 Gustav Mahler wrote his *Das klagende Lied* (Song of Lament), a rather noisy piece that enlists soprano, contralto, and tenor soloists, as well as chorus and orchestra, to articulate a text of the composer's creation.[14] Just a few years earlier, in 1887, Claude Debussy had written his strikingly beautiful *La Damoiselle élue* for women's voices (both solo and chorus), which enunciates texts from a poem (bearing the same name) by Dante Gabriel Rossetti (1828–1882). Originally written as incidental music for a miracle play by Gabriele d'Annunzio, Debussy's score to *Le Martyre de Saint Sebastien* (1911), scored for solo voices, chorus, and orchestra, is now invariably performed as a cantata. Others who have written representative cantatas in our era include Béla Bartók (*Cantata Profana*, 1930); Arnold Schoenberg (*A Survivor from Warsaw*, 1947); [15] and Igor Stravinsky (*Canticum sacrum*, 1956). Among those who have written contemporary cantatas for school, college, or church groups are George Kleinsinger (*I Hear America Singing*), Henry Hadley (*The Nightingale and the Rose*), and Randall Thompson (*The Peaceable Kingdom*).

J. S. BACH: *WACHET AUF! RUFT UNS DIE STIMME* (Sleepers Awaken! The Hour Strikes, Cantata No. 140)

Written for performance during Lutheran worship on the twenty-seventh Sunday after Trinity in 1731, Bach's *Wachet auf!* is a wedding cantata symbolic of the union between Christ and His people. As was often his practice when writing church cantatas, Bach based several of its numbers on a sturdy hymn sounded initially in the opening chorus.[16]

Scored for two oboes, a *taille* (probably *oboe da caccia*), two violin parts (including *violino piccolo*), viola, horn (used only in the first and last sections where it doubles the soprano voice), and continuo, this cantata employs a relatively small instrumental ensemble for accompanimental support. As was conventional, the chorus is marshalled into four parts (soprano, alto, tenor, and bass), and although the tenor recitative (number two) employs only continuo, a later declamation by the bass (number five) calls for the full string section. Particularly colorful instrumental writing appears: (1) in the soprano and bass duet (number three) where violino piccolo is used in an obbligato against the vocal lines; (2) in the tenor aria (number four) where violins and viola play an embellishing figure in unison; and (3) in the soprano and bass duet (number six) where an important ornamental part is sounded by oboe. As a finale, all voices as well as the orchestra (and probably the entire congregation) unite to sound the

---

[14] Dvořák had anticipated him somewhat by writing, in 1884, *The Spectre's Bride*, a secular cantata based on a text by Karel Erben.

[15] Schoenberg's sprawling *Gurre-Lieder* (Songs of Gurra, 1900–1911) is, in many respects, a spectacular secular cantata. Taking its textual material from Danish legendry, it is scored for five solo voices, three male choruses, a mixed chorus (in eight parts), a narrator, and orchestra. As might be expected, it is almost ear-shattering in intensity.

[16] Specifically, it reappears in the tenor chorale (number four in the sequence) and in the work's closing number.

dignified hymn that gives the cantata its name. This is an abstract of the text:

I. *Choral Fantasia for Four-Part Choir*

Sleepers awaken, the hour strikes; the watchman calls.
Awake, Jerusalem; midnight strikes, we can hear it sounding.
The watch cries out and asks: "Where are the wise virgins"?
Take cheer, for the Bridegroom comes. Let all arise;
Let the maids prepare a feast. May all go forth to meet Him.

II. *Tenor Recitative*

The Bridegroom comes; daughters of Zion shall rejoice.
He makes His choice and hastens to the home of the beloved.
The Bridegroom comes, He is handsome and sturdy,
And asks all to share in the marriage feast.
Let all arise, take lamps and go forth.

III. *Soprano and Baritone Duet*

Soprano: Come along with me quickly.
Baritone: Yes, I shall hasten to you.
Soprano: We are awaiting, with all the lamps lighted,
           The doors are open, come and claim your bride!
Baritone: With doors open, I rush to claim my bride.
           We shall live forever in joy and happiness.

IV. *Tenor Chorale*

Zion hears the call, and the faithful respond with joy.
All rise to greet their Lord; He comes, noble and victorious.
Supreme in Heaven and adored on earth, He is mighty and true.
May the Holy One come to us as Jehovah's Son.
We respond to the call, and join Him in the banquet hall.

V. *Bass Recitative*

May my lovely and chosen bride come to me,
And may the one I long to see remain forever at my side.
She rests in my heart with ties that can never be severed.
Forget your every care, my beloved, for I will protect you.
We are joined for better or worse, and share our lives in love.

VI. *Soprano and Bass Duet*

Soprano: Your love is mine.
Baritone: And I belong to you.
Soprano and Baritone: Faithful lovers are never parted.
Soprano: I am with you, and you with me.
Soprano and Baritone: Through fields of flowers we stray, forever united.

VII. *Chorale for Full Ensemble*

We sing *Gloria* with voices united; the angels rejoice.
We sound harps and strings, and place twelve pearls on His door.
He has gathered immortals, as angels surrounding the throne.
No mortal eye can see, or ear perceive, the joy we know.
Loudly we praise the Lord saying: *God in dulci jubilo.*

OTHER LARGE VOCAL FORMS

Along with the Mass, oratorio, and cantata, several other nonoperatic vocal forms, most of them religiously oriented, have developed during the last four centuries. In general, they have a *modus operandi,* an organizational scheme, and an expressive intent related to their associates. Each employs soloists, a chorus (sometimes two), and an orchestra; each is organized along additive lines and has a sequence of individual vocal or instrumental numbers linked by recitative or similar connectives. Included within this company of musical designs are (1) *Passion music,* (2) the *Te Deum,* (3) *Stabat Mater,* (4) *Magnificat,* (5) *Salve Regina,* and (6) *Sacred Service.*

Passion Music

Concerned with narrating details of Christ's Crucifixion, Passion music is an oratorio-like design filled with almost limitless emotional appeal. No less than painters, poets, and sculptors, composers have responded to the dramatic challenge inherent in this tragic act by commemorating it in highly moving music.

Actual backgrounds leading to a development of Passion music date from before the fifth century and are mainly based on the following:

1. The custom of making a musicodramatic presentation of events leading to Christ's death a part of observances for Holy Week. For centuries a narration of its details was carried out in chant, and a practice developed that presented the version by St. Matthew on Palm Sunday, by St. Mark on Tuesday of Holy Week, by St. Luke on Wednesday, and by St. John on Good Friday.
2. The Mystery or Miracle Plays that depict circumstances surrounding Christ's Nativity, Crucifixion, or Resurrection.

From the twelfth to the fifteenth centuries, a custom of intoning the Passion at Mass on Palm Sunday by three priests (rather than a single celebrant) became widespread. To enhance its impact, Christ's words were given to a low voice (bass); utterances of the Evangelist were assigned to a middle-range voice (tenor); and expressions from the crowd, known as a *turba,* were conveyed by an *alta,* or high-pitched voice. In addition to differences in pitch, each part was performed in a contrasted tempo; slow for bass, moderate for tenor, and fast for alta. Sometime between the fourteenth and sixteenth centuries, this monophonic practice was superseded by polyphonic works written for full chorus. Inevitably, polyphonic motets—in three, four, or five parts—began to appear in Passion music, just as they intermingled within the Mass, oratorio, and cantata. As a consequence, most of this period's Passion music used traditional chant melodies for those portions of the text enunciated by Christ or an Evangelist, while motets sung by the chorus were interwoven between. Invariably, both were performed *a cappella.*

With advent of the Reformation early in the sixteenth century, Passion music underwent some change. French Calvinists, of course, were little interested in a preservation of any religious customs held over from Catholicism; however, German Lutherans retained many long-established practices of the Roman church, which they modified to suit their new ritual. Accordingly, Passion music became an important adjunct of Easter observances wherever the Lutheran rite was observed, with these innovations:

1. A considerable use was now made of familiar chorale melodies.
2. Scriptural texts were given poetic treatment and cast in the form of arias, ensembles, and concerted numbers.
3. A continuo (usually played by harpsichord and gamba, that is, 'cello) supported the work's recitative.
4. Roles assigned to the chorus became greatly extended.
5. Most examples of Lutheran Passion music employed some sort of instrumental ensemble for accompaniment.

Luther preferred that a recitation of the Passion be given by a minister on either Palm Sunday or Good Friday. But the reformer's views did not prevail, and its musical rendition on these days became an accepted practice. Even Luther's lieutenant, Johann Walther (1496–1570), wrote for this Lenten service. Based on the Gospel of St. Matthew, Walther's composition is probably the earliest known example of Lutheran Passion music. Continuance was furthered when Heinrich Schütz returned to Germany in 1615 and became *Kapellmeister* to the Elector of Saxony at Dresden. Because of his training at Venice, Schütz was well informed about the latest innovations in vocal composition, and incorporated many advanced techniques of aria and recitative writing in his sacred works. His three Passions—according to St. Matthew, St. Luke, and St. John, written during 1665–1666 and scored for solo voice and chorus—are magnificent examples of this form, although they do not include orchestral accompaniment.[17] Equally distinguished are Schütz's Passion-oratorios, *Sieben Worte Jesu Christi am Kreuz* (Seven Words of Jesus Christ on the Cross, c. 1645) and *Historia des Leidens und Sterbens Unseres Herrn und Heylandes Jesu Christi* (Story of the Suffering and Death of Jesus Christ, c. 1665–1672). Closely akin to Passion music, the latter contains four settings of the text, one from each of the Evangelists. Important musically, they are also important connecting links between early Italian models and the later compositions of J. S. Bach.

In 1721, two years before Bach went to Leipzig, a tradition of performing Passion music at Vesper services on Good Friday was inaugurated by

---

[17] Some evidence exists, however, to show that Schütz intended the voices to be supported by organ.

Johann Kuhnau (1660–1722), the incumbent Cantor who contributed a work to begin this observance. From approximately 1:15 P.M. onward, the ritual followed a plan that included a singing of hymns, the preaching of a sermon and, finally, a performance of Passion music. In all, the service extended well into the early evening hours. Written while he was still resident in Cöthen (but preparing to leave for Leipzig), Bach's St. John Passion (1723), modeled on works by Schütz and Kuhnau, was his first venture into this form. Despite admitted limitations, it created a favorable impression at the first performance in Leipzig on Good Friday, 1723.

Passion music unquestionably reached an apogee with Bach. Although he was not a lone cultivator of the form—during this era Reinhard Keiser (1673–1739) and George Frideric Handel, for instance, also gained distinction—Bach unquestionably reached a pinnacle of near perfection in such religious compositions. His *St. Matthew Passion* (1729) is the finest example of Passion music in the literature, and because of its sublime musical language must be numbered among music's greatest works. With instinctive surety, Bach reconciled the nebulous but thorny differences between religious and secular styles of writing, coordinated the sprawling orchestral and vocal groups needed for such massive works, and restored integrity, dignity, and profundity to a design that heretofore had suffered from much maltreatment.

For the literary substance of his *St. Matthew Passion,* Bach turned to a version formulated by a local Leipzig citizen, Christian Friederich Henrici, who wrote under the pen name of "Picander." [18] Comparable in dimension and complexity with his celebrated Mass in B minor, this Passion music takes approximately three and a half hours to perform. It employs unusually large forces including soloists, double orchestra, double chorus, and organ. Roles for principal participants in this Biblical drama—Jesus, St. Peter, Judas, Pilate, and others—are assigned to soloists, and their utterances in both aria and recitative are linked by a narrator's (tenor) continuity. This is a listing of sections in an unusually massive work:

The Passion According to St. Matthew [19]
As set to music by J. S. Bach

Part One

1. *Chorus:* Come daughters, share my anguish
2. *Recit:* When Jesus finished these sayings
3. *Chorale:* Jesus, how have You offended
4. *Recit:* The elders, priests, and scribes consulted

[18] Textual material for the previously composed *St. John Passion* had been created by Barthold Hinrich Brockes. This version, incidentally, enjoyed considerable vogue in Bach's time and was used by more than twenty composers including Telemann, Keiser, Mattheson, and Handel.

[19] Much too long to be quoted in its entirety here, the full Passion text may be found in the New Testament where versions by St. Matthew, St. Mark, St. Luke, and St. John should be examined and compared.

5. *Chorus:*   Not on the feast day, lest an outbreak occur
6. *Recit:*   When Jesus was in Bethany, in the home of Simon
7. *Chorus:*   Why this waste
8. *Recit:*   When Jesus took notice, he said to them
9. *Recit:*   Blessed Saviour
10. *Aria* (Alto):   Grief and pain mend our hearts
11. *Recit:*   Then one of the twelve said to them
12. *Aria* (Sop.):   Your loving heart must bleed and break
13. *Recit:*   On the first day the disciples came
14. *Chorus:*   Where would you spend the Passover
15. *Recit. and Chorus:*   He said: Go into the city
16. *Chorale:*   You must bear these sorrows
17. *Recit:*   He gave them an answer
18. *Recit:*   Tears pour from our eyes
19. *Aria* (Sop.):   Lord, I offer my heart to you
20. *Recit:*   After singing a hymn together, they went out
21. *Chorale:*   May the Saviour defend me
22. *Recit:*   Peter answered
23. *Chorale:*   I will always stand close to you
24. *Recit:*   Jesus went to a place called Gethsemane
25. *Recit:*   Heavy is His grief
26. *Aria* (Tenor):   Let me watch beside my Lord
27. *Recit:*   He went aside and prayed
28. *Recit:*   The Saviour falls before His Father
29. *Aria* (Bass):   I would gladly endure the grief and pain
30. *Recit:*   And He came to his disciples
31. *Chorale:*   Let the will of God be done
32. *Recit:*   Again He came and found them sleeping
33. *Duet and Chorus:*   Behold, my Saviour now is taken
34. *Recit:*   See, one of them who was with Jesus
35. *Chorale:*   Man lament your grievous sin

Part Two

36. *Aria and Chorus:*   Is it possible that my Saviour is gone
37. *Recit:*   They led Jesus before the High Priest
38. *Chorale:*   This is a devious and crafty world
39. *Recit:*   Two false witnesses came forward and spoke
40. *Recit:*   But the Saviour did not answer
41. *Aria* (Tenor):   Be still, and rejoice
42. *Recit:*   The High Priest demanded an answer
43. *Chorus:*   He deserves to die
44. *Recit:*   And then they spat into His face
45. *Chorus:*   Tell us, Christ, who struck you
46. *Chorale:*   Who is it that dares to strike my Lord
47. *Recit. and Chorus:*   Peter was sitting in the courtyard
48. *Aria* (Alto):   May the Lord have mercy on me
49. *Chorale:*   Now I seek to see your face again
50. *Recit. and Chorus:*   In the morning, they took counsel

51. *Aria* (Bass):   I pray for my Lord's return
52. *Recit.:*   They took the gold
53. *Chorale:*   Give yourself to Jesus
54. *Recit. and Chorus:*   Jesus stood before the governor
55. *Chorale:*   The Shepherd shows a wonderful love
56. *Recit:*   What evil has He done
57. *Recit:*   Jesus has helped all men
58. *Aria* (Sop.):   My Saviour dies loving all men
59. *Recit. and Chorus:*   But they only cried out louder
60. *Recit:*   Gracious God beloved the Saviour
61. *Aria* (Alto):   Listen to my weeping
62. *Recit. and Chorus:*   The governor's soldiers took Jesus
63. *Chorale:*   Sacred head, grievously wounded
64. *Recit:*   After they had mocked Him
65. *Recit:*   Bear the Cross with honor
66. *Aria* (Bass):   By the Cross we are saved
67. *Recit. and Chorus:*   And then they came to Golgotha
68. *Recit:*   The thieves who were crucified also spoke
69. *Recit:*   The Lord hangs from the Cross
70. *Aria and Chorus:*   Look up there and see Jesus waiting
71. *Recit. and Chorus:*   There was darkness until the ninth hour
72. *Chorale:*   When death comes, and life begins to fail
73. *Recit. and Chorus:*   And then the veil of the temple was broken
74. *Recit:*   In the peace and quiet of evening
75. *Aria* (Bass):   May Jesus cleanse my heart
76. *Recit. and Chorus:*   Joseph took the body and wrapped it
77. *Recit:*   Now the Lord is laid to rest
78. *Chorus:*   With tears of grief, we lament His passing

Te Deum Laudamus

A jubilant prayer of thanksgiving whose authorship is often (but erroneously) attributed to St. Ambrose, Bishop of Milan, the *Te Deum* (that is, "To God," or more extensively "We Praise Thee, God") has been used for more than a thousand years to commemorate the coming of peace, deliverance from pestilence, or victory in battle. According to the Roman Catholic Breviary, a volume that contains prayers for the canonical hours, the *Te Deum* text originated when St. Augustine was baptized by St. Ambrose. At this time, so legend goes, the two saints expressed their joy by singing canticles (Biblical hymns of praise) to one another in an antiphonal discourse. Although it has quaint charm, this version of the hymn's origin, is undoubtedly apocryphal. More likely Nicetas, Bishop of Remesiana, was the originator (c. A.D. 400) of both the text and a chant melody originally associated with it.

Catholic in origin, the *Te Deum* text (quoted on p. 477) is also used by other religious denominations. Virtually all nations of Western Europe use *Te Deums* on occasions of coronations, festivals, or observances of thanks-

giving.[20] Initially a part of the liturgy at Matins (the first of a day's canonical hours), since the early eighteenth century musical settings of the
prayer have assumed a more public character and are characteristically
performed in cathedrals, the out-of-doors, or concert halls. Most require a
large performing body including soloists, chorus, and orchestra, and some
utilize such other groups as children's choirs, wind bands, and organ.

Originally, the *Te Deum* text was expressed in Latin and this practice
has continued in nearly all nations save England, where the vernacular is
preferred. One of the first English *Te Deums* was written in 1694 by Henry
Purcell to commemorate St. Cecilia's Day, she being the patron saint of music.
It employs an extremely small orchestra of two violins, two trumpets, and
a bass to support its singers, as does a companion piece by John Blow
written in 1695. While residing in England, the German-born Handel wrote
two similar works: the *Utrecht Te Deum* (1712, commemorating the Peace
of Utrecht) and the *Dettingen Te Deum* (1743, marking a victory for allied
forces under George II of England against the French in the Battle of
Dettingen). In later times, numerous other English-language *Te Deums*
have been written, of which those by Arthur Sullivan (1897, for Queen
Victoria's diamond jubilee); Charles V. Stanford (1898, in Latin); Walter
Damrosch (1898, hailing Admiral Dewey's victory at Manila); Hubert H.
Parry (1911, coronation of George V); Ralph Vaughan Williams (1936,
coronation of George VI); and William Walton (1953, coronation of Elizabeth II), are notable.

On the continent, Latin has been generally held inviolate, and aside
from early works (some listed at the end of this chapter, the *Te Deum* is
brilliantly represented in works by Hector Berlioz (1855, written for the
Paris Exhibition), an especially impressive piece that employs three choirs,
orchestra and organ; Anton Bruckner (1884); Antonín Dvořák (1896);
Giuseppe Verdi (1898); and Zoltán Kodály (1936). Here is the *Te Deum*
text in both Latin and English:

Te Deum
(A Hymn of Thanksgiving)

Te Deum laudamus: te Dominum confitemur.	We praise Thee O God; we acknowl-edge Thee to be the Lord.
Te aeternum Patrem omnis terra veneratur.	Thee, the Father everlasting, all the earth does worship.
Tibi omnes Angeli; tibi Caeli et universae Potestates.	To Thee all the angels, to Thee the heavens, and all the powers
Tibi Cherubim et Seraphim incessavili voce proclamant:	To Thee the cherubim and seraphim cry out without ceasing:
Sanctus, Sanctus, Sanctus Dominus Deus Sabaoth.	Holy, holy, holy, Lord God of hosts.

[20] And it is reported that George Washington directed a *Te Deum* be sung to
commemorate Lord Cornwallis' surrender at Yorktown (October 19, 1781), an event
that effectually terminated the American Revolution.

Pleni sunt caeli et terra majestatis gloriae tuae.	Full are the heavens and the earth of the majesty of Thy glory.
Te gloriosus Apostolorum chorus;	Thee, the glorious choir of the apostles,
Te Prophetarum laudabilis numerus;	Thee, the admirable company of the prophets,
Te Martyrum candidatus laudat exercitus.	Thee, the white-robed army of martyrs do praise.
Te per orbem terrarum sancta confitetur Ecclesia:	Thee, the holy Church throughout the world does confess.
Patrem immensae majestatis;	The Father of incomprehensible majesty,
Venerandum tuum verum, et unicum Filium;	Thine adorable, true and only Son,
Sanctum quoque Paracilitum Spirit Spiritum.	And the Holy Ghost the Paraclete.
Tu Rex gloriae, Christe.	Thou, O Christ, are the King of glory,
Tu Patris sempiternus es Filius.	Thou are the everlasting Son of the Father.
Tu ad liberandum suscepturus hominem, non horuisti Verginis uterum.	Thou, having taken upon Thee to deliver man, did not disdain the Virgin's womb.
Tu devicto mortis aculeo aperusiti credentibus regna caelorum.	Thou having overcome the sting of death, has opened to believers the kingdom of heaven.
Tu ad dexteram Dei sedes in gloria Patrix.	Thou sittest at the right hand of God, in the glory of the Father.
Judex crederis esse venturus,	Thou, we believe, are the Judge to come.
Te ergo quaesummus, tuis famulis subveni, quos pretios pretioso sanguine redemisti.	We beseech Thee, therefore, to help Thy servants, whom Thou hast redeemed with Thy precious Blood.
Aeterna fac cum Sanctis tuis in gloria numerari.	Make them to be numbered with Thy saints in glory everlasting.
Salvum fac populum tuum, Domine, et benedic haer editati tuae.	O Lord, save Thy people and bless Thine inheritance.
Et rege eos et extolle illos usque in aeternum.	And govern them, and exalt them forever.
Per singulos dies benedicimus te.	Day by day we bless Thee.
Et laudamus nomen tuum in saeculum, et in saeculum saeculi	And we praise Thy name forever; for ever and ever.
Dignare, Domine, die isto sine pecatto nos custodire.	Vouchsafe, O Lord, this day, to keep us without sin.
Miserere nostri, Domine, miserere nostri.	Have mercy on us, O Lord; have mercy on us.
Fiat misericordia tua, Domine, super nos, quemadmodum speravimus in te.	Let Thy Mercy, O Lord, be upon us; as we have trusted in Thee.

In te, Domine, speravi: non *confundar in aeternum.*	In Thee, O Lord, have I trusted; let me not be confounded for ever.
V. *Benedicamus Patrem et* *Filium cum, Sancto Spiritu,*	V. Let us bless the Father, and the Son, with the Holy Ghost.
R. *Laudemus et super-exaltemus* *eum in saecula.*	R. Let us praise and exalt Him for ever.

Stabat Mater

Based on a thirteenth-century religious poem, the musical *Stabat Mater* (literally, The Mother Was Standing) has grown into a design of poignant beauty. Its text (quoted in Latin and English on p. 480), generally credited to Jacopone da Todi (1228–1306), a Franciscan monk, describes the sorrow of Christ's Mother as she stands beneath the Cross on which He was crucified. Originally used as a *sequence,* a mnemonic device utilized during medieval times to assist choristers in remembering long florid chant melismas, the prayer has subsequently become part of the Mass of the Seven Sorrows of the Blessed Virgin Mary, read on the Friday of Passion Week (before Palm Sunday) and on September 15. Conventionally divided into twenty segments, it is organized in trochaic meter, which, in Latin, accords with an *aabccd* pattern.

Since the sixteenth century, this text has attracted many composers. Initially, Josquin des Prez and Giovanni Palestrina wrote polyphonic *Stabat Maters* of simple, eloquent beauty. Josquin's piece, which dates from the early part of the century, is based on a secular *cantus firmus* and scored for five voices. Palestrina's (c. 1590) employs eight voices in a double chorus and is intended for *a cappella* performance. For nearly two hundred years after its creation this latter work remained little-known to the world at large, for choristers at the Papal Chapel in Rome for whom the piece was composed were reluctant to share its sublime beauties with others. Ultimately, however, the piece was published in England in 1771, mostly because of efforts expended by Dr. Charles Burney, an eminent music historian. Although Palestrina was a masterful contrapuntist, this short work (performance time: eight minutes) shows few complexities and is rather striking in its simple loveliness.

Among other settings of the *Stabat Mater* that were created during ensuing generations, those by Giovanni Pergolesi (1736); Franz Joseph Haydn (1773); Franz Schubert (1815 and 1816); Gioacchino Rossini (1832, rewritten, 1842); Antonín Dvořák (1877); Giuseppe Verdi (1898); and Francis Poulenc (1951) are particularly outstanding. Like many other musical designs, by the late nineteenth century the *Stabat Mater* had become greatly expanded. Dvořák, for instance, divided his piece into ten distinctive numbers and scored it for four soloists (soprano, alto, tenor, and bass) and a sizeable chorus and orchestra. This is an outline of his architectural plan:

1. *Stabat Mater dolorosa:* quartet with chorus.
2. *Quis est homo, qui non fleret:* quartet.
3. *Eia Mater, fons amoris:* chorus.
4. *Fac, ut ardeat cor meum:* bass aria.
5. *Tui nati vulnerati:* chorus.
6. *Fac me tecum flere:* tenor solo with chorus.
7. *Virgo virginum praeclara:* chorus.
8. *Fac, ut portem Christi mortem:* soprano and tenor.
9. *Inflammatus et accensus:* alto aria.
10. *Quando corpus morietur:* quartet with chorus.

This is a bilingual quotation of the complete *Stabat Mater* text:

Stabat Mater

1. *Stabat Mater dolorosa,*
   Juxta crucem lacrimosa,
   Dum pendebat Filius.

   At the Cross her station keeping,
   Stood the mournful Mother, weeping,
   Close to Jesus to the last.

2. *Cujus animam gementem*
   Contristatam et colentem,
   Pertransivit gladius.

   Through her heart, bereaved of joy,
   Bowed with anguish and deeply
     grieved,
   Now at length the sword had passed.

3. *O quam tristis et afficta*
   Fuit illa benedicta
   Mater Unigeniti!

   O, that grief-laden, blessed one,
   Blessed Mother, blessed Maiden,
   Mother of the all-holy One!

4. *Quae maerebat, et dolebat,*
   Pia Mater dum videbat
   Nati poenas inclyti.

   O that silent and ceaseless mourning,
   O those dim eyes, never turning
   From that wondrous, suffering Son.

5. *Quis est homo, qui non*
     fleret,
   Matrem Christi si videret
   In tanto supplico?

   Who, in gazing on Christ's dear
     Mother,
   In her trouble so amazing,
   Would not weep?

6. *Quis non posset contristari,*
   Christi Matrem contemplari
   Dolentem cum Filio?

   Who, thinking of Christ's dear Mother
   Forced to drink such a cup of sorrow,
   Would not share her deep sorrow?

7. *Pro peccatis suae gentis*
   Vidit Jesum in tormentis
   Et flagellis subditum.

   For His people's sins,
   She saw the Victim in anguish,
   Saw Him bleed and die.

8. *Vidit suum dulcem natum*
   Moriendo desolatum,
   Dum emisit spiritum.

   Saw the Lord's Anointed taken;
   Saw her Child forsaken in death,
   Heard His last expiring cry.

9. *Eia Mater, fons amoris,*
   Me sentire vim doloris
   Fac, ut tecum lugeam.

   In the death of my Maker
   Let my sinful soul be sad,
   May I bear my part with her.

10. *Fac ut ardeat cor meum*
    In amando Christum Deum,
    Ut sibi complaceam.

    Of his death let me bear the blame,
    Of a spirit bowed and broken,
    And bear His death within my heart.

11. *Sancta Mater, istud agas,*
    Crucifixi fige plagas
    Cordi meo valide.

    You who bear on the Cross,
    All the pains I wish to share,
    My heart fills with love for Thee.

12. *Tui nati vulnerati,*	By Your glorious Death,
Tam dignati pro me pati,	You are saving me,
Poenas mecum divide.	Savior, turn my heart to Thee.
13. *Fac me tecum pie flere,*	At Your feet in adoration, I am
Crucifixo condolere,	Wrapt in earnest contemplation.
Donec ego vixero.	See, beneath Thy Cross I lie.
14. *Juxta crucem tecum stare,*	There, where all our sins you bear,
Et me tibi sociare	In full compassion, find them
In planctu desidero.	Hanging on a bitter Tree.
15. *Virgo virginum praeclara,*	You who are forever blessed,
Mihi jam non sis amara;	You who are confessed by all,
Fac me tecum plangere.	Now I lift my soul to Thee.
16. *Fac ut portem Christi mortem,*	Make me a bearer of your death,
Passionis fac consortem,	Let me share in your anguish,
Et plagas recolere.	And take to myself Thy pain.
17. *Fac me plagis vulnerari*	Let me be stricken with Thy stripes!
Fac me cruce inerbriari,	Let Thy Cross quicken me with hope,
Et cruore Filii.	That I may gain Thy love.
18. *Inflammatus et Accensus*	All my heart, inflamed and burning,
Per te, Virgo, sim defensus,	Savior, now is turning to Thee
In die judicii.	Shield me in the Judgment Day.
19. *Christe, cum sit hinc exire,*	By Thy Cross may I be guarded,
Da per Matrem me envire	Meritless—but yet rewarded
Ad plamam victoriae.	Through Thy precious grace.
20. *Quando corpus morietur,*	While my body is lying here
Fac ut animae donetur	Let my soul be swiftly flying
Paradisi gloria.	To Thy glorious Paradise.
Amen. Alleluia.	Amen.

Magnificat

Based on an utterance made by the Virgin Mary nearly two thousand years ago, the Magnificat has become a widely used Catholic prayer. According to St. Luke, Chapter I, Verses 46–55, it was enunciated by Mary when she met St. Elizabeth prior to Christ's birth. Subsequently, when this beautiful text became a part of the New Testament, it was taken into the Church's liturgy as a *canticle,* a hymn of praise chanted at one of the canonical hours. Now the Magnificat is used as a part of Vesper services, a ritual observed during early evening in Roman Catholic churches, where its Latin words are sung in Gregorian chant. In the Anglican service, where it is declaimed in English, the Magnificat is a part of Evening Prayer.

Although a chant melody is often employed for a recital of the Magnificat, it has also been given a number of composed settings. At first *descants* (decorative melodies imposed above the basic theme) were added, a practice that arose sometime after the tenth century. Subsequently, other polyphonic techniques were employed but, curiously enough, were applied only to alternate verses. When the Age of Polyphony was in its heyday during the fifteenth century and immediately thereafter, John Dunstable (England), Guillaume Dufay (Netherlands), Gilles Binchois (Burgundy), and Jacob Obrecht (Netherlands) wrote Magnificats whose soaring lines and florid counterpoint made them exquisite models of late Renaissance art. Later, such Baroque composers as Claudio Monteverdi (Italy) and Heinrich Schütz and Johann Sebastian Bach (Germany) wrote Magnificats in homophonic style.

Unquestionably, the elder Bach's work (his son, Carl Philipp Emanuel, also composed one) is a setting best-known to contemporary audiences. More extended than most companion pieces, it had an initial performance at Christmas time in 1723. Originally set in the key of E-flat major and interlarded with four extraneous compositions (as was a custom in Leipzig at the time), Bach's *Magnificat* was revised in 1730, transposed to D major, and established in the pattern known today. Organized along the lines of a church cantata, it employs the latter's conventional performing resources (that is, varied soloists, chorus, and orchestra) and is subdivided into these twelve contrasting sections:

1. *Magnificat anima mea:* five-part chorus (sopranos, I, II), with orchestra.
2. *Et exultavit:* soprano II (*solo or tutti*) with strings.
3. *Quia respexit:* soprano I with oboe *d'amore* and continuo.
4. *Omnes generationes:* chorus with orchestra (no trumpets).
5. *Quia fecit mihi magna:* bass aria with continuo.
6. *Et misericordia:* alto and tenor duet with flutes, violins, and continuo.
7. *Fecit potentiam:* chorus with full orchestra.
8. *Deposuit:* tenor aria with violins and continuo.
9. *Esurientes:* alto aria with two flutes and continuo.
10. *Suscepit Israel:* sopranos I and II and alto, with oboes and continuo.
11. *Sicut locutus est:* chorus accompanied only by continuo.
12. *Gloria:* chorus with full orchestra.

This is the *Magnificat's* complete text:

Magnificat

1. *Magnificat anima mea Dominum.*	My soul doth magnify the Lord
2. *Et exsultavit spiritus meus in Deo salutari meo.*	And my spirit hath rejoiced in God my Savior.
3. *Quia respecit humilitatem ancillae suae; ecce enim ex hoc beatam me dicent omnes generationes.*	He hath regarded the humility of his handmaid: for behold from henceforth all generations shall call me blessed.
4. *Quia fecit mihi magna qui potens est: et sanctum nomen ejus.*	For He that is mighty hath done great things to me: and holy is His name.
5. *Et misericordia ejus a progenie in progenies timentibus eum.*	And His mercy is from generation to generation, unto them that fear Him.

6. *Fecit potentiam in brachio suo: et dispersit superbos mente cordis sui.*

He hath showed strength with His arm: He hath scattered the proud in the conceit of their heart.

7. *Deposuit potentes de sede, et exaltavit humiles.*

He hath put down the mighty from their seat and hath exalted the humble.

8. *Esurientes implevit bonis: et divites dimisit inanes.*

He hath filled the hungry with good things; and the rich He hath sent empty away.

9. *Suscepit Israel puerum suum, recordatus misericordiae suae:*

He hath received His servant Israel, being mindful of His Mercy.

10. *Sicut locutus est ad patres nostros, Abraham, et semini ejus in saecula.*

As He spoke to our forefathers; to Abraham and his seed forever.

11. *Gloria Patri, et Filio, et Spiritui Sancto.*

Glory be to the Father, to the Son, and to the Holy Ghost.

12. *Sicut erat in principio, et nunc, et semper, et in saecula saeculorum.* Amen.

As it was in the beginning, is now, and ever shall be, world without end. Amen.

Salve Regina

Prayers to the Virgin Mary were begun by pious Catholics as early as the Middle Ages, and this devotion has increased with the passing centuries. A widely held belief in Roman Catholicism accepts Mary's intercession as an important aid in obtaining mercy, blessing, and salvation. As a consequence, such prayers as the *Alma Redemptoris Mater, Ave Maria, Magnificat,* or *Regina Coeli* have come into being, and all have been set to music at various times by diverse composers. Aside from the *Ave Maria* (Hail Mary, Full of Grace), the *Salve Regina, Mater Misericordiae* (Hail Holy Queen, Mother of Mercy) is undoubtedly the best-known of these supplications. Its words (quoted subsequently in their entirety) have been ascribed, but incorrectly, to Hermannus Contractus (1013–1054), a lame monk who worked at the monastery of St. Gall. More likely, Aymar, Bishop of Puy (d. 1098) was the author.

One of the four *antiphons* (a liturgical verse usually chanted in a responsorial manner) of the Virgin Mary, the *Salve Regina* has become part of the prayers recited at Compline, a canonical hour that closes the church day. Additionally, its text has been set by such composers as John Dunstable, Johannes Ockeghem, Giovanni Palestrina, Giovanni Pergolesi, Joseph Haydn, Franz Schubert, and Gabriel Fauré. This is a quotation of the prayer in Latin and English:

Salve Regina

Salve Regina, Mater misericordiae; vita dulcedo et spes nostra, salve. Ad te clamamus, excules filii

Hail, holy Queen, Mother of mercy; Our life, our sweetness and our hope. To thee do we cry, poor banished

Evae. Ad te suspiramus	children of Eve.
gementes et flentes in hac	To thee do we send up our sighs,
lacrimarum valle.	mourning and weeping in this
Eia ergo, advocata nostra,	valley of tears.
illos tuos misericordes oculos	Turn then, most gracious advocate,
ad mos converte.	thine eyes of mercy toward us.
Et Jesum, benedictum fructum	And after this our exile, show
ventris tui, nobis post hoc	us the blessed fruit of thy
excilium ostende	womb, Jesus.
O clemens, o pia, o dulcis	O clement, O loving, O sweet
Virgo Maria!	Virgin Mary!

Sacred Service

For untold centuries, music in the synagogue has consisted of a mono-phonic cantillation of sacred texts handed down orally from one generation to another. Although diffused throughout the world wherever the Jewish people traveled, venerable synagogal chant is still used at worship in orthodox Temples today. Early in the twentieth century, however, steps were taken to update the ritual in reformed synagogues, and the Sacred Service, a liturgical rite comparable, in many respects, with the Catholic Mass, was introduced. Deeply devotional, steeped in the life, culture, and thought of the Jewish people, this service combines silent prayer with verbally enunciated texts, music with spoken dialogue, and voices with instruments. Many of its prayers are more than two thousand years old, and some of the rituals it enshrines (for example, the removal of the Scroll from the Ark) were observed in the days of Moses. But music for the Sacred Service is of today's vintage, and such twentieth-century composers as Frederick Jacobi (1931), Ernest Bloch (1933), and Darius Milhaud (1949) have been motivated to set its texts to music.

Observed on a sabbath morning (Jacobi's work is called a *Sabbath Evening Service*), texts for a Sacred Service are contained within the Union Prayer Book, a collection of religious writings widely used in reformed synagogues. Characteristically, musical settings for the service use a solo baritone voice (in the role of cantor), a speaking voice who acts as prayer leader (rabbi), a four-part chorus, and orchestra.[21] This is the sequence of prayers normally observed:

1. *Mah Tovu:* How goodly are thy tents, O Jacob
2. *Bor'echu; Shema:* Bless the Lord
3. *Ve'ahavta:* And you shall love the Lord
4. *Mi Komocho:* Who is like unto Thee?
5. *Tzur Yisrael:* Rock of Israel, arise
6. *Prayer*

---

[21] For practical purposes, organ accompaniments (in lieu of the orchestra) are provided for most of these pieces.

7. *Kidusha:* We hallow Thy name
8. *Avinu:* Our Father, in Heaven
9. *Yiheyu l'ratzon:* Let the words
10. *Se'u She'arim:* Lift up your heads
11. *Havu:* Acknowledge the greatness of God
12. *Gad'lu:* Magnify the Lord
13. *Prayer*
14. *Etz Chayim:* It is a tree of life
15. *Adoration*
16. *Va Anachnu:* We bow the head
17. *Ba-Yom Ha-Hu:* On that day
18. *Kaddish:* Magnified and sanctified
19. *Adom Olam:* He is Lord of the world
20. *Yivarechecha:* The Lord shall bless you

Selected Large-Scale Vocal Works

(Including Masses, Requiems, Oratorios, Cantatas, Passions, Stabat Maters, Te Deums, and Salve Reginas)

Bach, Johann Sebastian (1685–1750)

Cantata No. 4, "Christ lag in Todesbanden" (c. 1724). Beginning with an instrumental sinfonia, this piece in seven sections for voices is based on a Luther text and effectively suggests pensive medieval mysticism.

Cantata No. 140, "Wachet auf!" (c. 1731). A symbolic "wedding" cantata in seven sections, it is based on a Nicolai chorale (1599) and employs soloists, chorus, and small orchestra.

Cantata No. 211, "Coffee Cantata" (1732). A humorous secular work that lampoons a craze for coffee drinking; based on a Picander text, it has ten sections and is witty and satiric.

Magnificat in D major (1723, revised, 1730). A superb choral piece in twelve sections, this work uses a five-part chorus and small orchestra to convey an unusually profound prayer.

Mass in B minor (1733–1738). One of music's greatest choral works, this lengthy, complex, and sublime piece in twenty-four sections uses a variety of soloists, large chorus, and orchestra.

The Passion According to St. Matthew (1729). Unusually long, with seventy-eight sections, this meditative and monumental work tells of Christ's death in profound and poignant terms.

Bartók, Béla (1881–1945)

Cantata Profana (The Giant Stags, 1930). A secular work based on Hungarian folk songs, it is organized in three sections and uses chorus, men soloists, and orchestra.

Beethoven, Ludwig van (1770–1827)

Christus am Oelberg (Christ on the Mount of Olives, 1803). With a German text by Huber, this sacred oratorio deals with Christ's suffering and agony.

Missa Solemnis in D major (1824): A towering orchestral Mass in five very large sections that uses four soloists, four-part chorus, and orchestra, this work is grandiose and almost spectacular.

Berlioz, Hector (1803–1869)

> *The Damnation of Faust* (1846). This oratorio is secular with a French text that has four subdivided sections; it is scored for orchestra, chorus, and three soloists.

> *L'Enfance du Christ* (1854). This sacred trilogy depicts young Christ's life in restrained, tender, and sublimely beautiful terms.

> Requiem, *Grand Messe des Morts* (1837). A commemorative and majestic work that uses huge performing forces, it has ten sections and is very impressive.

Bloch, Ernest (1880–1959)

> *Sacred Service, Avodath Hakodesh* (1930–1933). An eloquent and moving Sabbath synagogue service that has five divided sections and uses baritone, orchestra, and chorus.

Brahms, Johannes (1833–1897)

> *A German Requiem* (1867). Based on German texts taken from Scripture, this unusual work has seven sections and is a profound memoriam for the composer's mother.

> *Song of Destiny* (1871). Employing a Holderlin text, this work ponders life's futility; scored for orchestra-chorus, it has three sections and is warmly lyric.

Britten, Benjamin (b. 1913)

> *A Ceremony of Carols* (1942). Containing eleven medieval English carols and scored for boys' choir and harp, these pieces are fresh, vibrant, and different.

> *War Requiem* (1962). Intermingling a Wilfred Owen text with traditional Latin liturgy, this Requiem is an angry, large-scale denunciation of war.

Bruckner, Anton (1824–1896)

> Mass No. 3 in F minor (The Great, 1868). Seraphic and ecstatic and founded on the usual Latin text, this Mass is a warm, fervent, and Romantic work.

Byrd, William (1543–1623)

> *Mass for Five Voices* (c. 1610). Graceful, pure, and completely polyphonic, this is an excellent example of the early *a cappella* Mass.

Debussy, Claude (1862–1918)

> *La Damoiselle élue* (1888). A cantata for contralto, women's voices, and orchestra, this work employs a Rossetti text and is subtle and mystic.

> *Le Martyre de St. Sebastien* (1911). Written for a d'Annunzio mystery play, this music uses three women soloists, orchestra-chorus, has five sections, and is movingly celestial in spirit.

de Prez, Josquin (c. 1450–1521)

> *Missa Hercules dux Ferrariae* (c. 1475). This is a splendid Renaissance *a cappella work* with polyphonic texture that is based on a *cantus firmus*.

> *Missa de Beata Virgine* (c. 1500). Using Gregorian melodies, this music is contrapuntal and imitative in texture, has five sections, and is scored for five voices.

Dufay, Guillaume (c. 1400–1474)

> *Missa Caput* (c. 1450) and the Mass *Se la face ay pale*. These are excellent polyphonic Masses, each based on a *cantus firmus* and mostly scored for three voices.

Dvořák, Antonín (1841–1904)

Requiem (1890). A lengthy Romantic work that uses the traditional liturgical text and is scored for orchestra and chorus and solo voices, it is exalted and pious.

Stabat Mater (1877). Dividing the traditional prayer into ten sections, this is a lengthy, fervent, and extremely pensive piece.

Fauré, Gabriel (1845–1924)

Requiem (1887). Suggesting pensiveness and quiet resignation, this work has seven sections for soloists and orchestra-chorus.

Handel, George Frideric (1685–1759)

Dettingen Te Deum (1743). Written to celebrate a military victory, this is based on a text from the Book of Common Prayer and requires a large performing group.

Israel in Egypt (1739). A sacred oratorio in thirty-nine parts based on a Scriptural text that uses the English language, this is a fascinating and piquantly descriptive work.

Messiah (1742). This well-known oratorio, its text by Jennens and adapted from Scripture, is inspired, large-scale, and impressive.

Ode for St. Cecilia's Day (1739). Honoring music's patron saint, it divides a Dryden text (English) into twelve sections; the music is mostly consonant and lordly.

Haydn, Franz Joseph (1732–1809)

The Creation (1798). This outstanding oratorio, with a text taken mostly from Milton's *Paradise Lost*, is penetrating and sublime.

Mass No. 7, *Missa in Tempore Belli* (*Paukenmesse*, 1796). This is a fine Viennese orchestral Mass with a prominent part for timpani; it uses a liturgical text and has six sections.

Mass No. 11 in B-flat, *Missa Solemnis* (1801). Symphonic in character with a grandiose architectural pattern and Latin text, this music is warm and glowing.

The Seasons (1801). This is a secular oratorio employing an English-German text by Thomson. It has four large sections and is naive and pastorale.

Hindemith, Paul (1895–1963)

Requiem "For Those We Love" (1946). This is a contemporary, pungent, and dissonant oratorio in eleven sections that uses a Walt Whitman text, two soloists, and orchestra-chorus.

Honegger, Arthur (1892–1955)

Le Roi David (1921). A symphonic psalm in three parts with twenty-seven sections, this is vivid, occasionally stark, and relates the engrossing life of David.

Kodály, Zoltán (1882–1967)

Psalmus Hungaricus (1923). This is a Hungarian version of the Fifty-fifth Psalm; in one continuous section, it uses tenor, orchestra and chorus.

Te Deum (1936). This is a massive choral fresco with idiomatic Hungarian flavor, that requires four soloists and is opulent, climactic, and impressive.

Lassus, Orlandus (1532–1594)

Masses: *Bell' amfitrit' altera* and *In die tribulationis*. These Masses are late-

Renaissance contrapuntal works with Latin liturgical texts; they are soaring, ethereal, and heavenly.

Liszt, Franz (1811–1886)

Missa Solemnis (Gran Festival Mass, 1855). Radiant and warmly Romantic, this Mass uses four soloists, orchestra-chorus, and is expansive and occasionally pompous.

Machaut, Guillaume de (c. 1300–1377)

Mass: *Notre Dame* (c. 1364). The first known composed Mass. Ascetic, Gothic, almost stark in sound, and totally polyphonic, it is sung *a cappella.*

Mendelssohn, Felix (1809–1847)

Elijah (1846). A sacred oratorio in two parts and thirty-nine sections, with an English text taken from the Old Testament, it is exalted and fervent.

Milhaud, Darius (b. 1892)

Les Choëphores (The Libation-Bearers, 1916). Written for a Claudel-Aeschylus play, it has seven sections and is polytonal, stark, shocking, and amazingly different.

Sabbath Morning Service (1947). Based on a Hebrew text and intended for synagogical worship, it has twenty sections and is mostly reverential.

Monteverdi, Claudio (1567–1643)

Vespro della Beata Vergine (1610). This work includes psalms, hymns, and antiphons praising the Virgin. Scored for voices and orchestra, it is pious, adoring, and respectful.

Mozart, Wolfgang Amadeus (1756–1791)

Mass in C major, "Coronation," K. 317 (1779) and Mass in C minor, "The Great," K. 427 (1783). Splendid examples of the Viennese orchestral Mass, these are filled with sweetness and warmth.

Requiem, K. 626 (1791). The composer's final work, this Requiem reveals pathos and resignation. Structurally it is well balanced and very dramatic.

Vesperae Solennes de Confessore, K. 339 (1780). Three Psalms (110, 117, 113) written for *a cappella* chorus are included in this work; it glorifies, praises, and ennobles.

Obrecht, Jacob (1452–1505)

Missa Fortuna Desperata and Mass: *Sub Tuum Praesidium* (c. 1500). Liturgical works by the late-Renaissance Flemish master, these are polyphonic, sung *a cappella,* and other-worldly in expression.

Orff, Carl (b. 1895)

Carmina Burana (1935–1936). A lengthy secular cantata in three parts and twenty-five sections, it has driving rhythms and rather ribald thirteenth-century texts.

Palestrina, Giovanni (c. 1525–1594)

Missa Papae Marcelli (1563). Long associated with the Council of Trent, this is a polyphonic, *a cappella* work scored for six voices. It is one of music's best.

Stabat Mater (c. 1575). Written for eight voices and two choruses, this is a short (eight minutes) responsorial piece based on a Jacopone text.

Poulenc, Francis (1899–1963)

Gloria in G major (1961). While using a liturgical text this is not actually a Mass, but it has six sections and a contemporary, vivid musical syntax.

Stabat Mater (1951). Penitential, profound, and based on a Latin text, this employs a prominent soprano soloist and merges traditional and modern styles.

Prokofiev, Serge (1891–1953)

Alexander Nevsky (1939). A nationalistic secular oratorio that glorifies a folk hero and nation, it is noisy, long, and ornate.

Rachmaninoff, Sergei (1873–1943)

The Bells (1913). Based on a poem by Poe that describes life's cycle, this music is lyric, rich, and grandiose.

Schoenberg, Arnold (1874–1951)

Friede auf Erden (Peace on Earth, 1907). A short piece that continually verges on atonality. It is polyphonic and uses orchestra and chorus to implore the blessings of peace.

Schubert, Franz (1797–1828)

German Mass (1827). A *Missa brevis,* founded on a German text by J. P. Neumann, this work is pious, mystic, and uses solo voices.

Mass No. 6 in E-flat major (1828). Consistently lyric, homophonic, Romantic, and effusive, this is an excellent Viennese Mass.

Schütz, Heinrich (1585–1672)

"Christmas" Oratorio (c. 1665). This Baroque score of rare excellence details Christ's birth, has eight sections, and great amounts of polyphony.

Stainer, John (1840–1901)

The Crucifixion (1887). Exemplifying the British choral tradition, this music has an English text and is solid, secure, massive.

Stravinsky, Igor (b. 1882)

The Flood (1962). Telling the story of Noah with portions of the text from Genesis, this work uses a huge orchestra, soloists, narrator and chorus.

Mass (1948). This excellent modern work, with traditional Latin text, is scored for chorus and ten winds; it is clean, pungent, and strong.

Les Noces (1917–1923). A choreographic cantata concerned with a peasant wedding ritual, this is rhythmic, dissonant, and employs small orchestra-choral groups.

Oedipus Rex (1927). An opera-oratorio founded on a Cocteau text (Latin) that uses narrator, soloists, chorus, and orchestra, this is based on a well-known Greek tragedy.

Threni (Lamentations of Jeremiah, 1957–1958). An unusual cantata for six solo voices that use a Latin text, this is profound, precise, and pungent.

Vaughan Williams, Ralph (1872–1958)

Mass in G minor (1923). Contemporary in style but based on the traditional Latin text, this Mass is homophonic, sung *a capella,* and is unusually expressive.

Verdi, Giuseppe (1813–1901)

Requiem Mass, in memory of Manzoni (1874). Somewhat operatic and warmly sentimental in expression, this work is massive, melodic, and superbly written.

Vittoria, Tomás Luis de (1549–1611)

Messa da Requiem (*Officium Defunctorum,* c. 1600). A contrapuntal Spanish

Renaissance work that uses a Gregorian *cantus firmus,* it is mostly sung in a responsorial manner.

Vivaldi, Antonio (1678–1741)

Gloria in D major (c. 1715). Concerned with a single Mass prayer, this work has nine sections and is written in an ornate, fluent Baroque style.

Walton, William (b. 1902)

Belshazzar's Feast (1931). Bombastic and spectacular, with a Sitwell scriptural text, this is a pagan, vengeful, and jubilant contemporary choral work.

Chapter 17

Musical Logic: The Symphony

A bold, imaginative, and often excitingly dramatic instrumental design, the symphony swept to prominence in decades immediately after 1750 and, generally speaking, has held its pre-eminence to the present day. Not as venerable as the suite, overture, or concerto, it has benefited from the experimental endeavors applied to these earlier designs as well as the vicissitudes of shifting styles and tastes abroad during recent centuries. In its early stages during the Classic era, the symphony experienced careful nurturing and inquiring experimentation at the hands of Haydn, and, in turn, it was greatly enriched by the flowing lyricism of Mozart. In direct succession during the Romantic period, it came to know the dramatic eloquence of Beethoven, the gracious melodism of Schubert, the formal elegance of Mendelssohn, and the glowing ardor of Schumann. Subsequently, bold experimenters (Berlioz, Liszt, and the American, Charles Ives); capable craftsmen (Brahms, Bruckner, Dvořák, and Franck); enthusiastic tone poets (Tchaikowsky, Mahler, and Rachmaninoff); and a succession of gifted twentieth-century composers (Copland, Bernstein, and William Schuman) greatly expanded the symphonic concept and carried an enlarged version of the design into our own time.

During the more than two thousand years it has been in use, the word symphony has taken on widely separated connotations. Among ancient Greeks, for instance, *symphonia* was used to denote a concord of sound, and for more than ten centuries thereafter its general meaning was equivalent to what we now describe as harmony. By extension, it also identified the act of singing or playing together; thus, a symphonia resulted from group performance. This idea was still in force early in the seventeenth century when Giovanni Gabrieli in Venice composed several pieces for instruments and voices and called them *Sacre Symphoniae* (Sacred Symphonies). Subsequently, his pupil, Heinrich Schütz, then active in Dresden, wrote a collection of *Symphoniae Sacrae* and published them in three volumes (1629, 1647, and 1650). Shortly thereafter, the introductory section of a suite,

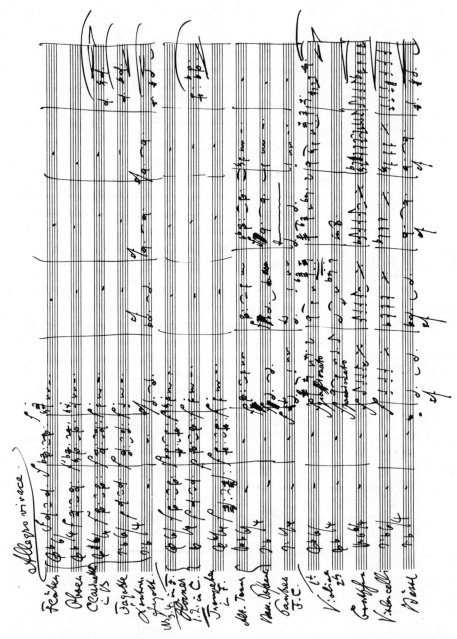

Figure 19. First page of Brahms' Symphony No. 3 in the composer's handwriting.

Symphony, No. 3

I

Allegro con brio

Johannes Brahms, Op. 90
1833 - 1897

Figure 20. First page of Brahms' Symphony No. 3 in printed form.

known to later generations as an overture, came to be called a *sinfonia*. Occasionally such sinfonias were inserted within oratorios or cantatas, as is demonstrated by the "Pastoral Symphony" in Handel's *Messiah* (1742). Even more significant to a development of the pattern we know today was the *sinfonia avanti l'opera* (symphony before the opera), a pattern employed as a curtain raiser by many Italian, French, and German opera composers shortly after 1650.

SOURCES FROM WHICH THE SYMPHONY AROSE

Few musical designs—perhaps none—spring into being full-blown. New ideas and techniques normally evolve from pre-existent forms and are leavened in large measure by prevailing stylistic currents. So it was, at any rate, with the symphony. Neither Johann Sebastian Bach (d. 1750) nor George Frideric Handel (d. 1759) wrote symphonies, although both were active in virtually all the then-known phases of musical creativity. But Carl Philipp Emanuel Bach (1714–1788), son of Johann Sebastian, became an important early symphonist whose works were closely studied (and occasionally emulated) by Haydn and Mozart. As a result of their efforts, sometime before 1780 the symphony's pattern became codified, a tradition was begun, and a literature was established. Then, the century's final decades witnessed a flowering of symphonic thought, occurring mostly within the environs of Vienna, unparalleled in the annals of music.

Of the several pre-existent designs that had a demonstrable influence on the symphony, these are especially important:

1. *Solo concerto* and *concerto grosso:* Antiphonal patterns that contributed the idea of tonal exchanges between instruments, or groups.
2. *Overture:* Italian-style works in particular that provided an outline of fast-slow-fast sections.
3. *Suite:* Multi-sectioned works from which the symphony absorbed its concept of disparate and contrasted movements, its adherence to a scheme of common or related keys in successive movements, and its regular employment of at least one dance pattern (typically a minuet).
4. *Serenade, cassation,* and *divertimento:* Suite-like designs that brought the idea of thematic manipulation to the fore.
5. *Sonata:* Well-known solo designs that suggested the manipulation of thematic material, an employment of contrasting themes and shifting tonalities, and a use of independent movements.

Prior to about 1770 the composing of symphonies was not considered a serious endeavor, primarily because writing for the period's ill-defined orchestras was a chanceful business. Unless employed as a household musician, as was Haydn, a composer could never be certain about available instruments or the adequacy of performers. On the other hand, writing opera could be both prestigious and lucrative. Consequently, astute composers directed their principal energies toward the theater, and symphonic writing became a secondary pursuit. Times were beginning to change, however, and the closing decades of the eighteenth century witnessed an unprecedented expansion of instrumental music. Styles, modes of expression, and performance techniques were in a state of flux during earlier years, but after the century's mid-point homophony gained a clear ascendancy over polyphony, chordal harmony triumphed over counterpoint, and secular music delivered a coup to the primacy heretofore accorded religious works. Previously uncertain in timbre, intonation, and mechanical operation, instruments were now perfected to an extent that performance on them could be both satisfactory and artistic. Consequently, a veritable avalanche of sonatas, concertos, serenades, divertimenti, and—finally—symphonies came pouring from composers' pens. Many were short-lived *pièces d'occasion*, but others proved more durable and are still being performed today.

PATTERNS FOR THE SYMPHONY

Good symphonies usually bear an imprint of universality. One is never the exact counterpart of another, of course, yet most display such general characteristics as these:

1. They are lengthy works whose performance time may extend from fifteen minutes to an hour or more.
2. Usually, symphonies are subdivided into independent and contrasted movements, typically three or four.
3. Although they are not devoid of melodic interest, sentimentality, or humor, symphonies are rarely trite, tawdry, or banal. Casual witticism usually finds a more congenial habitat elsewhere in music.
4. Normally, symphonic movements are separated by perceptible cadences, and each has its individual tempo, meter, melodic substance, formal pattern, key, and texture.
5. Although they may occasionally bear titles, most symphonic movements are numbered—first movement, second movement, and so on.
6. Nearly all symphonies are performed by the orchestra, although a few have been written for wind band. Those for organ are quite rare.

Most symphonies (for example, Symphony No. 5 in C minor by Beethoven, Symphony No. 4 in F minor by Tchaikowsky, or the "New World" Symphony by Dvořák) have four movements that disclose these qualities: [1]

---

[1] In general, these are comparable with the sonata's characteristics mentioned in Chapter 15.

1. *First movement:* Typically in a moderately fast tempo (although it may be prefaced by a slow introduction), a symphony's opening segment is usually organized in sonata form. Generally, it is epic, intense, dynamic, vigorous, mystic, or exultant in expression. As the keystone of a sizeable musical edifice, it establishes a general philosophic outlook for the entire work.

2. *Second movement:* Distinctively contrasted, the second section tends to be restrained rather than dynamic, lyric rather than terse. Such movements are usually slow in tempo and convey gentle languid melodies in a leisurely manner. Usually they are in a related key, or perhaps a minor tonality, and are organized in part form or variation form.

3. *Third movement:* Further contrast is provided by this section, which often displays the buoyant qualities of a dance. The gayest and shortest of symphonic movements, it may be a minuet, waltz, or scherzo. A return to the home key is typical at this point, and a utilization of part form in the ternary sequence is common.

4. *Fourth movement:* Affirming a buoyant, zestful, and invigorating spirit, a symphony's finale is usually fast and climactic. Early symphonies often employ rondo form here, whereas later pieces turn to sonata form, a combination of the two (sonata-rondo form), or even variation form. Regardless of structure, this epilogue usually sweeps over an exhilarating course at a brisk and rapid pace.

Four-movement symphonies are undoubtedly the most common, but others exist with fewer or more subdivisions. Here are some examples:

1. *In one movement:* Barber, Symphony No. 1 (1936); Harris, Symphony No. 3 (1938); Sibelius, Symphony No. 7 in C major (1924).
2. *In two movements:* Liszt, "Dante" Symphony; Schubert, Symphony No. 8 in B minor ("Unfinished").
3. *In three movements:* Franck, Symphony in D minor; Liszt, "Faust" Symphony; Stravinsky, *Symphony in Three Movements* (1945).
4. *In five movements:* Beethoven, Symphony No. 6 in F major ("Pastoral"); Berlioz, *Symphonie fantastique.*

PERFORMING MEDIA FOR SYMPHONIES

Basically, the symphony is an orchestral work. This was the group for which the early Viennese and Mannheim symphonists wrote and the body Haydn and Mozart had in mind as they scored their pieces. Very early symphonies (that is, those written shortly after 1750) were often marked "a 6," "a 8," "a 10," or "a 12," to indicate their number of musical parts (not to be confused with their participants). When, in about 1750, Johann Stamitz wrote his Symphony in B-flat major, Opus 8, No. 5, for instance, he inserted the designation "a 6" and scored the piece for first and second violins, viola, bass, and two horns. A "sinfonia a 8" added two oboes to this ensemble, "a 10" two bassoons, and "a 12" two flutes.

Mozart's late symphonies, which actually predate similar works by Haydn despite differences in the composers' ages, mostly follow the "a 12" plan but occasionally add particular instruments. Fundamentally, they include two each of flutes, oboes, bassoons, and horns, along with four string parts (first and second violins, viola, and bass). To illustrate, here is the instrumentation for Mozart's last six symphonies:

1. No. 35 in D: "a 12" group plus 2 clarinets, 2 trumpets, and timpani.
2. No. 36 in C: basic group (without flutes) plus 2 trumpets and timpani.[2]
3. No. 38 in A: basic group plus two trumpets and timpani.
4. No. 39 in E-flat: basic group (without oboes) plus two clarinets, two trumpets, and timpani.
5. No. 40 in G minor: basic group plus two clarinets.
6. No. 41 in C: basic group plus two trumpets and timpani.

Haydn's late symphonies (two sets of six works each written in 1791 and 1794) can be considered "a 15" works for they are scored for two each of flute, oboe, bassoon, horn, and trumpet, as well as the usual strings with timpani.[3] By about 1790, the orchestra's makeup had been reasonably well established. Henceforth it was to experience little drastic change save for an expansion of membership and the occasional addition of new instruments (that is, piccolo, English horn, bass clarinet, trombone, tuba, as well as varied percussion).[4]

Beethoven was one of the first to include voices within the symphony. Approaching the end of a brilliant career, he took an epochal step and wrote for solo voices (soprano, contralto, tenor, and bass) and chorus in the finale of his Symphony No. 9 in D minor (1823). In emulation, several subsequent symphonists—Berlioz in the Roméo et Juliette Symphony, Liszt in the "Faust" Symphony, and Mahler in his Symphony No. 2—also wrote for voices. Comparatively modest in his requirements, Liszt uses only one solo voice (tenor), but Berlioz and Mahler, particularly the latter, are much more demanding and employ several soloists, choirs, and choruses with orchestra.

While the French Revolution raged (c. 1789–1790), symphonies for winds were composed and played out-of-doors before huge crowds of people. Although wind bands do not have the myriad expressive resources of an orchestra, they do have full-sounding dynamic power and a nobility of utterance that make them very useful. François Gossec's "Military" Symphony, a modest little piece in three movements, was one of the first works to be written for band during the Terror. Although it can hardly be termed

[2] Mozart's presumed Symphony No. 37 was actually written by Michael Haydn.
[3] The second set also includes a pair of clarinets.
[4] For a detailed listing of the modern orchestra's instrumentation, see Chapter 5.

distinguished, this brief piece established a precedent that was subsequently followed by other more significant works (for example, Berlioz's *Symphonie funèbre et triomphale*, 1840). Later symphonies for winds have been written by such composers as: Paul Fauchet, (Symphony in B-flat, first performed in 1926); Paul Hindemith, (Symphony in B-flat, 1951); Morton Gould (Symphony No. 4 for Band, "West Point," 1952); Vincent Persichetti, (Symphony No. 6. 1956), and H. Owen Reed (*La Fiesta Mexicana*, 1956).

ABSOLUTE AND PROGRAM SYMPHONIES

Those who worked on the symphony prior to 1800, the Classicists, considered it a pure or absolute design. While most symphonies continue to remain within the absolute sphere, the claims of descriptive music were advanced with such persuasiveness early in the nineteenth century that program symphonies (illustrative works) began to appear in increasing number.

As with other descriptive pieces (suites, tone-poems, or rhapsodies), program symphonies have an intent of serving literary, pictorial, or narrative ends. Subjects treated within them are infinitely varied and may extend from a description of nature (e.g., Beethoven's *Pastoral Symphony*) to ventures into phantasmagoria (Berlioz's *Symphonie fantastique*). With the emergence of program symphonies, however, absolute works by no means disappeared. Alongside the flamboyant illustrative compositions of Berlioz and Liszt, for instance, the abstract symphonies of Mendelssohn and Schumann co-existed. And after 1850, when Brahms, Dvořák, Tchaikowsky, Bruckner, and others became prominent, the absolute symphony was reaffirmed as one of music's most distinguished designs.

While identifying titles and a correlative utilization of subtitles, poems, or essays on individual movements is a characteristic of descriptive compositions, it is not a sole criterion that distinguishes one kind of piece from another. Numerous abstract symphonies—e.g., Mozart's *Jupiter* Symphony (Symphony No. 41 in C major), Haydn's *Clock* Symphony (Symphony No. 101 in D major)—bear nicknames that have nothing to do with their avowed aesthetic content. On the other hand, Beethoven's *Pastoral* Symphony (1809), Berlioz's *Roméo et Juliette* Symphony (1839), Liszt's *Faust* Symphony (1854), Tchaikowsky's *Manfred* Symphony (1885), Vaughan Williams' *A London Symphony* (1914), or Stravinsky's *Symphony of Psalms* (1930), have titles that give a listener a meaningful idea of their expressive intent.

INTERRELATING SYMPHONIC MOVEMENTS

For several decades after the symphonic pattern was formulated, no one was apparently much concerned that its movements existed as individual entities. In effect, symphonies of this era were constituted from an association of disjunct parts connected by only two tenuous threads: a utilization of common or related keys and adherence to a conventional pattern of movement successives. Such a casual assemblage suggests that the symphony had serious internal weaknesses, of course, but it was not until the time of Beethoven (c. 1800–1825) that tangible steps were taken to rectify this condition. Then, partly as a result of his efforts and partly because kindred composers were similarly motivated, three techniques were introduced to engender greater synthesis:

1. A linking of movements by an avoidance of final cadences while progressing directly into succeeding sections over connecting bridge passes. An early example of this occurs between the third and fourth movements of Beethoven's Symphony No. 5 in C minor, where the *scherzo* (third movement) flows directly into an *allegro* (finale) over a bridge provided by strings and timpani.
2. Intermingling thematic material from one movement to another, so that melodies from a first movement may recur in the second, ideas from the first and second may appear in the third, and so on. César Franck's Symphony in D minor as well as Dvořák's "New World" Symphony exemplify thematic referral of this kind. Both Beethoven's Symphony No. 9 in D minor ("Choral") and Bruckner's Symphony No. 4 in E-flat major ("Romantic") adopt a modified plan when they present a summary of thematic material from the entire work in their finales (fourth movements).
3. Using a basic theme, sometimes in modified form, throughout a symphony so that it becomes a common factor in all the movements. Hector Berlioz, one of the first to use this device, termed his subject an *idée fixe* (a fixed idea); Tchaikowsky later called it a *motto* theme. Examples appear in Berlioz's *Symphonie fantastique* and Tchaikowsky's Symphony No. 5 in E minor.

UNUSUAL KINDS OF SYMPHONIES

Although the orchestra remains a primary body for symphonic performance, its membership has been occasionally altered to include unusual instruments. Aside from electronic devices, or the intermittent employment of piano, organ, harp, or saxophone, perhaps the most notable additions have been vocalists, singly and in chorus.

Many twentieth-century symphonies use voices in conjunction with the orchestra. When Ralph Vaughan Williams composed his "Sea" Symphony (1910), for instance, he employed choral resources to enunciate a Walt Whitman text, and he subsequently utilized a soprano soloist to sing wordless melismas in his "Pastoral" Symphony (1922). One of the most notable vocal-instrumental symphonies of recent times is Igor Stravinsky's *Symphony of Psalms* (1930), which uses orchestra (without violins or violas) and chorus to present texts from Psalms 38, 39, and 150. Similarly, Benjamin Britten's "Spring" Symphony (1949) relies on soloists, chorus, and orchestra. Very recently Leonard Bernstein followed this trend; only a single mezzo-soprano voice appears in the finale of his "Jeremiah" Symphony (1943), but sizeable choral forces and a narrator are required throughout the Symphony No. 3—*Kaddish* (1963).

Charles Widor (1844–1937), a prominent French organist, handled symphonic concepts in a unique manner when he composed ten large-scale works for his personal instrument and called them symphonies. More analogous to suites for a single instrument, these are not symphonies in an accepted sense but formidable pieces that greatly enrich organ literature. Among symphonic oddities, three works by Alexander Scriabin (1872–1915), his *Divine Poem* (1903), *Poem of Ecstasy* (1908), and *Prometheus: Poem of Fire* (1910) are strikingly bizarre. Scriabin's final "symphony" is particularly ostentatious, for it requires a large orchestra, piano, organ, choruses, color organ (a device that projects colors of variegated hues on an overhead screen), and another machine that wafts perfume into the air as the music is being played!

MODIFICATIONS OF THE SYMPHONIC CONCEPT

Arising as a composite form, the symphony later began to influence a number of associated patterns. Generally speaking, these peripheral designs retain some symphonic characteristics while asserting their own distinctive qualities. Chief among them are the sinfonietta, sinfonia concertante, symphonic suite, and symphonic poem.

Conceived for reduced performing forces (a string group, small orchestra, or wind ensemble) and expressing less exalted ideas than a full-scale composition, the sinfonietta is a symphony's diminutive off-shoot. Typically divided into movements—normally four—pieces of this kind are usually quite short and have few structural or aesthetic complexities. Among representative sinfoniettas are those by Leos Janáček (1925), Benjamin Britten (1932), Albert Roussel (1934), and Paul Hindemith (1950).

Utilizing one or more instruments in a solo capacity, the sinfonia concertante is normally a three-movement piece that judiciously contrasts solo timbre with full orchestral sonority. Both Haydn and Mozart, as well as numerous recent composers, have made excellent use of its format. Exemplificative are Mozart's Sinfonia Concertante in E-flat for Violin and Viola (K. 364), and his Sinfonia Concertante in E-flat for Oboe, Clarinet, Bassoon, Horn, and Strings (K. anh. 275b).

Occupying a position midway between suite and symphony, the symphonic suite combines the directness of an additive design with the complexities of symphonic manipulation. Freer in outline than a conventional symphony, it usually encompasses several movements (possibly four, five, or six), discloses some thematic manipulation, is scored for orchestra, and has an avowed descriptive intent. Rimsky-Korsakoff's *Scheherazade*, written in 1888 and based on four episodes from the celebrated *Arabian Nights Tales*, is a well-known example.

Only distantly related to the symphony, the symphonic poem, a single-movement design usually associated with illustrative music, became increasingly prominent after 1850. Quite akin to the overture, it is more fully discussed in Chapters 10 and 14.

WAYPOSTS IN THE RISE OF THE SYMPHONY

Formulating the Design (c. 1750)

Because it was primarily based on pre-existent forms, the symphony had to effectuate a distinctive break with the past and present a new face to the musical world in order to establish a claim to uniqueness. This was accomplished, in about 1750, by imposing a new façade over qualities inherited from its precursors. Some of the innovations of the symphony include:

1. A revised conception of the kind of melodic material considered suitable for inclusion within a serious instrumental design. Symphonic themes became more succinct than the florid melodies heretofore used in opera, and more memorable than the motivic subjects characteristically employed in Baroque suites and concertos.
2. A greater exploitation of thematic ideas was carried out, which, for the most part, was accomplished via the developmental process in sonata form.
3. A more colorful use of the orchestra was inaugurated, which was mainly accomplished by emphasizing newly discovered tonal resources in string and wind instruments.
4. Countermelodies were now frequently interwoven within the musical fabric to complement and enhance the beauty of primary subjects.

Most Baroque instrumental forms were concerned with thematic presentation, repetition, or digression from the principal subject. Coinciding with an emergence of sonata form, composers now began to turn toward the complexities, beauties, and expressive richness to be found in thematic transformation. At about this same time (that is, immediately prior to 1750) Pietro Locatelli (1695–1764) and G. B. Sammartini (1701–1775) inaugurated a trend when they began to write overture-like pieces free of association with opera. Thus, as a result of diverse efforts as the century reached its midpoint, Scarlatti's *sinfonia avanti l'opera* became the symphony. Now, however, unlike sections in an overture, the three contrasted movements, were both longer and clearly separated from one another. Within a quarter of a century, which is to say sometime around 1775, the symphony became expanded to a four-movement design when a minuet was typically incorporated as a third movement just before the finale.

Constituent sections in most Baroque suites were organized in binary part form (AB), but as it grew the symphony began to place greater reliance on ternary form, variation form, rondo form, and sonata form. Although it had not yet acquired thematic dualism (that is, an employment of two contrasting themes), the mid-eighteenth century version of sonata form had become an exceptionally important pattern. Within a decade or two, after a second melody had been introduced as the subordinate subject, it moved on to assume a dominant position in instrumental composition.

Far-reaching developments began to occur in orchestral scoring at about this time. Heretofore limited to supplying mere accompaniments for free-wheeling instruments of higher pitch, the orchestra's low strings now began to experience emancipation. As a tangible first step, the violas were assigned more interesting parts to play, and before another quarter of a century had passed, 'cellos and basses were divorced from a common line. Of course, the continuo had long since been abandoned, and wind instruments in increasing strength were given greater autonomy and used to provide contrast with the upper strings.

Much pioneering work on the early symphony was accomplished in Italy by native composers and in the environs of Vienna where such musicians as Georg Matthias Monn (1717–1750) and Georg Wagenseil (1715–1777) were active. In Germany, benefitting from the generous subsidy of a royal patron who assembled a fine orchestra for his personal pleasure, a group in Mannheim wrote symphonies in three or four movements that they scored in eight parts (two horns, two oboes, first and second violins, viola and "bass," usually played by 'cellos). Pioneers were Franz Richter (1709–1789) and Johann Stamitz (1717–1757), who were later succeeded by Karl Stamitz (1746–1801), Anton Stamitz (1753–1820), and Carl Cannabich (1771–1805).

Symphonism in the Classic Era

Few symphonies created between 1750 and 1775 can be considered more than historical curiosities. Although hundreds were written by dozens of composers, virtually none have maintained a fixed place in the repertoire. As an example of these early works, however, consider the "Sinfonia a 8" in A major by Anton Filtz (1730–1760).[5] A pupil of Johann Stamitz and leader of the Mannheim orchestra's 'cello section, Filtz wrote a great deal of

---

[5] Published by Chevardière in Paris as number two in a series of *Sinfonies périodiques* and subsequently reprinted in the *Mannheim Symphonists*, Vol. II (New York: Broude Bros., n.d.)

music during his comparatively short life. Scored for the usual Mannheim group (with eight parts), his brief Symphony in A major has these characteristics:

1. *First movement:* In the home key (A major), triple meter, and marked to be played *allegro*, the opening movement is divided into two sections of seventy-two and sixty-seven measures each. Two contrasting themes are introduced in the first section, which ultimately finds a cadence on the dominant. Fragments of the first theme experience a modicum of development for twenty-seven measures before the recapitulation reaffirms both subjects and concludes on the tonic.
2. *Second movement:* Shifting to the subdominant (D major), this *andante* is played in quadruple meter. It has two segments of thirty-four and forty-six measures, respectively, but no complexities appear to mar the simple beauty of this charming idyll.
3. *Third movement:* Back in the home key, this menuetto with trio follows a regular ternary pattern. Particularly notable in the trio is Filtz's virtuoso use of the flute.
4. *Fourth movement:* A vigorous *presto* in the home key and sextuple meter taken two beats to the measure, this epilogue in binary form has forty-nine measures in its first section and sixty-four in the second.

Symphonism, as this term is now understood, really began with Wolfgang Amadeus Mozart. The composer of forty-seven symphonies—of which forty-one are known, published, and recorded—this amazing genius brought unparalleled distinction to the form. Utilizing only the materials known to his predecessors, he infused the symphony with new ideas that were impressive, tender, and heroic, while leavening the symphony's rather austere formal beauty with passionate utterances learned in operatic composition. Among the most graceful and fluent works in the repertoire, his last six symphonies (composed between 1782–1788) are the earliest such pieces to remain in today's repertoire.[6]

Composed when his fortunes were at an unusually low ebb, in July, 1788, Mozart's Symphony No. 40 in G minor shows the remarkable state of perfection the design had attained by this time. Burdened with ever-mounting debts, worried about his wife's health, unable to secure a post worthy of his abilities, Mozart nevertheless composed as if he were entirely free of mundane care. Within three months, during the summer of 1788, he created three sublime symphonies (Nos. 39, 40, and 41); within three years he was dead at the age of thirty-five. These are details about his extremely tuneful Symphony in G minor:

[6] This is a listing of them: No. 35 in D major, K. 385 ("Haffner," 1782); No. 36 in C major, K. 425 ("Linz," 1783); No. 38 in A major, K. 504 ("Prague," 1786); No. 39 in E-flat, K. 545 (1788); No. 40 in G minor, K. 550 (1788); and No. 41 in C major, K. 551 ("Jupiter," 1788).

1. *First movement:* [7] An extremely quiet viola accompaniment provides a foundation over which first violins announce the principal theme:

Organized in sonata form, set in the home key, and pursuing a *molto allegro* course in duple meter, the movement also includes this subordinate theme:

Only the principal theme is used in the development, where it undergoes transformations that are clear, logical, and engrossing. Subsequently, the recapitulation reaffirms both subjects in their usual alignment, after which the movement concludes with a short coda.

2. *Second movement:* Continuing in sonata form but shifting to E-flat major, Mozart suggests quiet resignation in this graceful *andante.* These are its three themes:

---

[7] A brief analysis of this movement appeared earlier in Chapter 8.

Again, the development is concerned only with exploring potentials inherent in the principal subject.

3. *Third movement:* Lighthearted gaiety is clearly evident in this cleanly accented menuetto. As with nearly all Classic examples of this dance, the movement follows a *da capo* pattern in ternary form. This is its first theme:

4. *Fourth movement:* For a principal theme in the finale, Mozart employs a subject known as the "Mannheim skyrocket." Beginning in a comparatively low register, it surges upward in an arching trajectory to seemingly explode in a burst of tones. This is the theme:

Again sonata form is the movement's formal pattern, and duple meter in *allegro assai* tempo is employed. More restrained than the initial theme, the second subject is sounded by first violins:

With remarkable consistency, Mozart again limits himself to a perusal of the principal theme within this movement's development. Finally, after an orthodox recapitulation, a brief coda concludes.

Although he was older by twenty-four years, Joseph Haydn outlived Mozart by eighteen years, and it was during this final period that his best-known symphonies were written. Employed from 1760–1790 as a household musician to Prince Paul Anton of Esterhazy, Haydn was sequestered on a princely estate in rural Hungary and, as a result, wrote an amazingly large number of symphonies (104 have been authenticated). That Haydn's symphonies are greater than, or even equal to, Mozart's may be doubted. But he was a gifted musician whose prodigious creative feats, carried out with artistry, modesty, and devotion, have earned recognition and admiration throughout the musical world.

Haydn's final twelve symphonies are the capstones of an extremely busy career. Known as the "Salomon" Symphonies, they were written in two sets of six works each (numbers 93 through 98, 1791–1792, and numbers 99 through 104, 1794–1795), upon commission by an impresario who engaged Haydn to visit England and appear as conductor of the London Symphony Orchestra during these years. Although he lived for nearly a decade and a half after completing these works, Haydn never again returned to writing symphonies.

In company with Mozart, Haydn brought the classical symphony to a pinnacle of perfection. By now the orchestra's makeup had been firmly established, its sonority rested securely on the timbre of an enlarged string section, and roles assigned to winds and percussion were clearly postulated by pragmatic example. Furthermore, as the era came to a close, the standard four-movement symphony stood securely in all its finely chiseled elegance, and its expressive characteristics, as well as the formal outline for each subdivision, had been clearly delineated. Generations of symphonists were to build on this beautifully molded base.

The Romantic Symphony

Pronounced during the era of Classicism, a cultivation of the symphony continued during opening decades of the nineteenth century, but with an altered emphasis that brought fewer—but more strikingly individual—works to the desks of performing organizations. Then, as years wore on, fewer composers turned toward the design, so that when the final quarter of the century was reached, the symphony appeared to be uttering its last gasp. At a propitious moment, however, several distinguished musicians reversed the tide, renewed the pattern, and provided an orderly transition into the modern era.

As the Romantic century began, Ludwig van Beethoven, a young German from the Rhineland city of Bonn, who had lately taken up residence in Vienna, assumed the mantle handed down from Haydn and Mozart. Within a quarter of a century, he created nine monumental symphonies that almost totally overshadow all previous works in this category.[8] Generally

---

[8] Here is a listing: No. 1 in C major (1800); No. 2 in D major (1802); No. 3 in E-flat major ("Eroica," 1803); No. 4 in B-flat major (1806); No. 5 in C minor (1806); No. 6 in F major ("Pastoral," 1808); No. 7 in A major (1812); No. 8 in F major (1812); and No. 9 in D minor ("Choral," 1823).

Two curious works are also associated with Beethoven: the "Battle" Symphony, also known as *Wellington's Victory* (1813), a noisy pièce d'occasion written for the

speaking, Beethoven's first two symphonies follow the patterns of Classicism. Admirably fashioned, they suggest greatness rather than its actual attainment. But the Symphony No. 3, termed the "Eroica" because of its dedication "to the heroic nature of mankind," discloses the work of a fully mature symphonist. Longer than any previous symphony, it is founded on a wealth of memorable ideas handled with consummate architectural skill. After it, the Symphony No. 4, trim and tidy though it is, appears as a let-down; but the Symphony No. 5, with its knocking motive in the first movement, has become *the* symphony in music's literature. Symphony No. 6 ("Pastoral"), a lone excursion into descriptive writing within the symphonic idiom, eloquently discloses Beethoven's consuming love of nature. For Richard Wagner and innumerable others the Symphony No. 7 became "an apotheosis of the dance," for it progresses from one strongly marked rhythmic movement to another. Charming and graceful, Symphony No. 8 is somewhat overshadowed by the epochal D-minor Symphony that follows. With all the varied experience of a distinguished career on which to draw, Beethoven turned to an amalgamation of solo voices, chorus, and orchestra when he created the Symphony No. 9. Its complexities are formidable and tax the abilities of even the finest musicians, yet the sublimity of its message has never been surpassed. The "Choral" Symphony stands *sui generis*.

Beethoven's contributions to symphonic writing are so numerous as to defy a brief listing. Among his most significant innovations, however, are (1) a general broadening of the entire structure, as well as a lengthening of individual movements; (2) an enlargement of the orchestra—accomplished by requiring more strings, woodwinds, and brasses and adding such instruments as piccolo, trombone, and contra-bassoon; (3) an imposition of greater technical demands on the orchestra's musicians; (4) an increased emphasis on musical activity within development sections, as well as a manipulation of thematic material in other areas—particularly the closing sections of expositions and recapitulations; (5) a major expansion of codas; (6) an employment of idiomatic themes well able to withstand the vigorous buffeting of symphonic treatment; (7) a frequent use of wide-ranging modulatory schemes that shift boldly to foreign keys; (8) an incorporation of exotic harmonies and occasional dissonances within the musical fabric, and (9) an introduction of such patterns as the scherzo, funeral march, "Turkish" music, or expanded variation schemes within the symphonic design.

Living contemporaneously with Beethoven in Vienna, the era's second great symphonist, Franz Schubert, remained almost totally unrecognized during his lifetime. A shy and diffident man, Schubert moved within a closed circle of friends, but posterity has come to judge him an unusually capable composer. Like Beethoven, Schubert wrote nine symphonies. Al-

---

panharmonium and later orchestrated; and (2) the "Jena" Symphony, discovered in 1909 in Jena, Germany, and attributed to Beethoven—although it has since (in 1957) been ascribed to Friedrich Witt (1770–1837).

though thoroughly steeped in the precepts of Classicism, the tenets of Romanticism beckoned with such insistence that he is now universally acknowledged as one of the first (and in particular respects, one of the greatest) of Romantic composers. Where Beethoven is epic and monumental, Schubert is glowing and lyrical; where Beethoven is powerful, pre-emptory and brusque, Schubert is gentle, charming, and poetic. Their musical styles are individual and divergent, but between them Beethoven and Schubert brought Viennese symphonism to its golden age.

While still a student at the *konvict* (a school for choir boys attached to the Imperial Chapel), Schubert was introduced to the intricacies of symphonic writing. Composed between 1813 and 1818, his first six symphonies are works of charming beauty rather than profound import. The Symphony No. 4 in C minor, often termed the "Tragic," for instance, contains fascinating portents of ideas still to come. The Symphony No. 5 in B-flat major, almost Mozartean in essence, and the Symphony No. 6 in C major ("Little") show similar traceries. Unfortunately, the seventh symphony has been lost, but the Symphony No. 8 in B minor (1822), called the "Unfinished" because it has only two complete movements, is not only a splendid composition but the work for which Schubert is best-known today. Touched with autumnal sadness, beautifully organized and continually infused with tender lyricism, the "Unfinished" wends a gentle way through a sonata-form movement of classic proportions, and a sonatina-form structure of glowing beauty. Written in 1828, Schubert's final symphony, No. 9 in C major ("Great") indicates what might have been accomplished had fate permitted him longer life (he died in this year at the age of thirty-two). Cast in the grand mold of Beethoven, its ideas are nevertheless treated with Schubert's ineffable touch. After a lyric introduction, the first movement stresses a tightly knit motive as it unfolds in sonata form; the second movement is nostalgic and gracious; the agile scherzo (third movement) is neat, clear, and precise; and the driving finale shows that Schubert could be persuasively eloquent within the grand symphonic format without becoming eclectic.

Less a Romanticist than either Beethoven or Schubert, Felix Mendelssohn became their chronological successor. Fully indoctrinated in the philosophic principles of Classicism, Mendelssohn could not easily step outside their boundaries, nor did he seriously wish to do so. Disregarding preliminary symphonic essays, some written for strings alone, his most important works in this area are the Symphony No. 3 in A minor ("Scotch," 1842); Symphony No. 4 in A major ("Italian," 1833); and Symphony No. 5 in D major ("Reformation," 1835).[9] As befits the work of a man of impeccable taste, tender

---

[9] The numbers assigned to Mendelssohn's symphonies, as is also a circumstance with several other composers, are misleading. Actually the "Scotch" Symphony was his fifth work in this category; the "Reformation" his second; the "Italian," the third; and *Lobgesang* (1840), "Hymn of Praise"—a work that places divided reliance on choral forces and orchestra—the fourth.

sensibilities, and consummate musicianship, Mendelssohn's symphonies are carefully wrought, superbly tailored, and delightfully expressive. A masterful musical architect as well as a superlative melodist, the composer clearly reveals his indisputable gifts within them. At the same time, these symphonies appear to lack an inner depth; they are apparently little concerned with exploring profound human emotions. Seemingly, they soar and float on gossamer wings that are neither soiled nor burdened by the tragedies, conflicts, or tribulations of a workaday world.

A confidant and warm friend of Mendelssohn, Robert Schumann knew only too well the problems of human existence. Denied the opportunity to study music as a youth because of parental opposition, he was later forced to approach the problems of symphonic writing with a limited technique. A creative musician of great talent, Schumann nevertheles remained a neophyte in orchestral scoring, and his four symphonies consequently suffer from a lack of clarity and coloration. Still, with all their shortcomings, his Symphony No. 1 in B-flat major, the "Spring" (1841); Symphony No. 2 in C major (1846); Symphony No. 3 in E-flat major, the "Rhenish" (1850); and Symphony No. 4 in D minor (1841, revised 1851) are warm, radiant works that comprise important links in a chain of compositions that unites Beethoven's art with that of Brahms.

Except for sporadic efforts made during the Revolution (c. 1790) by Gossec, Mehul, and associates, up until 1830 the French were content to obtain their symphonies from abroad just as they imported opera. But in Hector Berlioz, France discovered a formidable creative talent admirably equipped to wrestle with the symphony's staggering problems. Berlioz's symphonies are five in number: the *Symphonie fantastique* (1830), a descriptive work based on a macabre narrative fashioned by the composer himself; *Harold in Italy* (1834), another illustrative piece that features a solo viola and relates episodes from Byron's "Childe Harold"; *Roméo et Juliette* (1839), a "dramatic symphony" of unusual dimensions scored for solo voices, three choruses, and orchestra; *Symphonie funèbre et triomphale* (1840), a commemorative work basically written for wind band, although voices and strings may be added; and *Lelio* (1831), a little-performed sequel to the *Symphonie fantastique*. Berlioz discloses startling originality in these compositions, for they require unusual performing groups and move with boldness and originality into new areas of symphonic thought. Possessed of an untrammeled disposition as well as evangelical zeal, until his death in 1869 this bellicose Frenchman stormed across the face of Europe in an unremitting effort to improve the state of music—and, incidentally, to propagandize his own works.

Beethoven, Schubert, Mendelssohn, Schumann, and Berlioz—in greater or lesser degrees—were Romanticists whose contributions to symphonic literature were, and still are, extremely significant. At their hands, the structure known to Haydn and Mozart became enormously expanded, its expres-

sive horizons were broadened, and its communicative powers greatly enlarged. But strangely enough, near midcentury, the symphony entered into
a period of decline. After 1840, other projects occupied most creative musicians, and some made no attempt to practice in the symphonic idiom at all.
Frederic Chopin, Giuseppe Verdi, and Richard Wagner are only three of the
period's prominent composers who ignored the symphony as though it did
not exist.

Franz Liszt might well have turned his abilities in other directions.
Creator of the symphonic poem, the greatest pianist of his era (and perhaps
of all time), an indefatigable arranger of countless works for the piano, and
a composer of much church music, he also found time and energy to write
the "Faust" Symphony (1854), a descriptive work that portrays three
characters in Goethe's drama, and the "Dante" Symphony (1856), based on
the Italian poet's *Divine Comedy*. Like Berlioz, Liszt was an unorthodox
symphonist, and these pieces show his penchant for the bizarre and unusual.
But his example did not inspire a group of disciples, nor did it reverse the
general trend of symphonic decline in Western Europe between 1850–1875.

Until after 1850, few Russian composers were known to the world at
large. Music in Russia (as opposed to Russian music) flourished, however,
for numerous Europeans (chiefly Italians) visited the land, composed, performed, and taught. But this had little to do with the formulation of a
national musical language. As the century moved onward, however, semblances of musical nationalism began to appear. Michael Glinka gave the
movement its initial impetus by writing two operas based on Russian subjects. Then the *Russian Five*, a group whose creed had to do with the creation and promulgation of Russian music, became active. Admitted dilet-
tantes, the "Five"—Mily Balakirev, Cesar Cui, Alexander Borodin, Modest
Mussorgsky, and Nicholas Rimsky-Korsakoff—were filled with indisputable
apostolic zeal and between them established a favorable climate in which
an idiomatic native music could grow. Aside from several descriptive works,
however, their most notable symphonic pieces were Borodin's Symphony
No. 2 in B minor (1876) and Rimsky's "Antar" Symphony (1868, revised in
1875 and 1897).

Working independently of the Five, the era's most notable Russian
symphonist, Peter I. Tchaikowsky, composed six excellent symphonies.[10]
Lengthy and discursive, they are extremely colorful and have eloquent
thematic lines that soar effortlessly over extensive reaches. Mostly, Tchaikowsky's symphonic movements are organized in sonata form or part form,
which he handles with the secure hand of a born architect. Throbbing with
emotionality, his Symphonies No. 4, 5, and 6, in particular, have become
unusually popular and are among the most frequently performed works in

[10] No. 1 in G minor "Winter Daydreams," (1866); No. 2 in C minor "Little
Russian," (1872); No. 3 in D major "Polish," (1875); No. 4 in F minor (1877); No. 5
in E minor (1888); and No. 6 in B minor (*Pathètique,* 1893).

the literature. In a sense, they epitomize the difficult task of pouring new wine into old bottles, for Tchaikowsky consistently clung to the standard symphonic pattern while infusing it with unabashed melodism and unrepressed emotional fervor. It was a virtuoso performance, and he carried it off with *élan*.

Heralded as a third B—Bach and Beethoven were the first two—Johannes Brahms became the most distinguished Germany symphonist of the late nineteenth century. Stoutly resisting the encroachments of novel devices—that is, voices, programmatic allusions, or the employment of unusual instruments—he maintained the symphony's traditional pattern (then more than one hundred years old) and wrote abstract instrumental works of rare beauty. Brahms approached the symphony with circumspection, for he was forty-three years old when his Symphony No. 1 in C minor (1876) appeared. Once the trail had been broken, however, others followed in quick succession, including the Symphonies No. 2 in D major (1877), No. 3 in F major (1883), and No. 4 in E minor (1885). A musician of unflagging integrity and unusual rectitude, Brahms remained steadfast in his adherence to conventional symphonic concepts. Scored for orchestra only, his pieces are filled with an abundance of emotional fervor but are totally devoid of illustrative associations. All follow the conventional four-movement sequence and show a grasp of musical procedures unknown since the time of Beethoven. Despite his veneration of the past, Brahms was a devout Romanticist, however, and his symphonies are suffused with melodies that only a matchless lyricist could create. Some argue the wisdom of associating Brahms with Bach and Beethoven (as suggested by the *bon mot* mentioned here), but none deny that his symphonies stand close to those of Beethoven in subtlety, complexity, and sublimity.

Occupying a position with Brahms comparable to the Beethoven-Schubert relationship of earlier years, Anton Bruckner lived and worked in the "musical city," Vienna, at the same time as his better-known associate. Almost as diffident and shy as Schubert, Bruckner was reluctant to enter into the cosmopolitan musical life of a great city; his years as a schoolmaster and church organist in upper Austria had ill-prepared him for the sophisticated activity in one of the world's great music centers. But he wrote symphonies, nine of them, that the Viennese understood and took warmly to their hearts. An organist of unusual ability, Bruckner often composed in terms of his personal instrument. Sustained pedal tones are common, and their scoring assigns a timbre to the orchestra commonly associated with the organ. But they have expansive *adagios* (second movements) that are almost ethereal in gentle lyricism, and vigorous scherzos (third movements) that effectively contrast incisive wind sonorities against the sensuous tonal qualities of strings. Unusually long, his pieces have melodic lines that seem to reach heavenward like the spires of medieval cathedrals. Not nearly as naive as his critics contended, Bruckner was a deeply religious man whose every act was motivated by a profound love of God. Written between 1866, when he was forty-two years old, and 1894, Bruckner's symphonies were continually revised by a composer readily willing to accommodate the well-intentioned advice of associates. Current critical opinion favors his original versions, however, and it is in this form that the Symphony No. 4 in E-flat major ("Romantic," 1874); the Symphony No. 7 in E major (1880); and the Symphony No. 9 in D minor (1894) have come into particular prominence.

Musical nationalism became rampant in Bohemia, an area now encompassed by the modern states of Czechoslovakia and Yugoslavia, shortly after 1850. Bedrich Smetana did much to further its course, but he was essentially an opera composer remembered in orchestral circles for his series of six symphonic poems entitled *Ma Vlast* (My Fatherland). But Smetana's disciple, Antonín Dvořák, became a symphonist of distinction whose most notable large-scale work is the Symphony No. 9 in E minor (1893), "From the New World." Like many symphonists before and after him (Beethoven, Schubert, Bruckner, and Mahler, for example), Dvořák wrote nine symphonies that, unfortunately, have become misnumbered.[11] Of these, the Symphonies No. 7 in D minor (1885), No. 8 in G major (1889), and, of course, No. 9 in E minor richly deserve their favored position.

After Berlioz's death in 1869, French symphonism fell on difficult days. But the ebullient Frenchman was more successful in proselytism than he realized, with a result that a younger generation of symphonists arose during the final quarter of the century whose output, unfortunately, was neither large nor distinguished. But between them, they sustained an orchestral tradition that bore a rich harvest during subsequent generations. Initially, César Franck, a Belgian-born organist and professor of composition at the Conservatoire, became their leader. Franck's Symphony in D minor (1888), a three-movement work that follows the cyclic method of thematic interrelationship, has become relatively well established in the literature. Among the younger men who surrounded Franck, who leaned on him for counsel, and who astutely followed his advice, were Ernest Chausson (Symphony in B-flat major, 1890); Vincent d'Indy (*Symphony on a French Mountain Air*, 1886); and Camille Saint-Saëns (Symphony No. 3 in C minor, 1886).

Symphonies in the Contemporary Era

A musical phenomenon without parallel, Viennese symphonism (which began in about 1750, prior to the age of Haydn and Mozart) continued into the twentieth century carried on the able shoulders of Gustav Mahler. Why

---

[11] Although quite confusing, this is the way the symphonies are now numbered: Symphony No. 1 in C minor ("Bells of Zlonice," 1865); Symphony No. 2 in B-flat major (1865); Symphony No. 3 in E-flat major (1873); Symphony No. 4 in D minor (1874); Symphony No. 5 in F major, old No. 3 (1875, revised 1887); Symphony No. 6 in D major, old No. 1 (1880); Symphony No. 7 in D minor, old No. 2 (1885); Symphony No. 8 in G major, old No. 4 (1889); and Symphony No. 9 in E minor, old No. 5 (1893).

this fabulous city should have become a focal point for so much unparalleled musical creativity is cause for quiet speculation. In Hapsburg times, of course, it resulted from an ingathering of talent at a seat of empire. But to have sustained such a distinguished tradition for so long—through the eras of Beethoven and Schubert, Brahms and Bruckner, and to ultimately culminate in the age of Mahler and later Schoenberg—is reason for no small wonder.

One of the most outstanding conductors of his time, Mahler was also a composer who wrote prodigiously (mostly during the summer) when not burdened with other professional tasks. In the span between 1888 and 1909 he created nine symphonies—a tenth remained unfinished at his death and has only recently been prepared for performance—that push the form toward its most lyric and, at the same time, most extravagant limits. A disciple of Bruckner, Mahler cultivated the same expansiveness as his mentor. Although his Symphony No. 1 in D major (1888) clings reasonably close to tradition, the Symphony No. 2 in C minor (1894), the "Resurrection," scored for soprano and contralto soloists, chorus, and orchestra, represents a major departure from orthodoxy. Symphony No. 3 in D minor (1895) is long, irregular in outline, and enlists a contralto soloist as well as a chorus of boys and women for performance; the Symphony No. 4 in G major (1900), which employs a soprano soloist in its finale, is more conventional in design. Symphony No. 5 in C-sharp minor joins a distinguished series of works bearing this number (by Beethoven, Dvořák, and Tchaikowsky) and is an impressive work scored for orchestra alone. Mahler's Symphony No. 8 in E-flat major (1907), "Symphony of a Thousand," is written for eight solo voices, double chorus, boys' choir, organ, and orchestra; however, his last completed symphony, No. 9 in D major (1909), returns to a more normal performing concept and employs only the usual orchestral body. Subjected to extremely sharp criticism, which occasionally amounted to virtual castigation, during his lifetime, Mahler has become a greatly admired composer in recent years. Sentimental and occasionally maudlin, his symphonies are unfailingly melodic, dramatic, and engrossing. In an era not particularly notable for musical excellence, he wrote in a way that carried symphonism to new heights.

That Mahler did not work entirely alone is principally because of the most eminent musician Scandinavia ever produced: the Finn, Jean Sibelius. Although he lived into recent times (d. 1957), Sibelius' period of symphonic composition belongs to the years between 1899 and 1924. During that time he composed seven symphonies whose compact substance, neatly chiseled outlines, and granitic facade remind many of Finland's austere natural beauty. Never sentimental, meretricious, or flaccid, these pieces are epic, noble, and monumental. All are conceived for orchestra, all are free of extraneous programmatic connotations, and each has an individual stamp that causes it to differ in some degree from other works in the repertoire.

Among them, Sibelius' Symphony No. 2 in D major (1901) and Symphony No. 5 in E-flat major (1915) are particularly notable.

Another Scandinavian, Carl Nielsen (1865–1931), a Dane, was also active in symphonic writing during these years. Progressive, adept, and acutely aware of the newer musical trends arising around him, Nielsen effectuated a workable liaison between the conventional and the experimental. Consequently, his six symphonies manage the dexterous feat of being both challenging and accessible. Occasionally majestic, they are lithe, terse, and exciting works that have only recently become reasonably well-known in the United States. Nielsen's Symphonies No. 3 ("Sinfonia Espansive," 1912); No. 4 ("Inextinguishable," 1916); and No. 5 (1922) are most representative.

Some twentieth-century composers did not write symphonies at all. Claude Debussy, for instance, followed a rhapsodic course in his orchestral pieces: *Images* (1909), *Nocturnes* (1899), and *La Mer* (1905). So did his compatriot, Maurice Ravel—*Boléro* (1927), *La Valse* (1920), and *Rapsodie espagnole* (1907)—and most of the Viennese atonalists, including Arnold Schoenberg, Alban Berg, and Anton von Webern. But others considered the symphony far from moribund. Serge Prokofiev, for instance, beginning with the *Classical Symphony* (1917) and concluding with the Symphony No. 7 (1953), created a brilliant series of orchestral compositions. His *Classical Symphony* is a sparkling and comparatively brief piece wherein the composer pokes sly fun at musical clichés abroad during the era of Mozart and Haydn, but thereafter his symphonic mien became more serious. Bold, brilliant, virtuosic, and occasionally brash, his Symphonies No. 4 (1930); No. 5 (1944); No. 6 (1947); and No. 7 (1952) are among the finest our times have known.

Somewhat older, by eighteen years, Sergei Rachmaninoff was another Russian symphonist who became active early in the twentieth century. Where Prokofiev was enterprising and audacious, however, Rachmaninoff was conservative and reactionary. Consequently, his symphonies (the best-known are No. 2 in E minor, 1907, and No. 3 in A minor, 1936) are so laden with out-of-date Romantic ardor as to be fulsome. Yet their luxuriant harmonies, rich-sounding sonorities, and extremely sentimental melodies initially earned them a warm audience. Time has caused the luster to fade, however, and modern ears often find them to be tedious, repetitive, and overweening.

Another Russian, Dmitri Shostakovich, is an important twentieth-century symphonist, who, to the present time, has written thirteen such works. Of these, his Symphony No. 1 in F major (1925); Symphony No. 5 (1937); and Symphony No. 7 ("Leningrad," 1941) are especially fine. Shostakovich unfailingly paints with a colorful brush; his works are vivid, tuneful, and strongly rhythmic. In the main he adheres to traditional patterns (so, too, does Prokofiev), but fills their outlines with an abundance of stunning innovational ideas. Few of his symphonies are "difficult" in a tonal sense, although sharply etched dissonant harmonies abound. Mostly, they present a freshly scrubbed countenance that many listeners find alluring.

Although a series of minor composers sustained a musical climate in England during the eighteenth and nineteenth centuries, it was not until the advent of Edward Elgar (d. 1934) that Britain acquired a gifted creative musician. Elgar's symphonies are not among the most laudable works in this category, but they did establish a precedent for Ralph Vaughan Williams, William Walton, Benjamin Britten, and other modern-day British composers. Vaughan Williams' nine symphonies range in expressive intent from poetic lyricism—Symphony No. 1 ("Sea," 1910), which employs soprano and baritone soloists, chorus, and orchestra to articulate a Walt Whitman text—through nostalgic nationalism—Symphony No. 2 ("London," 1942), which portrays life in a bustling urban metropolis—to acrid austerity conceived in a modern idiom—Symphony No. 6 in E minor (1948). All are vigorous, big, and pulsating works, filled with vibrant ideas that please and delight most discriminating ears. Neither Walton (Symphony No. 2, 1960) nor Britten disclose Vaughan Williams' apostolic zeal in cultivating the symphony, although the latter consistently reveals an imaginative approach to the design. Britten's "Simple" Symphony (1934), somewhat akin to Prokofiev's "Classical" Symphony, has a direct and basic appeal. And the "Spring" Symphony (1949), distinctly unconventional, is based on poems by twelve English writers and is performed by soloists, chorus, and orchestra. Britten's *Symphony for 'Cello and Orchestra* (1964) is also iconoclastic and naturally highlights a discourse that is almost concerto-like between the solo instrument and a chamber orchestra.

America's twentieth-century symphonists include expatriates from foreign shores who bring to their craft the traditions of a centuries-old culture, as well as native-born composers whose visions are unhampered by time-honored customs. Functioning so smoothly as to be virtually unnoticed, the nation's well-known "melting pot" has deftly intermingled these streams with a result that traditional concepts have been revitalized just as newer theories have been broadened. Consequently, in recent years a new kind of symphony has appeared in the United States that is bright, invigorating, kaleidoscopic, and occasionally jazzy.

With few peers in the field, the Russian-born Igor Stravinsky brought great originality to symphonic composition. His *Symphony of Psalms* (1930), a three-movement work for chorus and orchestra, is highly unusual, and so, too, is his pungently flavored *Symphony in Three Movements* (1945). Somewhat less distinguished are the *Symphonies of Wind Instruments* (1920), musical vignettes conceived on a greatly reduced scale, and the Symphony in C (1940), which tends to be turgid, rhetorical, and more than a little ponderous.

German-born Paul Hindemith, one of the century's most versatile composers, wrote symphonies that have a rather dense texture resulting from an interweaving of contrapuntal lines. His masterwork is *Mathis der Maler* (Mathias the Painter, 1934), a three-movement piece based on material abstracted from an opera of the same name. And his Symphony in B-flat for Band (1951), an unusually complex work for winds, is unquestionably one of the best pieces ever written for this performing group. But the Symphony in E-flat (1941) and *Symphonia Serena* (1947)—both orchestral works— lack clearly etched profiles, individuality, and color. Lumbering in gait and thick in texture, they have not been widely accepted.

Charles Ives, one of this land's most distinctive creative talents, worked in self-imposed obscurity since the early 1900s. An erstwhile businessman and part-time composer, he deliberately chose an anonymous path so there would be no need to cultivate popularity. Consequently, his symphonies, as well as virtually everything else he wrote, are piquant, unpredictable, and iconoclastic works occasionally infused with whimsy. Using popular American folk tunes when it suited his purpose, Ives consistently wrote with understated laconic terseness. His *Symphony: Holidays* (1913) depicts sentiments associated with such days of patriotic observance as Washington's Birthday, Decoration Day, July 4, and Thanksgiving. Additionally, his Symphonies No. 2 (1902), No. 3 (1904), and No. 4 (1916) display courageous unconventionality. Few composers of any nationality have written so uniquely.

Symphonies by other American-born composers tend to reflect traditions established by generations of European musicians. Walter Piston's Symphonies No. 3 (1947) and No. 4 (1949), four- and three-movement works, respectively, reveal this influence. Roy Harris, another native-born American, follows a modified course. His Symphony No. 3 (1938), a single-movement piece with five subdivisions, is lacking in symphonic succinctness, but the Symphony No. 4 ("Folksong," 1940), is quite unique. Separated into seven movements, scored for chorus and orchestra, and founded on a colorful sequence of well-known American folk songs, it is marvelously inventive. And the symphonic writings of William Schuman are new, direct, and different. Always vibrant, sometimes edgy, but mostly efficient and tidy, they are products of a superb craftsman. Best-known are the Symphonies No. 3 (1941), No. 6 (1948), and No. 8 (1962). Aaron Copland's fund of invention is fabulous. Writing in a bright, cheerful, and highly polished manner, he brings refreshing newness into the symphonic repertoire. Suggestive of the dazzling, high-strung pulsations of jazz, Copland's Symphony No. 3 (1946), is a fresh-sounding orchestral showpiece. So, too, are the symphonies of Leonard Bernstein. Scripturally oriented, his "Jeremiah" Symphony (1943) is a three-movement piece concerned with depicting prophecies contained in the *Book of Lamentations;* its finale requires a mezzo-soprano to sing Biblical texts. Bernstein's *Age of Anxiety* (1949) derives its expressive substance from a poem by W. H. Auden, and the Symphony No. 3—*Kaddish* (1963) is a huge, sprawling, and highly unconventional work that employs solo voices, chorus, and narrator as well as orchestral resources.

These, and many others, bespeak the symphony's current state of excellence. Because we live in an age of experimentation and change, it may be assumed that the symphonies still to be written will be even more unorthodox and challenging. Certainly, they should be fascinating to hear.

PARTICULAR EXAMPLES OF THE SYMPHONY

Franz Joseph Haydn (1732–1809), Symphony No. 103 in E-flat major

Obedient without being unduly servile, courtly in manner, and always deferential, Joseph Haydn was well-equipped personally and musically to fill his lengthy incumbency as *Kapellmeister* to the extremely wealthy Prince Anton Esterházy. Between 1761 and 1790, little disturbed by the distractions of metropolitan life, he supervised an always-active musical establishment on the huge estate his patron had built in emulation of Louis XIV's Versailles on a dreary swampland in rural Hungary. Prince Anton, an amateur musician himself, delighted so much in performance that he maintained a large orchestra, singers in sufficient number to staff an opera house, and a retinue of associated technicians at the palace of Esterház. Haydn was a general factotum who presided over this assemblage, wrote music for any occasion that might arise (weddings, funerals, festivals, parties, concerts, or church services), saw to rehearsals and performance, and looked after the general well-being of all musicians in the household. After nearly thirty years of service and upon the death of Prince Anton, in 1791, he accepted a pension settled on him by Prince Nicholas, successor in the Esterházy line. Thereafter, Haydn signed a contract that required him to visit England during an eighteen-month period in 1791–1792 and conduct the London Symphony Orchestra in a performance of six specially written symphonies. Subsequently, a return visit was arranged under the same terms for 1794–1795. In all, twelve symphonies, variously called the "Salomon" or "London" symphonies, were composed for use in England. One of these, the Symphony No. 103 in E-flat major, also known as the "Drumroll," had its premiere at London during the spring of 1795. These are its details:

1. *First movement:* An atmosphere of dignified nobility is suggested in the introduction's opening measures as low strings and bassoon, after a prefatory flourish by timpani, solemnly intone an *adagio* theme in triple meter. Subsequently, this subject is taken up by violins, and its extension involves strings, flutes, oboes, bassoons, and horns:

Marked *allegro con spirito,* the movement's main section is in sonata form and sextuple meter (with two beats to the measure). First violins announce the principal theme:

Haydn greatly extends this subject before first violins, supported by a single oboe, sound the subordinate theme, a waltz-like melody with an abundance of rhythmic verve:

Initially, the development becomes involved in a close scrutiny of the principal theme, which sounds in an overlapping manner before passing through a variety of keys. Held in abeyance during early measures, the subordinate theme is not entirely neglected and appears in the key of D-flat as the section nears its close.

More concise than the exposition, the recapitulation presents both subjects in their usual alignment. Before a brief sixteen-measure coda appears, a reminiscence of the *adagio* introduction, complete with drum roll, is heard.

2. *Second movement:* Shifting to the related tonalities of C minor and C major, the second movement is a variation design based on two themes. Written in duple meter, it is actually performed with four beats to the measure at an *allegretto* pace. Announced by violins in minor, the first theme is comparatively lengthy:

The second subject, somewhat akin to the first, shifts to major:

Haydn then presents two variations on each theme according to this plan:

a. Variation on the first theme, whose substance is little altered save for an addition of woodwind embellishments.

b. Variation on the second theme where a solo violin plays a kind of melodic embellishment of which Haydn was fond.

c. Another variation on the first theme, which uses brasses and timpani to sound reiterated fanfares while lower strings play descending scale passages.

d. A final variation on the second theme wherein Haydn treats the subject in a comparatively free manner.

3. *Third movement:* Suggesting a *ländler,* an Austrian rustic dance with strongly marked accents, and back in the key of E-flat major, this menuet with trio has the following plan:

Menuetto	Trio	Menuetto
a (10 measures, repeated)	*c* (8 measures, repeated)	*a* (without repeat)
b + *a* (38 measures, repeated)	*d* + *c* (24 measures, repeated)	*b* + *a* (without repeat)

First violins, doubled by flutes, announce the principal theme *a:*

In due time, violins supported by clarinet introduce a restrained subject *c* that opens the trio:

Recurrence of the menuetto is accomplished via a *da capo*.

4. *Fourth movement:* Vivacious, buoyant, and crisp, Haydn's finale is in duple meter and played at an *allegro con spirito* pace. As it begins, two horns sound a four-measure introduction, after which first violins present the movement's principal theme:

Virtually monothematic, the movement continually reaffirms this subject, which has been called a Croatian folk melody. In several of its subsequent appearances the theme gains harmonic support by being joined with the initial horn subject. Scored for the entire wind section, this idea is also paramount in the concluding coda.

Ludwig van Beethoven (1770–1827), Symphony No. 7 in A major

Conceived during turbulent 1812, when the legions of Napoleon were storming the face of Europe in a last futile effort on the Emperor's behalf, Beethoven's A major Symphony had its premiere at Vienna under the composer's direction in December, 1813. By this time, a progressive worsening of Beethoven's deafness had reached a point where he could hear only the score's loudest passages; indeed, contemporary chronicles reveal that he made a serious *faux pas* while conducting simply because he could not hear a quiet passage!

When he composed the seventh symphony, Beethoven was forty-two years of age, at the height of his career, and an acknowledged master of the pattern. Behind him lay the monumental "Eroica," the invigorating fifth symphony, and the epochal "Pastoral" (Symphony No. 6 in F major). Numerous chamber works, the opera *Fidelio*, several concertos, and a variety of other pieces reveal the breadth of his accomplishments. But even in the midst of this abundance, the Symphony No. 7 glistens as an especially brilliant piece. The succinctness of its themes, the exuberance of its rhythms, the finely chiseled elegance of its formal patterns, and the powerful masculinity of its expressiveness make it a symphony as timeless as the art of music itself. These are details about it:

1. *First movement:* A single crisp orchestral chord announces an introduction of such extensive dimensions as to be the near-equivalent of a movement itself. This is its first idea:

Marked to be played *poco sostenuto,* the introduction is punctuated by agile scale passages over which the initial subject floats with effortless ease. Later, the oboe announces a second idea:

Both themes appear in alternation until a partial cadence on a dominant chord draw the forces together in anticipation of important action to come. In sonata form, sextuple meter (with two beats in a measure), and *vivace* tempo, the movement's main section is almost obsessively concerned with this principal theme:

Over and over, in exposition, development, and recapitulation, this subject, or fragments from it, is reaffirmed; virtually no measure is free of its daemonic thrust. And this impetuous, imperious, and irresistible subject proves itself fully capable of sustaining the torrential flood of energies that ultimately mount to the level of an orchestral tour de force.

2. *Second movement:* Heralded by a sustained A-minor chord, this gentle and gracious section is a direct antipode of the ebullient opening. Marked *allegretto*—the composer later speculated whether it should have been designated *andante*—it moves in duple meter at a deliberate pace to disclose the outlines of a broadly conceived ternary design. The first subject is introduced by violas, 'cellos, and basses:

Subsequently, violas and 'cellos weave an important countermelody around it:

As the movement continues, both themes pass from one instrumental group to another while being continually heard in a masterful display of orchestral polyphony.

At midpoint, the movement shifts to A major as a new subject is announced by clarinets and bassoons over an undulating string accompaniment:

When the third section begins to reaffirm the first two themes, these subjects become embroiled in extensive polyphony. Ultimately, lines of fugal involvement are untangled, and a coda, which reaffirms ideas from both sections, concludes.

3. *Third movement:* One of the longest scherzos in symphonic literature with 653 measures, this movement ventures into the remote key of F major but adheres to a scherzo's conventional triple meter, part-form design, and *presto* tempo. First violins sound this opening theme:

Modulating to D major, the trio assumes a slightly slower pace as clarinets lead other winds in playing this subject:

More than two-thirds of the movement still remains ahead when the trio is concluded, for verbatim reappearances of both the scherzo and trio follow. Then, just prior to an extremely brief coda, the scherzo makes a third complete appearance. Finally, five crisp chords conclude.

4. *Fourth movement:* So frenetic as to suggest an orgiastic peasant dance, this finale sweeps forward with unbridled animation. Consisting of only four measures, its introduction establishes the key: A major; the tempo: *allegro con brio;* and the meter: duple. First violins sound a principal theme notable for its sequential extensions and frequent repetition over a heavily accented accompaniment:

Even more forthright, a second idea is announced by woodwinds:

Later, the subordinate theme, also an irrepressible subject, is sounded by strings and woodwinds:

Despite thematic abundance, the development is solely concerned with the first subject. Passing through a number of keys without losing its identity, this idea consistently displays all the adept nimbleness of a trained acrobat.

Back in major again (the development had shifted temporarily to minor), the recapitulation sounds each of the three themes in a regular sequence before the lengthy coda takes the still pulsating initial theme through more developmental activity. Finally, a tempestuous outpouring of sound closes the work on a series of A major chords.

Felix Mendelssohn (1809–1847), Symphony No. 4 in A major

On express orders from the composer, Mendelssohn's A major Symphony, which many consider a near-perfect work of art, was not published during his lifetime. Although this reticence is rather difficult to understand, numerous letters show that Mendelssohn was continuously dissatisfied with the piece, which undoubtedly accounts for it being called the fourth symphony, although it was written nearly ten years before his "Scotch" Symphony (No. 3 in A minor, 1842).

Surnamed the "Italian" Symphony, this buoyant work, which has now become a fixture in the repertoire, delightfully reflects the warmth and charm characteristically associated with a southern land. Actually, much of it was written in 1831 while Mendelssohn, an indefatigable traveler, sojourned at Rome. But even more to the point as far as the nickname is concerned, is the inclusion of a "Pilgrim's March" in the second movement and a saltarello—an Italian dance of spirited tempo and vigorous rhythm— in the finale. Strangely enough, however, the work had its premiere in England on March 13, 1833 under Mendelssohn's direction. At that time, the composer was twenty-four years of age.

1. *First movement:* Organized in a beautifully proportioned sonata form design, this opening segment begins with a crisp *pizzicato* chord articulated by strings. As woodwinds set up a chattering accompaniment in brisk tempo (marked *allegro vivace*) and compound duple meter (six-eighth time), octave-spaced violins announce an incisive first subject:

After considerable repetition and the appearance of some digressive material, the subordinate theme—more lyric and restrained than its companion—is introduced by clarinets and bassoons and repeated by flutes and oboes:

Because of its fleet nimbleness and comparative brevity, the exposition is usually repeated in performance, a circumstance Mendelssohn obviously desired for he provided lengthy first and second endings in the score.

Opening measures in the development announce a third theme, an unorthodox but delightful inclusion:

Despite its delayed appearance, this subject (which is initially treated in a *fugato* manner) exerts considerable influence on the piece. Indeed, with occasional reminiscences from the principal subject, it becomes a primary basis for the development.

Although foreshortened, the recapitulation runs a usual course. Now the subordinate theme is sounded by 'cellos and reiterated by first violins with, of course, a realignment of tonalities. And the third theme is appended as an integral part of the section. Finally, a rather lengthy coda concludes.

2. *Second movement:* Organized in short rondo form and progressing at a stately pace in quadruple meter, this section suggests a solemn ecclesiastical procession. Oboe, bassoon, and violas are used to announce the principal theme (in D minor) over a rhythmic *ostinato* conveyed by 'cellos and basses:

By way of digression strings present this brief crisp idea:

Subsequently, the clarinet presents an alternate theme that is later taken up by strings:

Relying mostly on its principal and alternate subjects, the movement occasionally uses a brief motive from the introduction. Its rhythmic pulse rests securely on the reiterated bass that continuously pursues a plodding course in a low register.

3. *Third movement:* In lieu of a crisp scherzo, Mendelssohn now employs a piece in ternary form that is a curious cross between a minuet and a waltz. First violins announce its initial idea in A major:

Shifting to E major, the dominant key, the trio features an interesting instrumental dialogue. Initially, bassoons and horns sound a gentle fanfare, embellished by first violins and flute:

Later, other instruments become involved in a similar discourse. After both strains in the trio have been presented and repeated, a near-verbatim reaffirmation of the first section is given. Then, a coda that includes thematic fragments from both parts of the movement concludes.

4. *Fourth movement:* Crisp and invigorating, the finale is a pulsating Italian folk dance. Founded on endlessly repeated dance figurations, this saltarello establishes a *presto* pace in A minor when two flutes announce the principal theme over a cleanly accented string accompaniment:

After this subject undergoes extensive repetition, it is succeeded by an innocuous subordinate theme as the general outlines of a sonata-rondo design unfold. Throughout the movement, orchestral sonority ranges from whisper-soft quietude to an opulent outpouring of sound. But everywhere the touch is incisive and masterly. Nothing could more effectively write *finis* to an especially radiant score.

Antonín Dvořák (1841–1904), Symphony No. 9 in E minor

Already well-established in his native Bohemia and a musician of growing international repute, shortly after 1890 Dvořák was importuned to become director of a newly founded National Conservatory of Music in New York City by Mrs. Jeanette Thurber, its benefactress. Unable to resist the temptation of an annual stipend of $15,000, he set aside a deeply rooted love of homeland and, in the autumn of 1892, with an entourage that included his wife, numerous progeny, a bevy of canaries, clothing, furniture, and servants, took up residence in an apartment at 327 East 17th Street, just east of the Conservatory's building. Dvořák remained on these shores until 1895 before returning to Prague, a comparatively wealthy man whose fame had now become truly international.

Setting about a self-imposed task in 1893 while in New York City, Dvořák composed his Symphony No. 9 in E minor, subtitled "From the New World." Actually the last of Dvořák's symphonies, it immediately aroused considerable discussion over the sources from which its themes were derived. Although he was enigmatic about the matter, and more than a little ambiguous, Dvořák tried, in 1900, to resolve the question by saying that he wrote in the spirit of native melodies—both Indian and Negro—but did not engage in any verbatim quotations. But melodic subjects in this symphony have such rich expressiveness that several—including the often-heard "Goin' Home" theme from the second movement—have been readily accepted within a world-wide treasury of beloved folk songs.

1. *First movement:* Opening quietly in E minor, 'cellos and woodwinds sustain a gentle discourse in *adagio* tempo that is occasionally enlivened by vigorous (and loud) interjections. When the tempo changes to *allegro molto,* the exposition presents this principal subject, sounded by horns and middle-voiced woodwinds:

After the usual repetitions and transitional passages have been heard, the subordinate subject, which includes two distinctive ideas, appears. The first has a narrow compass and could qualify as being in G minor if it did not use an occasional F-natural (the latter's presence places it in the Dorian mode):

A second member, clearly in G major, is announced by a lone flute in the low register:

In the development, this latter subject gains initial attention. Occasional quotations of the principal theme are interlarded, and the section soon becomes a musical battleground where continuous and sometimes near-frenetic action ensues. Almost precipitously the recapitulation appears, and the movement's three themes are heard in regular alignment, with, however, an altered scheme of tonalities as Dvořák engages his bent for wide-ranging modulations. Bold and brash, the coda has an ear-shattering terminus.

2. *Second movement:* Choosing the remote key of D-flat major as a tonal locus for this celebrated *largo,* Dvořák provides a progression of seven modulatory chords to lead into the movement. Sounded by brasses and low woodwinds, it begins in E major and concludes in D-flat. Then, with the tonality established, strings provide harmonic underpinnings for a lovely melody played by the English horn that many have likened to a spiritual:

Organized in a loosely conceived ternary design, the movement shifts to C-sharp minor and assumes a more rapid pace at its midpoint as flute and oboe sound this theme:

Considerable interest later rests on a flowing *legato* subject that clarinets with oboe support sound over a sturdy *pizzicato* bass:

Before the first section returns, a sonorous climax is attained wherein the first movement's principal theme is heard *fortissimo*. Subsequently, the spiritual-like English horn melody reappears, but its expanse is shortened and the instrumental hues altered. After the opening chordal progression has been sounded by winds, a conclusion is attained on an eerie-sounding D-flat chord assigned to string basses.

3. *Third movement:* A boisterous scherzo does duty in this portion of Dvořák's symphony. Some vacillation occurs, however, for the tempos vary (although triple meter remains constant throughout), and the tonality shifts from E minor to the parallel major as well as into adjacent keys. Basically a ternary design, the movement is founded on a crisp and

incisive first subject and a restrained and flowing second theme. Here is a quotation of both:

Before the midsection appears, a transitional passage again interpolates the principal theme from the first movement, sounded by the 'cellos in a deep register.

Presented by woodwinds over an undulating string figuration, this is the trio's principal idea:

Subsequently, a *da capo* brings back this movement's opening strains, after which an extended coda again reiterates the first movement theme as if to stress the symphony's over-all cohesiveness.

4. *Fourth movement:* Unrepressed vigor surges from this *allegro con fuoco* finale. After a spirited introduction, wherein strings literally rip heavily accented tones from their instruments, horns and trumpet sound this incisive principal theme:

Somewhat later, when a solo clarinet presents this theme as part of the subordinate subject, quietude pervades the movement:

Subsequently, strings announce a second subordinate idea:

Developmental activity initially becomes concerned with the principal theme, after which the lyric subject from the second movement and the first movement's principal theme are taken up.

Remarkably condensed, the recapitulation reaffirms each of the finale's subjects before a lengthy coda—which cites themes from both the first and second movements—brings the entire work to a climactic close.

Dmitri Shostakovich (b. 1906), Symphony No. 1

One of the Soviet Union's most outstanding contemporary composers, Shostakovich has clearly established himself as a symphonist of international renown. Since producing the Symphony No. 1 in his twentieth year (1926), he has published twelve others (the Symphony No. 13 dates from 1962), which shows that he is almost continually at work in this important musical domain.

Shostakovich unquestionably has a unique manner of writing. Many of his melodies are elfin-like subjects, often motivic in outline, that writhe, toss, turn, and gyrate with irrepressible abandon; but others—often assigned to high strings or solo flute—are expansive themes that soar and float like birds drifting effortlessly in a limitless sky. His orchestral colors are always piquant (solos for such distinctive voices as clarinet, oboe, trumpet, or solo violin abound), and he paints in vivid hues with the skill of a born orchestrator. Although his harmonic procedures are contemporary and extremely effective, like other musical qualities in his works they are adroitly fashioned and rarely shocking. And his fundamental aesthetic scheme is never so occult as to be incomprehensible. These are details about Shostakovich's Symphony No. 1, written just one year after he had received a graduation diploma from the Leningrad Conservatory:

1. *First movement:* Engaging in flip colloquy, the solo trumpet and bassoon sound a theme that is later taken up by other instruments, chiefly strings, as the movement's fifty-seven measure introductory section begins:

March-like in character, this pert whimsical subject played at an *allegretto* tempo in F minor by a solo clarinet becomes the movement's principal theme:

Immediately repeated by octave-spaced violins, and subsequently bandied about between other instruments, this subject soon gives way to the subordinate theme. Shifting to triple meter and assuming a slightly slower tempo, the second subject is presented by a solo flute in C minor:

Shostakovich's architectural plan in this movement hovers somewhere between sonata form and sonatina form. Apparently wishing to telescope the design, after a twenty-seven measure interlude between the exposition and recapitulation, he reaffirms portions of the principal theme in a new key and elaborates on them at the same time. In succession, the subordinate theme appears, this time in the unconventional key of A minor, after which the closing section reaffirms the principal theme in the home tonality of F minor. Based on the introduction's puckish subject, the coda concludes with an interesting interchange between several solo instruments.

2. *Second movement:* An extremely agile scherzo becomes a successor to the dynamic opening movement. Organized in large ternary form (*ABA*) and established in the key of A minor, it effectively uses a piano's dry percussive sounds in juxtaposition with conventional orchestral sonorities. After a thirteen-measure introduction, the first theme is sounded by first violins, reiterated by piano, and later passed to the bassoon:

For the midsection (trio), Shostakovich shifts to E minor and triple meter. Two flutes, and then two clarinets, sound this subject above an inverted pedal point on "E":

Subsequently, the rhythmic pulse shifts back to the original quadruple meter as bassoon and others cavort with uninhibited glee. Later, both subjects are combined as brasses intone the trio's somber theme against the fluent scherzo melody. Finally, the coda is quiet and pensive.

3. *Third movement:* Clinging to ternary form but shifting to the remote key of D-flat major, the third movement begins as a solo oboe sounds this restrained idea over a sustained string background:

Marked *lento,* the first section ultimately gives way to a slower *largo* as the movement enters its middle portion; again the solo oboe is spokesman and announces this second subject:

First violins, supported by other strings, bring the initial theme back to constitute the movement's third section. Near its close, both subjects are combined in a polyphonic discourse between solo trumpet and 'cellos and basses. The close is quiet except for a sustained snare drum roll that builds to a climax as it leads directly into the finale.

4. *Fourth movement:* Filled with abrupt changes in tempo, dynamics, and meter, this closing movement becomes a grand musical mélange. Following a subdued introduction, an *allegro molto* section in F minor presents this nimble subject:

After the principal theme has been heard repeatedly, a shift is made to A major where the entire ensemble sounds this expansive melody:

Later, the second subject is repeated by a solo violin and reiterated a third time by a solo horn. From this point, the movement pursues a course wherein its first theme is passed through the orchestra much as a basketball is tossed between players. After a pre-emptory pause, a solo 'cello reaffirms the second theme in restrained terms. But tranquility does not last, and both subjects are combined—with trombones playing the first and strings and woodwinds the second—in the key of F major as the movement builds to a climax. Moving in a vigorous *accelerando,* the finale ultimately comes to a tumultuous close.

Selected Symphonies

Beethoven, Ludwig van (1770–1827)
    Symphony No. 3 in E-flat major ("Eroica," 1803). An exalted, broadly conceived and excellent work dedicated to "the heroic nature of mankind," it is lengthy, architecturally superb, and powerfully assertive.

Symphony No. 5 in C minor (1807). This is the composer's best-known symphony. Unusually dynamic and aggressive, its first movement is founded on a celebrated "fate" motive. The third and fourth movements are linked.

Symphony No. 7 in A major (1812). Strong and impassioned with an abundance of dance-like rhythms, this piece is pulsating, vigorous, and memorable.

Symphony No. 9 in D minor ("Choral," 1823). An unusually long piece, three of its movements are instrumental but the finale uses chorus, orchestra, and vocal soloists to convey a Schiller text. It is splendidly epic and monumental.

Berlioz, Hector (1803–1869)

Symphonie fantastique (1830). Reputedly autobiographical, this symphony narrates a bizarre program about a would-be suicide. Extremely colorful, it has five movements.

Roméo et Juliette, Symphonie dramatique (1839). Cast in an unusual format, chorus, orchestra, and soloists are used to convey episodes from Shakespeare's drama. It is lengthy, discursive, and epochal.

Symphonie funèbre et triomphale (1840). Written to commemorate the nation's war dead, it is scored for wind band and chorus. It is grandiloquent, noisy, and impassioned.

Bernstein, Leonard (b. 1918)

"Jeremiah" Symphony (1943). A sweeping contemporary symphony that depicts three ideas from the Book of Lamentations, the music is glowing, mystical, and occasionally jazzy.

Symphony No. 3–*Kaddish* (1963). Also scripturally oriented, this massive work uses narrator, soloists, orchestra, and chorus to express ideas that are fervent, eloquent, and exalted.

Bizet, Georges (1838–1875)

Symphony No. 1 in C major (first performance 1935). "Lost" (on library shelves) for sixty years, it is classical in conception and elegant in design.

Borodin, Alexander (1833–1887)

Symphony No. 2 in B minor (1877). Obviously Russian in substance, this symphony is powerful and almost barbaric in expression; still, its melodies and harmonies have an attractive, pristine beauty.

Brahms, Johannes (1833–1897)

Symphony No. 1 in C minor (1876). Majestic, with a close-knit structure, this music has an abundance of captivating lyricism that makes it readily accessible.

Symphony No. 2 in D major (1877). This is a warm, sentimental, and structurally solid work that literally glows with the vibrance of musical Romanticism.

Symphony No. 3 in F major (1883). An epitome of symphonic lyricism, this symphony is regular in outline yet comparatively brief in expanse.

Symphony No. 4 in E minor (1885). By turns heroic, pensive, witty, and dynamic, this is a massive and noble work. Its finale is a brilliant passacaglia.

Britten, Benjamin (b. 1913)

A Simple Symphony for Strings (1934). Boisterous, playful, sentimental, and frolicsome, this symphony of recent vintage suggests a gay musical romp.

Spring Symphony (1949). Suite-like rather than symphonic, soloists and chorus are used to articulate fourteen poems by various English authors.

Bruckner, Anton (1824–1896)

Symphony No. 4 in E-flat major ("Romantic," revised 1880). Leisurely, flowing, and delightfully melodic, this symphony is almost seraphic in expression; the third movement is a splendid scherzo.

Symphony No. 7 in E major (1883). Angelic, serene, and abstract, this represents the traditional symphony in an unusually expansive format.

Chausson, Ernest (1855–1899)

Symphony in B-flat major (1890). Discursive and sometimes rambling, this three-movement symphony maintains an interesting cyclic thematic relationship between its sections.

Copland, Aaron (b. 1900)

Symphony No. 3 (1946). A bold and solidly constructed modern work in a traditional pattern; it is clean, clear, and colorful.

Dvořák, Antonín (1841–1904)

Symphony No. 8 in G major (old No. 4, 1889). Packed with warm Bohemian melodism, this is a poetic, splendidly constructed, and altogether satisfying piece.

Symphony No. 9 in E minor ("From the New World," old No. 5, 1893). Employing folk-like melodies and a magnificent pattern, this is a dynamic, ebullient symphony written while the composer resided in the United States.

Filtz, Anton (1726–1760)

Sinfonia a8 in A major, *Sinfonia periodique* No. 2 (c. 1750). A charming representative of the pre-Classical symphony, this piece has four movements and is scored for strings, two horns, and two flutes.

Franck, César (1822–1890)

Symphony in D minor (1889). Compact, in three movements, very melodic, and unusually opulent in sound, this symphony employs the cyclic method of thematic recurrence and frequent modulations.

Goldmark, Karl (1830–1915)

Symphony in E-flat major ("Rustic Wedding," 1860). Whimsical, charming, and somewhat peasant-like, it has five movements that depict a rural nuptial celebration.

Harris, Roy (b. 1898).

Symphony No. 3 (1938). Organized in a single movement that expresses a diversity of moods, it is new, different, and has a distinctly pungent timbre.

Symphony No. 4 ("Folksong," 1940). Employing a plethora of American folk melodies, it has seven movements and requires chorus and orchestra for performance. It is quaint and off-beat.

Haydn, Franz Joseph (1732–1809)

Symphonies Nos. 92–98 (1790–1792). Outstanding Classical works written to coincide with the composer's first London visit, these six pieces reflect the era's concept of musical elegance. Formal in outline and occasionally austere in expression, they are mostly buoyant, vivacious, and altogether charming.

Symphonies Nos. 99–104 (1793–1794). Comprising a second set of "London" symphonies, these are cast in the conventional four-movement pattern, employ a relatively large orchestra (for this period), are sunny and spirited in outlook, and are superbly written.

Hindemith, Paul (1895–1963)

Mathis der Maler (1934). A somewhat unusual contemporary symphony extracted from an opera score, this has three movements and is pungent, terse, and linear in substance and spirit.

Symphony in B-flat major for Band (1951). An impressive three-movement work for winds that has a complex texture, it is continually active and rarely melodic.

d'Indy, Vincent (1851–1931)

Symphony on a French Mountain Air (1886). Based on a Cévennes folk melody, this sparkling and animated work employs a solo piano and is cyclic in thematic usage.

Ives, Charles (1874–1954)

Symphony No. 2 (1897–1902). Combining hymns, college songs, national tunes in a bold and brash mélange, this is a distinctive and unique piece. Other works by this enterprising American (Symphony: "Holidays," 1904–1913 and Symphony No. 4, 1916) are similarly daring and imaginative.

Liszt, Franz (1811–1886)

Faust Symphony (after Goethe, 1857). This selection includes character studies of Faust, Gretchen, and Mephistopheles in the symphonic idiom. The piece is variegated, smooth, and very poetic.

Mahler, Gustav (1860–1911)

Symphony No. 1 in D major (1889). Nostalgic and melodic, the four movements in this piece abound with unusual instrumental effects; over all it is spacious and tranquil.

Symphony No. 2 in C minor ("Resurrection," 1894). Metaphysical, questioning, and daring, its five movements use various texts, soloists, chorus, and orchestra to express heaven-storming, spectacular ideas.

Symphony No. 4 in G major (1901). Atmospheric Viennese melodism appears here in richly hued symphonic robes; its finale uses a contralto to convey a gentle, haunting, folk text.

Symphony No. 5 in C-sharp minor (1902). By turns funereal, martial, and occasionally wild, this superb piece is organized in five movements and has themes that are mostly somber and brilliantly epic in expression.

Mendelssohn, Felix (1809–1847).

Symphony No. 3 in A minor ("Scotch," 1842). Radiant and buoyant, this splendid Romantic work has classic design and a fervent spirit; mostly it is whimsical, pictorial, and piquant.

Symphony No. 4 in A major ("Italian," 1833). Brilliant, sunny, and vital, with a superb architectural plan, it has an abundance of glittering themes and is virtually irresistible.

Mozart, Wolfgang Amadeus (1756–1791)

Symphony No. 35 in D major ("Haffner") K. 385 (1782); Symphony No. 36 in C major ("Linz") K. 425 (1783); Symphony No. 38 in D major ("Prague") K. 504 (1786). Reflecting the formal brilliance of Classicism, these are further warmed by the composer's glowing melodic ardor. Clinging to the established symphonic pattern, they are nonetheless individual, flowing, gracious, and suggestive of festive splendor. Unquestionably, they rank with the era's best.

Symphony No. 39 in E-flat major, K. 543; Symphony No. 40 in G minor, K. 550; Symphony No. 41 in C major, ("Jupiter") K. 551 (all 1788). The quintessence of Classic symphonism, these three pieces were written in less than two months. Permeated with compassion, pathos, and idealism, they follow the four-movement format but have such unique substance as to be absolutely nonpareil.

Nielsen, Carl (1865–1931)

Symphony No. 5 (1922). Startlingly different and occasionally grim, this epic masterwork by a little-known Danish composer is in two movements. Other notable pieces are his Symphonies No. 3 (1912); No. 4 (1916); and No. 6 (1925).

Piston, Walter (b. 1894)

Symphony No. 4 (1949). Folksy, full-blooded, but dignified in mien, this fine American work has four movements, is well-written, and is filled with buoyant gusto.

Prokofiev, Serge (1891–1953)

Symphony No. 1 in D major ("Classical," 1917). Deliberately anachronistic, glib, and puckishly antiquarian, this satirical piece is varicolored, crisp, and wittily insouciant.

Symphony No. 5 (1944). One of the twentieth century's best, this symphony is bold, powerful, occasionally dissonant, and architectonically excellent.

Symphony No. 7 (1953). Broadly melodic and surprisingly consonant for Prokofiev, this is a flowing, warm, and tender piece.

Rachmaninoff, Sergei (1873–1943)

Symphony No. 2 in E minor (1907). Evoking post-Romanticism in modern times, this is lush, tuneful, and pleasant. But it is almost overpowering in its emotionality.

Roussel, Albert (1869–1937)

Symphony No. 3 in G minor (1930). Aloof, recondite, and anti-Impressionistic, Roussel's symphony is both formal and cyclic, with a delicate outline and a well-balanced structure.

Saint-Saëns, Camille (1835–1921)

Symphony No. 3 in C minor ("Organ," 1886). Scored for orchestra, organ, and piano (two players), this piece in two segments is an eminently logical, lucid, and masterly disclosure of memorable ideas.

Schubert, Franz (1797–1828)

Symphony No. 4 in C minor ("Tragic," c. 1816); Symphony No. 5 in B-flat major (c. 1817); Symphony No. 6 in C major ("Little," 1818). Modest in dimension but filled with mature expressiveness, these surprisingly bold (in harmonic-thematic invention) works for Classical orchestra, written when the composer was in his late teens, are cleanly hewn, quietly restrained, and sweetly idyllic.

Symphony No. 8 in B minor ("Unfinished," 1822). Touched with autumnal sadness, this two-movement piece is unusually melodic, quietly resigned, and graciously tranquil in expression.

Symphony No. 9 in C major ("The Great," 1828). Magnificent, lengthy, and heroic, this full-scale work has a beautiful pattern, is wonderfully wrought, and is fervently Romantic in outlook.

Schuman, William (b. 1910)

Symphony No. 3 (1941). Bold, virtuosic, individual, and stunningly modern, this symphony follows a traditional pattern but employs a unique, contemporary syntax.

Schumann, Robert (1810–1856)

Symphony No. 1 in B-flat major ("Spring," 1841). Filled with vernal freshness and youthful exuberance, this is a songful, Romantic, and buoyant work.

Symphony No. 2 in C major (1846). Between a dynamic beginning and a powerful close, there is a riotous scherzo and an ingratiating adagio. The entire piece is tuneful and sweet.

Symphony No. 3 in E-flat major ("Rhenish," 1850). Almost folk-like, this gracious symphony suggests the character of hospitable Rhinelanders. It is broad, sweeping, and attractive.

Symphony No. 4 in D minor (revised 1851). Integrated by thematic means, the four movements, unfortunately, have a thick and heavy sound. Unquestionably, it is Schumann's least attractive symphony.

Shostakovich, Dmitri (b. 1906)

Symphony No. 1 in F major (1925). Irrepressible and bumptious, this symphony follows a normal four-movement pattern, but its material and expression are witty, biting, and dissonant.

Symphony No. 5 (1937). A contemporary masterwork, this is occasionally craggy and angular in melodic outline, with a pert scherzo and an almost barbaric finale.

Sibelius, Jean (1865–1957)

Symphony No. 1 in E minor (1899). Uncompromising in essence, this is a luminous piece with frequent touches of lyricism. Typically Nordic in outlook, it intermingles pathos with grandeur.

Symphony No. 2 in D major (1901). Filled with original ideas shaped in an unconventional manner, this piece nevertheless follows a symphony's usual pattern. But its procedures are bold, and its façade is unusually imposing.

Strauss, Richard (1864–1949)

Domestic Symphony (1903). An unusual one-movement piece with four subdivisions, this descriptive work is intended to depict family life. Coy, amusing, and written with prodigious skill, it is nevertheless artistically questionable.

Stravinsky, Igor (b. 1882)

Symphony of Psalms (1930). This is a spare, almost stark, rhetoric work in three movements. Within it chorus and orchestra convey a taut, immensely compelling discourse based on selected *Psalm* texts.

Symphony in Three Movements (1945). Devoid of conventional patterns, this contemporary work uses blocks of sound in a strong and invigorating way. It is ambitious, different, and iconcoclastic.

Tchaikowsky, Peter (1840–1893)

Symphony No. 1 in G minor ("Winter Dreams," 1868); Symphony No. 2

in C minor ("Little Russian," revised, 1881); Symphony No. 3 in D major ("Polish," 1875). These beguiling and gracious early works in the composer's symphonic output are formally perfect and splashed with glowing color. The Symphony No. 3 has five movements, the others have four. In all, they are little-known symphonic gems.

Symphony No. 4 in F minor (1878). Frenetic, unbridled, and occasionally raucous, this exciting work has a lyric second movement and a fine, scherzo-like third wherein much *pizzicato* is used. It is often performed.

Symphony No. 5 in E minor (1888). An exceptionally sentimental symphony that uses a motto theme to bind and relate its four movements, this is yielding, sweet, and unforgettable.

Symphony No. 6 in B minor (1893). Brooding, morbid, and weighty, with a deeply introspective finale, this piece strikes the ultimate in symphonic pensiveness.

Vaughan Williams, Ralph (1872–1958)

Symphony No. 2 ("London," 1920). Describing the topography and life of a great city in general terms, this big and rambling symphony is atmospheric, vibrant, and convincing.

Symphony No. 4 in F minor (1935). Acrid and seemingly disillusioned, this music is thickly scored, monumental, and epic; but it is hardly attractive.

Chapter 18

Opera: A Merger of Music and Drama

An unusually elaborate musicodramatic design that requires a large number of participants for adequate performance, opera has played an important part in the artistic life of virtually every civilized country of the world for more than three and a half centuries. Since about 1600, this composite form—which lays primary stress on poetry, drama, and music, but also includes such peripheral arts as scenic design, costuming, ballet, and lighting—has delighted countless thousands of theater-goers. Of course, its styles have changed considerably during the intervening years, and few works predating the time of Mozart (d. 1791) remain in our present-day repertoire. Still, modern opera (that written in the nineteenth and twentieth centuries) has much in common with the basic pattern formulated by Italian litterateurs who pioneered in devising *opera per musica* very late in the sixteenth century as the Renaissance was giving way to the Baroque.

Simply stated, opera is drama set to music, but its subtleties greatly transcend such a general comment. Both drama and opera are enacted in a theater by a cast of men, women, and occasionally children, who emote, gesticulate, declaim, and posture while portraying their roles. Where drama emphasizes the spoken word, however, opera stresses music, for nearly all who participate in its performance are called on to sing. Moreover, music's omnipresence in opera is sustained by an orchestra that accompanies singers, provides introductions, interludes, and epilogues for vocal pieces, and occasionally contributes selections of its own.

Despite an aura of grandeur that surrounds it, and a venerable tradition that sustains it, opera suffers from a number of problems. Works of this kind require a large number of participants and huge amounts of paraphernalia; they are, consequently, cumbersome and unwieldy in operation and almost prohibitively expensive to produce. Creating opera in the first place usually involves collaboration between several individuals (a librettist, composer, impresario, and others), and its performance necessarily enlists a phalanx of singers, instrumentalists, stagehands, designers, and theatrical technicians.

And although a string quartet can perform in a modest size room, a band in an athletic arena, or an orchestra in an auditorium, opera requires a theater and all the resources that go with it for adequate presentation.

Figure 21.   Scene from Act I of Puccini's *Tosca*.

OPERA'S COMPONENT ARTS

Some arts in the operatic complex engage one's visual sense, while others attract the ear. Among the principal ones are

1. *Poetry:* the linguistic portions of a piece that are sung, declaimed (usuall in recitative), or spoken. Often, this verbal material is rhymed, although poetic flow may be sacrificed occasionally to satisfy musical exigencies. In its totality, this literary material is known as the *libretto*.
2. *Drama:* the activities of movement, gesticulation, or pantomime that normally engage an opera-goer's eye. Directions concerning these are cited in the libretto.
3. *Music:* all the lyric aspects of a score including vocal and orchestral passages, bridges, entr'actes, ballet music, or overtures.

Of the subordinate arts that contribute color and enhanced communicativeness to opera, these are especially significant:

1. *Scenic design:* concerned with the conception, manufacture, and installation of props, curtains, backdrops, or furniture necessary to make stage action credible.

2. *Costuming:* designing, creating, and fitting the garments that members of a cast wear to make their dramatic enactment effective.
3. *Ballet:* pantomimic movements of the dance that bring beauty and environmental authenticity to many operatic situations.
4. *Lighting:* an enrichment of opera's visual aspects to accentuate dramatic scenes and minimize some of the theater's shortcomings.

Ways in which these resources may be utilized vary considerably from one opera to another. Some "grand" operas (Wagner's *Tannhaüser,* Verdi's *Aida*) emphasize lavish scenic effects, whereas others (Stravinsky's *Oedipus Rex,* Berg's *Wozzeck*) have settings that are stark to the point of barrenness. Debussy's *Pelléas et Mélisande* relies heavily on subdued lighting to establish an appropriate milieu, while such widely disparate works as Schoenberg's *Erwartung* and Mozart's *The Marriage of Figaro* use it as a means of localizing audience attention. Particular operas (Verdi's *La Traviata,* Gounod's *Faust,* Strauss' *Die Fledermaus*) contain scintillating ballet, but others (Beethoven's *Fidelio,* Wagner's "Ring" operas) ignore it.

THE DRAMATIC ESSENCE OF OPERA

Opera is at its best when probing diverse aspects of the human personality and depicting qualities that are virtuous or evil, selfish or generous, heroic or cowardly. Because the stage requires large-scale portrayal (because of distances involved), picayune sentiments and intimate gestures are usually avoided. Everything in the theater must be larger than life, and exaggeration in gesture, movement, rhetoric, or emotion is common. Even though the lyric stage is almost always concerned with humans, however, all that occurs thereon is not consistently credible.

Some operas are founded on pre-existent dramas: Verdi's *Rigoletto* (1851) is taken from Victor Hugo's *Le Roi s'amuse* (The Amusement of Kings); Mozart's *The Marriage of Figaro* (1786) is derived from a play of the same name by Beaumarchais (pseudonym for Pierre A. Caron); Puccini's *Tosca* (1900) is drawn from a play of the same title by Victorien Sardou; Verdi's *Otello* (1887) and *Falstaff* (1893) are from Shakespeare's *Othello* and *The Merry Wives of Windsor,* respectively; and Debussy's *Pélleas et Mélisande* (1902) is from a drama of the same name by Maurice Maeterlinck. Others find apt subjects for musicodramatic treatment in history (Mussorgsky's *Boris Godounov*); legend (Gounod's *Faust*); contemporary affairs (Beethoven's *Fidelio*); sociological circumstances (Gershwin's *Porgy and Bess*); personality studies (Bizet's *Carmen*); and Scripture (Saint-Saëns' *Samson et Dalila*).

Dramatically viewed, most opera hovers about the unfolding of a primary plot that may describe episodes in the life of a single individual, as in Mozart's *Don Giovanni,* Verdi's *Aida,* and Donizetti's *Lucia di Lammermoor.* So that some relief may be gained, subplots are often interposed.

These may be comic (as the interplay between Jacquino and Marcelline in Beethoven's *Fidelio*); tender and charming (as between Fenton and Anne in Verdi's *Falstaff*); or sinister (as the actions of Sparafucile in Verdi's *Rigoletto*). Sometimes several digressive lines are introduced, as in Mussorgsky's *Boris Godounov* where exchanges with the Czar's children, Xenia and Feodor; actions of two miscreant monks, Missail and Varlaam; and a love episode betwen Dmitri and Marina provide respite from the basic plot concerned with Boris' decline and death.

Almost inevitably, opera sweeps to a climax. Such a denouement normally occurs at the peak of rising tension, after which accumulated emotions are resolved and the work closes. Particular operas may have more than one climax. During the second act of Puccini's *Tosca*, for instance, the heroine kills Scarpia in an extremely tense scene, yet the principal climax is still to come, for it is only in the third act that both Tosca and her lover, Cavaradossi, meet an unfortunate end.

Opera naturally embraces a variety of dramatic ideas. Some are tragic in outcome (Verdi's *Otello*, Berg's *Wozzeck*, Leoncavallo's *I Pagliacci*), whereas others are farcical (Mozart's *The Marriage of Figaro*, Rossini's *The Barber of Seville*, Donizetti's *Don Pasquale*). Particular works take their substance from folk customs (Smetana's *The Bartered Bride*), others depict social mores in a particular stratum of society (Strauss' *Die Fledermaus*). Many portray self-sacrificing heroines (Wagner's *The Flying Dutchman*, Verdi's *Aida*); some are founded on a display of lust, violence and death (Richard Strauss' *Salome*, Mascagni's *Cavalleria Rusticana*, Stravinsky's *The Rake's Progress*). Seemingly, the sum total of human experience has been portrayed on the lyric stage.

THE PROBLEMS OF LANGUAGE

Sometimes taken for granted, the textual substance of opera is nevertheless extremely important, for it gives poignancy and meaning to a work's intellectual content. When creating a musicodramatic work, a composer must be at pains to consider the lilt and flow of language, the ideas it projects, the situations it creates, and how he can best employ all of music's materials to enlarge on the images that words arouse. Almost always the language employed in opera is native (or at least extremely well-known) to both librettist and composer, and it should be equally meaningful to the audience they are addressing. In recent times language barriers have been softened, but enough difficulties still remain to make it necessary for writers to consider their works as being German, French, Italian, Russian or (all too rarely) English in substance and style.

Several factors give stability to an opera's original language. As the primary text for which a musical score is created, it enjoys intimate relations with the melodic line in matters of syntax and nuance. Purists are not motivated by conservatism alone when they prefer opera in its original language, for an aura of authenticity, congruity, and charm is undeniably set aside when modifications are introduced.

When opera is exported, converting its language to a new tongue poses thorny problems. Translating any text so that it remains clear and meaningful is difficult, but a retention of versification in an operatic libretto is extremely troublous. Not only is a sustaining of alliteration problematic; subtleties of expression, allusions, and hints of *double-entendre* lose color, suggestiveness, and dramatic impact in the process of transliteration. Most burdensome of all, of course, is the task of merging a newly translated text with previously composed musical lines.

ORGANIZATIONAL PATTERNS IN OPERA

Plays are usually divided into acts and these, in turn, are subdivided into scenes. So, too, are operas. From a dramatic point of view, the differences between acts normally represent a major lapse in time or an important shift in setting, whereas scenes suggest minor changes in either. As a matter of course, the stage curtain is dropped between acts, but in theatrical performance scenes usually flow into one another separated only by altered lighting or minor adjustments in setting.

Operatic acts are often prefaced (before the curtain rises) by an overture, prelude, or entr'acte, and scenes may be bridged or set apart by similar orchestral passages. Many lyric dramas are "number operas," which is to say they are constituted from a series of autonomous units (that is, numbers) separated from one another by full cadences and a brief pause, which, in the theater, may be filled with audience applause. Depending on its style (see p. 550), an opera may interpose spoken dialogue, declamation, or recitative between musical numbers, which characteristically contrast with one another in melody, key, rhythmic qualities, expressive intent, and the performer or group who sings them.

The amount of set pieces (numbers) in an opera varies. Rossini's *Barber of Seville*, for instance, has twenty; Verdi's *Rigoletto* has only fourteen; and Mozart's *Don Giovanni* has twenty-four. Naturally, the length of individual numbers, as well as an opera's total expanse, has a bearing on their plentitude. Because numbers are usually autonomous, continuity for the entire work can be maintained by linking them with:

1. *Spoken dialogue:* a technique typically used in works for the light theater. An excellent means of furthering the dramatic narrative, prose insertions are common in German *singspiel* (see p. 551), French *opéra comique*, English-language operettas, comic operas, or musical comedies.
2. *Recitative:* a kind of declamation existing at a midpoint between intensified speech and sustained song. Employing rhythms, pitches, and rather

spare supportive harmonies, recitative is analogous to chant-like cantillation, but it does not have the symmetrical phrase structure of melody.
Two kinds of recitative are commonly used in opera, oratorio, and associated vocal works:

a. *recitativo secco* (dry recitative): which requires the voice to declaim
   over a sketchy accompaniment provided by a keyboard instrument,
   typically the harpsichord. Prior to 1800, *recitativo secco* enjoyed a heyday. Today's audiences, however, hear it only in such pieces as Mozart's
   The Marriage of Figaro and *Cosi fan tutti*, and Rossini's *The Barber
   of Seville*.

b. *recitativo accompagnato* (sometimes termed *recitativo stromentato*,
   accompanied recitative): which is more musically involved than its
   associate and requires orchestral support. Approximating the sustained
   lyricism of song, it does not include the memorable phrases of bona fide
   melody, as is shown by the connectives employed in Donizetti's *Lucia
   di Lammermoor*, Verdi's *La Traviata*, or Wagner's *Tannhaüser*.

3. *Orchestral passages:* which may act as introductions, interludes, or connectives. Because the orchestra is a noncommittal voice, its pronouncements can serve a variety of expressive purposes, as is demonstrated for
   instance, with *Siegfried's Rhine Journey* in Wagner's *Götterdämmerung*
   or the ballet music in Gounod's *Faust*.

To illustrate the architectural scheme of a typical number opera, here
is a listing of segments in the first act of Rossini's *The Barber of Seville*
(1816). After an overture has been played by the orchestra alone, these
individual pieces are heard:

1. *Piano, pianissimo*	tenor, baritone, men's chorus
2. *Ecco ridente in cielo*	tenor aria
3. *Ehi! Fiorello*	tenor, baritone, men's chorus
4. *Largo al factotum*	baritone aria
5. *Se il mio nome*	tenor aria
6. *All' idea di quel metallo*	tenor and baritone duet
7. *Una voce poco fa*	soprano aria
8. *La calunnia e un venticello*	bass aria
9. *Dunque io son*	soprano and baritone duet
10. *A un dottor della mia sorte*	bass aria
11. *Ehi, di casa*	finale by full ensemble

Number opera is quite easy to assimilate, but dramatic continuity unquestionably suffers in such a work. Consequently, to provide dramatically
cogent lyric drama, *through-composed opera* came into being. Within it, at
least in theory, individual numbers (arias, ensembles, and choruses) are
avoided, the musical flow is continuous, cadences are evaded or postponed,

and the textual line is sung in a free-flowing arioso. More than anyone else, Richard Wagner implemented through-composed opera when he formulated his *gesamtkunstwerk* (all-embracing art form) and demonstrated its theories in the Ring Cycle (written between 1854–1874). Although he did not consistently practice what he preached, Wagner expended herculean efforts to strengthen opera (he preferred to call it music drama). His technique is clearly demonstrated in the first act of *Die Walküre* (1856, part of the Ring Cycle), an operatic segment that is comparable in length to the portion from the Rossini opera already mentioned. This is its outline:

1. *Prelude and Scene I:* After an orchestral preface of modest length, two leading characters (Siegmund, tenor, and Sieglinde, soprano) appear and exchange comments in declamatory recitative. *Leitmotifs* (brief thematic incipits) are continually expressed by voices and orchestra during this lengthy discourse, but no pauses or separations occur.
2. *Scene II:* Joining these two, a third character (Hunding, bass) enters and assumes an important role in the conversation. The "endless melody" (Wagner's term) continues as before.
3. *Scene III:* Considerable dramatic conflict has now been built up, but the musical flow is unremitting. Much emphasis is given the orchestral line, and important pronouncements (in arioso) are continually made by the singers. From one end of the act to the other, however, no full cadences appear.

Revolutionary in its time, Wagner's thesis was far from faulty, and numerous subsequent composers have adopted his innovations. Although he worked in an entirely different cultural milieu, Giuseppe Verdi moved toward through-composed opera with *Otello* (1887) and *Falstaff* (1893). So, too, did such other Italians as Pietro Mascagni (*Cavalleria Rusticana*, 1890); Ruggiero Leoncavallo (*I Pagliacci*, 1892); and Giacomo Puccini (*La Bohème*, 1896, *Tosca*, 1900, and *Madama Butterfly*, 1904). Occasional individual numbers exist within these scores, but lines of continuity between them are so strong that, for the most part, a listener is taken from one to another with scarcely a perceptible break. In other lands during later years, integrated opera gained stature. In France, Gustave Charpentier (*Louise*, 1900) and Claude Debussy (*Pélleas et Mélisande*, 1904) employed its procedures, as did such Viennese Expressionists as Arnold Schoenberg (*Erwartung*, 1909, *Moses und Aron*, 1951) and Alban Berg (*Wozzeck*, 1921 and *Lulu*, 1934). Recently composed English-language operas, including Gian-Carlo Menotti's *The Medium* (1946), Benjamin Britten's *Peter Grimes* (1945), or Samuel Barber's *Vanessa* (1956) are similarly oriented.

THE OPERATIC CAST

For conveyance, opera is dependent on the men and women, the *cast,* who people its stage. Confronted with a formidable task, each must be visually appealing and capable of acting with conviction and authority, but most importantly, they must express themselves—artistically, fluently, and easily—in song. And these activities must be carried off with *élan,* sometimes under trying conditions.

"Principals" are those whose roles are absolutely essential to a further-ance of the plot, whose musical assignments are unusually important, and who are required to sing solo parts. Those serving in a minor capacity—in what is known as "B" roles, perhaps as servants, aides, parents, or similar associates—give authenticity to a work, but their function is subordinate, musically and dramatically. Members of the chorus fall within a third category. Lending the weight of numbers to a drama as townspeople, peasants, or soldiers, they usually perform as a group (that is, children's chorus, women's chorus, men's chorus, or mixed chorus). Finally, the super-numeraries, known colloquially as "supers," are an interesting appanage of opera where they act as spear bearers, villagers, or members of a retinue. Essentially, they add color and massivenes to an operatic scene, but do not sing; indeed, supers are specifically forbidden to do so.

The number of people in a cast varies. Some operas require a hundred or more participants (Wagner's *Die Meistersinger,* Verdi's *Aida*), while others use fewer than a dozen (Mozart's *Cosi fan tutti*). Poulenc's *La voix humaine* (1959) has only a single protagonist, Menotti's witty *The Tele-phone* (1947) uses two. Most operas employ principals with contrasting voice timbres (soprano, alto, tenor, or bass) in more or less equal num-bers, but some lean strongly in special directions. Wagner's *Die Meister-*

TABLE 24. *Voice Distribution in Three Well-known Operas.*

Voice Category	Mozart: *Marriage of Figaro* (1786)	Verdi: *La Traviata* (1853)	Bizet: *Carmen* (1875)
Soprano	Countess Almaviva Susanna Cherubino Barbarina	Violetta Annina	Micaela Frasquita Mercedes
Mezzo-soprano (Contralto)	Marcellina	Flora	Carmen
Tenor	Basilio	Alfredo	Don Jose Dancairo
Baritone	Count Almaviva	Germont Douphol	Remandado Escamillo Morales
Bass	Dr. Bartolo Antonio	Dr. Grenvil	Zuniga

singer, for instance, emphasizes men's voices, but Puccini's *Suor Angelica* has only women in its cast.

To show typical voice distribution in principal and subordinate roles, Table 24 gives a listing of the casts in three well-known operas.

Children occasionally appear in opera. Although their assignment to leading parts is comparatively rare, the use of a boy soprano in the title role of Menotti's *Amahl and the Night Visitors* (1951) shows how effective such an allocation can be. Similarly, important parts in Humperdinck's *Hansel and Gretel* could be performed by children but are more usually given to adults. Children's choruses appear in a number of operas, however, including Bizet's *Carmen,* Puccini's *La Bohème,* and Leoncavallo's *I Pagliacci.*

THE OPERATIC OVERTURE [1]

Virtually all operas begin with some sort of an instrumental preface, which is normally intended to attract audience attention and establish an appropriate emotional environment for subsequent dramatic action. Identified as overtures or preludes, these pieces differ rather considerably in substance, length, and organizational pattern. Overtures associated with early operas (those written prior to 1750) rarely have any thematic relationship with their parent work. After the mid-eighteenth century, however, steps were taken to link opera and overture by melodic means, as is shown in several of Mozart's works written between 1780 and 1791 (*Abduction from the Seraglio, Don Giovanni,* and *The Magic Flute*). Consequently, nearly all operatic overtures written after 1800 are founded on thematic material from the theatrical work. Wagner's Overture to *Tannhaüser* (1845), for instance, quotes substantial portions of the "Pilgrims' Chorus" and the "Venusberg Music," just as Bizet's Prelude to *Carmen* (1875) contains the "Bullring Music," portions of the "Toreador's Song," and the "Fate" motive. Such interdependence is even more pronounced between light theatrical works (operetta or musical comedy) and their preludes.

Some overtures may take from ten to fifteen minutes to perform (Beethoven's *Leonora Overture No. 3,* von Weber's *Oberon* Overture, or Wagner's *Tannhaüser* Overture), but others require only three, four, or five minutes (Glinka's Overture to *Ruslan and Ludmilla,* or Verdi's Prelude to *La Traviata*). In many cases, sonata form or part form (usually in the ABA sequence) are used, and sonatina form appears occasionally. Overtures to light opera are often mere potpourris of melodies from the parent score, as is demonstrated in Johann Strauss' Overture to *Die Fledermaus* and the preface to Sullivan's *The Mikado.*

A few operatic preludes are amazingly brief. Richard Strauss' *Salome* opens with a three-measure orchestral flourish, and Alban Berg's *Wozzeck*

[1] For further details on the overture, its style and background, see Chapter 10.

has a four-measure preface that leads directly into the onset of stage action. Lengthier overtures, on the other hand, terminate on a full cadence, usually with a discernible pause ensuing before dramatic activity begins. Nearly all overtures are orchestral, but a few incorporate brief vocal passages (the "Prologue" to Leoncavallo's *I Pagliacci,* which employs a baritone voice (Tonio) in its midportion, and the *Preludio* to Mascagni's *Cavalleria Rusticana,* which similarly utilizes a tenor (Turiddu). But these are exceptions.

BALLET IN OPERA

Since its formulation circa 1600, opera has consistently effectuated a liaison with the dance, and the colorful buoyancy of choreographic movement has enriched such large-scale works as Wagner's *Tannhaüser,* Ponchielli's *La Gioconda,* and Borodin's *Prince Igor.* Ballet serves best, of course, when it has a valid reason for being included within the operatic complex. And this occurs when festivals, pageants, victory celebrations, or gala parties are a part of the dramatic narrative.

Although principal singers may engage in rudimentary dance movements (as, for instance, in the title role of *Carmen*), a special ballet troupe comprised of men, women, and children is mostly employed for choreographic display. Because theirs is an art of pantomime, ballet dancers remain mute during performance and rely on gesture and movement for communicative purposes. Sometimes they follow the prescribed eurythmics of classical ballet; again they use the uninhibited and occasionally frenetic motions of folk and nationalistic dances. In either case, their plan of action, known as *choreography,* is carefully worked out beforehand.

No nation has been more assiduous in a cultivation of operatic ballet than France. Opera gained an initial foothold in Gallic lands during the time of Jean Baptiste Lully (1632–1687) when a composite design known as *opera-ballet* was formulated. And in subsequent years it has become an established practice to interpolate balletic display at particular points in virtually all French scores. Many, but not all, of their operas have five acts, and ballet divertissements are normally interpolated within Acts Two and Four. Although they do not precisely follow this plan, Massenet's *Manon,* Berlioz's *The Trojans,* Bizet's *Carmen,* and Gounod's *Faust* are representative French works that include a wealth of ballet music.

OPERATIC STYLE

Greatly influenced by the changing tastes of its public, opera has consistently reflected the prevalent cultural mores of the eras through which it passed. Less amenable to capricious alteration than modes of fashion, it is nevertheless demonstrably affected by popular trends, and this has resulted in a formulation of such operatic styles as:

Opera seria

Formulated early in the seventeenth century when composers began to employ subjects from Greek mythology (the tale of Orpheus and Euridice) in their operas, this style, lyric drama with the serious overtones of tragedy—which includes lengthy arias and ensembles, an elaborate orchestral score, and accompanied recitative—has been used in such diverse works as Donizetti's *Lucia di Lammermoor,* Verdi's *Rigoletto,* and Stravinsky's *Oedipus Rex.*

Opera buffa

Witty and spirited, opera buffa, which results when gay raillery, light-hearted cynicism, and casual whimsy are ensconced in a buoyant musical score (invariably employing *recitativo secco*), often suggests satire as individuals, groups, traditions, or social behavior are held up to ridicule. Popular during the eighteenth and early ninetenth century (Mozart's *The Marriage of Figaro, Cosi fan tutti,* and Rossini's *Barber of Seville*), the buffa style has only occasionally reappeared in more recent times.

Singspiel

German-language opera, which effectuates an interesting merger between folk art and the more recondite aspects of serious music, contains some short numbers that reflect the popular idiom. However, others tend to be complex, lengthy, and relatively difficult to sing. Notable examples are Mozart's *Abduction from the Seraglio,* Beethoven's *Fidelio,* and von Weber's *Der Freischutz.*

Opera comique

Akin to singspiel in the sense that it interposes spoken dialogue (in French) between arias, ensembles, and concerted choral numbers, this style should not be confused with comic opera, for its material—both musical and dramatic—can be profound and tragic. Bizet's *Carmen,* Gounod's *Faust,* and Offenbach's *Tales of Hoffman* are in comique style (although each has been provided with recitative since its premiere). In English-speaking countries, *ballad opera* (of which John Gay's *The Beggar's Opera* is an example) has appeared as a near-equivalent to both singspiel and comique.

Grand opera

Emphasizing lavish display and spectacular effects, grand opera employs a huge cast with numerous principals, sizeable choral groups, and a large orchestra. Processionals, mass scenes, pageantry, and ballet episodes abound. Among the best-known grand operas—which may have had an influence on the ultimate emergence of motion picture "spectaculars"—are Wagner's *Tannhaüser,* Verdi's *Aida,* and Meyerbeer's *Les Huguenots.*

Romantic opera

Surcharged with emotionalism and laden with sentiment, pieces in this style frequently depict a person as the pawn in a web of disquieting events, as in Verdi's *Rigoletto* or Wagner's *Lohengrin.* Usually, their musical scores are engagingly melodic, but the dramatic material may be tormented and murky. Although a final denouement is not always pleasing (Rigoletto's daughter is slain; Lohengrin must depart from Elsa), the resolution of conflict is usually so obvious as to appear inevitable.

Lyric opera

Sentimental and erotic, these are warm, songful, and touching works centering on the brief and tragic lives of young women whose romantic attachments lead to frustration, despair, and death. Such are the circumstances, at any rate, in Charpentier's *Louise,* Gounod's *Faust,* and Massenet's *Manon.* And in keeping with a prevalent mood of dramatic sensuousness, their musical scores are lush, sultry, and overblown.

Music drama

Wagner described the integrated works he began to compose shortly after 1850 as music drama, and in them combined the rhetoric of symphonic music with the visual beauties of stagecraft. His musical technique is founded on a system of leitmotifs wherein idiomatic (and brief) melodic ideas are continually sounded, transformed, and reaffirmed. Acting as his own librettist, Wagner wrote texts concerned with such historic-mythological figures as Wotan, Brunnhilde, Siegfried, Lohengrin, Tristan, and Parsifal. In this Wagnerian *gesamtkunstwerk*, all theatrical arts are presumably synthesized, but music is really dominant. Music dramas have "endless melody," a greatly expanded orchestra, swirling and continually shifting harmonies, and an adroit intermixture of instrumental and vocal lines. In the Wagner corpus, such pieces as *Tristan und Isolde,* the four "Ring" operas (*Das Rheingold, Die Walkure, Siegfried, Götterdämmerung*), and *Parsifal* are representative.

Verismo

Formulated in about 1890 by a group of Italian composers (although its roots go back to such earlier works as Verdi's *La Traviata* and Bizet's *Carmen*), this style brings an enactment of the emotions and passions from everyday life to the lyric stage. Some veristic operas display vengeance, lust, or murder (Leoncavallo's *I Pagliacci,* Mascagni's *Cavalleria Rusticana,* Puccini's *Tosca*), but others (Puccini's *La Bohème*) are almost blissful in their resigned acceptance of fate.

National or folk opera

Portraying events, personages or happenings of local interest, national opera is mostly founded on the lore of colorful ethnic groups. Although many are extremely popular on a local level, they tend to lose pertinancy when exported. Among those that have found international acceptance are Mussorgsky's *Boris Godounov*, Smetana's *The Bartered Bride*, and Gershwin's *Porgy and Bess*.

Operetta

Casual and engaging, these stage works are sparkling and witty, but their dramatic substance is often a mere trellis supporting a succession of tuneful numbers. Some composers have gained solid reputations (and sizeable fortunes) from writing for the light theater, including Victor Herbert, Sigmund Romberg, and Rudolph Friml. Among operettas, Johann Strauss' *Die Fledermaus,* the Gilbert and Sullivan *Yeoman of the Guard* and Offenbach's *La Perichole* are especially good.

Musical comedy

Only a step removed from operetta, musical comedy is even lighter than its associate. Its scores are constituted from a string of "pop tunes"— short, catchy, easily remembered melodies—linked by spoken dialogue. An abundance of dancing, witty repartee, and invigorating song make them attractive but shallow. Often, musical comedy can be performed by a musically untrained cast whose members have had only general experience in the theater as entertainers, dancers, or comedians. Such works as *South Pacific*, *Showboat, Brigadoon, My Fair Lady*, and *Carousel* are examples.

WAYPOSTS IN THE RISE OF OPERA

Operatic backgrounds

In primitive times many of the correlatives of present-day drama— pantomimic gestures, grotesque postures, and broadly framed grimaces accompanied by wailing and chanting—were a part of every rite. With the passing centuries these ceremonials were perfected and greatly refined, as is visually depicted in relics handed down from the ancient cultures of Egypt, Babylon, Mesopotamia, and China. Ultimately, in the dramatic art of ancient Greece, which predates the Christian era by approximately five hundred years, in the tragedies of Aeschylus, Sophocles, and Euripides or the comedies of Aristophanes, a demonstrable merger of pantomime, rhetoric, and music occurred that was unquestionably a direct precursor of contemporary opera. Theirs was primarily a verbal art, of course, but music, too, had a role to fulfill. As early Greek plays were enacted, musical interjections were provided by a chorus, a group of men and women who gathered at stage rear and commented on the unfolding dramatic events in rhymed incantation. They sang of lament, jubilation, compassion, or exultation and greatly assisted in establishing a credible environment for theatrical portrayal. Unfortunately, actual examples of Greek music have been irretrievably lost, but reliable historical documents attest to its manner of performance and general substance in rather complete detail.

With the gradual demise of Greek tragedy (culminating in the fourth and fifth centuries of the Christian era), almost all theatrical activity went into temporary eclipse during the so-called Dark Ages. Then, as the Middle Ages unfolded, vestiges of a renewed dramatic art began to appear in Western Europe in the skits and tableaus presented (mostly in the out-of-doors) by strolling bands of actors. Eventually, these became known as the Mystery or Miracle Plays, religious dramas enthusiastically sponsored by church officials and warmly greeted by the populace at large. Because theaters were then nonexistent (Greek drama had been given in out-of-door amphitheaters), the new dramas were given in improvised locales, often in, near, or about a church. Mostly performed by itinerant actors, they occasionally enlisted some local citizens who were coached in their roles by parish priests. Crude though they were, these simple dramas soon became powerful instruments by which an unlettered people were taught details about religious dogma. Although it again occupied a minor position, music was a tangible part of this undertaking, for actors sang and danced whenever the dramatic script provided an opportunity.

Between the tenth and sixteenth centuries, such church-sponsored religious plays became well-established in Italy, France, Spain, Germany, and England. Mostly their subjects dealt with events from Scripture marked by important feasts in the ecclesiastical year—Christmas, Easter, Corpus Christi, or the Massacre of the Holy Innocents. Initially presented in Latin, these liturgical dramas later began to use vernacular languages, and as they continued to attract increasingly larger audiences, performances were shifted from church courtyards to town squares. Players' guilds of laymen now assumed responsibility for enactment, although the dramas themselves continued to purvey religious topics. From these, fifteenth-century Morality Plays arose, of which *Everyman*, an English drama, is an excellent example. In time, secular subjects became increasingly important, and taverns or similar places of public assembly became makeshift theaters. More than ever, music was enlisted as a handmaiden of the undertaking, and songs that were good or bad, rowdy or refined, ominous or amorous, long or short, sung by audience or actor, became a regular part of the presentation. Developments like this made the birth of opera all but inevitable. Finally, in 1597 in Florence, Italy, the synthesis was accomplished when an integrated musico-dramatic work, combining aspects of Greek tragedy with elements from the contemporary theater and overlaying them with a monodic musical score, appeared. Then, like a conflagration in a high wind, *opera per musica* (a work with music), spread through the reaches of Italy; within a half century it had become firmly established in France, Germany, and England.

A child of the Renaissance, opera appeared at a time when intellectual interest in humanism was widespread. But the curiosity that led to its formulation was not mere antiquarianism, for new ideas were then being postulated everywhere, new worlds were being explored, and fascinating new vistas were continually unfolding before the gaze of bold and enterprising men. In science, government, geography, and literature, change was in the air. And in this exciting environment, opera became music's most distinguished *voyageur* on a venturesome path leading to the future.

Growth in the Seventeenth Century

Written in the *stile rappresentativo* (with declamatory vocal solos supported by instruments) and initially performed at the palace of Count Corsi (one of its co-creators) in Florence, *Dafne* (1597), with text by Rinuccini and music mostly by Jacopo Peri (1561–1633), was the first musico-dramatic work of operatic proportions to appear. Shortly thereafter, *Euridice*, also by Rinuccini and Peri and written to commemorate the marriage of Maria de' Medici with Henry IV of France, was produced at Florence on October 6, 1600. Another *Euridice*, based on the same libretto, but with music by Giulio Caccini (1550–1616), was composed late in 1600 but not produced until 1602.[2] All of these men were members of the *Camerata* (group), a band of litterateurs, artists, and musicians who gathered at the home of Count Giovanni Bardi in Florence to engage in speculation about the theater's past, present, and future. From their efforts, originally aimed at a reincarnation of ancient Greek tragedy, opera was created almost by happenstance.

Although hailed as artistic wonders, these early musicodramatic works differed greatly from later operas. Performed in a stilted manner, their plots dealt, for the most part, with mythology or the deities of ancient Greece. Each had an omnipresent chorus whose utterances were dramatically cogent but hardly momentous. Principal protagonists, usually few in number, intoned their lines in recitative while they "acted" in a stiff and unrealistic way. Orchestras of the time were a motley collection of available players who performed on such string instruments as theorboe, lute, viol, or viola da gamba. Scenery and costuming were not only minimal but, in keeping with the era's typical classical subjects, Hellenistic in style and decor. For all its shortcomings, however, early opera proved to be remarkably durable. By 1625, four distinctive styles—Florentine, Venetian, Neapolitan, and Roman—had been formulated, and before the midcentury had passed Italian

[2] Caccini's *Il rapimento di Cefalo* (The Abduction of Cefalo), very likely history's second genuine opera, was produced in this same city only three days after the premiere of Peri's epochal forerunner.

opera was being performed in such widely scattered cities as Vienna, Brussels, London, Paris, and Warsaw.

In Claudio Monteverdi opera met its first real master. *Orfeo*, produced at Mantua in 1607, was his first success, and inaugurated a series of works that included the tragedy *Arianna* (1608), ballet-opera *Il Ballo delle Ingrate* (1608); the dramatic scena *Il ... attimento di Tancredi e Clorinda* (1624); and finally *L'Incoronazi... 'oppea* (1642). Along with his technical innovations Monteverdi ... ra on a sound dramatic basis, realigned the orchestra's makeup ... tly ... nced its communicative power, and employed melodies, rhyt... and ... onies within his scores that sound bold and imaginative ev... mode ... ars.

In succeeding years numerous ... er hand ... ecame active in the lyric theater, but none were busier tha... those of ... essandro Scarlatti (1660–1725). Unusually prolific, Scarlatti wrote (in addition to more than five hundred cantatas, two hundred Masses, and fourteen oratorios) approximately 115 dramatic works for the Neapolitan stage. Not the least of his contributions was a perfecting of the Italian-style overture with fast-slow-fast subdivisions. Partly as a result of Monteverdi's pioneering efforts, and partly because of examples postulated by Scarlatti, opera now began to shift away from a preoccupation with declamatory recitative toward solo song expressed in the form of arias, particularly in the *da capo* form. At the same time, ensembles and choral numbers became increasingly important in the newer works then being composed.

In France, Jean Baptiste Lully, an Italian expatriate who had been taken to Paris as a boy, held opera in thrall. Equally adept in fashioning ballet scores as in gaining royal favor, he acquired letters of patent from Louis XIV in 1672 for establishing an *Academie royale de musique*, which was tantamount to acquiring absolute authority over all operatic activity in France. Although opera had been known in this land since before 1645, a Gallic predilection for classical tragedy, as exemplified in the plays of Racine, Corneille, and Quinault, and a deep-seated French partiality for ballet stifled its growth. With Quinault as librettist, however, Lully began to mold public acceptance as he astutely merged dramatic pathos with the visual beauties of ballet, and wrapped his theatrical works in sturdy and attractive musical scores. In addition he formulated a design for the French-style overture (with slow-fast-slow sections), mostly emphasized short and uncomplicated arias, stressed the vernacular language, and gave his audience plenty of dancing. As a result, from Lully's time onward, opera has remained an important corollary of French musical life.

Opera experienced many remarkable external developments during these years. In 1637 the first public opera house was opened at Venice, a step quickly emulated in other metropolitan centers. Its visual aspects were strengthened, and new kinds of scenery were designed using perspective to give an illusion of depth. Consequently, parks, groves of trees, even lakes, and rivers were readily simulated on stage. Costumes became more splendid than before, and props incidental to convincing stage action were skillfully manufactured and freely used. Most breathtaking of all, however, was a perfection of stage machinery (including a varied assortment of guys, winches, and pulleys) that enabled actors to engage in remarkably dexterous feats of physical activity. Needless to say, these innovations were warmly greeted by the opera-going public.

Textually, too, opera extended its scope. Although mythology continued to be a primary subject, historical events and personages began to appear in librettos. Vague references were occasionally made to religious subjects, although Scriptural topics were mostly considered the province of oratorio. But humor became increasingly important as witticism and even ribaldry appeared. In the serious times respite from the serious and sometimes tedious plots of *opera seria* came in the form of *intermezzi* interpolated between the several acts. Later, these grew into opera buffa.

Among the notable operatic events that occurred in the century's second half were (1) its growth in England, as evidenced by performances of John Blow's *Venus and Adonis* (1685) and the production of such works by Henry Purcell, the greatest musician in England's Restoration theater, as *Dido and Aeneas* (1689) and *King Arthur* (1691), with libretto by Dryden; (2) the spread of opera to Germany where Heinrich Schütz carried details concerning the Italian manner of writing when he returned from studies in Venice; (3) the opening of a public opera house at Hamburg in 1678 (tangible evidence of an interest in German opera), where Handel received his early training, and (4) a general flourishing of court opera in such northern cities as Hanover, Munich, and Dusseldorf. Although few—indeed, virtually none—of the operas composed during this age are regularly heard in the theater today, many are available in recorded form. Some are worthy of attention, and those by English composers (because their language is so readily assimilable) are certain to be enjoyed.

In the Eighteenth Century

By 1700, opera had developed to a point where most scores included three kinds of writing: (1) *secco* (dry) recitative, which was largely concerned with the rapid enunciation of semiverbal connecting passages over a sketchy harpsichord accompaniment; (2) *stromentato* (accompanied) recitative wherein a singer expressed a semilyric arioso with orchestral assistance; and (3) arias (solo songs) and vocal ensembles (duets, trios, and choruses) wherein the substance was both musical and lyric. Because the aria's melodic beauties and expressive range were almost unlimited, it soon became a cornerstone in operatic design and a favorite vehicle for virtuoso display. Three kinds were used: (1) the *aria cantabile*, a sweet and song-like piece well suited for expressions of tender sentiment; (2) the *aria parlante*, more declamatory in substance and extremely dramatic in expression; and (3) the *aria di bravura* (the most popular kind), a virtuoso piece filled with brilliant roulades and dazzling vocal acrobatics.

Most early eighteenth-century opera seria followed a carefully ordained plan. Almost invariably they were divided into three acts, and these, in turn, were subdivided into a sequence of autonomous segments called *scenas*. Each scena began with a lengthy recitative performed by one (sometimes more) of the principals, followed by a brilliant aria in *da capo* form. Casts consisted of six singers: three women and a like number of men. The leading woman singer (called the prima donna) was a high soprano, the third a contralto, and the second could be in either category. Men's roles were typically assigned to artificial sopranos (called *castrati*), although the third man was occasionally a tenor. Throughout, little use was made of concerted singing; apparently, vocalists of this era—with tacit approval from composers—were reluctant to share the limelight. Choral groups rarely appeared, a circumstance with undisputed economic advantages.

After 1750, opera buffa (whose origins rest with the previous century's comic intermezzi) appeared as a rival of opera seria. On the surface, opera buffa is casual, witty, and farcical, but works in this style often have satiric undercurrents where ostentation is mercilessly and cleverly lampooned. Buffa uses far more ensemble singing than its associate, particularly in the finales of acts, and it brought forward an interesting stock figure, the *basso buffo* (always enacted by a deep bass voice) who expresses ribaldry, dry humor, or overweening pomposity with side-splitting results, Giovanni Pergolesi's *La Serva padrona* (The Maid as Mistress), which first appeared at Naples in 1733 as an intermezzo, is a fine example of opera buffa. Using only three characters (one of them mute) it describes the clever machinations of a maid, Serpina, to ensnare and marry her wealthy bachelor-employer. Unquestionably, this piece greatly influenced a rising generation of opera composers, including Mozart.

Prominent creators of serious opera during this era were George Frideric Handel, Jean Philippe Rameau, and Christoph Willibald Gluck.

Born in Germany and trained in Italy, Handel ultimately gained lasting fame in England. Forced to act as an impresario as well as a composer, he was drastically affected by the fluctuating fortunes of operatic life. Masterfully adept in handling the then-popular Italian style, he gained considerable initial fame, but when this kind of opera fell to low estate in England after 1730, Handel became virtually destitute. With amazing versatility he turned to a new career in oratorio and became one of music's most distinguished creators of sacred music drama. Despite the caprice that either favored or disowned them, Handel's operas are far from negligible and several are finding favor in our own century including *Agrippina* (1709), *Giulio Cesare* (1724), *Rodelinda* (1725), and *Alcina* (1735).

Credited with being the formulator of a modern analytic approach to harmony, and in his day known as an unusually distinguished organist,

Rameau was also Lully's most illustrious operatic successor in France. For more than thirty years he dominated the nation's lyric theater and became a petrel about whom controversy continually raged. Lesser contemporaries pronounced his works unmelodic, their harmonies unintelligible, plots meaningless, and orchestration noisy. But Rameau treated this carping with indifference and continued to compose volumes of works. Of this staggering list, the ballet-opera *Les Indes galantes* (1735) and an opera seria *Castor et Pollux* (1737) are especially noteworthy.

Known in operatic annals as a reformer, the German-born Gluck spent years of rigorous apprenticeship in Italy after which he practiced his craft in Vienna and France. A simple statement of the reforms Gluck attempted to promulgate (although probably written by his librettist, Calzabigi), is included in the preface to *Alceste:*

I sought to reduce music to its true function, that of seconding poetry in order to strengthen the emotional impression and the impact of the dramatic situations without interrupting the action and without weakening it by superfluous ornaments.

Gluck initially tolerated the *castrati* (who, incidentally, were then going out of fashion), but the Paris versions of his works stipulate that, where possible, a tenor be substituted in their stead. Unfailingly dignified and lofty in dramatic substance, Gluck's operas have a serene musical loveliness that becomes deeply impassioned in moments of emotional stress. Their orchestral scores are magnificent, and such a master as Berlioz called Gluck a "poet" for the effects he elicited from this group. Especially important in his copious output are *Orfeo ed Euridice* (1762), *Alceste* (1767), *Iphigénie en Aulide* (1774), *Armide* (1777), and *Iphigénie en Tauride* (1779).

Throughout the Baroque era tongues were sharper and critical pens more waspish than ever before. One of the pithiest satires on opera, entitled *Il teatro alla moda* (1720), was written by a composer, Benedetto Marcello, who ridiculed the vanities, whims, and personal ambitions of all who placed personal aggrandizement above artistic veracity. Other critical essays were written during this time by the Englishman, Joseph Addison, and printed in *The Spectator.* Further vituperative polemics appeared in the Paris press during *La Guerre des Bouffons* (The War of the Comedians), a "newspaper war," in which the virtues of French opera seria or Italian opera buffa were extolled or castigated, depending on the writer's point of view.[3]

Of the composers active in writing opera during the Classic period (c. 1770–1810), none was so divinely inspired as Wolfgang Amadeus Mozart, who created a total of twenty-three dramatic works during a tragically brief life. His *The Marriage of Figaro* (1786) and *Cosi fan tutti* (1790),

[3] These, and similar essays on music and its practices, are contained within *Source Readings in Music History,* edited by Oliver Strunk and published by W. W. Norton & Company, Inc., 1950 (now available in paperback).

both with libretti by Lorenzo da Ponte, are Italian-language works that bring the buffa style to an apogee of excellence. Although termed a *dramma giocosa* by its composer, *Don Giovanni* (1787), also with a da Ponte libretto, is a complex and tragic work that has often been termed the world's most magnificent work of art. Mozart's *Abduction from the Seraglio* (1782) and *The Magic Flute* (1791) are singspiels written to implement the Emperor Franz Joseph's desire to found a national lyric theater in Hapsburg lands and are unquestionably the era's most important German-language operas. With few exceptions, such as the occasional appearance of a Gluck opera, Mozart's are the oldest lyric dramas to hold a fixed place in today's repertoire. Filled with occasional pathos, much good humor, and an abundance of sublime passion, they are consistently concerned with expressing universal sentiments. Although sometimes drawn larger than life, their characters are entirely credible, and many (for example, those in *Figaro*) step directly to the stage from the pathways of everyday life. In Mozart's scores every phrase is meaningful, every musical number is a model of classic beauty, and voices continually blend with instruments to create a gorgeous cantilena whose spirit is, like that of the composer, perennially youthful.

Other late eighteenth-century operas have been almost totally overshadowed by Mozart's faultless works. Domenico Cimarosa (1749–1801), creator of over sixty theatrical pieces—including the sprightly *Secret Marriage* (1792)—has been termed an "Italian Mozart," but he was merely facile with an adept touch for riotous comedy rather than genuinely distinguished. And Joseph Haydn, a gifted musician fully conversant with every phase of the craft, wrote an abundance of operas (all intended for performance at the private theater of his patron, Prince Esterházy), but they have proven to be ephemeral and are rarely heard today. Only in France, as the century neared its final decade, were there currents unique enough and creative spirits strong enough to formulate works that could survive the exacting rigors of operatic life. But even these are no match for the operas of Mozart.

As the French Revolution raged, Classicism's rationalism stood side-by-side with the spirit of terror, and no association was ever more incongruous. Throughout the nation chaos ran riot, but unrest was especially rampant in Paris where the guillotine stood ever-ready to go about its grisly business. Paradoxically, the theater flourished; seemingly, the *citoyens* wanted to wash daytime horrors from mind while enjoying an evening at the theater. Of composers active at the time, the most notable were (1) Andre Gretry (1741–1813), a Belgian who produced more than fifty French operas and whose *Richard Coeur-de-Lion* (1784) is a fine example of early opera comique; (2) Etienne Mehul (1763–1817), whose *Joseph* (1807) became a landmark in the French theater; and (3) Francois Gossec (1734–1829), an adept composer, an ardent revolutionist, and a founder of the Paris Conservatoire (1795).

Because composers avidly attempted to fulfill an apparently insatiable demand for new operas, *pasticcios* flourished. These were "pasteups" wherein a sequence of arias or other musical numbers were lifted from any available source and reassembled to constitute a new opera. Such a practice was tenable in these times for few works were published, and a typical opera was composed, played briefly (perhaps for a few weeks), and promptly forgotten. Performances were localized, borrowing widespread, and most composers were not overly scrupulous whence they derived their material. Good librettos were at a premium, and it was not unusual for a workable text to endure setting by a dozen or more composers.

Still quite removed from what the twentieth century expects as verisimilitude on the stage, the period's librettos nevertheless began to show distinct improvement. By now, emphasis had shifted from a concern with classical subjects to an emotive interplay betwen credible human beings. Although Gluck's figures retain their Hellenic abodes (and even venture to Hades on occasion), Mozart's men and women spring from the environs of Rome, Seville, or Vienna. And while the era's composers were important in effectuating this change, primary credit must go to such librettists as: Apostolo Zeno (1668–1750), a Venetian who became court poet to Charles VI in Vienna and established a formula for Italian operatic texts that endured for more than a century; Pietro Metastasio (1698–1782), successor to Zeno and a poet who collaborated with Mozart, Jommelli, Gluck, Handel, and Hasse (his *La Clemenza di Tito*, for instance, was set by Mozart and eighteen others); Ranieri di Calzabigi (1714–1795), a Parisian who provided Gluck with texts for *Orfeo, Alceste,* and *Paride ed Elena;* and Lorenzo da Ponte (1749–1838), librettist for Mozart's *The Marriage of Figaro, Don Giovanni,* and *Cosi fan tutti.*

In the Nineteenth Century

Operatic concepts did not shift abruptly as the new century began. Beethoven's *Fidelio* (1805), one of early Romanticism's most distinguished musicodramatic works, is a "rescue opera" whose roots are clearly imbedded in the French theater of Revolutionary times (c. 1790). Conceived as a singspiel, it is concerned with a heroine, Leonora, who saves her husband, Florestan, from an ignominious death in a prison where he is incarcerated for political reasons. Beethoven's vocal writing is often cruelly difficult to sing, but this score is little short of magnificent. Arias for Leonora (in the first act) and Florestan (in the second), some of the ensembles (the canonic quartet, *Mir ist so wunderbar,* and the "Prisoner's Chorus," both in the first act), and the concerted choral pieces that appear in the finale rank among the finest in operatic literature. Found faulty in its original version, *Fidelio* was revised in 1806 and only attained definitive form in 1814.

Nor did opera buffa pass quickly from the scene. Rossini's *Barber of Seville* (1816), one of the most glorious of buffas, contained so much wry humor that it soon convulsed all Europe (and, subsequently, most of the world) with laughter. Initially an extremely prolific composer (during one eight-year period, for instance, he wrote twenty operas), Rossini established a glowing reputation in Italy with *Tancredi* (1813), *La Cenerentola* (1817), and *La Gazza Ladra* (1817). After working briefly in London, he took up residence in Paris where he produced a grand opera, *William Tell* (1829). Thereafter, his wellspring of invention either ceased its flow or was deliberately diverted. At any rate, during his remaining thirty-eight years of life Rossini wrote only occasional nonoperatic pieces.

Gaetano Donizetti, another unusually facile musician, actually bettered Rossini's record by writing twenty-three operas in the seven-year span between 1822 and 1829. But his most important works were composed later, and include *Anna Bolena* (1830), *L'elisir di amore* (1832), *Lucrezia Borgia* (1833), and his masterpiece, *Lucia di Lammermoor* (1835). In later years, Donizetti fell an unfortunate prey to spells of depression that finally culminated in a paralytic stroke. *Don Pasquale* (1843), a gay and witty farce in buffa style, was his final work.

Another member in this triumvirate of Italian composers wrote brilliantly but briefly. When Vincenzo Bellini died in 1835 at the age of thirty-four, he had written (among others) *La Sonnambula* (1831), his masterwork *Norma* (1831), and *I Puritani* (1835). In company with Rossini and Donizetti, Bellini brought Italian bel canto opera to a peak of excellence. Vibrant melodies welled from their scores, and bravura vocal display—usually expressed in arias heavily interlarded with stunning roulades and cadenzas—reigned supreme. Sometimes so farcical as to appear ridiculous, comedy in their pieces (*The Barber of Seville, Don Pasquale*) occasionally soared to heights of timeless humor. Tragedy was not foreign to them, however, as is shown in *Lucia di Lammermoor* and *Norma*. Most importantly, of course, is an obvious fact that operatic writing advanced considerably at their hands. Accompanied recitative now supplanted the *secco* variety, novel and sometimes naive descriptive effects were elicited from the orchestra (for example, storm episodes in *The Barber of Seville* and *William Tell*), and the general musicodramatic fabric became more cogent, expressive, and intense than heretofore.

Early in the Romantic era, Carl Maria von Weber became Germany's most outstanding operatic composer. After serving a lengthy apprenticeship as an accompanist, conductor, and impresario, and after having created a series of fledgling works, Weber composed his masterpiece, *Der Freischütz* (1821). Based on a collection of eerie folk tales from the *Gespensterbuch* (Book of Ghost Stories) and organized in singspiel style, this opera is concerned with depicting a series of episodes in German bourgeois life. Two subsequent works by Weber, *Euryanthe* (1823) and *Oberon* (1826), were, however, less epochal.

Italian-born, Luigi Cherubini enjoyed considerable repute in Paris during these years, where he produced *Medea* (1797), based on a classical subject, and *Les Deux Journées* (The Two Days, 1800), a rescue opera. Subsequently he lost favor with the Emperor Napoleon and was replaced by another Italian, Gasparo Spontini. Sponsored by the Empress Josephine, Spontini's grand opera, *La Vestale* (1807), was chosen by three French judges (Gossec, Mehul, and Gretry) to receive an unusually lucrative prize, and shortly thereafter another successful work, *Fernand Cortez* (1809), was produced at Paris. Ever-mindful of dangers inherent in political upheaval, this wily composer managed to survive Napoleon's downfall and subsequently became a favorite of Louis XVIII. In time (1820), he moved to Berlin where he remained a veritable despot in charge of imperial opera for more than twenty years.

In Parisian esteem Spontini was replaced by a German expatriate, Giacomo Meyerbeer (1791–1864). Working with unusual foresight, Meyerbeer shrewdly assayed the operatic scene before he began to write a series of spectacular works. When *Robert le Diable* (1831) was produced, the Parisians were impressed; but when *Les Huguenots* (1836), *Le Prophète* (1849), and *L'Africaine* (1865) appeared, their adulation knew no limits. Grand in their every aspect, Meyerbeer's operas stress ostentatious effect and are filled with processions, prayers, and strikingly impressive scenes for chorus and ballet. Monumental in concept as well as epic in proportion, they are extremely lavish and spectacular. But like many other grandiose works of art, they tend to substitute pompous rhetoric and elaborate gesture for an expression of genuine sentiment. Still, despite their shortcomings, these colossal showcases dominated French opera until after the 1860s.

Hector Berlioz, a native-born son, waited in vain for success in France. Active in a variety of tasks at the Paris Opera (copying, editing, rehearsing, coaching, translating, and arranging), he finally persuaded the administration to mount his *Benvenuto Cellini* (1838). But the work was greeted with indifference and, according to Berlioz, "hissed with remarkable unanimity" by an audience accustomed to the elaborate panoply of Spontini and Meyerbeer. Nearly a quarter of a century later, another Berlioz opera *Béatrice and Bénédict* (1862, based on Shakespeare's *Much Ado About Nothing*), experienced a provincial premier (in German) at Baden-Baden. If anything, his masterwork, *Les Troyens,* suffered an even more ignominious fate. Its second section, called *Les Troyens à Carthage* (The Trojans at Carthage) was given at Paris in 1863, but the first portion, *La Prise de Troie* (The Taking of Troy), did not have a premiere until 1890 at Carlsruhe, in Germany, twenty-one years after Berlioz's death.

After 1850, the French lyric theater greeted a new generation of composers. In Charles Gounod it found a facile musician who easily satisfied the popular taste for opulent melody and emotion-tinged scores. His *Faust* (1859) has become one of the most frequently performed pieces in the repertoire, but such other Gounod works as *La Reine de Saba* (The

Queen of Sheba, 1862); *Mireille* (1864), and *Roméo et Juliette* (1867) have not fared as well.

Although he previously wrote *Les Pecheurs de perles* (The Pearl Fishers, 1863); *La Jolie fille de Perth* (The Fair Maid of Perth, 1867); and *Djamileh* (1872), enduring fame came to Georges Bizet for the biographic treatment he accorded a lusty, uninhibited gypsy girl in *Carmen* (1875). In comparison with other French works of the period, *Carmen* is rapier-like in the swiftness of its delineative strokes. Consistently exhibiting a genuine Gallic economy of means, *Carmen's* melodies have the timeless endurance of folk tunes; its vocal and orchestral colors sparkle with glowing incandescence, and its rhythms have the intoxicating verve typically associated with Spanish music.

Finally, this era of almost incessant operatic activity in France was brought to a close by Camille Saint-Saëns and Jules Massenet (1842–1912). *Samson et Dalila* (premiered at Weimar in 1877 and given at Paris in 1892) is Saint-Saëns' operatic masterpiece. Based on a Scriptural subject and employing a sensuous and at times overly saccharine musical language, it still retains an important place in the repertoire. Unabashedly melodic and more than a bit sentimental, Massenet's *Manon* (1884), *Werther* (1892), and *Thaïs* (1894) are distinctly dated pieces, but they continue to enjoy favor in French theaters.

With Giuseppe Verdi, Italian opera acquired its most articulate voice. Seemingly born to fulfill a creative destiny, Verdi became prominent at a time when Italy was embroiled in a bitter struggle for political hegemony. And he became popular both as a nationalist and an undisputed arbiter in its theater until the 1890s when such younger men as Puccini, Mascagni, and Leoncavallo appeared. During his lengthy career, Verdi composed over twenty-six operas, more than half of which continue to be heard in the twentieth century. Although some have fallen into comparative neglect— *Nabucco* (1842); *I Lombardi* (1843); *Ernani* (1844); *Macbeth* (1847); and *Luisa Miller* (1849)—*Rigoletto* (1851), *Il Trovatore* (1853), and *La Traviata* (1853) are extremely viable and can be considered three of the Italian theater's best-loved operas. Continuing to work with painstaking care, Verdi went on to produce *Les Vepres siciliennes* (1855); *Simon Boccanegra* (1857); *Un ballo in maschera* (1859); *La Forza del destino* (1862); *Don Carlos* (1867); and *Aida* (1872) during the century's third quarter. Finally, two works, both with librettos by Arrigo Boito and both based on Shakespeare, brought his brilliant career to its peak. *Otello* (1887), written when Verdi was seventy-four, and *Falstaff* (1893), when he was an octogenarian, are masterpieces with few peers.

As a composer, Verdi was ever in love with humans; he wrote for the heart, continually striving to excite the emotional sensibilities of his audience. The self-sacrificing Violetta in *La Traviata*, the tragic Rigoletto, the obese but humorous Falstaff, and the conniving Iago in *Otello* display passions that stimulate all mankind. Naturally, Verdi's true measure of genius is to be discovered in his music. Melodies soar and float, they caress the ear and enchant the mind; vocal virtuosity for its own sake is avoided, but moments of breathtaking lyricism bring the art of bel canto to penultimate heights. A master of cogent orchestral writing, Verdi never permitted its instruments to challenge the voice, and his operas—neatly balanced, lucid, yet passionately communicative—glow with the intense flame of Romantic ardor. Whether he spoke for Italian nationalism (as in *Les Vepres siciliennes*), portrayed a lovely Parisian courtesan (*La Traviata*), or described an anguished husband bereft of his senses (*Otello*), Verdi was consistently convincing. Italian opera never attained higher levels of excellence.

In Germany, Richard Wagner occupied a station comparable to Verdi's position in Italy. But their outlook, the artistic creed each professed, and the works they composed, are amazingly divergent. Wagner was an intellectual, a philosopher, a speculative musician forever formulating theories that he attempted to validate by pragmatic means. When he concluded during the 1840s that conventional opera had become exhausted, Wagner created the *gesamtkunstwerk*, an all-embracing design in which poetry, drama, and music, as well as other peripheral arts, would be intertwined in a new kind of super work. To prove his point, he began to compose a series of music dramas (Wagner's term) conceived along these lines. Because the Wagnerian aesthetic is amazingly complex, his pieces are lengthy, involved, and occasionally boring, but more often they are transcendentally beautiful. Aside from three preliminary works, the first to gain attention was *Rienzi* (1842), a grand opera that has since fallen from the repertoire. With *Der fliegende Holländer* (*The Flying Dutchman*, 1843), *Tannhaüser* (1845), and *Lohengrin* (1850), however, Wagner's important task was begun. In particular, the latter displays a new manner of writing wherein endless melody becomes important. Individual numbers are merged, final cadences are evaded, and bridges are continually employed to synthesize the opera into an indissoluble whole. Along the way, Wagner began to experiment with *leitmotifs* (leading motives): short, idiomatic thematic ideas associated with individuals, objects, or situations in his dramas. Manipulated in a symphonic manner, they greatly assist in limning a work's dramatic narrative.

In the midst of a tempestuous personal life marked by mounting debts, a second marriage (to a daughter of Liszt), and considerable political maneuvering, Wagner found the energy to create his magnum opus, a series of four interrelated operas known as *Der Ring des Nibelungen*, which includes *Das Rheingold* (1869), *Die Walküre* (1870), *Siegfried* (1876), and *Götterdämmerung* (1876). Acting as his own librettist (indeed, as his own impresario, conductor, manager, and general factotum), Wagner deliberately avoided conventional dramatic subjects to deal with superhuman deities and mythological figures taken from Norse, Celtic, Greek, and Teutonic legendry. Magic rings, dwarfs, Rhinemaidens, flying horses, dragons, and assorted unearthly objects abound in these works; their vocal lines are asymmetrical, and conventional arias, ensembles, or choruses are avoided in favor of a continuously flowing musical stream based on the system of leitmotifs. While creating the Ring Cycle—a task that occupied him between 1853 and 1874—Wagner found it possible to compose *Tristan und Isolde* (1865) and *Die Meistersinger von Nürnberg* (1868). Later, he closed a most brilliant theatrical career by writing *Parsifal* (1882).

More than anyone before his time, this unique genius raised the orchestra to a pinnacle of prominence. At his hands it portrays, suggests, and narrates in a manner that often supersedes the voice; indeed, many passages exist where the voice parts can be dispensed with entirely, as they usually are in concert performance. This, of course, is in marked distinction from the concept conventionally associated with opera. Wagner's personality was so powerful and the aesthetic creed he promulgated so all-encompassing, however, that almost no one could coexist with him in the German theatre. After 1850, a Wagnerian miasma totally overshadowed operatic life in the north, although his works were decidedly controversial and far from popular. Significantly, the only kind of opera that could arise in succession to music drama is exemplified by Engelbert Humperdinck's *Hansel und Gretel* (1893). Paradoxically, in German lyric theaters as the century drew to a close, metaphysical speculation gave way to a display of childlike simplicity.

For centuries Russia was content to import its opera from the West. Successive waves of French, German, and Italian (mostly the latter) composers arrived at St. Petersburg or Moscow, where they composed and produced opera for periods of time before returning home, enriched in fame and fortune. As late as 1862 this was still going on, for then Verdi's *La Forza del destino* had its premiere at the Court Opera in St. Petersburg. But inroads of native opera began to appear earlier when Michael Glinka produced his *A Life for the Czar* (1836). Based on an incident in Russian history and using the vernacular language as well as some native folk melodies (although in a fragmentary manner), Glinka's pioneering work was well received although a second, *Ruslan and Ludmilla* (1842), was less successful. But the die for Russian opera was cast, and as the century progressed, these composers produced a series of nationalistic works: Alexander Dargomijsky (1813–1869), who began but did not complete a Russian version of the Don Juan saga in *The Stone Guest* (1872); Alexander Borodin, whose colorful *Prince Igor* (1890) based on a twelfth-century historical subject also remained unfinished; Modest Mussorgsky, whose historically oriented, folk-laden score to *Boris Godounov* (1874) is probably the best Russian opera ever written; Peter I. Tchaikowsky, whose *Eugene Onegin* (1879) is based on Pushkin but musically is modeled after French examples; and Nicholas Rimsky-Korsakoff, whose *Ivan the Terrible* (1873) and *Le Coq d'or* (an opera-ballet, 1909) combine Slavic subjects with sensuous oriental imagery.

Never far removed from the mainstream of operatic creativity, the light musical theater reached peaks of unusual excellence during these years. In England, for instance, William S. Gilbert and Arthur Sullivan merged their very considerable talents for wit and satire to create a series of comic operas including *H. M. S. Pinafore* (1878), *Iolanthe* (1882), *The Mikado* (1885), and *The Gondoliers* (1889). Somewhat earlier, Jacques Offenbach enjoyed great popularity in Paris. With a calculating eye turned toward public acceptance, he wrote such scintillating works as *La Belle Hélène* (1864), *La Vie Parisienne* (1866), *Grande Duchesse de Gerolstein* (1867), and *La Perichole* (1868). His masterpiece, however, is a serious work, *Les Contes d'Hoffman* (The Tales of Hoffman, 1881), produced posthumously. In Vienna, Franz von Suppe (1819–1895) maintained the popular theater in a state of excitement with his *Poet and Peasant* (1846), *The Beautiful Galatea* (1865), *The Light Cavalry* (1866), and *Fatinitza* (1876). But it was Johann Strauss, the celebrated "waltz king," who gave Viennese operetta its distinctive flair as he brilliantly demonstrated in *Die Fledermaus* (1874), *One Night in Venice* (1883), and *The Gypsy Baron* (1885).

As the century moved into its final decade, *verismo* (operatic realism) was fostered by a group of Italian composers. Filling their scores with broad sweeping melodies and opulent orchestral colors carefully calculated to whip audiences into an emotional frenzy, Ruggiero Leoncavallo and Pietro Mascagni became primary spokesmen for the movement. Mascagni's *Cavalleria Rusticana* (Rustic Chivalry, 1890) narrates a tale of violence, deception, and death, incongruously set in a somnolent Sicilian village on an Easter Sunday morning. Leoncavallo's *I Pagliacci* (The Clowns, 1892) concerns itself with jealousy, infidelity, and murder among a band of itinerant actors. Considerably more excellence was brought to this style by Giacomo Puccini, who launched a distinguished theatrical career with *Manon Lescaut* (1893), *La Bohème* (1896), and *Tosca* (1900).

In the Twentieth Century

Verismo continued as the dominant operatic style in Italy early in the new century, and the redoubtable Puccini furthered its stylistic canons with *Madama Butterfly* (1904), an exotic opera based on the tale of an unfortunate liaison between an American naval lieutenant and a Japanese geisha. Puccini's *La fanciulla del West* (The Girl of the Golden West, 1910), has not been a popular success, although it treats with life in a Nevada mining camp and is replete with tinhorn gamblers, gold strikes, and shoot-outs. Subsequently, Puccini composed *Il Trittico* (1918), a group of one-act operas that includes *Il tabarro* (The Cloak), *Suor Angelica* (Sister Angelica), and *Gianni Schicchi*. Finally, a highly distinguished theatrical career was brought to a close with the unfinished *Turandot* (1926), whose dramatic milieu is set in ancient China. Others also at work in Italy during these years, include Umberto Giordano (1867–1948) best-known for *Andrea Chénier* (1896); Francesco Cilea (1866–1950), now remembered for *Adriana*

Lecouvreur (1902); the German-born Ermanno Wolf-Ferrari (1876–1948), whose witty *Jewels of the Madonna* (1911) is a light and sparkling work; and Ildebrando Pizzetti (b. 1880), creator of the tragic *Love of Three Kings* (1913).

As a principal legatee, it devolved on Richard Strauss to sustain the Wagnerian tradition in German opera during the new century. Equipped with an abundance of talent, a superb technique, and an adventuresome spirit, he rose brilliantly to the task and created a series of stunning works that initially aroused avid controversy before gaining ultimate acceptance. Between 1892 when he produced *Guntram* and 1941 when *Capriccio* appeared, Strauss wrote fifteen operas, of which the salacious *Salome* (1905), based on Oscar Wilde's play of the same name; the barbaric *Elektra* (1909), founded on Sophocles' classical tragedy; and the sumptuous *Der Rosenkavalier* (1911), expressive of the courtly Vienna of Maria Theresa's time, have become especially well-known. Although *Salome* and *Elektra* were deliberately conceived to stun and shock (both have been castigated, banned, and roundly denounced), Strauss' other operas (*Ariadne auf Naxos, Arabella,* and *Daphne*) are elegant, witty, and gracious. Through-composed, they express a continuous vocal cantilena supported by radiant orchestration.

When Claude Debussy produced his lone opera, *Pelléas et Mélisande* (1902), he brought an absolutely unique work to the lyric stage. Cloaked in the misty syntax of Impressionism, it seems to float in a musicodramatic limbo as it depicts in vague and nebulous terms a tragedy involving two brothers and a young girl. Encompassed within five acts, with numerous subscenes in each, Debussy's music runs continuously as it paints vaguely defined dramatic events in glistening iridescent hues.

Discreet allusiveness, however, is not a trait in the operas of Maurice Ravel, Debussy's successor in the French lyric theater. With urbane wit, cool detachment, and superb craftsmanship, Ravel endowed his *l'Heure espagnole* (The Spanish Hour, 1907) with all the gay jocosity of opera buffa. Laid in the Spanish city of Toledo, its plot concerns an elderly clockmaker, his young wife, and the flirtations she conducts while he is away adjusting the community's timepieces. Ravel's *l'Enfant et les sortileges* (The Bewitched Child, 1925), is similarly piquant, but the butt of its humor is a mischievous youngster who gets his comeuppance (and ultimate forgiveness) from the animals and objects he had previously tormented or broken. Provided with a ravishing orchestral score, this exquisitely shaped work is delightfully whimsical, extremely clever, and utterly captivating.

Traditions of Gallic opera have been sustained in the latest generation by Francis Poulenc, whose opera bouffe *Les Mamelles de Tiresias* (1947) is an extremely witty work and whose *Dialogues des Carmelites* (1956) sympathetically portrays temptations placed before a group of nuns during the French Revolution. Poulenc's *La voix humaine* (1959) is unusual in that it employs only a single protagonist (a soprano), who carries on an emotion-laden conversation via telephone with a lover who has recently deserted her.

Innovations more startling than those introduced by Richard Strauss appeared in German-language operas written by the Viennese Expressionists. Using the dissonant syntax of atonality, their pieces have an acrid sonority that indisputably expresses the turmoil, unrest, and disillusionment abroad before and after World War I. Although they are not often given public performance (but do exist in recorded form), two short operas by Arnold Schoenberg, *Ewartung* (1909) and *Die Gluckliche Hand* (1913), as well as the full-length *Moses und Aron* (produced, 1954), aptly represent this style. Even more significant, however, are two operas by Alban Berg. In *Wozzeck* (1925), he brought to the stage a tale, founded on the writings of Georg Büchner, of a desperately poor and wretchedly stupid soldier. Not at all pretty or tuneful in a conventional sense, *Wozzeck* is a splendidly organized work whose substance is awesome and murky, but deeply moving. Berg's *Lulu* (produced, 1937) is similarly concerned with a depiction of human depravity. Unfinished at the composer's death, it has now been sufficiently edited to warrant theatrical performance. This same cultural environment also gave rise to the bitter, satiric, and denunciatory works that Kurt Weill (1900–1950) conceived for the postwar German stage. Working in collaboration with Berthold Brecht, Weill established his reputation with an adaptation of the *Three Penny Opera* (1928) and went on to write *The Rise and Fall of the City of Mahagonny* (1930). After emigrating to the United States in 1935, he composed the lighter *Knickerbocker Holiday* (1938), several similar works for the American theater (for example, *One Touch of Venus*), and a folk opera *Down in the Valley* (1948). In recent years, Carl Orff (b. 1895) has become a prominent composer for the German stage. His *Der Mond* (1938), *Die Kluge* (1942), and *Antigonae* (1949) reveal a prodigious technique, an exquisite rhythmic sense, and a clarity of writing that few contemporary composers possess. Still, his operas tend to be remote, stilted, and almost dispassionate in dramatic substance; consequently, they have not attained an unqualified international stature.

For more than three centuries opera has been an essential part of Spanish musical life, and an idiomatic form, the *zarzuela* (comparable in many respects with French opera comique for it uses spoken dialogue as a connective between short, witty, and tuneful musical numbers), has become a national art form. Like most ethnic opera, however, the zarzuela languishes in a foreign environment, and representative pieces from this literature have rarely been successfully exported. Early in the twentieth century, however, Spain acquired two eminent musicians, Enrique Granados (1867–1916) and Manuel de Falla who were capable of writing for the international stage. Composer of seven operas, Granados is now remembered mostly for *Goyescas* (1916), whose characters and settings are drawn from tableaus fashioned by Goya (1746–1828), the great Spanish painter. Falla was more prodigious, and his works include the prize-winning *La Vida breve* (produced 1914); two ballets that incorporate important vocal passages, *El amor brujo* (1915) and the *Three Cornered Hat* (1919); and *Master Pedro's Puppet Show* (1923), a clever marionette-opera.

Content to import opera from the continent since the time of Henry Purcell (d. 1695), in the contemporary era England found an unusually gifted composer in Benjamin Britten. His operatic masterpiece is *Peter Grimes* (1945), the personality study of a morose and eccentric fisherman. However, such other works as *The Rape of Lucretia* (1946), based on classic tragedy; *Albert Herring* (1947), a comic opera derived from Maupassant; *Billy Budd* (1951), founded on Melville's tale of the same name; and *The Turn of the Screw* (1954), derived from the writings of Henry James, are also notable. Engrossing, powerfully expressive, and meticulously wrought, Britten's works are superb examples of English opera.

Perhaps the greatest creative musician of our era, Igor Stravinsky, an American resident since 1939 and a citizen since 1945, has written several works for the stage. Aside from his monumental ballet scores (*Firebird, Petrouchka,* and *Sacre du printemps*), *Rossignol* (1914), a "lyric tale" in three acts; *Renard* (1922), a one-act burlesque "to be sung and played"; *Marva* (1922), a comic opera taken from Pushkin; *Oedipus Rex* (staged in 1928), an opera-oratorio based on Sophocles; and an English-language work, *The Rake's Progress* (1951), dramatically founded on a series of Hogarth engravings, are impressive theatrical pieces. Reflective of modern compositional styles, Stravinsky's operas do not contain an abundance of pretty tunes, but the composer's lyric sense is impeccable, his concept of form flawless, and his dramatic instinct of surpassing excellence. In an era not noted for memorable dramatic scores, Stravinsky's operas elicit close attention.

George Gershwin's *Porgy and Bess* (1935), a work throbbing with a sense of sociological urgency, is probably the first lyric drama by a native-born American to win international recognition. Giving an authentic portrait of life on "Catfish Row"—the Negro quarter of a city in South Carolina—*Porgy and Bess* has a score more notable for tunefulness than complexity and combines the racy idioms of popular jazz with the sturdy simplicity of folk spirituals. When he wrote this opera, Gershwin was an experienced man of the theater (his previous Broadway musical comedies—most of them smash hits—include *Of Thee I Sing, Oh, Kay!,* and *Lady Be Good*), and his inventive flair, sensitivity for the subject he was portraying, and instinctive insight into the cultural mores of a minority group make *Porgy and Bess* a work of enduring beauty.

Steeped in the traditions of Italian opera—he was born there and still retains its citizenship while residing mostly in the United States—Gian-Carlo Menotti (b. 1911) composes operas that extend the concepts of Verdi and Puccini into our present era. An opera buffa entitled *Amelia Goes to the Ball*

(1937) established Menotti as a man worthy of attention, and this promise has been more than fulfilled in the humorous *Old Maid and the Thief* (1939); the eerie *The Medium* (1946); a witty farce, *The Telephone* (1947); the dramatic tale of homeless refugees, *The Counsel* (1950); a perennial Christmas favorite, *Amahl and the Night Visitors* (1951); a touching human-interest work, *The Saint of Bleecker Street* (1954); and the humorous *Last Savage* (1964). Acting as his own librettist, Menotti creates opera with a practical eye on the problems of performance. All employ English, are comparatively short, utilize a small orchestra and a limited cast, and are amenable to performance in regular theaters (as opposed to fully equipped opera houses) or on television.

As the United States lay in the toils of a great depression, Marc Blitzstein (1905–1964) created a sociological tract, *The Cradle Will Rock* (1937). Subsequently, he wrote music for *Regina* (1949), but a promise so brilliantly shown in the earlier piece has not been notably fulfilled. Other American composers who have had greater influence in shaping stylistic currents in the contemporary theater include Douglas Moore (b. 1893); Virgil Thomson (b. 1896); Aaron Copland (b. 1900); and Samuel Barber (b. 1910). Beginning with *The Headless Horseman* (1936), continuing with *The Devil and Daniel Webster* (1939) and several others, Moore ultimately produced his best-known work, *The Ballad of Baby Doe*, in 1956. For the most part concerned with depicting vignettes in American history, his scores are folkish, homespun, and engagingly simple. Thomson tends to be more sophisticated. His two operas, *Four Saints in Three Acts* (1934) and *The Mother of Us All* (1947), based on the life of Susan B. Anthony, an American suffragette, are founded on Gertrude Stein texts. As might be expected, their librettos are filled with bewildering literary inconsistencies as well as witty satire. But Thomson's music has a pristine clarity that is almost classic in outline, with a result that these pieces are novel, saucy, and enjoyable. Copland also composed two operas. One, *The Second Hurricane* (1937), was written for performance by high school students, while the second, a full-length work titled *The Tender Land* (1954) was conceived for the Metropolitan Opera Company. Fully conversant with the theater's vagaries and not inconsiderable demands, Copland has not really attained signal success in this area, and his shorter work (concerned with depicting the self-sacrificing heroism of young people living and working under extremely trying conditions) enjoys greater renown. Produced at New York City's Metropolitan Opera House in 1956, Barber's *Vanessa* (with a libretto by Menotti) is heavily laden with cloying dramatic clichés and tends to perpetuate post-Romantic traditions rather than strike out in new directions. Nevertheless, it has acquired considerable prestige. Barber's opulent *Antony and Cleopatra* (1966), a most recent arrival on the scene, is a commissioned work written to commemorate the opening of New York City's new Metropolitan Opera House at Lincoln Center.

Today, opera is obliged to vie for public acceptance with motion pictures, television, ballet, and drama. Confronted with formidable opposition, it admittedly does not claim the popular fancy known in the past. Still, this musicodramatic form not only endures but prospers. Operatic performances consistently draw large audiences, young and talented singers and instrumentalists press forward in search of recognition, new works are being continually produced, new (and extremely expensive) opera houses are being built, and the entire enterprise glows with vibrant vigor. That opera has been unable to effectuate a meaningful liaison with motion pictures and television and thus fulfill a promise that once seemed bright, is disappointing. Still, the future remains open, and the lyric theater—filled with glorious traditions and apparently inexhaustible resources—gives every evidence that it will flourish and grow for generations to come.

EXCERPTS FROM FIVE REPRESENTATIVE OPERAS

Wolfgang Amadeus Mozart (1756–1791), *The Marriage of Figaro*, Act I

Combining the abundant talents of Lorenzo da Ponte (1749–1838) as librettist and Mozart as composer, this jocose opera buffa (first performed at Vienna in May, 1786) is one of the lyric theater's most sparkling works. Based on a play by Beaumarchais, pseudonym for the French writer Pierre A. Caron, and a sequel to his better-known *Le Barbier de Seville*, it is concerned with young love (which, incidentally, does not always run smoothly), lecherous desire, wily deception, awakening passion, and just plain high spirits. Invidious enough to run afoul of official censorship in the original dramatic version, its satirical lampooning of the nobility was sufficiently blunted by Mozart's imaginative musical score to pass muster even in the conservative court circles of imperial Vienna.

Organized in four acts that, in turn, are subdivided into twenty-eight individual musical numbers, the opera is a succession of witty episodes. Yet moments of high comedy do not completely overshadow the plot's more serious aspects, as, for instance, when Figaro (a commoner) courageously determines to oppose the Count; nor do they obscure the Countess's deeply felt anguish over her husband's ridiculous behavior. Although some situations strain credibility (for example, Marcellina's wish to marry Figaro, who is ultimately proven her long-lost son), most depict fascinating and engrossing contrasts in human behavior ranging from extreme arrogance (the Count) to shrill cattiness (the inane rivalry between Marcellina and Susanna). Always and everywhere, of course, Mozart's sublime music portrays the human psyche in meaningful, compassionate, and highly perceptive terms.

The Cast

Count Almaviva, a wealthy landowner	baritone
Figaro, his valet	baritone
Countess Almaviva	soprano
Susanna, her maid	soprano
Dr. Bartolo, a physician	bass
Marcellina, Bartolo's housekeeper	mezzo-soprano
Cherubino, a page boy	soprano
Don Basilio, a music teacher	tenor

Time: The Eighteenth Century
Place: Near Seville

A BRIEF SYNOPSIS OF THE PLOT

Married to Rosina since the culmination of an eager courtship fully described in the author's *Barber of Seville,* Count Almaviva has now become deeply interested in the furtherance of a series of intrigues with his more comely feminine subjects. Chiefly, he covets Susanna, his wife's maid, who is soon to marry Figaro. Formerly an effective intermediary for his master in matters of amorous deception, Figaro is now cast as an adroit adversary who must protect the person and honor of his fiancée. Perhaps the most unfortunate victim of Almaviva's attempts at extramarital foray is his wife, the Countess. By shrewdly striking back, however, and assisting Susanna and Figaro in episodes that involve costume exchanges, purloined letters, false identities, and misplaced trinkets, she ultimately places her errant husband in a situation from which graceful extrication is impossible. Temporarily repentant (at least as far as this opera is concerned), the Count begs humble forgiveness and pledges to mend his ways. Further reconciliations are brought about as the opera nears its close between the several couples (Figaro and Susanna, Bartolo and Marcellina, and Cherubino and Barbarina) whose uninhibited antics make this opera such a good natured romp.

Here is the sequence of numbers that unfolds as the first act of *The Marriage of Figaro* is performed:

Act One: (An unfurnished room in the ducal palace)

1. *Overture:* Played by the orchestra in *presto* tempo, duple meter, and the key of D major; it is organized in sonatina form.
2. *Cinque, dieci, venti, trenta* (Two-foot, three-foot, four-foot, five-foot): While measuring their newly assigned apartment, Figaro converses with Susanna who has made a new hat and repeatedly asks his opinion of it. Pleased with these quarters, Figaro comments on their convenient location. Susanna, however, is less impressed.

3. *Se a caso madama la notte ti chiama* (Suppose my lady should require you at night): Because they will be close to chambers occupied by the Count and Countess, Susanna and Figaro can efficiently serve them day or night. However, Susanna discloses that numerous favors (including a dowry) Almaviva has been showing them have not been entirely innocent in intent. Summoned to duty, she leaves Figaro to mull over this latest bit of information.

4. *Se vuol ballare, signor Contino* (If you are after amusement, Mr. Count): Now aware of the Count's designs on Susanna, Figaro plans to outwit his master. Then, as he leaves, Bartolo and Marcellina enter. Speaking in recitative they disclose plans to interrupt the forthcoming nuptials between Susanna and Figaro.

5. *La vendetta* (Now for vengeance): Sullen because of a turn of past events, Bartolo considers this a fine opportunity to gain revenge. After expressing deep-seated animosity toward Figaro, he departs and Susanna enters to join Marcellina. During a brief recitative both women become bitingly sarcastic toward one another.

6. *Via resti, servita, madama brillante* (Your servant bids good day, illustrious lady): Despite obvious disparities in age, both women wish to marry Figaro; consequently, their conversational exchange is ironic and vituperative. Finally, Marcellina leaves and Susanna is joined by the page, Cherubino, who tells (in recitative) of his hopeless love for the Countess.

7. *Non so piu cosa son, cosa faccio* (Is it pain or pleasure that fills me): Cast in a "trouser role" (that is, a woman in man's attire) to sustain the image of a youth's unchanged voice, Cherubino sings of love and its problems. When the Count approaches to enter the room, Susanna hides the page by covering him with a bouffant dress. Within moments, however the Count himself is obliged to hide when Basilio enters. But the gossip Basilio brings (concerning Cherubino and the Countess) causes him to lose his temper and indignantly step forward.

8. *Cosa sento!* (It is disgraceful!): Using anger to cover his discomfiture, Almaviva demands that Cherubino be found. Then, in an amusing display of stage antics, he discovers the hidden page. Now Almaviva's ire becomes genuine enough, but it must be adroitly tempered, for Cherubino has heard his suggestive remarks to Susanna. What to do?

9. *Giovani liete, fiori spargete* (We come strewing flowers): Interrupting this farcical byplay, Figaro and a group of fellow workers enter to request that his lordship bless the proposed marriage. Although pretending to approve, Almaviva slyly defers the actual ceremony. Then, when the preceding argument breaks out anew, the Count says he will send Cherubino into military service.

10. *Non piu andrai, farfallone amoroso* (Say goodbye to fun and frolic):

Taking Cherubino by the arm, Figaro tells of the fun and pleasure awaiting him. War is glorious, he says, and Cherubino will return victorious, if he is not killed before! To the strains of martial music, all form an impromptu procession and march from the stage.

Figure 22.   Scene from Act III of Wagner's *Tannhäuser*.

Richard Wagner (1813–1883), *Tannhäuser* (highlights)

Wagner's *Tannhäuser* (1845), his fifth opera, shows much of the opulent ornateness conventionally associated with "grand" opera. It has a cast of over a hundred participants and an equally sizeable orchestra; it incorporates such set numbers as processionals, prayers, dances, and choruses; and virtually every episode over its considerable expanse is mounted in a spectacular way. As a matter of course, *Tannhäuser* employs the German language and discloses a rare degree of environmental authenticity by being based on a fragment from German history narrated in a medieval poem called *Der Sangerkrieg*. Moreover, it begins to show a totality of concept (the *gesamtkunstwerk*) that welds voices and orchestra, dancers and actors, scenery and lighting, rhetoric and pantomime into an indissoluble whole. Such a blending of forces was to become more complete in Wagner's subsequent works (the *Ring Cycle*, for instance), but preliminary techniques leading to the tremendous growth of German opera that was to occur over the next seventy years make an auspicious debut here.

The Cast (partial listing)

Tannhäuser, a minstrel	tenor
Wolfram, a knight	baritone
Elisabeth, niece of Hermann	soprano
Venus, a goddess	soprano
Hermann, Landgrave of Thuringia	bass

Time: Thirteenth century
Place: Thuringia, near Eisenach

A Brief Synopsis of the Plot

Laid in medieval Germany and invested with a panoply of ritualistic observances traditionally maintained in the households of petty noblemen, Wagner's *Tannhäuser* centers on the time-honored conflict between good and evil. Within it contending forces vie for the heart, mind, and personality of Heinrich Tannhäuser, a young knight-minstrel in the retinue of Hermann, Landgrave of Thuringia. Wanton lustfulness and a whole-hearted pursuit of pleasure are preoccupations at the court of Venus (on the Venusberg) where Tannhäuser has taken up residence prior to the opera's opening. But excessive licentiousness now begins to pall, and despite the very considerable distractions interposed by sirens, nymphs, and bacchantes (as well as Venus herself), the young knight resolutely departs from the Court of Love. Subsequently, while traveling through a forest near the Wartburg, Tannhäuser meets a hunting party and is taken back to the Landgrave's castle where he is warmly greeted, especially by Elisabeth, Hermann's niece. But when the young minstrel attempts to praise carnal love in a song contest held that evening at the castle, emotions flare and Tannhäuser is forced to rely for safe deliverance from sword-play on Elisabeth who acts as a staunch advocate in the face of overwhelming contrary opinion. Realizing that eternal damnation awaits unless heavenly forgiveness can be found, Tannhäuser undertakes a pilgrimage to Rome to seek absolution from the Pope. But the latter is powerless in the face of such grievous sinfulness, and the knight returns to Germany rebellious, hurt, and angry. Elisabeth, however, has remained steadfast. She prays continually for Tannhäuser, and ultimately offers her own life in expiation for his sins. As the opera enters into its final pages, both are dramatically released from the world to find eternal happiness in the broad vaults of heaven.

Act One (A spacious grotto within the Venusberg)

1. *Naht euch dem Strande!* (Come near the beach): Comfortably relaxed at the Court of Venus, Tannhäuser experiences at first hand the voluptuous delights of wanton pleasure. But his thoughts turn with recurrent insistence to the world of men, and he begs the goddess for release. Al-

though she thinks him mad, Venus assents. But, she says, one day he will return.

Act Two (In the Great Hall of the Wartburg Castle)

2. *Dich, teure Halle, gruss ich wieder* (I happily greet this beloved hall again): When Tannhäuser left for the Venusberg, Elisabeth fell into despondency; she seldom visited the castle and was rarely seen in public. Now that he has returned, she feels a renewal of spirit. Entering the manorial hall, she sings of new-found joy.

3. *Freudig begrussen wir di edle Halle* (We greet this noble hall): Townspeople, court retainers, and others also enter this huge room (in a section conventionally referred to as the "Entry of the Guests") and sing in honor of the Landgrave. Actually, they have come to witness a Tournament of Song between minstrels attached to the court.

4. *Gar viel und schon ward hier in dieser Halle* (Often we meet in this hall): Hermann graciously welcomes his subjects, reminds them of the noble traditions surrounding song contests, and assures them that pleasure awaits.

Act Three (On a roadside near the castle)

5. *Wohl wusst' ich hier sie im Gebet zu finden* (She can be found here deep in prayer): After having given offense at the song contest, Tannhäuser leaves for Rome. Spring and summer pass while Wolfram and Elisabeth vainly await his return. Observing Elisabeth kneeling in prayer at a wayside shrine, Wolfram comments on her devotion to God and her fidelity to Tannhäuser. Sounding faintly in the distance but growing in intensity with the passing moments, the familiar "Pilgrim's Chorus" sounds as supplicants pass returning from the Eternal City. But Tannhäuser is not among them.

6. *All macht'ge Jungfrau, hor mein Flehen* (Almighty Virgin, hear my prayer): Deeply disappointed, Elisabeth again kneels, and in "Elisabeth's Prayer" beseeches the Virgin's intercession. She gladly offers herself if only the knight might find redemption.

7. *Wie Todesahnung Dammrung deckt die Lande* (Almost like death, evening covers the land): Dusk has turned into evening, Elisabeth has gone to the castle, and only Wolfram remains. Accompanying himself on a minstrel's harp, in the familiar "Song to the Evening Star" he pleads with heaven to protect and sustain Elisabeth. At the aria's conclusion a dejected Tannhäuser appears and angrily reports on his experiences in Rome. Having lost all hope of salvation, he has determined to return to the Venusberg. In turn, Wolfram asks Tannhäuser to delay.

8. *Heil! Heil! Der Gnade Wunder Heil!* (Listen to an unbelievable wonder): A group of young pilgrims excitedly rush on the scene carrying a wooden

staff that has miraculously burst into bloom. God's will has become manifest (previously, the Pope had told Tannhäuser that only such a miracle
could save him), and all exult over this sign of divine blessing. Actually,
however, Elisabeth has given up her life, and when Tannhäuser sees her
bier being carried from the castle, he, too, collapses in death. Despite
the passing of Elisabeth and Tannhäuser religious fervor pervades the
assemblage, for it is obvious that God has blessed them, and that both
have found eternal salvation.

Figure 23.   Scene from Act I of Verdi's *La Traviata*.

Giuseppe Verdi (1813–1901), *La Traviata* (highlights)

When Verdi first became acquainted with *La Dame aux camelias* ("The
Woman of the Camelias"), a novel by Alexandre Dumas the younger that
was to become the literary substance of *La Traviata* (The Lost One), he
was already deep in work on *Il Trovatore*. But the dramatic possibilities of
Dumas' novel, which also gained widespread fame as a play, were so intriguing that Verdi forthwith directed Francesco Piave to prepare a libretto
for a new work with all possible speed. Then, in short order, he composed
his masterful score.

As with all of Verdi's operas, *La Traviata* (premiered in March, 1853) is
a passionate work, but its sentiments are quite different from the seething
emotions that so frequently appear in his other pieces. Here the predominant expression is restrained, tender, and gentle; and aside from occasional

passing moments of anger (that is, in the third act), the over-all feeling is one of loveliness, tender compassion, and deep pathos. Entirely credible, its characters consistently display emotions that motivate all humans. Love, despair, jealousy, and the tragedy of youthful death are portrayed with such conviction as to make their impact irresistible. And, of course, as one would expect from such a gifted musician, this musical score is one of opera's most lyric works. Melodism abounds, and the profusion of tunes given its singers is beautifully matched by the subtle harmonizations, adroit counterpoint, and incandescent colors assigned the orchestra. Rarely have the theater's resources been so convincingly, so effectively, and so compellingly united within a single opera.

The Cast (Partial Listing)

Violetta, a young Parisian courtesan	soprano
Annina, Violetta's maid	soprano
Flora, a friend of Violetta's	mezzo-soprano
Alfredo, a young man from Provence	tenor
Germont, father of Alfredo	baritone
(others, members of the chorus, ballet dancers, etc.)	

Time: About 1800
Place: Paris

A Brief Synopsis of the Plot

While attending a fashionable party in Paris, Alfredo is introduced to Violetta, a courtesan whom he has long admired from afar. Secretly impressed with Alfredo's protestations of love, Violetta is chary of having an affair with an impecunious youth. But the ways of love are inexplicable, and the heretofore calculating Violetta soon renounces her luxurious ways to live modestly on the city's outskirts with Alfredo. In the midst of their idyllic existence, Germont, father of Alfredo, appears with a request that Violetta break up this questionable liaison. Initially refusing to renounce the only genuine happiness she has known, Violetta is ultimately persuaded when Germont tells that his daughter is being denied marriage because of Alfredo's sinful life. After she agrees to separate from her lover, Violetta returns to Paris and, in company with friends, is enjoying a gay party when Alfredo appears. Becoming a cynosure of attention, gambling heavily and speaking uproariously, he offends everyone, especially Violetta. After a bitter exchange of words, the evening ends with all departing in downcast spirits. Shortly thereafter, illness forces Violetta to renounce her association with the smart set and, because of straitened financial circumstances, take up living in a tiny attic room. Death is not far away when Alfredo makes an unexpected return. Naturally, the lovers' reunion is rapturous, but the ravages of her sickness are so deeply implanted that even Alfredo's presence cannot restore Violetta. Gently, but inexorably, she slips from life.

Act One (A sumptuously furnished room in Violetta's house)

1. *Prelude:* Played by the orchestra in *adagio* tempo, quadruple meter, and the key of E major, it is relatively short, and is based on thematic fragments from the work that follows.
2. *Libiamo ne' lieti calici* (Let us drink from the joyous cup): After Alfredo has been importuned to offer a song, he responds with a lilting *brindisi* (drinking song). When he concludes, music sounds from an inner room (the ballroom), and Violetta urges her guests to enter and dance.
3. *Un di felice eterea* (One happy day): Because Violetta suffers a temporary fainting spell (an affliction that ultimately grows worse), she remains behind attended only by Alfredo. When she questions his interest, he responds by singing an impassioned love song. Violetta is touched but urges that he leave. An affair between them, she says, would be impossible.
4. *Ah fors'e lui che l'anima* (Is he my beloved?): After her guests have departed at daybreak, Violetta engages in a lengthy soliloquy. Alfredo's protestations have affected her, but to live without plenty of money is not in accord with the courtesan's plans. Accordingly, she launches into the brilliant *Sempre libera degg'io* (I shall fulfill a round of pleasure), firmly convinced that she should remain free.

Act Two (A comfortably furnished country home near Paris)

5. *Madamigella Valery? Son io* (Mademoiselle Valery? Yes, it is I): Despite her intentions, however, Violetta later capitulates to Alfredo's entreaties and takes up residence with him at a country retreat near Paris. Germont visits her one day and asks that she give up his son. Totally opposed at first, Violetta finally agrees and Germont, who had come prepared to despise the girl, departs with respect and even affection in his heart.
6. *Di Provenza il mar* (Come back to fair Provence): Germont is present when Alfredo receives Violetta's note saying that she is returning to Paris. When his son breaks down, the older man placates him by suggesting a return to their ancestral home in the south of France.

Act Three (A richly appointed room in Flora's house)

7. *Avrem lieta di maschere la notte* (Dancers will appear later): Members of the fashionable set are enjoying an evening at Flora's home when Alfredo enters. Obviously, trouble is brewing. Before long, he insults Violetta so grievously that everyone turns against him and Germont feels obliged to make a public apology (which he does in *Disprezzo degno*

se stesso rende—No man should offend a woman). Although Alfredo now laments his impetuous act, Violetta is so overcome she can scarcely hear the tender solicitations everyone offers. All leave with remorse and shame in their hearts.

Act Four (A sparsely funished room in a Parisian garret)

8. *Addio del passato bei sogni ridenti* (Farewell to happy dreams): Failing rapidly, Violetta awaits death attended only by Annina. But others have remembered, and Alfredo (accompanied by Germont) enters to rapturously greet his sweetheart.
9. *Parigi, o cara, noi lasceremo* (Dearest, we shall build a new life): Together again, Violetta and Alfredo are filled with happiness. But another weak spell warns Violetta that this is not to be; death awaits.
10. *Prendi quest'e l'immagine* (Take this locket): Resigned to her fate, Violetta gives Alfredo a locket to keep in remembrance, and (in *se una pudica vergine*—If you should find a gentle maiden) urges that he find a wife. Filled with remorse, Alfredo (and Annina, Germont, and the Doctor) weep openly as they watch life ebb from Violetta.

Georges Bizet (1838–1875), *Carmen,* Act Two

Written for performance at the *Opera comique* in Paris, the initial version of Bizet's *Carmen* observed a time-honored tradition of that theater by interspersing spoken dialogue between its musical numbers. This setting has continued to be used in French theaters, although a modified version that incorporates accompanied recitative is now more regularly employed elsewhere. Otherwise, one of the theater's most stunning works remains as Bizet prepared it for the premiere on March 3, 1875. Based on a notorious (and highly successful) novel by Prosper Merimée, and with a libretto prepared by Henri Meilhac and Ludovic Halevy (Bizet's father-in-law), *Carmen* imaginatively portrays a series of events in the short but tempestuous life of an uninhibited Gypsy girl. Although Bizet's previous acquaintance with the lore, music, and customs of Spain (the work's locale) or the Gypsies was casual at best, he very adroitly and persuasively captured a feeling for this exotic sociocultural milieu in his incandescent score.

Organized in four acts that encompass twenty-seven numbers, *Carmen* is an architectural masterpiece. Fairly bristling with melody of Bizet's own creativity, it is also radiant with authentic Iberian color. Shrewdly exploiting the captivating rhythms of several Spanish dances (the *habanera* and *seguidilla,* for example), the score also includes a wealth of related subjects including the pulsating "Gypsy Dance" (often called the *Chanson Bohème*), the energetic "Toreador's Song," and the boisterous "Bull Ring Music." Small wonder that *Carmen* has become one of the theater's most popular operas.

The Cast

Don José, a corporal of dragoons	tenor
Escamillo, a toreador	baritone
Zuniga, captain of dragoons	bass
Carmen, a Gypsy girl	mezzo-soprano
Frasquita ⎫ companions of Carmen Mercedes ⎭	soprano
Micaela, a village girl	soprano
Morales, a dragoon officer	baritone
El Dancairo ⎫ Gypsies and smugglers El Remandado ⎭	tenor

Time: 1820
Place: In and about Seville

A Brief Synopsis of the Plot

While on police duty in Seville with the Dragoons of Alcala, Don José falls in love with Carmen, a sultry, exciting Gypsy girl. After being arrested for assaulting a fellow-worker in a cigarette factory where they are employed, Carmen is remanded to jail, and José is ordered to escort her. Because he willfully allows the girl to escape, the unfortunate soldier is given a two-month term in the guardhouse. Subsequently, while gathered at a favorite rendevous on the city's outskirts, the Gypsies amuse themselves by singing and dancing. Escamillo, a popular toreador, enters and is warmly greeted. Attracted to Carmen he flirts with her briefly, but leaves after promising an early return. Now released from prison, José visits Carmen, but their reunion is interrupted by Zuniga who chides Carmen for preferring an enlisted man to an officer. Provoked, José unwisely assaults his superior and thereby becomes liable to execution; consequently, he reluctantly agrees to desert the dragoons and join the Gypsies.

Resting at a mountain camp preparatory to running contraband across the border, most of the Gypsies sleep while Frasquita, Mercedes, and Carmen attempt to foretell the future with playing cards. Fortune and happiness will favor the first two, it seems, but tragedy awaits Carmen. When Micaela brings news that José's mother is dying, he departs, but only after warning his now-truculent Gypsy sweetheart that she must remain faithful. Later, on a joyous festival day, everyone gathers near an arena in Seville preparatory to witnessing the bullfights. Resplendently dressed, Carmen enters on the arm of Escamillo, her latest conquest. Then, as events progress within the arena, José appears and demands that Carmen return to him. When she scornfully rejects his plea, he kills her as music from the bullring sounds incongruously in the background.

Act Two (At the inn of Lillas Pastia)

1. *Entr'acte:* Played by the orchestra. Sounding over a *pizzicato* accompaniment, two bassoons introduce a tune that is sung later in the act by José. Alternately shifting from minor to major, it prominently displays the sonorities of several woodwinds.

2. *Les tringles des sistres tintaient* (Gypsies dance to the sound of the sistrum): As members of the Gypsy band beam approval, Carmen, Frasquita, and Mercedes entertain. While they dance, repeated melodic strains mount in tempo and intensity until a near-orgiastic *presto* is attained. Breathlessly, the girls complete their performance with an animated flourish.

3. *Vivat! vivat le Torero!* (Hurrah! hurrah for the Toreador!): Shouts coming from a distance indicate that Escamillo, victor in the bullfights at Granada, is approaching. Accompanied by a sizeable entourage, he enters amidst applause and friendly greetings.

4. *Votre toast, je peux vous le rendre, Senors* (Sirs, your toast pleases me): Graciously responding to plaudits from the regimental officers, Escamillo sings his celebrated "Toreador's Song," and describes some of the adventures one in his profession must face. But there are rewards, too, for dark-eyed senoritas shower love on toreros.

5. *Nous avons en tête une affaire* (We are planning an affair): With the café cleared of patrons, the Gypsies' leaders begin to lay their plans to the strains of a brilliant quintet. Except for Carmen, all are enthusiastic over the possibilities of its success. Although they try to win her over, Carmen remains obdurate; she must remain behind to await the arrival of a lover.

6. *Haltela! Qui va la? Dragon d'Alcala!* (Be wary, for a Dragoon of Alcala approaches): As the Gypsies quibble, a regimental song sung (unaccompanied) by Don José is heard from the distance. Realizing that he will make a fine recruit, the Gypsies urge Carmen to win him for their ranks.

7. *Je vais danser en votre honneur* (Now I shall dance in your honor): After José arrives, Carmen begins to dance, accompanying herself with castanets. Within moments, however, bugles sound from a distance summoning the soldiers back to barracks. Not eager to suffer further reprimand, José prepares to leave. Stupefied with amazement, Carmen mocks the dragoon and angrily denounces his love. In response, José draws a wilted flower from his tunic, a memento from Carmen, and sings the impassioned "Flower Song." Somewhat mollified but still determined that he should remain, Carmen suggests that he desert the regiment and live with her in the mountains. But José is not about to dishonor his name; wresting loose, he reluctantly moves toward the door. At this moment a knock is heard.

8. *Holla! Carmen! Holla! holla!* (Hello! Carmen! Are you there?): Returning to meet Carmen, Zuniga sees her in José's company. After an angry

exchange, the corporal draws his sword (a treasonable act) and violence is about to ensue when the Gypsies intervene. Now José has no option. Reluctantly, he accepts admittance into the Gypsy band and all depart for the mountains, singing gaily.

George Gershwin (1898–1937), *Porgy and Bess* (highlights)

Breezy, brash, and occasionally profane, Gershwin's *Porgy and Bess* is refreshingly different from conventional opera. Reflecting the idioms of popular American tunes, jazz, the blues, and Negro folk music, it draws heavily on the experience Gershwin had acquired in writing such works as *Girl Crazy* (1930), *Strike Up the Band* (1930), and *Of Thee I Sing* (1931) for the Broadway theater. But it also shows a deep awareness of dramatic emotionalism, a careful concern for character delineation, and a determination to accurately and sympathetically depict the customs and mores of a tightly knit ethnic group. Written with obvious theatrical skill and a fine command over the rhetoric of music, it is a tautly conceived piece worthy of assuming a firm place in the repertoire.

Based on a book by DuBose Heyward that came to Gershwin's attention in 1929, *Porgy and Bess* deals with life on "Catfish Row," the Negro quarter in Charleston, South Carolina, and narrates a series of happenings in the lives of Row inhabitants. In particular, it is concerned with Porgy, a cripple, and Bess, a woman of dubious reputation easily dominated by anyone around her. After reading Heyward's book, Gershwin became convinced that its substance would make a fine musicodramatic work. He studied the volume carefully and even spent several months in South Carolina to become fully steeped in the environmental situation it depicts. Then, at the composer's urging, Heyward and Ira Gershwin shaped the book into an exciting operatic libretto. Produced in New York City in 1935, *Porgy and Bess* enchanted its opening night audience, and it has continued to please countless others during ensuing years.

The Cast

Porgy, a cripple	bass-baritone
Bess, Crown's girl	soprano
Crown, a tough stevedore	baritone
Serena, wife of Robbins	soprano
Clara, Jake's wife	soprano
Sportin' Life, a dope peddler	tenor
Frazier, a Negro "lawyer"	baritone

(and others including Maria, Jake, Mingo, Robbins, Peter, Annie, an Undertaker, Mr. Archdale, a Detective, and a Policeman)

Place: Charleston, S.C.
Time: The recent past

A Brief Synopsis of the Plot

On a languid summer evening, inhabitants of Catfish Row pass the time in a variety of pursuits. Some dance to the rhythms of Jasbo Brown's piano, Clara sings a lullaby to her fretful child, but most of the men—home from the day's laborious tasks—play dice. The game proceeds in a reasonably quiet way until Crown and Bess appear. Inflamed by alcohol and excited by gambling, the husky stevedore soon quarrels with Robbins and kills him. As police whistles sound, Bess sends Crown into hiding and finds sanctuary for herself in Porgy's room. After Robbins has been buried (with funds contributed by the neighbors), Catfish Row resumes a normal way of life and Bess becomes Porgy's accepted companion. "Lawyer" Frazier even gives her a "divorce" from Crown and a "marriage" to Porgy (for fifty cents each). On a gala day, everyone (except Porgy) leaves for a picnic on Kittiwah Island. As evening descends all return except Bess who has been abducted and held on the island by Crown. Ultimately she comes back to the Row in an incoherent state, but after regaining her senses humbly begs the forgiveness Porgy is only too anxious to extend. On the next morning when all gather to pray for fishermen caught in a fierce storm, Crown enters, mistreats Porgy, and insults everyone else. Later, Jake is lost at sea. Clara must now lament, and all gather to comfort her. After the stage clears, Crown steals furtively toward Porgy's room, but on the way a dagger is thrust into his back and Porgy emerges to throttle the husky stevedore. Inevitably, a police investigation ensues, and just as inevitably they learn nothing. Porgy is taken into custody, however, so he can identify Crown's body, and Sportin' Life uses the opportunity to urge that Bess run away. When Porgy is released, he returns to a strangely subdued Catfish Row. Learning of Bess' duplicity, he asks direction to New York and resolutely sets out in his goat cart to reclaim an errant sweetheart.

Act I (A street setting in Catfish Row)

1. "Introduction" (played by the orchestra) and "Summertime an' the Living Is Easy": Above the sounds of clinking coins and excited comments from dice players, Clara croons a soothing lullaby to her fretful baby. When her efforts prove unavailing, Jake cradles the child in his arms and sings the lilting "A Woman Is a Sometime Thing."
2. "Gone, Gone, Gone": Mourners gather in a poorly furnished room to pray for the soul of Robbins. With his body resting on a table before them, they sing a pensive spiritual. One by one, neighbors come forward to drop a few coins into a saucer resting on the dead man's chest. Monies collected will constitute a burial fund to assist in paying undertaking fees.

Act II (On Catfish Row a month later)

3. "I Got Plenty of Nuttin'": Ecstatically happy now that Bess is living with him, Porgy sings of the world's beauty. Although his goods are virtually nonexistent, he has his girl, his song, and heaven the whole day long, and is glad to be alive.
4. "Bess, You Is My Woman Now": Interrupting Sportin' Life as he attempts to pass "happy dust" to Bess, Porgy drives the unscrupulous peddler away and tells the humiliated woman of the happiness she has brought into his previously desolate life. Warmed by the ardor of Porgy's unselfish love, Bess joins in an eloquent duet.
5. "It Ain't Necessarily So": While Row inhabitants enjoy themselves at a picnic, Sportin' Life entertains with a song that irreverently refutes some time-honored aphorisms.
6. "What You Want Wid' Bess?": Last to leave the picnic grounds, Bess is intercepted by Crown. Vainly protesting that she is growing old and has found happiness with Porgy, Bess is forced into a thicket by Crown while others speed happily homeward.
7. "I Loves You, Porgy." After lying ill for days, a contrite Bess confesses her guilt to Porgy while expressing fear that Crown may return to claim her. Showing profound understanding, Porgy placates the troubled woman and says he will continually shield her.

Act III (On Catfish Row sometime later)

8. "There's a Boat Dat's Leavin' Soon for New York": After Porgy has been taken by the police, Sportin' Life approaches Bess and extolls the joys of living on upper Fifth Avenue in New York City. He promises plenty of clothes, furs, and jewelry and suggests they take the next northbound boat.
9. "Bess, Oh Where's My Bess," and "Oh Lawd, I'm on My Way": Released from jail, Porgy jubilantly returns to the Row. When Bess does not respond to repeated calls, he makes anxious inquiry of the neighbors. But the information he elicits is not pleasant: Bess has again taken to using dope and has gone to New York with Sportin' Life. But the redoubtable Porgy, having known love, will not allow it to be easily taken from him. Seated in a tiny goat-drawn cart, he starts in search of the wayward woman. As he rides from the scene, the final curtain falls.

Selected Operas

Bartók, Béla (1881–1945)
  Duke Bluebeard's Castle (1918). Balazs libretto based on Perrault. Using only two protagonists to portray a one-hour work, this highly unusual opera is stark, glowingly dissonant, but curiously sentimental.

Beethoven, Ludwig (1770–1827)

Fidelio (1805, 1806, 1814). Sonnleithner libretto. A rescue opera in singspiel style, this piece is architecturally superb, expressively heroic, noble, and lofty.

Bellini, Vincenzo (1801–1835)

Norma (1831). Romani libretto. Concerned with a love triangle in Gaul during pre-Christian times, it is dramatically stilted, filled with bravura vocal passages, and musically ornate.

La Sonnambula (1831). Romani libretto. With a brilliant role for coloratura soprano, it has a simple plot but a rather complex musical score.

Berg, Alban (1885–1935)

Wozzeck (1921). Berg libretto based on Büchner. A magnificent Expressionistic work founded on the atonal syntax; its plot tells of poverty, duplicity, wretchedness, and revenge.

Berlioz, Hector (1803–1869)

Les Troyens (produced in part, 1863; produced in entirety, 1898). Berlioz libretto based on Virgil. Actually divided into two parts, this huge and sprawling work requires a large cast; it has a good but magniloquent score.

Bizet, Georges (1838–1875)

Carmen (1875). Meilhac-Halevy libretto. Founded on a Hispanic-Gypsy plot, it is exciting, restless, and extremely tuneful.

Britten, Benjamin (b. 1913)

Peter Grimes (1945). Slater libretto. This is a macabre drama about an eccentric fisherman. Weighted with tragedy, it is turgid, intense, and unique.

Cilea, Francesco (1866–1950)

Adriana Lecouvreur (1902). Colautti libretto after Scribe. Describing the life and loves of a heroine at the *Comedie Française,* it has an intense, opulent, and taxing score.

Cimarosa, Domenico (1749–1801)

Il Matrimonio segreto (1792). Bertati libretto from Garrick. A witty spoof in buffa style that describes the rocky path of true love, its music is truly intoxicating.

Debussy, Claude (1862–1918)

Pélleas et Mélisande (1902). Composer libretto based on Maeterlinck. *Sui generis,* it is vague, allusive, and evanescent in both musical substance and plot.

Delibes, Leo (1836–1891)

Lakme (1883). Gondinet libretto. Heavy with violence, expressive of love and tragedy in colonial India, it has a sensuous but faded score.

Donizetti, Gaetano (1797–1848)

Lucia di Lammermoor (1835). Cammerano libretto after Walter Scott. Featuring a coloratura heroine and concerned with feuding in the Scottish highlands, this is a tragic, intense, and melodic piece.

Don Pasquale (1843). Ruffini libretto. Frothy and gay with particular emphasis given the basso buffo, it is a comic opera in superb bel canto style.

Falla, Manuel de (1876–1946)

La Vida breve (1913). C. F. Shaw libretto. Including numerous Flamenco melodies and Iberian dances, it is dramatically concerned with a love conflict between social castes.

Gay, John (1685–1732)

The Beggar's Opera (1728). This is a historically important ballad opera, with songs by Pepusch, that satirizes life among England's lower classes. Its latest adaptation is in Weill's *Three Penny Opera*.

Gershwin, George (1898–1937)

Porgy and Bess (1935). Ira Gershwin libretto based on Heyward. America's best-known lyric drama, it is sturdy, engrossing, and founded on a jazz-folk score.

Gilbert, William S. (1836–1911) and Sullivan, Arthur (1842–1900)

H. M. S. Pinafore (1878). First in a series of notable comic operas, it uproariously lampoons traditions in the British Navy.

Mikado (1885). Bubbling, silly, and irreverent, it spoofs life in Imperial Japan.

Yeoman of the Guard (1888). More romantic than its companions, it is sentimental and lyric.

Giordano, Umberto (1867–1948)

Andrea Chenier (1896). Illica libretto. Reflective of the unruly emotions aroused by the French Revolution, this is a richly melodic, exciting, and tempestuous opera.

Gluck, Christoph W. (1714–1787)

Orfeo ed Euridice (1762). Calzabigi libretto. A reform opera based on a classical legend, chorus and ballet have important roles within it. Its music is restrained and elegant.

Gounod, Charles (1818–1893)

Faust (1859). Barbier-Carré libretto based on Goethe. Overly sentimental but with enchanting melodies and fine dramatic characterizations, this work has become extremely well-known.

Handel, George Frideric (1685–1759)

Acis and Galatea (c. 1720). Probably a John Gay libretto. A masque with an English text, it is tender, dignified, and splendid.

Alcina (1735). Marchi libretto based on Ariosto. With an unusually ornate vocal line, it subordinates the orchestra, emphasizes the voice, and follows a precise formal pattern.

Humperdinck, Engelbert (1854–1921)

Hansel and Gretel (1893). Wette libretto based on Grimm's *Fairy Tales*. Considered a children's opera, it nevertheless has an interesting and rather complex musical score.

Leoncavallo, Ruggiero (1858–1919)

I Pagliacci (1892). Composer libretto. A veristic opera of modest length, it depicts the lives of traveling actors. Dramatically tense and tragic, its music is sweeping and eloquent.

Mascagni, Pietro (1863–1945)

Cavalleria Rusticana (1890). Menasci-Tozzetti libretto. Passionate and violent, this opera portrays flirtation and death in a Sicilian village on an Easter Sunday morning.

Massenet, Jules (1842–1912)

   Manon (1884). Meilhac-Gille libretto based on Prévost. Surcharged with emotionalism, it is passionate, artisan-like, but overly sweet.

Menotti, Gian-Carlo (b. 1911)

   Amahl and the Night Visitors (1951). Composer libretto. Written for television, this has become a traditional Christmas opera that tells of a crippled boy going to visit the Christ Child.

Monteverdi, Claudio (1567–1643)

   Orfeo (1607). Striggio libretto. One of music's first operas, it has a surprisingly viable score; its orchestration is especially notable.

Moore, Douglas (b. 1893)

   Ballad of Baby Doe (1956). La Touche libretto. Centering on the activities of a wealthy silver magnate, it depicts America's West during the 1890s; it is folkish in music, plot, and idiom.

Mozart, Wolfgang Amadeus (1756–1791)

   Die Entführung aus dem Serail (1782). Bretzner-Stephanie libretto. A comic opera in singspiel style, it is bright, engaging, whimsical, and happy.

   The Marriage of Figaro (1786). da Ponte libretto based on Beaumarchais. A sprightly opera buffa with satirical overtones, it has unexcelled arias and ensembles and is elegant, witty, and wise.

   Don Giovanni (1787). da Ponte libretto. One of the finest, this opera is beautifully endowed with complex arias and superb ensembles; it depicts the fate of an infamous libertine.

   Cosi fan tutti (1790). da Ponte libretto. An opera buffa lampooning the inconstancy of women, it has few ensembles, but many fine arias; dramatically it is racy and entertaining.

   The Magic Flute (1791). Schikaneder libretto. This is the composer's last opera. Based on occult text and in singspiel style, it intermingles simple airs with complex arias.

Mussorgsky, Modest (1839–1881)

   Boris Godounov (1874). Composer libretto. A superb Russian-language opera that employs a huge cast to convey an episode in the nation's history, its score is folkish, colorful, and Slavic.

Nicolai, Otto (1810–1849)

   The Merry Wives of Windsor (1849). Mosenthal libretto after Shakespeare. A comic opera replete with witticism and merry wisdom, its music is light, gay, and spontaneous.

Offenbach, Jacques (1819–1880)

   Tales of Hoffman (1881). Barbier-Carré libretto. Touchingly sentimental with more than a tinge of sadness, it concerns a poet's lost loves; the score is engagingly melodic.

Orff, Carl (b. 1895)

   Antigonae (1949). Holderlin libretto based on Sophocles. A classical subject in modern dress, the musical syntax is direct and deceptively simple.

Pergolesi, Giovanni (1710–1736)

   La Serva padrona (1733). Federico libretto. Originally an intermezzo and later a complete opera, it is gay and uninhibited with a light and fanciful score.

Ponchielli, Amilcare (1834–1886)

La Gioconda (1876). Boito libretto based on Hugo. Richly melodic and effectively dramatic, it concerns the ill-luck that continually pursues a lovely heroine.

Poulenc, Francis (1899–1963)

Dialogues des Carmelites (1956). Bernanos libretto. Depicting the plight of nuns who suffer martyrdom during the French Revolution, it emphasizes the spirituality of dedicated women.

Prokofiev, Serge (1891–1953)

War and Peace (1952). Composer libretto based on Tolstoy. An epic opera presenting a panoramic view of Russia during the Napoleonic invasion, it is vast, engrossing, and lyric.

Puccini, Giacomo (1858–1924)

La Bohème (1896). Giacosa-Illica libretto. This opera depicts young artists in Paris during the 1840s; it is a sentimental drama with an irresistible score.

Tosca (1900). Giacosa-Illica libretto from Sardou. Concerned with political intrigue, torture, violence, and death, its music is intense and fervent.

Madama Butterfly (1904). Giacosa-Illica libretto. Describing an ill-starred liaison between an American naval officer and a geisha, it is technically impeccable, exotic, and opulent.

Turandot (1926). Adami-Simoni libretto based on Gozzi. Extremely ornate in plot and staging, its music is semioriental, luxuriant, and magnificent.

Purcell, Henry (1659–1695)

Dido and Aeneas (1689). Tate libretto. An example of operatic antiquarianism, this is a historical landmark that depicts Virgil's tale; its music is quaint but expressive.

Ravel, Maurice (1875–1937)

l'Heure espagnole (1911). Franc-Nohain libretto. Racy tale of a clockmaker's amorous wife, it uses arioso throughout and has an extremely poignant orchestral score.

l'Enfant et les sortileges (1925). Colette libretto. A bemused child is effectively chastized in this fanciful and whimsical work; its scoring is superb.

Rossini, Gioacchino (1792–1868)

The Barber of Seville (1816). Sterbini libretto based on Beaumarchais. One of opera's most outstanding buffas, it bubbles and entertains with peerless arias and fine ensembles.

Saint-Saëns, Camille (1835–1921)

Samson and Delilah (1877). Lemaire libretto. Based on a Biblical episode, it has a sumptuous score. Some consider it overly luxuriant.

Schoenberg, Arnold (1874–1951)

Erwartung (1909) and *Die Gluckliche Hand* (1913). Marie Pappenheim and composer librettos. Stark, grim, brief, and convoluted works in Expressionistic style, they require a sizeable orchestra, a chorus of modest size, but only one singer in each.

Moses und Aron (1951). Composer libretto. This is a rarely performed Biblical drama concerned with the Exodus; spare, dissonant, and eloquent, it uses much rhythmic speech.

Smetana, Bedrich (1824–1884)

The Bartered Bride (1866). Sabina libretto. A gay folk-opera infused with zest and authentic nationalism, it employs numerous folk melodies and dances.

Strauss, Johann (1825–1899)

Die Fledermaus (1874). Haffner-Genee libretto. A scintillating operetta about wine, women, and song in Old Vienna, its plot is improbable, but the score is a gem.

Strauss, Richard (1864–1949)

Salome (1905). Lachmann libretto based on a Wilde play. Depicting a salacious Biblical narrative, it is extremely erotic but musically superb.

Elektra (1909). Hofmannsthal libretto after Sophocles. Brutal and violent, its plot is concerned with hate and murder; the music is cacophonous and unique.

Der Rosenkavalier (1911). Hofmannsthal libretto. Portraying youthful ardor, fading beauty, and sadness leavened by humorous buffoonery, it is one of opera's loveliest.

Stravinsky, Igor (b. 1882)

Le Renard (The Fox) (1922). Composer text. A one-act burlesque based on an amusing folk-tale, it can be performed by four singers, sundry dancers, and a small orchestra.

Oedipus Rex (1927). Cocteau-Danielou libretto from Sophocles. An opera-oratorio with Latin text, it employs a narrator, has much choral work, but has little action or stage decoration.

The Rake's Progress (1951). Auden-Kallman libretto inspired by Hogarth. Depicting dissolute life in eighteenth-century England, it is cleverly fashioned, tuneful, and spirited.

Tchaikowsky, Peter (1840–1893)

Eugene Onegin (1879). Shilovsky libretto. A disquisition on the vagaries of love, it is typically French in style and outlook; its melodies nevertheless have a Slavic tinge.

Verdi, Giuseppe (1813–1901)

Rigoletto (1851). Piave libretto based on Hugo. This is a sardonic, vengeful, remorseful, and tragic opera, whose music is dramatic, beautiful, and expressive.

La Traviata (1853). Piave libretto after Dumas. Lyric and touching in music and plot, it intermingles joy with sorrow; one of opera's most melodic works.

Aida (1871). Ghislanzoni libretto. This is lavish grand opera set in ancient Egypt the score of which is spectacular and magnificent.

Otello (1887). Boito libretto after Shakespeare. Concerned with passion, jealousy, and revenge, its music is eloquent, tender, and effective.

Falstaff (1893). Boito libretto after Shakespeare. The composer's final opera, it is fun-filled, witty, and complex; it is through-composed with few set numbers.

Wagner, Richard (1813–1883) (N.B. Wagner consistently acted as his own
  librettist)

  Tannhäuser (1845). A lengthy "grand" opera with dazzling arias and ensembles, it depicts the redemption of an errant knight by a self-sacrificing
  heroine.

  Tristan und Isolde (1865). Based on Celtic folk-legend and describing illicit
  love induced by magic potions, it is sensuous, ecstatic, and heavily laden
  with chromaticism.

  Lohengrin (1850). A Romantic opera that intermingles history with mysticism,
  it is lyric and sentimental and expresses threats of sinister evil.

  Die Meistersinger (1868). Humorous, warm, and sentimental, it depicts life
  in eighteenth-century Nuremburg; employing a huge cast, its score includes
  dances, pageantry, and processionals.

  The Ring Cycle: *Das Rheingold; Die Walküre; Siegfried; and Götterdämmerung.* (First full performance, 1876). Interconnected works that may
  very well constitute the theater's most monumental undertaking, the Cycle
  treats of gods, humans, dwarfs, monsters, and animals and merges legends,
  love stories, and magic with fantastic tales. Over all, it employs leitmotifs
  and enriched orchestral parts in a score that is incredibly complex,
  enormously expansive, and tremendously taxing.

Weber, Carl Maria (1786–1826)

  Der Freischütz (1821). Kind libretto. A Romantic singspiel concerned with
  peasant folk and the German forest, its melodies and arias are good but
  dated.

Weill, Kurt (1900–1950)

  The Threepenny Opera (1928). Brecht libretto. A reincarnation of the
  ballad-opera, this is based on Gay's "Beggar's Opera"; its text is ribald and
  its music is jazzy and witty.

APPENDIXES

Appendix A

Composer Glossary

Intended to be representative rather than all-inclusive, this compilation lists some of music's most distinguished composers. Further information about them and others who have been active in musical development can be found in (1) *The New College Encyclopedia of Music* by Westrup and Harrison (available in paperback); (2) *Baker's Biographical Dictionary of Musicians* (fifth edition), revised by Nicolas Slonimsky; and (3) the Grove *Dictionary of Music and Musicians* (fifth edition), edited by Eric Blom. (See the bibliography for a compendium of additional sources.)

Albeniz, Isaac (1860–1909). This Spanish composer-pianist brought modern Iberian music to international attention. His masterwork, *Iberia* (1906–1909), a flavorsome set of piano pieces, has been orchestrated in part.

Bach, Carl Phillip Emanuel (1714–1788). Unquestionably the most musically distinguished of Johann Sebastian's numerous progeny, C. P. E. Bach assisted greatly in effectuating an orderly transition from the Baroque to the Classic eras. Author of a celebrated treatise on keyboard playing, he was a fine harpsichordist and wrote over fifty concertos as well as an abundance of sonatas for this instrument. In addition, he composed two fine oratorios, much religious music, and a series of classically oriented symphonies.

Bach, Johann Sebastian (1685–1750). An extremely gifted German composer who brought Baroque music to its highest peak of excellence. Writing in virtually every form known to his time except opera, he created copious amounts of instrumental, keyboard (for organ and clavier), and sacred music. Particularly notable are his chorale preludes, fugues, toccatas, and fantasies for organ; suites, inventions, preludes, and fugues for clavichord or harpsichord; sonatas and suites (partitas) for solo strings (violin, 'cello); such orchestral works as the *Brandenburg Concertos* (1721), four orchestral suites, and several concertos for violin or harpsichord(s); nearly two hundred church cantatas; the Mass in B minor (1737); and the *St. Matthew Passion* (1729).

Balakirev, Mily (1837–1910). Credited with being founder of the "Russian Five," a group of nationalist-minded musicians, Balakirev made his greatest contribution to music as a mentor, pedagogue, and impresario. *Islamey,* an oriental fantasy for piano (later orchestrated), is his best-known work.

595

Barber, Samuel (b. 1910). A widely respected contemporary American composer who writes in the modern idiom with due recognizance of nineteenth-century traditions. His operas *Vanessa* (1958) and *Antony and Cleopatra* (1966) are widely discussed works that experience occasional performance, and such other works as the *Adagio for Strings* (1936), *Andromache's Farewell* (1963) for soprano and orchestra, and the *Concerto for Piano* (1962) have gained a firm place in the repertoire.

Bartók, Béla (1881–1945). An unusually distinguished Hungarian musician who was also a tireless collector of ethnic melodies. Greatly gifted as a pianist, he wrote a series of complex works for this instrument including concertos, suites, sonatas and *Mikrokosmos,* a collection of graded pieces couched in a modern syntax. An uncompromising modernist, Bartók consistently used traditional materials in a distinctive manner. For the stage he composed *Bluebeard's Castle* (1911), an opera with only two protagonists, and *The Miraculous Mandarin* (1919), a ballet. His six string quartets are complex, dissonant, and excellent; especially notable in his large body of works is the superb *Concerto for Orchestra* (1943).

Beethoven, Ludwig van (1770–1827). Renowned German symphonist who also composed superb concertos and overtures, prodigious amounts of chamber music (his sixteen string quartets are unexcelled), and a wealth of sonatas for piano, violin, and 'cello. His lone opera, *Fidelio* (1805; revised, 1806, 1814) stands as a splendid example of singspiel. Particularly outstanding among his other works are the Concerto No. 5 in E-flat major for Piano ("Emperor"); Concerto in D major for Violin; and Symphonies No. 3 in E-flat major ("Eroica"), No. 5 in C minor, No. 6 in F major ("Pastoral"), No. 7 in A major, and No. 9 in D minor ("Choral").

Bellini, Vincenzo (1801–1835). Short-lived but extremely fluent composer of Italian bel canto operas, who employed limpid melodic lines often embellished by soaring melismas to create "singers' operas" that were unfailingly filled with unexcelled opportunities for virtuoso display. His *Norma* (1831) is a fixture in the repertoire, and *I Puritani* (1835) and *La Sonnambula* (1831) make occasional appearances.

Berg, Alban (1885–1935). A distinguished practitioner in the atonal (twelve-tone) idiom, this fine Austrian composer was one of Schoenberg's most gifted disciples. Writing with consummate skill, he created an outstanding masterpiece in the opera *Wozzeck* (1914–1921), but left a later theatrical work, *Lulu* (1928–1934), unfinished. Other significant Berg pieces are the *Violin Concerto* (1935), the *Lyric Suite for String Quartet* (1926), and *Three Pieces for Orchestra* (1913–1914).

Berlioz, Hector (1803–1869). The colorful scores of this flamboyant French Romanticist reveal a strikingly unorthodox approach to creativity. Specializing in large-scale works that gave ample scope to his untrammeled imagination, he created the generally unsuccessful operas: *Benvenuto Cellini* (1838), *Béatrice and Bénédict* (1862), and *The Trojans* (1865–1869). Much more acclaimed were such orchestral compositions (some employing voices) as the *Symphonie fantastique, Harold in Italy* (with solo viola), *Roméo et Juliette* (a "dramatic symphony"), the *Requiem Mass,* and a *Te Deum.*

Bernstein, Leonard (b. 1918). Versatile American musician who excels as a conductor, pianist, and composer. A brilliant interpreter, he has been active as

Musical Director of the New York Philharmonic Orchestra and occasionally conducts opera in the United States and abroad. In the creative field Bernstein turns with surprising ease from writing scintillating music for the popular theater (*Fancy Free* and *West Side Story*) to composing symphonic works of the deepest and most probing complexity ("Jeremiah" Symphony, 1943; Symphony No. 3—*Kaddish*, 1963).

Bizet, Georges (1838–1875). An astute French opera composer, whose *Carmen* (1875) has become one of the most beloved works in the repertoire, consistently displays a well-considered frugality of means in his scores while exploiting vocal-orchestral resources to the hilt. In *Carmen*, Bizet adroitly fashioned a stunning piece based on Gypsy-Spanish idioms. Written earlier, his music for Daudet's *L'Arlésienne* (now mostly heard in orchestral suites) displays a similar tunefulness and a superb sense of form. Bizet's lone Symphony No. 1 in C major (1855) is Mozartean in cast and beautifully fashioned. Another opera, *Les Pecheurs de perles* (1863) is heard occasionally.

Borodin, Alexander (1833–1887). A physician-chemist, but also a member of the "Russian Five," Borodin's part-time musical activities bequeathed several delightful pieces to the literature. Incipits from his opera *Prince Igor* (unfinished at his death), particularly the buoyant "Polovtsian Dances," are often heard. His Symphony No. 2 in B minor is Russian to the core, and an evocative symphonic poem, "In the Steppes of Central Asia," is a widely played programmatic masterpiece.

Brahms, Johannes (1833–1897) Compositions by this important German Romanticist greatly assisted in bringing that important stylistic era to a close. A gifted pianist, Brahms wrote warm, lyric, but complex works for the instrument. His chamber music (two sonatas for clarinet, the Piano Quintet in F minor, Clarinet Quintet in B minor, and three string quartets are outstanding), four symphonies (in C minor, D major, F major, and É minor, respectively), the Violin Concerto in D major, and a double concerto (for violin and 'cello) mark him as a composer of distinction. And his "Hungarian Dances" (originally for piano duet) and *Academic Festival Overture* (for orchestra), comparatively light works, are perennially popular.

Britten, Benjamin (b. 1913). One of England's most brilliant contemporary composers. Strongly drawn to the lyric theater, Britten has written such operas (all employing English texts) as *Peter Grimes* (1945), *Albert Herring* (1947), and the *Turn of the Screw* (1954). Other facets of his creative bent are displayed in the pedagogically oriented *Young Person's Guide to the Orchestra* (1946), the pungently bitter *War Requiem* (1962), and the whimsical *Spring Symphony* (1949).

Bruckner, Anton (1824–1896). This religiously minded Austrian symphonist spent a lifetime as a church organist and composer of enormously expansive orchestral works. Other-worldly to the point of being naive, Bruckner cared little for acclaim. To him, music was a means of approaching God, and every effort was expended toward serving Him in a fitting manner. Bruckner's Mass No. 3 in F minor combines piety with a magnificent command of musical resources, and his Symphonies No. 4 in E-flat major ("Romantic"), No. 7 in E major, and No. 9 in D minor show the seraphic heights he could attain in purely instrumental writing.

Chopin, Frederic (1810–1849). Polish pianist-composer, whose works for that instrument have become a cornerstone in the present-day repertoire, concentrated on the smaller forms and devoted himself almost exclusively to the piano. Chopin created vast amounts of incredibly beautiful music. Representative are his seventeen waltzes, four scherzos, fifty-one mazurkas, twenty-seven etudes, twenty-five preludes, four ballades, and nineteen nocturnes. Large in scope, but less idiomatic, are his three piano sonatas, and two concertos (in E minor and F minor, respectively) for piano and orchestra.

Copland, Aaron (b. 1900). Sophisticated American composer whose works have a flair for revealing the latest in contemporary idioms. Often founded on jazzy rhythms as well as sparkling melodies, some of Copland's pieces deal with particular aspects of Americana, as is demonstrated in *Billy the Kid* (1938), *Rodeo* (1942), the *Lincoln Portrait* (1942, with narrator) and *Appalachian Spring* (1944). Particularly evocative is a fine descriptive work, *El Salón Mexico* (1936).

Corelli, Arcangelo (1653–1713). Widely emulated Italian violinist who became well-known as a composer of Baroque trio sonatas, concerti grossi, and works for solo strings. Best-known are his *Concerti Grossi*, Opus 6, which include the often-played "Christmas" concerto.

Couperin, François (1668–1733). French Baroque composer who was often called *le Grand* because of the beauty in his many fine works. Essentially a harpsichordist, Couperin also performed on the organ and wrote a great deal of religious music, as well as works for both of these keyboard instruments. His *Leçons de Ténèbres*, intended for church use, show a deep and pensive piety, while his *Apotheose de Lully*, for chamber ensemble, pays touching homage to a distinguished French predecessor. But the *ordres* (suites) for harpsichord most clearly represent his abundant talent, for they are elegant, wondrously poised, and precisely constructed.

Debussy, Claude (1862–1918). The sensuous, iridescent works of this greatly gifted French musician stand as exemplars of the Impressionistic style. Partly influenced by Mussorgsky and Wagner, Debussy continually sought to maintain Gallic traditions while perfecting a unique musical syntax. Suggestive and poetic, his piano works (*Preludes, Etudes, Images*) astutely exploit this instrument's evocative potentials, while his chamber music (Quartet in G minor, 1893, and sonatas for 'cello, violin, and the combined forces of viola, flute, and harp) reveal a superb grasp of musical architecture. His one opera, *Pelléas et Mélisande* (1902) is *sui generis,* and his orchestral compositions (*La Mer, Images, Nocturnes,* and *The Afternoon of a Faun*) attain unexampled pinnacles in musical symbolism.

Des Prez, Josquin (1450–1521). Flemish Renaissance composer who worked in Italy as a member of the Papal Chapel, and in France in the service of Louis XII, before spending his closing years at Condé in Flanders. A master of contrapuntal writing, Josquin composed more than thirty Masses, as well as a large number of motets and chansons in a beautifully conceived but polyphonically involved style. His *Missa Hercules dux Ferrariae* and *Missa Pange lingua* exemplify the richly ornamented beauties of his craft.

Donizetti, Gaetano (1797–1848). Prolific Italian operatic composer whose numerous operas make taxing virtuosic demands on executants. Musically brilliant and impressive, they are nevertheless sometimes shallow in dramatic subtance. Writing in the witty and spirited style of opera buffa, Donizetti created such comic works as *L'elisir d'amore* (1832) and *Don Pasquale* (1843), but his unquestioned masterwork is the tragic *Lucia di Lammermoor* (1835).

Dvořák, Antonín (1841–1904). Facile Bohemian composer who effectively merged the pristine loveliness of gracious folk lyricism with the involved procedures of symphonic writing. Equally active as a symphonist and operatic composer, Dvořák is now mostly acclaimed for his orchestral and chamber music. Among his choral works are a glowing *Stabat Mater* (1877) and a pensive *Requiem* (1890). Of his nine symphonies, No. 8 (formerly called No. 4) in G major, and No. 9 ("From the New World") in E minor, are especially fine. In chamber music, the Piano Trio in E minor ("Dumka"), and the String Quartet No. 6 in F major ("American") are favorites. His lilting *Slavonic Dances* are enjoyed everywhere.

Falla, Manuel De (1876–1946). Skilled Spanish composer whose operas and ballets combine Andalusian idioms with an admixture of Impressionism and Neo-classicism. An early opera, *La Vida breve* (1905) was a prize-winning work, and his ballets, *El amor brujo* (1915) and *El sombrero de tres picos* (1919) are frequently performed. Falla's best-known orchestral works are *Nights in the Gardens of Spain* (1916, with solo piano), and the Concerto for Harpsichord (1926).

Fauré, Gabriel (1845–1924). A somewhat neglected French musician whose numerous compositions intermingle vestiges of Romantic, Impressionistic, and modern styles, Fauré had considerable influence on a rising generation of French musicians as an organist and teacher. His cycle *La Bonne Chanson* represents French song at its best, and his *Requiem* is similarly excellent. In orchestral literature, *Pelléas et Mélisande* is his best-known work.

Franck, César (1822–1890). Belgium-born French musical mystic who spent most of his professional life as a choirmaster and organist at the Church of St. Clotilde in Paris. Adopting a warm Romantic style and a musical vocabulary laden with chromaticism and reiterated sequential figures, he wrote sparingly but well. His Symphony in D minor, Sonata for Violin in A major, Quintet in F minor for Piano and Strings, and *Symphonic Variations for Piano and Orchestra* are frequently performed.

Gershwin, George (1898–1937). One of America's most original creative musicians, Gershwin initially attracted attention as a writer of popular songs. Subsequently, he composed a series of musical comedies (*Girl Crazy, Oh, Kay!, Of Thee I Sing*), and the scores for a number of films. Meanwhile, signal success came with the jazzy *Rhapsody in Blue* (1924, for piano and orchestra), the Concerto in F for Piano (1925), and a brilliant symphonic poem *An American in Paris* (1928). Special attention must be accorded his lone opera, *Porgy and Bess* (1935), wherein folk idioms, jazz, and the socio-cultural mores of a minority ethnic group are poignantly intermingled.

Gilbert, William S. (1836–1911) and **Sullivan, Arthur S.** (1842–1900). Distinctive creators of comic opera whose irrepressible witticisms convulsed Victorian England, just as they have evoked gales of laughter since. Sullivan, a well-trained and thoroughly competent composer, provided scintillating scores, while Gilbert wrote the pungent, satirical verse that deflated pompous officialdom with incisive, rapier-like thrusts. Among their works are *H. M. S.*

Pinafore (1878), *Iolanthe* (1882), *The Mikado* (1885), and *Yeomen of the Guard* (1888).

Glinka, Mikhail (1804–1857). Venturesome Slavic composer often called the "Father of Russian Music." Reacting strongly against the importation of foreign music (chiefly Italian), he began to write scores that were nationally oriented and comparatively simple. His opera, *A Life for the Czar* (1836, now called *Ivan Sussanin*) established a trend that he subsequently followed in such other similarly conceived pieces as the opera *Ruslan and Ludmilla* (1842) and the orchestral fantasia *Kamarinskaya* (1848).

Gluck, Christoph Willibald (1714–1787). This Austrian-born composer became dissatisfied with the state of opera c. 1750–1760. In his view, theatrical works should be more cogent and logical, with their musical scores implementing dramatic veracity. And in such operas as *Orfeo* (1762), *Alceste* (1767), and *Iphigenie en Aulide* (1774) Gluck attempted to prove his thesis. Consequently, they are noble, elevating, and dignified in substance, but somewhat stilted and even ponderous in movement.

Grieg, Edvard (1843–1907). A Norwegian miniaturist unfailingly at his best in creating salon pieces for piano and songs that capture the ineffable charm of Nordic customs and lore. Widely known as the composer of music for Ibsen's drama, *Peer Gynt*, now mostly heard in orchestral suites, Grieg also gained international acclaim for his opulent Concerto in A minor for Piano.

Handel, George Frideric (1685–1759). Born in Germany, largely trained in Italy, and a practitioner in England, Handel was one of the Baroque era's most cosmopolitan composers. Extremely versatile, he wrote an abundance of concerti grossi and solo concerti for diverse instruments (his sixteen for organ are outstanding) and copious amounts of harpsichord music. Although he made his original reputation as a composer of opera (mostly in the Italian style), Handel is best remembered today as the creator of such oratorios (in English) as *Saul* (1739), *Israel in Egypt* (1739), *Messiah* (1742), *Samson* (1743), and *Solomon* (1748). His *Water Music* (1717) and *Royal Fireworks Music* (1749), originally scored for wind instruments, are now often performed by orchestra.

Haydn, Franz Joseph (1732–1809). An indefatigable symphonist active during the Classical era, Haydn turned out prodigious amounts of diverse music during a lengthy career. While in the service of a Count of Esterházy (1761–1790), he worked in nearly all fields and created an abundance of operas, Masses, quartets, sonatas for keyboard and other instruments, concertos, and symphonies. After retiring from this employment, Haydn wrote his most estimable pieces, the twelve "Salomon" Symphonies (numbered 93 through 104), six Masses (written between 1796 and 1802), and two oratorios, *The Creation* (1798) and *The Seasons* (1801).

Hindemith, Paul (1895–1963). An important twentieth-century musician whose teaching and writing greatly influenced a rising generation of composers. German-born, after 1937 Hindemith spent much of his time in the United States and Switzerland. Working freely and with an astute eye turned toward the practical exigencies of performance, he created, by modern standards, a large body of works. Among them are sonatas for a variety of instruments (for example, *Sonata for Clarinet and Piano*, 1940), a similar body of concertos (*Concerto for Violin and Orchestra*, 1940), much other chamber music, the *Mathis der Maler* Symphony (1934), and *Symphonic Metamorphosis on Themes by Weber* (for orchestra).

Ives, Charles (1874–1954). Iconoclastic American who may well be this country's most original composer. Recognizing that his style would never be popular, Ives became a businessman (insurance) and part-time composer. Working in almost complete obscurity, he created scores wherein naivete (exemplified in the use of well-known American folk melodies) is combined with extremely complex musical devices (polytonality, atonality, and polyrhythm). His *Three Places in New England* (1914) and the "Concord" Sonata for piano (1915) are epochal; his Variations on "America" (1891, for organ) is amusing; and his *Symphony: Holidays* (1913) is singularly fascinating.

Janáček, Leos (1854–1928). Czech composer whose works have been long neglected. Two operas *Jenufa* (1903) and *Kata Kabanová* (1921) have attracted attention in late years, however, and Janáček's *Slavonic Mass* (1927) has now become widely accepted as a masterwork that combines deep piety with a fine grasp of musical materials. The *Sinfonietta* (1926) is his best-known orchestral composition.

Khachaturian, Aram (b. 1903). The colorful compositions of this Tiflis-born Armenian composer have won warm acclaim in the Soviet Union. Combining facile melodism with brash and pulsating rhythms, his ballet music for *Gayne* (1942) and *Spartacus* (1953) has gained international attention. So, too, have the *Masquerade Suite* (1936), and a *Concerto for Violin and Orchestra* (1940).

Kodály, Zoltán (1882–1967). Versatile Hungarian musician long active in teaching, collecting native music, editing and composition. Although an avowed traditionalist, Kodály consistently invests his scores with new, distinctive ideas. Among his more notable orchestral compositions are a Suite from *Háry János* (1926), *Peacock Variations* (1939), *Concerto for Orchestra* (1939), and *Psalmus Hungaricus* (1923, for voices and orchestra).

Lassus, Orlandus (1532–1594). Trained in Italy, although born in the Flemish city of Mons, Lassus spent the last period of his life (after 1556) at Munich. Extremely prolific and a masterful contrapuntist, he wrote an abundance of Masses, motets, madrigals, chansons, and similar polyphonic choral works. Representative are the Masses *Bell'amfitrit altera* and *In die tribulationis*, and the lovely *Seven Pentitential Psalms*, all based on Latin texts.

Liszt, Franz (1811–1886). A fabulously talented pianist whose feats of dexterity fascinated the musical world of his time, Liszt wrote enormous amounts of curiously uneven music. Much of his output is flamboyant and tawdry, but particular compositions reveal a profound grasp of music's expressive possibilities. His Concertos No. 1 in E-flat major and No. 2 in A major for Piano are frequently performed, and such symphonic poems (a design he did much to perfect) as *Les Préludes* and *Tasso* are often heard. Liszt's "Hungarian Rhapsodies" (for piano or orchestra), as well as his "Mephisto Waltz," are repertoire fixtures.

Lully, Jean Baptiste (1632–1687). Italian-born composer-impresario who single-handedly established opera in France. Brought to Paris as a boy, he later entered the service of Louis XIV as a violinist. Shrewdly gaining the king's favor, he advanced rapidly in preferment to become royal composer. Comparatively few of Lully's works are heard today, but his historical significance is incalculable. Music from the comedy-ballet *Le Bourgeois gentilhomme* (written in 1670 and now mostly performed as a suite) gives some indication of his style.

MacDowell, Edward (1861–1908). Pioneering American musical Romanticist now best-remembered for his work in promulgating musical culture in the United States. Native-born, he was educated in Germany but later returned to New York City where, in 1896, he became a professor of music at Columbia University. Mostly a miniaturist (*Woodland Sketches*, 1896), he also created four piano sonatas and two distinctive piano concertos (1885, 1890).

Mahler, Gustav (1860–1911). Splendid Austrian symphonist whose lengthy and somewhat uneven scores often require voices, choirs, and sundry instrumental ensembles over and above the regular orchestra. Intermingling warm Viennese lyricism with melodies of folk or near-folk origin, Mahler wrote glowing pieces that consistently reflect strong emotionality. Well-known as a virtuoso conductor during his lifetime but often reviled as a composer, he was confident that his symphonies would one day be widely accepted. Seemingly, this era has now arrived, for his Symphonies No. 1 (1888), No. 2 (1894), No. 4 (1900), and No. 5 (1902), from a total of ten such pieces are often performed. As a composer of songs, some with orchestral accompaniment, Mahler is unsurpassed.

Mendelssohn, Felix (1809–1847). A German *wunderkind* who became one of Romanticism's best-known composers. Sensitive, refined, and amazingly versatile, he won renown as a conductor, pianist, and composer. Steeped in the tenets of Classicism, Mendelssohn nonetheless infused many of his works with the sweeping ardor of Romanticism. Outstanding are his Incidental Music for *A Midsummer Night's Dream* (for orchestra); Symphonies No. 3 ("Scotch") in A minor and No. 4 ("Italian") in A major; the Concertos in E minor for Violin and G minor for Piano; an oratorio, *Elijah;* the Octet in E-flat major for Strings; numerous overtures; and much piano music.

Milhaud, Darius (b. 1892). Prolific contemporary French composer whose numerous works range from chamber music to opera. Employing a bristling dissonant style and often utilizing melodies of a folkish cast, he has written ballets, sonatas, operas, and symphonies. Especially significant are the ballets *Création du monde* (1923) and *Le Boeuf sur le toit* (1919); the opera-oratorio *Les Choëphores* (1916) for voices and orchestra; and the *Suite provençale* (1937) for orchestra.

Monteverdi, Claudio (1567–1643). An outstanding pioneer in the creation of Italian opera, Monteverdi's example, postulated in a series of brilliant works, established paths on which that fledgling form traveled for generations. Although he wrote three Masses, numerous motets, madrigals, and other kinds of sacred music, mostly in the polyphonic style, Monteverdi gained lasting fame for his stage works (which he cloaked in the then newly emerging monodic-homophonic texture). Of more than twelve operas, only three survive: *Orfeo* (1607), *Il ritorno d'Ulisse in patria* (1641), and *L'incoronazione di Poppea* (1642).

Mozart, Wolfgang Amadeus (1756–1791). Unusually versatile Austrian composer whose more than six hundred compositions brilliantly epitomize the stylistic qualties of musical Classicism. Fluent and imaginative, he created quickly but always with artistry. Among his more notable works are the operas, *The*

Marriage of Figaro (1786), *Don Giovanni* (1787), *Cosi fan tutti* (1790), and *The Magic Flute* (1791); twenty-one concertos for piano, one for clarinet, two for flute, four for horn, five for violin; twenty-three string quartets, five string quintets, and sundry other kinds of chamber music; copious amounts of piano music including seventeen sonatas; eighteen Masses and the majestic *Requiem* (1791); and forty-one symphonies, of which No. 39 in E-flat, No. 40 in G minor, and No. 41 in C major (all written in 1788) are particularly fine.

Mussorgsky, Modest (1839–1881). This strikingly original Russian composer sought models worthy of emulation in the lore, music, and customs of his countrymen. Trained as a military officer, he served briefly in the Czar's army but resigned in 1858 to pursue a musical career. Espousing Russian artistic nationalism he wrote in a direct, evocative, and colorful manner. His masterwork is the opera *Boris Godounov* (1874), but a collection of piano pieces (subsequently orchestrated by Ravel and others) *Pictures at an Exhibition* and the descriptive *Night on Bald Mountain* are also very well-known.

Offenbach, Jacques (1819–1880). A German expatriate who gained fame and fortune by writing French comic opera, Offenbach combined the dual careers of impresario and composer when he became an important figure in musical affairs during Napoleon III's Second Empire. Now mostly remembered for *The Tales of Hoffman* (produced posthumously in 1881), Offenbach was adulated in his era as the composer of such sparkling operettas as *Orphée aux Enfers* (1858), *La Belle Hélène* (1864), and *La Vie Parisienne* (1866).

Orff, Carl (b. 1895). Contemporary German pedagogue-composer whose works often appear to be deceptively simple. Because Orff's melodies, rhythms, and harmonies are unfailingly clear-cut and his colors attractive, his compositions usually make a powerful and positive impression on a listener. Among them are the scenic cantata *Carmina Burana* (1936), the opera *Der Mond* (1938), and the musical play *Antigonae* (1949).

Palestrina, Giovanni (1525–1594). An Italian choirmaster and contrapuntist often called "the savior of church music." Presumably, the example of his magnificent Masses caused disputants at the Council of Trent (1545) to defer wholesale condemnation of such composed works (as opposed to those employing Gregorian Chant). Writing mostly in an imitative polyphonic style and employing a diatonic-modal vocabulary, Palestrina also created motets and madrigals, both sacred and secular, in abundance. Unusual beauty is to be found in his *Magnificat, Stabat Mater, Missa Papae Marcelli,* and the *Song of Solomon,* a collection of twenty-nine five-part motets.

Poulenc, Francis (1899–1963). A fecund modern French composer, Poulenc wrote beautifully balanced scores. Technically flawless, his pieces are warmly melodic and unfailingly reveal a fine sense of color. Chief among them is the Concerto in G minor for Organ, Strings, and Timpani (1938), the *Sextuor for Piano and Woodwind Quintet* (1932), a *Stabat Mater* (1951), and numerous exquisite songs.

Prokofiev, Serge (1891–1953). Composer-pianist who left his native Russia in 1918 only to return in 1934. Writing voluminously, Prokofiev has touched nearly all facets of musical creativity. His operatic setting of Tolstoy's *War and Peace* is of epic proportions, but the witty and ironic *Love for Three*

Oranges (1919) more clearly reflects his characteristic style. Notable among his seven symphonies are No. 1 ("Classical," 1917), No. 5 (1944), and No. 7 (1953). His five piano concertos (particularly Nos. 3 and 5) and the two violin concertos (in D major, 1913, and G minor, 1935) are often performed. *Alexander Nevsky* (1939), a secular oratorio, and the orchestral suite, *Lieutenant Kije* (1934), both taken from motion picture scores, are also notable.

Puccini, Giacomo (1858–1924). Facile Italian melodist who wrote a series of extremely popular operas. Using the *verismo* (realistic) style, Puccini brought situations from everyday life to the lyric stage and shrouded their tragic denouements with tonally opulent music. His *Manon Lescaut* (1893) received only modest acclaim, but *La Bohème* (1896), *Tosca* (1900), and *Madama Butterfly* (1904) were brilliantly successful. An epochal career in the theater, which reputedly made Puccini a millionaire, ended with the nearly completed *Turandot* (1926).

Purcell, Henry (1659–1695). Recognized as extremely gifted, the tragically short-lived Purcell brought unusual distinction to English music during the Restoration era. Amazingly versatile, he wrote for the theater, church, and court with an astounding fertility of invention. Chief among his works are the masque *Dido and Aeneas* (1689), the opera *King Arthur* (1691), and a number of anthems and odes.

Rachmaninoff, Sergei (1873–1943). The sweeping and lengthy scores of this Russian neo-Romanticist touch extremes of musical emotionalism ranging from murky introspection to seraphic exultation. Founded on long arching melodies, they are harmonically rich, rhythmically engaging, but traditionally oriented. Each of four concertos for piano is exemplificative (Concerto No. 2 in C minor is an especial favorite) of his style. Of three symphonies only No. 2 in E minor gains frequent performance, but the *Rhapsody on a Theme of Paganini* (1934, for piano and orchestra), has become a warmly received favorite.

Ravel, Maurice (1875–1937). The witty, occasionally sardonic, but always well-wrought pieces of this masterful French composer have gained a wide following. His *Boléro* (1928) is so well-known as to be notorious, but *Rapsodie espagnole* (1907), *La Valse* (1920), and two piano concertos (one for left hand alone and both composed in 1930–1931) are frequently performed. Ravel's two operas, *L' Heure espagnole* (1907) and *L'Enfant et les sortileges* (1925), are comparatively short but extremely humorous, and scores for the ballets, *Daphnis et Chloé* (1911) and *Ma Mère l'Oye* (1908) are often heard at orchestral concerts. And in the chamber music repertoire, his "Introduction and Allegro" (for harp, flute, clarinet, and string quartet, 1906) is highly regarded.

Respighi, Ottorino (1879–1936). Twentieth-century Italian composer whose operas (long an Italian specialty) have been singularly unsuccessful, although some of his orchestral tone poems have gained international acceptance. Following a descriptive course, Respighi has evocatively depicted portions of the Eternal City in such richly ornamented musical portraits as: *Fountains of Rome* (1917), *Pines of Rome* (1924), and *Feste Romane* (1929).

Rimsky-Korsakoff, Nikolai (1844–1908). Quondam Russian naval officer who renounced this career to become one of his country's most successful composers.

Appointed a professor at the St. Petersburg Conservatoire (1871) where he trained a number of embryonic Slavic musicians, Rimsky became a member of the "Russian Five" and ardently espoused the nationalist cause. But Oriental influences rather obviously dominate many of his works. Among his best-known compositions is *Scheherazade,* with *Capriccio espagnol* and the *Russian Easter* Overture close runners-up. Virtually none of Rimsky's numerous operas experience contemporary performance.

Rossini, Gioacchino (1792–1868). Prolific Italian operatic composer whose fund of invention poured forth in abundance until 1830, after which he virtually withdrew from public and musical life. Best-known for his *Barber of Seville* (1816) in opera buffa style, Rossini also wrote such other scintillating works as *La Cenerentola* and *Italiana in Algeri,* as well as the more serious *Semiramide, Tancredi,* and *William Tell.*

Saint-Saëns, Camille (1835–1921). This astute French composer wrote voluminously during an unusually lengthy career. Witty, urbane, and ironic, Saint-Saëns occasionally used his composer's pen in a satiric way (*Carnival of the Animals*). A virtuoso pianist, he wrote five concertos for this instrument, three violin concertos, a 'cello concerto, and much chamber music. His *Danse macabre* (for orchestra), the *Havanaise,* and *Introduction and Rondo Capriccioso* (both for violin and orchestra) are great favorites. An opera, *Samson et Dalila* (1877), and his Symphony No. 3 in C minor (with organ) are also in the standard repertoire.

Schoenberg, Arnold (1874–1951). Astonishing Austrian composer whose foresight, inventiveness, and ingenuity brought an entirely new vocabulary to music early in the current century. Convinced that conventional procedures had been exhausted, Schoenberg sought new means of expression and found them in a system of writing (often called atonality) founded on the twelve-tone (chromatic) scale. Avoiding standard notions of tonality (therefore, his works are called atonal), he wrote such startling but strangely beautiful works as *Pierrot Lunaire* (1912), four string quartets, and the opera *Moses und Aron* (1951). An earlier Romantic piece, *Verklarte Nacht* (1899), is much more conservative.

Schubert, Franz Peter (1797–1828). The sizeable body of works by this excellent Viennese composer mark an interesting confluence of Classic and Romantic styles. Perhaps the greatest of lieder composers, he was also an exemplary symphonist who demonstrated similar *élan* in the creation of chamber music, piano works, and Masses. Along with his more than six hundred art songs, Schubert is remembered for such orchestral works as the Symphonies No. 8 in B minor ("Unfinished") and No. 9 in C major; for such chamber music pieces as the Quartet No. 14 in D minor ("Death and the Maiden") and the Quintet in A major ("Trout"); as well as for large amounts of piano music.

Schuman, William (b. 1910). Contemporary American musician who has distinguished himself as a teacher (Juilliard), administrator (president, Lincoln Center in New York City), and composer. In his body of works, the Symphonies No. 3 (1941) and No. 8 (1962), the *New England Triptych* (1956), and the *Song of Orpheus* (for 'cello and orchestra, 1963) are outstanding.

Schumann, Robert (1810–1856). The sensitive musical scores and pronounced literary bent of this peerless German Romanticist brought distinction to that important artistic movement. With exquisite poetic insight he invested such collections of short piano works as *Carnaval, Kinderscenen* and *Fantasiestucke* with deeply felt emotional qualities. Richly communicative lieder (*Dichterliebe*, two sets of *Liederkreis*, and *Frauenliebe und Leben*) are veritable gems. And his four symphonies, although somewhat thick and massive in sonority, consistently display sweeping emotionalism and intense ardor. Schumann's Concerto for Piano, and his Concerto for 'Cello (both in A minor) are works of unparalleled beauty.

Schütz, Heinrich (1585–1672). Masterful German composer of the early Baroque whose professional career was mostly spent in Dresden after a period of study in Italy where he acquired insight into such southern specialties as polychoral writing and madrigal composition. Virtually all of Schütz's extant works are religiously oriented including the *Christmas Oratorio*, a *St. Matthew Passion*, and a depiction of the Crucifixion entitled *Seven Words from the Cross*.

Shostakovich, Dmitri (b. 1906). Versatile contemporary Russian composer whose brash but powerful works have attracted international attention. Often, he employs a seemingly timeless pulsating rhythmic figure over which long, sustained melodic lines float with effortless ease, but some of his other ideas are more restless, angular, and craggy in outline. Shostakovich has written copiously for a variety of media, but he is particularly well-known for his Symphonies No. 1 in F major (1925), No. 5 (1937), and No. 7 ("Leningrad," 1949).

Sibelius, Jean (1865–1957). This intrepid Finnish symphonist was writing large-scale works at a time (during the early twentieth century) when such pieces had elsewhere fallen into temporary neglect. Virtually all of Sibelius' compositions are orchestral. Particularly notable are such tone poems based on Scandinavian folk legends as *Swan of Tuonela, Finlandia, Valse triste, Lemminkainen's Return*, and *Tapiola*. Among his seven symphonies, No. 1 in E minor, No. 2 in D major, and No. 5 in E-flat major experience frequent performance, and his Concerto in D minor for Violin has become a repertoire stalwart.

Smetana, Bedrich (1824–1884). Zealous Bohemian nationalist who was obliged to endure exile, mostly spent in Sweden, for his musical and political views. Returning to Prague in 1863, he wrote his best-known opera, *The Bartered Bride* in 1866. His String Quartet in E minor, subtitled "From My Life," is unusual in being autobiographical. And in orchestral literature, his cycle of six symphonic poems entitled *Ma Vlast* (My Fatherland), of which the *Moldau* is a part, is significant.

Strauss, Johann (1825–1899). Fascinating melodies included within polkas, galops, and marches, as well as waltzes, brought fame and fortune to this internationally acclaimed "waltz king." One in a family of musicians (others were his father Johann and a brother Josef), he wrote a wealth of captivating three-quarter time pieces including "On the Beautiful Blue Danube," "Tales from the Vienna Woods," "Wine, Women, and Song," "Voices of Spring," and "Vienna Blood." Two operettas (from a total of sixteen), *Die Fledermaus* (1874) and *The Gypsy Baron* (1885), are regularly heard today.

Strauss, Richard (1864–1949). Programmatic realist whose orchestral tone poems interject a precise descriptive element into music. Glowing, bristling, occasionally dissonant, but always communicative, each attempts to narrate in musical terms details concerning a variety of events, circumstances, or personalities. Included are *Don Juan* (1888), *Till Eulenspiegel* (1895), *Don Quixote* (1897), *Ein Heldenleben* (1898), and several others. Also a superb composer of opera, Strauss could startle, shock, charm, or beguile as he demonstrated in *Salome* (1905), *Elektra* (1908), *Der Rosenkavalier* (1910), and *Arabella* (1932).

Stravinsky, Igor (b. 1882). Incomparable twentieth-century modernist whose numerous scores have set a standard of excellence for the era. Extremely versatile, Stravinsky attracted world-wide attention with the ballets, *The Firebird* (1910), *Petrouchka* (1911), and *Sacre du printemps* (1913). And during subsequent years a series of superior concertos, songs, chamber music, operas, and symphonies have appeared. Outstanding among them are the Suite from *l'Histoire du soldat* (1918), the opera-oratorio *Oedipus Rex* (1927), the *Symphony of Psalms* (1930), and an opera *The Rake's Progress* (1951).

Tartini, Giuseppe (1692–1770). The discovery of unusual performance techniques, which this Italian violinist-composer freely imparted to a succession of aspiring pupils, did much to further the development of string playing. The composer of more than one hundred violin concertos along with numerous trios, sonatas, and symphonies, he is best-known in the present day for his Sonata in G minor, often called the "Devil's Trill."

Tchaikowsky, Peter Ilich (1840–1893). Prodigious Russian Romanticist whose fluency enabled him to enter virtually every avenue of musical composition. Technically facile and an excellent master of orchestral coloration, he composed six symphonies (best-known are No. 4 in F minor, No. 5 in E minor, and No. 6 in B minor); a flamboyant Concerto in B-flat minor for Piano; and the hauntingly lovely Concerto in D major for Violin. His *Overture: 1812, Romeo and Juliet, Marche Slave,* and *Capriccio italien* are very popular, as are collections of excerpts from such ballets as *The Nutcracker, Swan Lake,* and *The Sleeping Beauty.* Of Tchaikowsky's numerous operas, only *Eugene Onegin* (1879) and *Pique Dame* (1890) gain an occasional hearing today.

Telemann, Georg Philipp (1681–1767). The enormous bulk of pieces by this productive German Baroque musician exceeds (but does not excel) that of his distinguished contemporary, J. S. Bach. Organist, kapellmeister, and cantor, Telemann wrote twelve sets of cantatas (each containing fifty-two works) for church use, an abundance of Passion music, oratorios, and similarly oriented church pieces, prodigious amounts of keyboard music, and a plethora of concerti for various instruments. Aside from sundry items in concerto literature, his Suite in A minor for Flute and Strings is a representative work.

Torelli, Giuseppe (1658–1709). Violinist and composer who, early in the Baroque era, assisted in bringing Italian string performance to a rare order of excellence. A pioneer in formulating definitive outlines for the concerto grosso, he also wrote numerous solo concerti for the violin. Among his better known pieces are the Concerti Grossi Opus 8, and a (solo) Concerto in D major for Trumpet.

Varèse, Edgard (1885–1965). Untrammeled contemporary musician whose unorthodox works, written between 1922 and 1965, have injected a new dimension into composition. Concerned with exploiting unusual sonorities—many found in bizarre percussion instruments—strident harmonies, and angular melodies, Varèse has written such shockingly dissonant pieces as *Octandre* (1924), *Ionisation* (1931), *Density 21.5* (1935), and *Deserts* (1954).

Vaughan Williams, Ralph (1872–1958). This English folk-lorist, teacher, conductor, and composer unstintingly devoted his enormous gifts toward a furtherance of British music. Versatile as well as fluent, he wrote nine uncompromising but attractive symphonies for orchestra. Vaughan Williams' Mass in G minor (1923), the oratorio *Sancta Civitas* (1926), and *Serenade to Music* (1938) are excellent choral works, and his operas, although not often performed, are of interest because of their subjects (for example, *The Pilgrim's Progress*, 1951).

Verdi, Giuseppe (1813–1901). Undoubtedly the greatest of Italian operatic composers, Verdi brought lyric drama in his native land to a point of unparalleled excellence during the Romantic era. Combining an infallible instinct for dramatic pathos with a ready fund of memorable Italianate melody, he created more than twenty-six operatic scores of imperishable beauty. Among these, *Rigoletto* (1851); *Il Trovatore* (1853); *La Traviata* (1853); *Aida* (1871); *Otello* (1887); and *Falstaff* (1893) stand supreme. But others—*Simon Boccanegra* (revised, 1881); *Un ballo in maschera* (1859); *La Forza del destino* (1862); and *Don Carlos* (1867)—are very worthy of attention and gain occasional contemporary performance.

Vittoria, Tomás Luis De (c. 1549–1611). Spanish priest-composer of the late Renaissance who devoted himself entirely to religious music. Working exclusively in the sixteenth-century *a cappella* polyphonic style, he created soaring compositions of incredible beauty. Many are Masses, Magnificats, and Requiems, but others are such smaller-scale pieces as motets, hymns, and settings of the Psalms.

Vivaldi, Antonio (1678–1741). The incredible creative output of this accomplished Italian Baroque composer is awesome. An ordained priest, Vivaldi wrote some sacred music—a *Gloria in D major* and a *Stabat Mater*—but his primary contributions were in the instrumental field. An excellent violinist, he wrote copiously for this instrument and associated strings; however, flute, oboe, bassoon, guitar, harp, trumpet, mandolin, and others were not neglected. Representative of this tremendous stream of productivity is a set of violin concertos issued under the title, *The Four Seasons*.

Wagner, Richard (1813–1883). Supreme creator of unexcelled German-language operas, wherein moments of transcendental beauty stand beside passages of almost unendurable tedium. Theoretician, scholar, impresario, poet, conductor, and author, Wagner expended his not inconsiderable abilities in only one direction: the lyric theater. Aside from early works now infrequently performed, his *Flying Dutchman* (1843), *Tannhäuser* (1845), *Lohengrin* (1850), *Tristan und Isolde* (1865), *Die Meistersinger* (1868), Ring Cycle—which includes *Das Rheingold* (performed, 1869), *Die Walküre* (1870), *Siegfried* (1871), *Götterdämmerung* (1876)—and *Parsifal* (1882) are monuments to his craft.

Weber, Carl Maria von (1786–1826). German Romantic pianist-conductor-composer now mostly remembered for his operas—particularly singspiel—although he was fluent in other areas as well. Virtually born in the theater, Weber attracted attention with *Der Freischutz* (1821) and followed it with the less successful *Euryanthe* (1823) and *Oberon* (1826). A fine melodist and master of orchestral form, he is also known for his sparkling overtures, two symphonies, a series of dazzling piano compositions, and several works for clarinet (a concertino; concertos in F minor and E major; a *Grand Duo Concertant*, with piano; and a quintet in B-flat major).

Webern, Anton (1883–1945). The compact works of this Viennese atonalist, pupil of Schoenberg and unique musical miniaturist, often suggest pointillistic texture. Emphasizing terseness and utilizing an extreme economy of means, he wrote pieces whose performance span lasts only a few moments. Dissonant, uncompromising, and often occult, they include *Five Movements for String Quartet* (1909), *Five Pieces for Orchestra* (1913), and *Six Pieces for Orchestra* (1910).

Wolf, Hugo (1860–1903). Austrian musician notable for his richly expressive lieder. Intense, moody, and unstable (he suffered from recurrent spells of insanity), Wolf merged music and poetry with impeccable taste and a fine sense of drama. Much of his work is encompassed within such collections as the *Goethe-Lieder, Italienisches Liederbuch,* and *Spanisches Liederbuch. His Italian Serenade,* for string quartet, is an exceptionally beautiful piece of chamber music.

Appendix B

A Glossary of Musical Terms

Some of the more commonly used musical terms are listed and briefly defined on these pages. For further information about them and other terminology in music's rather extensive vocabulary, see: (1) *The Harvard Dictionary of Music* (a brief version is available in paperback); (2) *The New College Encyclopedia of Music* (also available in paperback); (3) *The Oxford Companion to Music* (ninth edition); (4) *The Concise Oxford Dictionary of Music;* or (5) Grove's *Dictionary of Music and Musicians* (fifth edition).

a cappella. Singing without accompaniment; it is also used to identify music written for voices alone.

accelerando. Becoming faster—that is, gaining in tempo.

accent. Placing emphasis on particular tones or beats, usually by playing them with increased vigor.

accidental. A sign affecting the basic pitch of a tone; a sharp ($\sharp$), flat ($\flat$), or natural ($\natural$) are the most common of these; but a double sharp (x), or a double flat ($\flat\flat$), may occasionally appear.

accompaniment. A reiterated background commonly found in homophonic music that provides it with rhythmic thrust and harmonic depth.

ad libitum. Literally "at liberty," this designation allows a performer discretionary interpretative privileges.

affettuoso. Play with warmth and affection.

agitato. Play in an agitated or excited manner.

agréments. Ornaments in a melodic line that embellish its flow; their frequent employment is characteristic in pieces written during the Baroque and Rococo eras.

alla brève. Colloquially referred to as "cut time," it calls for a halving of common rhythmic valuations—that is, a half note receives one beat, two quarter notes make a beat, and so on.

allargando. A slowing of tempo with a simultaneous increase in volume; these changes often appear at the end of a piece

a piacere. To be played at will, freely.

arco. A term directing string instrumentalists to play with the bow as opposed to *pizzicato* (plucking).

610

aria. An extended piece for solo voice normally performed with orchestral accompaniment; arias are important constituents in such large vocal works as operas, oratorios, and cantatas.

arioso. A kind of recitative, more lyric than declamatory, that impinges on melody without partaking of the latter's memorable tonal flow.

arpeggio. Playing chord tones in a successive rather than a simultaneous manner; hence, they are often called broken chords.

assai. Literally "very"; often used in conjunction with other terms (*allegro assai*) to heighten their meaning.

a tempo. Revert to the original pace.

bar (or bar line). An upright line that separates one measure from another in written notation; often, the word is used colloquially to identify measures.

Baroque era. A significant stylistic period that extended from c. 1600–1750; outstanding among the creative musicians then active were J. S. Bach, Handel, Vivaldi, and Rameau. Mostly, pieces of this vintage are beautifully shaped, expressively austere, and melodically ostentatious.

basso ostinato. A continuous bass normally founded on a reiterated melodic-rhythmic figure.

bel canto. An especially expressive method of singing perfected in eighteenth-century Italy; it emphasizes beauty of vocal sound.

binary form. A bisectional pattern often employed in simple melodies or short pieces; its sections are usually designated *ab*.

bitonality. A simultaneous employment of two different keys whose coincidence may produce stridently dissonant effects.

bowing. A technique employed on such instruments as violin, viola, 'cello, or string bass, wherein strings are caused to vibrate by drawing the rosin-impregnated hair of a bow across them.

brio. Usually prefaced by con, it means to play with vigor and spirit.

broken chord. Playing the tones in a chord successively rather than simultaneously (as in an *arpeggio*).

cadence. A point of repose in a melodic line, or a harmonic sequence, that may be either temporary or final.

cadenza. An elaborate solo passage normally played (or sung) by a single individual; cadenzas occasionally appear in arias, and are near-fixtures in concertos.

cancrizans. Progressing in a retrograde manner, that is, from end to beginning.

canon. A contrapuntal design based entirely on the exact (or near-exact) imitation of a melody by one or more successive voices.

cantillation. Singing in a chant-like manner with particular emphasis on the syllabic declamation of a text.

cantus firmus. The basic melody (in medieval times often a Gregorian incipit) on which a polyphonic structure (*organum*, motet, and so on) is founded.

choir. A relatively small group of singers (as oppoesd to the larger-sized chorus) or a limited number of players (from five to ten) who perform on related instruments (for instance, a brass choir).

chorale. A hymn characteristically used in Lutheran (German Protestant) churches.

chord. A complex of three or more tones usually sounded simultaneously, although they may also be heard successively as broken chords or *arpeggios*. Many different kinds exist, and their creation, manipulation, and alignment falls within the province of harmony.

chromatic. Progressing by half steps (that is, from c to c♯, d to d♯, and so on).

Classicism. An important stylistic period extending from c. 1750–1810 that encompassed, in whole or part, the careers of Haydn, Mozart, Beethoven, and Schubert. Works written in this style are usually marked by formal elegance, emotional restraint, and superb workmanship.

clavier. A generic term used in the eighteenth century, and somewhat later, to identify such keyboard instruments as the clavichord, harpsichord, and piano.

clefs. Signs inscribed at the beginning of musical staves that assign names to the several lines and spaces; best-known are the treble (or G) clef, and the bass (or F) clef.

coda. A final epilogue in many pieces used to round off the design.

codetta. Diminutive of coda; such passages often conclude subdivisions within lengthy pieces.

con. Meaning "with," it is commonly used to modify another term—for example, *con spirito* means "with spirit."

consonance. A pleasing sound resulting from the simultaneous sounding of two or more compatible tones; its antipode is dissonance.

counterpoint. The process of setting one melodic line against another and thus creating a polyphonic structure; in common usage the words counterpoint, contrapuntal, and polyphonic have assumed a synonymous meaning.

crescendo. A gradual increase in volume.

da capo. A direction to return to the beginning of a piece and repeat previously played sections; it is often abbreviated merely to *D.C.*

dal segno. Return to the sign (:$:) and repeat; also written as *D.S.*

diatonic. Progressing in a scalar manner (c, d, e, f, and so on) as opposed to a chromatic succession (c, c♯, d, d♯).

diminuendo. A gradual decrease in volume.

dissonance. Cacophonous, harsh, and strident sonorities resulting from a simultaneous sounding of two or more incompatible tones.

dodecaphonic. Meaning "twelve," it is often applied to pieces employing the twelve-tone (atonal) system.

dolce. Play sweetly and softly.

dominant. The fifth degree of a scale or key; melodically and harmonically it is second in importance to the first degree (tonic).

dot. A dot placed after a note (♩.) prolongs its value by half (for example, a dotted half note receives three beats in quadruple meter); when placed under or over a note (♩ ♩̇), a dot signifies that a *staccato* (short, crisp) articulation is desired.

enharmonic. Applying two different names to the same tone (c-sharp and d-flat).

fermata. A hold or pause in the musical flow indicated by the sign ⌢

fine. The end of a composition.

giusto. Meaning "just" or "exact," it is normally used with basic tempo marks (*allegro giusto*) to suggest a precise pace.

glissando. Gliding rapidly from one tone to another, usually over a fairly wide expanse.

Gothic era. In a musical sense, the span betwen 1200 and 1450.

grace note. Perhaps the most common of melodic ornaments, it is a short auxiliary tone used to embellish principal members in a melody.

half tone. The smallest interval in Western music (often called a half step), it can be demonstrated by progressing upward from c to c♯, f to f♯, or downward from e to e♭, d to d♭, etc.

harmony. The substructural element in homophonic music normally provided by a progression of chords; similarly, the study of harmony has to do with a creation and manipulation of chords.

heterophony. Slight modifications introduced into a melody by individual performers, perhaps as rhythmic or thematic variants.

homophonic. Music that has a predominant melodic line supported by a complementary harmonic substructure.

hymn. A worshipful song in praise of God used by virtually all religious denominations; most employ Scriptural incipits as texts; those postdating 1700 are usually strophic in organization and founded on four-part harmony.

imitation. A frequently used device in polyphonic music concerned with restating a musical idea precisely (exact imitation) or on different scale levels (sequential imitation).

Impressionism. An idiomatic musical style whose vogue extended from c. 1890–1920; its most outstanding spokesman was Claude Debussy, although others (Maurice Ravel, Charles Griffes, Cyril Scott, and Frederick Delius) also used its vague, allusive, and suggestive syntax.

improvisation. The spontaneous (theoretically) creation of music while performing; it is often used in extemporizing variations on a theme.

incidental music. Pieces written to assist the communicativeness of some other art form such as drama, pantomime, motion pictures, television, or radio productions.

interval. The distance between two musical tones computed numerically—seconds, thirds, and so on; more precisely intervals may be major, minor, perfect, or augmented.

inversion. Altering the normal alignment of tones; melodically speaking, it infers a topsy-turvy turning of a tonal sequence; harmonically, it implies that some chord tone other than the root is lowermost.

K. An abbreviation for the name of Ludwig von Köchel (1800–1877), a Viennese botanist, who in 1862 published a chronological listing of Mozart's compositions that was almost error-free; subsequently, the composer's works have been almost unfailingly described as K. 331, K. 622, and so on.

key. The tonal locus in which a composition is laid—C major, F minor, and so on; or, it may be a lever on an instrument typically manipulated by a player's fingers.

key signature. The sharps or flats (or an absence of either) placed at the extreme left of a staff indicating a composition's tonality.

ledger lines. Short horizontal lines added above or below a staff to extend the range of tones the latter may indicate.

legato. Playing in a smooth and connected manner—that is, slurring from one tone to another.

leitmotiv. A German term (meaning "leading motif") used by Richard Wagner to describe the melodic fragments on which he based many of his music dramas.

libretto. The dramatic (that is, textual) substance of such choral works as operas, oratorios, and cantatas.

l'istesso tempo. To be played at the same pace as the preceding section.

maestoso. Play in a dignified and majestic manner.

major. A sequential scalar alignment of tones comprised of two whole steps, a half step, three whole steps, and a half step (1, 1, ½, 1, 1, 1, ½), used in a great deal of music written in recent centuries; the term is also applied to identify certain intervals and chords.

measure. Typically the smallest meaningful rhythmic unit in a piece, it contains the number of beats specified in a meter signature; in printed music, measures are separated from one another by bar lines.

meno. Meaning "less," it is often used as *meno mosso* (less fast).

meter. Patterns of stressed and unstressed beats collected and organized into measures; common meters are duple, triple, and quadruple, and each normally has an accent on its first pulse.

metronome. A mechanical device used to indicate precise rates of tempo.

middle C. A familiar point of orientation in music, it is a tone that rests approximately at the middle of a piano keyboard; in written scores it is notated on the first ledger line below the treble staff (or the first ledger line above the bass staff).

minor. Second only to major as a common scalar pattern used in the music of our time; several possibilities exist: natural, harmonic, or melodic. The intervallic sequence of harmonic minor is 1, ½, 1, 1, ½, 1½, ½.

modes. Scalar patterns that fall outside the major-minor system; known to the ancient Greeks and early Christians as Lydian, Phrygian, Dorian, and so on, each has a distinctive tonal pattern.

modulation. Changing key within a composition—for example, moving from C major to G major (tonic to dominant).

molto. Meaning "very," it is typically used in conjunction with other terms—for example, *molto adagio*, "very slow."

monophonic. That kind of music having only one line; characterized by playing or singing in unison, it is typified in much ancient music and most religious chant.

mosso. Meaning "animated," it is often combined with other terms—for example, *meno mosso*, "less fast."

moto. Meaning "motion," it is often combined with *con* (with).

movement. A major segment in a large musical structure (sonata, concerto, symphony, and so on); normally, each movement in a piece is autonomous and self-contained.

Neoclassicism. A reversion to eighteenth-century formal principles that became fashionable early in the twentieth century; the style is exemplified in Prokofiev's *Classical Symphony* (1918).

non troppo. Meaning "not too much," it is usually combined with other tempo terms—for example, *allegro non troppo*, not too fast.

notes. Written symbols for musical tones normally inscribed on a staff; to an executant, they prescribe: (1) the pitch of a tone and (2) its duration.

obbligato. An ornamental filigree, usually possessed of distinctive melodic characteristics, imposed above a primary tune.

opus. A numbering scheme applied by many composers to the successive issuance of their works—for example, Beethoven's Symphony No. 5 in C minor, Opus 67 is his fifth symphony but (presumably) his sixty-seventh composition.

parlando. Singing in a manner that approximates the manner of speech; usually, it is less impassioned than recitative.

partials. Members of an overtone series—that is, harmonics above a given fundamental tone.

pentatonic scale. A five-tone succession (as opposed to the eight steps characteristic of major-minor scales) frequently employed in ethnic music; it can be easily formulated by playing only the black keys on a piano (c♯, d♯, f♯, g♯, a♯).

phrase. A meaningful melodic idea extending for a number of measures (from three to eight is typical) that terminates on either a full or partial cadence; two phrases constitute a period, two periods a double period.

pitch. The highness or lowness of sounds, as determined by their vibrating cycles, that, in turn, gives rise to precise musical tones (a, b, c, and so on); minute gradations in the vibratory rate relate to the sharpness or flatness of a given tone, as in tuning a piano.

piu. Meaning "more," it is employed with common tempo marks—for example, *piu allegro*, faster.

pizzicato. A method of performing on string instruments (violin, viola, and others), wherein their strings are plucked rather than bowed.

poco. Meaning "little," it modifies various tempo, dynamic, or expressive marks.

polyphonic. Music constituted from an interweaving of two or more lines as is demonstrated in the canon, fugue, or motet.

polytonality. A simultaneous employment of two (rarely more) keys.

program music. Compositions based on the elucidation of extramusical ideas derived, perhaps, from literature, history, or geography.

quodlibet. A polyphonic piece wherein two (sometimes more) totally unrelated melodies, often of a popular or folkish nature, are sung or played simultaneously.

recitative. A declamatory method of vocal delivery by an individual singer wherein textual syllables are quickly enunciated; two kinds are fundamental: (1) *secco* (dry) and (2) *accompagnato* (accompanied).

refrain. A recurrent section (sometimes called the chorus) in popular, semiclassical, or folkish pieces.

Renaissance. In music history the period from c. 1400–1600 represented by a shift in style from the late Middle Ages (or Gothic era) to the Baroque; mostly, it was a period when *a cappella* polyphonic vocal music of rare excellence flourished.

responsorial. Performing in a dialogue-like manner, as in an exchange between a soloist (cantor, celebrant, lead-singer) and a group (choir, chorus, congregation).

rest. A period of organized silence; as with notes, the written symbols for musical tones, rests have a precise rhythmic valuation.

retrograde. Writing (and performing) from end to beginning—that is, starting on a composition's final tone and working toward the front as in cancrizans.

Rococo. A stylistic period, spanning the years between c. 1710 and 1780, that witnessed a merger of the Baroque and Classic eras.

Romanticism. One of music's most important stylistic movements, whose initial manifestations began as early as c. 1810 and whose final appearances date from as late as the 1920s. Fundamentally it stressed subjectivity and emotionalism, unbridled lyricism, opulent harmonization, and vivid coloration. Beethoven, Schubert, Mendelssohn, Schumann, Berlioz, Liszt, Wagner, Verdi, Chopin, Tchaikowsky, Brahms, Dvořák, and numerous others were important musical Romanticists.

sempre. Meaning "always," it modifies various tempo, dynamic, or expressive marks.

sequence. The repetition, either precise or modified, of a melodic or harmonic idea.

sforzando. Striking a single note or chord with a forced attack and then immediately diminishing.

sostenuto. To be played or sung in a sustained manner.

staccato. To be played detached, crisp, and short.

staff. A series of five parallel (horizontal) lines on which most music is printed (drum notation sometimes excepted).

strophic. Songs wherein several stanzas of text are sung to one basic melody; it is characteristic of hymns, simple songs, and folk melodies.

subdominant. The fourth degree of a scale and an important member (next to the tonic and dominant) in a composition's tonal hierarchy.

subito. Meaning "suddenly," it is often combined with *piano.*

supertonic. The second degree of a scale; one step above the tonic.

syncopation. A displacement of normal accentual stress either by (1) emphasizing an unstressed beat or (2) placing an accent between the beats.

tanto. Meaning "much," it is often used with *non*—that is, *non tanto* indicates not too much.

tempo. The pace or rate of speed at which a piece is performed.

ternary form. One of the basic patterns of musical organization consisting of three parts; commonly, the *aba* or *abc* alignments are used.

texture. The density of a composition's musical substance as reflected in the presence (or absence) of musical lines and harmonic substructure; basic kinds of texture are monophony, polyphony, and homophony.

theme. The melodic substance of a piece, sometimes called the tune or air.

through-composed. A composition, typically an art song or opera, wherein the melodic strand runs continuously with few interruptions, as opposed to a segmented or strophic organization.

timbre. The color, resonance, or characteristic sonority of musical tones.

time signature. More correctly described as the meter signature, it is a numerical quotation with numerator and denominator inscribed at the beginning of a piece; this sign indicates the number of beats in a measure and the kind of a note that receives a beat.

tonality. Often considered synonymous with key (that is, the tonal locus of a piece), it is more precisely concerned with relations between keys and any modulatory shifts that may occur from one to another.

tone. The actual musical substance that falls upon a listener's ear and an aural result of vibrations set up in a prepared body (that is, a musical instrument); musical tone has the qualities of pitch, intensity, duration, and timbre.

tonic. The first degree of a key or scale and normally its principal member.

transcription. The rearrangement of a piece so that it can be performed in a media other than the original—for example, an organ piece scored for orchestra, as in Bach's "Little" Fugue in G minor.

treble. The highest part in a composition; the name is often applied to the G (treble) clef on which music for violin, flute, clarinet, and other high-pitched instruments is written.

triad. The most common of simple chords consisting of three members—c-e-g, g-b-d, f-a-c.

troppo. Meaning "too much," it is often combined with *non*—for example, *adagio ma non troppo,* not too slow.

tutti. Meaning "all," it is applied to passages wherein all musicians perform.

unison. Playing precisely the same tones and melodies together and thus creating, in effect, monophonic music.

voice. The human apparatus for producing sounds and, by extension, an instrument on which music is sounded; often, it is applied to identify a musical line or a distinctive part.

whole tone. A primary interval in Western music (often called the whole step), as is demonstrated by progressing upward from c-d, g-a, and so on.

Appendix C

Suggested Bibliography

Consonant with the general purposes of this book (that is, to begin an investigation into music and its literature), no attempt has been made to compile a lengthy, or "scholarly," bibliography. And no effort has been expended to list foreign-language studies, although these are, indeed, both extensive and valuable. A particular feature, however, is the inclusion of books in paperback binding that may prove useful in building a personal, low-cost collection.

Books of General Reference

Apel, Willi, *Harvard Dictionary of Music* (Cambridge, Mass.: Harvard University Press, 1944).

Baker, Theodore, *Baker's Biographical Dictionary of Musicians*, fifth edition, edited by Nicolas Slonimsky (New York: G. Schirmer, 1958).

Cobbett, W. W., *Cyclopedic Survey of Chamber Music*, second edition with supplementary material, edited by Colin Mason, two volumes (London: Oxford University Press, 1963).

Grove, Sir George, *Grove's Dictionary of Music and Musicians*, fifth edition, edited by Eric Blom, ten volumes (New York: St. Martin's Press, Inc., 1955).

Parrish, Carl, and John F. Ohl, *Masterpieces of Music Before 1750* (New York: W. W. Norton & Company, Inc., 1951).

Parrish, Carl, *A Treasury of Early Music* (New York: W. W. Norton & Company, Inc., 1958).

Scholes, Percy A., *The Oxford Companion to Music*, ninth edition (New York: Oxford University Press, 1956).

Scholes, Percy A., *The Concise Oxford Dictionary of Music* (New York: Oxford University Press, 1952).

General Histories of Music

Abraham, Gerald, *A Hundred Years of Music*, third edition (Chicago: Aldine Publishing Company, 1964).

Chailley, Jacques, *40,000 Years of Music* (New York: Farrar, Strauss, and Giroux, 1964).

618

Crocker, Richard L., *A History of Musical Style* (New York: McGraw-Hill Book Company, 1966).

Ferguson, Donald N., *A History of Musical Thought* (New York: Appleton-Century-Crofts, Inc., 1948).

Grout, Donald J., *A History of Western Music* (New York: W. W. Norton and Company, Inc., 1960).

Harman, Alec (with Anthony Milner), and Wilfrid Mellers, *Man and His Music* (New York: Oxford University Press, 1962).

Lang, Paul Henry, *Music in Western Civilization* (New York: W. W. Norton and Company, Inc., 1941).

Ulrich, Homer and Paul Pisk, *A History of Music and Musical Style* (New York: Harcourt, Brace, and World, Inc., 1963).

Contemporary Music and Its Practice

Austin, William W., *Music in the 20th Century* (New York: W. W. Norton & Company, Inc., 1966).

Ewen, David, *The Complete Book of 20th Century Music* (Englewood Cliffs, N.J.: Prentice-Hall, Inc., 1952).

Hansen, Peter S., *An Introduction to Twentieth Century Music* (Boston: Allyn and Bacon, 1961).

Machlis, Joseph, *Introduction to Contemporary Music* (New York: W. W. Norton and Company, Inc., 1961).

Music in America

Chase, Gilbert, *America's Music from the Pilgrims to the Present* (New York: McGraw-Hill Book Company, Inc., 1955).

Mellers, Wilfred, *Music in a New Found Land* (New York: Alfred A. Knopf, 1965).

Opera and Its Aspects

Brockway, Wallace, and Herbert Weinstock, *The Opera, a History of Its Creation and Performance: 1600–1941* (New York: Simon and Schuster, 1941).

Brockway, Wallace, and Herbert Weinstock, *The World of Opera, the Story of Its Origins and the Lore of Its Performance* (New York: Pantheon Books, 1962).

Grout, Donald Jay, *A Short History of Opera* (New York: Columbia University Press, 1947).

Hamm, Charles, *Opera* (Boston: Allyn and Bacon, Inc., 1966).

Kobbe, C. W., *Kobbe's Complete Opera Book*, edited and revised by the Earl of Harewood (London: Putnam, reprinted 1958).

Weisstein, Ulrich, editor, *The Essence of Opera* (New York: Free Press of Glencoe, 1964).

Miscellaneous

Strunk, Oliver (editor), *Source Readings in Music History* (New York: W. W. Norton and Company, Inc., 1950). Also available in paperback.

Paperbacks [1]

Apel, Willi, and Ralph T. Daniel, *The Harvard Brief Dictionary of Music* (New York: Washington Square Press, Inc., 1961).

Bains, Anthony, editor, *Musical Instruments Through the Ages* (Baltimore: Penguin Books, Ltd., 1961).

Bamberger, Carl (editor), *The Conductor's Art* (New York: McGraw-Hill Book Company, Inc., 1965).

Barzun, Jacques, *Berlioz and His Century* (New York: Meridian Books, 1956)

Bentley, Eric, *Shaw on Music* (New York: Doubleday and Company, 1955).

Berlioz, Hector, *Evenings in the Orchestra* (Baltimore: Penguin Books, Ltd., 1963).

Blom, Eric, *Mozart* (New York: Collier Books, 1962).

Brockway, Wallace and Herbert Weinstock, *Men of Music* (New York: Simon and Schuster, 1958).

Bukofzer, Manfred, *Studies in Medieval and Renaissance Music* (New York: W. W. Norton and Company, Inc., 1950).

Copland, Aaron, *Copland on Music* (New York: W. W. Norton and Company, Inc., 1963).

Debussy, Claude, "Monsieur Croche the Dilettante Hater"; Ferruccio Busoni, "Sketch of a New Esthetic of Music"; and Charles Ives, "Essays Before a Sonata," all published together as *Three Classics in the Aesthetic of Music* (New York: Dover Publications, Inc., 1962).

Dent, Edward J., *Opera* (Baltimore: Penguin Books, 1945).

Donington, Robert, *The Instruments of Music* (New York: Barnes & Noble, Inc., 1962).

Haggin, B. H., *The Listener's Musical Companion* (New York: Doubleday and Company, 1959).

Harman, Carter, *A Popular History of Music* (New York: Dell Publishing Company, 1956).

Hill, Ralph, editor, *The Concerto* (Baltimore: Penguin Books, Ltd., 1961).

————, *The Symphony* (Baltimore: Penguin Books, Ltd., 1949).

Howard, John T. and James Lyons, *Modern Music* (New York: New American Library, 1957).

Hutchings, A. J. B., *The Baroque Concerto* (New York: W. W. Norton and Company, Inc., 1965).

Jacobs, Arthur, editor, *Choral Music* (Baltimore: Penguin Books, Ltd., 1963).

Lang, Paul Henry, editor, *Problems of Modern Music* (New York: W. W. Norton and Company, Inc., 1960).

Marliave, Joseph de, *Beethoven's Quartets* (New York: Dover Publications, Inc., 1961).

Miles, Russell H., *Johann Sebastian Bach* (Englewood Cliffs, N.J.: Prentice-Hall, Inc., 1962).

Moore, Douglas, *A Guide to Musical Styles* (New York: W. W. Norton and Company, Inc., 1962).

Newman, Ernest, *Great Operas*, Vols. I & II (New York: Vintage Books, 1959).

[1] Because most of these are biographies, collections of program notes, and articles on a common subject, they have not been separated into categories.

————, *Wagner as Man and Artist* (New York: Vintage Books, 1960).

Pauly, Reinhard, *Music in the Classic Period* (Englewood Cliffs, N.J.: Prentice-Hall, Inc., 1965).

Pincherle, Marc, *Vivaldi, Genius of the Baroque* (New York: W. W. Norton and Company, Inc., 1957).

Pleasants, Henry, *The Agony of Modern Music* (New York: Simon and Schuster, 1955).

Portnoy, Julius, *Music in the Life of Man* (New York: Holt, Rinehart, and Winston, 1963).

Robertson, Alex and Denis Stevens, editors, *The Pelican History of Music* (Baltimore: Penguin Books, Ltd., 1960).

Sachs, Curt, *The Wellsprings of Music* (New York: McGraw-Hill Book Company, Inc., 1965).

Seaman, Julius, editor, *Great Orchestral Music* (New York: Collier Books, 1962).

Seay, Albert, *Music in the Medieval World* (Englewood Cliffs, N.J.: Prentice-Hall, Inc., 1965).

Simon, Henry W., *100 Great Operas* (New York: Doubleday and Company, 1960).

Stravinsky, Igor, *An Autobiography* (New York: W. W. Norton and Company, Inc., 1962).

Tovey, Donald Francis, *The Forms of Music* (New York: Meridian Books, 1956).

Toye, Francis, *Rossini, a Study in Tragi-Comedy* (New York: W. W. Norton and Company, Inc., 1963).

Turner, W. J., *Mozart, The Man and His Works* (New York: Doubleday and Company, 1954).

Westrup, J. A. and Harrison, F. L., *The New College Encyclopedia of Music* (New York: W. W. Norton and Company, Inc., 1960).

Index

623